D1131182

college

Accounting

with Peachtree®

for Microsoft®
Windows®
Release 5.0

Judith M. Peters
College of DuPage

Robert M. Peters
DePaul University

Carol Yacht
Peachtree® Software Consultant

HOUGHTON MIFFLIN COMPANY   **Boston**   **New York**

Senior Sponsoring Editor: Anne Kelly
Associate Sponsoring Editor: Joanne Dauksewicz
Senior Project Editor: Nancy Blodget
Senior Manufacturing Coordinator: Florence Cadran
Associate Production/Design Coordinator: Jodi O'Rourke
Marketing Manager: Juli A. Bliss

This book is written to provide accurate and authoritative information concerning the covered topics. It is not meant to take the place of professional advice. The companies and financial information in this book have been created for instructional purposes. No reference to any specific company or person is intended or should be inferred. Any similarity with an existing company is purely coincidental.

Trademark Acknowledgments: IBM and IBM PC are registered trademarks of International Business Machines Corporation. Microsoft and Windows are registered trademarks of Microsoft Corporation. Peachtree is a registered trademark of Peachtree Software, Inc.

Peachtree® for Microsoft® Windows® screen shots reprinted with permission of Peachtree Software, Inc., an ADP Company.

Fc1

Printed in the U.S.A.

International Standard Book Numbers:
    Text: 0-395-94353-1
    Text and Data Disk: 0-395-94361-2

Library of Congress Card Catalog Number: 98-72073

1 2 3 4 5 6 7 8 9 — V H — 03 02 01 00 99 98

This book is dedicated
to our students.

Contents
in Brief

Contents

Preface

Until now, all introductory accounting textbooks taught students how to do manual accounting. Educational software, not commercial software, was used as an optional feature. Software instructions were found in an appendix or in a separate manual.

College Accounting with Peachtree® for Microsoft® Windows® is different because it teaches beginning accounting *using* general ledger software. The software instruction is seamlessly integrated into the accounting instruction. Software is not optional in this book; it is required. And not just any software! In addition to learning accounting, students are learning to use Peachtree Accounting for Windows—one of the most popular commercial software packages on the market.

Although the use of software is an important component of this textbook, accounting theory and manual practice are not neglected. All the topics covered in traditional college accounting books are covered in this book *in the same level of detail.* Beginning with Chapter 4, when Peachtree software is introduced, each chapter's homework requires both manual and computerized practice. The chapter demonstration problem and homework exercises are all done manually; Problem Sets A and B are computerized with Peachtree except for data entry sheets.

College Accounting with Peachtree is for students taking introductory accounting courses at two and four-year colleges, independent colleges, and in various kinds of training programs. It can be used in the single course model, traditional semester terms, and two and three-quarter sequences. We assume students have limited or no previous experience in accounting.

A Skills Emphasis

With traditional accounting books, students may "skim" chapters with little concentration before they complete the assignments. This results in minimal learning and inability to do the homework. Not in this book! Beginning in Chapter 4, most chapter examples require the student to actively participate through the use of Peachtree software. Participation in all chapter examples is a must because data saved to a disk at the end of one chapter becomes the beginning data for the next chapter. Misunderstandings do not "fall through the cracks" because errors must be corrected before beginning the next chapter. Printouts provide visible evidence that the chapter has been studied in detail. "Skimming" and superficial learning is no longer an option.

Textbook Features

Readability and Clarity

We present the material in a logical sequence and link key concepts with short transitions. New concepts are defined when they are introduced and demonstrated with simple examples. We strive for clarity and avoid loose rephrasing and synonyms that might confuse students. The tone of this book is businesslike but friendly. We want to make the learning process easy.

Consistency

You will find our word choice, phrasing, formats, and procedures consistent throughout the textbook and related materials. The account titles, transactions, phrasing, arithmetic requirements, and level of difficulty in the end-of-chapter assignments mirror those in the chapter.

Integration of Theory and Practice

As teachers, we understand the need for a clear and orderly presentation of accounting procedures with accounting theory. We provide a simple theoretical frame of reference to enhance students' understanding of accounting procedures. This frame of reference lays the groundwork for the development of accounting logic and reduces the need for memorization. The use of commercial accounting software motivates students; they know they are learning something useful. The integration of theory and computer practice means that students leave the accounting course ready for the contemporary world.

Unique Chapter Pedagogy

Learning Objectives

Learning objectives dictate the structure of each chapter. The chapter material is the basis for the end-of-chapter assignments, the Solutions Manual, the Instructor's Resource Manual, the Student Study Guide, and the Test Bank. The learning objectives are highlighted in the margin to indicate where they are discussed in the chapter.

Examples

Each new concept, term, or procedure is introduced with a readable definition and a clear example. Examples are used extensively to demonstrate, reinforce, and integrate important concepts.

Extended Example

One business is used as an extended example throughout the textbook. In Chapter 2, The Kitchen Taylor is introduced as a service business that refinishes kitchen cabinets. Then, in Chapter 8, The Kitchen Taylor becomes a merchandising business called TKT Products that sells new kitchen cabinets. Using the same business in Chapters 2 through 15 gives students a sense of continuity and confidence as they progress into more complex material.

Comments

The comment boxes, located at strategic points in the chapter, are designed to clarify and expand finer points. Timely clarification will ensure success with a difficult concept, method, or procedure.

Flow Charts

Flow charts provide visual summaries of procedures and relationships. The flow charts are simple to ensure clarity.

Peachtree Accounting for Windows Screen Captures

Starting in Chapter 1, there are Peachtree screen captures which show students what their screen displays should look like. These illustrations are used throughout the textbook to explain how to use the software. These screen captures give students feedback just when they need it most—when they are learning a new Peachtree feature.

End-of-Chapter Material

Chapter Summary

Each chapter ends with a summary that repeats the word choice and phrasing from the chapter. This repetition provides important reinforcement and consistency.

Pencil Logo

A pencil logo in the margin indicates that a manually prepared solution is required. All end-of-chapter demonstration problems and exercises require manual solutions. In addition, the data entry sheet portions of Problem Sets A and B are marked with pencil logos.

Demonstration Problems

After each chapter summary, there is a manually solved demonstration problem. These problems reinforce major chapter concepts in a format that prepares students for the homework problems and exercises. The demonstration problems can be used for extra practice by students or as in-class demonstrations by the instructor. Additional demonstration problems are provided in the Instructor's Resource Manual and Student Study Guide.

Chapter Glossary

New terms in each chapter are defined in an end-of-chapter glossary.

Self-Tests

Every chapter contains a short self-test located just before the homework material begins. Each self-test consists of five multiple-choice questions. The answers are provided as the final element of each chapter. These questions offer the student a quick review of the chapter.

Questions for Discussion

Each chapter includes eight questions for discussion. Students are asked to describe, define, or discuss these questions. The questions cover topics in the order in which they occur in the text, and they are phrased using the same terminology that is used in the chapter.

Exercises

Each chapter has approximately eight manually solved exercises. These exercises, labeled as to content and keyed to the chapter learning objectives, are simple applications of chapter material. Each exercise focuses on one new concept. The exercises are designed to parallel the examples used in the chapter.

Problems: Set A and Set B

Every chapter has an A and a B set of problems. The problems follow the sequence of the learning activities in the chapter. With the exception of data entry sheets, all of these problems require the use of Peachtree software.

Ace Cleaning Service, Problem Set A, is for use with chapters 4 through 7. Problem Set B, Loyal Lawn Service, is also for use with chapters 4 through 7. Ace Cleaning Service and Loyal Lawn Service are service businesses. In Chapter 4, students are instructed to load the data for Ace Cleaning Service and Loyal Lawn Service from the Company Data CD-ROM.

In Chapter 8, Ace Cleaning Service and Loyal Lawn Service evolve into merchandising businesses: ACS Products and LLS Products, respectively. In Chapter 8, students are instructed to load the data for ACS Products and LLS Products from the Company Data CD-ROM.

Mini-Cases

The mini-cases are business scenarios that ask students to make real-life business decisions.

A Case of Ethics

Each chapter ends with an ethics case. These cases promote discussions of ethical considerations related to accounting topics presented in the chapter. Since students can easily relate to the situations described, these cases should provoke some lively discussions.

Comprehensive Review Problems

The textbook contains two comprehensive review problems. Comprehensive Review Problem 1, Regal Dry Cleaners, reviews and reinforces material in Chapters 1 through 7. Students complete a two-month accounting cycle for a service business. Comprehensive Review Problem 2, Flashtec, reviews Chapter 8 through 15 topics through a one-month accounting cycle for a merchandising business. The data for each comprehensive review problem is in a directory on the Company Data CD-ROM.

Supplementary Materials

Our two goals in writing *College Accounting with Peachtree® for Microsoft® Windows®* are to (1) help students get ready for the world of work, and (2) provide students and faculty with a clear, readable, and consistent textbook. To ensure that these qualities appear in the supplemental materials, we wrote all of them ourselves.

For Instructors

Instructor's Solutions Manual

Answers to the questions for discussion, exercises, problems (sets A and B), mini-cases, ethics cases, and comprehensive review problems are provided for each chapter. Learning objectives are keyed to the exercises and problems.

Instructor's Resource Manual

The Instructor's Resource Manual, which is separate from the Solutions Manual, is designed to help busy professionals develop lectures and select homework assignments. There are chapter learning objectives keyed to the homework assignments, a chapter outline, the chapter summary from the text, a demonstration problem accompanied by a solution, and Peachtree tips. The Peachtree tips are designed to highlight software features and guide the instructor in the use of Peachtree and Windows.

Solution Transparencies

Acetate transparencies of solutions to all exercises, problems (sets A and B), and comprehensive problems are available.

Test Bank

The test bank for Chapters 1 through 15 consists of over 1,200 questions in true/false, multiple-choice, and short exercise formats. Each chapter has a separate set of questions to ensure instructor flexibility. If the instructor chooses not to use the computerized version, the test bank design and typography facilitate easy duplication. Students are questioned on their knowledge of accounting theory and Peachtree Software.

Computerized Test Bank

This computerized version of the test bank allows the instructor to select, alter, and add test items. The Computerized Test Bank is capable of generating different versions of the same test. It is available on 3 1/2 inch disks in Windows for IBM and compatible computers.

Houghton Mifflin also offers a call-in testing service to assist instructors. Contact Houghton Mifflin Testing Service at 800-225-1464, between 9:00 a.m. and 5:00 p.m. E.S.T.

For Students

Student Study Guide

Each chapter includes learning objectives, helpful hints, chapter outline, demonstration problems, true/false and multiple-choice questions (questions are different from those in the test bank), matching terms from the chapter glossary, completion questons, three exercises keyed to learning objectives, and solutions to the questions and exercises.

Working Papers

Working papers have been carefully reviewed to ensure coordination with the textbook. Account titles, forms, and notation conform with the text-book, the Instructor's Solutions Manual, the Instructor's Resource Manual, and transparencies.

Practice Sets

The following Practice Sets are available for use with the textbook. Data disks for use with Peachtree Accounting for Windows accompany each particular practice set.

Name	Type of Business	Chapter Coverage
Let's Party!	Service business, sole proprietorship	Chapters 1–7
The Rug Bug	Wholesale merchandising business, sole proprietorship	Chapters 8–15
Verde Audio & Video	Retail merchandising business, audio and video equipment, sole proprietorship	Chapters 8–15
Oak Creek Canyon Jewelers	Payroll, sole proprietorship	Chapters 12–13

Software

Peachtree Accounting for Windows, Release 5.0, Educational Version, is packaged with the text. In addition, there is a Company Data CD-ROM for use with Peachtree. The chart below shows when to start using the company data from the CD-ROM.

When Do You Use the Company Data CD-ROM?		
Company Data CD-ROM	Beginning of Chapter	End of Chapter
The Kitchen Taylor	4	
Ace Cleaning Service (Problem Set A)		4
Loyal Lawn Service (Problem Set B)		4
Regal Dry Cleaners (Comprehensive Review Problem 1)		7
TKT Products	8	
ACS Products (Problem Set A)		8
LLS Products (Problem Set B)		8
Flashtec (Comprehensive Review Problem 2)		15

System Requirements

To install Peachtree Accounting for Windows Release 5.0 you need the following:

- 100% IBM compatible 486 computer or higher
- Windows® 3.1 in enhanced mode or Windows® 95
- 16 MB RAM (recommended)
- Hard disk with at least 25 MB free disk space.
- VGA or better monitor
- CD-ROM drive
- Floppy disk drive
- Any Windows® supported printer
- Mouse

Acknowledgments

We are indebted to many individuals, faculty members, professional colleagues, and students who have contributed their knowledge and expertise. Particular acknowledgment should be given to the following:

Lee Cannell, El Paso Community College

Janet Caruso, Briarcliffe College

Sue Cook, Tulsa Junior College

Marilyn Fuller, Paris Junior College

Deborah J. Harper, Montgomery College

Andrea Johnson, Jefferson College

Bob Johnson, Jefferson College

William P. Logan, Middle Georgia Technical Institute

David Rasmussen, St. Martins's College

Kay Vinson Ruhland, Heald Business College

Francis Sakiey, Mercer Community College

Steve Teeter, Utah Valley State College

Jann Underwood-Holmes, Eldorado College

We wish to express special appreciation to Amy Dillon, Michael Gaiden, Bill Swiderski, Brian Swiderski, David Ribando, and William Vadbunker, all of DePaul University, for their helpful suggestions and meticulous attention to the Instructor's Solutions Manual and Test Bank. Many thanks go to LaTarsha Barnes, Kirsten Hansen, and Alan Kuska, also of DePaul University, for their help with the Study Guide.

We are particularly indebted to Anne Kelly, Bonnie Binkert, and Kristine Clerkin for their confidence in this textbook. Special thanks also go to Joanne Dauksewicz for her developmental support and to Linda Burkell, our accounting/technology "guru."

In addition, we wish to thank Maria Morelli and Ronna Weaver who skillfully guided us through a complicated production process. Many thanks also go to Margaret Haywood, a wonderful copy editor and a great friend.

Finally, we would like to extend sincere thanks to Susan Wells, Jan Woodhouse, and Bryan Ballard of Peachtree Software for their help and assistance. The ability to provide Peachtree Accounting for Windows for use with our text provides us with a valuable tool for accounting instruction.

Judith Peters
Robert Peters
Carol Yacht

The Computerized Accounting Environment

LEARNING OBJECTIVES

After studying this chapter, you should be able to:

1. Define the accounting process.

2. Describe the role of accountants.

3. Describe the use of Peachtree® Accounting for Windows® in business.

4. Describe the three major accounting career paths.

5. Discuss the business entity concept, matching principle, and historical cost principle.

6. Discuss accrual-basis versus cash-basis accounting.

7. Describe three ownership structures.

8. Classify businesses by their type of business activity.

9. Describe the users of accounting information.

10. Describe the importance of backup and restore.

veryone who makes economic decisions uses accounting. Accounting is
so essential to decision making that many refer to accounting and its terminology as the *language of business.* Accounting terms such as *net
income, accounts receivable, gross profit,* and *depreciation* are frequently
used by lawyers, engineers, doctors, investors, and creditors as well as management.

Even if you do not choose a business-related profession, you should be
comfortable with the language of business. You will be making economic
decisions throughout your life. For example: Is the company offering you a
job with financial security? Is the interest on your bank loan computed correctly? Should you take your stockbroker's advice? How is your business
doing? Are you able to prepare the financial information needed for your
automobile loan? These and other questions emphasize how a knowledge
of accounting will increase the quality of your personal economic decisions
and sharpen your understanding of the business environment.

This textbook begins with a brief study of the computerized accounting
environment. First we define the accounting process and explain the role
of accountants. Then, you are introduced to Peachtree® Accounting for Win-
dows®. Next, you will study the three major career paths available to
accountants. You will also take a look at three important accounting principles and a comparison of accrual-basis versus cash-basis accounting. This
is followed by a discussion of ownership structures, business activities, and
users of accounting information. The chapter concludes with a discussion
of the software that accompanies this textbook.

Accounting and Accountants

objective 1
Define the accounting process

Broadly defined, **accounting** is a process of analyzing, classifying, recording,
summarizing, and interpreting economic events. In accounting, these economic events are called *transactions.* A **business transaction** is an economic event that can be measured in dollars and affects the financial condition of a business. Common business transactions include selling goods
or services, buying land, renting equipment, and paying insurance premiums.
Although the resignation of a key executive may be a disruptive event for
a company, it is not a business transaction because this event cannot be
accurately measured in dollars. Persons known as *bookkeepers* often record
the most common daily transactions.

objective 2
Describe the role of
accountants

Accounting systems are set up, monitored, and operated by accountants.
However, an accountant's primary role is to provide accounting information
to interested parties on a timely basis. Modern accountants have the same
professional status as doctors and lawyers.

Peachtree® Accounting for Windows®

objective 3
Describe the use of Peachtree®
Accounting for Windows® in
business

Most businesses use computerized accounting systems. However, it is
important to note that the use of a computer does not eliminate the need
to understand the accounting process. In fact, it is impossible to use
accounting software without a basic knowledge of accounting. With that in
mind, this textbook combines the study of accounting with the use of
accounting software. More specifically, the software you will learn to use is

Peachtree® Accounting for Windows® (PAW). PAW is a commercial accounting package that is used by thousands of businesses. Because of its popularity, knowledge of Peachtree will be a great asset when you enter the job market.

The version of Peachtree that you will use is a Microsoft® Windows® application. Windows is a **graphical user interface (GUI).** A graphical user interface uses common symbols called **icons.** Icons or visual images appear on the screen. Examples of icons include a file folder, hourglass, and magnifying glass. What makes Windows software easy to use is its visual format. Besides using the keyboard in the traditional way, a *mouse* or *trackball* is also used.

The following screen capture shows how PAW uses a combination of text and icons. You will use the "General Journal Entry" window in subsequent chapters of this book. For now, this screen capture is an example of what a graphical user interface looks like on your computer screen.

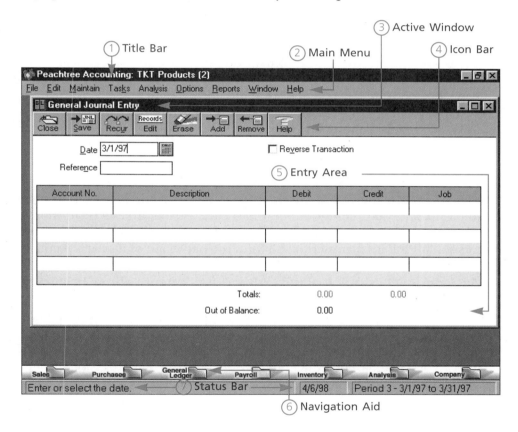

1. *Title bar:* The bar at the top of your screen. When a company is open in PAW, the name of the company is displayed on the title bar.

2. *Main menu:* When you click on the main menu headings, a submenu of options is pulled down, or opened. You can open these options with a mouse or by holding down the <Alt> key and pressing the underlined letter in the main menu option.

3. *Active window:* The "General Journal Entry" window has been chosen in order to record an entry. This bar shows what window is open or "active."

4. *Icon bar:* This icon bar shows visual images of information that pertain to the window. Some icons are common to all windows while other icons are specific to a particular window.

5. *Entry area:* This part of the screen is where you enter the information for the journal entry. You will learn how to do this in subsequent chapters.

6. *Navigation aid:* The navigation aid offers a graphical alternative to the main menu. The major functions of the program are represented as icons or pictures that show you how tasks flow through the system. You can click on an icon and perform that function.

7. *Status bar:* The bar (screen colors may vary) at the bottom of the window shows "help" information about the window, the current date, and the current accounting period.

One of the benefits of Windows software is that it standardizes terms and operations used in software programs. Once you learn how to use PAW, you will also know how to use other Windows applications. As you work through the chapters of this text, you will learn more about PAW and Windows. If you are already familiar with Windows®, that knowledge will make learning PAW even easier.

Now, let's consider career opportunities for accountants. Keep in mind that in today's job market, a knowledge of both accounting and computers is necessary in all of the fields described.

Accounting Careers

objective 4
Describe the three major accounting career paths

The need for accountants has existed since trading and commerce blossomed in the 15th and 16th centuries. In 1494, Luca Pacioli, a Franciscan monk, wrote a book describing the double-entry accounting process. The ideas expressed in Pacioli's manuscript still form the backbone of modern accounting. You will learn this double-entry process in the chapters that follow.

The Industrial Revolution of the 18th and 19th centuries brought an even greater need and opportunity for accountants as the factory system emerged and small companies became large manufacturing enterprises. Accountants became involved in solving management problems and providing all types of information to help company managers make decisions.

Today, aided by computers, accountants provide accurate decision-making data for almost every spectrum of our economic society. As a result, at least three major career paths are available to accountants: public accounting, managerial accounting, and government/not-for-profit accounting.

Public Accounting

To the average person, accountants in the field of public accounting are probably best known for the income tax service they provide individuals. In addition, public accountants provide auditing, tax, and consulting services to many different businesses and organizations for a fee.

Public accountants who pass an examination prepared and graded by the American Institute of Certified Public Accountants (AICPA) and fulfill other educational and work experience requirements are licensed as certified

public accountants (CPAs). CPAs provide an objective opinion on management reports to people not directly involved in managing the business. For example, stockholders, creditors, board members, trustees, and others rely on the opinions of CPAs.

A growing trend among public accounting firms is to hire para-accountants. These individuals usually have certificates or degrees in accounting but are not CPAs. They work under the direction of a CPA and perform a variety of functions in the areas of bookkeeping, auditing, and taxation.

Managerial Accounting

Accountants working in the field of **managerial accounting** are employed by one company and provide services for only that company. They perform general accounting, tax, budget, and cost accounting services for a single employer.

The role of managerial accountants is to provide business managers with accounting information that will help them make decisions. The accountants who provide this decision-making information gain a more professional status when they pass a rigorous examination that gives them the title of **certified management accountant (CMA).**

Government/Not-for-Profit Accounting

Government/not-for-profit accounting careers involve employment with the federal, state, or local government in such positions as auditors, revenue agents, or contract supervisors. Not-for-profit organizations such as churches, schools, clubs, and charities also employ accountants for various accounting duties ranging from general accounting to specialized accounting services.

Accountants employed in the three accounting fields—public, managerial, and government/not-for-profit—frequently specialize in certain aspects of their particular accounting field. Some accountants work in two or three accounting fields during their careers. Also, accountants often move into other professions. Many of today's executives and senior managers began their careers as accountants in public, managerial, and government/not-for-profit accounting.

Now that you have a general idea about the career opportunities for accountants as well as the nature of accounting and accountants, you are ready for an introduction to three accounting principles that guide many of the accounting procedures presented in this textbook.

Accounting Principles

In the United States, accountants follow **generally accepted accounting principles (GAAP)**—the official concepts, rules, procedures, and guidelines of accounting. GAAP are essentially developed by the **Financial Accounting Standards Board (FASB)**, which was organized in 1973 and consists of seven independent, full-time members. These principles provide a common frame of reference so that similar accounting treatment is given to similar situations. We introduce GAAP in Chapter 1 so that you become aware of them at the beginning of your study of accounting. Understanding these

objective 5
Discuss the business entity concept, matching principle, and historical cost principle

principles also gives you a starting point in making decisions when you later use accounting in actual business situations that may be different from those presented in this textbook.

Accountants use many generally accepted accounting principles. This textbook—your introduction to accounting—concentrates on the business entity concept, matching principle, and historical cost principle. In the chapters that follow, you will find yourself frequently referring back to these three principles.

Business Entity Concept

In accounting, a business entity is an economic unit that is separate from its owner(s) and from other businesses. The **business entity concept** requires the separation of the owner's personal and business transactions. If an owner owns two or more businesses, each business is treated as a separate entity.

To separate the personal transactions of the owner from those of the business, probably the first thing the owner of a new business does is to open a checking account in the name of the business. Only business-related money is deposited in this account, and only business-related checks are written against this account. The personal affairs of the owner are transacted through the owner's personal account. Should the owner own two or more businesses, each business would have its own checking account.

Matching Principle

All profit-seeking businesses expect to earn revenues. **Revenue** is the amount that a business charges a customer for a service performed or a product provided. Businesses also expect to have **expenses,** which are the costs incurred in the process of earning revenues.

The **matching principle** requires that these revenues and expenses be recorded in the time period in which they occur. When a business wants to determine its income or loss for a specific period of time, it compares, or matches, the revenues and expenses recorded during that period of time. An excess of revenues over expenses results in net income. An excess of expenses over revenues results in a net loss. Thus, through a proper matching of revenues and expenses, a business is able to compute its income or loss for a specified period of time. In Chapter 2, the matching principle is illustrated with more specific examples of revenues and expenses.

Historical Cost Principle

The **historical cost principle** requires that accountants record items, such as equipment and land, at their original cost. This acquisition cost, known as *historical cost,* is not changed as the current value of the item changes. For example, a business does not adjust its records upward if land purchased several years ago at a cost of $100,000 has increased in current market value to $125,000.

In addition to the business entity concept, matching principle, and historical cost principle, you should be introduced to the accrual basis of accounting before beginning your study of the accounting process in Chapter 2. As you will see in the next section, GAAP require the use of the accrual basis of accounting.

Accrual-Basis versus Cash-Basis Accounting

There are two bases of accounting: the accrual basis and the cash basis. Under **accrual-basis accounting**, revenues must be recorded when they are earned, regardless of whether the cash has been received. When the product or service has been provided to the customer, the revenue has been earned and must be recorded. Expenses also must be recorded in the period in which they are incurred, regardless of whether the cash is paid out at that time or later. When we have accepted a product or service from someone else, the expense has been incurred and must be recorded. Under **cash-basis accounting**, revenues are recorded when the cash is received and expenses are recorded when the cash is paid out.

objective 6
Discuss accrual-basis versus cash-basis accounting

Let's look at a comparison of how the same business transaction is handled under each basis.

Transaction	Accrual Basis	Cash Basis
Sold product to customer on credit.	Since product was provided to customer, revenue is recorded.	Since cash was not received, revenue is not recorded.
Had office painted but have not yet paid the bill.	Since service was accepted from someone else, expense is recorded.	Since cash was not paid out, expense is not recorded.

Cash-basis accounting works well for individuals and small service-oriented businesses, but most companies use the accrual basis. It is generally agreed that accrual-basis accounting results in a more timely measurement of income. In fact, GAAP require the use of accrual-basis accounting. The matching principle, as you will recall, requires that revenues and expenses be recorded in the time period they occurred. Unless otherwise instructed, you can assume the use of the accrual basis throughout this textbook.

So far, our environment of accounting has included the accounting process, Peachtree Accounting for Windows, career opportunities, accounting principles, and accrual-basis versus cash-basis accounting. Now, we are going to shift gears and direct our attention to ownership structures and business activities.

Ownership Structures

A business may be organized as a sole proprietorship, partnership, or corporation. The accounting process is similar under each of these ownership structures.

objective 7
Describe three ownership structures

Sole Proprietorship

A **sole proprietorship** is a business owned by one person and usually managed by the same person. It is the most common type of business organization. A sole proprietorship is easy to organize and gives the owner the opportunity to be his or her own boss. Under this structure, the owner receives all the income but must also assume all the risk—a risk that can go beyond the owner's investment in the business. Should the business be unable to pay its bills, creditors can seize personal assets of the owner such as a personal savings account, a car, or even the owner's home.

Partnership

A business owned by two or more persons is a partnership. It is a multiple proprietorship in which income, risk, and responsibility are shared by the partners. These individuals must agree on such things as the amount of money each is to invest in the partnership, how the work of the partnership is to be divided, and how partnership income or loss is to be divided.

Although a partnership can be organized with a verbal agreement, a written partnership agreement is preferred. This agreement is dissolved when a current partner leaves or a new partner wants to join. For the business to continue, a new partnership must be formed. Although a partnership has limited life, the partners have unlimited personal liability. If the partnership has financial difficulty, the personal assets of the partners may be used to pay the debts of the business.

Corporations

A corporation is a business owned by many individuals whose participation in the business is often limited. Unlike a sole proprietorship or partnership, a corporation issues shares of stock that allow for the division of ownership into many parts. Owners (stockholders) may transfer their ownership by transferring their shares of stock. If the corporation has financial difficulty, stockholders usually cannot lose more than their original investment.

The unique stock ownership structure of corporations makes them a popular form of investment for individuals. The distribution of income, risk, and responsibility depends on the number of shares owned. Since stockholders are not generally involved in the day-to-day activities of the corporation, the responsibility for daily operations is usually given to professional managers. The stockholders' interests are monitored by a board of directors and reviewed annually by public accountants hired by the stockholders.

Business Activities

objective 8
Classify businesses by their type of business activity

Accountants also classify businesses by their type of business activity. Most businesses sell either a service or a product. This leads to the following classification:

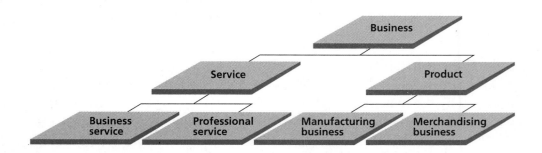

A **service business** sells a skill or technique that has no physical existence. As shown on page 8, service businesses sell either a business service or a professional service. Examples of business services include the services of dry cleaners, stockbrokers, realtors, and insurance agents. Professional services are provided by physicians, attorneys, public accountants, and educators.

A business that sells a product either makes the product or buys it ready-made from a supplier. A **manufacturing business** buys various components, such as cloth, thread, and buttons, and makes a product, such as coats. A **merchandising business,** such as your local discount store, buys ready-made products from suppliers and resells them to its own customers.

Some businesses sell both products and services. For example, an automobile repair shop is primarily a service business, but the shop also sells automotive parts.

We have almost completed our discussion of the accounting environment except for a quick look at the users of accounting information and a brief discussion of the accounting software that accompanies this textbook.

Users of Accounting Information

Accounting information is used by many individuals and groups with diverse needs. The many users of accounting information can be divided into two general groups: internal users and external users.

objective 9
Describe the users of accounting information

Internal Users

Those who manage the business, collectively known as *management,* are the **internal users** of accounting information. Managers are decision makers who are constantly faced with such questions as:

What products or services are the most profitable?

Will the business have enough cash to pay its debts as they come due?

Should the company borrow money to expand its facilities?

Are the sales greater this month than last?

Are customers paying their bills on time?

To answer these questions, managers depend on a steady flow of reliable accounting information.

External Users

Individuals or groups outside the business who have either a direct or indirect financial interest in the business are known as **external users.** Examples of those with a direct interest include present or potential investors, bankers, and suppliers. Those with an indirect interest include taxing authorities, regulatory agencies, labor unions, financial advisers, and customers.

To satisfy the needs of external users, accountants prepare general-purpose financial statements that summarize the activities of the business. The information contained in these statements is used to evaluate the company's past performance as well as to predict its future performance. You will become familiar with these financial statements as you study the chapters in this textbook.

Software

College Accounting with Peachtree® for Microsoft® Windows® requires the use of Peachtree Accounting for Windows, Release 5.0, Batch 03. The Company Data CD-ROM contains the company information that you will use in Chapters 4 through 15.

Company Data CD-ROM

The Company Data CD-ROM contains a directory for each of the eight sets of company data files. You will use this data in Set A and Set B Problems, the Comprehensive Review Problems, and in the extended example.

Loading Peachtree Accounting for Windows (PAW)

Your instructor may have already loaded Peachtree Accounting for Windows (PAW) on your computer or network. If not, directions for loading PAW are in Appendix A at the back of this textbook.

Backup and Restore

objective 10
Describe the importance of backup and restore

Beginning in Chapter 4, you will be reminded to backup each chapter's data. What is meant by a backup? Why is it so important?

When using PAW, information is automatically saved to the hard drive of the computer. In a classroom setting, a number of students may be using the same computer. Of course, this means that when you return to the computer, your data will probably be gone. **Backing up** your data simply means saving it on a floppy disk, so that it will be available when you want to work again.

You will backup all your data to a floppy disk in drive A (or B). When backing up, **it is extremely important that you always use a blank formatted disk.** This means that the disk you use to backup should not have any other information on it. PAW requires a **separate** blank formatted disk for each backup.

It is important to backup each chapter's data so that you can start where you left off the next time you use PAW. To start again, you will need to **restore** your data. For example, at the end of Chapter 4, you will backup your Chapter 4 data. Then, at the beginning of Chapter 5, you will need to restore your Chapter 4 data. The restored data provides a starting point for the new chapter.

Remember, you are backing up to a floppy disk in drive A (or B). Then, you are restoring from the floppy disk to the computer's hard drive. The PAW "Backup" command allows you to save your work to a floppy disk in drive A (or B). The PAW "Restore" command allows you to start where you left off.

If you are using your own computer, it is still important to backup to a floppy disk. You might want to go back to a previous chapter and, if you have a backup, that will be easy to do. A handy thing to remember is to "backup early and often!"

Looking Ahead

Before using Peachtree Accounting for Windows, you must acquire some basic accounting skills that do not directly involve the computer. In Chapter 2, you will study the accounting equation. In Chapter 3, you will learn how to use debits and credits to record transactions. Then, in Chapter 4, you will be ready to begin the accounting cycle using PAW.

We know that you are eager to use your software, but be patient! Study Chapters 2 and 3 very carefully. A good understanding of the material contained in those chapters is *crucial* to your success in using Peachtree Accounting for Windows.

Chapter One Summary

We began our study of the computerized accounting environment by broadly defining accounting as a process of analyzing, classifying, recording, summarizing, and interpreting economic events. Business transactions are economic events that can be measured in dollars and affect the financial condition of a business.

All accounting systems are based on the same accounting principles and are set up, monitored, and operated by accountants. The primary role of accountants is to provide accounting information in a usable form to interested parties on a timely basis.

Peachtree Accounting for Windows, commonly referred to as PAW, is a popular commercial accounting package. The version of Peachtree that you will use is a Windows application. Windows is a graphical user interface (GUI). It uses symbols that are called icons.

Almost every spectrum of our economic society requires accounting information. As a result, three major career paths are open to accountants: public accounting, managerial accounting, and government/not-for-profit accounting.

This chapter introduced three important accounting principles—the business entity concept, matching principle, and historical cost principle. You also received your first glimpse of accrual-basis accounting. This was followed by a brief introduction to ownership structures and business activities. The differences between the internal and external users of accounting information was also discussed.

College Accounting with Peachtree for Microsoft Windows includes a Company Data CD-ROM. The CD-ROM contains the company information that you will use in Chapters 4 through 15. Peachtree Accounting for Windows, Release 5.0, Batch 01 is required.

Beginning in Chapter 4, you will backup your data to a floppy disk in drive A (or B). It is important that you always use a blank formatted disk to backup. When you begin the next chapter, you will have to restore your data.

Glossary

accounting The process of analyzing, classifying, recording, summarizing, and interpreting economic events. *2*

accrual-basis accounting A system of recording financial information that requires revenues to be recorded when they are earned (product sold or service provided) and expenses to be recorded when they are incurred (product or service accepted), regardless of whether cash has been received or paid. *7*

backing up Saving data to a floppy disk. *10*

business entity concept An accounting rule requiring that a business entity be treated as an economic unit that is separate from its owner(s) and other businesses; it requires a separation of personal and business transactions. *6*

business transaction An economic event that can be measured in dollars and affects the financial condition of a business. *2*

cash-basis accounting A system of recording financial information that requires revenues to be recorded only when cash is received and expenses to be recorded only when cash is paid out. *7*

certified management accountant (CMA) A title given to managerial accountants who pass a rigorous examination. *5*

certified public accountant (CPA) A title given to public accountants who pass an examination prepared and graded by the American Institute of Certified Public Accountants (AICPA) and who also fulfill other educational and work experience requirements. *4, 5*

corporation A business owned by many individuals whose participation in the business is often limited; ownership is evidenced by shares of stock. *8*

expense A cost incurred in the process of earning revenue. *6*

external users Accounting information users who are individuals and groups outside the business and who have either a direct or indirect financial interest in the business. *9*

Financial Accounting Standards Board (FASB) A group consisting of seven independent, full-time members that is influential in the development of GAAP. *5*

generally accepted accounting principles (GAAP) The official concepts, rules, procedures, and guidelines followed by accountants. *5*

graphical user interface (GUI) A graphical user interface uses common symbols called icons. *3*

historical cost principle A principle of accounting that requires accountants to record items at their original cost. The cost figure is not changed as the current value of the item changes. *6*

icons Visual or graphical images that appear on the screen. Examples of icons include a file folder, hourglass, and magnifying glass. *3*

internal users Users of accounting information that are business managers who need a steady flow of reliable accounting information in order to function as decision makers. *9*

managerial accounting A field of accounting that provides general accounting, tax, budget, and cost accounting services for a single employer. *5*

manufacturing business A business that buys various components and makes a product that it sells. *9*

matching principle A principle that requires revenues and expenses to be recorded in the same time period they occur. *6*

merchandising business A business that buys ready-made products from suppliers and resells them to its own customers. *9*

partnership A business owned by two or more persons; a multiple proprietorship. *8*

public accounting A field of accounting that provides auditing, tax, and consulting services to many different individuals, businesses, and organizations for a fee. *4*

restore Using backed up data to begin where you previously left off. *10*

revenue The amount that a business charges a customer for a service performed or a product provided. *6*

service business A business that sells a skill or technique that has no physical existence. *9*

sole proprietorship A business owned by one person and usually managed by the same person. *7*

Self-Test

Select the best answer.

1. Common business transactions do *not* include
   a. the resignation of a key executive.
   b. buying land.
   c. selling goods or services.
   d. paying insurance premiums.

2. CMA stands for
   a. chartered management accountant.
   b. certified management accountant.
   c. certified municipal accountant.
   d. certified master accountant.

3. Historical cost is
   a. increased monthly for changes in current market value.
   b. increased only at year-end for changes in current market value.
   c. increased for changes in appraised value.
   d. not increased for changes in current market value.

4. Which of the following statements is *not* true under accrual-basis accounting?
   a. Revenues must be recorded when earned.
   b. Revenues are recorded only when the cash is received.
   c. Revenue must be recorded when a product or service is provided to the customer.
   d. An expense is recorded when a product or service is accepted from someone else.

5. A service business sells
   a. a product that it manufactures.
   b. a product that it purchases ready-made from a supplier.
   c. a skill or technique that has no physical existence.
   d. both products and services.

Answers to the self-test can be found after the case at the end of this chapter.

Questions for Discussion

1. Define accounting.
2. Describe the role of accountants.
3. Describe the three major career paths open to accountants.
4. *a.* GAAP is an abbreviation for what phrase?
   b. FASB is an abbreviation for what organization?
5. What is the purpose of GAAP?
6. *a.* Discuss the business entity concept.
   b. Discuss the matching principle.
   c. Discuss the historical cost principle.
7. Discuss the concept of accrual-basis accounting.
8. Describe three types of ownership structures.
9. Discuss the differences among a service business, a manufacturing business, and a merchandising business.
10. Describe the users of accounting information.

A Case of Ethics

Your friend owns a small business. He frequently brags about how much money he saves by charging home cleaning supplies to his business. What do you think about this practice?

Answers to Self-Test

1. *a*   2. *b*   3. *d*   4. *b*   5. *c*

Analyzing Transactions

The Accounting Equation

LEARNING OBJECTIVES

After studying this chapter, you should be able to:

1. Discuss the concept of the accounting equation.

2. Use the accounting equation to analyze basic transactions in terms of increases and decreases.

3. Describe the purpose and content of the three basic financial statements.

4. Describe how the three basic financial statements are related.

You will recall from Chapter 1 that accounting was defined as a process of analyzing, classifying, recording, summarizing, and interpreting economic events called *business transactions.* The entire accounting process operates within the framework of one equation—the accounting equation. This chapter begins with an explanation of the accounting equation. Next you will learn to analyze, classify, and record business transactions within the framework of the accounting equation. Then you will study financial statements that summarize transactions that have occurred over a specified period of time.

The Accounting Equation

objective 1
Discuss the concept of the
accounting equation

As defined in Chapter 1, a business transaction is an economic event that can be measured in dollars and affects the financial condition of a business. Typical business transactions include making sales, purchasing supplies, and paying employees' wages. The basic accounting equation is the framework in which all business transactions are analyzed. This basic equation is:

Assets = Liabilities + Owner's Equity

Let's begin our study of the accounting equation by defining its components.

Assets are all the things of value owned by a business, whether paid for or not. Assets include such things as cash, supplies, land, buildings, and equipment. A separate record, known as an account, is kept for each individual asset. We do not have an account titled *assets.* The term *asset* refers to a classification or type of account.

Liabilities are the amounts owed (debts) to people outside the business known as creditors. The term *liability,* like *asset,* refers to a classification or type of account. Liability accounts include Accounts Payable, Notes Payable, and Mortgage Payable. Most liability accounts have the word *payable* in their title. This reminds us that these are the amounts we have agreed to pay in the future.

Owner's equity represents the net worth of a business—the difference between all a business owns (assets) and all it owes (liabilities). We might also think of owner's equity in terms of rights to assets. The left side of the accounting equation contains all the things of value (assets) owned by a business. Who has rights to those assets? The right side of the equation answers this question. The liability component expresses the rights, or equity, of creditors in those assets. Remember that we must pay liabilities out of assets, so our creditors have certain rights to our assets. The remaining rights, or equity, in assets is expressed in the owner's equity component of the equation. In other words, owner's equity describes the rights of the owner to business assets. The term capital means the same thing as owner's equity. These two terms are often used interchangeably by accountants.

Owner's equity is a classification or type of account. An example of a specific owner's equity account is Mary Jones, Capital. In a sole proprietorship, the title of the owner's equity account is always the owner's name followed by a comma and the word *Capital.*

The accounting equation (A = L + OE) must always be in balance. The total of everything to the left of the equal sign must always equal the total of everything to the right of the equal sign. In other words, the total of all assets must always equal the total of all rights to assets (creditors' plus owners').

Analyzing Transactions

As we have noted, all business transactions must be analyzed within the framework of the accounting equation. The analysis process involves three steps. Let's study this three-step process before considering any specific transactions.

objective 2
Use the accounting equation to analyze basic transactions in terms of increases and decreases

step 1:   Read and think.

The analysis process always begins with a thorough understanding of the event that has taken place. Before picking up a pencil:

- Read the given data carefully.
- Think about the data using good, old-fashioned common sense.

This step is crucial. You cannot analyze what you don't understand and you cannot understand what you haven't read and thought about carefully. So remember to read and think before you write!

step 2:   Identify accounts, classifications, and effect.

- Accounts. Name the specific accounts involved in each transaction (Cash, Supplies, Equipment, etc.).
- Classifications. Classify each account (asset, liability, or owner's equity).
- Effect (+ or −). Determine the effect (increase or decrease) on each account.

step 3:   Check the accounting equation (A = L + OE) for balance.

The accounting equation is in balance if the total of everything on the left side of the equation is equal to the total of everything on the right side of the equation. A lack of balance indicates an error in Step 1 and/or Step 2.

Let's practice our analytical skills by considering the case of Dennis Taylor. Dennis decided to convert his hobby, refinishing wooden surfaces, into a profit-making business specializing in refinishing old kitchen cabinets. Dennis named his new business The Kitchen Taylor and organized it as a sole proprietorship. The Kitchen Taylor is a service business because it sells a service (refinishing) rather than a product. Let's analyze some basic transactions that occurred during the first month of operations.

December 1 Transaction

step 1:   *Dennis invested $10,000 cash in his new business in a checking account in the name of The Kitchen Taylor.*

Comment

Always start your analysis with the easiest part of the transaction, saving the most difficult for last. Most students easily understand the flow of cash, so it's usually the best place to begin. Is cash (including checks) involved in a transaction? In other words, is cash changing hands (being received or paid out) in the current transaction? Be aware that a dollar sign does not necessarily indicate that cash is changing hands.

step 2:   Account?   Cash
                Classification?   Asset
                Effect?   +$10,000

                Account?   Dennis Taylor, Capital
                Classification?   Owner's Equity
                Effect?   +$10,000

Comment   Remember the business entity concept. The accounting equation represents the status of The Kitchen Taylor, not Dennis Taylor.

step 3:

	Assets	=	Liabilities	+	Owner's Equity
	Cash	=			Dennis Taylor, Capital
Before	–0–	=	–0–	+	–0–
Dec. 1	+10,000				+10,000
After	10,000	=	–0–	+	10,000

December 2 Transaction

step 1:   **The Kitchen Taylor purchased a truck for which $6,000 in cash was paid, Check No. 101.**

Comment   The word **paid** indicates that cash is involved.

step 2:   Account?   Cash
                Classification?   Asset
                Effect?   –$6,000

                Account?   Truck
                Classification?   Asset
                Effect?   +$6,000

Comment   Notice that all the activity in this transaction occurs in the assets section of the equation. The pool of assets is being rearranged, but total assets remain the same. Notice also that owner's equity is not affected by this transaction. The Kitchen Taylor's net worth is unchanged.

step 3:

	Assets			=	Liabilities	+	Owner's Equity
	Cash	+	Truck	=			Dennis Taylor, Capital
Before	10,000			=	–0–	+	10,000
Dec. 2	– 6,000		+6,000				
After	4,000	+	6,000	=	–0–	+	10,000

10,000   10,000

December 3 Transaction

step 1:   *The Kitchen Taylor paid a 24-month insurance premium, $1,200, Check No. 102.*

step 2:
Account?   Cash
Classification?   Asset
Effect?   –$1,200

Account?   Prepaid Insurance
Classification?   Asset
Effect?   +$1,200

step 3:

		Assets				=	Liabilities	+	Owner's Equity
					Prepaid				Dennis Taylor,
	Cash	+	Truck	+	Ins.	=			Capital
Before	4,000	+	6,000	+		=	–0–	+	10,000
Dec. 3	–1,200				+1,200				
After	2,800	+	6,000	+	1,200	=	–0–	+	10,000

10,000   10,000

December 4 Transaction

step 1:   *The Kitchen Taylor purchased $425 worth of sandpaper, steel wool, chemicals, and various other supplies, promising to pay in the near future.*

> *Comment*
>
> No cash is involved in this transaction. The Kitchen Taylor is buying supplies with a promise to pay in the future. This promise represents a liability. More specifically, the promise is recorded as an increase in a liability account known as *Accounts Payable*. This type of transaction is frequently described as a purchase on account.

step 2:
Account?   Accounts Payable
Classification?   Liability
Effect?   +$425

Account?   Supplies
Classification?   Asset
Effect?   +$425

step 3:

	Assets							=	Liabilities	+	Owner's Equity
	Cash	+	Truck	+	Prepaid Ins.	+	Supplies	=	Accounts Payable	+	Dennis Taylor, Capital
Before	2,800	+	6,000	+	1,200			=	–0–	+	10,000
Dec. 4							+425		+425		
After	2,800	+	6,000	+	1,200	+	425	=	425	+	10,000

10,425   10,425

December 7 Transaction

step 1: *The Kitchen Taylor refinished several cabinets for a customer receiving $1,500 in cash.*

Comment

Revenue is the amount that a business charges a customer for the service performed or the product provided. The $1,500 in this transaction represents revenue earned by The Kitchen Taylor. Revenue is a classification or type of account. Revenue accounts have various titles such as Sales, Fares Earned, or Fees Earned. Dennis has chosen Fees Earned as the title for The Kitchen Taylor's revenue account.

step 2: Account?   Cash
Classification?   Asset
Effect?   +$1,500

Account?   Fees Earned
Classification?   Revenue   (Owner's Equity)
Effect?   +$1,500   (+$1,500)

step 3:

	Assets							=	Liabilities	+	Owner's Equity		
	Cash	+	Truck	+	Prepaid Ins.	+	Supplies	=	Accounts Payable	+	Dennis Taylor, Capital	+	Fees Earned
Before	2,800	+	6,000	+	1,200	+	425	=	425	+	10,000		
Dec. 7	+1,500												+1,500
After	4,300	+	6,000	+	1,200	+	425	=	425	+	10,000	+	1,500

11,925   11,925

Comment

It should be noted that revenue has a special relationship to owner's equity. **The basic relationship between revenue and owner's equity is that revenue increases total owner's equity.**

$$A = L + OE$$
$$+ R$$

In view of this relationship, whenever revenue is earned, the balance in a specific revenue account increases. That, in turn, means that total owner's equity also increases.

December 10 Transaction

step 1: *The Kitchen Taylor paid $425 to a creditor on account, Check No. 103.*

step 2:

Account?	Cash
Classification?	Asset
Effect?	−$425

Account?	Accounts Payable
Classification?	Liability
Effect?	−$425

> **Comment**
>
> In the December 4 transaction, The Kitchen Taylor made a purchase on account. That promise to pay in the future was recorded as a liability. The Kitchen Taylor is now paying that liability. This is frequently described as making a payment on account.

step 3:

	Assets						=	Liabilities	+	Owner's Equity		
	Cash	+	Truck	+	Prepaid Ins.	+	Supplies	=	Accounts Payable	+	Dennis Taylor, Capital	+	Fees Earned
Before	4,300	+	6,000	+	1,200	+	425	=	425	+	10,000	+	1,500
Dec. 10	−425								−425				
After	3,875	+	6,000	+	1,200	+	425	=	–0–	+	10,000	+	1,500

11,500   11,500

December 15 Transaction

step 1: *The Kitchen Taylor refinished several cabinets, charging the customer $1,400 for the completed work. The customer promised to pay The Kitchen Taylor in the near future.*

> **Comment**
>
> In place of cash, The Kitchen Taylor has received a promise to pay from the customer. This promise has value and is therefore considered to be an asset. More specifically, it is recorded as an increase in an asset account known as *Accounts Receivable*. This type of transaction is frequently referred to as a sale on account.

step 2:

Account?	Fees Earned	
Classification?	Revenue	(Owner's Equity)
Effect?	+$1,400	(+$1,400)

Account?	Accounts Receivable
Classification?	Asset
Effect?	+$1,400

Comment

Notice that revenue has been recorded even though The Kitchen Taylor has not yet been paid. Why? The Kitchen Taylor is on the accrual basis of accounting as described in Chapter 1. This means that revenue must be recorded when it is earned, regardless of whether the cash has been received. We consider the revenue to be earned when the product or service has been provided to the customer.

step 3:

		Assets									=	Liabilities	+	Owner's Equity		
	Cash	+	Truck	+	Prepaid Ins.	+	Supplies	+	Accts. Rec.	=	Accounts Payable	+	Dennis Taylor, Capital	+	Fees Earned
Before Dec. 15	3,875	+	6,000	+	1,200	+	425			=	–0–	+	10,000	+	1,500
									+1,400						+1,400
After	3,875	+	6,000	+	1,200	+	425	+	1,400	=	–0–	+	10,000	+	2,900
					12,900								12,900		

December 17 Transaction

step 1:   **The Kitchen Taylor paid $600 monthly rent for a small office and storage space, Check No. 104.**

Comment

Expenses are costs incurred in the process of earning revenue. Expenses represent a classification or type of account. Examples of specific expense accounts include Rent Expense, Salary Expense, and Utilities Expense.

step 2:   Account?   Cash
            Classification?   Asset
            Effect?   −$600

            Account?   Rent Expense
            Classification?   Expense   (Owner's Equity)
            Effect?   +$600   (−$600)

Comment

It should be noted that expenses, like total revenue, have a special relationship to owner's equity. **Expenses decrease total owner's equity.**

$$A = L + OE$$
$$+ R - E$$

Whenever an expense is incurred, the balance in a specific expense account increases. However, as the expense account balance increases, it causes total owner's equity to decrease.

step 3:

					Assets					=	Liabilities	+	Owner's Equity		
	Cash	+	Truck	+	Prepaid Ins.	+	Supplies	+	Accts. Rec.	=	Accts. Pay.	+	Dennis Taylor, Capital	+ Fees Earned	− Rent Expense
Before Dec. 17	3,875 −600	+	6,000	+	1,200	+	425	+	1,400	=	−0−	+	10,000	+ 2,900	+600
After	3,275	+	6,000	+	1,200	+	425	+	1,400	=	−0−	+	10,000	+ 2,900	− 600
					12,300								12,300		

December 21 Transaction

step 1:   **The Kitchen Taylor received a $500 payment on account from a charge customer.**

> **Comment**
>
> On December 15, The Kitchen Taylor made a sale on account and received a promise to pay from the customer. At that time, the customer's promise was recorded as an account receivable. On December 21, the customer is making good on that promise. This means that, in addition to recording the receipt of cash, we must return to the Accounts Receivable account and record a decrease. Observe that no revenue is recorded in this transaction because the related revenue has already been recorded on December 15.

step 2:   Account?   Cash
Classification?   Asset
Effect?   +$500

Account?   Accounts Receivable
Classification?   Asset
Effect?   −$500

step 3:

					Assets					=	Liabilities	+	Owner's Equity		
	Cash	+	Truck	+	Prepaid Ins.	+	Supplies	+	Accts. Rec.	=	Accts. Pay.	+	Dennis Taylor, Capital	+ Fees Earned	− Rent Expense
Before Dec. 21	3,275 +500	+	6,000	+	1,200	+	425	+	1,400 −500	=	−0−	+	10,000	+ 2,900	− 600
After	3,775	+	6,000	+	1,200	+	425	+	900	=	−0−	+	10,000	+ 2,900	− 600
					12,300								12,300		

December 26 Transaction

step 1:   **A small repair, costing $65, had to be made on the truck. Such routine maintenance and repairs to assets are considered expenses of doing business. The Kitchen Taylor promised to pay for this in the near future.**

step 2:   Account?   Repair Expense
             Classification?   Expense   (Owner's Equity)
             Effect?   +$65   (−$65)

             Account?   Accounts Payable
             Classification?   Liability
             Effect?   +$65

Comment

Observe that The Kitchen Taylor has recorded this expense even though the bill has not been paid. Why? Accrual-basis accounting requires that expenses be recorded when they are incurred, regardless of whether the cash is paid out now or later. An expense has been incurred when a product or service is accepted from someone else.

step 3:

	Assets						=	Liabilities	+		Owner's Equity		
	Cash	+ Truck +	Prepaid Ins.	+ Supplies +	Accts. Rec.	=	Accts. Pay.	+	Dennis Taylor, Capital	+ Fees Earned	− Rent Expense	− Repair Expense
Before Dec. 26	3,775	+ 6,000 +	1,200	+ 425 +	900	=	−0− +65	+	10,000	+ 2,900	− 600	− +65
After	3,775	+ 6,000 +	1,200	+ 425 +	900	=	65	+	10,000	+ 2,900	− 600	− 65
			12,300							12,300		

December 28 Transaction

step 1:   **Dennis withdrew $200 in cash from the business for personal use, Check No. 105.**

Comment

Dennis is the owner of The Kitchen Taylor. He is *not* an employee. Only amounts paid to employees are recorded as salary expense. Since the owner is not an employee, amounts withdrawn by the owner cannot be recorded as salary expense. In fact, amounts withdrawn by the owner for personal use cannot be recorded as any type of expense. Remember, expenses, by definition, are incurred to earn revenue. Withdrawals by the owner for personal use are recorded in a separate account known as a *drawing account*. The drawing account title contains the owner's name followed by a comma and the word *Drawing* (Dennis Taylor, Drawing).

step 2:   Account?   Cash
             Classification?   Asset
             Effect?   −$200

             Account?   Dennis Taylor, Drawing
             Classification?   Drawing   (Owner's Equity)
             Effect?   +$200   (−$200)

> *Comment*
>
> Just as revenue and expense accounts have special relationships to owner's equity, so does the drawing account. **The basic relationship between drawing and owner's equity is that withdrawals by the owner decrease total owner's equity.**
>
> $$A = L + OE$$
> $$+R - E - D$$
>
> Whenever the owner makes a withdrawal for personal use, the balance in the drawing account is increased. However, as the balance in the drawing account increases, it causes total owner's equity to decrease.

step 3:

	Assets					= Liabilities	+	Owner's Equity				
	Cash + Truck +	Prepaid Ins. +	Supplies +	Accts. Rec. =	Accts. Pay. +	Dennis Taylor, Capital −	Dennis Taylor, Draw. +	Fees Earn. −	Rent Exp. −	Repair Exp.		
Before	3,775 + 6,000 +	1,200 +	425 +	900 =	65 +	10,000		+ 2,900 −	600 −	65		
Dec. 28	−200						+200					
After	3,575 + 6,000 +	1,200 +	425 +	900 =	65 +	10,000 −	200 +	2,900 −	600 −	65		

12,100   12,100

December 29 Transaction

step 1: **The Kitchen Taylor paid a utility bill, $80, Check No. 106.**

step 2:

Account?	Cash
Classification?	Asset
Effect?	−$80

Account?	Utilities Expense	
Classification?	Expense	(Owner's Equity)
Effect?	+$80	(−$80)

step 3:

	Assets					= Liabilities	+	Owner's Equity				
	Cash + Truck +	Prepaid Ins. +	Supplies +	Accts. Rec. =	Accts. Pay. +	Dennis Taylor, Capital −	Dennis Taylor, Draw. +	Fees Earn. −	Rent Exp. −	Repair Exp. −	Util. Exp.	
Before	3,575 + 6,000 +	1,200 +	425 +	900 =	65 +	10,000 −	200 +	2,900 −	600 −	65		
Dec. 29	−80										+80	
After	3,495 + 6,000 +	1,200 +	425 +	900 =	65 +	10,000 −	200 +	2,900 −	600 −	65 −	80	

12,020   12,020

December 30 Transaction

step 1: **The Kitchen Taylor received a $300 payment on account from a charge customer.**

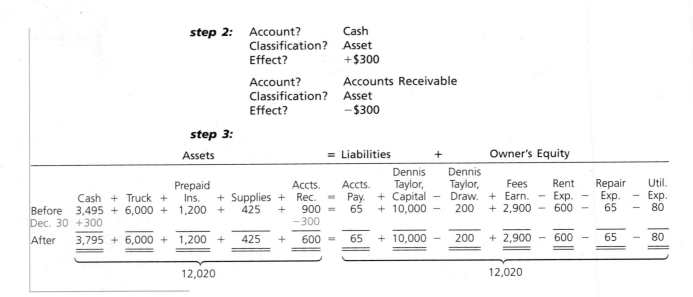

step 2:

Account?	Cash
Classification?	Asset
Effect?	+$300
Account?	Accounts Receivable
Classification?	Asset
Effect?	−$300

step 3:

	Assets					=	Liabilities	+		Owner's Equity				
	Cash +	Truck +	Prepaid Ins. +	Supplies +	Accts. Rec.	=	Accts. Pay. +	Dennis Taylor, Capital −	Dennis Taylor, Draw. +	Fees Earn. −	Rent Exp. −	Repair Exp. −	Util. Exp.	
Before	3,495 +	6,000 +	1,200 +	425 +	900	=	65 +	10,000 −	200 +	2,900 −	600 −	65 −	80	
Dec. 30	+300				−300									
After	3,795 +	6,000 +	1,200 +	425 +	600	=	65 +	10,000 −	200 +	2,900 −	600 −	65 −	80	

12,020   12,020

Summary of December Transactions

Figure 2.1 summarizes our analyses of the December 1 through 30 transactions and their effect on the accounting equation. Use this summary to review each transaction by briefly describing the event being recorded in each transaction. When necessary, return to the explanation given earlier in the chapter to refresh your memory.

Figure 2.1

	Assets				=	Liabilities +	Owner's Equity					
	Cash +	Truck +	Prepd. Ins. +	Sup. +	Accts. Rec. =	Accts. Pay. +	Dennis Taylor, Capital −	Dennis Taylor, Draw. +	Fees Earned −	Rent Exp. −	Repair Exp. −	Util. Exp.
Bal. 12/1	−0− 10,000				= −0−	−0−	10,000					
Bal. 12/2	10,000 −6,000	+6,000			= −0−		10,000					
Bal. 12/3	4,000 −1,200	6,000	+1,200		= −0−		10,000					
Bal. 12/4	2,800	6,000	1,200	+425	= −0−	+425	10,000					
Bal. 12/7	2,800 +1,500	6,000	1,200	425	= 425		10,000		+1,500			
Bal. 12/10	4,300 −425	6,000	1,200	425	= 425	−425	10,000		1,500			
Bal. 12/15	3,875	6,000	1,200	425	= −0−	+1,400	10,000		1,500 +1,400			
Bal. 12/17	3,875 −600	6,000	1,200	425	1,400 = −0−		10,000		2,900	+600		
Bal. 12/21	3,275 +500	6,000	1,200	425	1,400 = −0− −500		10,000		2,900	600		
Bal. 12/26	3,775	6,000	1,200	425	900 = −0− +65		10,000		2,900	600		+65

Figure 2.1 *(concluded)*

	Assets					=	Liabilities +	Owner's Equity					
	Cash +	Truck +	Prepd. Ins. +	Sup. +	Accts. Rec. =	Accts. Pay. +	Dennis Taylor, Capital −	Dennis Taylor, Draw. +	Fees Earned −	Rent Exp. −	Repair Exp. −	Util. Exp.
Bal. 12/28	3,775 −200	6,000	1,200	425	900 =	65	10,000	+200	2,900	600	65	
Bal. 12/29	3,575 −80	6,000	1,200	425	900 =	65	10,000	200	2,900	600	65	+80
Bal. 12/30	3,495 +300	6,000	1,200	425	900 = −300	65	10,000	200	2,900	600	65	80
Bal.	3,795 +	6,000 +	1,200 +	425 +	600 =	65 +	10,000 −	200 +	2,900 −	600 −	65 −	80

Cash	$ 3,795		Accounts Payable	$ 65
Truck	6,000		Dennis Taylor, Capital.	10,000
Prepaid Insurance	1,200		Dennis Taylor, Drawing.	−200
Supplies	425		Fees Earned	2,900
Accounts Receivable . .	600		Rent Expense	−600
			Repair Expense	−65
			Utilities Expense	−80
			Total Liabilities and	
Total Assets.	$12,020		Owner's Equity	$12,020

Financial Statements

One of the basic functions of accounting is to summarize financial data. Day to day, we analyze, classify, and record transactions as they occur. Periodically (usually monthly or yearly), those data must be summarized in a format that is more helpful to users of financial data such as owners, creditors, or government agencies. Financial statements provide that format.

objective 3
Describe the purpose and content of the three basic financial statements

In this text, we will use Peachtree Accounting for Windows to prepare three basic financial statements:

1. Income statement
2. Balance sheet
3. Statement of cash flow

As a group, these statements present a financial picture of the business. It is important to understand that no single statement presents the whole picture. Each statement presents only a part of the total picture.

Figures 2.2, 2.3, and 2.4 show The Kitchen Taylor's financial statements for its first month of operations. Remember that these statements summarize the data recorded in the December transactions. The summary of the December 1 through 30 transactions, shown in Figure 2.1, provides the information necessary to prepare The Kitchen Taylor's financial statements. Observe the relationship between the column totals shown at the bottom of Figure 2.1 and the account balances shown on the financial statements in Figures 2.2, 2.3, and 2.4.

In this chapter, you will study the purpose and content of each statement and their interrelationships. In a later chapter, you will learn how to prepare financial statements using Peachtree.

Income Statement

The purpose of the income statement is to compute net income or loss for a specified period of time. Only revenue and expense accounts are displayed on the income statement. Net income is computed by subtracting total expenses from total revenues. An excess of expenses over revenues results in a net loss.

Peachtree was used to print out the income statement shown in Figure 2.2. Observe that the date line on the income statement reflects a period of time, usually a month or year. Since net income is a summary figure representing a combination of revenue earned and expenses incurred over a period of time, it is important that the date line reflect the period of time covered by the statement. It would be impossible, for example, to draw any valid conclusions about net income being "good" or "bad" without knowing whether the income statement reflected results for a month or a year.

If the reporting period is a month, Peachtree automatically prints out figures for the current month and also cumulative figures for the year to date. Because The Kitchen Taylor has only been in business for one month, the current month and year-to-date figures shown in Figure 2.2 are the same.

In addition to dollar figures, you will observe that the income statement also includes percentage of revenue columns for both the current month and the year to date. The percentages shown for each expense, total expenses, and net income indicate the relationship of each item to total revenues. For example, in the current month column, we can easily see that total expenses represent 25.69 percent of total revenues.

$$\frac{\$745}{\$2,900} = .2569 = 25.69\%$$

Peachtree automatically makes these computations and prints them out on every income statement. This information is very useful in analyzing relationships between revenues and expenses and in making comparisons between different time periods and even different companies.

Figure 2.2

The Kitchen Taylor
Income Statement
For the Twelve Months Ending December 31, 1995

	Current Month		Year to Date	
Revenues				
Fees Earned	2,900.00	100.00	2,900.00	100.00
Total Revenues	2,900.00	100.00	2,900.00	100.00
Expenses				
Rent Expense	600.00	20.69	600.00	20.69
Repair Expense	65.00	2.24	65.00	2.24
Utilities Expense	80.00	2.76	80.00	2.76
Total Expenses	745.00	25.69	745.00	25.69
Net Income	$ 2,155.00	74.31	$ 2,155.00	74.31

Balance Sheet

As its name implies, the balance sheet proves that the accounting equation is in balance as of a specified date. Because of this, the date line on the balance sheet indicates a specific day, not a period of time.

Only asset, liability, and owner's equity accounts are shown on this statement. As you will recall, the terms capital and owner's equity mean the same thing. Both terms are commonly used in financial statements. Referring to The Kitchen Taylor's balance sheet shown in Figure 2.3, you will observe that Peachtree uses the term capital.

Peachtree lists two categories of assets on the balance sheet as well as total assets. Assets that The Kitchen Taylor will use up within a year are called current assets. Assets that last longer than a year are listed under property and equipment.

Figure 2.3

The Kitchen Taylor
Balance Sheet
December 31, 1995

ASSETS

Current Assets		
Cash	$ 3,795.00	
Accounts Receivable	600.00	
Supplies	425.00	
Prepaid Insurance	1,200.00	
Total Current Assets		6,020.00
Property and Equipment		
Truck	6,000.00	
Total Property and Equipment		6,000.00
Total Assets		$ 12,020.00

LIABILITIES AND CAPITAL

Current Liabilities		
Accounts Payable	$ 65.00	
Total Current Liabilities		65.00
Long-Term Liabilities		
Total Long-Term Liabilities		0.00
Total Liabilities		65.00
Capital		
Dennis Taylor, Capital	10,000.00	
Dennis Taylor, Drawing	<200.00>	
Net Income	2,155.00	
Total Capital		11,955.00
Total Liabilities & Capital		$ 12,020.00

Under liabilities, Peachtree lists two categories as well as total liabilities. Current liabilities are those due within a year. Long-term liabilities are due beyond one year.

The last section shown on the balance sheet is capital or owner's equity. If the balance sheet is going to balance, the capital section must be brought up to date. As you will recall, revenue, expense, and drawing transactions have an effect on total capital but are recorded daily in separate accounts. In Figure 2.3, capital is updated for these transactions. Since revenues and expenses are combined on the income statement to compute net income (loss), it is convenient to use this composite figure on the balance sheet. In summary, the capital or owner's equity section of the balance sheet must be updated for the following items:

+   Net income
−   Net loss
−   Drawing

Comment

In manual accounting systems, there is a fourth financial statement known as the statement of owner's equity. It is prepared after the income statement but before the balance sheet. The purpose of the statement of owner's equity is to update the owner's capital account for net income or loss and withdrawals by the owner.

Beginning capital account balance
+ Net income (or minus net loss)
− Withdrawals by the owner
Ending capital account balance

The up-to-date capital account balance is then displayed as a single figure on the balance sheet. In Peachtree Accounting for Windows, however, a statement of owner's equity is *not* prepared because PAW updates capital for these items within the capital section of the balance sheet.

Statement of Cash Flow

The statement of cash flow describes the flow of cash in and out of the business during a specific period of time. It provides the answers to three important questions:

1. From where did cash receipts come?
2. For what were cash payments used?
3. What was the overall change in cash?

As you already know, The Kitchen Taylor uses the accrual basis of accounting. Under the accrual basis, revenue is recorded when it is earned and expenses are recorded when they are incurred, regardless of whether the cash has been received or paid. Over the long run, the accrual basis is generally the most useful way to measure revenues and expenses. Over the short run, however, The Kitchen Taylor must have sufficient cash to pay its bills as they come due.

When the accrual basis of accounting is used, the balance sheet and income statement provide very little information about the flow of cash. It is possible that The Kitchen Taylor might have net income but could be short of cash, or have a net loss and have excess cash. Therefore, the information provided by the statement of cash flow is extremely useful to Dennis Taylor.

Referring to Figure 2.4, you will observe that Peachtree automatically separates The Kitchen Taylor's cash flows (both receipts and payments) into three basic groups: operating activities, investing activities, and financing activities. You will study these activities in more detail in a later chapter.

Figure 2.4

The Kitchen Taylor
Statement of Cash Flow
For the twelve Months Ended December 31, 1995

	Current Month	Year to Date
Cash Flows from operating activities		
Net Income	$ 2,155.00	$ 2,155.00
Adjustments to reconcile net income to net cash provided by operating activities		
Accounts Receivable	<600.00>	<600.00>
Supplies	<425.00>	<425.00>
Prepaid Insurance	<1,200.00>	<1,200.00>
Accounts Payable	65.00	65.00
Total Adjustments	<2,160.00>	<2,160.00>
Net Cash provided by Operations	<5.00>	<5.00>
Cash Flows from investing activities		
Used For		
Truck	<6,000.00>	<6,000.00>
Net cash used in investing	<6,000.00>	<6,000.00>
Cash Flows from financing activities		
Proceeds From		
Dennis Taylor, Capital	10,000.00	10,000.00
Dennis Taylor, Drawing	0.00	0.00
Used For		
Dennis Taylor, Capital	0.00	0.00
Dennis Taylor, Drawing	<200.00>	<200.00>
Net cash used in financing	9,800.00	9,800.00
Net increase <decrease> in cash	$ 3,795.00	$ 3,795.00
Summary		
Cash Balance at End of Period	$ 3,795.00	$ 3,795.00
Cash Balance at Beginning of Period	0.00	0.00
Net Increase <Decrease> in Cash	$ 3,795.00	$ 3,795.00

Interrelationship of the Financial Statements

objective 4
Describe how the three basic
financial statement are related

Observe that the three financial statements shown in Figures 2.2, 2.3, and 2.4 are separate but related. The year-to-date net income figure ($2,155) is taken from the income statement and used on the balance sheet to update the capital section. The Cash account balance ($3,795) shown on the balance sheet is explained in detail on the statement of cash flow using information from both the income statement and the balance sheet.

As mentioned earlier, it is important to remember that no single statement tells the whole story. For example, the income statement indicates how much revenue a business has earned during a specific period of time, but it says nothing about how much of that amount has or has not been received in cash. For information about cash and accounts receivable, we have to look at the balance sheet and statement of cash flow.

Chapter Two Summary

The basic accounting equation is the framework in which all business transactions are analyzed.

Assets = Liabilities + Owner's Equity

This equation must always be kept in balance. The total of everything on the left side of the equation must always equal the total of everything on the right side of the equation.

In analyzing each transaction, we should:

step 1:   Read and think carefully before writing.

step 2:   Identify accounts, classifications, and effect (+ or −).

step 3:   Check the accounting equation for balance.

Day to day, we analyze, classify, and record transactions as they occur. Periodically, these accumulated data are summarized in the form of financial statements: income statement, balance sheet, and statement of cash flow. The purpose of each statement may be summarized as follows:

Statement	Purpose
Income statement	Computes net income. (Revenue − Expense = Net income or loss)
Balance sheet	Proves that the accounting equation is in balance.
Statement of cash flow	Describes the flow of cash in and out of the business.

As a group, financial statements present a financial picture of the business. Individual statements present only a part of the total picture.

The following chart illustrates the flow of data through the business:

In Chapter 3, you will learn to use debits and credits to record increases and decreases in the accounts.

Demonstration Problem

On January 1, 1995, Barb Hoagland started a pet-grooming business, Pampered Pets. Transactions for the first month of operations were as follows:

   a. Barb invested cash in the business, $20,000.

   b. Paid for equipment, $8,000.

   c. Purchased supplies on account, $900.

   d. Performed grooming services for cash, $1,500.

   e. Paid a creditor on account, $300.

   f. Performed grooming services for a customer who promised to pay in the near future, $200.

   g. Paid monthly rent for office and store space, $800.

   h. Received payment on account from a charge customer, $100.

   i. Paid for a small repair to equipment, $50.

   j. Barb withdrew cash from the business for personal use, $500.

   k. Paid utility bill, $100.

Instructions

Analyze the preceding transactions by identifying the following for each transaction:

   1. Accounts.

   2. Classifications.

   3. Effect.

Solution to Demonstration Problem

Transaction	Account	Classification	Effect
a	Cash Barb Hoagland, Capital	Asset Owner's Equity	+$20,000 +$20,000
b	Cash Equipment	Asset Asset	−$ 8,000 +$ 8,000
c	Supplies Accounts Payable	Asset Liability	+$ 900 +$ 900
d	Fees Earned Cash	Revenue (Owner's Equity) Asset	+$ 1,500 (+$1,500) +$ 1,500
e	Cash Accounts Payable	Asset Liability	−$ 300 −$ 300
f	Fees Earned Accounts Receivable	Revenue (Owner's Equity) Asset	+$ 200 (+$200) +$ 200
g	Cash Rent Expense	Asset Expense (Owner's Equity)	−$ 800 +$ 800 (−$800)
h	Cash Accounts Receivable	Asset Asset	+$ 100 −$ 100
i	Repair Expense Cash	Expense (Owner's Equity) Asset	+$ 50 (−$50) −$ 50

j	Barb Hoagland,
	  Drawing
	Cash
		Drawing
		  (Owner's Equity)
		Asset
			+$ 500 (−$500)
			
			−$ 500

k	Utilities Expense Cash	Expense (Owner's Equity) Asset	+$ 100 (−$100) −$ 100

Glossary

account   A record used to record increases and decreases within each component of the accounting equation.   *16*

accounting equation   The framework in which all business transactions are analyzed.   *16*

$$\text{Assets} = \text{Liabilities} + \text{Owner's Equity}$$

accrual-basis accounting   A system of recording financial information that requires revenues to be recorded when they are earned (product or service provided) and expenses to be recorded when they are incurred (product or service accepted), regardless of whether cash has been received or paid.   *22, 24*

assets   Things of value owned by a business.   *16*

business transaction   An economic event that can be measured in dollars and that affects the financial condition of a business.   *16*

capital   The net worth of a business (assets minus liabilities); defines the owner's rights to assets. Also known as owner's equity.   *16*

cash   An asset; includes coin, currency, and checks.   *17*

creditor   A person or company to whom a debt is owed.   *16*

expenses Costs incurred in the process of earning revenue. *22*

liabilities Amounts owed to creditors; debts. *16*

net income The excess of revenues over expenses. *28*

net loss The excess of expenses over revenues. *28*

owner's equity The net worth of a business (assets minus liabilities); defines the owner's rights to business assets. Also known as *capital.* *16*

paid Indicates an outflow of cash. *18*

payment on account Paying for something previously purchased with a promise to pay in the future. *21*

purchase on account Buying something with a promise to pay in the future. *19*

revenue The amount that a business charges a customer for a service performed or a product provided. *20*

sale on account The provision of a product or service to a customer in exchange for the customer's promise to pay in the future. *21*

Self-Test

Select the best answer.

1. The accounting equation is the framework in which
   a. only revenue transactions are analyzed.
   b. only expense transactions are analyzed.
   c. only owner's equity transactions are analyzed.
   d. all business transactions are analyzed.

2. A sale on account increases
   a. revenue and increases assets.
   b. revenue and increases liabilities.
   c. assets and decreases owner's equity.
   d. assets and decreases liabilities.

3. The purchase of an asset for cash
   a. increases assets and increases owner's equity.
   b. has no effect on total assets.
   c. increases expenses and decreases assets.
   d. increases assets and decreases liabilities.

4. Revenue and expense account balances are displayed on the
   a. income statement.
   b. statement of cash flow.
   c. balance sheet.
   d. All of the above.

5. Asset and liability account balances are displayed on the
   a. income statement.
   b. statement of cash flow only.
   c. the balance sheet.
   d. All of the above.

Answers to the self-test can be found after the cases at the end of this chapter.

Questions for Discussion

1. What is the definition of each of the following five types of accounts: asset, liability, owner's equity, revenue, and expense?

2. How does the right side of the accounting equation express who has rights to the assets of a business?

3. What three questions must be answered when analyzing a business transaction within the framework of the accounting equation?

4. *a.* Which liability account is used to record a purchase on account?
   b. Which asset account is used to record a sale on account?

5. Why are withdrawals by the owner of a business not recorded as salary expense?

6. What three types of accounts have a special relationship to owner's equity?

7. What are the three basic financial statements and the purpose of each?

8. How are the three basic financial statements related to one another?

Exercises

Exercise 2.1

Complete Accounting Equation
L.O. 1

Use the accounting equation to solve the following:

Company 1:	A = $170,000	L = $66,000	OE = ?
Company 2:	A = $46,000	L = ?	OE = $30,000
Company 3:	A = ?	L = $68,000	OE = $126,000

Exercise 2.2

Provide Missing Number
L.O. 1

Solve the following:

a. Company A owns assets totaling $144,000 and owes $68,000 to creditors. What is its owner's equity?

b. Company B has owner's equity of $106,000 and assets totaling $180,000. How much do liabilities total?

c. During the month, Company C's assets increased by $56,000 while liabilities decreased by $4,000. What is the change in owner's equity?

Exercise 2.3

Calculate Year-End Liabilities
L.O. 1

Valdez Company begins 1995 with assets totaling $280,000 and liabilities totaling $170,000. During 1995 assets decreased by $40,000 while owner's equity decreased by $30,000. What is the amount of Valdez's total liabilities at the end of 1995?

Exercise 2.4

Classify Accounts
L.O. 2

Classify the following accounts. Use the letter codes given.

A = Asset   L = Liability   O = Owner's equity   R = Revenue   E = Expense

1. Accounts Receivable
2. Equipment
3. Truck
4. Accounts Payable
5. Prepaid Insurance

6. Rent Expense
7. Fees Earned
8. Supplies
9. S. Martin, Capital
10. Cash

Exercise 2.5

Indicate whether the following accounts appear on the income statement or the balance sheet. Use the following abbreviations.

Income Statement or Balance Sheet Account
L.O. 3

I = Income Statement   B = Balance Sheet

1. Supplies
2. Fees Earned
3. Susan King, Capital
4. Accounts Receivable
5. Repair Expense
6. Accounts Payable
7. Building
8. Utilities Expense
9. Truck
10. Cash

Exercise 2.6

The following transactions are for Wang's Print Shop:

Transaction Analysis
L.O. 1, 2

1. Received cash for printing services performed.
2. Purchased supplies on account.
3. Performed printing services for customers on account.
4. Paid for minor repair to printing equipment.
5. Made a payment on account to a creditor.
6. Received a payment on account from a charge customer.
7. Mary Wang, the owner, withdrew cash from the business for personal use.
8. Paid utility bill.

Indicate the effect of each transaction on the accounting equation by selecting A, B, C, D, or E:

A. Increases assets, increases liabilities.
B. Increases assets, increases owner's equity.
C. Increases one asset, decreases another asset.
D. Decreases assets, decreases liabilities.
E. Decreases assets, decreases owner's equity.

Exercise 2.7

Indicate the effect of each of the following transactions on total assets, total liabilities, and owner's equity using the chart format given. The transactions will increase (+), decrease (−), or have no effect (NE) on each of the account classifications.

Transaction Analysis
L.O. 1, 2

Transaction	Total Assets	Total Liabilities	Owner's Equity
1. Performed services on account.			
2. Purchased equipment for cash.			
3. Purchased supplies on account.			
4. Received payment on account.			
5. Paid creditor on account.			
6. Paid employees' salaries.			
7. Paid 12-month insurance premium.			
8. Owner withdrew cash for personal use.			

Problems—Set A

Problem 2.1A

Transaction Analysis
L.O. 1, 2

On January 1, 1995, Sarah Jackson started a small service business known as Jackson Accounting Services. Transactions for the first month of operations were as follows:

1. Sarah invested cash in the business, $20,000.
2. Paid cash for equipment, $12,000.
3. Purchased supplies on account, $800.
4. Performed accounting services for cash, $600.
5. Paid a creditor on account, $400.
6. Performed accounting services for a customer who promised to pay in the near future, $500.
7. Paid monthly rent for office space, $750.
8. Received a payment on account from a charge customer, $250.
9. Paid for a small repair to equipment, $60.
10. Sarah withdrew cash from the business for personal use, $375.
11. Paid 12-month insurance premium, $1,200.

Instructions

Analyze the preceding transactions by identifying the following for each transaction:

a. Accounts. Name the specific accounts involved in each transaction.

b. Classifications. Classify each account (asset, liability, owner's equity, revenue, expense, or drawing).

c. Effect. Determine the effect (+ or −) on each account.

Problem 2.2A

Accounting Equation;
Transaction Analysis
L.O. 1, 2

On June 1, 1995, Michael Parker started a data processing business known as Parker Data Services. Transactions for the first month of operations were as follows:

1. Michael invested cash in the business, $10,000.
2. Purchased supplies on account, $400.
3. Paid cash for equipment, $6,000.
4. Performed services for cash, $500.

5. Paid a creditor on account, $200.

6. Performed services for a customer who promised to pay in the near future, $700.

7. Paid monthly rent for office space, $800.

8. Paid for a small repair to equipment, $50.

9. Received a payment on account from a charge customer, $350.

10. Michael withdrew cash from the business for personal use, $275.

11. Paid utility bill, $90.

Instructions

Record transactions 1 through 11 in columnar form using the following format. To verify that the accounting equation is in balance after each transaction, be sure to subtotal each column after every transaction.

	Assets			= Liabilities	+	Owner's Equity					
Trans. No.	Cash +	Accounts Receivable +	Supplies +	Equipment =	Accounts Payable +	Parker, Capital −	Parker, Draw. +	Fees Earned −	Rent Exp. −	Rep. Exp. −	Utilities Exp.

Problem 2.3A

The following accounts and balances appear on the books of Colombo Associates on December 31, 1995:

Financial Statements
L.O. 3, 4

Accounts Payable	$ 8,000
Office Furniture	6,000
Catherine Colombo, Capital	26,850
Commissions Earned	39,000
Salary Expense	12,000
Cash	14,000
Rent Expense	3,000
Accounts Receivable	12,700
Office Supplies	650
Utilities Expense	1,500
Equipment	9,000
Catherine Colombo, Drawing	15,000

Instructions

Compute the following:

1. Net income or loss

2. Total assets

3. Total liabilities

4. Total capital

5. Total liabilities and capital

Problem 2.4A

Ron Novak opened Ron's TV Repairs, a sole proprietorship, on July 1, 1995. Business transactions for the first month of operations were as follows:

Accounting Equation;
Transaction Analysis; Financial
Statements
L.O. 1–4

1. Ron transferred cash from his personal savings account to the company checking account, $10,000.

2. Purchased equipment on account, $3,500.

3. Purchased supplies for cash, $500.

4. Performed repair services for customers on account, $1,200.

5. Paid for a small repair to equipment, $90.

6. Paid cash for a used delivery truck, $5,000.

7. Paid monthly rent, $900.

8. Received payment on account from a charge customer, $325.

9. Paid employee's salaries, $800.

10. Performed repair services for cash, $1,400.

11. Paid 24-month insurance premium, $360.

12. Ron withdrew cash from the business for personal use, $200.

Instructions

1. Record transactions *1* through *12* in columnar form using the following format. Be sure to subtotal after each transaction.

Assets						= Liabilities	+	Owner's Equity				
Trans. No.	Accts.		Ppd.			Accts.	Novak,	Novak,	Fees	Rent	Rep.	Sal.
Cash + Rec.	+ Supplies	+ Ins.	+ Truck	+ Equip.	= Pay.	+ Capital	− Draw.	+ Earned	− Exp.	− Exp.	− Exp.

2. Compute the following:
   a. Net income or loss
   b. Total assets
   c. Total liabilities
   d. Total capital
   e. Total liabilities and capital

Problems—Set B

Problem 2.1B

Transaction Analysis
L.O. 1, 2

On January 1, 1995, Carol Carter started a data processing business known as Carter Data Services. Transactions for the first month of operations were as follows:

1. Carol invested cash in the business, $15,000.

2. Paid cash for equipment, $6,000.

3. Purchased supplies on account, $350.

4. Performed processing services for cash, $400.

5. Paid a creditor on account, $200.

6. Performed processing services for a customer who promised to pay in the near future, $500.

7. Paid monthly rent for office space, $700.

8. Received a payment on account from a charge customer, $250.

9. Paid for a small repair to equipment, $70.

10. Carol withdrew cash from the business for personal use, $300.

11. Paid 12-month insurance premium, $420.

Instructions

Analyze the preceding transactions by identifying the following for each transaction:

a. Accounts. Name the specific accounts involved in each transaction.

b. Classifications. Classify each account (asset, liability, owner's equity, revenue, expense, or drawing).

c. Effect. Determine the effect (+ or −) on each account.

Problem 2.2B

Record Transactions 1 through 11 from Problem 2.1B in columnar form using the following format. To verify that the accounting equation is in balance after each transaction, be sure to subtotal each column after every transaction.

Accounting Equation;
Transaction Analysis
L.O. 1, 2

			Assets				= Liabilities	+		Owner's Equity			
Trans. No.	Cash +	Accounts Receivable +	Supplies +	Ppd. Ins. +	Equip. =	Accounts Payable +	Carol Carter, Cap. −	Carol Carter, Draw. +	Fees Earned −	Rent Exp. −	Rep. Exp.

Problem 2.3B

The following accounts and balances appear on the books of Corona Advertising Agency on December 31, 1995:

Financial Statements
L.O. 3, 4

Accounts Payable	$12,300
Office Furniture	5,200
Fees Earned.	30,000
Salary Expense	9,000
Jose Corona, Capital	23,900
Cash	12,000
Rent Expense.	6,000
Accounts Receivable	11,200
Office Supplies.	600
Utilities Expense	1,200
Equipment	7,500
Jose Corona, Drawing	13,500

Instructions

Compute the following:

1. Net income or loss
2. Total assets
3. Total liabilities
4. Total capital
5. Total liabilities and capital

Problem 2.4B

Wanda Grabow opened Grabow Interiors, a sole proprietorship, on July 1, 1995. Business transactions for the first month of operations were as follows:

Accounting Equation;
Transaction Analysis; Financial Statements
L.O. 1–4

1. Wanda transferred cash from her personal savings account to the company checking account, $20,000.
2. Purchased equipment on account, $7,000.
3. Purchased supplies for cash, $1,000.
4. Performed decorating services for customers on account, $1,000.
5. Paid for a small repair to equipment, $140.

6. Paid cash for a delivery truck, $10,000.

7. Paid monthly rent, $900.

8. Received payment on account from a charge customer, $400.

9. Paid employees' salaries, $500.

10. Performed decorating services for cash, $300.

11. Paid utility bill, $160.

12. Wanda withdrew cash from the business for personal use, $1,200.

Instructions

1. Record transactions *1* through *12* in columnar form using the following format.

		Assets				= Liabilities	+		Owner's Equity					
Trans. No.	Cash +	Accounts Receivable +	Supp. +	Truck +	Equip. =	Accounts Payable =	Grabow, Cap. +	Grabow, Draw. -	Fees Earned +	Rent Exp. -	Rep. Exp. -	Utilities Exp. -	Sal. Exp. -

2. Compute the following:
   a. Net income or loss
   b. Total assets
   c. Total liabilities
   d. Total capital
   e. Total liabilities and capital

Mini-Cases

Case 2–1

Hampton Painting and Decorating has earned more revenue this year than last. However, this year's net income is lower than last year's. Mark Hampton, the owner, does not understand how this could be possible. How would you explain this situation to him?

Case 2–2

Each month Hilda Wasser, owner of Hilda's Hair Boutique, withdraws $1,000 for personal use. She records these withdrawals as salary expense. As Hilda's new accountant, how would you respond to this situation?

Case 2–3

You are the accountant for Lamb Real Estate. Gary Lamb, the owner, observes that you have recorded some unpaid bills as expenses for this year. He questions recording these items as expenses since no cash has been paid out. Explain this situation to Gary.

A Case of Ethics

Your neighbor, Charles, recently bought his wife a new car for her birthday. While showing you the car, Charles indicated that he had purchased it in the name of his business and planned to charge all the gas, insurance, and other related expenses to the business. "It's one of the 'perks' of owning your own business," says Charles. Comment.

Answers to Self-Test

1. *d*   2. *a*   3. *b*   4. *a*   5. *c*

Analyzing Transactions
Debits and Credits

LEARNING OBJECTIVES

After studying this chapter, you should be able to:

1. Work with T-accounts.

2. Use debits and credits to record increases and decreases.

3. Analyze transactions using debits and credits.

4. Prepare a data entry sheet.

chapter 3

In the last chapter, you learned to analyze transactions within the framework of the accounting equation. In Chapter 3, you will study debits and credits, which are a simple extension of that process of analysis. First you will be introduced to T-accounts. Next, you will study debits and credits. Then, returning to The Kitchen Taylor, you will learn to record transactions on a data entry sheet and in T-accounts using debits and credits.

The T-Account

objective 1
Work with T-accounts

In Chapter 2, you learned to record increases and decreases in The Kitchen Taylor's accounts. In this chapter, you will learn to record those increases and decreases using debits and credits. However, in order to understand debits and credits, you must first learn about T-accounts. An example of a T-account is shown below. In view of its "T" shape, its name seems appropriate.

Account Title	
Debit (Dr.)	Credit (Cr.)

Observe that the left side of the T-account is always the debit side and the right side is always the credit side. This never changes regardless of the type of account. Although arbitrary, this is a rule observed by all accountants, just like the rule of stopping for red and advancing on green lights is observed by all drivers.

The balance in a T-account is computed as follows:

step 1: **Total the debit amounts.**

step 2: **Total the credit amounts.**

step 3: **Subtract the smaller total from the larger total. The difference is called the balance.**

step 4: **The balance is written on the side of the account with the larger total.**

For practice, let's compute the balance in the following T-account:

	Account Title	
	Debit	Credit
	500	350
	1,200	500
	125	**850** (step 2)
(step 1)	**1,825**	
(steps 3 and 4)	**975**	

In this example, the credit total ($850) is smaller and is subtracted from the debit total ($1,825), resulting in a debit balance of ($975). Totals are written in small pencil figures known as footings.

Now that you know about T-accounts, we are ready to study debits and credits. Keep in mind, though, that a T-account is just a rough draft version of the formal account that you will study in Chapter 4.

Debits and Credits

In the previous chapter, you analyzed transactions by identifying accounts, classifying those accounts, and deciding the effect in terms of increases and decreases. Debits and credits are simply the tools accountants use to record those increases and decreases in the accounts.

objective 2
Use debits and credits to record increases and decreases

Debits may be used to both increase and decrease account balances. Credits may also be used to both increase and decrease account balances. So how do you know which to use? Usage is determined by account classifications and the accounting equation.

To demonstrate, let's set up a T-account for each account classification. Each T-account represents the way that all the individual accounts within each classification function.

Assets		=	Liabilities		+	Owner's Equity	
Dr.	Cr.		Dr.	Cr.		Dr.	Cr.
+	−		−	+		−	+

Observe that assets appear on the *left* side of the equation. Assets are increased with debits, which are always recorded on the *left* side of a T-account. To decrease asset accounts, we credit—the only remaining possibility.

Observe that liabilities and owner's equity both appear on the *right* side of the equation. Both are increased with credits, which are always recorded on the *right* side of a T-account. To decrease liability and owner's equity accounts, we debit—the only remaining possibility.

You learned in Chapter 2 that revenue, expense, and drawing accounts have special relationships to total owner's equity, also known as *total capital.* Let's review those relationships.

- Revenue increases total owner's equity.
- Expenses decrease total owner's equity.
- Withdrawals for personal use decrease total owner's equity.

Revenue accounts are increased with credits and decreased with debits based on the relationship of revenue to total owner's equity.

1. Revenue increases total owner's equity.
2. Credits increase total owner's equity.
3. Therefore, as the balance on the credit side of a revenue account increases, this credit indirectly increases total owner's equity.

Owner's Equity	
Dr.	Cr.
−	+

Revenue	
Dr.	Cr.
−	+

Expense accounts are increased with debits and decreased with credits based on the relationship of expenses to total owner's equity.

1. Expenses decrease total owner's equity.

2. Debits decrease total owner's equity.

3. Therefore, as the balance on the debit side of an expense account increases, this debit indirectly decreases total owner's equity.

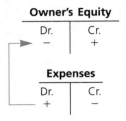

Drawing accounts are increased with debits and decreased with credits based on the relationship of drawing to total owner's equity.

1. Withdrawals by the owner for personal use decrease total owner's equity.

2. Debits decrease total owner's equity.

3. Therefore, as the balance on the debit side of the drawing account increases, this debit indirectly decreases total owner's equity.

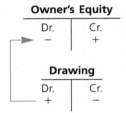

Debit and Credit Review

The rules of debit and credit are summarized in the following chart. Use it to review the debit and credit relationships described earlier in this chapter.

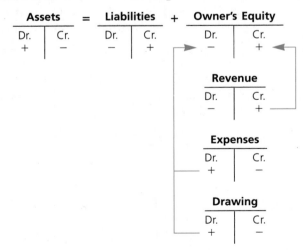

Normal Balances

Accountants frequently use the term *normal balance*. The normal balance side of an account is simply the side on which increases are recorded.

Classification	Normal Balance
Asset	Debit
Liability	Credit
Owner's Equity	Credit
Revenue	Credit
Expenses	Debit
Drawing	Debit

It is possible for an account to have a balance on its decrease side. Such abnormal balances, however, are relatively infrequent and usually of short duration.

Chart of Accounts

The Kitchen Taylor's **chart of accounts** is shown in Figure 3.1. In Chapter 4, you will use Peachtree Accounting for Windows to print out this chart of accounts.

Figure 3.1

The Kitchen Taylor
Chart of Accounts
As of Dec. 31, 1995

Account ID	Account Description	Active?	Account Type
110	Cash	Yes	Cash
111	Accounts Receivable	Yes	Accounts Receivable
112	Supplies	Yes	Inventory
113	Prepaid Insurance	Yes	Other Current Assets
120	Truck	Yes	Fixed Assets
210	Accounts Payable	Yes	Accounts Payable
310	Dennis Taylor, Capital	Yes	Equity—doesn't close
320	Dennis Taylor, Drawing	Yes	Equity—gets closed
330	Retained Earnings	Yes	Equity—Retained Earnings
410	Fees Earned	Yes	Income
510	Rent Expense	Yes	Expenses
511	Repair Expense	Yes	Expenses
512	Utilities Expense	Yes	Expenses

Under the heading Account Description, Peachtree lists the titles of all the accounts used by The Kitchen Taylor. Under the heading, Account ID, it lists the account number of each account. The Kitchen Taylor numbers accounts according to the following system:

Account No.	Account Classification
100–199	Assets
200–299	Liabilities
300–399	Owner's Equity
400–499	Revenue
500–599	Expenses

Numbering systems may vary from company to company. However, account numbers generally indicate classifications of accounts and placement within a particular classification.

The other information shown on the chart of accounts will be discussed in later chapters.

Data Entry Sheet

In a computerized accounting system, each transaction is analyzed and recorded by hand on a data entry sheet before the information is placed in the accounts. This forces us to organize our information before going to the computer. A partial data entry sheet is shown in Figure 3.2.

Figure 3.2

DATA ENTRY SHEET The Kitchen Taylor					
Date	Account ID	Reference	Trans Description	Debit Amt	Credit Amt
12/1/95	110		Cash	10,000.00	
	310		Dennis Taylor, Capital		10,000.00
12/2/95	120		Check No. 101, Truck	6,000.00	
	110		Check No. 101, Cash		6,000.00

Observe that each transaction recorded on the data entry sheet includes the following:

- Date.
- Debit and credit account numbers (Account ID).
- Debit account title (Trans Description) and amount.
- Credit account title (Trans Description) and amount.

The reference column is usually blank, but it could be used for special notations.

Be sure to note the order of the required information. Within each transaction, the date and the debit account information always come first; the credit information is always second. **Within each transaction, the debits must equal the credits.** This is extremely important because total debits must equal total credits for the accounting equation to be in balance.

Looking ahead to Chapter 4, the order and accuracy of the information on the data entry sheet will be very important when you use Peachtree to record journal entries.

Analyzing Transactions Using Debits and Credits

Let's practice our expanded analytical skills by returning to The Kitchen Taylor and again considering the December transactions from Chapter 2. We will continue to use the three-step process studied in the previous chapter. However, at the end of step 2, we will determine how to record the increases and decreases using debits and credits. In step 3, we will record the debits and credits on a data entry sheet and also in T-accounts. We will check the accounting equation for balance by checking the equality of debits and credits within each transaction.

objective 3
Analyze transactions using debits and credits

December 1 Transaction

step 1: *Dennis invested $10,000 cash in his new business in a checking account in the name of The Kitchen Taylor.*

step 2:
Account?	Cash
Classification?	Asset
Effect?	+$10,000
How?	Debit

Account?	Dennis Taylor, Capital
Classification?	Owner's Equity
Effect?	+$10,000
How?	Credit

step 3:

DATA ENTRY SHEET The Kitchen Taylor					
Date	**Account ID**	**Reference**	**Trans Description**	**Debit Amt**	**Credit Amt**
12/1/95	110		Cash	10,000.00	
	310		Dennis Taylor, Capital		10,000.00

Comment

Remember that for the accounting equation to be in balance, **total debits must equal total credits.**

Using T-accounts, the December 1 transaction is recorded as shown below. *It is important to remember that these T-accounts are rough-draft accounts.* You will learn about formal accounts in Chapter 4.

Cash		Dennis Taylor, Capital	
Dr. 10,000.00	Cr.	Dr.	Cr. 10,000.00

December 2 Transaction

step 1: **The Kitchen Taylor paid $6,000 for a truck, Check No. 101.**

step 2:
Account?	Cash
Classification?	Asset
Effect?	−$6,000
How?	Credit

Account?	Truck
Classification?	Asset
Effect?	+$6,000
How?	Debit

step 3:

DATA ENTRY SHEET The Kitchen Taylor					
Date	Account ID	Reference	Trans Description	Debit Amt	Credit Amt
12/2/95	120		Check No. 101, Truck	6,000.00	
	110		Check No. 101, Cash		6,000.00

Comment

The Kitchen Taylor, like most businesses, pays all bills by check. Observe that on the data entry sheet, the check number is recorded before both the debit and credit account titles in the Trans Description column. This will be important in Chapter 4 when you use PAW to record transactions.

Using T-accounts, the December 2 transaction is recorded as follows:

Truck		Cash	
Dr. 6,000.00	Cr.	Dr.	Cr. 6,000.00

December 3 Transaction

step 1: **The Kitchen Taylor paid a 24-month insurance premium, $1,200, Check No. 102.**

step 2:   Account?   Cash
           Classification?   Asset
           Effect?   −$1,200
           How?   Credit

           Account?   Prepaid Insurance
           Classification?   Asset
           Effect?   +$1,200
           How?   Debit

step 3:

DATA ENTRY SHEET The Kitchen Taylor					
Date	Account ID	Reference	Trans Description	Debit Amt	Credit Amt
12/3/95	113		Check No. 102, Prepaid Insurance	1,200.00	
	110		Check No. 102, Cash		1,200.00

Using T-accounts, the December 3 transaction is recorded as follows:

Prepaid Insurance			Cash	
Dr. 1,200.00	Cr.		Dr.	Cr. 1,200.00

December 4 Transaction

step 1:   **The Kitchen Taylor purchased $425 worth of sandpaper, steel wool, chemicals, and various other supplies, promising to pay in the near future.**

step 2:   Account?   Supplies
           Classification?   Asset
           Effect?   +$425
           How?   Debit

           Account?   Accounts Payable
           Classification?   Liability
           Effect?   +$425
           How?   Credit

step 3:

DATA ENTRY SHEET The Kitchen Taylor					
Date	Account ID	Reference	Trans Description	Debit Amt	Credit Amt
12/4/95	112		Supplies	425.00	
	210		Accounts Payable		425.00

Using T-accounts, the December 4 transaction is recorded as follows:

Supplies		Accounts Payable	
Dr. 425.00	Cr.	Dr.	Cr. 425.00

December 7 Transaction

step 1: **The Kitchen Taylor refinished several cabinets for a customer receiving $1,500 in cash.**

step 2:
Account?	Cash
Classification?	Asset
Effect?	+$1,500
How?	Debit

Account?	Fees Earned
Classification?	Revenue
Effect?	+$1,500
How?	Credit

step 3:

DATA ENTRY SHEET The Kitchen Taylor					
Date	Account ID	Reference	Trans Description	Debit Amt	Credit Amt
12/7/95	110		Cash	1,500.00	
	410		Fees Earned		1,500.00

Using T-accounts, the December 7 transaction is recorded as follows:

Cash		Fees Earned	
Dr. 1,500.00	Cr.	Dr.	Cr. 1,500.00

December 10 Transaction

step 1: **The Kitchen Taylor paid $425 to a creditor on account, Check No. 103.**

step 2:
Account?	Cash
Classification?	Asset
Effect?	−$425
How?	Credit

Account?	Accounts Payable
Classification?	Liability
Effect?	−$425
How?	Debit

step 3:

			DATA ENTRY SHEET The Kitchen Taylor		
Date	Account ID	Reference	Trans Description	Debit Amt	Credit Amt
12/10/95	210		Check No. 103, Accounts Payable	425.00	
	110		Check No. 103, Cash		425.00

Using T-accounts, the December 10 transaction is recorded as follows:

Accounts Payable			Cash	
Dr. 425.00	Cr.		Dr.	Cr. 425.00

December 15 Transaction

step 1: **The Kitchen Taylor refinished several cabinets, charging the customer $1,400 for the completed work. The customer promised to pay The Kitchen Taylor in the near future.**

step 2:

Account?	Fees Earned
Classification?	Revenue
Effect?	+$1,400
How?	Credit

Account?	Accounts Receivable
Classification?	Asset
Effect?	+$1,400
How?	Debit

step 3:

			DATA ENTRY SHEET The Kitchen Taylor		
Date	Account ID	Reference	Trans Description	Debit Amt	Credit Amt
12/15/95	111		Accounts Receivable	1,400.00	
	410		Fees Earned		1,400.00

Using T-accounts, the December 15 transaction is recorded as follows:

Accounts Receivable			Fees Earned	
Dr. 1,400.00	Cr.		Dr.	Cr. 1,400.00

December 17 Transaction

step 1:   *The Kitchen Taylor paid $600 monthly rent for a small office and storage space, Check No. 104.*

step 2:   Account?   Cash
          Classification?   Asset
          Effect?   −$600
          How?   Credit

          Account?   Rent Expense
          Classification?   Expense
          Effect?   +$600
          How?   Debit

step 3:

DATA ENTRY SHEET The Kitchen Taylor					
Date	Account ID	Reference	Trans Description	Debit Amt	Credit Amt
12/17/95	510		Check No. 104, Rent Expense	600.00	
	110		Check No. 104, Cash		600.00

Using T-accounts, the December 17 transaction is recorded as follows:

Rent Expense		Cash	
Dr.	Cr.	Dr.	Cr.
600.00			600.00

December 21 Transaction

step 1:   *The Kitchen Taylor received a $500 payment on account from a charge customer.*

step 2:   Account?   Cash
          Classification?   Asset
          Effect?   +$500
          How?   Debit

          Account?   Accounts Receivable
          Classification?   Asset
          Effect?   −$500
          How?   Credit

step 3:

DATA ENTRY SHEET The Kitchen Taylor					
Date	Account ID	Reference	Trans Description	Debit Amt	Credit Amt
12/21/95	110		Cash	500.00	
	111		Accounts Receivable		500.00

Using T-accounts, the December 21 transaction is recorded as follows:

Cash		Accounts Receivable	
Dr.	Cr.	Dr.	Cr.
500.00			500.00

December 26 Transaction

step 1: *A small repair, costing $65, had to be made on the truck. The Kitchen Taylor promised to pay for this in the near future.*

step 2:
Account?	Repair Expense
Classification?	Expense
Effect?	+$65
How?	Debit

Account?	Accounts Payable
Classification?	Liability
Effect?	+$65
How?	Credit

step 3:

			DATA ENTRY SHEET The Kitchen Taylor		
Date	Account ID	Reference	Trans Description	Debit Amt	Credit Amt
12/26/95	511		Repair Expense	65.00	
	210		Accounts Payable		65.00

Using T-accounts, the December 26 transaction is recorded as follows:

Repair Expense		Accounts Payable	
Dr.	Cr.	Dr.	Cr.
65.00			65.00

December 28 Transaction

step 1: *Dennis withdrew $200 in cash from the business for personal use, Check No. 105.*

step 2:
Account?	Cash
Classification?	Asset
Effect?	−$200
How?	Credit

Account?	Dennis Taylor, Drawing
Classification?	Drawing
Effect?	+$200
How?	Debit

step 3:

DATA ENTRY SHEET The Kitchen Taylor					
Date	Account ID	Reference	Trans Description	Debit Amt	Credit Amt
12/28/95	320		Check No. 105, Dennis Taylor, Drawing	200.00	
	110		Check No. 105, Cash		200.00

Using T-accounts, the December 28 transaction is recorded as follows:

Dennis Taylor, Drawing			Cash	
Dr.	Cr.		Dr.	Cr.
200.00				200.00

December 29 Transaction

step 1: **The Kitchen Taylor paid a utility bill, $80, Check No. 106.**

step 2:

Account?	Cash
Classification?	Asset
Effect?	−$80
How?	Credit

Account?	Utilities Expense
Classification?	Expense
Effect?	+$80
How?	Debit

step 3:

DATA ENTRY SHEET The Kitchen Taylor					
Date	Account ID	Reference	Trans Description	Debit Amt	Credit Amt
12/29/95	512		Check No. 106, Utilities Expense	80.00	
	110		Check No. 106, Cash		80.00

Using T-accounts, the December 29 transaction is recorded as follows:

Utilities Expense			Cash	
Dr.	Cr.		Dr.	Cr.
80.00				80.00

December 30 Transaction

step 1:   **The Kitchen Taylor received a payment on account from a charge customer, $300.**

step 2:

Account?	Cash
Classification?	Assets
Effect?	+$300
How?	Debit

Account?	Accounts Receivable
Classification?	Asset
Effect?	−$300
How?	Credit

step 3:

DATA ENTRY SHEET The Kitchen Taylor					
Date	Account ID	Reference	Trans Description	Debit Amt	Credit Amt
12/30/95	110		Cash	300.00	
	111		Accounts Receivable		300.00

Using T-accounts, the December 30 transaction is recorded as follows:

Cash			Accounts Receivable	
Dr. 300.00	Cr.		Dr.	Cr. 300.00

Summary of Transactions

The Kitchen Taylor's December transactions are summarized on the data entry sheet shown in Figure 3.3. In the next chapter, you will be referring to this data entry sheet as you use Peachtree to record journal entries for The Kitchen Taylor.

objective 4
Prepare a data entry sheet

Figure 3.3

DATA ENTRY SHEET The Kitchen Taylor					
Date	Account ID	Reference	Trans Description	Debit Amt	Credit Amt
12/1/95	110		Cash	10,000.00	
	310		Dennis Taylor, Capital		10,000.00
12/2/95	120		Check No. 101, Truck	6,000.00	
	110		Check No. 101, Cash		6,000.00
12/3/95	113		Check No. 102, Prepaid Insurance	1,200.00	
	110		Check No. 102, Cash		1,200.00
12/4/95	112		Supplies	425.00	
	210		Accounts Payable		425.00
12/7/95	110		Cash	1,500.00	
	410		Fees Earned		1,500.00
12/10/95	210		Check No. 103, Accounts Payable	425.00	
	110		Check No. 103, Cash		425.00
12/15/95	111		Accounts Receivable	1,400.00	
	410		Fees Earned		1,400.00
12/17/95	510		Check No. 104, Rent Expense	600.00	
	110		Check No. 104, Cash		600.00
12/21/95	110		Cash	500.00	
	111		Accounts Receivable		500.00
12/26/95	511		Repair Expense	65.00	
	210		Accounts Payable		65.00
12/28/95	320		Check No. 105, Dennis Taylor, Drawing	200.00	
	110		Check No. 105, Cash		200.00
12/29/95	512		Check No. 106, Utilities Expense	80.00	
	110		Check No. 106, Cash		80.00
12/30/95	110		Cash	300.00	
	111		Accounts Receivable		300.00

Chapter Three Summary

T-accounts are a rough-draft version of the formal account that you will study in Chapter 4. The debit side of a T-account is always the left side. The credit side of a T-account is always the right side. The account balance is the difference between total debits and credits and is always written on the side of the account with the larger total.

Debits and credits are simply the tools used by accountants to record increases and decreases in the accounts. Debits may be used to both increase and decrease account balances. Credits may also be used to both increase and decrease account balances. Knowing which to use is determined by account classifications and the accounting equation.

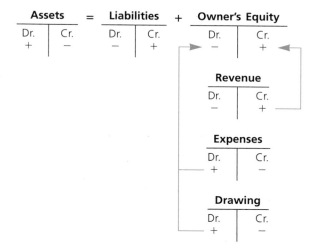

In the next chapter, you will learn to record transactions using a journal and ledger accounts.

Demonstration Problem

Ted Clingner established a sole proprietorship known as Clingner Designs. The following transactions are from the first month of operations.

a. Ted invested cash in the new business.
b. Paid the monthly rent.
c. Paid cash for equipment.
d. Purchased supplies on account.
e. Performed interior design services for cash.
f. Paid a creditor on account.
g. Performed interior design services on account.
h. Ted made a withdrawal of cash for personal use.
i. Received a payment on account from a charge customer.
j. Paid a one-year insurance premium.

Instruction

Analyze each transaction by determining:

1. Account?
2. Classification (asset, liability, owner's equity, revenue, expense, or drawing)?
3. Effect (+ or −)?
4. How (dr. or cr.)?

Solution to Demonstration Problem

Transaction	Account	Classification	Effect (+ or −)	How (dr. or cr.)
a	Cash	Asset	+	dr.
	Ted Clingner, Capital	Owner's Equity	+	cr.
b	Rent Expense	Expense	+	dr.
	Cash	Asset	−	cr.
c	Equipment	Asset	+	dr.
	Cash	Asset	−	cr.
d	Supplies	Asset	+	dr.
	Accounts Payable	Liability	+	cr.
e	Cash	Asset	+	dr.
	Fees Earned	Revenue	+	cr.
f	Accounts Payable	Liability	−	dr.
	Cash	Asset	−	cr.
g	Accounts Receivable	Asset	+	dr.
	Fees Earned	Revenue	+	cr.
h	Ted Clingner, Drawing	Drawing	+	dr.
	Cash	Asset	−	cr.
i	Cash	Asset	+	dr.
	Accounts Receivable	Asset	−	cr.
j	Prepaid Insurance	Asset	+	dr.
	Cash	Asset	−	cr.

Glossary

balance—account The difference between total debits and total credits. Written on side with larger total. *44*

balance—accounting equation Total debits equal total credits. *48*

chart of accounts A listing of the account titles and account numbers used by a particular business. *47*

credit Used to increase liability, owner's equity, and revenue accounts. Used to decrease asset, expense, and drawing accounts. Abbreviation: cr. *44*

data entry sheet In a computerized accounting system, it is used to record transactions by hand before going to the computer. It is an organizational tool. *48*

debit Used to increase asset, expense, and drawing accounts. Used to decrease liability, owner's equity, and revenue accounts. Abbreviation: dr. *44*

footing A total placed in small pencil figures at the bottom of a column of figures. *44*

normal balance The increase side of an account. *47*

T-account A simple T-shaped account form with debits on the left and credits on the right. It is a rough draft version of a formal account. *44*

Self-Test

Select the best answer.

1. In T-accounts, credits are recorded
   a. on the right side.
   b. on the left side.
   c. on both sides.
   d. only in certain accounts.

2. In T-accounts, the balance is written on
   a. the credit side of the account.
   b. the side with the smaller total.
   c. the side with the larger total.
   d. the debit side of the account.

3. Debits increase
   a. liability, owner's equity, and revenue accounts.
   b. asset, owner's equity, and revenue accounts.
   c. revenue, expense, and drawing accounts.
   d. asset, expense, and drawing accounts.

4. For the accounting equation to be in balance,
   a. total debits must be larger than total credits.
   b. total credits must be larger than total debits.
   c. total debits must equal total credits.
   d. all accounts must have a debit balance.

5. Which of the following statements is *not* true?
   a. Revenue increases total owner's equity.
   b. Expenses increase total owner's equity.
   c. Expenses decrease total owner's equity.
   d. Withdrawals for personal use decrease total owner's equity.

Answers to the self-test can be found after the cases at the end of this chapter.

Questions for Discussion

1. What four questions must be answered when analyzing business transactions using debits and credits?
2. Describe the structure of a T-account.
3. Debits are used to increase which classifications of accounts?
4. Debits are used to decrease which classifications of accounts?
5. Credits are used to increase which classifications of accounts?
6. Credits are used to decrease which classifications of accounts?
7. Why must total debits always equal total credits?
8. a. As the balance on the debit side of an expense account increases, does total owner's equity indirectly increase or decrease?
   b. As the balance on the credit side of a revenue account increases, does total owner's equity indirectly increase or decrease?

Exercises

Exercise 3.1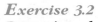

Debit or Credit
L.O. 2

Indicate whether a debit or credit is needed to accomplish the following:

1. Increase assets.
2. Decrease assets.
3. Increase liabilities.
4. Decrease liabilities.
5. Increase owner's equity.
6. Decrease owner's equity.

7. Increase revenue.
8. Decrease revenue.
9. Increase expenses.
10. Decrease expenses.
11. Increase drawing.
12. Decrease drawing.

Exercise 3.2

Effect of Debit or Credit
L.O. 2

Determine whether the following will increase or decrease the account specified:

1. Debit to Truck.
2. Credit to Fees Earned.
3. Credit to Accounts Receivable.
4. Debit to Utilities Expense.
5. Credit to Denise Jones, Capital.
6. Debit to Rent Expense.
7. Debit to Denise Jones, Drawing.
8. Debit to Prepaid Insurance.
9. Credit to Cash.

Exercise 3.3

T-accounts
L.O. 1, 2

Referring to the following T-accounts, describe Transactions (a) through (g):

Cash		
Dr.	Cr.	
(a) 10,000	(b) 4,000	
(f) 375	(e) 450	
	(g) 150	

Accounts Receivable		
Dr.	Cr.	
(c) 500	(f) 375	

Truck	
Dr.	Cr.
(b) 4,000	

Accounts Payable		
Dr.	Cr.	
(g) 150	(d) 150	

Robert Gross, Capital	
Dr.	Cr.
	(a) 10,000

Robert Gross, Drawing	
Dr.	Cr.
(e) 450	

Fees Earned	
Dr.	Cr.
	(c) 500

Repair Expense	
Dr.	Cr.
(d) 150	

Exercise 3.4

Determine whether the following transactions will increase or decrease total assets, total liabilities, and total owner's equity. Use a format with the following column headings:

Effect of Debit or Credit
L.O. 2, 3

Transaction	Assets	Liabilities	Owner's Equity

Transaction

1. Dr. Rent Expense, Cr. Cash.
2. Dr. Karen Brown, Drawing; Cr. Cash.
3. Dr. Cash, Cr. Fees Earned.
4. Dr. Accounts Receivable, Cr. Fees Earned.
5. Dr. Prepaid Insurance, Cr. Cash.
6. Dr. Cash, Cr. Accounts Receivable.
7. Dr. Accounts Payable, Cr. Cash.
8. Dr. Supplies, Cr. Cash.

Exercise 3.5

For each of the following transactions, determine:

Transaction Analysis
L.O. 2, 3

1. Accounts?
2. Classification (asset, liability, owner's equity, revenue, expense, or drawing)?
3. Effect (+ or −)?
4. How (dr. or cr.)?

Use the following format:

Transaction	Account	Classification	Effect (+ or −)	How (dr. or cr.)

Transaction

1. Made a sale on account.
2. Paid monthly rent.
3. Received payment on account from charge customer.
4. Purchased supplies on account.
5. Purchased truck for cash.
6. Richard Moore, owner, withdrew cash for personal use.
7. Paid one-year insurance premium.
8. Paid creditor on account.

Exercise 3.6

T-accounts
L.O. 1

On March 31, 1995, the accounts of Martin Miller, M. D., appear as follows:

Cash		Accounts Receivable	
Dr.	Cr.	Dr.	Cr.
30,000	880	3,500	4,800
250	1,320	1,000	
3,350	1,600		

Supplies		Equipment	
Dr.	Cr.	Dr.	Cr.
600		5,160	
300			

Accounts Payable		Martin Miller, Capital	
Dr.	Cr.	Dr.	Cr.
350	900		30,000
1,450	5,160		

Martin Miller, Drawing		Fees Earned	
Dr.	Cr.	Dr.	Cr.
1,600			250
200			4,500
			550

Rent Expense		Salary Expense	
Dr.	Cr.	Dr.	Cr.
1,320		440	
		440	

Compute the balance in each T-account. Be sure to indicate whether each balance is a debit or credit balance.

Exercise 3.7

Abnormal Balance
L.O. 1

Referring to your account balances from Exercise 3.6, list any accounts with an abnormal balance and explain what transaction might have produced the abnormal balance.

Exercise 3.8

Data Entry Sheet
L.O. 4

What is wrong with the following data entry sheet?

DATA ENTRY SHEET Carter Services					
Date	Account ID	Reference	Trans Description	Debit Amt	Credit Amt
	110		Cash		500.00
	210		Accounts Payable	5,000.00	

Problems—Set A

Problem 3.1A

Transaction Analysis
L.O. 2, 3

Clarence Jones, an attorney, established a sole proprietorship known as Jones Legal Associates. Following are transactions for June 1995, the first month of operations:

June   1   Clarence invested cash in his new business, $18,000.

        3   Paid cash for equipment, $10,800, Check No. 101.

        4   Purchased supplies on account, $765.

        6   Performed legal services for cash, $3,750.

        9   Paid a creditor on account, $525, Check No. 102.

      12   Paid for a small repair to the equipment, $84, Check No. 103.

      15   Performed legal services on account, $2,775.

      19   Paid the monthly rent, $1,000, Check No. 104.

      21   Received a payment on account from a charge client, $1,800.

      22   Paid secretary's salary, $975, Check No. 105.

      25   Clarence made a withdrawal for personal use, $1,200, Check No. 106.

      28   Paid electric bill, $160, Check No. 107.

The following accounts are used by Jones Legal Associates:

110	Cash		320	Clarence Jones, Drawing
111	Accounts Receivable		410	Fees Earned
112	Supplies		510	Rent Expense
120	Equipment		511	Repair Expense
210	Accounts Payable		512	Salary Expense
310	Clarence Jones, Capital		513	Utilities Expense

Instructions

1. Analyze each transaction by determining:
   a. Accounts? (Note: Insert check number in parentheses whenever Cash is credited.)
   b. Classification (asset, liability, owner's equity, revenue, expense, or drawing)?
   c. Effect (+ or −)?
   d. How (dr. or cr.)?

2. Use the following columnar format:

Transaction	Account	Classification	Effect (+ or −)	How (dr. or cr.)

Problem 3.2A

Instructions

Record the transactions described in Problem 3.1A on a data entry sheet.

Data entry sheet
L.O. 4

Problem 3.3A

Ann Prada, a dentist, established a sole proprietorship known as Prada Dental Services. Following are transactions for the month of January 1995, the first month of operations:

Jan 1   Ann invested cash in the business, $17,000.

    3   Purchased a small computer on account, $2,800.

    5   Billed a patient for dental services performed on account, $1,200.

    6   Paid cash for letterhead paper, $250, Check No. 101.

    9   Paid a creditor on account, $560, Check No. 102.

  10   Performed dental services for cash, $720.

  12   Paid monthly rent, $975, Check No. 103.

  14   Received payment on account from a charge patient, $750.

  15   Paid a one-year insurance premium covering the period January 15, 1995, through January 14, 1996, $336, Check No. 104.

  18   Purchased printer ink cartridges on account, $54.

  21   Ann made a withdrawal for personal use, $1,000, Check No. 105.

  25   Paid dental assistant's salary, $865, Check No. 106.

  29   Paid electric bill, $150, Check No. 107.

The following accounts are used by Prada Dental Services:

110	Cash		310	Ann Prada, Capital
111	Accounts Receivable		320	Ann Prada, Drawing
112	Office Supplies		410	Fees Earned
113	Prepaid Insurance		510	Rent Expense
120	Office Equipment		511	Salary Expense
210	Accounts Payable		512	Utilities Expense

Instructions

1. Analyze each transaction by determining:
   a. Accounts? (Note: Insert check number in parentheses whenever Cash is credited.)
   b. Classification (asset, liability, owner's equity, revenue, expense, or drawing)?
   c. Effect (+ or −)?
   d. How (dr. or cr.)?

2. Use the following format:

Transaction	Account	Classification	Effect (+ or −)	How (dr. or cr.)

Problem 3.4A

Instructions

Record the transactions described in Problem 3.3A on a data entry sheet.

Problems—Set B

Problem 3.1B

Diane Stamps, an architect, established a sole proprietorship known as Classic Design Services. Following are transactions for May 1995, the first month of operations:

Transaction Analysis
L.O. 2, 3

May 1 Diane invested cash in her new business, $9,000.

2 Paid cash for equipment, $5,400, Check No. 101.

5 Purchased supplies on account, $380.

6 Performed design services for cash, $1,875.

8 Paid a creditor on account, $260, Check No. 102.

10 Paid for a small repair to the equipment, $42, Check No. 103.

13 Performed design services on account, $1,350.

15 Paid monthly rent, $600, Check No. 104.

19 Received a payment on account from a charge client, $900.

22 Paid secretary's salary, $480, Check No. 105.

26 Diane made a withdrawal for personal use, $750, Check No. 106.

30 Paid electric bill, $195, Check No. 107.

The following accounts are used by Classic Design Services:

110	Cash		320	Diane Stamps, Drawing
111	Accounts Receivable		410	Fees Earned
112	Supplies		510	Rent Expense
120	Equipment		511	Repair Expense
210	Accounts Payable		512	Salary Expense
310	Diane Stamps, Capital		513	Utilities Expense

Instructions

1. Analyze each transaction by determining:
   a. Accounts? (Note: Insert check number in parentheses whenever Cash is credited.)
   b. Classification (asset, liability, owner's equity, revenue, expense, or drawing)?
   c. Effect (+ or −)?
   d. How (dr. or cr.)?

2. Use the following format:

Transaction	Account	Classification	Effect (+ or −)	How (dr. or cr.)

Problem 3.2B

Instructions

Record the transactions described in Problem 3.1B on a data entry sheet.

Data Entry Sheet
L.O. 4

Problem 3.3B

Hector Ramos, an accountant, established a sole proprietorship known as Ramos Accounting Services. Following are transactions for the month of October 1995, the first month of operations:

Oct. 1 Hector invested cash in the business, $9,000.

3 Purchased computer equipment on account, $1,275.

4 Billed a client for accounting services performed on account, $1,385.

6 Paid cash for letterhead paper, $400, Check No. 101.

9 Paid a creditor on account, $600, Check No. 102.

10 Performed accounting services for cash, $900.

12 Paid monthly rent, $1,000, Check No. 103.

15 Received payment on account from a charge client, $925.

16 Paid a one-year insurance premium covering the period October 16, 1995, through October 15, 1996, $315, Check No. 104.

19 Purchased office supplies on account, $63.

24 Hector made a withdrawal for personal use, $1,250, Check No. 105.

29 Paid employee's salary, $825, Check No. 106.

The following accounts are used by Ramos Accounting Services:

110	Cash	310	Hector Ramos, Capital
111	Accounts Receivable	320	Hector Ramos, Drawing
112	Office Supplies	410	Fees Earned
113	Prepaid Insurance	510	Rent Expense
120	Computer Equipment	511	Salary Expense
210	Accounts Payable		

Instructions

1. Analyze each transaction by determining:
   a. Accounts? (Note: Insert check number in parentheses whenever Cash is credited.)
   b. Classification (asset, liability, owner's equity, revenue, expense, or drawing)?
   c. Effect (+ or −)?
   d. How (dr. or cr.)?

2. Use the following format:

Transaction	Account	Classification	Effect (+ or −)	How (dr. or cr.)

Problem 3.4B

Instructions

Record the transactions described in Problem 3.3B on a data entry sheet.

Mini-Cases

Case 3–1

Your friend Michael Roberts is taking a beginning accounting course. He is having some difficulty understanding debits and credits and asks you for assistance. How would you explain debits and credits?

Case 3–2

Your boss is a very successful architect but has had no training in accounting. He thinks that you are wasting time by recording every transaction with both a debit and a credit. "One of those things should be enough," he says. How would you convince him that you are correct?

Case 3–3

DuPage Laundry and Dry Cleaning uses only one revenue account. Revenue, however, is derived from two sources: laundry and dry cleaning. The owner, Ron Maguire, would like more detailed revenue information from his accounting records. What would you suggest?

A Case of Ethics

Jennifer, who owns her own business, makes an additional investment in her business in the form of an antique desk for her office. She has owned the desk for about five years but has been using it in her home. Jennifer believes that the true market value of the desk is probably around $3,500 but has recorded it at $5,000 on the books. "It'll help to dress up my balance sheet as well as my office," says Jennifer. Comment.

Answers to Self-Test

1. *a*   2. *c*   3. *d*   4. *c*   5. *b*

Journalizing and Posting

LEARNING OBJECTIVES

After studying this chapter, you should be able to:

1. Start Peachtree Accounting for Windows.

2. Print the chart of accounts.

3. Record journal entries using the "General Journal Entry" window.

4. Print the general journal.

5. Post to the general ledger.

6. Print the general ledger.

7. Print the trial balance.

8. Back up your data.

In Chapter 3, you analyzed transactions and recorded the debits and credits on a data entry sheet. Although useful, a data entry sheet is only a preparatory device. You are now ready to study how transactions are formally recorded in the journal and ledger using Peachtree Accounting for Windows (PAW).

The General Journal

In previous chapters, you learned to analyze transactions using a three-step process that ends with a data entry sheet. In this chapter, you will use the data entry sheet to record a journal entry for each transaction. The formal accounting cycle begins with this journal entry.

Journal entries must always be recorded in a journal. The journal is often referred to as the *book of original entry* because this is where the formal recording process begins. The two-column journal (one debit column and one credit column) we will be using is known as a general journal. Any transaction, no matter how complex, can be recorded in a general journal. Later in the text, we will consider more specialized types of journals.

A separate journal entry must be prepared for each transaction. Each journal entry must:

- Include a **debit** part and a **credit** part.
- Balance—meaning the debits must equal the credits.

Balance between debits and credits is necessary if we are to keep the accounting equation in balance. To maintain balance, each journal entry requires the use of at least two accounts: the account being debited and the account being credited. This system is often referred to as double-entry accounting. An entry requiring debits to more than one account and/or credits to more than one account is known as a compound journal entry. As in all journal entries, total debits must equal total credits.

The process of recording entries is known as journalizing. In this chapter, you will learn how to journalize transactions using Peachtree.

Starting Peachtree Accounting for Windows

objective 1
Start Peachtree Accounting for Windows

To start Peachtree, follow these easy steps:

Comment

These steps assume that Peachtree has already been installed on your computer. If that is *not* the case, go to Appendix A, "Installing Peachtree Accounting Software."

step 1: Before going to step 2, you **must** go to Appendix B and load The Kitchen Taylor company data from the CD-ROM that came with this text. It is extremely important that you follow the directions in Appendix B to load the *original* Kitchen Taylor company data for use in PAW.

step 2: Start Windows. If you are using Windows 3.1*x*, double-click on the Peachtree Accounting folder in File Manager. For Windows 95, click on the "Start" icon, then "Programs."

step 3: Double-click on the "Peachtree Accounting" icon. The hourglass symbol displays on your screen while the program is loading. This may take a few moments.

step 4: The "Presenting Peachtree Accounting" screen displays.

step 5: Click once with your left mouse button on the Open folder. Again, the hourglass symbol displays on your screen while the program is loading.

step 6: The "Open Company" window displays. The Kitchen Taylor is listed in the Company <u>N</u>ame box. Click once on "The Kitchen Taylor" to highlight it.

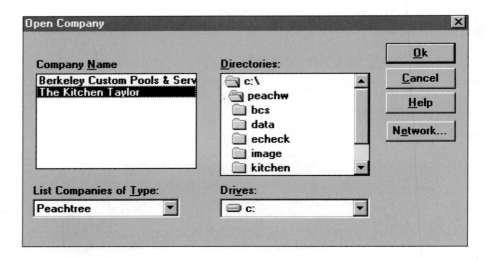

Comment

If The Kitchen Taylor is not listed in the Company <u>N</u>ame box or *if it appears but you did not load it* (some other student did), you **must** go to Appendix B to load the *original* Kitchen Taylor company data from the CD-ROM that came with this text. *This is extremely important.*

step 7: Click on <u>O</u>k.

step 8: The "Convert Company Files" window pops up.

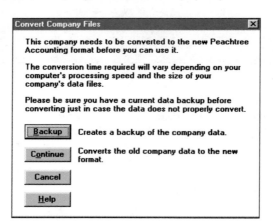

step 9: Click on C<u>o</u>ntinue. A series of screens pop up. The program is converting your data for use with Peachtree Accounting for Windows Release 5.0.

step 10: The main menu for "Peachtree Accounting: The Kitchen Taylor" should be displayed across the top of your screen.

Peachtree Accounting: The Kitchen Taylor

<u>F</u>ile <u>E</u>dit <u>M</u>aintain Ta<u>s</u>ks <u>A</u>nalysis <u>O</u>ptions <u>R</u>eports <u>W</u>indow <u>H</u>elp

Printing the Chart of Accounts

Follow these steps to print The Kitchen Taylor's chart of accounts:

objective 2
Print the chart of accounts

step 1:   Click on Reports. The Reports pull-down menu displays. Select General Ledger. The "Select a Report" window displays. "Chart of Accounts" is highlighted.

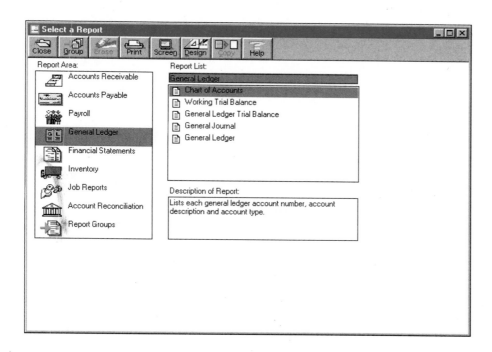

step 2:   Click on the Print icon ⬛. The "Chart of Accounts Filter" window displays.

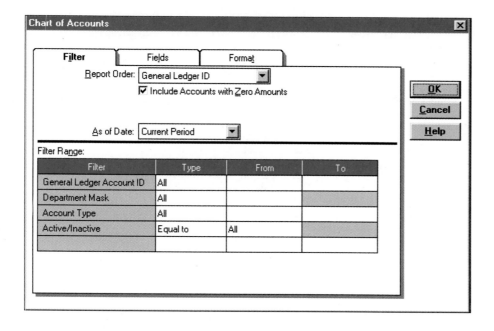

step 3:   Click on <u>O</u>K and the "Print" window pops up.

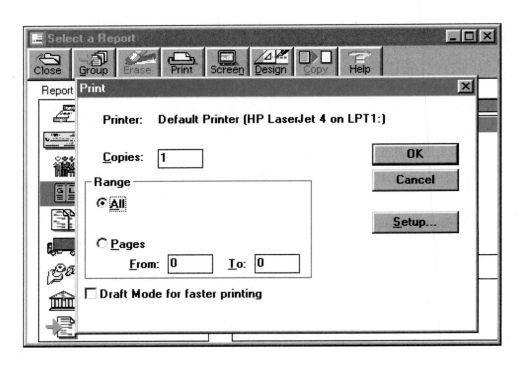

step 4:   Click on OK and the chart of accounts starts to print. Compare your printout with Figure 4.1.

Figure 4.1

The Kitchen Taylor
Chart of Accounts
As of Dec 31, 1995

Filter Criteria includes: Report order is by ID. Report is printed with Accounts having Zero Amounts and in Detail Format.

Account ID	Account Description	Active?	Account Type
110	Cash	Yes	Cash
111	Accounts Receivable	Yes	Accounts Receivable
112	Supplies	Yes	Inventory
113	Prepaid Insurance	Yes	Other Current Assets
120	Truck	Yes	Fixed Assets
210	Accounts Payable	Yes	Accounts Payable
310	Dennis Taylor, Capital	Yes	Equity-doesn't close
320	Dennis Taylor, Drawing	Yes	Equity-gets closed
330	Retained Earnings	Yes	Equity-Retained Earnings
410	Fees Earned	Yes	Income
510	Rent Expense	Yes	Expenses
511	Repair Expense	Yes	Expenses
512	Utilities Expense	Yes	Expenses

step 5:   Click on the Close icon 🔲 to close the "Select a Report" window and return to the main menu.

Recording Journal Entries Using the "General Journal Entry" Window

You are now ready to journalize. Remember every journal entry contains the following information:

objective 3
Record journal entries using the "General Journal Entry" window

- Date
- Debit account number, title, and amount
- Credit account number, title, and amount

As you will recall, you learned to prepare a data entry sheet in Chapter 3. A data entry sheet should always be prepared before transactions are journalized. It allows us to rough draft transactions and hopefully avoid errors. Referring to The Kitchen Taylor's data entry sheet, let's use PAW to journalize the December 1 transaction.

			DATA ENTRY SHEET The Kitchen Taylor		
Date	Account ID	Reference	Trans Description	Debit Amt	Credit Amt
12/1/95	110		Cash	10,000.00	
	310		Dennis Taylor, Capital		10,000.00

step 1: Click on Tasks, then click on General Journal Entry. The "General Journal" window displays.

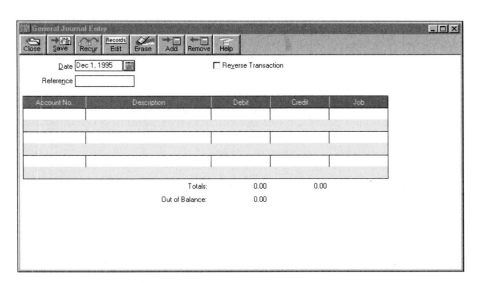

In this textbook, we will *not* use the **"Smart Guide"** that is displayed at the bottom of your "General Journal Entry" window. **Follow these steps to turn it off: From the Main Menu click on Options, then click on Smart Guide.** The check mark next to the words "Smart Guide" is deleted and the "Smart Guide" is turned off.

Comment

step   *2:*   Enter the date in the <u>D</u>ate text box. In PAW, there are two ways to enter December 1, 1995. One way is to click on the calendar icon next to the <u>D</u>ate box and select a day. Or, if the <u>D</u>ate text box does not display 12/1/95, type **1**, then press <Enter>.

step   *3:*   Click once on the "Account No." column.

step   *4:*   Click on the magnifying glass icon in the "Account No." column. A chart of accounts list pops up.

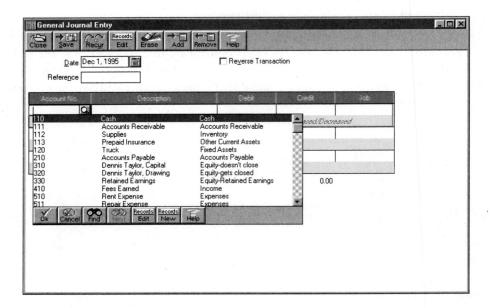

step   *5:*   Account No. 110, Cash, is highlighted because it is the first account in the list. If it is not highlighted, click once with your left mouse button to highlight Account No. 110, Cash. Click on the ✔ Ok button at the bottom of the chart of accounts list to select Account No. 110.

step   *6:*   Your cursor goes to the "Description" column. Type the word **Cash** and press the <Enter> key.

step   *7:*   Your cursor is in the "Debit" column. Type **10000.** being sure to type the decimal point. Do not use commas when entering dollar amounts. Press the <Enter> key three times.

Comment

The steps in this textbook assume that you will type the decimal point. However, if you would like PAW to set the decimal point automatically, follow these steps:

a. From the main menu, select <u>O</u>ptions, then <u>G</u>lobal.

b. In the <u>D</u>ecimal Point Entry box, click on "Manual." When "Manual" is selected, a black circle is placed within a circle.

c. In the "Number of decimal places" box, make sure the number **2** is selected.

d. Click on <u>O</u>k.

When global options are selected for automatic placement of the decimal point, this feature is in effect for all companies.

***step* 8:**   Your cursor is in the "Account No." column. Click on the magnifying glass icon and select Account No. 310, Dennis Taylor, Capital. Click on the ✔ Ok button.

***step* 9:**   In the "Description" column, type **Dennis Taylor, Capital.** When you start typing, the highlighted word *Cash* will be erased. Press the <Enter> key two times. If you make a mistake while typing, just press the Backspace key to erase the incorrect character(s).

***step* 10:**   Your cursor is in the "Credit" column. Type **10000.** being sure to type the decimal point. Press the <Enter> key. When you press the <Enter> key, a box with a magnifying glass icon forms around the "Job" column. You will not be typing anything in the "Job" column.

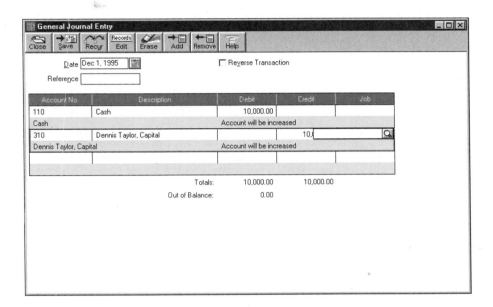

Observe that the "Out of Balance" line shows "0.00." This is important because it means that your debits equal your credits.

***step* 11:**   Click on the Save icon [icon]. The "General Journal Entry" window is ready for the next transaction. **Remember to click on the Save icon after each transaction.**

Using the data entry sheet shown in Figure 4.2, you can now journalize the remaining transactions for the month of December by repeating steps 2–11 for each transaction. As you will recall, this data entry sheet was prepared in Chapter 3. Since you have already journalized The Kitchen Taylor's December 1 transaction, it is not shown again in Figure 4.2.

Figure 4.2

			DATA ENTRY SHEET The Kitchen Taylor		
Date	Account ID	Reference	Trans Description	Debit Amt	Credit Amt
12/2/95	120		Check No. 101, Truck	6,000.00	
	110		Check No. 101, Cash		6,000.00
12/3/95	113		Check No. 102, Prepaid Ins.	1,200.00	
	110		Check No. 102, Cash		1,200.00
12/4/95	112		Supplies	425.00	
	210		Accounts Payable		425.00
12/7/95	110		Cash	1,500.00	
	410		Fees Earned		1,500.00
12/10/95	210		Check No. 103, Accts. Pay.	425.00	
	110		Check No. 103, Cash		425.00
12/15/95	111		Accounts Receivable	1,400.00	
	410		Fees Earned		1,400.00
12/17/95	510		Check No. 104, Rent Exp.	600.00	
	110		Check No. 104, Cash		600.00
12/21/95	110		Cash	500.00	
	111		Accounts Receivable		500.00
12/26/95	511		Repair Expense	65.00	
	210		Accounts Payable		65.00
12/28/95	320		Check No. 105, Dennis Taylor, Drawing	200.00	
	110		Check No. 105, Cash		200.00
12/29/95	512		Check No. 106, Utilities Exp.	80.00	
	110		Check No. 106, Cash		80.00
12/30/95	110		Cash	300.00	
	111		Accounts Receivable		300.00

Printing the General Journal

objective 4
Print the general journal

Follow these steps to print The Kitchen Taylor's general journal:

step 1: From the main menu, select Reports, then General Ledger. The "Select a Report" window displays.

step 2: In the "Report List," highlight "General Journal." Click on the Print icon. The "General Journal Filter" screen displays.

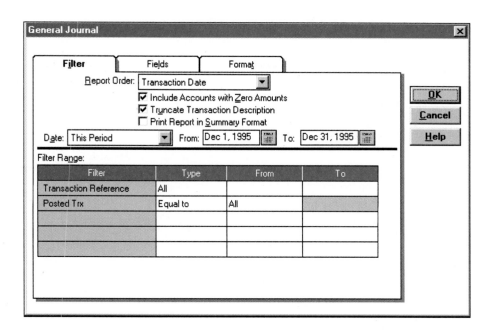

step 3: Click on OK.

step 4: The "Print" window pops up. Click on OK. The General Journal starts to print. Compare your printout to Figure 4.3.

Figure 4.3

The Kitchen Taylor

General Journal

For the Period From Dec 1, 1995 to Dec 31, 1995

Filter Criteria includes: Report order is by Date. Report is printed with Accounts having Zero Amounts and with Truncated Transaction Descriptions and in Detail

Date	Account ID	Reference	Trans Description	Debit Amt	Credit Amt
12/1/95	110		Cash	10,000.00	
	310		Dennis Taylor, Capital		10,000.00
12/2/95	120		Check No. 101, Truck	6,000.00	
	110		Check No. 101, Cash		6,000.00
12/3/95	113		Check No. 102, Prepaid Insurance	1,200.00	
	110		Check No. 102, Cash		1,200.00
12/4/95	112		Supplies	425.00	
	210		Accounts Payable		425.00
12/7/95	110		Cash	1,500.00	
	410		Fees Earned		1,500.00
12/10/95	210		Check No. 103, Accounts Payable	425.00	
	110		Check No. 103, Cash		425.00
12/15/95	111		Accounts Receivable	1,400.00	
	410		Fees Earned		1,400.00
12/17/95	510		Check No. 104, Rent Expense	600.00	
	110		Check No. 104, Cash		600.00
12/21/95	110		Cash	500.00	
	111		Accounts Receivable		500.00
12/26/95	511		Repair Expense	65.00	
	210		Accounts Payable		65.00
12/28/95	320		Check No. 105, Dennis Taylor, Drawing	200.00	
	110		Check No. 105, Cash		200.00
12/29/95	512		Check No. 106, Utilities Expense	80.00	
	110		Check No. 106, Cash		80.00
12/30/95	110		Cash	300.00	
	111		Accounts Receivable		300.00
		Total		22,695.00	22,695.00

Troubleshooting: What if your General Journal printout does not match Figure 4.3? **Comment**
Follow these steps to edit the General Journal:

1. From the main menu, select Tas<u>k</u>s, <u>G</u>eneral Journal Entry.

2. Click on the "Records Edit" icon ⊞ . The "Select General Journal Entry" window displays.

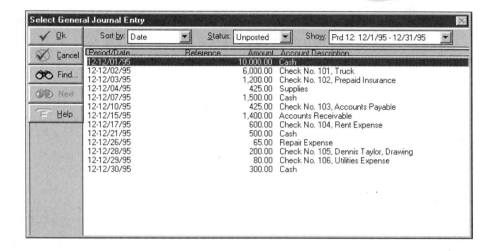

3. Highlight the General Journal entry that needs editing. Click on <u>O</u>k.

4. The "General Journal Entry" window displays the journal entry that you selected. Make the needed corrections, then click on <u>S</u>ave. When you have completed editing, click on the Close icon ⊞ to return to the main menu.

Posting to the General Ledger

objective 5
Post to the general ledger

Journalizing transactions is the first step in our recording process. The journal contains information grouped by transaction and arranged in chronological order. The second step in our recording process is to transfer this information from the journal to the ledger. The **general ledger** is simply a group of accounts such as Cash, Accounts Receivable, Supplies, Truck, Accounts Payable, and so on. It contains all the accounts shown on the chart of accounts. The process of transferring information from the journal to the ledger is known as **posting.**

As we post from the journal to the ledger, the information in the journal is sorted by account. This is important because it would be very difficult to determine account balances by looking at the journal alone.

For example, how would you determine your current cash balance if you had only a journal as a source of information? It would not be easy! You would have to scan each line in the journal, looking for debits and credits to Cash. You would have to write them down and, then, add and subtract. Hoping, of course, that you did not overlook any cash items. The process of posting, on the other hand, brings all those cash debits and cash credits to one place—the Cash account. If you want to know your cash balance, you simply look at the Cash account in the ledger.

Probably one of the best reasons to use accounting software is that it makes posting so fast and easy. Before accounting software was available, posting was a time consuming (and boring!) task because each debit and each credit had to be hand posted one at a time. In PAW, however, everything is posted automatically with only a few quick steps.

Although accounting software makes posting easy, it is important to note the significance of accurate journal entries. Right or wrong, PAW will post whatever you journalize. PAW cannot tell that you meant to debit Account No. 111 instead of Account No. 110. So, use your data entry sheet, proofread your journal entries, and edit your entries when you find errors.

Now, let's see how easy it is to post using PAW.

Comment

PAW includes two types of posting methods: *batch posting* and *real-time posting*. In batch posting, transactions are saved by the program then posted in a group. In real-time posting, transactions are posted to the general ledger as they are entered and saved. *This textbook uses batch posting.*

Follow these steps to post The Kitchen Taylor's general journal:

step 1: Click on the Close icon to close all windows before you post. Click on Tasks, then System. A pull-down menu displays.

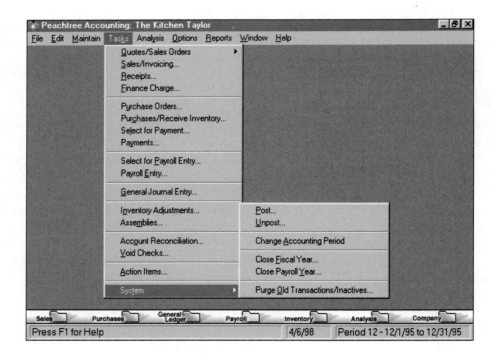

step 2: Click once on Post. The "Post" window displays.

step 3: Click once on the box next to General Journal. A check mark is placed in the box.

```
┌─────────────────────────────────────────────────────┐
│ Post                                              [X] │
├─────────────────────────────────────────────────────┤
│                    Select which Journal(s) to post:   │
│                    ─────────────────────────────────  │
│   ┌────────┐       ☐ All Journals                     │
│   │   OK   │                                          │
│   └────────┘       ☐ Cash Disbursements Journal       │
│   ┌────────┐                                          │
│   │ Cancel │       ☐ Cash Receipts Journal            │
│   └────────┘                                          │
│   ┌────────┐       ☑ General Journal                  │
│   │  Help  │                                          │
│   └────────┘       ☐ Inventory Adjustments Journal    │
│                                                       │
│                    ☐ Assemblies Journal               │
│                                                       │
│                    ☐ Payroll Journal                  │
│                                                       │
│                    ☐ Purchase Journal                 │
│                                                       │
│                    ☐ Sales Journal                    │
│                                                       │
└─────────────────────────────────────────────────────┘
```

step 4: Click on OK.

After The Kitchen Taylor's December 1 transaction is posted, the Cash and Dennis Taylor, Capital accounts appear as displayed in Figure 4.4. Study the arrows in Figure 4.4 showing the transfer of information from the journal to the ledger.

Figure 4.4

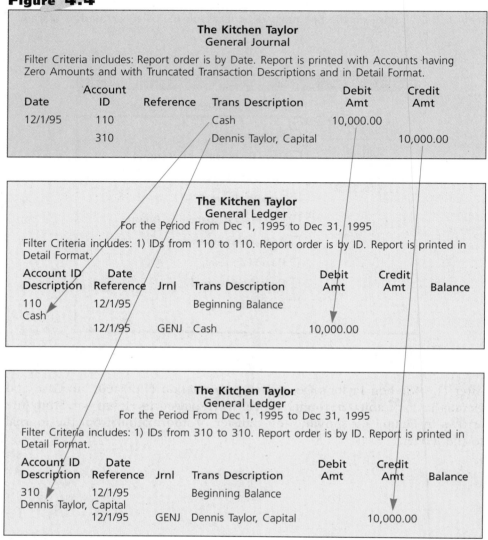

After completing the journalizing and posting, the same information is in two places and in two different kinds of order:

Journal → Chronological (date) order

Ledger → Account order

Posting to the individual accounts in the ledger is simple and fast. PAW does all the work for you. As noted earlier, this is one of the greatest benefits of accounting software.

Printing the General Ledger

To print The Kitchen Taylor's general ledger, follow these steps:

objective 6
Print the general ledger

step 1: From the main menu, select Reports, then General Ledger.

step 2: In the "Report List," highlight "General Ledger."

step 3: Click on the Print icon.

step 4: The "General Ledger Filter" screen displays. Click on OK.

step 5: The "Print" window pops up. Click on OK. A window pops up that shows you how many general ledger pages will print. It will take a few moments to load the data before printing actually begins.

Figure 4.5 shows The Kitchen Taylor's general ledger after all the December transactions have been posted. Compare your general ledger with Figure 4.5.

Figure 4.5

The Kitchen Taylor
General Ledger
For the Period From Dec 1, 1995 to Dec 31, 1995

Filter Criteria includes: Report order is by ID. Report is printed in Detail Format.

Account ID Account Description	Date Reference	Jrnl	Trans Description	Debit Amt	Credit Amt	Balance
110 Cash	12/1/95		Beginning Balance			
	12/1/95	GENJ	Cash	10,000.00		
	12/2/95	GENJ	Check No. 101, Cash		6,000.00	
	12/3/95	GENJ	Check No. 102, Cash		1,200.00	
	12/7/95	GENJ	Cash	1,500.00		
	12/10/95	GENJ	Check No. 103, Cash		425.00	
	12/17/95	GENJ	Check No. 104, Cash		600.00	
	12/21/95	GENJ	Cash	500.00		
	12/28/95	GENJ	Check No. 105, Cash		200.00	
	12/29/95	GENJ	Check No. 106, Cash		80.00	
	12/30/95	GENJ	Cash	300.00		
			Current Period Change	12,300.00	8,505.00	3,795.00
	12/31/95		Ending Balance			3,795.00
111 Accounts Receivable	12/1/95		Beginning Balance			
	12/15/95	GENJ	Accounts Receivable	1,400.00		
	12/21/95	GENJ	Accounts Receivable		500.00	
	12/30/95	GENJ	Accounts Receivable		300.00	
			Current Period Change	1,400.00	800.00	600.00
	12/31/95		Ending Balance			600.00
112 Supplies	12/1/95		Beginning Balance			
	12/4/95	GENJ	Supplies	425.00		
			Current Period Change	425.00		425.00
	12/31/95		Ending Balance			425.00

Figure 4.5 *(continued)*

The Kitchen Taylor
General Ledger
For the Period From Dec 1, 1995 to Dec 31, 1995
Filter Criteria includes: Report order is by ID. Report is printed in Detail Format.

Account ID Account Description	Date Reference	Jrnl	Trans Description	Debit Amt	Credit Amt	Balance
113 Prepaid Insurance	12/1/95		Beginning Balance			
	12/3/95	GENJ	Check No. 102, Prepaid Insurance	1,200.00		
			Current Period Change	1,200.00		1,200.00
	12/31/95		Ending Balance			1,200.00
120 Truck	12/1/95		Beginning Balance			
	12/2/95	GENJ	Check No. 101, Truck	6,000.00		
			Current Period Change	6,000.00		6,000.00
	12/31/95		Ending Balance			6,000.00
210 Accounts Payable	12/1/95		Beginning Balance			
	12/4/95	GENJ	Accounts Payable		425.00	
	12/10/95	GENJ	Check No. 103, Accounts Payable	425.00		
	12/26/95	GENJ	Accounts Payable		65.00	
			Current Period Change	425.00	490.00	-65.00
	12/31/95		Ending Balance			-65.00
310 Dennis Taylor, Capital	12/1/95		Beginning Balance			
	12/1/95	GENJ	Dennis Taylor, Capital		10,000.00	
			Current Period Change		10,000.00	-10,000.00
	12/31/95		Ending Balance			-10,000.00
320 Dennis Taylor, Drawing	12/1/95		Beginning Balance			
	12/28/95	GENJ	Check No. 105, Dennis Taylor, Drawing	200.00		
			Current Period Change	200.00		200.00
	12/31/95		Ending Balance			200.00

Figure 4.5 *(continued)*

The Kitchen Taylor
General Ledger
For the Period From Dec 1, 1995 to Dec 31, 1995
Filter Criteria includes: Report order is by ID. Report is printed in Detail Format.

Account ID Account Description	Date Reference	Jrnl	Trans Description	Debit Amt	Credit Amt	Balance
410 Fees Earned	12/1/95		Beginning Balance			
	12/7/95	GENJ	Fees Earned		1,500.00	
	12/15/95	GENJ	Fees Earned		1,400.00	
			Current Period Change		2,900.00	-2,900.00
	12/31/95		Ending Balance			-2,900.00
510 Rent Expense	12/1/95		Beginning Balance			
	12/17/95	GENJ	Check No. 104, Rent Expense	600.00		
			Current Period Change	600.00		600.00
	12/31/95		Ending Balance			600.00
511 Repair Expense	12/1/95		Beginning Balance			
	12/26/95	GENJ	Repair Expense	65.00		
			Current Period Change	65.00		65.00
	12/31/95		Ending Balance			65.00
512 Utilities Expense	12/1/95		Beginning Balance			
	12/29/95	GENJ	Check No. 106, Utilities Expense	80.00		
			Current Period Change	80.00		80.00
	12/31/95		Ending Balance			80.00

You probably noticed that some of the accounts have a minus sign in front of the "Ending Balance" amount; for example, Account No. 410, Fees Earned, shows −2,900.00. This indicates a credit balance. The accounts that do not have a minus sign in front of the "Ending Balance" amount have debit balances.

The Kitchen Taylor's General Ledger includes all the accounts in the Chart of Accounts. Observe that each account includes:

- Account ID and Description: For example, 110, Cash; 111, Accounts Receivable; 112, Supplies, etc. This is the Account ID (account number) and Description (account title) from the chart of accounts.

- Date and Reference: The date of the transaction. This is the date that was recorded in the journal for this transaction.
- Jrnl: For example, GENJ is the abbreviation for General Journal. This is the journal that was used to record the transaction.
- Debit Amt: This amount comes from the debit amount column in the journal.
- Credit Amt: This amount comes from the credit amount column in the journal.
- Balance: The account balance is the difference between the "Debit Amt" total and "Credit Amt"total. For the Cash account, the calculation is 12,300 − 8,505 = 3,795. For the Accounts Payable account, the calculation is 425 − 490 = −65. The minus sign in front of this account balance indicates that it is a credit balance.

Printing the Trial Balance

After completing the journalizing and posting for the month, we are ready to prepare a **trial balance.** The purpose of a trial balance is to verify that our accounting equation is in balance. The trial balance is a "trial" to test the overall equality of the debits and credits in the ledger. It is easy to prepare.

objective 7
Print the trial balance

Follow these steps to print a trial balance:

step 1: From the "Select a Report" window, highlight "General Ledger Trial Balance."

step 2: Click on the Print icon.

step 3: At the Filter window, click on OK.

step 4: At the "Print" window, click on OK. The trial balance starts to print. Compare your printout with Figure 4.6.

Figure 4.6

The Kitchen Taylor
General Ledger Trial Balance
As of Dec 31, 1995
Filter Criteria includes: Report order is by ID. Report is printed in Detail Format.

Account ID	Account Description	Debit Amt	Credit Amt
110	Cash	3,795.00	
111	Accounts Receivable	600.00	
112	Supplies	425.00	
113	Prepaid Insurance	1,200.00	
120	Truck	6,000.00	
210	Accounts Payable		65.00
310	Dennis Taylor, Capital		10,000.00
320	Dennis Taylor, Drawing	200.00	
410	Fees Earned		2,900.00
510	Rent Expense	600.00	
511	Repair Expense	65.00	
512	Utilities Expense	80.00	
	Total:	12,965.00	12,965.00

Observe that The Kitchen Taylor's debits and credits both total $12,965. This proves that the accounting equation is in balance on December 31, 1995.

Backing Up Your Chapter 4 Data

objective 8
Back up your data

Beginning in Chapter 4, you are reminded to back up each chapter's data. It is important that you understand why and how this is done.

When using PAW, information is automatically saved to the hard drive of the computer. In a classroom setting, a number of students may be using the same computer. Of course, this means that when you return to the computer, your data will probably be gone. Backing up your data simply means saving it to a floppy disk, so that it will be available when you want to work again.

You will back up all your data to a floppy disk in drive A (or B). When backing up, **it is extremely important that you always use a blank formatted disk.** This means that the disk you use to back up should *not* have any other information on it. PAW requires a **separate** blank formatted disk for each backup.

It is important to back up each chapter's data so that you can start where you left off the next time you use PAW. To start again, you will need to restore your data. For example, at the end of Chapter 4, you are going to back up your Chapter 4 data. Then, at the beginning of Chapter 5, you will need to restore your Chapter 4 data. The restored data provides a starting point for the new chapter.

Remember, you are backing up to a floppy disk in drive A (or B). Then, you are restoring from the floppy disk to the computer's hard drive. The Backup command allows you to save your work to a floppy disk in drive A (or B). The Restore command allows you to start where you left off.

Comment

If you are using your own computer (not the one in the school's computer lab or classroom), follow these steps to back up to drive C:

step 1: From the main menu, select File, Backup.

step 2: Type **chapter4** in the Destination box.

step 3: Click on the Backup button. (Your data is backed up to drive C. (c:\peachw\kitchen\chapter4 is the complete filename or path.)

step 4: When all the files are backed up to drive C, you are returned to the main menu.

step 5: As an "insurance policy," also back up to a blank formatted disk in drive A. Follow the steps below.

Follow these steps to back up your Kitchen Taylor data for Chapter 4:

step 1: Insert a blank formatted disk in drive A.

step 2: From PAW's main menu, select File, then Backup.

step 3: Type **a:\chapter4** in the Destination text box. When you start typing, the characters in the Destination text box will be deleted.

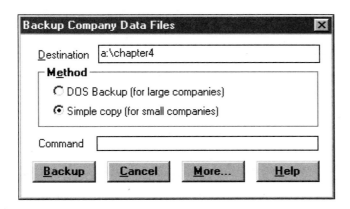

step 4: Click on the <u>B</u>ackup button [Backup] . Your files begin to copy. When all the files have been saved to drive A, you are automatically returned to the main menu.

step 5: Click on <u>F</u>ile, E<u>x</u>it to exit PAW.

This backup disk provides a starting point for your work in Chapter 5. Take good care of it!

Chapter Four Summary

In this chapter, we further refined our process of recording transactions. We are now able to use PAW to journalize transactions—make journal entries in a general journal to formally record transactions in the financial records of a business. Each transaction requires a separate journal entry. Each entry must:

- Include a debit part and a credit part.
- Balance—the debits must equal the credits.

Journalizing is the first step in our recording process. The second step is to transfer the information from the journal to the ledger (a group of accounts). This process is known as *posting*. As we post, the information is sorted by account.

At the end of the month, after all transactions have been journalized and posted, we print out a trial balance. The purpose of a trial balance is to check the overall equality of debits and credits in the ledger.

Accounting data flow through a business in an orderly pattern. The following flowchart demonstrates the pattern as studied up to this point.

When using PAW, one of the most important steps is to back up, or save, your data. Use a blank formatted disk for backing up your Chapter 4 data.

Demonstration Problem

Steve Duffy opened his own engineering business known as Duffy Associates in June 1995.

Duffy Associates Chart of Accounts As of June 30, 1995			
Account ID	Account Description	Active?	Account Type
110	Cash	Yes	Cash
111	Accounts Receivable	Yes	Accounts Receivable
112	Supplies	Yes	Inventory
210	Accounts Payable	Yes	Accounts Payable
310	Steve Duffy, Capital	Yes	Equity—doesn't close
320	Steven Duffy, Drawing	Yes	Equity—gets closed
410	Professional Fees	Yes	Income
510	Salary Expense	Yes	Expenses

The following transactions occurred during the first month of operations.

June	1	Steve Duffy invested cash in the business, $50,000.
	2	Performed services on account, $12,000.
	5	Performed services for cash, $4,000.
	9	Purchased supplies on account, $1,300.
	10	Received payment on account from charge customer, $2,000.
	15	Paid employees' salaries, $2,500, Check No. 101.
	20	Steve Duffy withdrew cash for personal use, $1,000, Check No. 102.
	28	Paid creditor on account, $800, Check No. 103.

Instructions

1. Record Duffy's transactions for June 1995 on a data entry sheet.
2. Referring to Duffy's chart of accounts, set up a T-account for each account inserting the account title at the top.
3. Referring to Duffy's data entry sheet, hand post the transactions to the T-accounts.
4. Compute and record the balance in each T-account.
5. Prepare a handwritten trial balance that includes a three-line heading (company name, trial balance, date) and account description, debit amount, and credit amount columns.

Solution to Demonstration Problem

1.

				Debit	Credit

		DATA ENTRY SHEET Duffy Associates			
Date	**Account ID**	**Reference**	**Trans Description**	**Debit Amt**	**Credit Amt**
6/1/95	110		Cash	50,000.00	
	310		Steve Duffy, Capital		50,000.00
6/2/95	111		Accounts Receivable	12,000.00	
	410		Professional Fees		12,000.00
6/5/95	110		Cash	4,000.00	
	410		Professional Fees		4,000.00
6/9/95	112		Supplies	1,300.00	
	210		Accounts Payable		1,300.00
6/10/95	110		Cash	2,000.00	
	111		Accounts Receivable		2,000.00
6/15/95	510		Check No. 101, Salary Expense	2,500.00	
	110		Check No. 101, Cash		2,500.00
6/20/95	320		Check No. 102, Steve Duffy, Drawing	1,000.00	
	110		Check No. 102, Cash		1,000.00
6/28/95	210		Check No. 103, Accounts Payable	800.00	
	110		Check No. 103, Cash		800.00

2, 3 & 4.

```
            Cash           110              Accounts Receivable  111
         Dr.          Cr.                  Dr.          Cr.
  6/1   50,000  6/15   2,500       6/2   12,000  6/10   2,000
  6/5    4,000  6/20   1,000       Bal.  10,000
  6/10   2,000  6/28     800
         56,000         4,300
  Bal.  51,700
```

```
          Supplies         112              Accounts Payable    210
         Dr.          Cr.                  Dr.          Cr.
  6/9    1,300                     6/28     800  6/9    1,300
                                                 Bal.     500
```

```
     Steve Duffy, Capital  310          Steve Duffy, Drawing  320
         Dr.          Cr.                  Dr.          Cr.
                6/1   50,000      6/20   1,000
```

```
     Professional Fees     410              Salary Expense      510
         Dr.          Cr.                  Dr.          Cr.
                6/2   12,000      6/15   2,500
                6/5    4,000
                Bal.  16,000
```

5.

	Duffy Associates General Ledger Trial Balance As of June 30, 1995	
Account Description	Debit Amt	Credit Amt
Cash	51,700.00	
Accounts Receivable	10,000.00	
Supplies	1,300.00	
Accounts Payable		500.00
Steve Duffy, Capital		50,000.00
Steve Duffy, Drawing	1,000.00	
Professional Fees		16,000.00
Salaries Expense	2,500.00	
Total:	**66,500.00**	**66,500.00**

Glossary

backing up   Saving data to a floppy disk.   *92*

balance—journal entry   Debits equal credits.   *72*

compound journal entry   A journal entry requiring debits and/or credits to more than one account.   *72*

double-entry accounting   A system requiring a minimum of two accounts in each journal entry: the account debited and the account credited. This is necessary to keep the accounting equation in balance.   *72*

general journal   A two-column journal, one Debit column and one Credit column.   *72*

general ledger   A group of accounts.   *83*

journal   The place where journal entries are recorded. It is frequently referred to as the *book of original entry* because this is where the formal recording process begins.   *72*

journal entry   Formally records a transaction in the financial records of a business. It must include a debit part and a credit part. Debits must equal credits.   *72*

journalizing   The process of recording journal entries.   *72*

posting   The process of transferring information from the journal to the ledger.   *83*

restore   Using backed up data to begin where you previously left off.   *92*

trial balance   A list of accounts and balances to test the overall equality, or balance, of debits and credits in the ledger.   *91*

Self-Test

Select the best answer.

1. Each journal entry must
   - *a.* include a debit part.
   - *b.* include a credit part.
   - *c.* balance.
   - *d.* All of the above.

2. A ledger is a group of
   - *a.* accounts.
   - *b.* journals.
   - *c.* transactions.
   - *d.* trial balances.

3. The process of transferring information from the journal to the ledger is known as
   - *a.* journalizing.
   - *b.* ledgerizing.
   - *c.* posting.
   - *d.* balancing.

4. Transactions are recorded first in the
   - *a.* trial balance.
   - *b.* journal.
   - *c.* ledger.
   - *d.* financial statements.

5. The trial balance
   - *a.* tests the overall equality of debits and credits in the ledger.
   - *b.* tests the overall equality of debits and credits in the journal.
   - *c.* proves that all transactions have been journalized and posted.
   - *d.* All of the above.

Answers to the self-test can be found after the cases at the end of this chapter.

Questions for Discussion

1. Briefly describe the seven steps required to start PAW.

2. Why is the journal often referred to as the book of original entry?

3. What is a compound journal entry?

4. Why must every journal entry balance?

5. Is it more convenient to use the journal or the ledger for the following?
   - *a.* To access information by account.
   - *b.* To access information by date.

6. Briefly describe the eleven steps required to record a journal entry using PAW.

7. In PAW, what are four basic steps for posting to the ledger?

8. What is the purpose of the trial balance?

Exercises

Exercise 4.1

Data entry sheet
L.O. 3

Jane Moy started Moy Company in August 1995.

	Moy Company Chart of Accounts As of Aug 31, 1995		
Account ID	Account Description	Active?	Account Type
110	Cash	Yes	Cash
111	Accounts Receivable	Yes	Accounts Receivable
112	Supplies	Yes	Inventory
113	Equipment	Yes	Fixed Assets
210	Accounts Payable	Yes	Accounts Payable
310	Jane Moy, Capital	Yes	Equity—doesn't close
320	Jane Moy, Drawing	Yes	Equity—gets closed
410	Fees Earned	Yes	Income
510	Rent Expense	Yes	Expenses
511	Utilities Expense	Yes	Expenses

Record Moy Company's transactions for August 1995 on a data entry sheet:

August 1   Jane Moy invested cash in the business, $5,000.

1   Paid cash for supplies, $900, Check No. 101.

2   Purchased equipment on account, $8,250.

6   Paid monthly rent, $1,000, Check No. 102.

9   Performed services on account, $18,000.

15   Paid creditor on account, $400, Check No. 103.

19   Jane Moy withdrew cash for personal use, $2,500, Check No. 104.

23   Performed services for cash, $2,600.

27   Received payment on account from charge customer, $950.

31   Paid electric bill, $190, Check No. 105.

Exercise 4.2

Posting
L.O. 5

1. Referring to the chart of accounts given in Exercise 4.1, set up a T-account for each account inserting the account title at the top. For example:

Cash	110
Dr.	Cr.

If necessary, review the Chapter 4 demonstration problem to refresh your memory about T-accounts.

2. Referring to your data entry sheet from Exercise 4.1, hand post the transactions to the T-accounts. For example:

Cash	110		Jane Moy, Capital	310

	Dr.	Cr.		Dr.	Cr.	
8/1	5,000				8/1	5,000

3. Compute and record the balance in each T-account.

Exercise 4.3

Referring to your T-accounts from Exercise 4.2, prepare a handwritten trial balance that includes a three-line heading (company name, trial balance, date) and account description, debit amount and credit amount columns.

Trial Balance
L.O. 7

Exercise 4.4

Herbert Cohen started Cohen Medical Associates in April 1995.

Data entry sheet
L.O. 3

Cohen Medical Associates Chart of Accounts As of April 30, 1995			
Account ID	**Account Description**	**Active?**	**Account Type**
110	Cash	Yes	Cash
111	Accounts Receivable	Yes	Accounts Receivable
112	Supplies	Yes	Inventory
113	Equipment	Yes	Fixed Assets
210	Accounts Payable	Yes	Accounts Payable
310	Herbert Cohen, Capital	Yes	Equity—doesn't close
320	Herbert Cohen, Drawing	Yes	Equity—gets closed
410	Professional Fees	Yes	Income
510	Salary Expense	Yes	Expenses
511	Utilities Expense	Yes	Expenses
512	Repair Expense	Yes	Expenses

Record Cohen Medical Associates transactions for April 1995 on a data entry sheet.

April 1 Herbert Cohen invested cash in the business, $15,000.

   3 Performed services on account, $7,500.

   6 Performed services for cash, $2,250.

   8 Purchased supplies on account, $1,854.

  10 Received payment on account from charge customer, $7,500.

  13 Paid employees' salaries, $1,310, Check No. 101.

  16 Herbert Cohen withdrew cash for personal use, $3,000, Check No. 102.

  20 Paid gas bill, $390, Check No. 103.

  23 Paid creditor on account, $1,100, Check No. 104.

  27 Paid for small plumbing repair, $60, Check No. 105.

  30 Purchased equipment for $7,000, paying $2,000 in cash and the remainder on account, Check No. 106.

Exercise 4.5

Posting
L.O. 5

1. Referring to the chart of accounts given in Exercise 4.4, set up a T-account for each account inserting the account title at the top. For example:

Cash	110
Dr.	Cr.

Review the Chapter 4 demonstration problem if you need to refresh your memory about T-accounts.

2. Referring to your data entry sheet from Exercise 4.4, hand post the transactions to the T-accounts. For example:

Cash	110	Herbert Cohen, Capital 310	
Dr.	Cr.	Dr.	Cr.
4/1 15,000			4/1 15,000

3. Compute and record the balance in each T-account.

Exercise 4.6

Trial Balance
L.O. 7

Referring to your T-accounts from Exercise 4.5, prepare a handwritten trial balance that includes a three-line heading (company name, trial balance, date) and account description, debit amount, and credit amount columns.

Problems—Set A

Problem 4.1A

Start PAW; Chart of Accounts
L.O. 1, 2

Ace Cleaning Service was established by Joan Haywood on December 1, 1995.

Ace Cleaning Service
Chart of Accounts
As of Dec 31, 1995

Account ID	Account Description	Active?	Account Type
110	Cash	Yes	Cash
111	Accounts Receivable	Yes	Accounts Receivable
112	Supplies	Yes	Inventory
113	Prepaid Insurance	Yes	Other Current Assets
114	Equipment	Yes	Fixed Assets
210	Accounts Payable	Yes	Accounts Payable
310	Joan Haywood, Capital	Yes	Equity—doesn't close
320	Joan Haywood, Drawing	Yes	Equity—gets closed
330	Retained Earnings	Yes	Equity—Retained Earnings
410	Cleaning Revenue	Yes	Income
510	Rent Expense	Yes	Expenses
511	Repair Expense	Yes	Expenses
512	Salary Expense	Yes	Expenses
513	Utilities Expense	Yes	Expenses

Instructions to load the Ace Cleaning Service company data and print the chart of accounts.

1. Start Windows. If you are running Windows 3.1*x*, choose File, Run in Program Manager. If you are running Windows 95, choose Start, Run.

2. Place the Company Data CD-ROM in drive D (or the appropriate drive for your CD-ROM).

3. Type **d:\setup.exe** in the dialog box. (This text assumes drive D is your CD-ROM drive. Use the appropriate drive letter if your CD-ROM is located in a different location.)

4. Click on the OK button. A screen pops up that says "One moment please. . . ."

5. The "Company Data to accompany College Accounting with Peachtree" window pops up. Click on Continue.

6. Accept the default for the "Path: C:\PEACHW" by clicking on Continue. (If Peachtree was installed in a different directory, type that location in the "Path" dialog box.)

7. The next screen, "Companies", shows the data that is included on the Company Data CD-ROM.

8. Since you are loading data for Ace Cleaning Service only, click on the box next to Aceclean.

9. Click on Continue. A scale shows what percentage of the data has been copied. All files have been copied to the hard drive of your computer when the scale is completed. The "Success" window displays.

10. Click on OK. You are returned to Program Manager in Windows 3.1*x* or the desktop in Windows 95.

11. Remove the Company Data CD-ROM from drive D (or the appropriate drive for your CD-ROM).

12. Double-click on the Peachtree Accounting icon. At the "Presenting Peachtree Accounting" window, click on Open.

13. Click once on Ace Cleaning Service to highlight it.

> **Comment**
>
> If Ace Cleaning Service is not listed in the Company Name box or if *it appears but you did not load it* (some other student did), you **must** go back to Instruction 1 to load the *original* Ace Cleaning Service company data from the CD-ROM that came with this text. *This is extremely important.*

14. Click on Ok. The main menu for Ace Cleaning Service displays.

15. Follow these steps to print Ace Cleaning Service's chart of accounts.
    a. From the main menu, select Reports, then General Ledger. In the "Report List," the "Chart of Accounts" is highlighted.
    b. On the "Icon Bar," click on the Print icon 🖷. The "Chart of Accounts Filter" window displays.
    c. Click on OK and the "Print" window pops up.
    d. Click on OK and the chart of accounts starts to print. Compare your printout with the one shown at the beginning of this problem.
    e. On the "Icon Bar," click on Close. You are returned to the main menu.
    f. To exit PAW, select File, Exit.

Problem 4.2A

Data entry sheet
L.O. 3

Ace Cleaning Service completed the following transactions during its first month of operations:

Dec. 1　Joan Haywood invested cash in the business, $7,500.

　　2　Paid monthly rent, $625, Check No. 1001.

　　5　Purchased $5,000 worth of equipment, $1,000 in cash, Check No. 1002, and the remainder on account.

　　8　Performed cleaning services for cash, $450.

　　10　Paid a one-year insurance premium covering the period December 10, 1995, through December 9, 1996, $648, Check No. 1003.

　　11　Paid creditor on account, $800, Check No. 1004

　　14　Performed cleaning services on account, $2,800.

　　17　Paid employees' salaries, $645, Check No. 1005.

　　19　Received payment on account from charge customer, $325.

　　21　Paid cash for supplies, $180, Check No. 1006.

　　22　Performed cleaning services: $800 cash, $600 on account.

　　25　Had equipment repaired, agreeing to pay in the near future, $260.

　　26　Paid creditor on account, $935, Check No. 1007.

　　28　Paid electric bill, $136, Check No. 1008.

　　29　Joan Haywood withdrew cash for personal use, $540, Check No. 1009.

　　30　Received payment on account from charge customer, $800.

Instructions

Record these transactions on a data entry sheet. Number data entry sheet pages.

Problem 4.3A

Journalize, post, trial balance
L.O. 3–7

Use PAW's "General Journal Entry" feature to journalize and post the December transactions for Ace Cleaning Service.

Instructions

1. Start PAW and open Ace Cleaning Service. The "Open Company" screen displays. In the Company Name box, highlight Ace Cleaning Service, then click on Ok. The main menu is displayed across the top of your screen.

2. Using your completed data entry sheet from Problem 4.2A, record general journal entries using PAW's "General Journal Entry" feature.

3. Print the general journal.

4. Proofread your general journal. If necessary, make corrections using PAW's "Edit Records" feature. If you made any corrections, reprint the general journal.

5. Post to the general ledger.

6. Print the general ledger.

7. Print a trial balance.

Problem 4.4A

Your Ace Cleaning Service data **must** be backed up. You will restore it in Chapter 5. Follow these steps:

Back up
L.O. 8

step 1: Insert a blank formatted disk in drive A.

step 2: From PAW's main menu, select File, then Backup.

step 3: Type a:\acedec.44a in the Destination text box.

step 4: Click on the Backup button. Your files begin to copy. When all the files have been saved to drive A, you are automatically returned to the main menu.

step 5: Click on File, Exit to exit PAW.

Problems—Set B

Problem 4.1B

Chris Canon established Loyal Lawn Service on December 1, 1995.

Start PAW; Chart of Accounts
L.O. 1, 2

	Loyal Lawn Service Chart of Accounts As of Dec 31, 1995		
Account ID	Account Description	Active?	Account Type
110	Cash	Yes	Cash
111	Accounts Receivable	Yes	Accounts Receivable
112	Supplies	Yes	Inventory
113	Prepaid Insurance	Yes	Other Current Assets
114	Equipment	Yes	Fixed Assets
210	Accounts Payable	Yes	Accounts Payable
310	Chris Canon, Capital	Yes	Equity—doesn't close
320	Chris Canon, Drawing	Yes	Equity—gets closed
330	Retained Earnings	Yes	Equity—Retained Earnings
410	Lawn Service Revenue	Yes	Income
510	Rent Expense	Yes	Expenses
511	Repair Expense	Yes	Expenses
512	Salary Expense	Yes	Expenses
513	Utilities Expense	Yes	Expenses

Instructions to load the Loyal Lawn Service company data and print the chart of accounts.

1. Start Windows. If you are running Windows 3.1*x*, choose File, Run in Program Manager. If you are running Windows 95, choose Start, Run.

2. Place the Company Data CD-ROM in drive D (or the appropriate drive for your CD-ROM).

3. Type **d:\setup.exe** in the dialog box. (This text assumes drive D is your CD-ROM drive. Use the appropriate drive letter if your CD-ROM is located in a different location.)

4. Click on the OK button. A screen pops up that says "One moment please. . . ."

5. The "Company Data to accompany College Accounting with Peachtree" window pops up. Click on <u>C</u>ontinue.

6. Accept the default for the "Path: C:\PEACHW" by clicking on <u>C</u>ontinue. (If Peachtree was installed in a different directory, type that location in the "Path" dialog box.)

7. The next screen, "Companies", shows the data that is included on the Company Data CD-ROM.

8. Since you are loading data for Loyal Lawn Service only, click on the box next to Loyal.

9. Click on <u>C</u>ontinue. A scale shows what percentage of data has been copied. All files have been copied to the hard drive of your computer when the scale is completed. The "Success" window displays.

10. Click on O<u>K</u>. You are returned to Program Manager in Windows 3.1*x* or the desktop in Windows 95.

11. Remove the Company Data CD-ROM from drive D (or the appropriate drive for your CD-ROM).

12. Double-click on the Peachtree Accounting icon. At the "Presenting Peachtree Accounting" window, click on <u>O</u>pen.

13. Click once on Loyal Lawn Service to highlight it.

Comment

If Loyal Lawn Service is not listed in the Company <u>N</u>ame box or if *it appears but you did not load it* (some other student did), you **must** go back to Instruction 1 to load the *original* Loyal Lawn Service company data from the CD-ROM that came with this text. *This is extremely important.*

14. Click on <u>O</u>k. The main menu for Loyal Lawn Service displays.

15. Follow these steps to print Loyal Lawn Service's chart of accounts.
   a. From the main menu, select <u>R</u>eports, then <u>G</u>eneral Ledger. In the "Report List," the "Chart of Accounts" is highlighted.
   b. On the "Icon Bar," click on the Print icon 🖨. The "Chart of Accounts Filter" window displays.
   c. Click on <u>O</u>K and the "Print" window pops up.
   d. Click on OK and the chart of accounts starts to print. Compare your printout with the one shown at the beginning of this problem.
   e. On the "Icon Bar," click on Close. You are returned to the main menu.
   f. To exit PAW, select <u>F</u>ile, E<u>x</u>it.

Problem 4.2B

Data entry sheet
L.O. 3

Loyal Lawn Service completed the following transactions during its first month of operations:

Dec. 1   Chris Canon invested cash in the business, $7,000.

2   Paid monthly rent, $595, Check No. 1001.

4   Purchased equipment for $5,000, paying $2,000 in cash, Check No. 1002, and the remainder on account.

6   Performed lawn services for cash, $637.

10   Paid a one-year insurance premium covering the period December 10, 1995, through December 9, 1996, $600, Check No. 1003.

12   Paid creditor on account, $730, Check No. 1004.

15   Performed lawn services on account, $2,150.

17   Paid employees' salaries, $690, Check No. 1005.

18   Received payment on account from charge customer, $375.

20   Paid cash for supplies, $225, Check No. 1006.

22   Performed lawn services: $400 cash, $800 on account.

25   Had equipment repaired, agreeing to pay in the near future, $145.

26   Paid creditor on account, $980, Check No. 1007.

28   Paid electric bill, $162, Check No. 1008.

29   Chris Canon withdrew cash for personal use, $420, Check No. 1009.

30   Received payment on account from charge customer, $710.

Instructions

Record these transactions on a data entry sheet. Number data entry sheet pages.

Problem 4.3B

Use PAW's "General Journal Entry" feature to journalize and post the December transactions for Loyal Lawn Service.

Journalize, post, trial balance
L.O. 3–7

Instructions

1. Start PAW and open Loyal Lawn Service. The "Open Company" screen displays. In the Company Name box, highlight "Loyal Lawn Service," then click on Ok. The main menu is displayed across the top of your screen.

2. Using your completed data entry sheet from Problem 4.2B, record general journal entries using PAW's "General Journal Entry" feature.

3. Print the general journal.

4. Proofread your general journal. If necessary, make corrections using PAW's "Edit Records" feature. If you made any corrections, reprint the general journal.

5. Post to the general ledger.

6. Print the general ledger.

7. Print a trial balance.

Problem 4.4B

Your Loyal Lawn Service data **must** be backed up. You will restore it in Chapter 5. Follow these steps:

Back up
L.O. 8

step 1:   Insert a blank formatted disk in drive A.

step 2:   From PAW's main menu, select File, then Backup.

step 3:   Type **a:\loyaldec.44b** in the Destination text box.

step 4:   Click on the Backup button. Your files begin to copy. When all the files have been saved to drive A, you are automatically returned to the main menu.

step 5:   Click on File, Exit to exit PAW.

Mini-Cases

Case 4–1

You have been hired as a consultant to suggest improvements in Hager Corporation's accounting procedures. In looking through Hager's journal, you observe that transaction descriptions indicating account titles are never used. What would you suggest relative to the use of transaction descriptions in journal entries?

Case 4–2

Bob Koval owns a travel agency and does his own accounting work. Bob claims that he never prints a trial balance because this saves him a lot of time. How would you respond to this situation?

Case 4–3

You are the sole proprietor of a small business. You notice that your bookkeeper does not use data entry sheets before recording journal entries. How would you respond to this situation?

A Case of Ethics

Your neighbor, Chris, owns a small business. At a neighborhood party, he reveals that in the future he does not intend to record all business transactions. "It's difficult to obtain bank loans if your income statement shows a net loss, so I told my accountant to stop journalizing expense transactions whenever expenses begin to exceed revenues." Chris's accountant is threatening to quit rather than carry out this new policy. What is your opinion of Chris's new policy?

Answers to Self-Test

1. *d*　2. *a*　3. *c*　4. *b*　5. *a*

Adjusting Entries

LEARNING OBJECTIVES

After studying this chapter, you should be able to:

1. Describe the purpose of adjusting entries.
2. Describe the adjustments for supplies, insurance, wages, and depreciation.
3. Restore data from the previous chapter.
4. Add new accounts to Peachtree's chart of accounts.
5. Journalize the adjusting entries.
6. Print the adjusting entries.
7. Post the adjusting entries.
8. Print the general ledger.
9. Print the adjusted trial balance.
10. Back up your data.

After studying the appendix at the end of this chapter, you should be able to:

11. Compute depreciation using four different methods.

In previous chapters, you learned to journalize, post, and prepare an unadjusted trial balance. In this chapter you will learn to make adjusting entries that update some of the ledger account balances. You will also learn to prepare an adjusted trial balance.

The Purpose of Adjusting Entries

Figure 5.1 shows the trial balance you prepared for The Kitchen Taylor at the end of Chapter 4.

Figure 5.1

The Kitchen Taylor
General Ledger Trial Balance
As of Dec 31, 1995
Filter Criteria includes: Report order is by ID. Report is printed in Detail Format.

Account ID	Account Description	Debit Amt	Credit Amt
110	Cash	3,795.00	
111	Accounts Receivable	600.00	
112	Supplies	425.00	
113	Prepaid Insurance	1,200.00	
120	Truck	6,000.00	
210	Accounts Payable		65.00
310	Dennis Taylor, Capital		10,000.00
320	Dennis Taylor, Drawing	200.00	
410	Fees Earned		2,900.00
510	Rent Expense	600.00	
511	Repair Expense	65.00	
512	Utilities Expense	80.00	
	Total:	**12,965.00**	**12,965.00**

Although this trial balance verified the equality of the debits and credits in the ledger, some of the accounts need to be updated. The need to update exists because a few **internal transactions** have occurred that have not been recorded (journalized). This is possible because internal transactions do not involve anyone outside the business.

It is acceptable to allow these internal transactions to go unrecorded on a daily basis, but we cannot prepare an income statement or a balance sheet with incorrect account balances. Therefore, before preparing financial statements, we must update some of the accounts. Accountants refer to this updating process as adjusting the accounts. The updating is accomplished through entries known as **adjusting entries.** It is easy to remember that adjusting entries are simply updating entries.

The trial balance shown in Figure 5.1 is referred to as an *unadjusted* trial balance. Now, let's return to The Kitchen Taylor to study the adjustments for supplies, insurance, wages, and depreciation. After these accounts have been updated, we will prepare an *adjusted* trial balance.

The Adjustment for Supplies

objective 2
Describe the adjustments for supplies, insurance, wages, and depreciation

As you will recall, when supplies are purchased, the asset account Supplies is debited (increased). As long as supplies are unused, they are considered to be an asset. Day to day, however, they are used. The cost of used supplies is an expense—Supplies Expense.

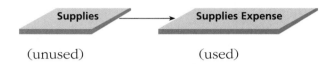

(unused)   (used)

It is not practical to update the accounts (Supplies and Supplies Expense) on a daily basis as the supplies are actually used. Because the dollar amounts involved in such daily transactions tend to be small, the cost of the paperwork would greatly exceed the benefit of such daily updating. Consequently, we wait until the end of the accounting period to update.

The unadjusted trial balance in Figure 5.1 shows that the Supplies account has a debit balance of $425. However, an inventory, or physical count, of supplies on hand on December 31 indicates that only $115 worth of unused supplies are left in the storeroom. The $310 difference ($425 − $115 = $310) represents the cost of used supplies.

$ 425	Unused—beginning (asset)
−115	Unused—ending (asset)
$ 310	Used (expense)

Based on this information, the following accounts must be adjusted:

- The asset account, Supplies, must be decreased by a credit of $310.
- The Supplies Expense account must be increased by a debit of $310.

The adjustment for supplies must now be recorded on The Kitchen Taylor's data entry sheet.

DATA ENTRY SHEET The Kitchen Taylor					
Date	Account ID	Reference	Trans Description	Debit Amt	Credit Amt
12/31/95	513		Supplies Expense	310.00	
	112		Supplies		310.00

Comment

As you will recall from Chapters 3 and 4, a data entry sheet is used to draft entries before they are recorded in the general journal. Later in this chapter, after all The Kitchen Taylor's adjustments are recorded on a data entry sheet, you will use PAW to journalize all the adjustments and post to the general ledger.

After the adjustment for supplies is journalized and posted, the December 31 financial statements will include:

Balance Sheet	Income Statement
Supplies $115 (unused)	Supplies Expense $310 (used)

The Adjustment for Insurance

Insurance coverage, like supplies, is always purchased in advance. The cost of the unexpired future coverage is something of value to the business and is recorded as an asset—Prepaid Insurance. As time goes by, however, the coverage is used up (expires). The cost of the expired coverage is now an expense—Insurance Expense.

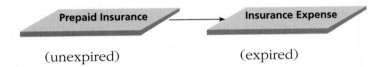

(unexpired)   (expired)

As with supplies, it is not practical to update the accounts (Prepaid Insurance and Insurance Expense) on a daily basis. Instead, we wait until the end of the accounting period.

The unadjusted trial balance in Figure 5.1 shows that the Prepaid Insurance account has a debit balance of $1,200. This $1,200 represents the cost of a two-year, or 24-month, premium paid early in December. By December 31, one month of that prepaid coverage has expired.

$$\$1{,}200/24 \text{ months} = \$50 \text{ per month}$$

$$1 \text{ month} \times \$50 \text{ per month} = \underline{\$50}$$

Based on this information, the following accounts must be adjusted:

- The asset account, Prepaid Insurance, must be decreased by a credit of $50.
- The Insurance Expense account must be increased by a debit of $50.

Comment

You will notice that some new accounts are introduced in the adjusting entries. Later in this chapter, you will learn how to add new accounts to Peachtree's chart of accounts.

The adjustment for insurance must now be recorded on The Kitchen Taylor's data entry sheet.

DATA ENTRY SHEET The Kitchen Taylor					
Date	Account ID	Reference	Trans Description	Debit Amt	Credit Amt
12/31/95	514		Insurance Expense	50.00	
	113		Prepaid Insurance		50.00

After the adjustment for insurance is journalized and posted, the December 31 financial statements will include:

Balance Sheet	Income Statement
Prepaid Insurance $1,150 (unexpired)	Insurance Expense $50 (expired)

The Adjustment for Wages

The Kitchen Taylor, a new business, has only one part-time employee. That employee works a five-day week (Monday through Friday) and is paid $100 per week ($20 per day times five days). Payday is every Friday. The usual payroll entry recorded each Friday is:

```
Dr. Wages Expense . . . . . . . . . . . . . . . . . . . . . . . . . . . . 100
        Cr. Cash . . . . . . . . . . . . . . . . . . . . . . . . . . . . . . . . . 100
```

Let's assume that December 31, 1995 falls on a Wednesday. That means three days (Monday, Tuesday, and Wednesday) of this pay period fall in December and two days (Thursday and Friday) fall in January. As usual, Friday is payday (January 2, 1996).

1995 December			1996 January	
Monday 29	Tuesday 30	Wednesday 31	Thursday 1	Friday 2
$60 ($20 × 3 days)			$40 ($20 × 2 days)	

Accrual-basis accounting requires that expenses be recorded in the period in which they are incurred regardless of when they are paid. Therefore, the $60 of wages expense incurred on December 29, 30, and 31 must be recorded in December even though the wages will not actually be paid until January 2. As of December 31, this $60 represents wages expense that has been incurred but not yet paid.

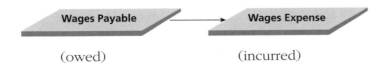

Wages Payable   Wages Expense

(owed)   (incurred)

Based on this information, the following adjustment must be recorded on December 31:

- The Wages Expense account must be increased by a debit of $60.
- As of Wednesday, December 31, $60 is owed to the employee. To record this liability, the Wages Payable account must be increased by a credit of $60.

The adjustment for wages must now be recorded on The Kitchen Taylor's data entry sheet.

			DATA ENTRY SHEET The Kitchen Taylor			
Date	Account ID	Reference	Trans Description	Debit Amt	Credit Amt
12/31/95	515		Wages Expense	60.00	
	211		Wages Payable		60.00

Comment

Observe that a separate liability account—Wages Payable—is used to record this liability. The Accounts Payable account is not used for wages owed to employees.

After journalizing and posting the adjustment for wages, the December 31 financial statements will include:

Balance Sheet	Income Statement
Wages Payable $60 (owed)	Wages Expense $60 (incurred)

The Adjustment for Depreciation

Assets are used to generate revenue, but how long are they useful? This period of usefulness is referred to as an asset's useful life. Of course, useful life varies greatly from asset to asset.

Some assets, such as supplies, are used up quickly. They are used to generate revenue for a period of less than a year. Assets with a useful life of one year or less are known as current assets. Other assets, such as equipment, are used up more slowly. They are used to generate revenue for a period greater than one year—perhaps 5, 10, 20 years or even longer. Assets that have a useful life of more than one year are known as fixed assets. Other examples of fixed assets include cars, trucks, and buildings.

Fixed assets are also called plant assets. Although both terms mean the same thing, you will notice that PAW refers to these assets as fixed assets.

We know from earlier discussions that as an asset is used, its cost is transferred to an appropriate expense account. To properly match revenue and expense on the income statement, the cost of a fixed asset must be spread over its useful life. This process of spreading the cost of a fixed asset over its useful life of more than one year is known as depreciation. There is one exception—land. Land is not depreciated because it is not used up like other fixed assets.

Now that you understand the need to depreciate fixed assets, let's consider how to record depreciation.

> **Comment**
>
> For now, we will not worry about how to compute depreciation. You will be given the dollar amount. At this time, our goal is to understand the nature of depreciation and to correctly record the given amount. If your instructor wishes to cover depreciation methods at this time, the appendix at the end of this chapter explains how to compute depreciation.

The purchase of a fixed asset is recorded with a debit (increase) to an asset account—Equipment, Truck, Building, and so on. As the asset is used up, the cost associated with the used-up portion is transferred to an expense account—Depreciation Expense.

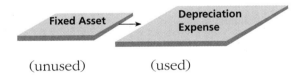

(unused)   (used)

Let's assume that The Kitchen Taylor wishes to record $100 of depreciation on its truck (fixed asset). The following adjustment is recorded on December 31:

- The Depreciation Expense account is increased by a debit of $100.
- The $6,000 cost of the truck must be preserved in the Truck account until the truck is discarded, sold, or traded, as required by the principle of historical cost discussed in Chapter 1. Therefore, instead of reducing the asset account directly with a credit of $100, we reduce it indirectly by crediting an account known as *Accumulated Depreciation*. The purpose of the Accumulated Depreciation account is to keep a cumulative record of all the depreciation ever recorded on a particular asset.

Comment

Accumulated depreciation is a contra-asset account. A contra-asset account is contrary to assets—it is a subtraction from assets. The Accumulated Depreciation account (contra asset) has a normal balance on the credit side. As the credit balance in the Accumulated Depreciation account increases, it indirectly decreases total assets.

Asset

Dr.	Cr.
+	−

Accumulated Depreciation

Dr.	Cr.
−	+

The adjustment for depreciation must now be recorded on The Kitchen Taylor's data entry sheet.

DATA ENTRY SHEET The Kitchen Taylor					
Date	Account ID	Reference	Trans Description	Debit Amt	Credit Amt
12/31/95	516		Depreciation Expense	100.00	
	121		Accum. Depreciation		100.00

After the adjustment for depreciation, the December 31 financial statements will include:

Balance Sheet		Income Statement
Truck $6,000		Depreciation Expense
Less accumulated depreciation 100 $5,900		$100
(unused)		(used)

Although unlabeled on the balance sheet, $5,900 is referred to as the **book value** of the truck.

$$\text{Book Value} = \text{Cost} - \text{Accumulated Depreciation}$$

Comment

Be careful not to confuse the terms *book value* and *market value*. Book value refers to the undepreciated cost of an asset; book value can only decrease over time. Market value refers to the current price of an asset if it were bought or sold today; market value can increase or decrease over time depending on market conditions.

Figure 5.2 shows The Kitchen Taylor's data entry sheet after all the December 31 adjustments have been recorded. We will refer to this data entry sheet as we use PAW to journalize the adjustments. However, before we can journalize, we must restore The Kitchen Taylor's data from Chapter 4.

Figure 5.2

			DATA ENTRY SHEET The Kitchen Taylor		
Date	Account ID	Reference	Trans Description	Debit Amt	Credit Amt
12/31/95	513		Supplies Expense	310.00	
	112		Supplies		310.00
12/31/95	514		Insurance Expense	50.00	
	113		Prepaid Insurance		50.00
12/31/95	515		Wages Expense	60.00	
	211		Wages Payable		60.00
12/31/95	516		Depreciation Expense	100.00	
	121		Accum. Depreciation		100.00

Restoring Data from Chapter 4

At the end of Chapter 4, you backed up (saved) The Kitchen Taylor's December transactions. Before you can journalize the adjusting entries, you must restore your Kitchen Taylor data from Chapter 4. That will allow you to start where you left off at the end of Chapter 4.

objective 3
Restore data from the previous chapter

Follow these steps to restore your Chapter 4 data:

step 1: Start Windows, then PAW. Open The Kitchen Taylor.

> Be sure that you insert your **backup disk,** *not* The Kitchen Taylor data that came on the CD-ROM with this textbook. That disk should be stored in a safe place.

Comment

step 2: Place your Kitchen Taylor backup disk in drive A.

step 3: From the main menu, select <u>F</u>ile, then <u>R</u>estore.

step 4: Type **a:\chapter4** in the Source box. (Use the same file name that you used when you backed up The Kitchen Taylor in Chapter 4.)

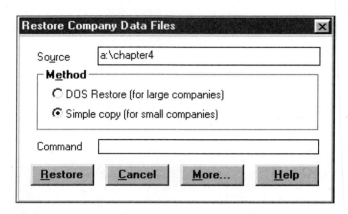

step 5: Click on the Restore button. Read the "Warning" screen, then click on OK. Restoring the files will take a few moments. When the files are restored, you are returned to the main menu.

step 6: Remove disk from drive A.

step 7: To check that your files are restored, display the "General Ledger Trial Balance" screen. Follow these steps:
 a. From the main menu, select Reports, then General Ledger.
 b. Highlight "General Ledger Trial Balance."
 c. Click on the Screen 🖥 icon, then click on OK.

Compare your screen to Figure 5.1 shown at the beginning of this chapter.

Now that you have restored The Kitchen Taylor's data, you are ready to journalize the adjustments shown on the data entry sheet in Figure 5.2.

Journalizing the Adjusting Entries and Adding New Accounts

In Chapter 4, you learned to journalize transactions using PAW's "General Journal Entry" window. In this chapter, you will use the same "General Journal Entry" window to journalize The Kitchen Taylor's adjustments. Let's begin by bringing up the "General Journal Entry" window to our screen. (HINT: From the main menu, select Tasks, then General Journal Entry.)

objective 4
Add new accounts to Peachtree's chart of accounts

As you journalize the adjustments, you will need to add some new accounts to The Kitchen Taylor's chart of accounts. With the "General Journal Entry" window on your screen, let's practice this procedure by adding the Supplies Expense account to The Kitchen Taylor's chart of accounts.

step 1: In the Date box, type **31** and press <Enter> two times.

step 2: In the "Account No." box, click on the magnifying glass icon 🔍. The chart of accounts list pops up.

step 3: At the bottom of the chart of accounts list, click on the Records New icon.

step 4: The "Maintain Chart of Accounts" window displays.

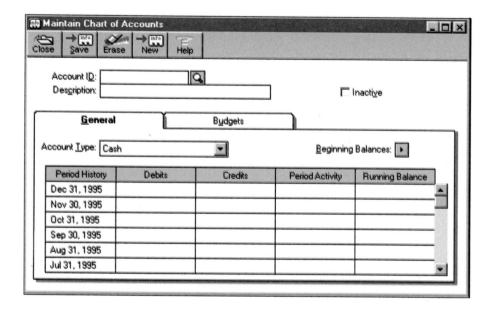

step 5:   In the Account ID box, type **513** and press <Enter>.

step 6:   In the Description box, type **Supplies Expense** and press <Enter>.

step 7:   In the Account Type box, click on the down arrow. Scroll down the list and highlight "Expenses," then press <Enter>.

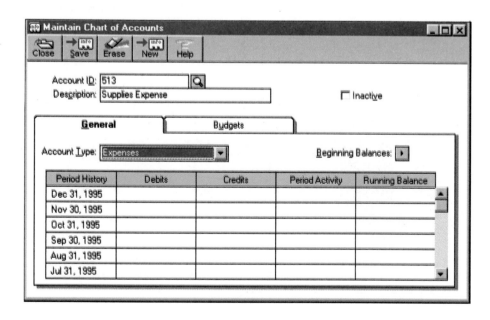

step 8:   Click on the info Save icon. You have added Account No. 513, Supplies Expense, to the chart of accounts.

Following the same procedure, add the accounts shown at the top of page 118 to The Kitchen Taylor's chart of accounts. When you are finished, click on the Close icon.

Account ID	Description	Account Type
121	Accumulated Depreciation	Accumulated Depreciation
211	Wages Payable	Other Current Liabilities
514	Insurance Expense	Expenses
515	Wages Expense	Expenses
516	Depreciation Expense	Expenses

objective 5
Journalize the adjusting entries

Referring to the data entry sheet shown in Figure 5.2, you are now ready to journalize The Kitchen Taylor's adjusting entries for supplies, insurance, wages, and depreciation. *Remember to save after each entry.*

Printing the Adjusting Entries

objective 6
Print the adjusting entries

Follow these steps to print the December 31 adjusting entries:

step 1:   From the main menu, select Reports, then General Ledger.

step 2:   In the "Report List," highlight General Journal.

step 3:   Click once on the "Print" icon. The "General Journal Filter" window displays.

step 4:   In the "From" box, click on the Calendar icon 📅. Select **31** as the date.

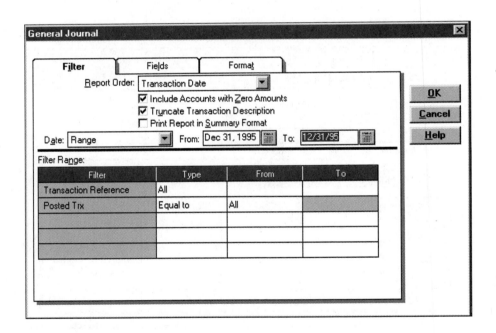

step 5:   Click on OK. When the "Print" window pops up, click on OK. The December 31 adjusting entries start to print. Compare your screen to Figure 5.3.

Figure 5.3

The Kitchen Taylor
General Journal
For the Period From Dec 31, 1995 to Dec 31, 1995

Filter Criteria includes: Report order is by Date. Report is printed with Accounts having Zero Amounts and with Truncated Transaction Descriptions and in Detail

Date	Account ID	Reference	Trans Description	Debit Amt	Credit Amt
12/31/95	513		Supplies Expense	310.00	
	112		Supplies		310.00
	514		Insurance Expense	50.00	
	113		Prepaid Insurance		50.00
	515		Wages Expense	60.00	
	211		Wages Payable		60.00
	516		Depreciation Expense	100.00	
	121		Accumulated Depreciation		100.00
		Total		520.00	520.00

Posting the Adjusting Entries

After the adjusting entries have been journalized, they must be posted to the general ledger. Follow these steps to post the adjusting entries.

objective 7
Post the adjusting entries

step 1: Click on the Close icon to close all windows before you post. Click on Tasks, then System. A pull-down menu displays.

step 2: Click once on Post. The "Post" window displays.

step 3: Click once on the box next to "General Journal." A check mark is placed in the box.

step 4: Click on OK.

Printing the General Ledger

Follow these steps to print The Kitchen Taylor's general ledger:

objective 8
Print the general ledger

step 1: From the main menu, select Reports, then General Ledger.

step 2: In the "Report List," highlight "General Ledger."

step 3: Click on the Print icon.

step 4: The "General Ledger Filter" screen displays. Click on OK.

step 5: The "Print" window pops up. Click on OK. A window pops up that shows you how many general ledger pages will print. It will take a few moments to load the data before printing actually begins.

Figure 5.4 shows The Kitchen Taylor's general ledger after the adjusting entries have been posted. Compare your printout with Figure 5.4.

Figure 5.4

The Kitchen Taylor
General Ledger
For the Period From Dec 1, 1995 to Dec 31, 1995
Filter Criteria includes: Report order is by ID. Report is printed in Detail Format.

Account ID Account Description	Date Reference	Jrnl	Trans Description	Debit Amt	Credit Amt	Balance
110 Cash	12/1/95		Beginning Balance			
	12/1/95	GENJ	Cash	10,000.00		
	12/2/95	GENJ	Check No. 101, Cash		6,000.00	
	12/3/95	GENJ	Check No. 102, Cash		1,200.00	
	12/7/95	GENJ	Cash	1,500.00		
	12/10/95	GENJ	Check No. 103, Cash		425.00	
	12/17/95	GENJ	Check No. 104, Cash		600.00	
	12/21/95	GENJ	Cash	500.00		
	12/28/95	GENJ	Check No. 105, Cash		200.00	
	12/29/95	GENJ	Check No. 106, Cash		80.00	
	12/30/95	GENJ	Cash	300.00		
			Current Period Change	12,300.00	8,505.00	3,795.00
	12/31/95		Ending Balance			3,795.00
111 Accounts Receivable	12/1/95		Beginning Balance			
	12/15/95	GENJ	Accounts Receivable	1,400.00		
	12/21/95	GENJ	Accounts Receivable		500.00	
	12/30/95	GENJ	Accounts Receivable		300.00	
			Current Period Change	1,400.00	800.00	600.00
	12/31/95		Ending Balance			600.00
112 Supplies	12/1/95		Beginning Balance			
	12/4/95	GENJ	Supplies	425.00		
	12/31/95	GENJ	Supplies		310.00	
			Current Period Change	425.00	310.00	115.00
	12/31/95		Ending Balance			115.00

Figure 5.4 *(continued)*

The Kitchen Taylor
General Ledger
For the Period From Dec 1, 1995 to Dec 31, 1995
Filter Criteria includes: Report order is by ID. Report is printed in Detail Format.

Account ID Account Description	Date Reference	Jrnl	Trans Description	Debit Amt	Credit Amt	Balance
113 Prepaid Insurance	12/1/95		Beginning Balance			
	12/3/95	GENJ	Check No. 102, Prepaid Insurance	1,200.00		
	12/31/95	GENJ	Prepaid Insurance		50.00	
			Current Period Change	1,200.00	50.00	1,150.00
	12/31/95		**Ending Balance**			**1,150.00**
120 Truck	12/1/95		Beginning Balance			
	12/2/95	GENJ	Check No. 101, Truck	6,000.00		
			Current Period Change	6,000.00		6,000.00
	12/31/95		**Ending Balance**			**6,000.00**
121 Accumulated Depreciation	12/1/95		Beginning Balance			
	12/31/95	GENJ	Accumulated Depreciation		100.00	
			Current Period Change		100.00	-100.00
	12/31/95		**Ending Balance**			**-100.00**
210 Accounts Payable	12/1/95		Beginning Balance			
	12/4/95	GENJ	Accounts Payable		425.00	
	12/10/95	GENJ	Check No. 103, Accounts Payable	425.00		
	12/26/95	GENJ	Accounts Payable		65.00	
			Current Period Change	425.00	490.00	-65.00
	12/31/95		**Ending Balance**			**-65.00**

Figure 5.4   *(continued)*

The Kitchen Taylor
General Ledger
For the Period From Dec 1, 1995 to Dec 31, 1995
Filter Criteria includes: Report order is by ID. Report is printed in Detail Format.

Account ID Account Description	Date Reference	Jrnl	Trans Description	Debit Amt	Credit Amt	Balance
211 Wages Payable	12/1/95		Beginning Balance			
	12/31/95	GENJ	Wages Payable		60.00	
			Current Period Change		60.00	-60.00
	12/31/95		Ending Balance			-60.00
310 Dennis Taylor, Capital	12/1/95		Beginning Balance			
	12/1/95	GENJ	Dennis Taylor, Capital		10,000.00	
			Current Period Change		10,000.00	-10,000.00
	12/31/95		Ending Balance			-10,000.00
320 Dennis Taylor, Drawing	12/1/95		Beginning Balance			
	12/28/95	GENJ	Check No. 105, Dennis Taylor, Drawing	200.00		
			Current Period Change	200.00		200.00
	12/31/95		Ending Balance			200.00
410 Fees Earned	12/1/95		Beginning Balance			
	12/7/95	GENJ	Fees Earned		1,500.00	
	12/15/95	GENJ	Fees Earned		1,400.00	
			Current Period Change		2,900.00	-2,900.00
	12/31/95		Ending Balance			-2,900.00
510 Rent Expense	12/1/95		Beginning Balance			
	12/17/95	GENJ	Check No. 104, Rent Expense	600.00		
			Current Period Change	600.00		600.00
	12/31/95		Ending Balance			600.00

Figure 5.4 *(continued)*

The Kitchen Taylor
General Ledger
For the Period From Dec 1, 1995 to Dec 31, 1995
Filter Criteria includes: Report order is by ID. Report is printed in Detail Format.

Account ID Account Description	Date Reference	Jrnl	Trans Description	Debit Amt	Credit Amt	Balance
511 Repair Expense	12/1/95		Beginning Balance			
	12/26/95	GENJ	Repair Expense	65.00		
			Current Period Change	65.00		65.00
	12/31/95		Ending Balance			65.00
512 Utilities Expense	12/1/95		Beginning Balance			
	12/29/95	GENJ	Check No. 106, Utilities Expense	80.00		
			Current Period Change	80.00		80.00
	12/31/95		Ending Balance			80.00
513 Supplies Expense	12/1/95		Beginning Balance			
	12/31/95	GENJ	Supplies Expense	310.00		
			Current Period Change	310.00		310.00
	12/31/95		Ending Balance			310.00
514 Insurance Expense	12/1/95		Beginning Balance			
	12/31/95	GENJ	Insurance Expense	50.00		
			Current Period Change	50.00		50.00
	12/31/95		Ending Balance			50.00
515 Wages Expense	12/1/95		Beginning Balance			
	12/31/95	GENJ	Wages Expense	60.00		
			Current Period Change	60.00		60.00
	12/31/95		Ending Balance			60.00
516 Depreciation Expense	12/1/95		Beginning Balance			
	12/31/95	GENJ	Depreciation Expense	100.00		
			Current Period Change	100.00		100.00
	12/31/95		Ending Balance			100.00

Printing the Adjusted Trial Balance

objective 9
Print the adjusted trial balance

After you have journalized and posted the adjusting entries, you should print an adjusted trial balance. This trial balance tests the overall equality of the debits and credits in the ledger after the accounts have been adjusted.

Follow these steps to print The Kitchen Taylor's adjusted trial balance.

step 1: From the main menu, select Reports, then General Ledger.

step 2: Highlight General Ledger Trial Balance.

step 3: Click on the Print icon.

step 4: At the "General Ledger Trial Balance Filter" window, click on OK.

step 5: At the "Print" window, click on OK. The general ledger trial balance begins to print. Compare your printout with Figure 5.5.

Figure 5.5

The Kitchen Taylor
General Ledger Trial Balance
As of Dec 31, 1995
Filter Criteria includes: Report order is by ID. Report is printed in Detail Format.

Account ID	Account Description	Debit Amt	Credit Amt
110	Cash	3,795.00	
111	Accounts Receivable	600.00	
112	Supplies	115.00	
113	Prepaid Insurance	1,150.00	
120	Truck	6,000.00	
121	Accumulated Depreciation		100.00
210	Accounts Payable		65.00
211	Wages Payable		60.00
310	Dennis Taylor, Capital		10,000.00
320	Dennis Taylor, Drawing	200.00	
410	Fees Earned		2,900.00
510	Rent Expense	600.00	
511	Repair Expense	65.00	
512	Utilities Expense	80.00	
513	Supplies Expense	310.00	
514	Insurance Expense	50.00	
515	Wages Expense	60.00	
516	Depreciation Expense	100.00	
	Total:	13,125.00	13,125.00

Backing Up Your Chapter 5 Data

objective 10
Back up your data

As noted in Chapter 4, you must back up your data at the end of every chapter. Follow these steps to back up your Chapter 5 data:

step 1: Insert a blank formatted disk in drive A.

step 2: From PAW's main menu, select File, then Backup.

step 3: Type a:\chapter5 in the Destination text box.

step 4: Click on the Backup button. Your files begin to copy. When all the files have been saved to drive A, you are automatically returned to the main menu.

step 5: Click on File, Exit to exit PAW.

This backup disk provides a starting point for your work in Chapter 6. *Treat it well!*

Chapter Five Summary

Adjusting entries update account balances in the ledger. The need to update exists because a few internal transactions have occurred that have not been journalized. Typical adjusting entries include adjustments for supplies, insurance, wages, and depreciation. Adjusting entries sometimes require the addition of new accounts to the chart of accounts.

After adjusting entries are journalized and posted, an adjusted trial balance is printed. The adjusted trial balance tests the equality of debits and credits in the ledger after adjusting entries have been journalized and posted.

The accounting cycle, as studied to this point, is summarized in the following flowchart:

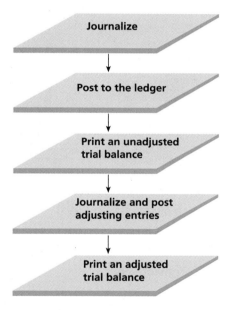

Demonstration Problem

The unadjusted trial balance and end-of-month adjustment data for Foth Data Services are as follows:

Foth Data Services
General Ledger Trial Balance
As of Dec 31, 1995

Filter Criteria includes: Report order is by ID. Report is printed in Detail Format.

Account ID	Account Description	Debit Amt	Credit Amt
110	Cash	8,000.00	
111	Accounts Receivable	7,000.00	
112	Supplies	900.00	
113	Prepaid Insurance	2,000.00	
120	Equipment	10,000.00	
121	Accumulated Depreciation		1,400.00
210	Accounts Payable		5,300.00
310	Ed Foth, Capital		17,200.00
320	Ed Foth, Drawing	5,000.00	
410	Fees Earned		35,000.00
510	Advertising Expense	2,500.00	
511	Rent Expense ·	12,000.00	
512	Utilities Expense	1,300.00	
513	Wages Expense	9,500.00	
514	Depreciation Expense	700.00	
	Total:	**58,900.00**	**58,900.00**

Adjustment Data

a. Inventory of supplies at December 31, $300.

b. Insurance expired during the month, $1,400.

c. Wages expense incurred but not yet paid as of December 31, $800.

d. Depreciation on the equipment, $900.

Instructions:

Record the adjustments on a data entry sheet. The following new accounts will be needed:

Account ID	Account Title
211	Wages Payable
515	Supplies Expense
516	Insurance Expense

Solution to Demonstration Problem

			DATA ENTRY SHEET Foth Data Services		
Date	Account ID	Reference	Trans Description	Debit Amt	Credit Amt
12/31/95	515		Supplies Expense	600.00	
	112		Supplies		600.00
12/31/95	516		Insurance Expense	1,400.00	
	113		Prepaid Insurance		1,400.00
12/31/95	513		Wages Expense	800.00	
	211		Wages Payable		800.00
12/31/95	514		Depreciation Expense	900.00	
	121		Accum. Depreciation		900.00

Glossary

adjusting entries   Entries that update internal transactions that have occurred but have not yet been record (journalized).   *108*

book value   Equals cost minus accumulated depreciation.   *114*

contra-asset account   An account that is contrary to assets. It is a subtraction from assets.   *114*

current asset   An asset used to generate revenue for a period of one year or less.   *112*

depreciation   The process of spreading the cost of a fixed asset over its useful life of more than one year.   *113*

fixed asset   An asset used to generate revenue for a period longer than one year. Also known as a *plant asset.*   *113*

internal transaction   A transaction occurring within a business that does not involve anyone outside of the business.   *108*

market value   The current price of an asset if it were bought or sold today.   *114*

plant asset   An asset used to generate revenue for a period longer than one year. Also known as a fixed asset.   *113*

useful life   Period of time over which an asset will help generate revenue.   *112*

Self-Test

Select the best answer.

1. The purpose of adjusting entries is to
   a. update accounts.
   b. add new accounts.
   c. delete accounts.
   d. All of the above.

2. The cost of unused supplies and insurance is
   a. an asset.
   b. a liability.
   c. an expense.
   d. None of the above.

3. The cost of employee wages that have been incurred but not yet paid is considered to be
   a. a liability.
   b. an expense.
   c. Both a and b.
   d. None of the above.

4. The adjusting entry to record expired insurance requires a
   a. debit to Prepaid Insurance and a credit to Insurance Expense.
   b. debit to an asset and credit to a fixed asset.
   c. debit to Insurance Expense and a credit to Accumulated Depreciation.
   d. debit to Insurance Expense and credit to Prepaid Insurance.

5. The adjusting entry to record depreciation requires a
   a. debit to Depreciation Expense and a credit to Accumulated Depreciation.
   b. debit to Accumulated Depreciation and a credit to Depreciation Expense.
   c. debit to Depreciation Expense and a credit to Depreciation Payable.
   d. debit to Accumulated Depreciation and a credit to a plant asset account.

Answers to the self-test can be found after the cases at the end of this chapter.

Questions for Discussion

1. What is the purpose of adjusting entries?
2. Why is it necessary to adjust for supplies? How is the adjustment recorded?
3. Why is it necessary to adjust for insurance? How is the adjustment recorded?
4. Why is it necessary to adjust for wages? How is the adjustment recorded?
5. What is depreciation? How is it recorded?
6. What is the main menu selection to record journal entries in PAW?
7. What is the main menu selection to print a chart of accounts in PAW?
8. What is the difference between an unadjusted trial balance and an adjusted trial balance?

Exercises

Exercise 5.1

Accounting cycle
L.O. 1-9

Arrange the following steps in the accounting cycle in their proper order:

a. Post to the ledger.
b. Print an adjusted trial balance.
c. Journalize and post the adjusting entries.
d. Journalize.
e. Print an unadjusted trial balance.

Exercise 5.2

Match the following terms with the definitions shown below:

Terminology
L.O. 1, 2

1. Book value
2. Useful life
3. Market value
4. Contra-asset account
5. Fixed asset
6. Internal transaction
7. Adjusting entries
8. Current asset
9. Depreciation

Definitions

a. An asset used to generate revenue for a period longer than one year.

b. Entries that update internal transactions that have occurred but have not yet been recorded (journalized).

c. Period of time over which an asset will help generate revenue.

d. Equals cost minus accumulated depreciation.

e. The current price of an asset if it were bought or sold today.

f. An asset used to generate revenue for a period of one year or less.

g. A transaction occurring within a business that does not involve anyone outside the business.

h. The process of spreading the cost of a fixed asset over its useful life of more than one year.

i. An account that is contrary to assets. It is a subtraction from assets.

Exercise 5.3

The December 1, 1995, balance in the Supplies account is $525. On December 31, 1995, an inventory indicates that $270 worth of supplies is left unused in the storeroom.

Adjustment for Supplies
L.O. 2

a. In data entry sheet format, what is the necessary adjusting entry on December 31?

b. Relative to this situation, the December 31 balance sheet will show what account and balance?

c. Relative to this situation, the December 31 income statement will show what account and balance?

Exercise 5.4

On September 1, 1995, Pronto Company paid a $360 premium for one year of insurance coverage. This future insurance coverage was recorded in the Prepaid Insurance account.

Adjustment for Insurance
L.O. 2

a. In data entry sheet format, what is the necessary adjusting entry on December 31?

b. Relative to this situation, the December 31 balance sheet will show what account and balance?

c. Relative to this situation, the December 31 income statement will show what account and balance?

Exercise 5.5

Iglesias Company pays its employees a total of $1,500 for a five-day workweek (Monday through Friday). Payday is each Friday. Assume that December 31, 1995, falls on Tuesday.

Adjustment for Wages
L.O. 2

a. In data entry sheet format, what is the necessary adjusting entry on December 31?

b. Relative to this situation, the December 31 balance sheet will show what account and balance?

c. Relative to this situation, the December 31 income statement will show what account and balance?

Exercise 5.6

Adjustment for Depreciation
L.O. 2

On December 31, 1995, Woo Associates wishes to record $975 of depreciation on its equipment.

a. In data entry sheet format, what is the necessary adjusting entry on December 31?

b. Relative to this situation, the December 31 balance sheet will show what account and balance?

c. Relative to this situation, the December 31 income statement will show what account and balance?

Exercise 5.7

Adjustment for Selected
Accounts
L.O. 2

Based on the following information, record the necessary April 30 adjusting entries in data entry sheet format:.

a. Supplies used during April, $280.

b. Insurance expired during April, $630.

c. Wages expense incurred but not paid as of April 30, $1,750.

d. Depreciation on the truck for April, $390.

Exercise 5.8

Adjustment for Selected
Accounts
L.O. 2

Based on the following information, record the necessary September 30 adjusting entries in data entry sheet format:

a. Prior to adjustment the Supplies account had a balance of $340. On September 30, 1995, an inventory indicates that $160 worth of supplies is left unused in the storeroom.

b. Prior to adjustment, the Prepaid Insurance account had a balance of $750. On September 30, unexpired insurance coverage amounts to only $320.

c. The payroll each Friday totals $2,000 for a five-day workweek (Monday through Friday). September 30 falls on Thursday.

d. Depreciation on the building for September, $1,800.

Problems—Set A

Problem 5.1A

Restore data, trial balance
L.O. 3

In Chapter 4, Problem Set A, you journalized and posted the December transactions for Ace Cleaning Service. The December 31, 1995, unadjusted trial balance for Ace Cleaning Service is shown in Figure 5.6.

Figure 5.6

Ace Cleaning Service
General Ledger Trial Balance
As of Dec 31, 1995
Filter Criteria includes: Report order is by ID. Report is printed in Detail Format.

Account ID	Account Description	Debit Amt	Credit Amt
110	Cash	4,366.00	
111	Accounts Receivable	2,275.00	
112	Supplies	180.00	
113	Prepaid Insurance	648.00	
114	Equipment	5,000.00	
210	Accounts Payable		2,525.00
310	Joan Haywood, Capital		7,500.00
320	Joan Haywood, Drawing	540.00	
410	Cleaning Revenue		4,650.00
510	Rent Expense	625.00	
511	Repair Expense	260.00	
512	Salary Expense	645.00	
513	Utilities Expense	136.00	
	Total:	**14,675.00**	**14,675.00**

Instructions

1. Start Windows, then PAW. Open Ace Cleaning Service.

2. Follow these steps to restore your Ace Cleaning Service data:
   a. Place your Ace Cleaning Service backup disk in drive A.

> Be sure that you insert your **backup disk,** *not* the Ace Cleaning Service data that came on the CD-ROM with this textbook. That disk should be stored in a safe place.   ***Comment***

   b. From the main menu, select <u>F</u>ile, then <u>R</u>estore.
   c. Type **a:\acedec.44a** in the So<u>u</u>rce box. (Use the same file name that you used when you backed up Problem 4.4A in Chapter 4.)
   d. Click on the <u>R</u>estore button. Read the "Warning" screen, then click on OK. Restoring the files will take a few moments. When the files are restored, you are returned to the main menu.
   e. Remove the disk from drive A.

3. To check that your files are restored, print the general ledger trial balance and compare it to the unadjusted trial balance shown in Figure 5.6.

Problem 5.2A

Ace Cleaning Service has the following adjustment data on December 31, 1995:   Data entry sheet

L.O. 5

a. Supplies used during December, $80.

b. Insurance expired during December, $54.

c. Salary expense incurred but not yet paid as of December 31, $258.

d. Depreciation on the equipment for December, $75.

Instructions

Record these adjustments on a data entry sheet.

Problem 5.3A

Adjusting entries; adjusted trial balance
L.O. 5–9

Instructions

1. Using PAW's "General Journal Entry" feature and your completed data entry sheet from Problem 5.2A, journalize the Ace Cleaning Service adjustments. Add new accounts to the chart of accounts as needed using the account titles and numbers shown below.

115	Accumulated Depreciation
215	Salaries Payable
514	Supplies Expense
515	Insurance Expense
516	Depreciation Expense

2. Print the chart of accounts.
3. Print the December 31, 1995, general journal.
4. Proofread your general journal. If necessary, make corrections using PAW's "Edit Records" feature. If you made any corrections, reprint the general journal.
5. Post to the ledger.
6. Print the general ledger.
7. Print the adjusted trial balance.

Problem 5.4A

Back up
L.O. 10

Your Ace Cleaning Services data **must** be backed up. You will restore it in Chapter 6. Follow these steps:

step 1: Insert a blank formatted disk in drive A.

step 2: From PAW's main menu, select File, then Backup.

step 3: Type **a:\acedec.54a** in the "Destination" text box.

step 4: Click on the Backup button. Your files begin to copy. When all the files have been saved to drive A, you are automatically returned to the main menu.

step 5: Click on File, Exit to exit PAW.

Problems—Set B

Problem 5.1B

Restore data
L.O. 3

In Chapter 4, Problem Set B, you journalized and posted December entries for Loyal Lawn Service. The December 31, 1995, unadjusted trial balance for Loyal Lawn Service is shown in Figure 5.7.

Figure 5.7

Loyal Lawn Service
General Ledger Trial Balance
As of Dec 31, 1995

Filter Criteria includes: Report order is by ID. Report is printed in Detail Format.

Account ID	Account Description	Debit Amt	Credit Amt
110	Cash	2,720.00	
111	Accounts Receivable	1,865.00	
112	Supplies	225.00	
113	Prepaid Insurance	600.00	
114	Equipment	5,000.00	
210	Accounts Payable		1,435.00
310	Chris Canon, Capital		7,000.00
320	Chris Canon, Drawing	420.00	
410	Lawn Service Revenue		3,987.00
510	Rent Expense	595.00	
511	Repair Expense	145.00	
512	Salary Expense	690.00	
513	Utilities Expense	162.00	
	Total:	**12,422.00**	**12,422.00**

Instructions

1. Start Windows, then PAW. Open Loyal Lawn Service.
2. Follow these steps to restore your Loyal Lawn Service data:
   a. Place your Loyal Lawn Service backup disk in drive A.

> *Comment*
>
> Be sure that you insert your **backup disk,** *not* the Loyal Lawn Service data that came on the CD-ROM with this textbook. That disk should be stored in a safe place.

   b. From the main menu, select File, then Restore.
   c. Type **a:\loyaldec.44b** in the Source box. (Use the same file name that you used when you backed up Problem 4.4B in Chapter 4.)
   d. Click on the Restore button. Read the "Warning" screen, then click on OK. Restoring the files will take a few moments. When the files are restored, you are returned to the main menu.
   e. Remove the disk from drive A.
3. To check that your files are restored, print the general ledger trial balance and compare it to the unadjusted trial balance shown in Figure 5.7.

Problem 5.2B

Loyal Lawn Service has the following adjustment data on December 31, 1995:

Data entry sheet
L.O. 5

a. Supplies used during December, $90.
b. Insurance expired during December, $50.

c. Salary expense incurred but not yet paid as of December 31, $414.

d. Depreciation on the equipment for December, $75.

Instructions

Record these adjustments on a data entry sheet.

Problem 5.3B

Adjusting entries; adjusted trial
balance
L.O. 5–9

Instructions

1. Using PAW's "General Journal Entry" feature and your completed data entry sheet from Problem 5.2B, journalize the Loyal Lawn Service adjustments. Add new accounts to the chart of accounts as needed using the account titles and numbers shown below.

115	Accumulated Depreciation
215	Salaries Payable
514	Supplies Expense
515	Insurance Expense
516	Depreciation Expense

2. Print the chart of accounts.

3. Print the December 31, 1995, general journal.

4. Proofread your general journal. If necessary, make corrections using PAW's "Edit Records" feature. If you made any corrections, reprint the general journal.

5. Post to the ledger.

6. Print the general ledger.

7. Print the adjusted trial balance.

Problem 5.4B

Back up
L.O. 10

Your Loyal Lawn Service data **must** be backed up. You will restore it in Chapter 6. Follow these steps:

step 1:   Insert a blank formatted disk in drive A.

step 2:   From PAW's main menu, select File, then Backup.

step 3:   Type a:\loyaldec.54b in the Destination text box.

step 4:   Click on the Backup button. Your files begin to copy. When all the files have been saved to drive A, you are automatically returned to the main menu.

step 5:   Click on File, Exit to exit PAW.

Mini-Cases

Case 5–1

Your friend, Michael O'Brien paid a $900 insurance premium for three years of coverage beginning December 1 of this year. He complains to you about all that insurance expense in one year having a terrible effect on his current year's net income. Would you agree?

Case 5–2

A client is thinking of buying a building. She calls and says she may pay for the building over 5 years rather than over 15 years. That way, she says, she will be able to depreciate the building over a five-year period. She asks for your opinion of her plan.

Case 5–3

You notice that your new assistant did not journalize any adjusting entries on December 31. When asked about this, he replied, "The adjustments are on the data entry sheet." How would you respond?

A Case of Ethics

An accountant friend brags to you that whenever it looks like his boss's company is going to show a net loss for the month, he boosts net income by not making any adjustments for supplies, insurance, wages, or depreciation. "My boss thinks I'm a genius!" says your friend. What do you think?

Answers to Self-Test

1. *a*   2. *a*   3. *c*   4. *d*   5. *a*

Appendix 5A—Depreciation

Depreciation Terminology

Before studying the methods used to depreciate fixed assets, we must define some terms that are essential to the understanding of depreciation methods. These terms are *cost, residual value, depreciable base, useful life,* and *book value.*

Cost is an abbreviated version of the term *historical cost,* which was defined in Chapter 1. Cost includes all the outlays necessary to acquire an asset and make it useful to the business.

Residual value is the trade-in or salvage value that the fixed asset will have at its anticipated disposal date. The residual value is an estimate provided by management or others who are familiar with the values of used fixed assets. The accountant assigns a zero residual value if the asset will have little or no value at the end of its useful life or if the asset will be used until it is discarded.

Depreciable base is that part of the fixed asset's cost that will be expended during its useful life. Depreciable base is equal to the cost minus residual value.

$$\text{Depreciable Base} = \text{Cost} - \text{Residual Value}$$

Useful life is an estimate of the total service the fixed asset will provide. This estimate depends on many factors such as use, climate, and technological change. Because of varying circumstances, different estimates of useful life for the same asset are possible. Useful life can be measured in units of time, number of units produced, operating hours, miles driven, and so on. Having the estimate of useful life, the accountant knows over what time period the depreciable base will be expensed.

Book value is the unused or undepreciated cost of a fixed asset. As discussed earlier, book value is equal to cost minus accumulated depreciation.

Book Value = Cost − Accumulated Depreciation

Now we are ready to study the various methods of computing depreciation.

Depreciation Methods

Compute depreciation using
four different methods
L.O. 11

There are four commonly used methods of depreciation. The four methods are:

- Straight line.
- Units of production.
- Sum-of-the-years' digits.
- Double-declining balance.

Let's consider each method in greater detail.

Straight-Line Method

The following formula is used to compute straight-line depreciation.

$$\frac{\text{Cost} - \text{Residual Value}}{\text{Useful life}} = \text{Annual Depreciation}$$

Let's try an example. Satellite Services acquired a fixed asset on January 2, 1995, for a total cost of $150,000. The useful life was estimated to be five years. At the anticipated disposal date, it is estimated that the fixed asset will have a residual value of $12,000. Using the straight-line method, the first year's depreciation is computed as follows:

$$\frac{150,000 - \$12,000}{5 \text{ years}} = \$27,600 \text{ Depreciation for } 1995$$

A depreciation schedule for the entire useful life of the asset appears as follows:

		Depreciation Schedule—Straight-Line Method		
Year	Book Value (beginning of year)	Annual Depreciation Expense	Accumulated Depreciation	Book Value (end of year)
1995	$150,000	($150,000 − 12,000) ÷ 5 = $27,600	$ 27,600	$122,400
1996	122,400	(150,000 − 12,000) ÷ 5 = 27,600	55,200	94,800
1997	94,800	(150,000 − 12,000) ÷ 5 = 27,600	82,800	67,200
1998	67,200	(150,000 − 12,000) ÷ 5 = 27,600	110,400	39,600
1999	39,600	(150,000 − 12,000) ÷ 5 = 27,600	138,000	12,000

Comment

Each full year's depreciation expense is the same. The Accumulated Depreciation account balance increases by the same amount each year. At the end of its useful life, the book value of the fixed asset is equal to its estimated residual value.

Units-of-Production Method

Under the units-of-production method, depreciation is computed in two steps:

step 1: $\dfrac{\text{Cost} - \text{Residual Value}}{\text{Useful Life (defined in units)}} = \text{Depreciation per Unit}$

step 2: $\text{Depreciation per Unit} \times \begin{array}{c}\text{Number of Units}\\ \text{Produced in}\\ \text{Current Year}\end{array} = \text{Annual Depreciation}$

The units-of-production method results in depreciation that varies from year to year. The amount of the annual depreciation reflects the extent to which the fixed asset is used. Usage may be measured in such things as units produced, hours of use, or miles driven.

Let's demonstrate the units-of-production method using Satellite Services's asset information: the asset cost $150,000, had a residual value of $12,000, and was estimated to have the capacity to produce 30,000 units during its life. In 1995, the asset produced 8,000 units. The first year's depreciation is computed as follows:

step 1: $\dfrac{\$150,000 - \$12,000}{30,000 \text{ Units}} = \$4.60 \text{ Depreciation per Unit}$

step 2: $\$4.60 \times 8,000 \text{ Units} = \$36,800 \text{ Depreciation for 1995.}$

Assuming that the asset produced 4,000 units in 1996, depreciation for the second year is computed as follows:

$$\$4.60 \times 4,000 \text{ Units} = \$18,400 \text{ Depreciation for 1996}$$

Although the number of units produced in 1996 has changed, observe that the depreciation per unit remains constant at $4.60 per unit. Under the units-of-production method, the depreciation per unit is computed in the first year and remains constant through the entire useful life of the asset.

A depreciation schedule for the entire useful life of the asset, given the indicated annual production, appears as follows:

		Depreciation Schedule—Units-of-Production Method		
Year	Book Value (beginning of year)	Annual Depreciation Expense	Accumulated Depreciation	Book Value (end of year)
1995	$150,000	($4.60 × 8,000) = $36,800	$ 36,800	$113,200
1996	113,200	($4.60 × 4,000) = 18,400	55,200	94,800
1997	94,800	($4.60 × 7,000) = 32,200	87,400	62,600
1998	62,600	($4.60 × 5,000) = 23,000	110,400	39,600
1999	39,600	($4.60 × 6,000) = 27,600	138,000	12,000

Comment

Each year's depreciation expense is different. The Accumulated Depreciation account balance increases by these different amounts. At the end of its useful life, the book value of the fixed asset is equal to its estimated residual value.

Sum-of-the-Years'-Digits Method

The following formula is used to compute sum-of-the-years'-digits depreciation:

$$(\text{Cost} - \text{Residual Value}) \times \frac{\text{Remaining Years of Useful Life}}{\text{Sum-of-the-Years' Digits}} = \text{Annual Depreciation}$$

The fraction in this formula is called the sum-of-the-years'-digits fraction. This fraction is like a countdown clock indicating the time remaining. The numerator (top number) represents the remaining years of useful life at the beginning of the current year. The numerator decreases as the asset's remaining life becomes smaller. The denominator (bottom number) represents the sum of the years' digits and will not change. The denominator, the sum of the years' digits, is calculated by adding the digit 1 for the first year of useful life to the digit 2 for the second year of useful life to the digit 3 . . . finally, adding the digit for the last year of the asset's useful life. For example, the sum of the years' digits for a five-year useful life is computed as follows:

$$1 + 2 + 3 + 4 + 5 = \underline{15}$$

The sum of-the-years' digits (SYD) may also be calculated by using the following formula:

$$\text{SYD} = \frac{\text{Total Useful Life in Years}^2 + \text{Total Useful Life in Years}}{2}$$

For example, assuming a five-year useful life:

$$\frac{(5)^2 + 5}{2} = \frac{30}{2} = 15$$

Let's demonstrate the sum-of-the-years'-digits method using Satellite Services's asset information. The asset cost $150,000, had a residual value of $12,000, and was estimated to have a useful life of five years. The first year's depreciation is computed as follows:

$$(\$150,000 - \$12,000) \times \frac{5}{15} = \$46,000 \text{ Depreciation for 1995}$$

To continue the example, the depreciation for the second year is computed as follows:

$$(\$150,000 - \$12,000) \times \frac{4}{15} = \$36,800 \text{ Depreciation for 1996}$$

A depreciation schedule for the entire useful life of the asset appears as follows:

Depreciation Schedule—Sum-of-the-Year's-Digits Method				
Year	Book Value (beginning of year)	Annual Depreciation Expense	Accumulated Depreciation	Book Value (end of year)
1995	$150,000	($150,000 − 12,000) × 5/15 = 46,000	$ 46,000	$104,000
1996	104,000	(150,000 − 12,000) × 4/15 = 36,800	82,800	67,200
1997	67,200	(150,000 − 12,000) × 3/15 = 27,600	110,400	39,600
1998	39,600	(150,000 − 12,000) × 2/15 = 18,400	128,800	21,200
1999	21,200	(150,000 − 12,000) × 1/15 = 9,200	138,000	12,000

Each year's depreciation expense is smaller than the previous year's. The Accumulated Depreciation account increases by these different amounts. At the end of the asset's useful life, the book value of the fixed asset is equal to its estimated residual value. The SYD method is referred to as an *accelerated depreciation method* because the annual depreciation in the early years is greater than under the straight-line method.

Double-Declining-Balance Method

The following formula is used to compute double-declining-balance depreciation:

Book Value $\times$ (2 $\times$ Straight-Line Rate) = Annual Depreciation

To determine the straight-line rate of depreciation, divide 100 percent by the useful life in years:

$$\frac{100\%}{\text{Useful Life in Years}} = \text{Straight-Line Rate}$$

For example, an asset with a 10-year useful life would have a straight-line rate calculated as follows:

$$\frac{100\%}{10 \text{ Years}} = 10\%$$

Let's demonstrate the double-declining-balance method using Satellite Services's asset information. The asset cost $150,000, had a residual value of $12,000, and had an estimated useful life of five years. The first year's depreciation is computed as follows:

$150,000 \times 40\% = 60,000$ Depreciation for 1995

The book value used in this formula is always the book value as of the beginning of the current period. In the first year, the book value is always the full cost of the asset since there is no accumulated depreciation on the first day of the first year. The straight-line rate in our example is 20 percent (100%/5 years), which results in a double-declining rate of 40 percent (2 $\times$ 20%).

To continue the example, the depreciation for the second year is computed as follows:

$90,000 \times 40\% = 36,000$ Depreciation for 1996

In the second year of our example, the book value on the first day of the second year is $90,000 ($150,000 − $60,000). The double-declining rate is still 40 percent. This rate remains constant through the useful life of the asset.

A depreciation schedule for the entire useful life of the asset appears as follows:

Depreciation Schedule—Double-Declining-Balance Method				
Year	Book Value (beginning of year)	Annual Depreciation Expense	Accumulated Depreciation	Book Value (end of year)
1995	$150,000	($150,000 × .40) = $60,000	$ 60,000	$ 90,000
1996	90,000	(90,000 × .40) = 36,000	96,000	54,000
1997	54,000	(54,000 × .40) = 21,600	117,600	32,400
1998	32,400	(32,400 × .40) = 12,960	130,560	19,440
1999	19,440	(19,440 − 12,000) = 7,440	138,000	12,000

It is important to note that book value cannot be allowed to fall below residual value. Although this is true of all depreciation methods, the double-declining-balance method is the only method that does not use residual value in the formula for calculating depreciation expense. Therefore, the depreciation expense for the last year of useful life is always the amount necessary to adjust the book value to the asset's residual value. Since the residual value is $12,000 in this example, the depreciation for the last year is $7,440 ($19,440 − $12,000), which brings the book value to exactly $12,000 at the end of 1999.

Comment

Observe that the rate of depreciation is the same each year (40 percent in this example). However, that constant rate is applied to a book value that is decreasing each year. Also observe that annual depreciation expense gets smaller each year. This large-to-small pattern indicates that the double-declining-balance method is another example of an accelerated depreciation method.

Depreciation and Federal Income Taxes

The depreciation methods presented in this appendix are commonly used for financial reporting purposes. The phrase *for financial reporting purposes* refers to the way transactions are recorded daily and ultimately reported in the financial statements used by investors, potential investors, creditors, and others outside the business. Many businesses use one method of depreciation for financial reporting purposes and a different method for income tax purposes. This is acceptable to both the accountant and the taxing authorities. Ultimately, the total amount of depreciation expense recorded over the entire useful life of an asset is the same regardless of the method of depreciation. Many businesses use an accelerated method of depreciation for income tax purposes.

Any of the depreciation methods discussed can be used for tax purposes as long as the fixed asset was acquired before 1981. Fixed assets acquired between 1981 and 1986 must be depreciated using the **Accelerated Cost Recovery System (ACRS)** described in the Internal Revenue Code. Assets acquired after December 31, 1986, must be depreciated using the **Modified Accelerated Cost Recovery System (MACRS)** required by the Tax Reform Act of 1986. Both the ACRS and the MACRS systems result in the accelerated depreciation of fixed assets.

Exercises

Appendix 5A Exercise 1

On January 2, 1995, Compton Associates purchased a piece of equipment at a cost of $18,000. The estimated useful life is four years and the residual value is $2,000.

Prepare a depreciation schedule for each of the following methods:

a. Straight-line.
b. Sum-of-the-years' digits.
c. Double declining balance.

Appendix 5A Exercise 2

On March 12, 1995, Collins Company acquired a new truck at a cost of $16,000. This asset has an estimated residual value of $4,000 and an estimated useful life of 80,000 miles. Collins selected the units-of-production method of depreciation. The truck is driven 15,000 miles in 1995, 19,000 miles in 1996, 25,000 miles in 1997, and 21,000 miles in 1998.

Prepare a depreciation schedule for 1995–1998.

Appendix 5A Exercise 3

On July 1, 1995, Alexos Associates acquired a copy machine at a cost of $10,600. The estimated useful life is four years and the estimated residual value is $1,000.

Prepare a depreciation schedule for each of the following methods:

a. Straight line.
b. Sum-of-the years' digits.
c. Double declining balance.

Internal Control
Focus on Cash

LEARNING OBJECTIVES

After studying this chapter, you should be able to:

1. Explain the basic concept of internal control.

2. Establish, use, and replenish a petty cash fund.

3. Restore data from the previous chapter.

4. Establish and use a change fund.

5. Account for shortages and overages using Cash Short and Cash Over accounts.

6. Describe the basic forms and procedures related to the use of a checking account.

7. Prepare a bank reconciliation and the related journal entries.

8. Back up your data.

Every business is concerned with safeguarding its cash from loss or theft. In this chapter, you will study the use of a checking account to safeguard cash. Many of you probably use a personal checking account in managing your own cash. Since many of the procedures involved in opening and maintaining business and personal accounts are similar, much of this discussion may sound familiar. You will begin your study of cash management with a discussion of internal controls and special cash funds.

Internal Controls

objective 1
Explain the basic concept of internal control

The procedures used by management to control business operations are known as internal controls. The broad topic of internal control can be divided into two subtopics: internal administrative controls and internal accounting controls.

Although some overlap exists between the two, internal administrative controls are primarily concerned with:

1. Promoting efficiency.
2. Encouraging employee compliance with company policies.

Internal accounting controls are primarily concerned with:

1. Protecting assets.
2. Ensuring the accuracy of accounting data.

We will focus our attention on internal accounting controls specifically dealing with cash. In this discussion, *cash* is defined in the broad sense to include currency, coin, checks, bank drafts, and money orders.

The Petty Cash Fund

objective 2
Establish, use, and replenish a petty cash fund

Paying bills by check is certainly an important way to safeguard cash. However, this is not practical in the case of bills for small amounts. For example, writing a check for $0.75 to cover postage due on incoming mail does not make sense. The cost of writing a check for such a small amount exceeds the face amount of the check. Instead, most businesses pay small bills in cash out of a petty cash fund.

The petty cash fund is established for a fixed amount. The size of the fund depends on the needs of the business. Day to day, small bills are paid in cash directly out of the fund. Periodically, the fund is replenished, usually on a weekly or monthly basis.

Establishing the Petty Cash Fund

The petty cash fund is established by writing a check for the fixed amount of the fund. Next, the check is cashed, and the cash is placed in a petty cash box.

To demonstrate the accounting for such a transaction, let's assume that on December 29 The Kitchen Taylor issues Check No. 107 to establish a $100 petty cash fund. This transaction is recorded on a data entry sheet as shown in Figure 6.1.

Figure 6.1

			DATA ENTRY SHEET The Kitchen Taylor		
Date	Account ID	Reference	Trans Description	Debit Amt	Credit Amt
12/29/95	109		Check No. 107, Petty Cash	100.00	
	110		Check No. 107, Cash		100.00

The Petty Cash account is an asset account. It appears on the balance sheet immediately before the Cash account. The Petty Cash account is not debited or credited again unless the business decides to change the fixed size of the fund.

Making Payments from the Petty Cash Fund

For internal control purposes, one person should be designated as custodian of the petty cash fund. This should be the only person disbursing cash from the fund. The custodian makes payments from the fund based on a company policy describing such things as acceptable purposes for payments and limits on the size of individual payments.

The custodian should prepare a petty cash voucher for each payment from the fund. The voucher describes the amount, date, and purpose of each payment. Most petty cash vouchers also categorize the payment by account and require the signatures or initials of the parties making and receiving the payment. Figure 6.2 shows a completed petty cash voucher.

Figure 6.2

PETTY CASH VOUCHER

NO.   1   DATE   December 29, 1995

PAID TO   U. S. Postal Service $ .65

FOR   Postage Due

ACCOUNT   Miscellaneous Expense

Received by: Approved by Custodian:
J. avalos   *D. Taylor*

Comment

> The custodian should be advised that the fund will be balanced on an unannounced basis. To balance the petty cash fund, the supervisor will:
>
> 1. Count the cash in the box.
> 2. Total the petty cash vouchers.
> 3. Add the cash in the box to the total of the vouchers; this sum should equal the fixed size of the petty cash fund.

In addition to vouchers, some companies use a petty cash record to summarize all the petty cash voucher information on a single sheet. The columnar format of the petty cash record makes it convenient to sort voucher information by account. This, in turn, makes it convenient to compile the information needed to replenish the fund at the end of the month. Figure 6.3 shows The Kitchen Taylor's petty cash record for the month of December.

Figure 6.3

Petty Cash Record
For the Month of December 1995

| | | | | | Distribution of Payments | | | |
| | | | | | | | Other | |
Date	Voucher No.	Explanation	Payments	Supplies	Delivery Expense	Misc. Expense	Account	Amount
Dec. 29		Established Fund, $100						
29	1	Postage due	.65			.65		
29	2	Star Delivery Service	4.30		4.30			
30	3	Felt-tip pens	2.75	2.75				
30	4	Withdrawal by owner	10.00				D. Taylor, Drawing	10.00
30	5	Star Delivery Service	4.75		4.75			
30	6	Scratch pads	3.80	3.80				
31	7	Sent telegram	4.90			4.90		
31	8	Withdrawal by owner	6.50				D. Taylor, Drawing	6.50
31	9	Postage due	.22			.22		
31	10	Small repair	8.50				Repair Expense	8.50
		Totals	46.37	6.55	9.05	5.77		25.00
		Bal., 12-31 $ 53.63						
		Replenished 46.37						
		Bal., 1-1 $100.00						

Replenishing the Petty Cash Fund

If a petty cash record is used, the information to replenish the fund is taken directly from the petty cash record. Otherwise, the information comes directly from the petty cash vouchers.

The Kitchen Taylor's petty cash fund is replenished based on the petty cash record shown in Figure 6.3. This transaction is recorded on a data entry sheet as shown in Figure 6.4.

Figure 6.4

			DATA ENTRY SHEET The Kitchen Taylor		
Date	Account ID	Reference	Trans Description	Debit Amt	Credit Amt
12/31/95	112		Check No. 108, Supplies	6.55	
	517		Check No. 108, Delivery Expense	9.05	
	518		Check No. 108, Miscellaneous Expense	5.77	
	320		Check No. 108, Dennis Taylor, Drawing	16.50	
	511		Check No. 108, Repair Expense	8.50	
	110		Check No. 108, Cash		46.37

The credit to the Cash account represents Check No. 108, written in the amount of $46.37. This check is cashed, and the cash is placed in the petty cash box. This brings the fund up to its fixed size ($100). After replenishment on December 31, the actual cash in the box ($100) is equal to the Petty Cash account balance ($100) shown on the December 31 balance sheet.

Comment

As noted earlier, replenishing petty cash does *not* change the fixed size of the fund. Therefore, the replenishment entry does *not* involve the Petty Cash account.

The petty cash fund may be replenished any time cash in the box gets low. However, the fund should always be replenished at the end of the month. This is necessary for the monthly financial statements to reflect up-to-date account balances. Remember, payments from the petty cash fund are not journalized until the fund is replenished.

Restoring Data from Chapter 5

Before you can use PAW to journalize The Kitchen Taylor's petty cash transactions, you must restore your data from Chapter 5. Follow these steps:

objective 3
Restore data from previous chapter

step 1: Start Windows, then PAW. Open The Kitchen Taylor.

step 2: Place your Kitchen Taylor backup disk in drive A.

step 3: From the main menu, select File, then Restore.

step 4: Type **a:\chapter5** in the "Source" box. (Use the same file name that you used when you backed up The Kitchen Taylor in Chapter 5.)

step 5: Click on the Restore button. Read the "Warning" screen, then click on OK. Restoring the files will take a few moments. When the files are restored, you are returned to the main menu.

step 6: Remove disk from drive A.

Using PAW to Journalize and Post the Petty Cash Transactions

You probably noticed that some new accounts need to be added to The Kitchen Taylor's chart of accounts: Petty Cash, Account No. 109; Delivery Expense, Account No. 517; and Miscellaneous Expense, Account No. 518. Using the Tasks pull-down menu, you can add these accounts while recording the journal entries in the "General Journal Entry" window. Or, you can add these new accounts by selecting the Maintain pull-down menu and clicking on Chart of Accounts. In PAW, the account type for the Petty Cash account is Cash.

Journalize the transaction shown on the data entry sheet in Figure 6.1 to establish the Petty Cash Fund. Then, journalize the transaction to replenish the petty cash fund shown on the data entry sheet in Figure 6.4. *Remember to post your journal entries.*

The Change Fund

objective 4
Establish and use a change fund

Businesses that regularly receive cash (currency and coin) from customers need to be able to make change. If all cash inflows are deposited into a checking account at the end of each day, an empty cash drawer the following morning could present a problem. This problem is easily solved by establishing a change fund.

A change fund is a fixed amount of cash that is kept in the cash drawer on a permanent basis for the purpose of making change. How large the fund should be depends on the needs of the individual business. Once the size of the fund has been determined, the business must decide on the denominations of the bills and coins to be used in the change fund.

Let's assume that on December 31 The Kitchen Taylor issues Check No. 109 to establish a $75 change fund. This transaction is recorded on a data entry sheet as shown in Figure 6.5.

Figure 6.5

DATA ENTRY SHEET The Kitchen Taylor					
Date	Account ID	Reference	Trans Description	Debit Amt	Credit Amt
12/31/95	108		Check No. 109, Change Fund	75.00	
	110		Check No. 109, Cash		75.00

The credit to the Cash account represents Check No. 109, written in the amount of $75. This check is cashed, requesting the desired denominations of bills and coins, and the cash is placed in the cash drawer.

At the end of each business day, all the cash in the cash drawer is deposited in the checking account *except* for the amount of the change fund. The $75 change fund is counted out and immediately placed back in the cash drawer.

The Change Fund account is an asset account. It appears on the balance sheet before Cash or the Petty Cash account.

The Change Fund account is not debited or credited again unless the business decides to change the size of the fund. Otherwise, the $75 balance remains in the account, and the $75 in cash remains in the cash drawer.

> The change fund and the petty cash fund are separate funds with separate purposes. The change fund is used to make change for customers. The petty cash fund is used to pay small bills.
>
> ***Comment***

Using PAW to Journalize and Post the Change Fund Transaction

You probably noticed that Change Fund, Account No. 108, needs to be added to The Kitchen Taylor's chart of accounts. Using the Tas<u>k</u>s pull-down menu, you can add this account while recording the journal entry in the "General Journal Entry" window. Or, you can add this new account by selecting the <u>M</u>aintain pull-down menu and clicking on Chart of <u>A</u>ccounts. In PAW, the account type for the Change Fund account is Cash.

Journalize the transaction to establish the Change Fund shown on the data entry sheet in Figure 6.5. *Then, post this journal entry.*

Cash Short and Cash Over

Businesses recording large numbers of cash sales generally use a cash register. As each sale is registered, the tape inside the cash register keeps a cumulative record of the day's sales. At the end of the day, the cash in the drawer (minus the change fund) should be equal to the total on the cash register tape. However, even with careful and honest employees, small errors in making change do occur from time to time. Such errors cause the cash in the drawer to be unequal to the total on the tape.

objective 5
Account for shortages and overages using Cash Short and Cash Over accounts

If the cash in the drawer is less than the tape total, the difference is referred to as a *shortage*. On the other hand, if the cash in the drawer is more than the tape total, the difference is referred to as an *overage*. An expense account titled Cash Short is used to record shortages; a revenue account titled Cash Over is used to record overages.

Since The Kitchen Taylor's December sales have already been journalized and posted, the following cash short and over examples will *not* be formally recorded on The Kitchen Taylor's books.

To demonstrate a shortage, let's assume the following facts about The Kitchen Taylor's December 7 cash sales:

Tape	=	$1,500
Cash	=	1,498
Shortage	=	$ 2

Figure 6.6 shows how the cash sales for December 7 are recorded in the general journal using the Cash Short account.

Figure 6.6

The Kitchen Taylor
General Journal
For the Period From Dec 7, 1995 to Dec 7, 1995
Filter Criteria includes: Report order is by Date. Report is printed with Accounts having Zero Amounts and with Truncated Transaction Descriptions and in Detail Format.

Date	Account ID	Reference	Trans Description	Debit Amt	Credit Amt
12/7/95	110		Cash	1,498.00	
	520		Cash Short	2.00	
	410		Fees Earned		1,500.00

To demonstrate an overage, let's alter the facts as follows:

Tape	=	$1,500
Cash	=	1,501
Overage	=	$ 1

Figure 6.7 shows how the cash sales for December 7 are recorded in the general journal using the Cash Over account.

Figure 6.7

The Kitchen Taylor
General Journal
For the Period From Dec 7, 1995 to Dec 7, 1995
Filter Criteria includes: Report order is by Date. Report is printed with Accounts having Zero Amounts and with Truncated Transaction Descriptions and in Detail Format.

Date	Account ID	Reference	Trans Description	Debit Amt	Credit Amt
12/7/95	110		Cash	1,501.00	
	410		Fees Earned		1,500.00
	411		Cash Over		1.00

Comment

> The Cash Short and Cash Over accounts may also be used to account for occasional shortages or overages in the petty cash fund.

Checking Account

objective 6
Describe the basic forms and procedures related to the use of a checking account

A checking account is one of the most important ways to safeguard cash. It provides both a secure place to store cash as it flows into the business and a safe way to pay bills. In general, all cash received should be deposited daily into a checking account, and all cash payments should be made by check. Exceptions to this general policy involve the use of special cash funds, such as the petty cash and change funds. Let's review some of the basic forms and procedures related to the use of a checking account.

Signature Card

When a checking account is opened, the bank requires that a signature card be signed by each person authorized to sign checks. This card should be signed exactly the way checks will be signed. In the future, the bank can use the signature card to detect forgeries by comparing signatures on checks with signatures on the card. This procedure also limits the number of employees allowed to sign checks and thus reduces the risk of improper disbursements of cash.

Deposit Tickets

A deposit ticket must accompany each deposit. This provides a record of each deposit. Blank deposit tickets are furnished by the bank but must be prepared by the depositor. An example of a deposit ticket is shown in Figure 6.8.

Figure 6.8

Currency, coin, and checks are listed separately on the deposit ticket. Each check being deposited should be identified by its American Banking Association (ABA) number. This number is printed in the upper right corner of each check in the form of a fraction. The numerator indicates the city or state and the specific bank; the denominator indicates the Federal Reserve district and the routing number.

$$\frac{70\text{-}492}{719}$$

70—City or state
492—Specific bank
7—Federal Reserve district
19—Routing number

The information contained in the numerator is all that is necessary on the deposit ticket (example: 70-492).

Endorsements

The depositor must endorse each check being deposited. The endorsement transfers ownership and guarantees payment of the check; it may be handwritten or stamped on the back of the check. There are essentially two types of endorsements:

- A blank endorsement includes only the signature of the depositor. It is not a very safe type of endorsement because the check can be paid to anyone who might subsequently endorse the check.

- A restrictive endorsement includes such words as *for deposit only.* This protects against theft by restricting further circulation of the check. The check with the restrictive endorsement in Figure 6.9 can be deposited only at Wheaton Valley Bank. It is a good practice to endorse all incoming checks with a restrictive endorsement.

Figure 6.9

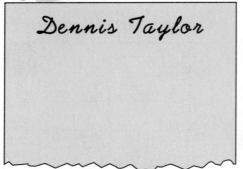

Blank Endorsement   Restrictive Endorsement

Checks

A check is a document signed by the depositor that orders the bank to pay a certain amount of money to a certain party. The following three parties are named on the face of every check:

1. Drawer—the party who signs the check.
2. Drawee—the drawer's bank.
3. Payee—the party being paid.

Checks are usually attached to a check stub. The amount of each check, the date, the check number, and the payee's name are recorded on the stub. The purpose of each check as well as the previous balance and the new balance in the checking account are also filled in on each stub. The check stub later provides the information necessary for the journal entry to formally record the cash payment that each check represents. To avoid omissions, the check stub should be completed before the check is written. This is important because we cannot make a journal entry without the proper information. Figure 6.10 shows a properly written check and check stub.

Figure 6.10

Bank Statement

Each month a **bank statement** is sent to the depositor. This statement includes the following information:

> Balance—beginning of the month
>
> Additions—deposits and credit memos
>
> Deductions—checks, debit memos
>
> Balance—end of the month

Bank credit memos are brief forms, prepared by the bank, explaining additions to the depositor's account for items other than regular deposits. Bank debit memos explain subtractions from the depositor's account for items other than checks written by the depositor.

> *Comment*
>
> From the bank's point of view, the depositor's account is a liability (credit balance), since the bank owes the depositor the balance in the account. Therefore, the bank records additions to the account with credits and deductions with debits.

Canceled checks are often returned to the depositor along with the bank statement. These are the checks that have actually been presented to the bank for payment during the period covered by the bank statement. Other checks may have been written but have not yet been presented for payment by the payee. Of course, the bank has no record of these checks. Figure 6.11 shows The Kitchen Taylor's bank statement for December.

Figure 6.11

WHEATON VALLEY BANK			
Wheaton, Illinois			

The Kitchen Taylor		Statement Date: 12-31-95	
2400 Main Street		Account No. 0200098250	
Wheaton, Illinois 60187		12-1-95 to 12-31-95	

REGULAR CHECKING			
Previous Balance			0.00
3 Deposits (+)			12,000.00
7 Checks (−)			8,101.37
Nonsufficient funds (−)			500.00
Service charges (−)			15.00
Ending Balance			**3,383.63**

DEPOSITS			
	12/3/95	10,000.00	
	12/7/95	1,500.00	
	12/21/95	500.00	

CHECKS (Asterisk * indicates break in check number sequence)			
	12/9/95	101	6,000.00
	12/10/95	102	1,200.00
	12/20/95	*104	600.00
	12/29/95	*106	80.00
	12/29/95	107	100.00
	12/31/95	108	46.37
	12/31/95	109	75.00

OTHER ITEMS			
	12/25/95	NSF (−)	500.00

Bank Reconciliation

The Need for a Bank Reconciliation

objective 7
Prepare a bank reconciliation and the related journal entries

If all cash received is deposited in the checking account and all cash disbursed is paid out of the checking account, the balance in the checking account should be equal to the balance in the depositor's Cash account. On any given day, however, these two balances are rarely the same. Although the difference could be the result of an error, it usually is the result of timing. Sometimes the depositor has access to information before the bank and other times the bank has access to information before the depositor. When the information becomes known to both the bank and the depositor, the differences usually disappear. On any given day, the true balance usually lies somewhere between the bank's balance and the depositor's Cash account balance.

Each month when the bank statement is received, the depositor should compare the ending balance according to the bank statement with the general ledger Cash account balance as of the same date. To obtain the true or adjusted balance as of the end of the month, the reasons for any difference must be identified. This requires a careful comparison of the bank statement and the depositor's records. In PAW, this monthly process of bringing the two balances into agreement is known as account reconciliation. Bank reconciliation is another term commonly used to describe this process.

Typical Reconciliation Items

Any item appearing on the bank statement but not in the depositor's records is creating a difference and is, therefore, a reconciliation item. Conversely, any item appearing in the depositor's records but not on the bank statement is also a reconciliation item. Let's review some of the most common reconciliation items.

Outstanding checks. These are checks that have been written but not yet presented to the bank for payment. These checks were deducted by the depositor when written. The bank has not deducted for them since they have not been presented for payment. Since the depositor's records are already up to date, no journal entry is required for outstanding checks.

Deposits in transit. These are deposits that were made before the end of the month but were not processed by the bank in time to appear on the bank statement. The depositor has already added these deposits to the Cash account; the bank has not. Again, no journal entry is required for deposits in transit because the depositor's records are already up to date.

Service charges. Banks charge for the routine processing of checks and deposits as well as for other special services. Routine charges are frequently based on the number of checks processed or the average daily balance in the account. The bank reports deductions for service charges on the bank statement. A debit memo explaining the charges is enclosed with the statement. Since the depositor's records do not yet include the service charges, a journal entry is required to record them.

NSF (nonsufficient funds) checks. These are previously deposited checks that the bank has returned to the depositor because the drawer's account did not contain enough cash. Notice that these are *not* checks that the depositor has written. In this textbook, it is assumed that all NSF checks are checks written to the depositor by customers. Added by both the bank and the depositor when deposited, an NSF check must be deducted by both when returned. The bank shows an NSF check as a deduction on the bank statement. The depositor must now make a journal entry to record the NSF check.

Collections. If requested, most banks will collect payments for a depositor on such items as installment sales, charge accounts, and promissory notes. Such collections are added to the depositor's balance on the bank statement. A credit memo explaining each collection is enclosed with the statement. Since the depositor's records do not include such collections, a journal entry is required.

Errors.   In the process of reconciliation, errors are sometimes discovered. The appropriate adjustment must be made on the side of the party responsible for the error. In the case of a bank error, the depositor's records are correct and no journal entry is required. However, if the error was made by the depositor, a correcting entry is required.

The Reconciliation Process

Updating Journal Entries

On December 31, 1995, The Kitchen Taylor's Cash account in the general ledger shows a balance of $3,573.63. The bank statement displayed in Figure 6.11 shows an ending balance on December 31, 1995 of $3,383.63. To reconcile these two amounts, we must identify the reasons for the discrepancy. We begin this process by reviewing the bank statement for items that have not been recorded on The Kitchen Taylor's books. Journal entries are required to update for these items.

The bank statement shown in Figure 6.11 indicates that The Kitchen Taylor must record journal entries for an NSF check ($500) and service charges ($15). The other items shown on the bank statement (checks and deposits) do not require entries because they have already been recorded on The Kitchen Taylor's books.

In data entry sheet format, the required entries are recorded as follows:

		DATA ENTRY SHEET The Kitchen Taylor			
Date	Account ID	Reference	Trans Description	Debit Amt	Credit Amt
12/31/95	111		NSF, Accounts Receivable	500.00	
	110		NSF, Cash		500.00
12/31/95	519		Service Charge Expense	15.00	
	110		Cash		15.00

Referring to the data entry sheet, use PAW to journalize these two entries. You will need to add Service Charge Expense, Account No. 519. *Then, post these journal entries.*

Now let's print the Cash account, Account No. 110, so we can determine the updated ending balance on December 31, 1995.

step 1:   Click on Reports, then General Ledger.

step 2:   On the "Report List," highlight "General Ledger."

step 3:   Click on the Print icon.

step 4:   In the "Filter, Type From, To" table, click on the first row (General Ledger Account ID) of the "From" column. The magnifying glass icon is shown. Select Account No. 110, Cash, and click on OK.

step 5: In the "To" column, select Account No. 110, Cash, and click on OK.

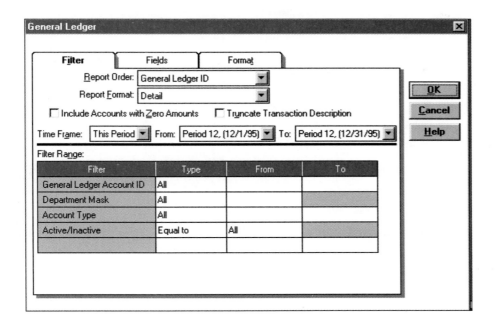

step 6: Click on OK.

step 7: The "Print" window pops up. Click on OK. The Cash account begins to print. Compare your printout with Figure 6.12.

Observe that the general ledger Cash account balance on December 31, 1995, is $3,058.63.

Figure 6.12

The Kitchen Taylor
General Ledger
For the Period From Dec 1, 1995 to Dec 31, 1995

Filter Criteria includes: 1) IDs from 110 to 110. Report order is by ID. Report is printed in Detail Format.

Account ID / Account Description	Date / Reference	Jrnl	Trans Description / Trans Description	Debit Amt	Credit Amt	Balance
110 / Cash	12/1/95		Beginning Balance			
	12/1/95	GENJ	Cash	10,000.00		
	12/2/95	GENJ	Check No. 101, Cash		6,000.00	
	12/3/95	GENJ	Check No. 102, Cash		1,200.00	
	12/7/95	GENJ	Cash	1,500.00		
	12/10/95	GENJ	Check No. 103, Cash		425.00	
	12/17/95	GENJ	Check No. 104, Cash		600.00	
	12/21/95	GENJ	Cash	500.00		
	12/28/95	GENJ	Check No. 105, Cash		200.00	
	12/29/95	GENJ	Check No. 106, Cash		80.00	
	12/29/95	GENJ	Check No. 107, Cash		100.00	
	12/30/95	GENJ	Cash	300.00		
	12/31/95	GENJ	Check No. 108, Cash		46.37	
	12/31/95	GENJ	Check No. 109, Cash		75.00	
	12/31/95	GENJ	NSF, Cash		500.00	
	12/31/95	GENJ	Cash		15.00	
			Current Period Change	12,300.00	9,241.37	3,058.63
	12/31/95		Ending Balance			3,058.63

Using PAW's Account Reconciliation Feature

In PAW, the "Account Reconciliation" feature makes it easy to complete a bank reconciliation. Let's practice by reconciling The Kitchen Taylor's account.

step 1:   From the main menu, select Tasks, then Account Reconciliation.

step 2:   In the "Account to Reconcile" box, select Account No. 110, Cash.

step 3:   Type **3383.63** in the "Statement Ending Balance" box, in the lower right corner of your screen. This is the ending balance on The Kitchen Taylor's bank statement.

step 4:   In the "Checks and Credits" table, click on the box in the "Clear" column to place a check mark next to each check, nonsufficient funds, and service charge transaction that is shown on the bank statement. Do *not* check off any outstanding checks (Nos. 103 and 105).

step 5:   In the "Deposits & Debits" table, place a check mark in the "Clear" column for each deposit that is listed on the bank statement. Do *not* check off any deposits in transit (December 30, $300). Your reconciliation is complete if the "Unreconciled Difference" shown in the lower right corner of the screen is zero.

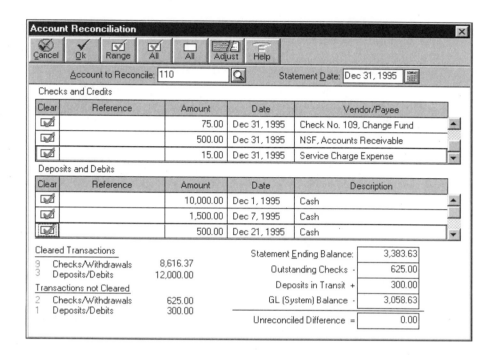

step 6:   Click on Ok.

Printing the Account Reconciliation Report

Follow these steps to print an account reconciliation report:

step 1:   From the main menu, select Reports, Account Reconciliation.

step 2:   In the "Report List," highlight "Account Reconciliation."

step 3:   Click on the Print icon.

step 4:   The "Account Reconciliation Filter" window displays. Make sure that Account No. 110 is shown as the GL Account ID. If 110 is not displayed in the GL Account ID box, click on the magnifying glass icon and select Account No. 110, Cash.

step 5:   Click on OK.

step 6:   At the "Print" window, click on OK. The Account Reconciliation Report starts to print. Compare your printout to Figure 6.13.

Observe that the "Ending GL Balance" on the account reconciliation is the same as the updated ending balance in the Cash account shown in Figure 6.12. The true or adjusted balance on December 31, 1995, is $3,058.63.

Figure 6.13

The Kitchen Taylor
Account Reconciliation
As of Dec 31, 1995
110 - Cash
Bank Statement Date: December 31, 1995
Filter Criteria includes: Report is printed in Detail Format.

Beginning GL Balance		
Add: Cash Receipts		
Less: Cash Disbursements		
Add <Less> Other		3,058.63
Ending GL Balance		3,058.63
Ending Bank Balance		3,383.63
Add back deposits in transit		
Total deposits in transit		
<Less> outstanding checks		
Total outstanding checks		
Add <Less> Other		
	Dec 10, 1995	<425.00>
	Dec 28, 1995	<200.00>
	Dec 30, 1995	300.00
Total other		<325.00>
Unreconciled difference		
Ending GL Balance		3,058.63

Printing the Trial Balance

At this point, we again need to check the overall equality of the debits and credits in the ledger by printing a trial balance.

Follow these steps to print The Kitchen Taylor's trial balance:

step 1: From the "Select a Report" window, highlight "General Ledger." (Hint: General Ledger is in the "Report Area" list.)

step 2: Highlight "General Ledger Trial Balance," then make the selections to print. (Hint: Click on the Print icon, then click on OK. When the "Print" window pops up, click on OK.)

Compare your printout to Figure 6.14.

If you notice any discrepancies, you must locate your error(s) and make the necessary correction(s) since this data will provide your starting point in Chapter 7. You can edit your general journal entries by selecting Tasks,

General Journal Entry, then the Records Edit icon. Since your general journal entries are posted, click on the down arrow in the "Status" box, then select "Posted." Your general journal entries are listed on the screen. Double-click on the entry that needs editing, make the necessary change(s), then post. Reprint your Trial Balance and again compare it to Figure 6.14.

Figure 6.14

The Kitchen Taylor
General Ledger Trial Balance
As of Dec 31, 1995
Filter Criteria includes: Report order is by ID. Report is printed in Detail Format.

Account ID	Account Description	Debit Amt	Credit Amt
108	Change Fund	75.00	
109	Petty Cash	100.00	
110	Cash	3,058.63	
111	Accounts Receivable	1,100.00	
112	Supplies	121.55	
113	Prepaid Insurance	1,150.00	
120	Truck	6,000.00	
121	Accumulated Depreciation		100.00
210	Accounts Payable		65.00
211	Wages Payable		60.00
310	Dennis Taylor, Capital		10,000.00
320	Dennis Taylor, Drawing	216.50	
410	Fees Earned		2,900.00
510	Rent Expense	600.00	
511	Repair Expense	73.50	
512	Utilities Expense	80.00	
513	Supplies Expense	310.00	
514	Insurance Expense	50.00	
515	Wages Expense	60.00	
516	Depreciation Expense	100.00	
517	Delivery Expense	9.05	
518	Miscellaneous Expense	5.77	
519	Service Charge Expense	15.00	
	Total:	**13,125.00**	**13,125.00**

Backing Up Your Chapter 6 Data

You must back up your Chapter 6 data because it will provide your starting point for the next chapter. Follow these steps:

objective 8
Back up your data

step 1: Insert a blank formatted disk in drive A.

step 2: From PAW's main menu, select File, then Backup.

step 3: Type **a:\chapter6** in the Destination text box.

step 4: Click on the Backup button. Your files begin to copy. When all the files have been saved to drive A, you are automatically returned to the main menu.

step 5: Click on File, Exit to exit PAW.

Innovations in Banking

Automated Teller Machines

Through the use of **automated teller machines (ATMs)**, depositors enjoy the convenience of being able to make deposits and withdrawals 24 hours a day. To use an ATM, the depositor must have a plastic bank card (resembling a credit card) and a password expressed as a number or letter code. Banks introduced ATMs several years ago in an effort to reduce labor costs. These days, they are so heavily used that many banks charge a fee for each transaction processed by an ATM.

Electronic Funds Transfer

Banks are increasingly offering services that allow customers to transfer funds by computer, without the use of a check. This process is generally referred to as *electronic funds transfer* or *EFT.* Examples of such services include the direct deposit of payroll and social security checks, as well as the use of debit cards. A debit card looks like a charge card; however, when it is used to pay for a purchase, the amount is instantly subtracted from the customer's checking account. Of course, ATMs are another example of electronic funds transfer.

Check Truncation

Traditionally, banks have returned canceled checks to depositors along with their monthly statements. In an effort to cut costs, some financial institutions have stopped this practice. Instead, they maintain microfilm copies of each check that are available to depositors upon request. This procedure is referred to as *check truncation.*

Chapter Six Summary

In this chapter, we focused our attention on internal accounting controls dealing with cash. These controls are primarily concerned with protecting assets and ensuring the accuracy of accounting data.

Most businesses pay small bills in cash out of a petty cash fund. This fund is established for a fixed amount and is periodically replenished, usually on a weekly or monthly basis. Payments from the petty cash fund are not formally journalized until the fund is replenished. Replenishing petty cash does not change the fixed size of the fund. Therefore, the replenishment entry does not involve the Petty Cash account. Petty Cash is an asset account and appears on the balance sheet above Cash.

Businesses that regularly receive cash (currency and coin) from customers need a change fund. A change fund is a fixed amount of cash that is kept in the cash drawer on a permanent basis for the purpose of making change. The Change Fund is an asset account and appears on the balance sheet above Cash or Petty Cash.

Businesses recording large numbers of cash sales generally use a cash register. At the end of the day, the cash in the drawer (minus the change fund) should be equal to the total on the cash register tape. However, small errors in making change do occur from time to time. An expense account titled Cash Short is used to record shortages. A revenue account titled Cash Over is used to record overages.

The use of a checking account is one of the most important ways to safeguard cash. To use a checking account, the depositor must become familiar with signature cards, deposit tickets, checks, endorsements, and bank statements. Cash receipts should be deposited into a checking account, and cash payments should be made by check.

Due to timing differences and the possibility of errors, a bank reconciliation should be prepared at the end of each month to obtain the adjusted or true balance. In reconciling the bank statement balance and the Cash account balance, the reasons for any differences are identified. Common reconciliation items include outstanding checks, deposits in transit, service charges, NSF checks, collections, and errors.

Some reconciliation items require journal entries to update or correct the Cash account. After these entries have been journalized and posted, the Cash account balance equals the adjusted or true balance as of the end of the period. This is the Cash account balance that appears on the balance sheet.

Demonstration Problem

Part A

After receiving its monthly bank statement, Kim Enterprises identified the following reconciliation items:

- *a.* Outstanding checks:
  - No. 1245 . . . .$150
  - No. 1260 . . . .$375
- *b.* Deposit in transit, $600.
- *c.* Bank debit memo for service charges, $25.
- *d.* An NSF check for $90 from Chris Martin.
- *e.* Bank credit memo for a collection from a charge customer, $235.
- *f.* Check No. 1248 written for $405 was recorded in the journal as $450. (This check was a payment on account to a creditor.)

Instructions

Record the necessary journal entries on a data entry sheet. In the Date column, insert the letter of the item to which the journal entry relates. Leave the Account ID column blank.

Part B

Flores Associates, a newly formed business, had the following selected transactions during December 1995:

Dec. 1   Established a petty cash fund, $150.

      1   Established a change fund, $50.

      7   Recorded cash sales: total cash in drawer, $1,250; cash register tape, $1,195.

    21   Recorded cash sales: total cash in drawer, $1,690; cash register tape, $1,655.

    31   Replenished the petty cash fund: Delivery Expense, $25; Supplies, $42; Jose Flores, owner, for personal use, $70.

Instructions

Record these transactions on a data entry sheet. Leave the Account ID column blank.

Solution to Demonstration Problem

Part A

				DATA ENTRY SHEET Kim Enterprises		
Date	Account ID	Reference	Trans Description		Debit Amt	Credit Amt
c.			Service Charge Expense		25.00	
			Cash			25.00
d.			Accounts Receivable		90.00	
			Cash			90.00
e.			Cash		235.00	
			Accounts Receivable			235.00
f.			Cash (450-405)		45.00	
			Accounts Payable			45.00

Items a and b do *not* require journal entries.

Part B

				DATA ENTRY SHEET Flores Associates		
Date	Account ID	Reference	Trans Description		Debit Amt	Credit Amt
12/1/95			Petty Cash		150.00	
			Cash			150.00
12/1/95			Change Fund		50.00	
			Cash			50.00
12/7/95			Cash (1,250-50*)		1,200.00	
			Sales			1,195.00
			Cash Over			5.00
12/21/95			Cash (1,690-50*)		1,640.00	
			Cash Short		15.00	
			Sales			1,655.00
12/31/95			Delivery Expense		25.00	
			Supplies		42.00	
			Jose Flores, Drawing		70.00	
			Cash			137.00

*The $50 change fund must be subtracted.

Glossary

account reconciliation   In PAW, the process of bringing the bank statement balance and the Cash account balance into agreement. This is also known as bank reconciliation.   *155*

American Banking Association (ABA) number   The number printed in the upper right corner of each check in the form of a fraction. The numerator indicates the city or state and the specific bank; the denominator indicates the Federal Reserve District and the routing number.   *151*

automated teller machines (ATMs)   Allows banking customers to make electronic deposits and withdrawals.   *162*

bank reconciliation   The process of bringing the bank statement balance and the Cash account balance into agreement. In PAW, it is known as account reconciliation.   *155*

bank statement   A statement prepared by the bank showing account activity for a specified period of time.   *153*

blank endorsement   Includes only the signature of the depositor.   *152*

canceled checks   Checks that have been presented to the bank for payment. They are often returned to the depositor along with the bank statement.   *153*

change fund   A fixed amount of cash kept in the cash drawer on a permanent basis for the purpose of making change.   *148*

check   A document signed by the depositor ordering the bank to pay a certain amount of money to a certain party.   *152*

collections   Payments collected for the depositor by the bank.   *155*

deposit in transit   A deposit made before the end of the month but not processed by the bank in time to appear on the bank statement.   *155*

deposit ticket   A form supplied by the bank but prepared by the depositor that must accompany each deposit. Currency, coin, and checks being deposited are listed separately.   *151*

endorsement   A signature or stamp on the back of a check transferring ownership and guaranteeing payment of the check.   *152*

errors   In the process of reconciliation, the appropriate adjustment must be made on the side of the party responsible for the error.   *156*

internal accounting controls   Procedures primarily concerned with protecting assets and ensuring the accuracy of accounting data.   *144*

internal administrative controls   Procedures primarily concerned with promoting efficiency and encouraging employee compliance with company policies.   *144*

internal controls   Procedures used by management to control business operations. They can be divided into internal administrative controls and internal accounting controls.   *144*

NSF (nonsufficient funds) check   A previously deposited check that has been returned to the depositor because the drawer's account did not contain enough cash.   *155*

outstanding checks   Checks that have been written but not yet presented to the bank for payment.   *155*

petty cash fund   A cash fund used to pay small bills.   *144*

petty cash record   A columnar form that summarizes all petty cash voucher information on a single sheet.   *146*

petty cash voucher   A form prepared for each payment from a petty cash fund. The form contains the amount, date, and purpose of each payment, as well as signatures acknowledging approval and receipt.   *145*

restrictive endorsement   Protects against theft by restricting further circulation of a check.   *152*

service charge   A fee charged by the bank for the routine processing of checks and deposits as well as for other special services.   *155*

signature card   A card that must be signed by each person authorized to sign checks drawn on a particular checking account. The bank uses the card to verify signatures on checks.   *151*

Self-Test

Select the best answer.

1. In preparing a bank reconciliation, a journal entry is required for
   a. outstanding checks.
   b. deposits in transit.
   c. service charges.
   d. All of the above.

2. After the entries required by a bank reconciliation have been journalized and posted, the Cash account balance is
   a. equal to the Ending GL Balance shown on the account reconciliation report.
   b. the up-to-date balance shown on the balance sheet.
   c. Both a and b.
   d. None of the above.

3. The Petty Cash account is debited to
   a. establish the petty cash fund.
   b. replenish the petty cash fund.
   c. eliminate the petty cash fund.
   d. All of the above.

4. A fund that contains a fixed amount of cash that is kept in the cash drawer on a permanent basis for the purpose of making change is known as a(n)
   a. allowance fund.
   b. petty cash fund.
   c. change fund
   d. cash short and cash over fund.

5. The Cash Short account
   a. appears on the income statement.
   b. is an expense account.
   c. indicates a shortage.
   d. All of the above.

Answers to the self-test can be found after the cases at the end of this chapter.

Questions for Discussion

1. What is the definition of each of the following?
   a. Internal control.
   b. Internal accounting control.
   c. Internal administrative control.

2. *a.* What is the purpose of a petty cash fund?
   b. What is a petty cash voucher?
   c. How is the petty cash fund replenished?

3. *a.* What is the purpose of a change fund?
   b. When is the change fund debited or credited?

4. *a.* What type of account is Cash Short?
   b. What type of account is Cash Over?

5. *a.* What is the purpose of an endorsement?
   b. What is a restrictive endorsement?

6. What is the purpose of a bank reconciliation?

7. What are some typical reconciliation items?

8. Which reconciliation items require the depositor to record journal entries?

Exercises

Exercise 6.1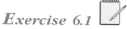

Match the following terms with the definitions shown below:

Terminology
L.O. 1–7

1. Restrictive endorsement.
2. Bank reconciliation.
3. Petty cash record.
4. Canceled checks.
5. Petty cash voucher.
6. Change fund.
7. Petty cash fund.
8. Check.
9. Outstanding check.
10. Deposit in transit.
11. NSF check.
12. Internal accounting controls.
13. Endorsement.

Definitions

a. Procedures primarily concerned with protecting assets and ensuring the accuracy of accounting data.

b. A document signed by the depositor ordering the bank to pay a certain amount of money to a certain party.

c. A signature or stamp on the back of a check, transferring ownership and guaranteeing payment of a check.

d. A form prepared for each payment from a petty cash fund. The form contains the amount, date, and purpose of each payment, as well as signatures acknowledging approval and receipt.

e. A deposit made before the end of the month but not processed by the bank in time to appear on the bank statement.

f. Protects against theft by restricting further circulation of a check.

g. The process of bringing the bank statement balance and the Cash account balance into agreement.

b. A cash fund used to pay small bills.

i. A check that has been written but not yet presented to the bank for payment.

j. A fixed amount of cash kept in the cash drawer on a permanent basis for the purpose of making change.

k. Checks that have been presented to the bank for payment. They are often returned to the depositor along with the bank statement.

l. A columnar form that summarizes all petty cash voucher information on a single sheet.

m. A previously deposited check that has been returned to the depositor because the drawer's account did not contain enough cash.

Exercise 6.2

Petty Cash
L.O. 2

a. Record the following transactions on a data entry sheet:

Aug. 1   Established a petty cash fund, $80.

   31   Replenished petty cash based on the following payment information taken from the Petty Cash Record:

Supplies	$26.75
Delivery expense	11.50
Miscellaneous expense	32.90

b. What type of account is Petty Cash and on what financial statement does it appear?

Exercise 6.3

Change Fund
L.O. 4

Budget Shoe Repair has decided to establish a change fund in the amount of $65.

a. On a data entry sheet, record the general journal entry to establish the change fund.

b. When will another entry debiting or crediting the Change Fund account be necessary?

c. At the end of the day, the cash in Budget's cash drawer totals $489.25. The tape shows sales totaling $424.25. How much cash should be deposited in the checking account?

d. What type of account is the Change Fund and on what financial statement does it appear?

Exercise 6.4

Cash Short/Over
L.O. 5

At the end of the day on May 15, 1995, the cash in Quick Copy Shop's cash drawer totals $834.65. The cash register tape shows sales totaling $782.25. Quick Copy maintains a $50 change fund.

On a data entry sheet, record the cash sales for May 15.

Exercise 6.5

Bank Reconciliation
L.O. 7

For each of the reconciliation items shown below indicate:

a. Whether the item requires a journal entry (yes or no).

b. Whether the item is added to or deducted from the ending bank balance on PAW's account reconciliation report (+ or −). Or, "no" if it does not appear on the account reconciliation report.

	(a)	(b)
Reconciliation item	Journal Entry	Add or Deduct
1. Service charge.		
2. Deposit in transit.		
3. Outstanding check.		
4. NSF check.		

Exercise 6.6

Costello Company's bank statement shows an ending balance of $3,076.70 on June 30, 1995. On the same date, Costello's Cash account balance is $4,161.40. The following reconciliation items have been identified;

Bank Reconciliation
L.O. 7

- Outstanding checks:

    No. 437 $859.80

    No. 438   723.50

- Deposit in transit, $2,025.

- Bank memo for service charges, $18.

- An NSF check for $625 from Pat Murphy.

Record the necessary entries on a data entry sheet.

Exercise 6.7

Based on the information presented in Exercise 6.6, compute the ending general ledger Cash account balance after reconciliation. Begin your computations with the June 30 bank statement balance. Show all your work.

Bank Reconciliation
L.O. 7

Exercise 6.8

Apple Associates wrote Check No. 1245 to Becker Company for $463.90. However, this payment on account was recorded as $436.90 in the journal.

Bank Reconciliation
L.O. 7

   Record the necessary entry on a data entry sheet. Hint: Remember that the amount on the check represents the amount actually paid out of Apple's account at the bank.

Problems—Set A

Problem 6.1A

In Chapter 5, Problem Set A, you journalized and posted adjusting entries for Ace Cleaning Service. The December 31 adjusted trial balance for Ace Cleaning Service is shown in Figure 6.15. Follow these steps to restore your Chapter 5 data and print Ace's trial balance.

Restore data, trial balance
L.O. 3

Ace Cleaning Service
General Ledger Trial Balance
As of Dec 31, 1995
Filter Criteria includes: Report order is by ID. Report is printed in Detail Format.

Account ID	Account Description	Debit Amt	Credit Amt
110	Cash	4,366.00	
111	Accounts Receivable	2,275.00	
112	Supplies	100.00	
113	Prepaid Insurance	594.00	
114	Equipment	5,000.00	
115	Accumulated Depreciation		75.00
210	Accounts Payable		2,525.00
215	Salaries Payable		258.00
310	Joan Haywood, Capital		7,500.00
320	Joan Haywood, Drawing	540.00	
410	Cleaning Revenue		4,650.00
510	Rent Expense	625.00	
511	Repair Expense	260.00	
512	Salary Expense	903.00	
513	Utilities Expense	136.00	
514	Supplies Expense	80.00	
515	Insurance Expense	54.00	
516	Depreciation Expense	75.00	
	Total:	**15,008.00**	**15,008.00**

Instructions

step 1: Start Windows, then PAW. Open Ace Cleaning Service.

step 2: Place your Ace Cleaning Service backup disk in drive A.

step 3: From the main menu, select File, then Restore.

step 4: Type **a:\acedec.54a** in the Source box. (Use the same file name that you used when you backed up Ace Cleaning Service in Chapter 5.)

step 5: Click on the Restore button. Read the "Warning" screen, then click on OK. Restoring the files will take a few moments. When the files are restored, you are returned to the main menu.

step 6: Remove disk from drive A.

step 7: Check that your files are restored by displaying or printing the trial balance. Compare it to the adjusted trial balance shown in Figure 6.15.

Problem 6.2A

Petty Cash and Change Fund
L.O. 2, 4

Ace Cleaning Service completed the following transactions in December, 1995:

Dec. 29   Established a $50 petty cash fund, Check No. 1010. Petty Cash is Account No. 109.

      30   Established a $30 change fund, Check No. 1011. Change Fund is Account No. 108.

      31   Issued Check No. 1012 to replenish the petty cash fund based on the following information taken from Ace's petty cash record:

Supplies	$12.50
Repair Expense	10.00
Joan Haywood, Drawing	15.00
Total Payments	$37.50

Instructions

1. Record the above transactions on a data entry sheet.
2. Referring to your data entry sheet, use PAW's "General Journal Entry" feature to *journalize* and *post* the transactions.

Problem 6.3A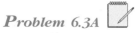

Ace Cleaning Service's bank statement is shown in Figure 6.16.

Data entry sheet
L.O. 7

Figure 6.16

First National Bank			
Chicago, Illinois			
Ace Cleaning Service		Statement Date: 12-31-95	
452 Mountain Drive		Account No. 0267018556	
Evanston, Illinois 60522		12-1-95 to 12-31-95	
REGULAR CHECKING			
Previous Balance			0.00
4 Deposits (+)			9,075.00
6 Checks (−)			4,653.00
Nonsufficient funds (−)			325.00
Service charges (−)			15.00
Ending Balance			**4,082.00**
DEPOSITS			
	12/4/95	7,500.00	
	12/8/95	450.00	
	12/19/95	325.00	
	12/22/95	800.00	
CHECKS (Asterisk * indicates break in check number sequence)			
	12/9/95	1001	625.00
	12/12/95	1002	1,000.00
	12/16/95	1003	648.00
	12/20/95	1004	800.00
	12/26/95	1005	645.00
	12/28/95	*1007	935.00
OTHER ITEMS			
	12/29/95	NSF (−)	325.00

Instructions

1. Record the necessary entries on a data entry sheet. Date all the transactions December 31, 1995.

2. Using PAW's "General Journal Entry" feature, *journalize* and *post* the entries shown on your data entry sheet. (Hint: Add Account No. 517 Service Charge Expense.)

Problem 6.4A

Bank Reconciliation
L.O. 7

Instructions

1. Use PAW's account reconciliation feature to reconcile the Cash account.

2. Print the account reconciliation report.

Problem 6.5A

Chart of accounts, journal, trial balance
L.O. 2-7

Instructions

1. Print the chart of accounts.

2. Print the general journal for December 29 through 31.

3. Print the general ledger trial balance.

Problem 6.6A

Back up
L.O. 8

Your Ace Cleaning Service data **must** be backed up. You will restore it in Chapter 7. Follow these steps:

step 1:   Insert a blank formatted disk in drive A.

step 2:   From PAW's main menu, select File, then Backup.

step 3:   Type **a:\acedec.66a** in the Destination text box.

step 4:   Click on the Backup button. Your files begin to copy. When all the files have been saved to drive A, you are automatically returned to the main menu.

step 5:   Click on File, Exit to exit PAW.

Problems—Set B

Problem 6.1B

Restore data, trial balance
L.O. 3

In Chapter 5, Problem Set B, you journalized and posted adjusting entries for Loyal Lawn Service. The December 31 adjusted trial balance for Loyal Lawn Service is shown in Figure 6.17. Follow these steps to restore your Chapter 5 data and print Loyal's trial balance.

Figure 6.17

Loyal Lawn Service
General Ledger Trial Balance
As of Dec 31, 1995
Filter Criteria includes: Report order is by ID. Report is printed in Detail Format.

Account ID	Account Description	Debit Amt	Credit Amt
110	Cash	2,720.00	
111	Accounts Receivable	1,865.00	
112	Supplies	135.00	
113	Prepaid Insurance	550.00	
114	Equipment	5,000.00	
115	Accumulated Depreciation		75.00
210	Accounts Payable		1,435.00
215	Salaries Payable		414.00
310	Chris Canon, Capital		7,000.00
320	Chris Canon, Drawing	420.00	
410	Lawn Service Revenue		3,987.00
510	Rent Expense	595.00	
511	Repair Expense	145.00	
512	Salary Expense	1,104.00	
513	Utilities Expense	162.00	
514	Supplies Expense	90.00	
515	Insurance Expense	50.00	
516	Depreciation Expense	75.00	
	Total:	**12,911.00**	**12,911.00**

Instructions

step 1: Start Windows, then PAW. Open Loyal Lawn Service.

step 2: Place your Loyal Lawn Service backup disk in drive A.

step 3: From the main menu, select File, then Restore.

step 4: Type **a:\loyaldec.54b** in the Source box. (Use the same file name that you used when you backed up Loyal Lawn Service in Chapter 5.)

step 5: Click on the Restore button. Read the "Warning" screen, then click on OK. Restoring the files will take a few moments. When the files are restored, you are returned to the main menu.

step 6: Remove disk from drive A.

step 7: Check that your files are restored by displaying or printing the trial balance. Compare it to the adjusted trial balance shown in Figure 6.17.

Problem 6.2B

Loyal Lawn Service completed the following transactions in December 1995:

Petty Cash and Change Fund
L.O. 2, 4

Dec. 29 Established a $75 petty cash fund, Check No. 1010. Petty Cash is Account No. 109.

30 Established a $25 change fund, Check No. 1011. Change Fund is Account No. 108.

31 Issued Check No. 1012 to replenish the petty cash fund based on the following information taken from Loyal's petty cash record:

Supplies	$15.00
Repair Expense	8.75
Chris Canon, Drawing	50.00
Total Payments	$73.75

Instructions

1. Record the above transactions on a data entry sheet.

2. Referring to your data entry sheet, use PAW's "General Journal Entry" feature to *journalize* and *post* the transactions.

Problem 6.3B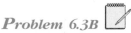

Data entry sheet
L.O. 7

Loyal Lawn Service's bank statement is shown in Figure 6.18.

Figure 6.18

Federated Bank & Trust Wheaton, Illinois				
Loyal Lawn Service 1823 King Drive Wheaton, Illinois 60221			Statement Date: 12-31-95 Account No. 0367418221 12-1-95 to 12-31-95	
REGULAR CHECKING				
Previous Balance				0.00
4 Deposits (+)				8,412.00
6 Checks (−)				5,595.00
Nonsufficient funds (−)				375.00
Service charges (−)				20.00
Ending Balance				**2,422.00**
DEPOSITS				
	12/2/95	7,000.00		
	12/6/95	637.00		
	12/18/95	375.00		
	12/22/95	400.00		
CHECKS (Asterisk * indicates break in check number sequence)				
	12/9/95	1001	595.00	
	12/12/95	1002	2,000.00	
	12/16/95	1003	600.00	
	12/20/95	1004	730.00	
	12/26/95	1005	690.00	
	12/28/95	*1007	980.00	
OTHER ITEMS				
	12/31/95	NSF (−)	375.00	

Instructions

1. Record the necessary entries on a data entry sheet. Date all the transactions December 31, 1995.

2. Using PAW's "General Journal Entry" feature, *journalize* and *post* the entries shown on your data entry sheet. (Hint: Add Account No. 517 Service Charge Expense.)

Problem 6.4B

Instructions

1. Use PAW's account reconciliation feature to reconcile the Cash account.

2. Print the account reconciliation report.

Bank Reconciliation
L.O. 7

Problem 6.5B

Instructions

1. Print the chart of accounts.

2. Print the general journal for December 29 through 31.

3. Print the general ledger trial balance.

Chart of accounts, journal, trial balance
L.O. 2–7

Problem 6.6B

Your Loyal Lawn Service data **must** be backed up. You will restore it in Chapter 7. Follow these steps:

Back up
L.O. 8

step 1: Insert a blank formatted disk in drive A.

step 2: From PAW's main menu, select File, then Backup.

step 3: Type a:\loyaldec.66b in the Destination text box.

step 4: Click on the Backup button. Your files begin to copy. When all the files have been saved to drive A, you are automatically returned to the main menu.

step 5: Click on File, Exit to exit PAW.

Mini-Cases

Case 6–1

Your new client, Jerry Eberhart, established a petty cash fund about six months ago. When you asked him for a copy of the petty cash voucher form, he stated that petty cash vouchers were not used. "We don't need anything that fancy. We simply pay out the cash, and when the cash in the box gets low, we throw in a few bucks," said Mr. Eberhart. When you asked how the debit portion of the replenishment entry was determined without a voucher, he replied: "We always debit Miscellaneous Expense." Comment on Mr. Eberhart's petty cash procedure.

Case 6–2

Your neighbor, Maxine Reamy, owns her own business. As checks are received, she places them in an envelope that she keeps in her desk. After several accumulate, she endorses the checks and deposits them in her business checking account. Maxine's new accountant is unhappy with these procedures and has suggested several changes but Maxine is reluctant to change. Knowing you are an accountant, she asks for your opinion.

Case 6–3

Your friend Carol Johanson claims that it takes her only five minutes to reconcile her business checking account. "I don't prepare a formal reconciliation," says Carol. "I simply debit or credit my Cash account to bring it into agreement with the ending bank statement balance. After all, the bank never makes any errors and all the adjustments would be on my side anyway." Comment on Carol's method of bank reconciliation.

A Case of Ethics

Henry is a cashier at a small, local business. The owner also owns several other businesses. Because the owner is busy, she trusts Henry to balance his own cash register drawer at the end of the day. Henry pockets small amounts of cash whenever there is an overage. "The books still balance, and the owner is rich and doesn't need that money as much as I do," says Henry. Comment.

Answers to Self-Test

1. *c*   2. *c*   3. *a*   4. *c*   5. *d*

Financial Statements and Closing the Fiscal Year

LEARNING OBJECTIVES

After studying this chapter, you should be able to:

1. Describe the purpose and content of financial statements.

2. Restore data from previous chapter.

3. Print the financial statements.

4. Describe the concept of fiscal years and interim periods.

5. Describe the need for closing entries.

6. Use Peachtree Accounting for Windows to close the fiscal year.

7. Print a post-closing trial balance.

8. Backup your data.

The **accounting cycle,** as studied to this point, is summarized in the following flowchart:

Journalize

↓

Post to the ledger

↓

Print an unadjusted trial balance

↓

Journalize and post adjusting entries

↓

Print an adjusted trial balance

In this chapter, you will complete the basic accounting cycle with financial statements and the closing process.

Financial Statements

objective 1
Describe the content and
purpose of financial statements

In Chapters 4, 5, and 6, you used PAW to journalize and post daily transactions, adjust accounts at the end of the month, and reconcile the Cash account. The trial balance displayed in Figure 7.1 was prepared at the end of Chapter 6 and shows The Kitchen Taylor's up-to-date general ledger account balances on December 31, 1995.

Figure 7.1

The Kitchen Taylor
General Ledger Trial Balance
As of Dec 31, 1995

Filter Criteria includes: Report order is by ID. Report is printed in Detail Format.

Account ID	Account Description	Debit Amt	Credit Amt
108	Change Fund	75.00	
109	Petty Cash	100.00	
110	Cash	3,058.63	
111	Accounts Receivable	1,100.00	
112	Supplies	121.55	
113	Prepaid Insurance	1,150.00	
120	Truck	6,000.00	
121	Accumulated Depreciation		100.00
210	Accounts Payable		65.00
211	Wages Payable		60.00
310	Dennis Taylor, Capital		10,000.00
320	Dennis Taylor, Drawing	216.50	
410	Fees Earned		2,900.00
510	Rent Expense	600.00	
511	Repair Expense	73.50	
512	Utilities Expense	80.00	
513	Supplies Expense	310.00	
514	Insurance Expense	50.00	
515	Wages Expense	60.00	
516	Depreciation Expense	100.00	
517	Delivery Expense	9.05	
518	Miscellaneous Expense	5.77	
519	Service Charge Expense	15.00	
	Total:	13,125.00	13,125.00

Periodically (usually monthly or yearly), the information contained in the accounts must be summarized in a format that is more helpful to users of financial data such as owners, creditors, or government agencies. Financial statements provide that format.

As you will recall from Chapter 2, there are three basic financial statements.

1. Income statement

2. Balance sheet

3. Statement of cash flow

Comment

In manual accounting systems, there is a fourth financial statement known as the statement of owner's equity. It is prepared after the income statement but before the balance sheet. The purpose of the statement of owner's equity is to update the owner's capital account for net income or loss and withdrawals by the owner.

Beginning capital account balance
+ Investments by the owner
+ Net income (or minus net loss)
− Withdrawals by the owner
─────────────────────────────
Ending capital account balance

The up-to-date capital account balance is then displayed as a single figure on the balance sheet. In PAW, however, a statement of owner's equity is not prepared because PAW updates capital for these items within the capital section of the balance sheet.

As a group, these statements present a financial picture of the business. It is important to understand that no single statement presents the whole picture. Each statement presents only a part of the total picture.

Let's review the purpose and content of each statement and their interrelationships. Then, we will use Peachtree to print The Kitchen Taylor's financial statements.

Income Statement

The purpose of the income statement is to compute net income or loss for a specified period of time. Only revenue and expense accounts are displayed on the income statement. **Net income** is computed by subtracting total expenses from total revenues. An excess of expenses over revenues results in a net loss.

Peachtree was used to print out the income statement shown in Figure 7.2. Observe that the date line on the income statement reflects a period of time, usually a month or year. Since net income is a summary figure representing a combination of revenue earned and expenses incurred over a period of time, it is important that the date line reflect the period of time covered by the statement. It would be impossible, for example, to draw any valid conclusions about net income being "good" or "bad" without knowing whether the income statement reflected results for a month or a year.

Figure 7.2

	Current Month		Year to Date	
The Kitchen Taylor				
Income Statement				
For the Twelve Months Ending December 31, 1995				
Revenues				
Fees Earned	2,900.00	100.00	2,900.00	100.00
Total Revenues	2,900.00	100.00	2,900.00	100.00
Expenses				
Rent Expense	600.00	20.69	600.00	20.69
Repair Expense	73.50	2.53	73.50	2.53
Utilities Expense	80.00	2.76	80.00	2.76
Supplies Expense	310.00	10.69	310.00	10.69
Insurance Expense	50.00	1.72	50.00	1.72
Wages Expense	60.00	2.07	60.00	2.07
Depreciation Expense	100.00	3.45	100.00	3.45
Delivery Expense	9.05	0.31	9.05	0.31
Miscellaneous Expense	5.77	0.20	5.77	0.20
Service Charge Expense	15.00	0.52	15.00	0.52
Total Expenses	1,303.32	44.94	1,303.32	44.94
Net Income	$ 1,596.68	55.06	$ 1,596.68	55.06

If the reporting period is a month, Peachtree automatically prints out figures for the current month and also cumulative figures for the year to date. Since The Kitchen Taylor has only been in business for one month, the current month and year-to-date figures shown in Figure 7.2 are the same.

In addition to dollar figures, you will observe that the income statement also includes percentage of revenue columns for both the current month and the year to date. The percentages shown for each expense, total expenses, and net income indicate the relationship of each item to total revenue. For example, in the current month column, we can easily see that total expenses represent 44.94 percent of total revenues.

$$\frac{\$1,303.32}{\$2,900.00} = .4494 = 44.94\%$$

Peachtree automatically makes these computations and prints them out on every income statement. This information is very useful in analyzing relationships between revenues and expenses and in making comparisons between different time periods and even different companies.

Balance Sheet

As its name implies, the balance sheet proves that the accounting equation is in balance as of a specified date. Only asset, liability, and owner's equity accounts are shown on this statement. As you will recall, the terms *capital* and *owner's equity* mean the same thing. Both terms are commonly used in financial statements. Referring to The Kitchen Taylor's balance sheet shown in Figure 7.3, you will observe that Peachtree uses the term capital. You will also notice that the date line indicates a specific day, not a period of time.

Figure 7.3

The Kitchen Taylor
Balance Sheet
December 31, 1995

ASSETS

Current Assets			
Change Fund	$	75.00	
Petty Cash		100.00	
Cash		3,058.63	
Accounts Receivable		1,100.00	
Supplies		121.55	
Prepaid Insurance		1,150.00	
Total Current Assets			5,605.18
Property and Equipment			
Truck		6,000.00	
Accumulated Depreciation		<100.00>	
Total Property and Equipment			5,900.00
Total Assets		$	11,505.18

LIABILITIES AND CAPITAL

Current Liabilities			
Accounts Payable	$	65.00	
Wages Payable		60.00	
Total Current Liabilities			125.00
Long-Term Liabilities			
Total Long-Term Liabilities			0.00
Total Liabilities			125.00
Capital			
Dennis Taylor, Capital		10,000.00	
Dennis Taylor, Drawing		<216.50>	
Net Income		1,596.68	
Total Capital			11,380.18
Total Liabilities & Capital		$	11,505.18

Peachtree lists two categories of assets on the balance sheet as well as total assets. Assets that The Kitchen Taylor will use up within a year are called *current assets.* Assets that last longer than a year are listed under property and equipment.

Under liabilities, Peachtree also lists two categories as well as total liabilities. *Current liabilities* are those due within a year. Long-term liabilities are due beyond one year.

The last section shown on the balance sheet is capital or owner's equity. If the balance sheet is going to balance, the capital or owner's equity section must be brought up to date. As you will recall, revenue, expense, and drawing transactions have an effect on total capital but are recorded daily in separate accounts. On the balance sheet, capital is updated for these transactions. Because revenues and expenses are combined on the income statement to compute net income (loss), it is convenient to use this composite figure on the balance sheet. In summary, the capital or owner's equity section of the balance sheet must be updated for the following items:

> \+ Net income
>
> − Net loss
>
> − Drawing

Statement of Cash Flow

The statement of cash flow describes the flow of cash in and out of the business during a specific period of time. It provides the answers to three important questions:

1. From where did cash receipts come?
2. For what were cash payments used?
3. What was the overall change in cash?

As you already know, The Kitchen Taylor uses the accrual basis of accounting. Under the accrual basis, revenue is recorded when it is earned and expenses are recorded when they are incurred, regardless of whether the cash has been received or paid. Over the long run, the accrual basis is generally the most useful way to measure revenue and expenses. Over the short run, however, The Kitchen Taylor must have sufficient cash to pay its bills as they come due.

When the accrual basis of accounting is used, the balance sheet and income statement provide very little information about the flow of cash. It is possible that The Kitchen Taylor might have net income but be short of cash, or have a net loss but have excess cash. Therefore, the information provided by the statement of cash flow is extremely useful to Dennis Taylor.

Referring to Figure 7.4, you will observe that Peachtree automatically separates The Kitchen Taylor's cash flows (both receipts and payments) into three basic groups: operating activities, investing activities, and financing activities.

Figure 7.4

The Kitchen Taylor
Statement of Cash Flow
For the twelve Months Ended December 31, 1995

	Current Month	Year to Date
Cash Flows from operating activities		
Net Income	$ 1,596.68	$ 1,596.68
Adjustments to reconcile net income to net cash provided by operating activities		
Accumulated Depreciation	100.00	100.00
Accounts Receivable	<1,100.00>	<1,100.00>
Supplies	<121.55>	<121.55>
Prepaid Insurance	<1,150.00>	<1,150.00>
Accounts Payable	65.00	65.00
Wages Payable	60.00	60.00
Total Adjustments	<2,146.55>	<2,146.55>
Net Cash provided by Operations	<549.87>	<549.87>
Cash Flows from investing activities		
Used For		
Truck	<6,000.00>	<6,000.00>
Net cash used in investing	<6,000.00>	<6,000.00>
Cash Flows from financing activities		
Proceeds From		
Dennis Taylor, Capital	10,000.00	10,000.00
Used For		
Dennis Taylor, Drawing	<216.50>	<216.50>
Net cash used in financing	9,783.50	9,783.50
Net increase <decrease> in cash	$ 3,233.63	$ 3,233.63
Summary		
Cash Balance at End of Period	$ 3,233.63	$ 3,233.63
Cash Balance at Beginning of Period	0.00	0.00
Net Increase <Decrease> in Cash	$ 3,233.63	$ 3,233.63

The chart shown in Figure 7.5 includes only the types of operating, investing, and financing activities that The Kitchen Taylor needs at this time. In later chapters, we will add more activities within each category.

Figure 7.5

Operating Activities
Cash received from: Net income adjusted to net cash provided by operations

Investing Activities
Cash received from: Sale of fixed assets
Cash paid for: Purchase of fixed assets

Financing Activities
Cash received from: Investments by owner
Cash paid for: Withdrawals by owner

Interrelationship of the Financial Statements

Observe that the three financial statements shown in Figures 7.2, 7.3, and 7.4 are separate but related. The net income figure ($1,596.68) is taken from the income statement and used on the balance sheet to update the capital section. The total of the Change Fund, Petty Cash, and Cash account balances ($3,233.63) shown on the balance sheet is explained in detail on the statement of cash flow using information from both the income statement and the balance sheet.

As mentioned earlier, it is important to remember that no single statement tells the whole story. For example, the income statement indicates how much revenue a business has earned during a specific period of time, but it says nothing about how much of that amount has or has not been received in cash. For information about cash and accounts receivable, we have to look at the balance sheet and statement of cash flow.

Restoring Data from Chapter 6

objective 2
Restore data from previous chapter

Before you can use PAW to print The Kitchen Taylor's financial statements, you must restore your data from Chapter 6. Follow these steps:

step 1: Start Windows, then PAW. Open The Kitchen Taylor.

step 2: Place your Kitchen Taylor backup disk in drive A.

step 3: From the main menu, select File, then Restore.

step 4: Type **a:\chapter6** in the Source box. (Use the same file name that you used when you backed up The Kitchen Taylor in Chapter 6.)

step 5: Click on the Restore button. Read the "Warning" screen, then click on OK. Restoring the files will take a few moments. When the files are restored, you are returned to the main menu.

step 6: Remove disk from drive A.

Printing the Financial Statements

objective 3
Print the financial statements

Now that you have reviewed their content and purpose, you are ready to print The Kitchen Taylor's income statement, balance sheet, and statement of cash flow.

Follow these easy steps:

step 1:   Start Windows, then PAW. Open The Kitchen Taylor. From the main menu, select Reports, then Financial Statements.

step 2:   Highlight "Income Statement."

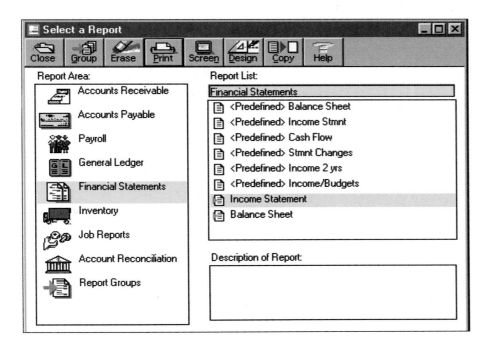

step 3:   Click on the Print icon. The "Income Statement" window displays.

step 4:   Click once on the check mark in the box next to "Show Zero Amounts" to deselect it.

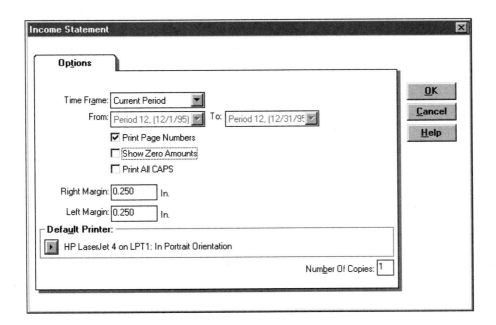

step 5:   Click on OK. When the "Print" window pops up, click on OK. The income statement starts to print. Compare your printout with Figure 7.2.

step 6: To print the balance sheet, highlight "Balance Sheet," then make the selections to print. Compare your printout to Figure 7.3.

step 7: To print the statement of cash flow, highlight "<Predefined> Cash Flow," deselect "Show Zero Amounts," then make the selections to print. Compare your printout to Figure 7.4.

Comment

Predefined refers to formats that PAW has established. We printed a statement of cash flow using a predefined format. However, formats can be changed. We did *not* use predefined formats to print the income statement and balance sheet.

Fiscal Year and Interim Periods

objective 4
Describe the concept of fiscal years and interim periods

The basic accounting cycle is completed over a period of 12 consecutive months. A **calendar year** consists of 12 consecutive months always beginning in January and ending in December. A **fiscal year** also consists of 12 consecutive months. However, a fiscal year (financial year) can be any grouping of 12 consecutive months. The most popular fiscal year is the calendar year (January 1 through December 31), but a fiscal year could begin July 1 and end the following June 30, or it could begin October 1 and end the following September 30.

A fiscal year usually ends at a slow time of year for the business, allowing extra time for special year-end activities. Once a new business chooses a fiscal year, it continues to use that same fiscal year in the future. Consistency enables users of financial statements to make year-to-year comparisons.

Any period of time shorter than a fiscal year is known as an **interim period.** Statements prepared for periods less than a fiscal year (monthly, quarterly, semiannually) are known as **interim statements.**

Closing the Fiscal Year

As The Kitchen Taylor's fiscal year is the calendar year, the books must be closed on December 31, 1995.

Comment

Because The Kitchen Taylor is a new business, its first fiscal year consists of only one month (December). All future fiscal years will consist of 12 consecutive months beginning in January and ending in December.

The Need for Closing Entries

objective 5
Describe the need for closing entries

As you will recall from earlier chapters, revenue, expense, and the owner's drawing account have special relationships to total owner's equity. Those relationships are summarized in the following chart.

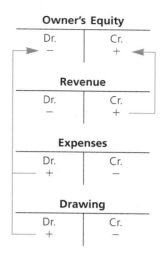

Revenue increases total owner's equity.

Expenses decrease total owner's equity

Drawing decreases total owner's equity.

Day to day, as revenue, expense, and drawing transactions occur, they are recorded in separate accounts. However, at year-end, the balances in these individual revenue, expense, and drawing accounts must be moved to a different location.

Why? These accounts are all income statement accounts, except for drawing. As you will recall, an income statement covers a specific period of time—not more than one year. At year-end, these accounts must be **closed** (brought to a zero balance) to be ready to start accumulating data for the next year. The drawing account, although not an income statement account, also accumulates data for only one year and must be brought to a zero balance at year-end.

How to Close an Account

Closing an account means bringing the account balance to zero. For example, if Account A has a $500 debit balance, it is closed with a $500 credit, leaving a zero balance.

Account A

Dr.		Cr.	
Balance	500	Closing	500

If Account C has an $825 credit balance, it is closed with an $825 debit, leaving a zero balance.

Account C

Dr.		Cr.	
Closing	825	Balance	825

When an account is closed, the debit or credit balance that has been removed is not thrown away but is simply moved to a different account.

Account A				**Account B**			
Dr.		Cr.		Dr.		Cr.	
Balance	500	Closing	500	Closing	500		

Observe that we have not lost the $500 debit; we have simply moved it from Account A to Account B.

Account C			Account D	
Dr.	Cr.		Dr.	Cr.
Closing 825	Balance 825			Closing 825

Again, observe that we have not lost the $825 credit; we have moved it from Account C to Account D.

Because revenue, expense, and drawing accounts are closed at the end of each year, they are often referred to as temporary owner's equity accounts. They are temporary in the sense that there is no carryover of their balances from one year to the next. They are closed at the end of every year and therefore begin every new year with a zero balance.

On the other hand, balance sheet accounts (assets, liabilities, and capital) are not closed at year-end. Asset, liability, and capital accounts are often referred to as permanent accounts. They are permanent in the sense that their year-end balances carry over and become beginning balances in the new year.

The Closing Procedure

At the end of every fiscal year, the temporary owner's equity accounts (revenue, expense, drawing) must be closed to a permanent owner's equity account. In PAW, there are two permanent owner's equity accounts: the owner's capital account and the Retained Earnings account. PAW closes the temporary accounts to the Retained Earnings account.

The procedure used to close the temporary accounts consists of three steps:

step 1:   Close all revenue accounts to the Retained Earnings account.

step 2:   Close all expense accounts to the Retained Earnings account.

step 3:   Close the owner's drawing account to the Retained Earnings account.

Referring to The Kitchen Taylor's trial balance shown in Figure 7.1 for account titles and balances, let's use T-accounts to demonstrate the closing procedure.

step 1:   Close all revenue accounts to the Retained Earnings account.

Fees Earned			Retained Earnings	
Dr.	Cr.		Dr.	Cr.
Closing 2,900	Balance 2,900			Closing 2,900

step 2: Close all expense accounts to the Retained Earnings account.

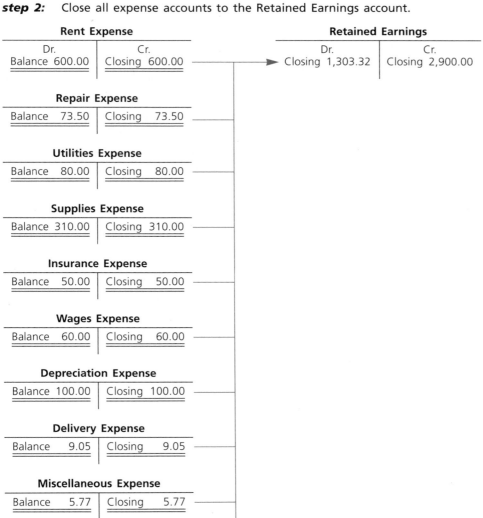

Rent Expense		
Dr.	Cr.	
Balance 600.00	Closing 600.00	

Retained Earnings	
Dr.	Cr.
Closing 1,303.32	Closing 2,900.00

Repair Expense	
Balance 73.50	Closing 73.50

Utilities Expense	
Balance 80.00	Closing 80.00

Supplies Expense	
Balance 310.00	Closing 310.00

Insurance Expense	
Balance 50.00	Closing 50.00

Wages Expense	
Balance 60.00	Closing 60.00

Depreciation Expense	
Balance 100.00	Closing 100.00

Delivery Expense	
Balance 9.05	Closing 9.05

Miscellaneous Expense	
Balance 5.77	Closing 5.77

Service Charge Expense	
Balance 15.00	Closing 15.00

step 3: Close the owner's drawing account to the Retained Earnings account.

Dennis Taylor, Drawing	
Dr.	Cr.
Balance 216.50	Closing 216.50

Retained Earnings	
Dr.	Cr.
Closing 1,303.32	Closing 2,900
Closing 216.50	

Each of the three steps in the closing procedure requires a journal entry. In data entry sheet format, The Kitchen Taylor's **closing entries** are recorded as follows:

			DATA ENTRY SHEET The Kitchen Taylor		
Date	Account ID	Reference	Trans Description	Debit Amt	Credit Amt
12/31/95	410		Fees Earned	2,900.00	
	330		Retained Earnings		2,900.00
12/31/95	330		Retained Earnings	1,303.32	
	510		Rent Expense		600.00
	511		Repair Expense		73.50
	512		Utilities Expense		80.00
	513		Supplies Expense		310.00
	514		Insurance Expense		50.00
	515		Wages Expense		60.00
	516		Depreciation Expense		100.00
	517		Delivery Expense		9.05
	518		Miscellaneous Expense		5.77
	519		Service Charge Expense		15.00
12/31/95	330		Retained Earnings	216.50	
	320		Dennis Taylor, Drawing		216.50

After the closing entries have been journalized and posted, all the temporary accounts (revenue, expense, drawing) have *zero* balances. They are *closed.*

Comment

You may have noticed that prior to closing on December 31, 1995, The Kitchen Taylor's Retained Earnings account had a zero balance. Why? Because December 31, 1995, marks the end of The Kitchen Taylor's *first* fiscal year. After closing the 1995 fiscal year, the Retained Earnings account has a $1,380.18 credit balance computed as follows:

	Beginning Retained Earnings balance	$ -0-
+	Revenues	2,900.00 Cr.
−	Expenses	−1,303.32 Dr.
−	Drawing	− 216.50 Dr.
	Ending Retained Earnings balance	$ 1,380.18 Cr.

Using **PAW** to **C**lose the **F**iscal **Y**ear

objective 6
Use PAW to close the fiscal year

Earlier in the chapter, you recorded The Kitchen Taylor's closing entries on a data entry sheet. Normally, the next step would be to journalize and post these entries. In the case of closing entries, however, you do *not* need to do this because PAW automatically completes the closing procedure with a few simple steps. We prepared the data entry sheet so that you would understand what PAW does "behind the scenes."

To demonstrate how easy it is when using PAW, let's close The Kitchen Taylor's fiscal year. Follow these steps:

step   1:   From the main menu, select Tas**k**s, S**y**s**t**em, Close **F**iscal Year. A "Warning" screen with three choices displays.

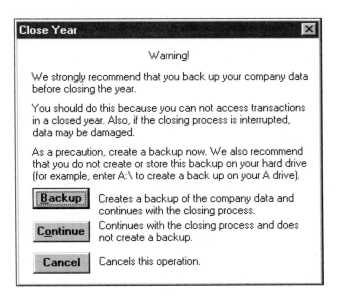

step   2:   Click on C**o**ntinue.

step   3:   The next screen is a Peachtree Accounting Question "If Payroll or 1099s are being used, the Payroll Year should be closed first. If you are using Peachtree Fixed Assets, all General Journal entries for depreciation should be posted first. Do you want to continue?"

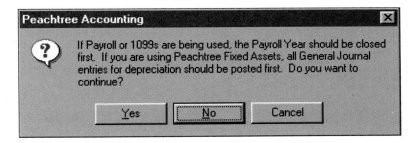

step   4:   Click on **Y**es.

step   5:   The next window displays "Would you like to print your reports before continuing?"

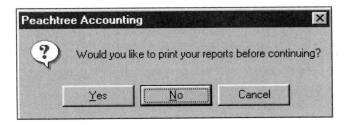

Comment   The "Would you like to print your reports before continuing?" window will display if the general journal has been modified since printing your reports. If all reports printed correctly, without having to modify the general journal, PAW will skip this screen. Step 7 shows the next screen display.

step 6: Click on <u>N</u>o.

step 7: The next screen displays "You are closing to the retained earnings account: '330'."

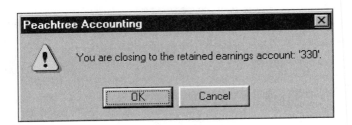

step 8: Click on OK.

step 9: The "Close Fiscal Year" window displays.

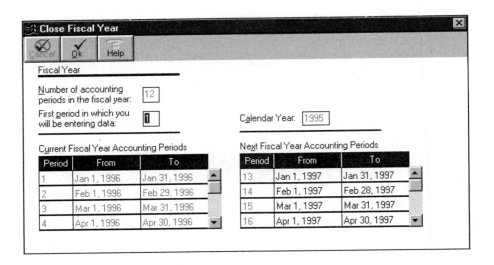

step 10: Click on <u>O</u>k.

step 11: The "Fiscal Year close completed; Do you want to purge?" window displays.

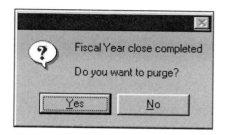

step 12: Click on <u>N</u>o. You are returned to the main menu.

Printing the Post-Closing Trial Balance

After the fiscal year is closed, a post-closing trial balance is printed. This completes the basic accounting cycle.

The post-closing trial balance is a final check on the overall equality of debits and credits in the general ledger. Only permanent accounts appear on the post-closing trial balance because all temporary accounts have been closed.

objective 7
Print a post-closing trial balance

Follow these steps to print The Kitchen Taylor's post-closing trial balance:

step 1: From the main menu, select <u>R</u>eports, <u>G</u>eneral Ledger, General Ledger Trial Balance.

step 2: Make the selections to print the post-closing trial balance. Compare your screen to Figure 7.6.

Figure 7.6

The Kitchen Taylor
General Ledger Trial Balance
As of Jan 31, 1996
Filter Criteria includes: Report order is by ID. Report is printed in Detail Format.

Account ID	Account Description	Debit Amt	Credit Amt
108	Change Fund	75.00	
109	Petty Cash	100.00	
110	Cash	3,058.63	
111	Accounts Receivable	1,100.00	
112	Supplies	121.55	
113	Prepaid Insurance	1,150.00	
120	Truck	6,000.00	
121	Accumulated Depreciation		100.00
210	Accounts Payable		65.00
211	Wages Payable		60.00
310	Dennis Taylor, Capital		10,000.00
330	Retained Earnings		1,380.18
	Total:	11,605.18	11,605.18

Observe that the post-closing trial balance is dated January 31, 1996. All the permanent account balances are brought forward to the next account period: January 1 through 31, 1996.

Backing Up Your Chapter 7 Data

objective 8
Back up your data

As noted in previous chapters, you must back up your data at the end of every chapter. Follow these steps to back up your Chapter 7 data:

step 1:   Insert a blank formatted disk in drive A.

step 2:   From PAW's main menu, select File, then Backup.

step 3:   Type a:\chapter7 in the Destination text box.

step 4:   Click on the Backup button. Your files begin to copy. When all the files have been saved to drive A, you are automatically returned to the main menu.

step 5:   Click on File, Exit to exit PAW.

Chapter Seven Summary

Periodically (usually monthly or yearly), the information contained in the accounts must be summarized in a format that is more helpful to users of financial data such as owners, creditors, or government agencies. Financial statements provide that format. There are three basic financial statements.

1. Income statement
2. Balance sheet
3. Statement of cash flow

The basic accounting cycle is completed over a period of 12 consecutive months. A calendar year consists of 12 consecutive months always beginning in January and ending in December. A fiscal year (financial year) also consists of 12 consecutive months, but it can be any grouping of 12 consecutive months.

At the end of each fiscal year, the temporary owner's equity accounts (revenue, expense, drawing) must be closed to a permanent owner's equity account. In PAW, there are two permanent owner's equity accounts: the owner's capital account and the Retained Earnings account. PAW closes temporary accounts to the Retained Earnings account in three steps.

step 1:   Close all revenue accounts to the Retained Earnings account.

step 2:   Close all expense accounts to the Retained Earnings account.

step 3:   Close the owner's drawing account to the Retained Earnings account.

After the fiscal year is closed, a post-closing trial balance is printed. The post-closing trial balance is a final check on the overall equality of debits and credits in the ledger. Only permanent accounts appear on the post-closing trial balance because all temporary accounts have been closed.

This completes the basic accounting cycle.

Journalize
↓
Post to the ledger
↓
Print an unadjusted trial balance
↓
Journalize and post adjusting entries
↓
Print an adjusted trial balance
↓
Print financial statements
↓
Close the fiscal year
↓
Print a post-closing trial balance

Demonstration Problem

Drake Associates' adjusted trial balance is shown in Figure 7.7.

Figure 7.7

Drake Associates
General Ledger Trial Balance
As of Dec 31, 1995

Filter Criteria includes: Report order is by ID. Report is printed in Detail Format.

Account ID	Account Description	Debit Amt	Credit Amt
110	Cash	5,000.00	
111	Accounts Receivable	7,000.00	
112	Supplies	200.00	
113	Prepaid Insurance	700.00	
120	Equipment	10,000.00	
121	Accumulated Depreciation		1,800.00
210	Accounts Payable		2,000.00
215	Wages Payable		900.00
310	Henry Drake, Capital		17,300.00
320	Henry Drake, Drawing	8,000.00	
410	Fees Earned		40,000.00
510	Advertising Expense	2,000.00	
511	Rent Expense	13,000.00	
512	Utilities Expense	1,100.00	
513	Wages Expense	12,900.00	
514	Insurance Expense	300.00	
515	Depreciation Expense	600.00	
516	Supplies Expense	700.00	
517	Miscellaneous Expense	500.00	
	Total:	**62,000.00**	**62,000.00**

Instructions

Use T-accounts to demonstrate the three-step closing procedure needed to close Drake Associates' accounts.

Solution to Demonstration Problem

step 1: Close all revenue accounts to the Retained Earnings account.

Fees Earned			Retained Earnings	
Dr.	Cr.		Dr.	Cr.
Closing 40,000	Balance 40,000			Closing 40,000

step 2: Close all expense accounts to the Retained Earnings account.

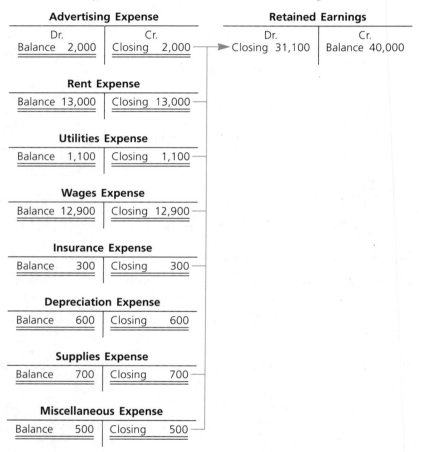

Advertising Expense			Retained Earnings	
Dr.	Cr.		Dr.	Cr.
Balance 2,000	Closing 2,000		Closing 31,100	Balance 40,000

Rent Expense	
Balance 13,000	Closing 13,000

Utilities Expense	
Balance 1,100	Closing 1,100

Wages Expense	
Balance 12,900	Closing 12,900

Insurance Expense	
Balance 300	Closing 300

Depreciation Expense	
Balance 600	Closing 600

Supplies Expense	
Balance 700	Closing 700

Miscellaneous Expense	
Balance 500	Closing 500

Step 3: Close the owner's drawing account to the Retained Earnings account.

Henry Drake, Drawing			Retained Earnings	
Dr.	Cr.		Dr.	Cr.
Balance 8,000	Closing 8,000		Closing 31,100	Closing 40,000
			Closing 8,000	

Glossary

accounting cycle   The accounting process completed during each fiscal year: journalizing; posting to ledger; printing an unadjusted trial balance, journalizing and posting adjusting entries; printing an adjusted trial balance; printing financial statements; closing fiscal year; printing post-closing trial balance.   *178*

calendar year A year consisting of 12 consecutive months always beginning in January and ending in December. *186*

closed account An account with a zero balance. *187*

closing entries Three entries prepared at the end of the fiscal year to close the temporary owner's equity accounts (revenue, expense, and drawing) to the Retained Earnings account. *189*

fiscal year A financial year consisting of 12 consecutive months. The most popular fiscal year is the calendar year (January through December), but it could be any grouping of 12 consecutive months—for example, July 1 though the following June 30. *186*

interim period A period of time shorter than one fiscal year. *186*

interim statement A statement prepared for a period of less than one fiscal year. *186*

permanent accounts Assets, liability, and capital accounts are permanent in the sense that their year-end balances carry over and become beginning balances in the new fiscal year. *188*

temporary owner's equity accounts Accounts that accumulate data for only one fiscal year (revenue, expense, and drawing). At the end of each fiscal year, they are closed to retained earnings. They are temporary in the sense that there is no carryover of their balances from one year to the next. They begin every new year with a zero balance. *188*

Self-Test

Select the best answer.

1. The purpose of the closing procedure is to close
   a. the permanent owner's equity accounts to the temporary owner's equity accounts.
   b. all accounts to permanent owner's equity.
   c. the temporary owner's equity accounts to the Retained Earnings account.
   d. all accounts.

2. In what order are the temporary accounts closed?
   a. Assets, liabilities, capital.
   b. Revenue, expenses, drawing.
   c. Retained earnings, assets, liabilities.
   d. Liabilities, drawing, revenue, expenses.

3. A post-closing trial balance
   a. is prepared after the fiscal year is closed.
   b. checks the overall equality of debits and credits in the ledger.
   c. completes the basic accounting cycle.
   d. All of the above.

4. A fiscal year
   a. is any grouping of 12 consecutive months.
   b. is always a calendar year.
   c. is an interim period.
   d. All of the above.

5. In PAW, closing entries
   a. are not part of the accounting cycle.
   b. must be journalized.
   c. must be posted.
   d. are processed automatically by selecting "Close Fiscal Year."

Answers to the self-test can be found after the cases at the end of this chapter.

Questions for Discussion

1. Why is it necessary to close the fiscal year?
2. Use a T-account to demonstrate how an account is closed.
3. Define the following terms:
   a. Temporary owner's equity accounts.
   b. Permanent owner's equity accounts.
   c. Interim period.
   d. Interim statement.
4. What are the three steps in the closing procedure?
5. How are the financial statements interrelated?
6. How do you close the fiscal year using PAW?
7. What is the basic accounting cycle?
8. What is the difference between a calendar year and a fiscal year?

Exercises

Exercise 7.1

Terminology
L.O. 1–7

Match the following terms with the definitions shown below:

1. Calendar year
2. Accounting cycle
3. Temporary owner's equity accounts
4. Closed account
5. Interim period
6. Permanent owner's equity accounts
7. Closing entries
8. Fiscal year
9. Interim statement

Definitions

a. Accounts that accumulate data for only one fiscal year.
b. A statement prepared for a period of less than one fiscal year.
c. A year consisting of 12 consecutive months always beginning in January and ending in December.
d. Accounts whose balances are carried over to the new fiscal year.
e. The accounting process completed during each fiscal year: journalizing, posting, and so on.
f. Three entries prepared at the end of the fiscal year to close the temporary owner's equity accounts to the Retained Earnings account.
g. A financial year consisting of 12 consecutive months.
h. A period of time shorter than one fiscal year.
i. An account with a zero balance.

Exercise 7.2

Arrange the following steps in the accounting cycle in their proper order:

Accounting cycle
L.O. 1–7

   a. Post to the ledger.

   b. Journalize and post adjusting entries.

   c. Journalize.

   d. Print unadjusted trial balance.

   e. Print post-closing trial balance.

   f. Print financial statements.

   g. Close fiscal year.

   h. Print adjusted trial balance.

Exercise 7.3

Classify each of the accounts listed below as one of the following:

Account classification
L.O. 1

     CA—Current Asset
     FA—Fixed Asset
     CL—Current Liability
     TOE—Temporary Owner's Equity
     POE—Permanent Owner's Equity

  1. Prepaid Insurance

  2. Retained Earnings

  3. Rent Expense

  4. John Gargaro, Drawing

  5. Wages Payable

  6. Fees Earned

  7. Accounts Payable

  8. Equipment

Exercise 7.4

Indicate on which statement the accounts listed below are shown.

Financial statements
L.O. 1

     IS—Income Statement
     BS—Balance Sheet

  1. Fees Earned

  2. Accounts Payable

  3. Depreciation Expense

  4. Retained Earnings

  5. Mary Avalos, Drawing

  6. Mary Avalos, Capital

  7. Building

  8. Prepaid Insurance

  9. Cash

  10. Accumulated Depreciation

Exercise 7.5

Indicate whether each of the following accounts should be closed at year-end (yes or no):

Closing entries
L.O. 5

a. Prepaid Insurance

b. Accumulated Depreciation

c. Depreciation Expense

d. Amy Lee, Drawing

e. Supplies Expense

f. Accounts Payable

g. Amy Lee, Capital

h. Fees Earned

i. Supplies

j. Rent Expense

Exercise 7.6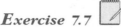

Closing entries
L.O. 5

Arrange the following steps in the closing procedure in their proper order:

a. Close expense accounts to Retained Earnings.

b. Close the owner's drawing account to Retained Earnings.

c. Close revenue to Retained Earnings.

Exercise 7.7

Closing entries
L.O. 5

After the three-step closing procedure is complete, the Retained Earnings account appears as follows:

Retained Earnings

Closing	8,390	Closing 11,320
Closing	2,930	

From this information, answer the following questions:

a. What was total revenue?

b. What were total expenses?

c. How much did the owner withdraw for personal use?

Exercise 7.8

Time periods
L.O. 4

Indicate which of the following terms best describes the time frame listed below:

- Calendar year

- Fiscal year

- Interim period

1. July 1, 1995–June 30, 1996.

2. June 1, 1995–June 30, 1995.

3. January 1, 1996–December 31, 1996.

Problems—Set A

Problem 7.1A

Restore data
L.O. 2

Follow these steps to restore your Ace Cleaning Service data from Chapter 6 and print a trial balance:

step 1:   Start Windows, then PAW. Open Ace Cleaning Service.

step 2: Place your Ace Cleaning Service backup disk in drive A.

step 3: From the main menu, select File, then Restore.

step 4: Type **a:\acedec.66a** in the Source box. (Use the same file name that you used when you backed up Ace Cleaning Service in Chapter 6.)

step 5: Click on the Restore button. Read the "Warning" screen, then click on OK. Restoring the files will take a few moments. When the files are restored, you are returned to the main menu.

step 6: Remove disk from drive A.

step 7: Follow these steps to print the trial balance:
  a. From the main menu, select Reports, then General Ledger.
  b. The "Select a Report" window displays. Highlight General Ledger Trial Balance.
  c. Make the selections to print. Compare your printout to Figure 7.8.

Figure 7.8

Ace Cleaning Service
General Ledger Trial Balance
As of Dec 31, 1995
Filter Criteria includes: Report order is by ID. Report is printed in Detail Format.

Account ID	Account Description	Debit Amt	Credit Amt
108	Change Fund	30.00	
109	Petty Cash	50.00	
110	Cash	3,908.50	
111	Accounts Receivable	2,600.00	
112	Supplies	112.50	
113	Prepaid Insurance	594.00	
114	Equipment	5,000.00	
115	Accumulated Depreciation		75.00
210	Accounts Payable		2,525.00
215	Salaries Payable		258.00
310	Joan Haywood, Capital		7,500.00
320	Joan Haywood, Drawing	555.00	
410	Cleaning Revenue		4,650.00
510	Rent Expense	625.00	
511	Repair Expense	270.00	
512	Salary Expense	903.00	
513	Utilities Expense	136.00	
514	Supplies Expense	80.00	
515	Insurance Expense	54.00	
516	Depreciation Expense	75.00	
517	Service Charge Expense	15.00	
	Total:	**15,008.00**	**15,008.00**

Problem 7.2A

Instructions

Follow these steps to print Ace Cleaning Service's financial statements:

Financial statements
L.O. 3

step 1: From the main menu, select Reports, then Financial Statements.

step 2: Highlight "Income Statement."

step 3: Click on the Print icon. The "Income Statement" window displays.

step 4: Click once on the check mark in the box next to "Show Zero Amounts" to deselect it.

step 5: Click on OK. When the "Print" window pops up, click on OK. The income statement starts to print.

step 6: To print the balance sheet, highlight "Balance Sheet" and make the selections to print.

step 7: To print the statement of cash flow, highlight "<Predefined> Cash Flow," deselect "Show Zero Amounts," then make the selections to print.

Problem 7.3A

Closing entries
L.O. 5

Referring to your Ace Cleaning Service trial balance from Problem 7.1A, record the necessary closing entries on a data entry sheet.

Problem 7.4A

Closing the fiscal year, trial balance
L.O. 5, 6, 7

1. Follow these steps to close the fiscal year for Ace Cleaning Services:

    step 1: From the main menu, select Tasks, System, Close Fiscal Year.

    step 2: Click on Continue.

    step 3: The next screen is a "Peachtree Accounting Question" window.

    step 4: Read the question, then click on Yes.

    step 5: The next window displays "Would you like to print your reports before continuing?"

Comment

The "Would you like to print your reports before continuing?" window will display if the general journal has been modified since printing your reports. If all reports printed correctly, without having to modify the general journal, PAW will skip this screen. Step 7 shows the next screen display.

    step 6: Click on No.

    step 7: The next screen displays "You are closing to the Retained Earnings account: '330'."

    step 8: Click on OK.

    step 9: The "Close Fiscal Year" window displays.

    step 10: Click on Ok.

    step 11: The "Fiscal Year close completed; Do you want to purge?" window displays.

    step 12: Click on No. You are returned to the main menu.

2. Print a post-closing trial balance.

Problem 7.5A

Your Ace Cleaning Service data **must** be backed up. Follow these steps:

Back up
L.O. 8

step 1: Insert a blank formatted disk in drive A.

step 2: From PAW's main menu, select File, then Backup.

step 3: Type **a:\acedec.75a** in the Destination text box.

step 4: Click on the Backup button. Your files begin to copy. When all the files have been saved to drive A, you are automatically returned to the main menu.

step 5: Click on File, Exit to exit PAW.

Problems—Set B

Problem 7.1B

Follow these steps to restore your Loyal Lawn Service data from Chapter 6 and print a trial balance:

Restore data
L.O. 2

step 1: Start Windows, then PAW. Open Loyal Lawn Service.

step 2: Place your Loyal Lawn Service backup disk in drive A.

step 3: From the main menu, select File, then Restore.

step 4: Type **a:\loyaldec.66b** in the Source box. (Use the same file name that you used when you backed up Loyal Lawn Service in Chapter 6.)

step 5: Click on the Restore button. Read the "Warning" screen, then click on OK. Restoring the files will take a few moments. When the files are restored, you are returned to the main menu.

step 6: Remove disk from drive A.

step 7: Follow these steps to print the trial balance:

   a. From the main menu, select Reports, then General Ledger.
   b. The "Select a Report" window displays. Highlight General Ledger Trial Balance.
   c. Make the selections to print. Compare your printout to Figure 7.9.

Figure 7.9

Loyal Lawn Service
General Ledger Trial Balance
As of Dec 31, 1995
Filter Criteria includes: Report order is by ID. Report is printed in Detail Format.

Account ID	Account Description	Debit Amt	Credit Amt
108	Change Fund	25.00	
109	Petty Cash	75.00	
110	Cash	2,151.25	
111	Accounts Receivable	2,240.00	
112	Supplies	150.00	
113	Prepaid Insurance	550.00	
114	Equipment	5,000.00	
115	Accumulated Depreciation		75.00
210	Accounts Payable		1,435.00
215	Salaries Payable		414.00
310	Chris Canon, Capital		7,000.00
320	Chris Canon, Drawing	470.00	
410	Lawn Service Revenue		3,987.00
510	Rent Expense	595.00	
511	Repair Expense	153.75	
512	Salary Expense	1,104.00	
513	Utilities Expense	162.00	
514	Supplies Expense	90.00	
515	Insurance Expense	50.00	
516	Depreciation Expense	75.00	
517	Service Charge Expense	20.00	
	Total:	**12,911.00**	**12,911.00**

Problem 7.2B

Instructions

Financial statements
L.O. 3

Follow these steps to print Loyal Lawn Service's financial statements:

step 1: From the main menu, select <u>R</u>eports, then <u>F</u>inancial Statements.

step 2: Highlight "Income Statement."

step 3: Click on the Print icon. The "Income Statement" window displays.

step 4: Click once on the check mark in the box next to "Show Zero Amounts" to deselect it.

step 5: Click on <u>O</u>K. When the "Print" window pops up, click on OK. The income statement starts to print.

step 6: To print the balance sheet, highlight "Balance Sheet" and make the selections to print.

step 7: To print the statement of cash flow, highlight "<Predefined> Cash Flow," deselect "Show Zero Amounts," then make the selections to print.

Problem 7.3B

Closing entries
L.O. 5

Referring to your Loyal Lawn Service trial balance from Problem 7.1B, record the necessary closing entries on a data entry sheet.

Problem 7.4B

1. Follow these steps to close the fiscal year for Loyal Lawn Service:

Closing the fiscal year, trial balance
L.O. 5, 6, 7

step 1: From the main menu, select Tasks, System, Close Fiscal Year.

step 2: Click on Continue.

step 3: The next screen is a "Peachtree Accounting Question" window.

step 4: Read the question, then click on Yes.

step 5: The next window displays "Would you like to print your reports before continuing?"

The "Would you like to print your reports before continuing?" window will display **Comment** if the general journal has been modified since printing your reports. If all reports printed correctly, without having to modify the general journal, PAW will skip this screen. Step 7 shows the next screen display.

---

step 6: Click on No.

step 7: The next screen displays "You are closing to the Retained Earnings account: '330'."

step 8: Click on OK.

step 9: The "Close Fiscal Year" window displays.

step 10: Click on Ok.

step 11: The "Fiscal Year close completed; Do you want to purge?" window displays.

step 12: Click on No. You are returned to the main menu.

2. Print a post-closing trial balance.

Problem 7.5B

Your Loyal Lawn Service data **must** be backed up. Follow these steps:

Back up
L.O. 8

step 1: Insert a blank formatted disk in drive A.

step 2: From PAW's main menu, select File, then Backup.

step 3: Type a:\loyaldec.75b in the Destination text box.

step 4: Click on the Backup button. Your files begin to copy. When all the files have been saved to drive A, you are automatically returned to the main menu.

step 5: Click on File, Exit to exit PAW.

Mini-Cases

Case 7–1
Scott Foreman, a friend of yours, says he does not need to close the fiscal year because he does not use any temporary accounts. Instead, he records all revenue, expense, and drawing transactions directly in the Retained Earnings account as they occur. Is this a good idea?

Case 7–2
Harry Haynes, your new accounts receivable clerk, asks, "How is it possible for Accounts Receivable to be a permanent account? Our customers have to pay in 30 days." What is your reply?

Case 7–3
Chris Bayne, a client, complains that the post-closing trial balance you prepared is incomplete. Chris says, "You left out my drawing account, as well as all the revenue and expense accounts." Did you make a mistake?

A Case of Ethics

The owner of Sorena Company has asked her accountant not to close the revenue accounts at the end of the fiscal year. "Our year-end income statement will look a lot better if we can fatten up those revenue figures with a couple extra days of revenue," she says. What do you think of this plan?

Answers to Self-Test

1. *c*   2. *b*   3. *d*   4. *a*   5. *d*

Comprehensive Review Problem 1

Covering Chapters 1–7

Part A

Regal Dry Cleaners began operations in November 1995. Their chart of accounts is shown in Figure 7.10.

Figure 7.10

Regal Dry Cleaners
Chart of Accounts
As of Nov 30, 1995

Filter Criteria includes: Report order is by ID. Report is printed with Accounts having Zero Amounts and in Detail Format.

Account ID	Account Description	Active?	Account Type
110	Cash	Yes	Cash
111	Accounts Receivable	Yes	Accounts Receivable
112	Supplies	Yes	Inventory
113	Prepaid Insurance	Yes	Other Current Assets
114	Equipment	Yes	Fixed Assets
115	Accumulated Deprec.--Equipment	Yes	Accumulated Depreciation
116	Truck	Yes	Fixed Assets
117	Accumulated Deprec.--Truck	Yes	Accumulated Depreciation
210	Accounts Payable	Yes	Accounts Payable
211	Salaries Payable	Yes	Other Current Liabilities
310	James Regal, Capital	Yes	Equity-doesn't close
320	James Regal, Drawing	Yes	Equity-gets closed
330	Retained Earnings	Yes	Equity-Retained Earnings
410	Dry Cleaning Revenue	Yes	Income
510	Advertising Expense	Yes	Expenses
511	Deprec. Expense--Equipment	Yes	Expenses
512	Deprec. Expense--Truck	Yes	Expenses
513	Insurance Expense	Yes	Expenses
514	Rent Expense	Yes	Expenses
515	Salary Expense	Yes	Expenses
516	Supplies Expense	Yes	Expenses
517	Telephone Expense	Yes	Expenses
518	Utilities Expense	Yes	Expenses

Instructions to load the Regal Dry Cleaners company data and print the chart of accounts.

1. Start Windows. If you are running Windows 3.1x, choose File, Run in Program Manager. If you are running Windows 95, choose Start, Run.

2. Place the Company Data CD-ROM in drive D (or the appropriate drive for your CD-ROM).

3. Type **d:\setup.exe** in the dialog box. (This text assumes drive D is your CD-ROM drive. Use the appropriate drive letter if your CD-ROM is located in a different location.)

4. Click on the OK button. A screen pops up that says "One moment please. . . ."

5. The "Company Data to accompany College Accounting with Peachtree" window pops up. Click on Continue.

6. Accept the default for the "Path: C:\PEACHW" by clicking on Continue. (If Peachtree was installed in a different directory, type that location in the "Path" dialog box.)

7. The next screen, "Companies", shows the data that is included on the Company Data CD-ROM.

8. Since you are loading data for Regal Dry Cleaners only, click on the box next to Regal.

9. Click on Continue. A scale shows what percentage of data has been copied. All files have been copied to the hard drive of your computer when the scale is completed. The "Success" window displays.

10. Click on OK. You are returned to Program Manager in Windows 3.1x or the desktop in Windows 95.

11. Remove the Company Data CD-ROM from drive D (or the appropriate drive for your CD-ROM).

12. Double-click on the Peachtree Accounting icon. At the "Presenting Peachtree Accounting" window, click on Open.

13. Click once on Regal Dry Cleaners to highlight it.

Comment

If Regal Dry Cleaners is not listed in the Company Name box or if *it appears but you did not load it* (some other student did), you **must** go back to Instruction 1 to load the *original* Regal Dry Cleaners company data from the CD-ROM that came with this text. *This is extremely important.*

---

14. Click on Ok. The main menu for Regal Dry Cleaners displays.

15. Follow these steps to print Regal Dry Cleaners' chart of accounts.
    a. From the main menu, select Reports, then General Ledger. In the "Report List," the "Chart of Accounts" is highlighted.
    b. On the "Icon Bar," click on the Print icon 🖶 . The "Chart of Accounts Filter" window displays.
    c. Click on OK and the "Print" window pops up.
    d. Click on OK and the chart of accounts starts to print. Compare your printout with Figure 7.10.
    e. On the "Icon Bar," click on "Close." You are returned to the main menu.
    f. To exit PAW, select File, Exit.

Part B

Regal Dry Cleaners completed the following transactions during its first month of operations:

Nov. 1 The owner, James Regal, invested cash in the business, $24,000.

1 Paid monthly rent, $600, Check No. 101.

2 Purchased equipment for $3,600, paying $1,000 in cash, Check No. 102, and the remainder on account.

2 Established a $30 change fund, Check No. 103. (Add Account No. 108, Change Fund.)

3 Purchased cleaning fluids and other supplies on account, $280.

4 Purchased a truck for cash, $13,800, Check No. 104.

5 Paid a one-year insurance premium covering the period November 5, 1995, through November 4, 1996, $864, Check No. 105.

6 Established a $50 petty cash fund, Check No. 106. (Add Account No. 109, Petty Cash.)

7 Paid bill for newspaper advertising, $108, Check No. 107.

9 Recorded revenue from dry cleaning services: $300 cash and $750 on account.

12 Paid employees' salaries, $435, Check No. 108.

14 Paid creditor on account, $114, Check No. 109.

17 Recorded revenue from dry cleaning services: $205 cash and $970 on account.

20 Received payment on account from charge customer, $520.

22 Paid electric bill, $106, Check No. 110.

24 Paid creditor on account, $600, Check No. 111.

26 Paid employees' salaries, $492, Check No. 112.

27 Received payment on account from charge customer, $435.

28 The owner withdrew $300 to pay for personal expenses, Check No. 113.

29 Recorded revenue from dry cleaning services: $246 cash and $940 on account.

29 Issued Check No. 114 to replenish the petty cash fund based on the following information taken from Regal's petty cash record:

Supplies	$12.50
Advertising Expense	10.00
James Regal, Drawing	15.00
Total payments	$37.50

Instructions

1. Record these transactions on a data entry sheet. Number the data entry sheet pages.

2. Referring to your completed data entry sheet, record the general journal entries using PAW's "General Journal Entry" feature.

3. Print the general journal.

4. Proofread your general journal. If necessary, make corrections using PAW's "Edit Records" feature. If you make any corrections, reprint the general journal.

5. Post to the general ledger.

6. Print a trial balance.

7. Follow these steps to back up your work up to this point:
   a. Insert a blank formatted disk in drive A.
   b. From PAW's main menu, select File, then Backup.
   c. Type **a:\novutb.reg** in the Destination text box.
   d. Click on the Backup button. Your files begin to copy. When all the files have been saved to drive A, you are automatically returned to the main menu.

Part C

Regal's accounts need to be adjusted based on the following data:

a. Supplies used during November, $157.

b. Expired insurance, $72.

c. Salary expense incurred but not yet paid as of November 30, $280.

d. Depreciation on equipment, $90.

e. Depreciation on truck, $360.

Instructions

1. Record these adjustments on a data entry sheet.

2. Use PAW's "General Journal Entry" feature to journalize the adjustments.

3. Print the November 30, 1995, general journal. Proofread your general journal and make any necessary corrections.

4. Post to the general ledger.

5. Print an adjusted trial balance.

6. Follow these steps to back up your work up to this point:
    a. Insert a blank formatted disk in drive A.
    b. From PAW's main menu, select File, then Backup.
    c. Type **a:\novatb.reg** in the Destination text box.
    d. Click on the Backup button. Your files begin to copy. When all the files have been saved to drive A, you are automatically returned to the main menu.

Part D

Regal Dry Cleaners' bank statement is shown in Figure 7.11.

Figure 7.11

VALLEY NATIONAL BANK Wheaton, Illinois				
Regal Dry Cleaners 1206 Broadway Wheaton, Illinois 60187			Statement Date: 11-30-95 Account No. 0311098245 11-1-95 to 11-30-95	
REGULAR CHECKING				
Previous Balance				0.00
4 Deposits (+)				25,025.00
10 Checks (−)				17,387.50
Nonsufficient funds (−)				300.00
Service charges (−)				15.00
Ending Balance				**7,322.50**
DEPOSITS				
	11/3/95	24,000.00		
	11/9/95	300.00		
	11/21/95	205.00		
	11/25/95	520.00		
CHECKS (Asterisk * indicates break in check number sequence)				
	11/7/95	101	600.00	
	11/10/95	102	1,000.00	
	11/10/95	103	30.00	
	11/10/95	104	13,800.00	
	11/11/95	105	864.00	
	11/12/95	106	50.00	
	11/29/95	*110	106.00	
	11/30/95	111	600.00	
	11/30/95	*113	300.00	
	11/30/95	114	37.50	
OTHER ITEMS				
	11/25/95	NSF (−)	300.00	

Instructions

1. Record any necessary entries on a data entry sheet. Date these entries November 30, 1995.
2. Use PAW's "General Journal Entry" feature to journalize the entries. (Add Account No. 519, Service Charge Expense.)
3. Post to the general ledger.
4. Use PAW's "Account Reconciliation" feature to reconcile the Cash account.
5. Print the Account Reconciliation Report. Immediately continue to Part E.

Part E
Complete the following end-of-month activities:

1. Print the general ledger.

2. Print the general ledger trial balance.

3. Print the financial statements:
   a. Income statement
   b. Balance sheet
   c. Statement of cash flow

4. Follow these steps to back up your November data:
   a. Insert a blank formatted disk in drive A.
   b. From PAW's main menu, select File, then Backup.
   c. Type **a:\regal.nov** in the Destination text box.
   d. Click on the Backup button. Your files begin to copy. When all the files have been saved to drive A, you are automatically returned to the main menu.

5. If you want to immediately begin Regal's December transactions, go directly to Section 2, Part A, Instruction 2.

6. If you want to quit now and return later, then click on File, Exit to exit PAW.

Section 2—December

Part A

Regal Dry Cleaners completed the following transactions during December 1995:

Dec. 1 Paid monthly rent, $600, Check No. 115.

4 Received payment on account from charge customer, $537.

9 Paid employees' salaries, $480, Check No. 116. (HINT: Debit Salary Expense $200 ($480−280) and debit Salaries Payable $280—recall November's adjusting entries.)

11 Recorded revenue from dry cleaning services: $430 cash and $1,030 on account.

15 Paid creditor on account, $1,200, Check No. 117.

18 Purchased supplies on account, $86.

21 The owner withdrew $360 to pay for personal expenses, Check No. 118.

23 Paid employees' salaries, $430, Check No. 119.

24 Paid telephone bill, $176, Check No. 120.

26 Paid electric bill, $120, Check No. 121.

28 Received payment on account from charge customer, $940.

30 Recorded revenue from dry cleaning services: $570 cash and $1,092 on account.

Instructions

1. Follow these steps to restore your Regal Dry Cleaners data from November:
   a. Start Windows, then PAW. Open Regal Dry Cleaners.
   b. Place your Regal Dry Cleaners backup disk in drive A.

 c. From the main menu, select File, then Restore.

 d. Type **a:\regal.nov** in the Source box. (Use the same file name that you used when you backed up Regal Dry Cleaners in November.)

 e. Click on the Restore button. Read the "Warning" screen, then click on OK. Restoring the files will take a few moments. When the files are restored, you are returned to the main menu.

 f. Remove disk from drive A.

2. It is necessary to change accounting periods since you have completed November and are beginning the month of December. In PAW, this updates the general journal and the reports to the next month. Follow these steps to change accounting periods:

 a. From the main menu, select Tasks, then System.

 b. From the System pull-down menu, select Change Accounting Period.

 c. In the accounting period box, click on the down arrow, then, select "12—Dec 1, 1995 to Dec. 31, 1995."

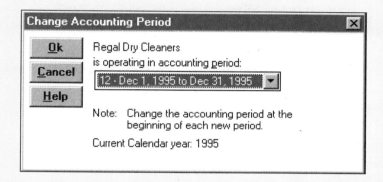

 d. Click on Ok. Since you have already printed reports, click on No at the next screen.

3. Record the December transactions on a data entry sheet. Number the data entry sheet pages.

4. Referring to your completed data entry sheet, record the general journal entries using PAW's "General Journal Entry" feature.

5. Print the general journal.

6. Proofread your general journal. If necessary, make corrections using PAW's "Edit Records" feature. If you make any corrections, reprint the general journal.

7. Post to the general ledger.

8. Print a trial balance.

9. Follow these steps to back up your work up to this point.
   a. Insert a blank formatted disk in drive A.
   b. From PAW's main menu, select File, then Backup.
   c. Type **a:\decutb.reg** in the Destination text box.
   d. Click on the Backup button. Your files begin to copy. When all the files have been saved to drive A, you are automatically returned to the main menu.

Part B

Regal's accounts need to be adjusted based on the following December 31 data:

a. Supplies used during December, $120.

b. Expired insurance, $72.

c. Salary expense incurred but not yet paid as of December 31, $280.

d. Depreciation on equipment, $90.

e. Depreciation on truck, $360.

Instructions

1. Record these adjustments on a data entry sheet.

2. Use PAW's "General Journal Entry" feature to journalize the adjustments.

3. Print the December 31, 1995, general journal. Proofread your general journal and make any necessary corrections.

4. Post to the general ledger.

5. Print an adjusted trial balance.

6. Follow these steps to back up your work up to this point:
   a. Insert a blank formatted disk in drive A.
   b. From PAW's main menu, select File, then Backup.
   c. Type **a:\decatb.reg** in the Destination text box.
   d. Click on the Backup button. Your files begin to copy. When all the files have been saved to drive A, you are automatically returned to the main menu.

Part C

Regal Dry Cleaners' bank statement is shown in Figure 7.12.

Figure 7.12

VALLEY NATIONAL BANK			
Wheaton, Illinois			

Regal Dry Cleaners 1206 Broadway Wheaton, Illinois 60187			Statement Date: 12-31-95 Account No. 0311098245 12-1-95 to 12-31-95
REGULAR CHECKING			
Previous Balance				7,322.50
4 Deposits (+)				1,648.00
7 Checks (−)				2,659.00
Nonsufficient funds (−)				537.00
Service Charges (−)				15.00
Ending Balance				**5,759.50**

DEPOSITS			
	12/1/95	435.00	
	12/7/95	246.00	
	12/12/95	537.00	
	12/30/95	430.00	

CHECKS (Asterisk * indicates break in check number sequence)			
	12/1/95	107	108.00	
	12/2/95	108	435.00	
	12/10/95	109	114.00	
	12/10/95	*112	492.00	
	12/15/95	*115	600.00	
	12/20/95	116	480.00	
	12/30/95	*119	430.00	

OTHER ITEMS			
	12/20/95	NSF (−)	537.00	

Instructions

1. Record any necessary entries on a data entry sheet. Date these entries December 31, 1995.
2. Use PAW's "General Journal Entry" feature to journalize the entries.
3. Post to the general ledger.
4. Use PAW's "Account Reconciliation" feature to reconcile the Cash account.
5. Print the Account Reconciliation Report. Immediately continue to Part D.

Part D

Complete the following end-of-month activities:

1. Print the general ledger.
2. Print the general ledger trial balance.
3. Print the financial statements:

     a. Income statement

     b. Balance sheet

     c. Statement of cash flow

4. Follow these steps to back up your data up to this point:

     a. Insert a blank formatted disk in drive A.

     b. From PAW's main menu, select File, then Backup.

     c. Type **a:\regal.dec** in the Destination text box.

     d. Click on the Backup button. Your files begin to copy. When all the files have been saved to drive A, you are automatically returned to the main menu.

Part E

Instructions

1. Close the fiscal year for Regal Dry Cleaners.

2. Print a post-closing trial balance.

3. Follow these steps to back up your December data:

     a. Insert a blank formatted disk in drive A.

     b. From PAW's main menu, select File, then Backup.

     c. Type **a:\regalend.95** in the Destination text box.

     d. Click on the Backup button. Your files begin to copy. When all the files have been saved to drive A, you are automatically returned to the main menu.

4. Click on File, Exit to exit PAW.

Merchandising Business

Accounting for Purchases

8

In previous chapters, we focused our attention on accounting for businesses that sell a service. In this chapter, we will apply our knowledge of the accounting cycle to businesses that sell a product. More specifically, we will focus our attention on the purchasing activities of such a business. After studying the purchasing process, you will learn about a vendor ledger and a purchase journal as well as how to record other purchase-related transactions.

A Merchandising Business

objective 1
Describe the nature of a merchandising business

Businesses that sell products can be divided into two groups: manufacturing and merchandising. A manufacturing business makes the product that it sells. A merchandising business purchases the product ready-made from a vendor and then resells it to customers. Units purchased by a merchandising business for resale are referred to as merchandise. Such items as office supplies or equipment are *not* merchandise because they are *not* purchased for resale but are to be used by the business. However, an office supply or equipment company would consider office supplies or equipment to be merchandise because the company purchases these items for resale.

In this chapter, Dennis Taylor decides that it is more profitable to sell ready-made kitchen cabinets than to refinish old cabinets. Dennis also changes the name of his business to TKT Products. In other words, TKT Products is a merchandising business. To TKT Products, cabinets and related items are merchandise.

The Purchasing Process

objective 2
Describe the purchasing process

As noted earlier, merchandising businesses purchase the merchandise they sell from suppliers known as *vendors.* Purchasing procedures often vary based on the size of the business. Our discussion describes the typical purchasing process for a moderate to large-sized firm. This process is illustrated in Figure 8.1.

Figure 8.1

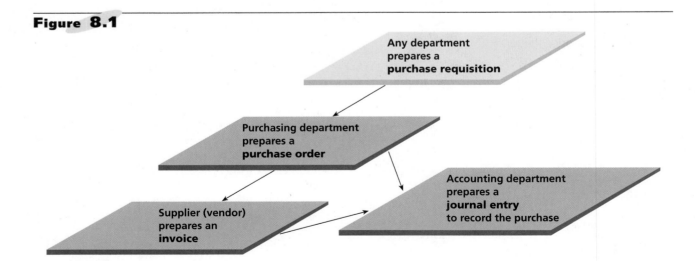

Generally, departmental requests to buy merchandise must be in writing. The form used for such requests is known as a purchase requisition. As shown in Figure 8.2, the purchase requisition is sent to the purchasing department and indicates what is needed and when it is needed. After the purchase requisition has been approved, the purchasing department prepares a purchase order, as shown in Figure 8.3, which is sent to a vendor. A copy of the purchase order is also sent to the purchaser's accounting department. The purchase order is an offer to purchase the requested goods from the vendor. If the offer is accepted, the vendor will prepare an invoice like the one shown in Figure 8.4. This invoice is sent to the purchaser's accounting department about the time the goods are shipped. The accounting department compares the purchase order with the invoice to be sure that the company is being billed for what was ordered and that the price is correct. After comparing the purchase order with the invoice, the accounting department makes a journal entry to record the purchase.

Figure 8.2

TKT PRODUCTS 2400 Main Street Wheaton, Illinois 60187	PURCHASE REQUISITION NO. H534
To: Purchasing Department	Date Requested: November 2, 1996
From: Hardware Department	Date Required: December 1, 1996

Quantity	Description
100	Hinges for cabinets (2")

Requested by: *Mary Grant*   Approved by: *Dennis Taylor*

Date Ordered: Nov. 23, 1996, P. O. No. 1283

Figure 8.3

TKT PRODUCTS 2400 Main Street Wheaton, Illinois 60187	PURCHASE ORDER NO. 1283
To: Saroya Corporation 1741 West River Road Milwaukee, Wisconsin 53217	Date: December 1, 1996 FOB: Destination Terms: n/30

Quantity	Description	Unit Price	Total
100	Hinges for cabinets (2")	9.00	900.00

Ordered by: *Kevin Barker*

Figure 8.4

SAROYA CORPORATION 1741 West River Road Milwaukee, Wisconsin 53217		INVOICE NO. 941	

Sold to: TKT Products
2400 Main Street
Wheaton, Illinois 60187

Date: December 1, 1996
Terms: n/30
F.O.B.: Destination

Quantity	Description	Unit Price	Total
100	Hinges for cabinets (2")	9.00	900.00

The Merchandise Inventory Account

objective 3
Describe the Merchandise Inventory account

As TKT Product sells cabinets and related items, it must maintain an inventory of these products. This creates the need for a new asset account titled Merchandise Inventory. The balance in the Merchandise Inventory account represents the cost of all merchandise in inventory and available for sale. It is important to note that only transactions involving merchandise, units for resale, are recorded in this account.

The Merchandise Inventory account is a permanent account that appears under current assets on the balance sheet.

Types of Inventory Systems

objective 4
Describe perpetual and periodic inventory systems

An inventory system refers to the accounting, procedures, and records used by a business to control its inventory. There are two major types of inventory systems: the periodic inventory system and the perpetual inventory system. The basic difference between the two systems is reflected in how often the Merchandise Inventory account is updated.

In a periodic inventory system, the Merchandise Inventory account is updated periodically. The updating occurs just before financial statements are prepared. The balance in the Merchandise Inventory account remains the same between financial statement dates. Businesses with manual accounting systems often use a periodic inventory system.

In a perpetual inventory system, the Merchandise Inventory account is continuously updated. Because the Merchandise Inventory account is increased or decreased for every purchase, sale, or return of merchandise, its balance in the general ledger is always current.

Peachtree requires the use of a perpetual inventory system which is preferable because of its constantly up-to-date information. In PAW, the Merchandise Inventory account contains summary information about the total cost of the merchandise on hand and available for sale. In addition, PAW keeps a detailed inventory record for each item of merchandise in stock. PAW automatically updates these subsidiary records every time there is a change in the Merchandise Inventory account caused by a purchase, sale, or return of merchandise. This detailed information about each product in inventory can be accessed by printing out an item costing report.

Figure 8.5 shows an example of an item costing report for TKT Products.

Figure 8.5

TKT Products
Item Costing Report
For the Period From Dec 1, 1996 to Dec 31, 1996

Filter Criteria includes: Report order is by ID.

Item ID Item Description	Date	Qty Received	Item Cost	Actual Cost	Assembly Qty Assembly ($)	Adjust Qty Adjust ($)	Quantity Sold	Cost of Sales	Remaining Qty	Remain Value
666dr cabinet doors	12/5/96	14.00	150.00	2,100.00					14.00	2,100.00
	12/8/96	-3.00	150.00	-450.00					11.00	1,650.00
	12/10/96						8.00	1,200.00	3.00	450.00
	12/12/96						-2.00	-300.00	5.00	750.00
	12/21/96						2.00	300.00	3.00	450.00
777gl wood glue	12/9/96	30.00	4.80	144.00					30.00	144.00
	12/11/96	-5.00	4.80	-24.00					25.00	120.00
	12/14/96						5.00	24.00	20.00	96.00
	12/15/96						-2.00	-9.60	22.00	105.60
888cab kitchen cabinets	12/3/96						3.00	810.00	-3.00	-810.00
	12/4/96	12.00	270.00	3,240.00					9.00	2,430.00
	12/7/96						-1.00	-270.00	10.00	2,700.00
	12/13/96	28.00	270.00	7,560.00					38.00	10,260.00
	12/16/96	-6.00	270.00	-1,620.00					32.00	8,640.00
	12/18/96						20.00	5,400.00	12.00	3,240.00
	12/23/96						-4.00	-1,080.00	16.00	4,320.00
999hin hinges for cabinets	12/1/96	100.00	9.00	900.00					100.00	900.00
	12/2/96						70.00	630.00	30.00	270.00
	12/3/96	-5.00	9.00	-45.00					25.00	225.00
	12/4/96						-10.00	-90.00	35.00	315.00
	12/28/96						8.00	72.00	27.00	243.00
	12/30/96						-2.00	-18.00	29.00	261.00

The Vendor Ledger

objective 5
Describe the vendor ledger

In the past, you have recorded transactions involving accounts payable by simply debiting or crediting the Accounts Payable account. The balance in the Accounts Payable account indicated the total amount owed to all the business's creditors. Common sense tells us that this accounts payable information is not adequate. A business must know its creditors by name. All purchases and payments on account must be identified with a creditor's name. This information is easily added to our existing accounting system through the use of a vendor ledger.

Up to this time, we have worked with only one group of accounts, known as a general ledger. The Accounts Payable account found in the general ledger will now be referred to as a control or controlling account. The Accounts Payable account will continue to function as it has in the past; it will contain only summary information. The vendor ledger, another group of accounts, will provide the detail. The vendor ledger will contain a separate account for each creditor (vendor). This type of ledger is known as a subsidiary ledger. The entire vendor ledger supports or explains just one general ledger account—the Accounts Payable (control) account. The Accounts Payable account is a controlling account because it *controls* the vendor ledger. Some businesses use the term *accounts payable ledger* instead of vendor ledger.

When journalizing, the creditor's (vendor's) name must be indicated whenever the Accounts Payable account is debited or credited. In posting, PAW automatically posts all debits and credits to accounts payable twice; once to the Accounts Payable (control) account in the general ledger and again to the creditor's account in the vendor ledger.

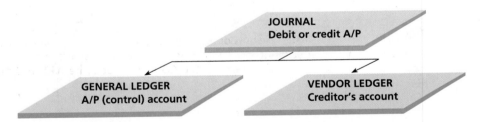

After all journalizing and posting are completed, the balance in the Accounts Payable (control) account should equal the total of the creditor (vendor) account balances in the vendor ledger. We will print out TKT Products' vendor ledger later in this chapter.

Loading the TKT Products Company Data

objective 6
Load the data for TKT Products

You are almost ready to use PAW to journalize a purchase on account. First, however, you need to load the data for TKT Products. Follow these steps to load the company data:

step   1:   Start Windows. If you are running Windows 3.1x, choose File, Run in Program Manager. If you are running Windows 95, choose Start, Run.

step 2: Place the Company Data CD-ROM in drive D (or the appropriate drive for your CD-ROM).

step 3: Type **d:\setup.exe** in the dialog box. (This text assumes drive D is your CD-ROM drive. Use the appropriate drive letter if your CD-ROM is located in a different location.)

step 4: Click on the OK button. A screen pops up that says "One moment please. . . ."

step 5: The "Company Data to accompany College Accounting with Peachtree" window pops up. Click on Continue.

step 6: Accept the default for the "Path: C:\PEACHW" by clicking on Continue. (If Peachtree was installed in a different directory, type that location in the "Path" dialog box.)

step 7: The next screen, "Companies", shows the data that is included on the Company Data CD-ROM.

step 8: Since you are loading data for TKT Products only, click on the box next to TKT.

step 9: Click on Continue. A scale shows what percentage of the data has been copied. All files have been copied to the hard drive of your computer when the scale is completed. The "Success" window displays.

step 10: Click on OK. You are returned to Program Manager in Windows 3.1*x* or the desktop in Windows 95.

step 11: Remove the Company Data CD-ROM from drive D (or the appropriate drive for your CD-ROM).

step 12: Double-click on the Peachtree Accounting icon. At the "Presenting Peachtree Accounting" window, click on Open.

step 13: Click once on TKT Products to highlight it.

> **Comment**
>
> If TKT Products is not listed in the Company Name box or if *it appears but you did not load it* (some other student did), you **must** go back to Instruction 1 to load the *original* TKT Products company data from the CD-ROM that came with this text. *This is extremely important.*

step 14: Click on Ok. When the "Convert Company Files" screen displays, click on Continue. The main menu for TKT Products displays.

step 15: Print TKT's chart of accounts.
- a. From the main menu, select Reports, then General Ledger. In the "Report List," the "Chart of Accounts" is highlighted.
- b. On the "Icon Bar," click on the Print icon. The "Chart of Accounts Filter" window displays.
- c. Click on OK and the "Print" window pops up.
- d. Click on OK and the chart of accounts starts to print.
- e. On the "Icon Bar," click on "Close." You are returned to the main menu.

Compare your chart of accounts with the one shown in Figure 8.6. You will notice that there are a lot of new accounts listed on TKT Products' chart of accounts. You will learn more about these new accounts in the next several chapters.

Figure 8.6

TKT Products
Chart of Accounts
As of Dec 31, 1996

Filter Criteria includes: Report order is by ID. Report is printed with Accounts having Zero Amounts and in Detail Format.

Account ID	Account Description	Active?	Account Type
108	Change Fund	Yes	Cash
109	Petty Cash	Yes	Cash
110	Cash	Yes	Cash
111	Accounts Receivable	Yes	Accounts Receivable
112	Merchandise Inventory	Yes	Inventory
113	Supplies	Yes	Inventory
114	Prepaid Insurance	Yes	Other Current Assets
120	Truck	Yes	Fixed Assets
121	Accumulated Depreciation	Yes	Accumulated Depreciation
210	Accounts Payable	Yes	Accounts Payable
211	Wages Payable	Yes	Other Current Liabilities
213	Sales Tax Payable	Yes	Other Current Liabilities
214	Federal Income Tax Payable	Yes	Other Current Liabilities
215	FICA--Soc. Sec. Tax Payable	Yes	Other Current Liabilities
216	FICA--Medicare Tax Payable	Yes	Other Current Liabilities
217	State Income Tax Payable	Yes	Other Current Liabilities
220	FUTA Tax Payable	Yes	Other Current Liabilities
221	SUTA Tax Payable	Yes	Other Current Liabilities
223	Health Insurance Payable	Yes	Other Current Liabilities
224	Union Dues Payable	Yes	Other Current Liabilities
310	Dennis Taylor, Capital	Yes	Equity-doesn't close
320	Dennis Taylor, Drawing	Yes	Equity-gets closed
330	Retained Earnings	Yes	Equity-Retained Earnings
410	Fees Earned	Yes	Income
411	Sales	Yes	Income
412	Sales Returns and Allowances	Yes	Income
413	Sales Discount	Yes	Income
501	Cost of Sales	Yes	Cost of Sales
610	Depreciation Expense	Yes	Expenses
611	FICA--Soc. Sec. Tax Expense	Yes	Expenses
612	FICA--Medicare Tax Expense	Yes	Expenses
613	FUTA Tax Expense	Yes	Expenses
614	SUTA Tax Expense	Yes	Expenses
615	Insurance Expense	Yes	Expenses
616	Rent Expense	Yes	Expenses
617	Repair Expense	Yes	Expenses
618	Service Charge Expense	Yes	Expenses
619	Supplies Expense	Yes	Expenses
620	Utilities Expense	Yes	Expenses
621	Wages Expense	Yes	Expenses
622	Miscellaneous Expense	Yes	Expenses

Special Journals

objective 7
Describe special journals

Up to this point, all journal entries have been recorded in a general journal. Although effective, this is not the most efficient way to handle repetitive types of transactions.

In a merchandising business, purchases on account, sales on account, receipts of cash, and disbursements of cash occur over and over again. In most businesses, these four types of transactions represent more than 90 percent of the daily activity. If these transactions could be recorded more efficiently, the savings in time and effort would be substantial. This increased efficiency can be achieved through the use of **special journals.**

In this and the next several chapters, you will be introduced to four special journals. Each of these special journals will accommodate only certain types of transactions.

Journal	Transactions
Purchase journal	Purchases on account and returns on account
Cash disbursements journal	All payments of cash
Sales journal	Sales on account and returns on account
Cash receipts journal	All receipts of cash

Any transaction that does not fit into a special journal is recorded in the general journal. *It is important to note that a transaction is recorded in only one journal.* Since you will ultimately be working with five journals (four special journals and one general journal), *a choice must be made for each transaction.* In this chapter, we will focus our attention on the **purchase journal** which accommodates only purchases and returns on account. In Chapter 9, you will learn to record cash purchases and transportation charges relating to purchases.

The Purchase Invoice

The information necessary to record a transaction in the purchase journal comes from a purchase invoice similar to the one shown earlier in Figure 8.4. The purchase invoice contains the vendor's name and address, invoice number, date, transportation terms, description of the merchandise, and the purchase price.

The vendor's credit terms are also displayed on the invoice. Net 30 days, or n/30, means that the full invoice amount is due 30 days from the invoice date. If the vendor is offering a discount to the purchaser for early payment, the terms might read 2/10, n/30. This means that a 2 percent discount is deducted if the invoice is paid within 10 days of the invoice date; the full amount is due in 30 days. These terms of credit will be studied in greater detail in Chapter 9.

In this text, for practical reasons, the actual purchase invoice is not presented for each purchase transaction. In most cases, the transaction is described in sentence form as in previous chapters.

Recording Purchases

In PAW, all the information about a purchase is recorded in a "Purchases/Receive Inventory" window. Then, PAW takes the necessary information from the window and automatically journalizes the transaction in the purchase journal. Later, we can view the purchase journal on our screen or by printing it out. Some of the information from this "Purchases/Receive Inventory" window will be used later when the invoice is paid. You will study the payment process in the next chapter. For now, we will concentrate on recording the purchase.

objective 8
Use PAW to record purchases on account

For some practice in recording a purchase of merchandise, let's use PAW to journalize the following transaction for TKT Products:

December 1, 1996   Purchased 100 hinges on account, $9.00 each, from Saroya Corporation, Invoice No. 941, terms n/30, total cost $900. (This invoice is shown in Fig. 8.4.)

As usual, we start by recording the information on a data entry sheet. This forces us to read the transaction carefully and organize the information before going to the "Purchases/Receive Inventory" window.

DATA ENTRY SHEET TKT Products					
Date	Account ID	Reference	Trans Description	Debit Amt	Credit Amt
12/1/96	112		Merchandise Inventory	900.00	
	210		Accounts Payable, Saroya Corporation, Invoice No. 941		900.00

Referring to the data entry sheet, follow these steps to journalize the purchase of merchandise on account in the purchase journal:

step 1:   From the Tasks menu, click on Purchases/Receive Inventory. The "Purchases/Receive Inventory" window displays.

step 2:   Your cursor is in the "Vendor ID" box. Click on the magnifying glass icon and select Saroya Corporation.

step 3:   In the "Invoice #" box, type **941** and press the <Enter> key.

step 4:   In the "Date" box, type **1** or accept the default for 12/1/96 by pressing the <Enter> key. Notice that the "Terms" are "Net 30 Days."

step 5:   Observe that the "A/P Account" box displays "210." This is the TKT Products Accounts Payable account. Notice that the "Ship Via" box is completed. United Parcel Service (UPS) is the carrier used by this vendor to ship merchandise to TKT Products.

step 6:   Go to the "Quantity" column and type **100,** then press the <Enter> key.

step 7:   In the "Item" column, click on the magnifying glass icon and select "hinges for cabinets." The description, "hinges for cabinets," is automatically completed. Press the <Enter> key. Notice that the "GL Account 112, Merchandise Inventory" is automatically selected and debited.

Comment   Click on the "Journal" icon to see the Purchase Journal transaction that you just entered.

The "Accounting Behind the Screens" window for the Purchases Journal allows you to see what accounts were debited and credited for Invoice No 941. Observe that Account No. 112, Merchandise Inventory, was debited and that Account No. 210, Accounts Payable, was credited. Although the vendor account, Saroya Corporation, is not shown, it was credited to the vendor ledger. Click on Ok to return to the "Purchases/Receive Inventory" window.

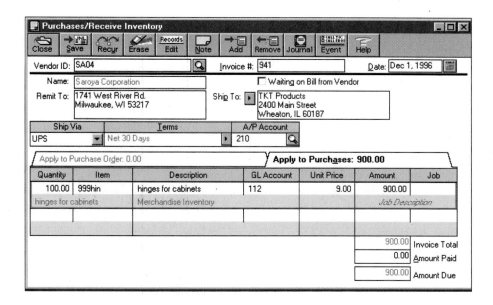

step 8: Click on the "Save" icon.

step 9: Close the "Purchases/Receive Inventory" window.

As we recorded information in the "Purchases/Receive Inventory" window, you probably observed that PAW supplied some basic information about Saroya Corporation such as the item description, unit price, and credit terms. In a real situation, we would have previously stored in PAW the items, prices, and credit terms of vendors from whom we purchase frequently. Then when recording transactions, this information is automatically supplied by PAW. In this text, the TKT Products company data contained this information.

Recording Purchases Returns and Allowances

To the purchaser, a return of merchandise to a vendor is a purchase return. An allowance granted by the vendor to the purchaser for damaged but usable merchandise is a purchase allowance. Since returns are more common, that is where we will focus our attention.

objective 9
Use PAW to record purchases returns and allowances

> To the purchaser, a return of merchandise to the vendor is a purchase return. To the vendor, this returned merchandise represents a sales return. These transactions are opposite sides of the same coin. We will look at sales returns in a later chapter.
>
> *Comment*

To demonstrate how to account for a purchase return, let's assume that TKT Products returns a portion of the merchandise that was purchased on December 1 from Saroya Corporation, Invoice No. 941. This is considered to be a return on account because the purchase on account has not yet been paid. The vendor, Saroya Corporation, prepared the credit memo shown below and sent a copy to TKT Products. This credit memo contains the basic facts about the return and serves as the source document for TKT's purchase return journal entry.

SAROYA CORPORATION 1741 West River Road Milwaukee, WI 53217	CREDIT MEMORANDUM NO. 143
Credit to: TKT Products 2400 Main Street Wheaton, Illinois 60187	Date: December 3, 1996 Terms: n/30

Your account is being credited as follows:		
5	Hinges for cabinets (2")	$45.00

Since a purchase return decreases the level of inventory on hand, the Merchandise Inventory account must be decreased with a credit. In addition, the Accounts Payable account must be decreased with a debit since TKT does not owe Saroya for the cost of the merchandise returned. This information is recorded on a data entry sheet as follows:

DATA ENTRY SHEET TKT Products					
Date	Account ID	Reference	Trans Description	Debit Amt	Credit Amt
12/3/96	210		Accounts Payable—Saroya Corporation, Invoice No. 941	45.00	
	112		Merchandise Inventory		45.00

Referring to the data entry sheet, we are now ready to use PAW to journalize this transaction. Using the "Purchases/Receive Inventory" window, we will record this purchase return as a "negative" invoice by placing a minus sign before the invoice number (−941) and the quantity (−5) as we enter the necessary information.

Follow these steps to journalize this purchase return on account in the purchase journal:

step 1: From the main menu, select Ta*sks*, then Pu*r*chases/Receive Inventory.

step 2: In the "Vendor ID" box, click on the magnifying glass icon, then select Saroya Corporation.

step 3: In the "*I*nvoice ID" box, type **-941** and press the <Enter> key.

step 4: In the "*D*ate" box, type **3**.

step 5: Go to the "Quantity" column and type **-5** and press the <Enter> key.

step 6: In the "Item" column, select "hinges for cabinets."

step 7: In the "Description" column, type **returned five cabinet hinges** and press the <Enter> key.

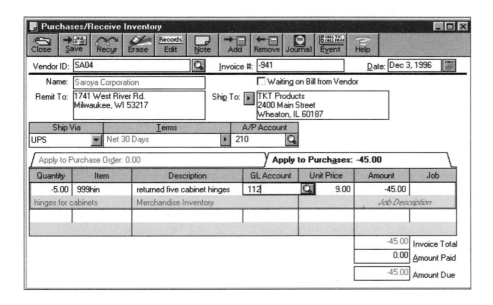

step 8: Accept the "GL Account" default. The default is what PAW automatically places in the box.

step 9: Click on the "Journal" icon to see the Purchases Journal. Then, click on Ok to return to the "Purchases/Receive Inventory" window.

step 10: Click on the Save icon.

Additional TKT Products Transactions

Now you are ready to journalize the following additional TKT transactions for the month of December 1996. First, record the transactions on a data entry sheet, then use PAW to journalize them. If necessary, refer back to the appropriate steps given earlier in this chapter. As you journalize, you will notice a higher than normal number of returns. This is meant to give you extra practice and does not reflect a normal pattern of purchases and returns. **Be sure to save after each transaction.**

Comment

In step 4 of recording a purchase, you may notice that the vendor's credit terms appear in the "Terms" box. Since most vendors offer TKT a discount for early payment, PAW automatically computes the amount.

Dec. 4 Purchased 12 kitchen cabinets on account at $270 each from Kavan Manufacturing; Invoice No. A623; terms 2/10, n/30; $3,240.

5 Purchased 14 cabinet doors on account at $150 each from Avery Products; Invoice No. 4837; terms 1/10, n/30; $2,100.

6   Purchased supplies on account from Wheaton Supplies, Invoice No. W310, terms net 30 days, $114. (HINT: Type **1** in the "Quantity" column; in the "Description" column, type **letterhead paper, business cards, envelopes**; accept the default for Account No. 113 in the "GL Account" column, and type **114** in the "Unit Price" column. Remember, supplies are *not* merchandise.)

8   Returned 3 cabinet doors purchased on December 5 from Avery Products, Invoice No. 4837, $450.

9   Purchased 30 tubes of wood glue on account at $4.80 each from Franklin Products; Invoice No. 1489; terms 2/10, n/30; $144.

11 Returned 5 tubes of wood glue purchased on December 9 from Franklin Products, Invoice No. 1489, $24.

13 Purchased 28 kitchen cabinets on account at $270 each from Kavan Manufacturing; Invoice No. A658; terms 2/10, n/30; $7,560.

16 Returned 6 kitchen cabinets purchased on December 13 from Kavan Manufacturing, Invoice No. A658, $1,620.

When you have finished journalizing, close the "Purchases/Receive Inventory" window.

Printing the Purchase Journal

objective 10
Print the purchase journal

Follow these steps to print the purchase journal:

step 1:   From the main menu, select Reports, Accounts Payable.

step 2:   In the "Report List" highlight "Purchase Journal."

step 3:   Click on the "Print" icon.

step 4:   At the "Filter" screen, click on OK.

step 5:   At the "Print" screen, click on OK.

Compare your purchase journal with Figure 8.7. If you need to make any corrections, go back to the "Purchases/Receive Inventory" window. Click on the "Edit Records" icon and make any needed corrections.

Figure 8.7

TKT Products
Purchase Journal
For the Period From Dec 1, 1996 to Dec 31, 1996
Filter Criteria includes: 1) Invoices only. Report order is by Date. Report is printed in Detail Format.

Date	Account ID Account Description	Invoice #	Line Description	Debit Amount	Credit Amount
12/1/96	112 Merchandise Inventory 210 Accounts Payable	941	hinges for cabinets Saroya Corporation	900.00	900.00
12/3/96	112 Merchandise Inventory 210 Accounts Payable	-941	returned five cabinet hinges Saroya Corporation	45.00	45.00
12/4/96	112 Merchandise Inventory 210 Accounts Payable	A623	kitchen cabinets Kavan Manufacturing	3,240.00	3,240.00
12/5/96	112 Merchandise Inventory 210 Accounts Payable	4837	cabinet doors Avery Products	2,100.00	2,100.00
12/6/96	113 Supplies 210 Accounts Payable	W310	letterhead paper, business cards, envelopes Wheaton Supplies	114.00	114.00
12/8/96	112 Merchandise Inventory 210 Accounts Payable	-4837	returned three cabinet doors Avery Products	450.00	450.00
12/9/96	112 Merchandise Inventory 210 Accounts Payable	1489	wood glue Franklin Products	144.00	144.00
12/11/96	112 Merchandise Inventory 210 Accounts Payable	-1489	returned five tubes of wood glue Franklin Products	24.00	24.00
12/13/96	112 Merchandise Inventory 210 Accounts Payable	A658	kitchen cabinets Kavan Manufacturing	7,560.00	7,560.00
12/16/96	112 Merchandise Inventory 210 Accounts Payable	-A658	returned six kitchen cabinets Kavan Manufacturing	1,620.00	1,620.00
				16,197.00	16,197.00

Posting the Purchase Journal

objective 11
Post the purchase journal

Follow these steps to post the purchase journal.

step 1:   From the main menu, select Tasks, then System, then Post.

step 2:   Select the Purchase Journal.

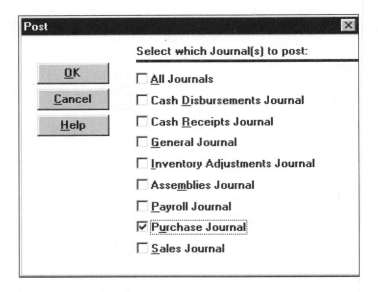

step 3:   Click on OK. A screen displays that says "Now posting Purchase Journal."

Printing the Vendor Ledger

objective 12
Print the vendor ledger

Follow these steps to print the vendor ledger:

step 1:   From the main menu, select Reports, Accounts Payable.

step 2:   Highlight "Vendor Ledgers."

step 3:   Click on the "Print" icon.

step 4:   At the "Filter" screen, click on OK.

step 5:   At the "Print" screen, click on OK.

Compare your printout with Figure 8.8. Observe that the "Type" column in the vendor ledger indicates that the posted information came from the purchase journal, which is abbreviated PJ.

Figure 8.8

TKT Products
Vendor Ledgers
For the Period From Dec 1, 1996 to Dec 31, 1996
Filter Criteria includes: Report order is by ID.

Vendor ID Vendor	Date	Trans No	Type Paid	Debit Amt	Credit Amt	Balance
AV01	12/5/96	4837	PJ		2,100.00	2,100.00
Avery Products	12/8/96	-4837	PJ	450.00		1,650.00
FR02	12/9/96	1489	PJ		144.00	144.00
Franklin Products	12/11/96	-1489	PJ	24.00		120.00
KA03	12/4/96	A623	PJ		3,240.00	3,240.00
Kavan Manufacturing	12/13/96	A658	PJ		7,560.00	10,800.00
	12/16/96	-A658	PJ	1,620.00		9,180.00
SA04	12/1/96	941	PJ		900.00	900.00
Saroya Corporation	12/3/96	-941	PJ	45.00		855.00
WH05	12/1/96	Balance Fwd				125.00
Wheaton Supplies	12/6/96	W310	PJ		114.00	239.00

Backing Up Your Data

It is crucial to back up your TKT Products data. You will need it when you begin Chapter 9. Follow these steps to back up your data:

objective 13
Back up your data

step 1: Put a blank formatted disk in drive A.

step 2: From the main menu, select File, then Backup.

step 3: Type **a:\chapter8.tkt** in the Destination text box. When you start typing, the characters in the Destination text box will be deleted.

step 4: Click on the Backup button ▐ **Backup** ▐ . When all the files have been saved to drive A, you are automatically returned to the main menu.

step 5: Click on File, Exit to exit PAW.

Chapter Eight Summary

In this chapter, we studied the purchasing activities of a merchandising business. The purchasing process is summarized in the following flowchart:

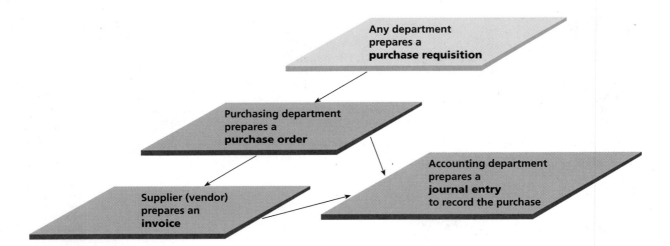

PAW uses a perpetual inventory system. Therefore, purchases of merchandise on account are recorded by debiting Merchandise Inventory and crediting Accounts Payable and the vendor's account in the vendor ledger.

Through the use of a vendor ledger, we can conveniently keep track of how much we owe to each of our creditors. The Accounts Payable (control) account in the general ledger contains summary information, while the vendor ledger provides the detail.

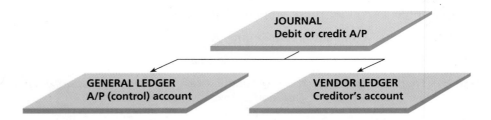

In a merchandising business, purchases on account occur frequently. A purchase journal greatly reduces the time and effort required to record and post these repetitive transactions. In PAW, all the information about a purchase is recorded in a "Purchases/Receive Inventory" window. Then, PAW takes the necessary information from the window and automatically journalizes the transaction in the purchase journal.

The "Purchases/Receive Inventory" window is also used to record purchase returns and allowances. The return is treated as a "negative" invoice by inserting a minus sign in front of the invoice number and quantity.

Demonstration Problem

Nguyen Company, a new business, completed the following transactions during July 1996.

July   1   Purchased merchandise on account from Kramer Corporation, Invoice No. 465, $530.

      5   Purchased merchandise on account from Bianco Company, Invoice No. 4596, $1,200.

    10   Returned a portion of the merchandise purchased on July 1 from Kramer Corporation, Invoice No. 465, $95.

15 Purchased merchandise on account from Kramer Corporation, Invoice No. 791, $420.

20 Purchased office equipment on account from Wilson Equipment, Invoice No. 721, $1,560. (Remember, office equipment is *not* merchandise.)

25 Returned a portion of the merchandise purchased on July 5 from Bianco Company, Invoice No. 4596, $480.

Instructions

1. Record these transactions on a data entry sheet. Leave "Account ID" blank.
2. How much is owed to Kramer Corporation?
3. How much is owed to Bianco Company?
4. How much is owed to Wilson Equipment?

Solution to Demonstration Problem

1.

		DATA ENTRY SHEET Nguyen Company			
Date	**Account ID**	**Reference**	**Trans Description**	**Debit Amt**	**Credit Amt**
7/1			Merchandise Inventory	530.00	
			Accounts Payable— Kramer Corp., Invoice No. 465		530.00
7/5			Merchandise Inventory	1,200.00	
			Accounts Payable— Bianco Co., Invoice No. 4596		1,200.00
7/10			Accounts Payable— Kramer Corp., Invoice No. 465	95.00	
			Merchandise Inventory		95.00
7/15			Merchandise Inventory	420.00	
			Accounts Payable— Kramer Corp., Invoice No. 791		420.00
7/20			Office Equipment	1,560.00	
			Accounts Payable— Wilson Equipment, Invoice No. 721		1,560.00
7/25			Accounts Payable— Bianco Co., Invoice No. 4596	480.00	
			Merchandise Inventory		480.00

2. Kramer Corporation is owed $855.00 ($530 − 95 + 420).
3. Bianco Company is owed $720.00 ($1,200 − 480).
4. Wilson Equipment is owed $1,560.

Glossary

controlling account   A general ledger account containing summary information, which is supported by a subsidiary ledger.   *222*

credit memo   A business document prepared by the seller (vendor) containing information relevant to a return or allowance. A copy is sent to the purchaser. *228*

inventory system   The accounting, procedures, and records used by a business to control its inventory.   *220*

invoice   A business document prepared by the seller containing all the relevant information about a sale. To the seller, it is a sales invoice. To the purchaser it is a purchase invoice.   *219*

merchandise   Units purchased by a merchandising business for resale to its customers.   *218*

merchandising business   A business that purchases a ready-made product from a supplier and resells it to its own customers.   *218*

periodic inventory system   A type of inventory system under which the accountant periodically updates the Merchandise Inventory account. The updating must precede the issuance of financial statements.   *220*

perpetual inventory system   A type of inventory system under which the accountant continuously updates the Merchandise Inventory account for purchases, sales, and returns of merchandise.   *220*

purchase allowance   A reduction in the price of previously purchased merchandise. The seller (vendor) "allows" for defective merchandise by reducing the price to the purchaser.   *227*

purchase journal   A special journal used to record all purchases on account. *225*

purchase order   An offer to purchase goods from a vendor.   *219*

purchase requisition   A form used by departments to request the purchase of necessary items. It is sent to the purchasing department.   *219*

purchase return   The return of previously purchased merchandise to the vendor.   *227*

special journal   A journal designed to facilitate the recording and posting of repetitive transactions.   *225*

subsidiary ledger   A group of accounts that supports or explains one general ledger account (controlling account.)   *222*

vendor ledger   A subsidiary ledger containing a separate account for each creditor (vendor). This ledger supports or explains one general ledger account—the Accounts Payable (control) account. Also known as an *accounts payable ledger.* *222*

Self-Test

Select the best answer.

1. The Merchandise Inventory account is used to record the purchase of
   a. supplies.
   b. equipment.
   c. merchandise.
   d. All of the above.

2. The balance in the Accounts Payable (control) account
   a. indicates the total amount owed to all creditors.
   b. should equal the total of the creditor account balances in the vendor ledger.
   c. is a summary figure.
   d. All of the above.

3. Which type of inventory system is used in PAW?
   a. Periodic inventory system.
   b. Perpetual inventory system.
   c. PAW does not use an inventory system.
   d. None of the above.

4. The entry to record a purchase return requires
   a. recording a negative invoice.
   b. putting a minus sign in front of the invoice number.
   c. putting a minus sign in front of the quantity.
   d. All of the above.

5. In PAW, which of the following windows is used to record a purchase on account?
   a. General journal entry window.
   b. Payments window.
   c. Purchases/Receive Inventory window.
   d. None of the above.

Answers to the self-test can be found after the cases at the end of this chapter.

Questions for Discussion

1. What is the purpose of the following?
   a. Purchase requisition.
   b. Purchase order.
   c. Purchase invoice.

2. The Merchandise Inventory account
   a. is used to record what type of transaction?
   b. has a normal balance on the debit or credit side?
   c. is a temporary or permanent account?

3. What is the relationship between the Accounts Payable (control) account and the vendor ledger?

4. The purchase journal accommodates what type(s) of transaction(s)?

5. In posting the purchase journal, describe where debits and credits to Accounts Payable are posted.

6. What is a merchandising business?

7. What is the difference between a purchase return and a purchase allowance?

8. What is the difference between a perpetual inventory system and a periodic inventory system?

Exercises

Exercise 8.1

Terminology
L.O. 1–12

Match the following terms with the definitions shown below:

1. Purchase requisition
2. Special journal
3. Purchase journal
4. Purchase allowance
5. Controlling account
6. Purchase order
7. Purchase return
8. Vendor ledger
9. Merchandise
10. Perpetual inventory system

Definitions

a. The return of previously purchased merchandise to the vendor.

b. A form used by departments to request the purchase of necessary items. It is sent to the purchasing department.

c. A journal designed to facilitate the recording and posting of repetitive transactions.

d. An offer to purchase goods from a supplier.

e. A reduction in the price of previously purchased merchandise. The seller "allows" for defective merchandise by reducing the price to the purchaser.

f. A type of inventory system under which the accountant continuously updates the Merchandise Inventory account for purchases, sales, and returns of merchandise.

g. A subsidiary ledger containing a separate account for each creditor.

h. A special journal used to record the purchase of merchandise on account.

i. A general ledger account containing summary information, which is supported by a subsidiary ledger.

j. Units purchased by a merchandising business for resale to its customers.

Exercise 8.2

Invoice Information
L.O. 2

Referring to the purchase invoice that is shown at the top of page 239, answer the following questions:

a. Who is the purchaser?

b. Who is the vendor?

c. What is the invoice number?

d. What are the credit terms?

e. What is the price per unit?

f. What is the total amount due?

```
DUFFY CORPORATION                                         INVOICE NO. 486
409 Dearborn Circle
Lutherville, Maryland 21093

Sold to: Maxwell Products                    Date:    January 8, 1996
         1545 Bay Drive                      Terms:   Net 30 days
         Baltimore, Maryland 21204           P.O. No.: 256
```

Quantity	Description	Unit Price	Total
130	#T-62 Metal hooks	1.24	161.20

Exercise 8.3

Using the invoice shown in Exercise 8.2, record this purchase of merchandise in data entry sheet format.

Entry for Purchase Using Invoice
L.O. 2, 3, 8

Exercise 8.4

Describe transactions (a) and (b) as indicated by the following T-accounts:

Purchase and Purchase Return
L.O. 3, 4, 8, 9

Accounts Payable			Merchandise Inventory		
Dr.		Cr.	Dr.		Cr.
(b)	225	(a)	800	(a)	800	(b)	225

Exercise 8.5

Vendor Ledger
L.O. 5

Garnet Company
Vendor Ledgers

Filter Criteria includes: Report order is by ID.

Vendor ID Vendor	Date	Trans No	Type	Paid	Debit Amt	Credit Amt	Balance
AN01 Andrews Company	11/1/96	Balance Fwd					1,049.00
	11/17/96		PJ			210.00	
CH02 Chang & Assoc.	11/1/96	Balance Fwd					684.00
	11/3/96		PJ		250.00		
	11/6/96		PJ			127.00	
PR03 Prairie Products	11/1/96	Balance Fwd					273.00
	11/5/96		PJ			136.00	
	11/10/96		PJ			98.00	
RI04 Ricardo Corp.	11/1/96	Balance Fwd					1,490.00
	11/15/96		PJ			375.00	
	11/18/96		PJ		500.00		

Instructions

a. Compute the balance for each vendor's account.

b. The balance in the Accounts Payable (control) account should be what amount?

Exercise 8.6

Entries for Purchases and
Purchase Return
L.O. 5, 8, 9

Assuming the use of a vendor ledger, record the following transactions on a data entry sheet:

June 1　Purchased merchandise on account from Lang Company, Invoice No. 844, $372.

2　Purchased merchandise on account from Benjamin Products, Invoice No. Z12, $477.

6　Returned a portion of the merchandise purchased on June 2 from Benjamin Products, Invoice No. Z12, $200.

Exercise 8.7

Entries for Purchases and
Purchase Return
L.O. 5, 8, 9

Assuming the use of a vendor ledger, record the following transactions on a data entry sheet:

July 1　Purchased office furniture on account from Z-Gallerie, Invoice No. 9244, $892.

2　Purchased merchandise on account from Norrie Manufacturing, Invoice No. X62, $1,477.

6　Returned a portion of the merchandise purchased on July 2 from Norrie Manufacturing, Invoice No. X62, $450.

Exercise 8.8

Select Journal
L.O. 7

Indicate which journal (purchase journal or general journal) is used to record each of the following transactions:

a. Purchase of merchandise on account.

b. Return of defective merchandise purchased on account.

c. Adjusting entry for prepaid insurance.

d. Adjusting entry for depreciation.

e. Purchase of office equipment on account.

Problems—Set A

Problem 8.1A

Load Data
L.O. 6

The owner, Joan Haywood decided to expand Ace Cleaning Service into a merchandising business selling various types of cleaning products. She also renamed the business ACS Products. The chart of accounts for ACS Products is shown in Figure 8.9.

Figure 8.9

ACS Products
Chart of Accounts
As of Dec 31, 1996
Filter Criteria includes: Report order is by ID. Report is printed with Accounts having Zero Amounts and in Detail Format.

Account ID	Account Description	Active?	Account Type
108	Change Fund	Yes	Cash
109	Petty Cash	Yes	Cash
110	Cash	Yes	Cash
111	Accounts Receivable	Yes	Accounts Receivable
112	Merchandise Inventory	Yes	Inventory
113	Supplies	Yes	Inventory
114	Prepaid Insurance	Yes	Other Current Assets
120	Equipment	Yes	Fixed Assets
121	Accumulated Depreciation	Yes	Accumulated Depreciation
210	Accounts Payable	Yes	Accounts Payable
211	Wages Payable	Yes	Other Current Liabilities
213	Sales Tax Payable	Yes	Other Current Liabilities
214	Federal Income Tax Payable	Yes	Other Current Liabilities
215	FICA--Soc. Sec. Tax Payable	Yes	Other Current Liabilities
216	FICA--Medicare Tax Payable	Yes	Other Current Liabilities
217	State Income Tax Payable	Yes	Other Current Liabilities
220	FUTA Tax Payable	Yes	Other Current Liabilities
221	SUTA Tax Payable	Yes	Other Current Liabilities
223	Health Insurance Payable	Yes	Other Current Liabilities
224	Union Dues Payable	Yes	Other Current Liabilities
310	Joan Haywood, Capital	Yes	Equity-doesn't close
320	Joan Haywood, Drawing	Yes	Equity-gets closed
330	Retained Earnings	Yes	Equity-Retained Earnings
410	Cleaning Revenue	Yes	Income
411	Sales	Yes	Income
412	Sales Returns and Allowances	Yes	Income
413	Sales Discount	Yes	Income
501	Cost of Sales	Yes	Cost of Sales
610	Depreciation Expense	Yes	Expenses
611	FICA--Soc. Sec. Tax Expense	Yes	Expenses
612	FICA--Medicare Tax Expense	Yes	Expenses
613	FUTA Tax Expense	Yes	Expenses
614	SUTA Tax Expense	Yes	Expenses
615	Insurance Expense	Yes	Expenses
616	Rent Expense	Yes	Expenses
617	Repair Expense	Yes	Expenses
618	Service Charge Expense	Yes	Expenses
619	Supplies Expense	Yes	Expenses
620	Utilities Expense	Yes	Expenses
621	Wages Expense	Yes	Expenses
622	Miscellaneous Expense	Yes	Expenses

Instructions to load the ACS Products company data and print the chart of accounts.

1. Start Windows. If you are running Windows 3.1*x*, choose File, Run in Program Manager. If you are running Windows 95, choose Start, Run.

2. Place the Company Data CD-ROM in drive D (or the appropriate drive for your CD-ROM).

3. Type **d:\setup.exe** in the dialog box. (This text assumes drive D is your CD-ROM drive. Use the appropriate drive letter if your CD-ROM is located in a different location.)

4. Click on the OK button. A screen pops up that says "One moment please. . . ."

5. The "Company Data to accompany College Accounting with Peachtree" window pops up. Click on Continue.

6. Accept the default for the "Path: C:\PEACHW" by clicking on Continue. (If Peachtree was installed in a different directory, type that location in the "Path" dialog box.)

7. The next screen, "Companies", shows the data that is included on the Company Data CD-ROM.

8. Since you are loading data for ACS Products only, click on the box next to ACS.

9. Click on Continue. A scale shows what percentage of the data has been copied. All files have been copied to the hard drive of your computer when the scale is completed. The "Success" window displays.

10. Click on OK. You are returned to Program Manager in Windows 3.1*x* or the desktop in Windows 95.

11. Remove the Company Data CD-ROM from drive D (or the appropriate drive for your CD-ROM).

12. Double-click on the Peachtree Accounting icon. At the "Presenting Peachtree Accounting" window, click on Open.

13. Click once on ACS Products to highlight it.

Comment

> If ACS Products is not listed in the Company Name box or if *it appears but you did not load it* (some other student did), you **must** go back to Instruction 1 to load the *original* ACS Products company data from the CD-ROM that came with this text. *This is extremely important.*

14. Click on Ok. The main menu for ACS Products displays.

15. To be sure that your ACS Products data was loaded properly, print ACS's chart of accounts and compare it to Figure 8.9. Follow these steps:
    a. From the main menu, select Reports, then General Ledger. In the "Report List," the "Chart of Accounts" is highlighted.
    b. On the "Icon Bar," click on the Print icon [Print]. The "Chart of Accounts Filter" window displays.
    c. Click on OK and the "Print" window pops up.
    d. Click on OK and the chart of accounts starts to print. Compare your printout with Figure 8.9.
    e. On the "Icon Bar," click on "Close." You are returned to the main menu.

16. To exit PAW, select File, Exit.

Problem 8.2A

Data Entry Sheet
L.O. 5, 7, 8, 9

ACS Products completed the following transactions during December 1996:

Dec. 1 Purchased 250 boxes of window cleaner from Alsip Industries; Invoice No. P913; terms 2/10, n/30; $4,192.50.

2 Purchased 300 packages of dust cloths from Prado Products; Invoice No. 8762; terms 2/10, n/30; $2,331.00.

4 Returned 50 packages of dust cloths purchased on December 2 from Prado Products, Invoice No. 8762, $388.50.

5 Purchased 200 mop refills from Taft Corporation; Invoice No. EL93; terms net 30 days; $2,634.00.

6   Purchased supplies (letterhead paper, business cards, envelopes) on account from XYZ Supplies; Invoice No. X13; terms net 30 days; $265.95. (Remember, supplies are *not* merchandise.)

7   Returned 40 mop refills purchased on December 5 from Taft Corporation, Invoice No. EL93, $526.80.

10   Purchased 150 boxes of window cleaner from Alsip Industries; Invoice No. P996; terms 2/10, n/30; $2,515.50.

Instructions

Record these transactions on a data entry sheet.

Problem 8.3A

Instructions

Referring to your data entry sheet from Problem 8.2A, use PAW to journalize the transactions in the purchase journal. (Hint: Use the "Purchases/Receive Inventory" window.)

Use PAW To Record Purchases
L.O. 5, 7, 8, 9

Problem 8.4A

Instructions

1. Print the purchase journal. Check your journal entries for accuracy. If necessary, make corrections and reprint the purchase journal.

2. Post the purchase journal.

3. Print the vendor ledgers.

Post; Print Journal and Vendor Ledger
L.O. 10, 11, 12

Problem 8.5A

Your ACS Products data **must** be backed up. You will restore it in Chapter 9. Follow these steps:

Back Up
L.O. 13

step 1:   Insert a blank formatted disk in drive A.

step 2:   From PAW's main menu, select File, then Backup.

step 3:   Type **a:\acsdec.85a** in the Destination text box.

step 4:   Click on the Backup button. Your files begin to copy. When all the files have been saved to drive A, you are automatically returned to the main menu.

step 5:   Click on File, Exit to exit PAW.

Problems—Set B

Problem 8.1B

The owner, Chris Canon, decided to expand Loyal Lawn Service into a merchandising business selling various types of lawn and garden products. He also renamed the business LLS Products. The chart of accounts for LLS Products is shown in Figure 8.10.

Load Data
L.O. 6

Figure 8.10

LLS Products
Chart of Accounts
As of Dec 31, 1996

Filter Criteria includes: Report order is by ID. Report is printed with Accounts having Zero Amounts and in Detail Format.

Account ID	Account Description	Active?	Account Type
108	Change Fund	Yes	Cash
109	Petty Cash	Yes	Cash
110	Cash	Yes	Cash
111	Accounts Receivable	Yes	Accounts Receivable
112	Merchandise Inventory	Yes	Inventory
113	Supplies	Yes	Inventory
114	Prepaid Insurance	Yes	Other Current Assets
120	Equipment	Yes	Fixed Assets
121	Accumulated Depreciation	Yes	Accumulated Depreciation
210	Accounts Payable	Yes	Accounts Payable
211	Wages Payable	Yes	Other Current Liabilities
213	Sales Tax Payable	Yes	Other Current Liabilities
214	Federal Income Tax Payable	Yes	Other Current Liabilities
215	FICA--Soc. Sec. Tax Payable	Yes	Other Current Liabilities
216	FICA--Medicare Tax Payable	Yes	Other Current Liabilities
217	State Income Tax Payable	Yes	Other Current Liabilities
220	FUTA Tax Payable	Yes	Other Current Liabilities
221	SUTA Tax Payable	Yes	Other Current Liabilities
223	Health Insurance Payable	Yes	Other Current Liabilities
224	Union Dues Payable	Yes	Other Current Liabilities
310	Chris Canon, Capital	Yes	Equity-doesn't close
320	Chris Canon, Drawing	Yes	Equity-gets closed
330	Retained Earnings	Yes	Equity-Retained Earnings
410	Lawn Service Revenue	Yes	Income
411	Sales	Yes	Income
412	Sales Returns and Allowances	Yes	Income
413	Sales Discount	Yes	Income
501	Cost of Sales	Yes	Cost of Sales
610	Depreciation Expense	Yes	Expenses
611	FICA--Soc. Sec. Tax Expense	Yes	Expenses
612	FICA--Medicare Tax Expense	Yes	Expenses
613	FUTA Tax Expense	Yes	Expenses
614	SUTA Tax Expense	Yes	Expenses
615	Insurance Expense	Yes	Expenses
616	Rent Expense	Yes	Expenses
617	Repair Expense	Yes	Expenses
618	Service Charge Expense	Yes	Expenses
619	Supplies Expense	Yes	Expenses
620	Utilities Expense	Yes	Expenses
621	Wages Expense	Yes	Expenses
622	Miscellaneous Expense	Yes	Expenses

Instructions to load the LLS Products company data and print the chart of accounts.

1. Start Windows. If you are running Windows 3.1*x*, choose File, Run in Program Manager. If you are running Windows 95, choose Start, Run.

2. Place the Company Data CD-ROM in drive D (or the appropriate drive for your CD-ROM).

3. Type **d:\setup.exe** in the dialog box. (This text assumes drive D is your CD-ROM drive. Use the appropriate drive letter if your CD-ROM is located in a different location.)

4. Click on the OK button. A screen pops up that says "One moment please. . . ."

5. The "Company Data to accompany College Accounting with Peachtree" window pops up. Click on <u>C</u>ontinue.

6. Accept the default for the "Path: C:\PEACHW" by clicking on <u>C</u>ontinue. (If Peachtree was installed in a different directory, type that location in the "Path" dialog box.)

7. The next screen, "Companies", shows the data that is included on the Company Data CD-ROM.

8. Since you are loading data for LLS Products only, click on the box next to LLS.

9. Click on <u>C</u>ontinue. A scale shows what percentage of the data has been copied. All files have been copied to the hard drive of your computer when the scale is completed. The "Success" window displays.

10. Click on O<u>K</u>. You are returned to Program Manager in Windows 3.1*x* or the desktop in Windows 95.

11. Remove the Company Data CD-ROM from drive D (or the appropriate drive for your CD-ROM).

12. Double-click on the Peachtree Accounting icon. At the "Presenting Peachtree Accounting" window, click on <u>O</u>pen.

13. Click once on LLS Products to highlight it.

Comment

If LLS Products is not listed in the Company <u>N</u>ame box or if *it appears but you did not load it* (some other student did), you **must** go back to Instruction 1 to load the *original* LLS Products company data from the CD-ROM that came with this text. *This is extremely important.*

---

14. Click on O<u>k</u>. The main menu for LLS Products displays.

15. To be sure that your LLS Products data was loaded properly, print LLS's chart of accounts and compare it to Figure 8.10. Follow these steps:
    a. From the main menu, select <u>R</u>eports, then <u>G</u>eneral Ledger. In the "Report List," the "Chart of Accounts" is highlighted.
    b. On the "Icon Bar," click on the Print icon. The "Chart of Accounts Filter" window displays.
    c. Click on <u>O</u>K and the "Print" window pops up.
    d. Click on OK and the chart of accounts starts to print. Compare your printout with Figure 8.10.
    e. On the "Icon Bar," click on "Close." You are returned to the main menu.
16. To exit PAW, select <u>F</u>ile, E<u>x</u>it.

Problem 8.2B

LLS Products completed the following transactions during December 1996:

Data Entry Sheet
L.O. 5, 7, 8, 9

Dec. 1   Purchased 210 compost buckets from Bertel Company; Invoice No. BR79; terms 2/10, n/30; $2,520.00.

2   Purchased 250 planters from Lance Company; Invoice No. 1662; terms 2/10, n/30; $2,392.50.

3   Returned 20 compost buckets purchased on December 1 from Bertel Company, Invoice No. BR79, $240.00.

5 Purchased 350 topiary forms from Safer Brothers; Invoice No. 4498; terms net 30 days; $4,189.50.

6 Purchased supplies (letterhead paper, business cards, envelopes), on account from Stanton Supplies; Invoice No. ST32; terms net 30 days; $242.85. (Remember, supplies are *not* merchandise.)

7 Returned 60 topiary forms purchased on December 5 from Safer Brothers, Invoice No. 4498, $718.20.

8 Purchased 100 planters from Lance Company; Invoice No. 1736; terms 2/10, n/30; $957.00.

Instructions

Record these transactions on a data entry sheet.

Use PAW To Record Purchases and Returns
L.O. 5, 7, 8, 9

Problem 8.3B

Referring to your data entry sheet from Problem 8.2B, use PAW to journalize the transactions in the purchase journal. (Hint: Use the "Purchases/Receive Inventory" window.)

Post, Print Journal and Vendor Ledger
L.O. 10, 11, 12

Problem 8.4B

Instructions

1. Print the purchase journal. Check your journal entries for accuracy. If necessary, make corrections and reprint the purchase journal.

2. Post the purchase journal.

3. Print the vendor ledgers.

Back Up
L.O. 13

Problem 8.5B

Your LLS Products data **must** be backed up. You will restore it in Chapter 9. Follow these steps:

step 1: Insert a blank formatted disk in drive A.

step 2: From PAW's main menu, select File, then Backup.

step 3: Type **a:\llsdec.85b** in the Destination text box.

step 4: Click on the Backup button. Your files begin to copy. When all the files have been saved to drive A, you are automatically returned to the main menu.

step 5: Click on File, Exit to exit PAW.

Mini-Cases

Case 8–1

Your friend, Pat Dealy, owns a successful merchandising business. Her accountant has complained about not receiving copies of purchase orders from the purchasing department. As the accounting department receives the purchase invoice from the vendor, Pat does not understand why the accountant needs a copy of the purchase order. Explain.

Case 8–2

Your boss, the owner of a new merchandising business, has a weak background in accounting. Because he finds the financial statements confusing, he thinks having fewer accounts would make them easier to understand. For starters, he suggests that you eliminate the Supplies account and instead record supplies in the Merchandise Inventory account. What is your response to this suggestion?

Case 8–3

Because you use PAW, your business has a perpetual inventory system. Your friend, Chris, does his accounting manually and uses a periodic system. Chris doesn't understand the difference between these two inventory systems. Explain the difference to Chris.

A Case of Ethics

Joe works as a purchasing agent for a large company. Although it is against company policy, he regularly accepts expensive personal gifts from sales representatives hoping to obtain purchase orders from his company. "Everybody does it," he says. "It's like a fringe benefit for purchasing agents!" Comment.

Answers to Self-Test

1. *c*   2. *d*   3. *b*   4. *d*   5. *c*

Merchandising Business

Cash Payments

LEARNING OBJECTIVES

After studying this chapter, you should be able to:

1. Describe transportation charges.

2. Compute cash discounts.

3. Restore data from the previous chapter.

4. Describe PAW's Payments Task.

5. Use PAW to pay specific invoices.

6. Print checks in payment of invoices.

7. Use PAW to pay specific invoices less returns.

8. Use PAW to record cash purchases.

9. Print the cash disbursements journal.

10. Post the cash disbursements journal.

11. Print the vendor ledger.

12. Back up your data.

In Chapter 8, you learned about merchandising businesses and how to use PAW to record purchases on account in a purchase journal. In this chapter, you will learn to use PAW to record cash payments in a cash disbursements journal. But first you will study transportation charges and cash discounts.

Transportation Charges

objective 1
Describe transportation charges

When a business purchases merchandise, or any other asset, it must consider transportation charges. Does the seller (vendor) pay the transportation charges or does the purchaser pay them? In negotiating the purchase, this question must be settled.

If the seller is to pay, the invoice indicates that the transportation terms are FOB destination. This means that the goods will be shipped "free on board" to the purchaser's place of business (destination). If the purchaser is to pay, the invoice indicates FOB shipping point. This means that the purchaser must pay to transport the goods from the seller's place of business (shipping point).

Either way, the purchaser ultimately pays the transportation charges. If the terms are FOB destination, the purchaser pays indirectly through a higher purchase price. If the terms are FOB shipping point, the purchaser pays the carrier directly or is billed by the seller for the cost of transportation.

From an accounting point of view, the transportation charges are considered to be part of the cost of the item being purchased. For example, let's assume that on December 17, TKT Products purchases $1,200 worth of merchandise on account from Kavan Manufacturing, Invoice No. 660, FOB destination. In data entry sheet format, this transaction is recorded as follows:

			DATA ENTRY SHEET TKT Products		
Date	Account ID	Reference	Trans Description	Debit Amt	Credit Amt
12/17/96	112		Merchandise Inventory	1,200.00	
	210		Accounts Payable, Kavan Mfg., Invoice No. 660		1,200.00

In this case, we assume that the cost of transportation is part of the $1,200 purchase price that is debited to the Merchandise Inventory account.

Let's try another example. This time, let's assume that on December 19, TKT Products purchases $800 worth of merchandise on account from Franklin Products, Invoice No. 1495, FOB shipping point. In data entry sheet format, this transaction is recorded as follows:

DATA ENTRY SHEET TKT Products					
Date	Account ID	Reference	Trans Description	Debit Amt	Credit Amt
12/19/96	112		Merchandise Inventory	800.00	
	210		Accounts Payable, Franklin Products, Invoice No. 1495		800.00

On December 20, the merchandise arrives. On receipt, TKT Products pays the carrier $50 in cash to cover the cost of transportation. Again, in data entry sheet format, this transaction is recorded as follows:

DATA ENTRY SHEET TKT Products					
Date	Account ID	Reference	Trans Description	Debit Amt	Credit Amt
12/20/96	112		Merchandise Inventory	50.00	
	110		Cash		50.00

Since the transportation costs increase the cost of the merchandise being purchased, they are debited to the Merchandise Inventory account.

Now let's consider the purchase of something other than merchandise. On December 21, TKT Products purchases supplies on account from Wheaton Supplies, Invoice No. W312, FOB shipping point, $775. This transaction is recorded as follows:

DATA ENTRY SHEET TKT Products					
Date	Account ID	Reference	Trans Description	Debit Amt	Credit Amt
12/21/96	113		Supplies	775.00	
	210		Accounts Payable, Wheaton Supplies, Invoice No. W312		775.00

The supplies are received on December 23. On arrival, TKT Products pays the carrier $65 in cash to cover the cost of transportation. This transaction is recorded as follows:

DATA ENTRY SHEET TKT Products					
Date	Account ID	Reference	Trans Description	Debit Amt	Credit Amt
12/23/96	113		Supplies	65.00	
	110		Cash		65.00

The cost of transportation is considered to be part of the cost of the supplies. The transportation charges are therefore debited to the Supplies account.

Now that we know how transportation charges affect the cost of merchandise and other assets, we are ready to study the effect of a purchases discount on the cost of merchandise.

Cash Discounts

objective 2
Compute cash discounts

As noted in Chapter 8, the vendor's **credit terms** are displayed in an abbreviated format at the top of each purchase invoice. For example, "net 30 days," or "n/30," means that the full invoice amount is due 30 days from the invoice date; "n/EOM" means that the full amount is due by the end of the month. The time between the invoice date and the date full payment is due is known as the **credit period.**

Comment

Usually the term *net* refers to a figure after deductions. However, when used to describe credit terms, the word *net* refers to the full amount.

To encourage charge customers to pay quickly, a vendor may offer the purchaser a **cash discount.** This is an amount that may be deducted from the bill if it is paid within a specified time known as the **discount period.** For example, credit terms of 2/10, n/30 indicate that a 2 percent discount may be deducted if the invoice is paid within 10 days of the invoice date or the full amount is due 30 days from the invoice date.

To the vendor, the cash discount is a **sales discount.** To the purchaser, the cash discount is a **purchases discount.** In Chapters 8 and 9, we are concentrating on accounting for the purchaser. In Chapters 10 and 11, we will look at these topics from the seller's (vendor's) point of view.

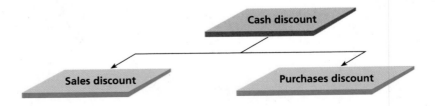

To demonstrate a purchase discount, we will return to TKT Products. Let's assume that on December 2, 1996, TKT purchased 5 cabinet doors from Avery Products, Invoice No. 4679, terms 1/10, n/30, total cost $750. In data entry sheet format, this transaction would be recorded as follows:

		DATA ENTRY SHEET TKT Products			
Date	**Account ID**	**Reference**	**Trans Description**	**Debit Amt**	**Credit Amt**
12/2/96	112		Merchandise Inventory	750.00	
	210		Accounts Payable, Avery Products, Invoice No. 4679		750.00

Observe that this invoice was recorded at the full amount even though TKT intends to take the purchases discount. Now, let's assume that on December 7, TKT returns 1 of the cabinet doors purchased on December 2, Invoice No. 4679, $150. In data entry sheet format, this transaction is recorded as follows:

		DATA ENTRY SHEET TKT Products			
Date	**Account ID**	**Reference**	**Trans Description**	**Debit Amt**	**Credit Amt**
12/7/96	210		Accounts Payable, Avery Products, Invoice No. 4679	150.00	
	112		Merchandise Inventory		150.00

Since the purchases discount has not yet been recorded, the full cost of the returned merchandise is subtracted from both the Accounts Payable and Merchandise Inventory accounts.

On December 12, the last day of the discount period, TKT pays Avery Products the amount due on Invoice No. 4679. When recording this type of transaction, PAW automatically does the necessary arithmetic but it is still important for us to understand the process. With that in mind, let's review the following computations:

a.
$750.00	Accounts payable
−150.00	Less returned merchandise
$600.00	Updated accounts payable

b.
$600.00	Merchandise
×.01	
$ 6.00	Purchases discount

c.
$600.00	Updated accounts payable
−6.00	Less purchases discount
$594.00	Cash payment

In data entry sheet format, this payment is recorded as follows:

DATA ENTRY SHEET TKT Products					
Date	Account ID	Reference	Trans Description	Debit Amt	Credit Amt
12/12/96	210		Accounts Payable, Avery Products, Invoice No. 4679	600.00	
	110		Cash		594.00
	112		Merchandise Inventory		6.00

It is important to observe that the purchases discount is credited to the Merchandise Inventory account. This is necessary because the discount reduces the cost of the merchandise.

Comment

If an invoice includes the cost of merchandise plus transportation charges, the discount can be applied only to the cost of the merchandise. For example, if an invoice showed merchandise costing $100 plus transportation charges of $25, the discount could only be taken on the $100 cost of the merchandise. Cash discounts do *not* apply to transportation charges.

In this textbook, TKT's vendors ship FOB destination or else TKT pays the carrier directly for the transportation charges.

If the credit terms had been n/30 or the invoice had *not* been paid by the end of the discount period, $600 would have to be paid to Avery Products. This transaction would be recorded with a debit to Accounts Payable, Avery Products, and a credit to Cash for the full amount.

Now, we are ready to use PAW to record payments of cash.

Restoring Data from Chapter 8

objective 3
Restore data from the previous chapter

Before you can use PAW to record TKT's cash payments, you must restore your TKT data from Chapter 8. Then you will print the vendor ledger to be sure that you loaded your data properly. Follow these steps:

step 1: Start Windows, then PAW. Open TKT Products.

step 2: Place your Chapter 8 backup disk in drive A.

Comment

Be sure that you are inserting your backup disk from Chapter 8 *not* the Company Data CD-ROM that came with this textbook. That disk should be stored in a safe place.

step 3:   From the main menu, select File, then Restore.

step 4:   Type a:\chapter8.tkt in the "Source" box. (Use the same file name that you used when you backed up in Chapter 8.)

step 5:   Click on the Restore button. Read the "Warning" screen, then click on OK. When the files are restored, you are returned to the main menu.

step 6:   Remove disk from drive A.

step 7:   Follow these steps to print the vendor ledger.
a. From the main menu, click on Reports, Accounts Payable.
b. Highlight vendor ledgers.
c. Make the selections to print. Compare your printout with Figure 9.1.

Figure 9.1

TKT Products
Vendor Ledgers
For the Period From Dec 1, 1996 to Dec 31, 1996
Filter Criteria includes: Report order is by ID.

Vendor ID Vendor	Date	Trans No	Type Paid	Debit Amt	Credit Amt	Balance
AV01	12/5/96	4837	PJ		2,100.00	2,100.00
Avery Products	12/8/96	-4837	PJ	450.00		1,650.00
FR02	12/9/96	1489	PJ		144.00	144.00
Franklin Products	12/11/96	-1489	PJ	24.00		120.00
KA03	12/4/96	A623	PJ		3,240.00	3,240.00
Kavan Manufacturing	12/13/96	A658	PJ		7,560.00	10,800.00
	12/16/96	-A658	PJ	1,620.00		9,180.00
SA04	12/1/96	941	PJ		900.00	900.00
Saroya Corporation	12/3/96	-941	PJ	45.00		855.00
WH05	12/1/96	Balance Fwd				125.00
Wheaton Supplies	12/6/96	W310	PJ		114.00	239.00

> If your vendor ledger does *not* agree with Figure 9.1, you will need to make corrections to your Chapter 8 data. Check with your instructor if you need help editing the purchase journal.   ***Comment***

The Payments Task

In Chapter 8, you learned to use PAW to record purchases on account. Through the Purchases/Receive Inventory Task, PAW took the information from the "Purchases/Receive Inventory" window and automatically journalized the transaction in the purchase journal. In recording the purchase, you specified the vendor's name, invoice number, inventory item, and the description and price of the item being purchased. PAW uses this information when the bill is paid.

objective 4
Describe PAW's Payments Task

In PAW, the Payments Task is used to pay bills. When the vendor's name and invoice number are recorded in the "Payments" window, PAW is able to access the information previously recorded through the Purchases/Receive Inventory Task and automatically journalize the payment in the cash disbursements journal. All payments of cash are recorded in the **cash disbursements journal.** It is another example of a special journal that can be viewed on our screen or printed out.

The following flowchart shows how the Purchases Task and the Payments Task work together in PAW.

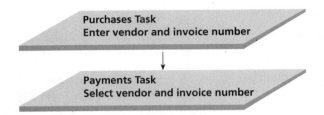

Paying Specific Vendor Invoices

objective 5
Use PAW to pay specific invoices

Once you have entered vendor invoices in the "Purchases/Receive Inventory" window, you can easily use the "Payments" window to pay specific invoices. Remember, with information from the "Payments" window, PAW automatically journalizes all cash payments in the cash disbursements journal.

Let's practice by returning to TKT Products. As you will recall from Chapter 8, on December 4, TKT purchased merchandise on account from Kavan Manufacturing, Invoice No. A623, terms 2/10, n/30, $3,240. On December 14, the last day of the discount period, TKT is ready to pay this invoice.

Follow these steps to journalize this payment on account in the cash disbursements journal:

step 1:   From the Tasks menu, select Payments. The "Select a Cash Account" window displays.

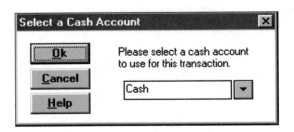

step 2:   Accept the default for "Cash" by clicking on Ok.

step 3:   Select "Kavan Manufacturing" as the "Vendor." Press the <Enter> key twice.

step 4:   In the "Date" box, type **14** and press <Enter>.

step 5: The "Apply to Invoices" folder tab should already be selected. Click once on the "Pay" box for Invoice No. A623. A check mark is placed in the "Pay" box and a red line is placed around the row for Invoice No. A623. The amount of the check, $3,175.20 ($3,240 − 64.80), is shown in the "dollars" box.

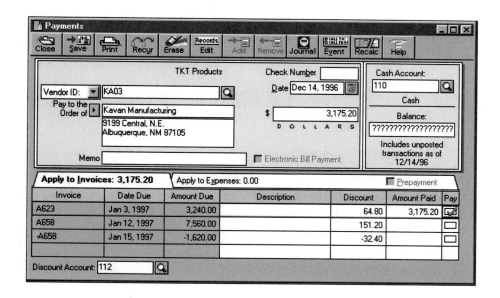

Printing the Check

Follow these steps to print the check:

step 1: The "Payments" window with Kavan Manufacturing's check should be displayed as shown in the previous screen.

step 2: Click on the "Print" icon.

step 3: The "Print Forms: Disbursement Checks" window pops up. "AP Preprint 1 Stub" is highlighted. You must select "AP Preprint 1 Stub" if you are using the working papers.

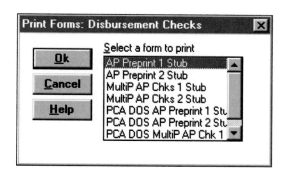

step 4: Click on Ok.

step 5: At the "Print Forms" window, click on Real.

objective 6
Print checks in payment of invoices

step 6:   Type **1650** in the First check number box.

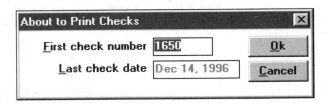

step 7:   Click on Ok. The check starts to print.

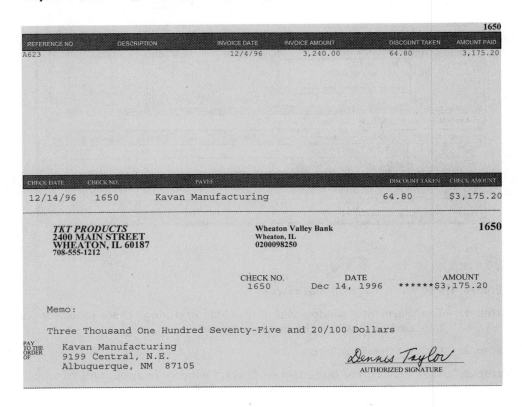

Comment   If your check does *not* show the same amount as the check shown above, go back to the "Payments" window and click on the Edit Records icon. Select December 14, Kavan Manufacturing. Make sure you select the correct invoice to pay.

     When you reprint Check No. 1650, "Duplicate" will be shown on the reprinted check.

Paying Specific Invoices Less Returns

objective 7
Use PAW to pay specific invoices less returns

In Chapter 8, TKT Products purchased merchandise on December 5 from Avery Products, Invoice No. 4837, terms 1/10, n/30, $2,100. Then on December 8, $450 of that merchandise was returned to Avery. As you will recall, the purchase return was entered as "negative" Invoice No. 4837. On December 15, the last day of the discount period, TKT wishes to pay the balance on this invoice less the purchases discount.

Follow these steps to record this transaction in the cash disbursements journal:

step 1: The "Payments" window should be displayed on your screen.

step 2: In the "Vendor ID" lookup box, select Avery Products. Press the <Enter> key twice.

step 3: Type **15** in the "Date" box, then press <Enter>.

step 4: Click on the "Pay" box for **negative** Invoice No. −4837. *It is important to note that you must "pay" negative invoices first.*

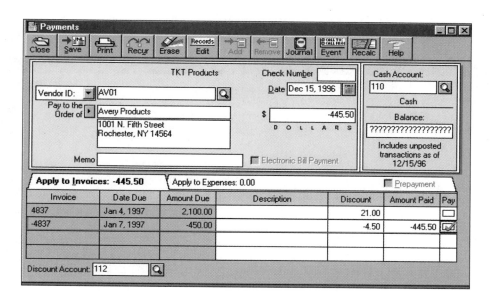

step 5: Click on the "Pay" box of the **positive** Invoice No. 4837.

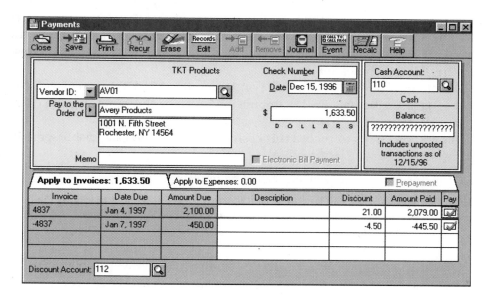

step 6: Make the selections to print the check. (Hint: Click on the Print icon; accept the default for "AP Preprint 1 Stub" by clicking on O̲K; select R̲eal; the next check number, 1651, automatically displays; click on O̲k.)

REFERENCE NO	DESCRIPTION	INVOICE DATE	INVOICE AMOUNT	DISCOUNT TAKEN	AMOUNT PAID
4837		12/5/96	2,100.00	21.00	2,079.00
-4837		12/8/96	-450.0	-4.50	-445.5

CHECK DATE	CHECK NO.	PAYEE	DISCOUNT TAKEN	CHECK AMOUNT
12/15/96	1651	Avery Products	16.50	$1,633.50

TKT PRODUCTS
2400 MAIN STREET
WHEATON, IL 60187
708-555-1212

Wheaton Valley Bank
Wheaton, IL
0200098250

1651

CHECK NO. 1651   DATE Dec 15, 1996   AMOUNT ******$1,633.50

Memo:

One Thousand Six Hundred Thirty-Three and 50/100 Dollars

PAY TO THE ORDER OF   Avery Products
1001 N. Fifth Street
Rochester, NY 14564

Dennis Taylor
AUTHORIZED SIGNATURE

Cash Purchases

objective 8
Use PAW to record cash purchases

TKT Products pays cash for some purchases. Usually these cash disbursements are for expenses. Since these cash purchases involve payments of cash, they are also recorded in the cash disbursements journal through the "Payments" window. They are not recorded in the purchase journal because they are not purchases on account.

To demonstrate, let's assume that on December 15 TKT issues Check No. 1652 to Jackson Rentals in the amount of $600 for the monthly rent (Rent Expense, Account No. 616).

Follow these steps to record this cash purchase in the cash disbursements journal:

step 1: The "Payments" window should be displayed.

step 2: Click on the "Pay to the Order of" box. Type **Jackson Rentals** in the "Pay to the Order of" box. Press the <Enter> key two times.

step 3: Type **15** in the "D̲ate" box.

step 4: The "Apply to Expenses" folder tab should be selected. If not, select it.

step 5: Click on the "Quantity" column. Then type **1** and press the <Enter> key twice.

step 6: In the "Description" column, type **monthly rent** and press <Enter>.

step 7: In the "GL Account" column, select Account No. 616, Rent Expense.

step 8: In the "Unit Price" column, type **600** and press <Enter>.

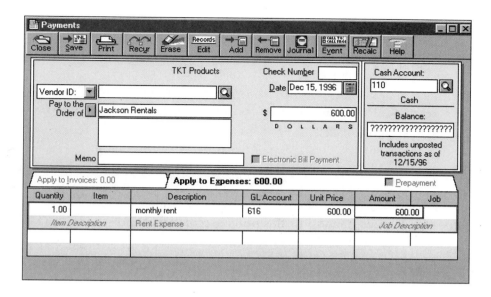

step 9: Print Check No. 1652.

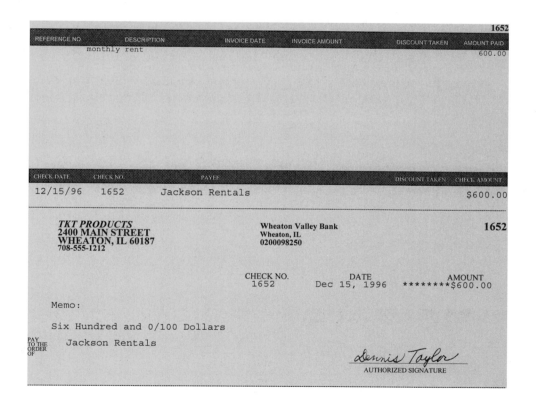

Additional TKT Products Transactions

Now you are ready to journalize the following additional TKT cash payment transactions and print the checks. Most of these transactions relate to TKT's December 1996 purchases on account from Chapter 8. As necessary, refer back to the appropriate steps given earlier in this chapter. **Be sure to print the check after journalizing each transaction.** PAW automatically saves the transaction when each check is printed.

Dec. 17   Issued Check No. 1653 to Federal Freight for transportation charges relating to the purchase of merchandise, $265. This was a cash purchase. (Hint: In the "GL Account" column, select Account No. 112, Merchandise Inventory.)

19   Issued Check No. 1654 to Franklin Products to pay Invoice No. 1489 dated 12/9/96; terms 2/10, n/30; less purchase return.

21   Issued Check No. 1655 to Archer Plumbing for a repair (Repair Expense), $65. This was a cash purchase.

23   Issued Check No. 1656 to Kavan Manufacturing to pay Invoice No. A658 dated 12/13/96; terms 2/10, n/30; less purchase return.

26   Issued Check No. 1657 to Morton Trucking for transportation charges relating to the purchase of merchandise, $382. This was a cash purchase.

27   Issued Check No. 1658 to Saroya Corporation to pay Invoice No. 941 dated 12/1/96; terms net 30 days; less purchase return.

29   Issued Check No. 1659 to Wheaton Supplies to pay Invoice No. W212, terms net 30 days, $125. (This pays a November 30 invoice which is shown as the December 1 balance forward in the vendor ledger.)

30   Issued Check No. 1660 to Fox Valley Power for electric bill (Utilities Expense), $198. This was a cash purchase.

As you journalized TKT's cash payments transactions, you printed the check for each transaction. Take a moment and compare your checks with Figure 9.2.

Figure 9.2

REFERENCE NO	DESCRIPTION	INVOICE DATE	INVOICE AMOUNT	DISCOUNT TAKEN	AMOUNT PAID
	transportation charges				265.00

CHECK DATE	CHECK NO.	PAYEE		DISCOUNT TAKEN	CHECK AMOUNT
12/17/96	1653	Federal Freight			$265.00

TKT PRODUCTS
2400 MAIN STREET
WHEATON, IL 60187
708-555-1212

Wheaton Valley Bank
Wheaton, IL
0200098250

1653

CHECK NO.	DATE	AMOUNT
1653	Dec 17, 1996	********$265.00

Memo:

Two Hundred Sixty-Five and 0/100 Dollars

PAY TO THE ORDER OF   Federal Freight

Dennis Taylor
AUTHORIZED SIGNATURE

Figure 9.2 *(continued)*

						1654
REFERENCE NO	DESCRIPTION	INVOICE DATE	INVOICE AMOUNT		DISCOUNT TAKEN	AMOUNT PAID
1489		12/9/96	144.00		2.88	141.12
-1489		12/11/96	-24.00		-0.48	-23.52

CHECK DATE	CHECK NO.	PAYEE		DISCOUNT TAKEN	CHECK AMOUNT
12/19/96	1654	Franklin Products		2.40	$117.60

TKT PRODUCTS
2400 MAIN STREET
WHEATON, IL 60187
708-555-1212

Wheaton Valley Bank
Wheaton, IL
0200098250

1654

CHECK NO.	DATE	AMOUNT
1654	Dec 19, 1996	********$117.60

Memo:

One Hundred Seventeen and 60/100 Dollars

PAY TO THE ORDER OF

Franklin Products
890 Aspen Dr.
Los Angeles, CA   90046

Dennis Taylor
AUTHORIZED SIGNATURE

Figure 9.2 *(continued)*

						1655
REFERENCE NO	DESCRIPTION	INVOICE DATE	INVOICE AMOUNT		DISCOUNT TAKEN	AMOUNT PAID
repair						65.00

CHECK DATE	CHECK NO.	PAYEE		DISCOUNT TAKEN	CHECK AMOUNT
12/21/96	1655	Archer Plumbing			$65.00

TKT PRODUCTS
2400 MAIN STREET
WHEATON, IL 60187
708-555-1212

Wheaton Valley Bank
Wheaton, IL
0200098250

1655

CHECK NO.	DATE	AMOUNT
1655	Dec 21, 1996	*********$65.00

Memo:

Sixty-Five and 0/100 Dollars

PAY TO THE ORDER OF

Archer Plumbing

Dennis Taylor
AUTHORIZED SIGNATURE

Figure 9.2 (continued)

1656

REFERENCE NO	DESCRIPTION	INVOICE DATE	INVOICE AMOUNT	DISCOUNT TAKEN	AMOUNT PAID
A658		12/13/96	7,560.00	151.20	7,408.80
-A658		12/16/96	-1,620.00	-32.40	-1,587.60

CHECK DATE	CHECK NO.	PAYEE	DISCOUNT TAKEN	CHECK AMOUNT
12/23/96	1656	Kavan Manufacturing	118.80	$5,821.20

TKT PRODUCTS
2400 MAIN STREET
WHEATON, IL 60187
708-555-1212

Wheaton Valley Bank
Wheaton, IL
0200098250

1656

CHECK NO.   DATE   AMOUNT
1656   Dec 23, 1996   ******$5,821.20

Memo:

Five Thousand Eight Hundred Twenty-One and 20/100 Dollars

PAY
TO THE   Kavan Manufacturing
ORDER   9199 Central, N.E.
OF   Albuquerque, NM 87105

Dennis Taylor
AUTHORIZED SIGNATURE

Figure 9.2 (continued)

1657

REFERENCE NO	DESCRIPTION	INVOICE DATE	INVOICE AMOUNT	DISCOUNT TAKEN	AMOUNT PAID
	transportation charges				382.00

CHECK DATE	CHECK NO.	PAYEE	DISCOUNT TAKEN	CHECK AMOUNT
12/26/96	1657	Morton Trucking		$382.00

TKT PRODUCTS
2400 MAIN STREET
WHEATON, IL 60187
708-555-1212

Wheaton Valley Bank
Wheaton, IL
0200098250

1657

CHECK NO.   DATE   AMOUNT
1657   Dec 26, 1996   ********$382.00

Memo:

Three Hundred Eighty-Two and 0/100 Dollars

PAY
TO THE   Morton Trucking
ORDER
OF

Dennis Taylor
AUTHORIZED SIGNATURE

Figure 9.2 *(continued)*

1658

REFERENCE NO.	DESCRIPTION	INVOICE DATE	INVOICE AMOUNT	DISCOUNT TAKEN	AMOUNT PAID
941		12/1/96	900.00		900.00
-941		12/3/96	-45.00		-45.00

CHECK DATE	CHECK NO.	PAYEE	DISCOUNT TAKEN	CHECK AMOUNT
12/27/96	1658	Saroya Corporation		$855.00

TKT PRODUCTS
2400 MAIN STREET
WHEATON, IL 60187
708-555-1212

Wheaton Valley Bank
Wheaton, IL
0200098250

1658

CHECK NO.	DATE	AMOUNT
1658	Dec 27, 1996	*******$855.00

Memo:

Eight Hundred Fifty-Five and 0/100 Dollars

PAY TO THE ORDER OF

Saroya Corporation
1741 West River Rd.
Milwaukee, WI 53217

Dennis Taylor
AUTHORIZED SIGNATURE

Figure 9.2 *(continued)*

1659

REFERENCE NO.	DESCRIPTION	INVOICE DATE	INVOICE AMOUNT	DISCOUNT TAKEN	AMOUNT PAID
W212		11/30/96	125.00		125.00

CHECK DATE	CHECK NO.	PAYEE	DISCOUNT TAKEN	CHECK AMOUNT
12/29/96	1659	Wheaton Supplies		$125.00

TKT PRODUCTS
2400 MAIN STREET
WHEATON, IL 60187
708-555-1212

Wheaton Valley Bank
Wheaton, IL
0200098250

1659

CHECK NO.	DATE	AMOUNT
1659	Dec 29, 1996	*******$125.00

Memo:

One Hundred Twenty-Five and 0/100 Dollars

PAY TO THE ORDER OF

Wheaton Supplies
475 Drake Rd.
Wheaton, IL 60187

Dennis Taylor
AUTHORIZED SIGNATURE

Figure 9.2   *(concluded)*

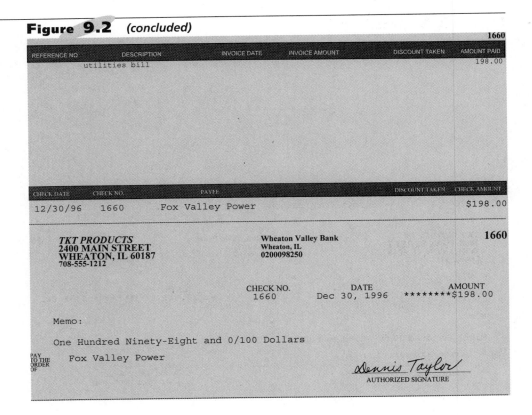

Close the "Payments" window when you are finished.

Printing the Cash Disbursements Journal

objective 9
Print the cash disbursements journal

Follow these steps to print the cash disbursements journal.

step 1:   From the Reports menu, select Account Payable.,

step 2:   Highlight Cash Disbursements Journal.

step 3:   Make the selections to print.

Compare your printout to Figure 9.3. If you need to make any corrections, go back to the "Payments" window. Click on the Edit Records icon and make any needed corrections.

Figure 9.3

TKT Products
Cash Disbursements Journal
For the Period From Dec 1, 1996 to Dec 31, 1996

Filter Criteria includes: Report order is by Date. Report is printed in Detail Format.

Date	Check #	Account ID	Line Description	Debit Amount	Credit Amount
12/14/96	1650	112	Discounts Taken		64.80
		210	Invoice: A623	3,240.00	
		110	Kavan Manufacturing		3,175.20
12/15/96	1651	112	Discounts Taken		16.50
		210	Invoice: 4837	2,100.00	
		210	Invoice: -4837		450.00
		110	Avery Products		1,633.50
12/15/96	1652	616	monthly rent	600.00	
		110	Jackson Rentals		600.00
12/17/96	1653	112	transportation charges	265.00	
		110	Federal Freight		265.00
12/19/96	1654	112	Discounts Taken		2.40
		210	Invoice: 1489	144.00	
		210	Invoice: -1489		24.00
		110	Franklin Products		117.60
12/21/96	1655	617	repair	65.00	
		110	Archer Plumbing		65.00
12/23/96	1656	112	Discounts Taken		118.80
		210	Invoice: A658	7,560.00	
		210	Invoice: -A658		1,620.00
		110	Kavan Manufacturing		5,821.20
12/26/96	1657	112	transportation charges	382.00	
		110	Morton Trucking		382.00
12/27/96	1658	210	Invoice: 941	900.00	
		210	Invoice: -941		45.00
		110	Saroya Corporation		855.00
12/29/96	1659	210	Invoice: W212	125.00	
		110	Wheaton Supplies		125.00
12/30/96	1660	620	utilities bill	198.00	
		110	Fox Valley Power		198.00
	Total			15,579.00	15,579.00

Posting the Cash Disbursements Journal

objective 10
Post the cash disbursements journal

Follow these steps to post the cash disbursements journal:

step 1: From the main menu, select Tasks, then System, then Post.

step 2: Select the Cash Disbursements Journal.

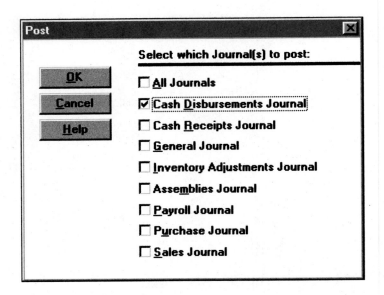

step 3: Click on OK.

Printing the Vendor Ledger

objective 11
Print the vendor ledger

As you will recall from Chapter 8, TKT Products has a vendor ledger. PAW automatically updates the appropriate vendor's account whenever a debit or credit to the Accounts Payable account is journalized. Since most of the cash payment transactions journalized in this chapter involved changes in Accounts Payable, the vendor balances have changed.

Follow these steps to print an up-to-date copy of the vendor ledger:

step 1: From the main menu, Select Reports, Accounts Payable.

step 2: Highlight "Vendor Ledgers."

step 3: Click on the Print icon.

step 4: At the Filter screen, click on OK.

step 5: At the "Print" screen, click on OK.

Compare your printout with Figure 9.4. Observe that the "Type" column in the vendor ledger indicates that the posted information came from the purchase journal (PJ) and the cash disbursements journal (CDJ).

Figure 9.4

TKT Products
Vendor Ledgers
For the Period From Dec 1, 1996 to Dec 31, 1996

Filter Criteria includes: Report order is by ID.

Vendor ID Vendor	Date	Trans No	Type	Paid	Debit Amt	Credit Amt	Balance
AV01 Avery Products	12/5/96	4837	PJ	*		2,100.00	2,100.00
	12/8/96	-4837	PJ	*	450.00		1,650.00
	12/15/96	1651	CDJ		16.50	16.50	1,650.00
	12/15/96	1651	CDJ		1,650.00		0.00
FR02 Franklin Products	12/9/96	1489	PJ	*		144.00	144.00
	12/11/96	-1489	PJ	*	24.00		120.00
	12/19/96	1654	CDJ		2.40	2.40	120.00
	12/19/96	1654	CDJ		120.00		0.00
KA03 Kavan Manufacturing	12/4/96	A623	PJ	*		3,240.00	3,240.00
	12/13/96	A658	PJ	*		7,560.00	10,800.00
	12/14/96	1650	CDJ		64.80	64.80	10,800.00
	12/14/96	1650	CDJ		3,240.00		7,560.00
	12/16/96	-A658	PJ	*	1,620.00		5,940.00
	12/23/96	1656	CDJ		118.80	118.80	5,940.00
	12/23/96	1656	CDJ		5,940.00		0.00
SA04 Saroya Corporation	12/1/96	941	PJ	*		900.00	900.00
	12/3/96	-941	PJ	*	45.00		855.00
	12/27/96	1658	CDJ		855.00		0.00
WH05 Wheaton Supplies	12/1/96	Balance Fwd					125.00
	12/6/96	W310	PJ			114.00	239.00
	12/29/96	1659	CDJ		125.00		114.00

Backing Up Your Chapter 9 Data

As noted previously, it is crucial to back up your Chapter 9 data. You will need it when you begin Chapter 10. Follow these steps to back up your data:

objective 12
Back up your data

step 1: Place a blank formatted disk in drive A.

step 2: From the main menu, select File, Backup.

step 3: The Destination text box displays the last backup name that was typed; for example, a:\chapter8.tkt. Type **a:\chapter9.tkt** in the Destination text box.

step 4: Click on the Backup button. Your files begin to copy. When all the files have been saved to drive A, you are automatically returned to the main menu.

Chapter Nine Summary

FOB destination means that the seller is paying the transportation charges. FOB shipping point means that the purchaser is paying the transportation charges. These charges are considered to be part of the cost of the item being purchased.

The vendor's credit terms are displayed in an abbreviated format at the top of each purchase invoice. For example, "net 30 days," or "n/30," means that the full invoice amount is due 30 days from the invoice date; "n/EOM" means that the full amount is due by the end of the month. Credit terms of 2/10, n/30 indicate that a 2 percent discount may be deducted if the invoice is paid within 10 days of the invoice date or the full amount is due 30 days from the invoice date.

In PAW, the "Payments" window is used to pay bills. All the information about a cash payment is recorded in the "Payments" window. Then PAW takes the necessary information from this window and automatically journalizes the transaction in the cash disbursements journal which is another example of a special journal. All payments of cash are recorded in the cash disbursements journal. This journal can be viewed on your screen or printed out.

Demonstration Problem

Pershing Enterprises completed the following selected transactions during July 1996. Assume all payments are on account unless otherwise specified.

July 1 Issued Check No. 1275 to Brennan Manufacturing to pay Invoice No. 4278, no discount, $2,588.

5 Issued Check No. 1276 to Atlantic Freight for transportation charges relating to the purchase of merchandise, $134. This was a cash purchase.

10 Issued Check No. 1277 to Armor Plumbing for a repair (Repair Expense), $152. This was a cash purchase.

16 Issued Check No. 1278 to Krane Products to pay Invoice No. 7781, $1,200 less a 2% cash discount.

21 Issued Check No. 1279 to Ramos Office Supplies for the purchase of computer paper and ink cartridges, $125. This was a cash purchase.

27 Issued Check No. 1280 to Lang Industries to pay Invoice No. M896, $1,800 less a 1% cash discount.

Instructions

Record these transactions on a data entry sheet. Leave the "Account ID" column blank.

Solution to Demonstration Problem

			DATA ENTRY SHEET Pershing Enterprises		
Date	Account ID	Reference	Trans Description	Debit Amt	Credit Amt
7/1			Accounts Payable, Brennan Mfg., Invoice No. 4278	2,588.00	
			Cash, Check No. 1275		2,588.00
7/5			Merchandise Inventory	134.00	
			Cash, Check No. 1276		134.00
7/10			Repair Expense	152.00	
			Cash, Check No. 1277		152.00
7/16			Accounts Payable, Krane Products, Invoice No. 7781	1,200.00	
			Merchandise Inventory		24.00
			Cash, Check No. 1278		1,176.00
7/21			Supplies	125.00	
			Cash, Check No. 1279		125.00
7/27			Accounts Payable, Lang Ind., Invoice No. M896	1,800.00	
			Merchandise Inventory		18.00
			Cash, Check No. 1280		1,782.00

Glossary

cash discount   A discount offered by the seller to encourage charge customers to pay promptly.   *252*

cash disbursements journal   A special journal used to record outflows of cash. *256*

credit period   The time between the invoice date and the date full payment is due.   *252*

credit terms   Terms of payment determined by the seller (vendor).   *252*

discount period   A specified time during which a cash discount may be taken. *252*

FOB destination   The goods are shipped free on board (FOB) to the purchaser's place of business (destination). The seller (vendor) pays the transportation charges. *250*

FOB shipping point   The purchaser pays to transport goods from the seller's place of business (shipping point).   *250*

purchases discount   The term used to describe a cash discount from the purchaser's point of view.   *252*

sales discount   The term used to describe a cash discount from the seller's (vendor's) point of view.   *252*

Self-Test

Select the best answer.

1. FOB destination means that
    a. the seller (vendor) pays the transportation costs.
    b. the purchaser pays the transportation costs.
    c. the seller and purchaser share the transportation costs.
    d. there are no transportation costs.

2. Sellers (vendors) offer cash discounts to
    a. reduce transportation costs.
    b. encourage the purchaser to pay quickly.
    c. require the net amount in 30 days.
    d. All of the above.

3. Every transaction in the cash disbursements journal requires a
    a. debit to Cash.
    b. credit to Cash.
    c. debit to Accounts Receivable.
    d. credit to Accounts Payable.

4. In PAW, transportation charges related to the purchase of merchandise are debited to the
    a. Transportation Expense account.
    b. Cost of Freight account.
    c. Accounts Payable account.
    d. Merchandise Inventory account.

5. In PAW, a purchases discount is recorded with a credit to the
    a. Purchases Expense account.
    b. Cost of Sales account.
    c. Merchandise Inventory account.
    d. Merchandise Expense account.

Answers to the self-test can be found after the cases at the end of this chapter.

Questions for Discussion

1. Who pays the transportation charges under the following terms?
    a. FOB destination
    b. FOB shipping point

2. a. What is the purpose of a cash discount?
    b. A cash discount to the seller is what type of discount?
    c. A cash discount to the purchaser is what type of discount?

3. What do the following credit terms mean?
    a. n/30
    b. 1/15, n/30
    c. n/EOM

4. Why does the purchaser ultimately pay the transportation charges regardless of the transportation terms?

5. Why is the purchases discount credited to the Merchandise Inventory account?

6. What information must you record in the "Payments" window?

7. In PAW, how are the Purchases and Payments Tasks related?

8. How are the cash disbursements journal and the vendor ledger related?

Exercises

Exercise 9.1

Match the following terms with the definitions shown below:

Terminology
L.O. 1–12

1. Purchases discount
2. Cash discount
3. FOB shipping point
4. Cash disbursements journal
5. Discount period
6. FOB destination
7. Credit terms
8. Credit period

Definitions

a. A discount offered by the seller to encourage charge customers to pay promptly.

b. A specified time during which a cash discount may be taken.

c. A special journal used to record all outflows of cash.

d. Terms of payment determined by the seller (vendor).

e. The goods are shipped free on board (FOB) to the purchaser's place of business.

f. The time between the invoice date and the date full payment is due.

g. The term used to describe a cash discount from the purchaser's point of view.

h. The purchaser pays to transport goods from the seller's place of business.

Exercise 9.2

Indicate which task in PAW (Purchases/Receive Inventory Task or Payments Task) is used to record each of the following transactions.

Purchases and Payments Tasks
L.O. 4, 5, 7, 8

1. Purchase of merchandise on account.
2. Purchase of supplies for cash.
3. Purchase of supplies on account.
4. Payment to creditor on account.
5. Return of merchandise on account to vendor.

Exercise 9.3

Indicate which special journal (purchase journal or cash disbursements journal) is used to record each of the transactions in Exercise 9.2.

Special Journals
L.O. 4, 5, 7, 8

Exercise 9.4

For each purchase described at the top of page 274, determine the cash payment necessary to settle the account, assuming all purchases discounts are taken if paid within the discount period.

Payment; Cash Discount
L.O. 2, 5

Transaction	Invoice Date	Credit Terms	Date Paid	Merchandise
A	June 1	n/30	June 28	$500
B	June 7	2/10, n/30	June 17	$785
C	June 12	1/10, n/30	June 22	$570
D	June 18	2/10, n/30	June 26	$864
E	June 19	1/10, n/30	June 30	$265

Exercise 9.5

Payment with Discount
L.O. 2, 5

COLOMBO CORPORATION   **INVOICE NO. 8674**
816 Farnham Lane
Westport, CT 06880

Sold to: Johnson Enterprises   Date: 7/18/96
        458 Adams Road   Terms: 1/10, n/30
        Oneonta, NY 13820   F.O.B.: Shipping point

Quantity	Description	Unit Price	Total
300	Part No. 323-B	1.75	525.00

In reference to Invoice No. 8674, record the following transactions in data entry sheet format on the books of Johnson Enterprises:

1. The purchase of merchandise on account.

2. The payment on account within the 10-day discount period.

Exercise 9.6

Transportation Charges;
Discount
L.O. 1, 2, 5

Record the following transactions in data entry sheet format:

March 12   Purchased merchandise on account from Buggs Corporation; 1/10, n/30; FOB shipping point; $1,500.

      14   Issued Check No. 472 to Fast Freight for transportation costs related to the March 12 purchase, $85.

Exercise 9.7

Payment Less Purchase Return
L.O. 2, 7

Record the following transactions in data entry sheet format:

June 5   Purchased merchandise on account from Burton Company; 2/10, n/30; FOB destination; $784.

      9   Returned defective merchandise to Burton Company for credit, $60.

     15   Issued Check No. 365 to Burton Company in settlement of the account.

Exercise 9.8

Transportation Charges;
Discount
L.O. 1, 2

HARMON PRODUCTS
498 Susan Lane
Fort Thomas, KY 41075

INVOICE NO. 7632

Sold to: Theodore Company
       121 Lake Street
       Eau Claire, WI 57401

Date: 3/16/96
Terms: 2/10, n/30
F.O.B.: Shipping point

Quantity	Description	Unit Price	Total
280	Part No. 176-K Transportation Charges	6.50	1,820 195 2,015

Theodore Company received a bill from Harmon Products indicating that
Theodore still owes $3.90 on Invoice No. 7632 (as shown). Theodore claims
it paid this invoice promptly within the 10-day discount period with Check
No. 457 in the amount of $1,974.70. Does Theodore owe Harmon Products
an additional $3.90? Explain.

Problems—Set A

Problem 9.1A

In Chapter 8, Problem Set A, you recorded purchases on account for ACS
Products. ACS's vendor ledger is shown in Figure 9.5. Follow these steps to
restore your data and print ACS's vendor ledger:

Restore Data; Vendor Ledger
L.O. 3, 11

step 1:   Start Windows, then PAW, open ACS Products.

step 2:   Place your ACS Products backup disk in drive A.

> **Comment**
>
> Be sure that you are inserting your ACS backup disk from Chapter 8 *not* the Company Data CD-ROM that came with this textbook. That disk should be stored in a safe place.

step 3:   From the main menu, select File, then Restore.

step 4:   Type a:\acsdec.85a in the Source box. (Use the same file name that you
used in Chapter 8.)

step 5:   Click on the Restore button. Read the "Warning" screen, then click on
OK. Restoring the files will take a few moments. When the files are
restored, you are returned to the main menu.

step 6:   Remove disk from drive A.

step 7:   Follow these steps to print ACS's vendor ledger from Chapter 8:
a. From the main menu, select <u>R</u>eports, Accounts <u>P</u>ayable.
b. Highlight vendor ledgers.
c. Make the selections to print. Compare your vendor ledger with Figure 9.5.

Figure 9.5

ACS Products
Vendor Ledgers
For the Period From Dec 1, 1996 to Dec 31, 1996
Filter Criteria includes: Report order is by ID.

Vendor ID Vendor	Date	Trans No	Type Paid	Debit Amt	Credit Amt	Balance
001AL	12/1/96	P913	PJ		4,192.50	4,192.50
Alsip Industries	12/10/96	P996	PJ		2,515.50	6,708.00
002PR	12/2/96	8762	PJ		2,331.00	2,331.00
Prado Products	12/4/96	-8762	PJ	388.50		1,942.50
003TA	12/5/96	EL93	PJ		2,634.00	2,634.00
Taft Corporation	12/7/96	-EL93	PJ	526.80		2,107.20
004XY	12/1/96	Balance Fwd				1,300.00
XYZ Supplies	12/6/96	X13	PJ		265.95	1,565.95

Problem 9.2A

Data Entry Sheet
L.O. 5, 7, 8

ACS Products completed the following selected transactions during December 1996. Assume all payments are on account unless otherwise indicated.

Dec. 1   Issued Check No. 1425 to Kerr Rentals for monthly rent (Rent Expense), $625. This was a cash purchase.

10   Issued Check No. 1426 to Alsip Industries to pay Invoice No. P913; dated 12/1/96; terms 2/10, n/30.

11   Issued Check No. 1427 to American Freight for transportation charges related to the purchase of merchandise, $72. This was a cash purchase.

12   Issued Check No. 1428 to Prado Products to pay Invoice No. 8762 dated 12/2/96; terms 2/10, n/30; less purchase return on 12/4/96.

16   Issued Check No. 1429 to Commonwealth Power for electric bill (Utilities Expense), $206. This was a cash purchase.

20   Issued Check No. 1430 to Alsip Industries to pay Invoice No. P996, dated 12/10/96; terms 2/10, n/30.

28   Issued Check No. 1431 to Taft Corporation to pay Invoice No. EL93 dated 12/5/96; terms net 30 days; less purchase return on 12/7/96.

29   Issued Check No. 1432 to XYZ Supplies to pay Invoice No. X12; terms net 30 days; $1,300. (This pays a November 30 invoice which is shown as the December 1 balance forward in the vendor ledger.)

30   Issued Check No. 1433 to Grant Repairs for a minor repair to the equipment (Repair Expense), $84. This was a cash purchase.

Instructions

Record these transactions on a data entry sheet. In some cases, you will have to refer to ACS's Chapter 8 transactions.

Problem 9.3A

Referring to your data entry sheet from Problem 9.2A, use PAW's Payments Task to *journalize* ACS's transactions in the cash disbursements journal and *print* Check Nos. 1425 through 1433.

Payments Task
L.O. 4–8

Problem 9.4A

Follow these steps to print and post the cash disbursements journal:

Print and Post CDJ
L.O. 9, 10

step 1: From the main menu, select Reports, Accounts Payable.

step 2: Highlight the "Cash Disbursements Journal."

step 3: Make the selections to print. Proofread your cash disbursements journal. If necessary, make any needed corrections, then reprint the cash disbursements journal.

step 4: Post the cash disbursements journal.

Problem 9.5A

Follow these steps to print ACS's vendor ledger:

Print Vendor Ledger
L.O. 11

step 1: From the main menu, select Reports, Accounts Payable.

step 2: Highlight vendor ledgers.

step 3: Make the selections to print.

Problem 9.6A

Your ACS Products data **must** be backed up. You will restore it in Chapter 10. Follow these steps:

Back Up
L.O. 12

step 1: Insert a blank formatted disk in drive A.

step 2: From PAW's main menu, select File, then Backup.

step 3: Type a:\acsdec.96a in the Destination text box.

step 4: Click on the Backup button. Your files begin to copy. When all the files have been saved to drive A, you are automatically returned to the main menu.

step 5: Click on File, Exit to exit PAW.

Problems—Set B

Problem 9.1B

In Chapter 8, Problem Set B, you recorded purchases on account for LLS Products. LLS's vendor ledger is shown in Figure 9.6. Follow these steps to restore your data and print LLS's vendor ledger:

Restore Data; Vendor Ledger
L.O. 3, 11

step 1: Start Windows, then PAW. Open LLS Products.

step 2: Place your LLS Products backup disk in drive A.

Comment

> Be sure that you are inserting your LLS backup disk from Chapter 8 *not* the Company Data CD-ROM that came with this textbook. That disk should be stored in a safe place.

step 3: From the main menu, select File, then Restore.

step 4: Type a:\llsdec.85b in the Source box. (Use the same file name that you used in Chapter 8.)

step 5: Click on the Restore button. Read the "Warning" screen, then click on OK. Restoring the files will take a few moments. When the files are restored, you are returned to the main menu.

step 6: Remove disk from drive A.

step 7: Follow these steps to print LLS's vendor ledger from Chapter 8:
  a. From the main menu, select Reports, Accounts Payable.
  b. Highlight vendor ledgers.
  c. Make the selections to print. Compare your vendor ledger with Figure 9.6.

Figure 9.6

LLS Products
Vendor Ledgers
For the Period From Dec 1, 1996 to Dec 31, 1996

Filter Criteria includes: Report order is by ID.

Vendor ID Vendor	Date	Trans No	Type Paid	Debit Amt	Credit Amt	Balance
111BER	12/1/96	BR79	PJ		2,520.00	2,520.00
Bertel Company	12/3/96	-BR79	PJ	240.00		2,280.00
222LAN	12/2/96	1662	PJ		2,392.50	2,392.50
Lance Company	12/8/96	1736	PJ		957.00	3,349.50
333SAF	12/5/96	4498	PJ		4,189.50	4,189.50
Safer Brothers	12/7/96	-4498	PJ	718.20		3,471.30
444STA	12/1/96	Balance Fwd				1,380.00
Stanton Supplies	12/6/96	ST32	PJ		242.85	1,622.85

Problem 9.2B

Data Entry Sheet
L.O. 5, 7, 8

LLS Products completed the following transactions during December 1996. Assume all payments are on account unless otherwise indicated.

Dec. 1 Issued Check No. 1240 to Haley Rentals for monthly rent (Rent Expense), $595. This was a cash purchase.

3 Issued Check No. 1241 to Rapid Freight for transportation charges relating to the purchase of merchandise, $115. This was a cash purchase.

6 Issued Check No. 1242 to Brown Repairs for minor repair to the equipment (Repair Expense), $97. This was a cash purchase.

10 Issued Check No. 1243 to Bertel Company to pay Invoice No. BR79 dated 12/1/96; terms 2/10, n/30; less purchase return on 12/3/96.

12 Issued Check No. 1244 to Lance Company to pay Invoice No. 1662 dated 12/2/96; terms 2/10, n/30.

18 Issued Check No. 1245 to Lance Company to pay Invoice No. 1736 dated 12/8/96; terms 2/10, n/30.

20 Issued Check No. 1246 to Lakeshore Power for electric bill (Utilities Expense), $215. This was a cash purchase.

28 Issued Check No. 1247 to Safer Brothers to pay Invoice No. 4498 dated 12/5/96; terms net 30 days; less purchase return on 12/7/96.

30 Issued Check No. 1248 to Stanton Supplies to pay Invoice ST21; terms net 30 days; $1,380. (This pays a November 30 invoice which is shown as the December 1 balance forward in the vendor ledger.)

Instructions

Record these transactions on a data entry sheet. In some cases, you will have to refer to LLS' Chapter 8 transactions.

Problem 9.3B

Referring to your data entry sheet from Problem 9.2B, use PAW's Payments Task to *journalize* LLS's transactions in the cash disbursements journal and *print* Check Nos. 1240 through 1248.

Payments Task
L.O. 4–8

Problem 9.4B

Follow these steps to print and post the cash disbursements journal:

Print and Post CDJ
L.O. 9, 10

step 1: From the main menu, select Reports, Accounts Payable.

step 2: Highlight the "Cash Disbursements Journal."

step 3: Make the selections to print. Proofread your cash disbursements journal. If necessary, make any needed corrections, then reprint the cash disbursements journal.

step 4: Post the cash disbursements journal.

Problem 9.5B

Follow these steps to print LLS's vendor ledger:

Print Vendor Ledger
L.O. 11

step 1: From the main menu, select Reports, Accounts Payable.

step 2: Highlight vendor ledgers.

step 3: Make the selections to print.

Problem 9.6B

Your LLS Products data **must** be backed up. You will restore it in Chapter 10. Follow these steps:

Back Up
L.O. 12

step 1: Insert a blank formatted disk in drive A.

step 2: From PAW's main menu, select File, then Backup.

step 3: Type **a:\llsdec.96b** in the Destination text box.

step 4: Click on the Backup button. Your files begin to copy. When all the files have been saved to drive A, you are automatically returned to the main menu.

step 5: Click on File, Exit to exit PAW.

Mini-Cases

Case 9–1

Your purchasing agent has received two price quotations on the same merchandise.

Supplier A:　$275 per unit, FOB destination.
Supplier B:　$265 per unit, FOB shipping point.

Why might Supplier A be the better choice even though the price per unit is higher?

Case 9–2

As your friend Richard Moy uses PAW in his new business, you have suggested that he use the Purchases and Payments Tasks to record purchases on account and cash disbursements. Richard thinks it is easier to record all transactions in the general journal. How would you convince him that you are correct?

Case 9–3

Your neighbor, Mary Norville, owns her own business. Many of Mary's vendors offer purchase discounts, but Mary thinks it is too much trouble to keep track of the due dates in order to save such a small amount of money. What do you think?

A Case of Ethics

Jeff, an employee in the accounting department, received a purchase invoice for 5.25″ disks. He is curious about this invoice because he knows that all of the company's computers use 3.5″ disks. Jeff calls the purchasing department and determines that the purchase requisition was initiated by his friend, Ralph. Jeff also knows that Ralph's home computer is old and uses 5.25″ disks. Rather than "make waves" for Ralph, Jeff pays the invoice. "This is a big company," says Jeff. "The cost of a couple of boxes of disks won't put the owner in the poor house." Comment.

Answers to Self-Test

1. *a*　　2. *b*　　3. *b*　　4. *d*　　5. *c*

Merchandising Business

Accounting for Sales

10

LEARNING OBJECTIVES

After studying this chapter, you should be able to:

1. Compute trade discounts.

2. Describe the customer ledger.

3. Describe how to assign the cost of merchandise inventory.

4. Restore data from the previous chapter.

5. Use PAW to record sales on account.

6. Print the sales invoice.

7. Use PAW to record sales to a retail customer.

8. Use PAW to record sales returns.

9. Post the sales journal.

10. Print the sales journal.

11. Print the customer ledger.

12. Back up your data.

In Chapters 8 and 9, you learned to use PAW's Purchases/Receive Inventory and Payments Tasks. Now that TKT Products has merchandise available for sale, we are ready to record sales. To do that, you will learn to use PAW's Sales/Invoicing Task. You will also study several related topics such as trade discounts, sales returns and allowances, the customer ledger, and how to assign cost to the units sold and in inventory. Because sales and purchases are opposite sides of the same coin, many of the transactions presented in this chapter present the seller's point of view on topics previously covered in the purchases chapter.

Trade Discounts

objective 1
Compute trade discounts

Some businesses distribute catalogs listing their products and prices to their customers. These prices, however, are not selling prices. They are known as list prices. The actual selling price consists of the list price minus an amount known as a trade discount.

$$\boxed{\text{List Price}} - \boxed{\text{Trade Discount}} = \boxed{\text{Selling Price}}$$

The use of a trade discount allows the seller to change the selling price without reprinting the catalog. The list price printed in the catalog remains fixed, but the trade discount and, consequently, the selling price can be changed as often as necessary. Because printing and distributing a catalog are expensive processes, the use of trade discounts represents quite a savings to the seller.

To demonstrate the use of a trade discount, let's assume that product KX-16 is currently selling at a list price of $1,000 less a 15 percent trade discount. The selling price is computed as follows:

```
List price . . . . . . . . . . . . . . . . . .$1,000
Less 15% trade discount
      ($1,000 × .15) . . . . . . . . . . . .− 150
Selling price . . . . . . . . . . . . . . . .$  850
```

Math Tip

To calculate a trade discount, the discount must be converted from a percentage to either a decimal or a fraction. Since most people prefer to use decimals, we will convert to a decimal. This is accomplished in two steps:

step 1: Move the decimal point two places to the left.

step 2: Drop the percentage sign.

For example, let's convert 25 percent from a percent to a decimal:

step 1: .25.%

step 2: .25

The trade discount does *not* appear in the accounts of either the purchaser or the seller. Trade discounts are used only to compute the selling price, which is the significant figure to the accountant.

The Customer Ledger

In Chapter 8, you were introduced to the concept of a controlling account and a subsidiary ledger. You applied that concept to accounts payable. Now we will apply that concept to accounts receivable.

objective 2
Describe the customer ledger

In the past, you recorded transactions involving accounts receivable by simply debiting or crediting the Accounts Receivable account. The resulting balance in the Accounts Receivable account indicated the total amount due from all charge customers. This information, although useful, is not adequate. Just as a business must be able to identify its creditors, it must also know how much is due from each of its customers. Another subsidiary ledger, called the customer ledger, conveniently adds this information to our accounting system.

The Accounts Receivable account in the general ledger will now be referred to as a *control* or *controlling account.* As in the past, the Accounts Receivable account contains only summary information. The customer ledger provides the necessary detail. It contains a separate account for each customer.

When journalizing, the customer's name must be indicated when the Accounts Receivable account is debited or credited. PAW automatically posts all debits and credits to accounts receivable to the Accounts Receivable (control) account in the general ledger and to the customer's account in the customer ledger. Although PAW uses the term *customer ledger,* this ledger is also commonly known as the *accounts receivable ledger.*

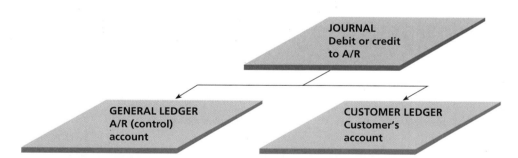

After all journalizing and posting are completed, the balance in the Accounts Receivable (control) account should equal the total of the customer account balances in the customer ledger. We will print out TKT Products' customer ledger later in this chapter.

From now on, we will assume that every company has both a customer ledger and a vendor ledger.

Assigning the Cost of Merchandise Inventory (FIFO)

objective 3
Describe how to assign the cost
of merchandise inventory

To have merchandise available for sale to customers, TKT Products must purchase merchandise from a vendor. The price that TKT pays to purchase each unit is known as the *cost* of that unit. The cost of all the units sold during a specific period of time is known as the *cost of sales*. On the income statement of a merchandising business, the cost of sales is subtracted from the total revenues generated from selling those units to arrive at a subtotal known as *gross profit*.

To generate a gross profit, the selling price (revenue) of the merchandise sold must be higher than its cost. For example:

Total revenues	$16,579.00
− Cost of sales	−10,008.00
Gross profit	$ 6,571.00

As you already know from Chapter 8, when merchandise is purchased, the cost is recorded in the Merchandise Inventory account. Over a period of time, what happens to that merchandise?

There are only two basic outcomes: it is sold or it remains unsold. The cost of the sold merchandise appears on the income statement as the cost of sales. The cost of the unsold merchandise remains in the Merchandise Inventory account and is reported on the balance sheet in the current assets section.

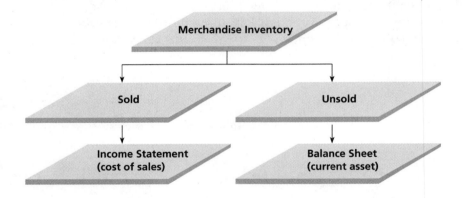

Most businesses, like TKT Products, purchase merchandise many times throughout the year. If the purchase price was always the same, assigning a cost to the units sold would be easy (quantity times the cost per unit). Most of the time, however, a business's inventory is composed of merchandise purchased at different prices. This makes it more difficult to assign a cost to the units sold and the remaining inventory.

From several commonly used methods, TKT Products has chosen the first-in, first-out (FIFO) method to assign these costs. Under the FIFO method, the cost of merchandise purchased first (first in) is assigned to the merchandise sold first (first out). The unsold units, or ending inventory, are assigned the last or remaining costs.

Referring to the item costing report in Figure 10.1, the cost of the units sold is shown in the Cost of Sales column. The cost of the unsold units (ending inventory) is shown in the Remain Value column. Once TKT Products chooses the FIFO method, PAW automatically makes the necessary computations.

Inventory methods, such as FIFO, are covered in detail in more advanced accounting courses.

Figure 10.1

TKT Products
Item Costing Report
For the Period From Dec 1, 1996 to Dec 31, 1996

Filter Criteria includes: Report order is by ID.

Item ID / Item Description	Date	Qty Received	Item Cost	Actual Cost	Assembly Qty / Assembly ($)	Adjust Qty / Adjust ($)	Quantity Sold	Cost of Sales	Remaining Qty	Remain Value
666dr cabinet doors	12/5/96	14.00	150.00	2,100.00					14.00	2,100.00
	12/8/96	-3.00	150.00	-450.00					11.00	1,650.00
	12/10/96						8.00	1,200.00	3.00	450.00
	12/12/96						-2.00	-300.00	5.00	750.00
	12/21/96						2.00	300.00	3.00	450.00
777gl wood glue	12/9/96	30.00	4.80	144.00					30.00	144.00
	12/11/96	-5.00	4.80	-24.00					25.00	120.00
	12/14/96						5.00	24.00	20.00	96.00
	12/15/96						-2.00	-9.60	22.00	105.60
888cab kitchen cabinets	12/3/96						3.00	810.00	-3.00	-810.00
	12/4/96	12.00	270.00	3,240.00					9.00	2,430.00
	12/7/96						-1.00	-270.00	10.00	2,700.00
	12/13/96	28.00	270.00	7,560.00					38.00	10,260.00
	12/16/96	-6.00	270.00	-1,620.00					32.00	8,640.00
	12/18/96						20.00	5,400.00	12.00	3,240.00
	12/23/96						-4.00	-1,080.00	16.00	4,320.00
999hin hinges for cabinets	12/1/96	100.00	9.00	900.00					100.00	900.00
	12/2/96						70.00	630.00	30.00	270.00
	12/3/96	-5.00	9.00	-45.00					25.00	225.00
	12/4/96						-10.00	-90.00	35.00	315.00
	12/28/96						8.00	72.00	27.00	243.00
	12/30/96						-2.00	-18.00	29.00	261.00

Restoring Data from Chapter 9

Your TKT Products data from Chapter 9 must be restored before you can use PAW to record sales. Follow these steps to restore your data:

objective 4
Restore data from previous chapter

step 1:   Start Windows, then PAW. Open TKT Products.

step 2:   Place your Chapter 9 backup disk in drive A.

step 3:   From the main menu, select File, then Restore.

step 4:   Type **a:\chapter9.tkt** in the "Source" box. (Use the same file name that you used when you backed up in Chapter 9.)

step 5:   Click on the Restore button. Read the "Warning" screen, then click on OK. When the files are restored, you are returned to the main menu.

step 6:   Remove disk from drive A.

To be sure that your data has been loaded properly, let's print TKT's customer master file list. Follow these steps:

step 1:   From the main menu, click on Reports, Accounts Receivable.

step 2:   Highlight the "Customer Master File List."

step 3:   Make the selections to print. Compare your printout with Figure 10.2.

Figure 10.2

TKT Products
Customer Master File List

Filter Criteria includes: Report order is by ID.

Customer ID Customer	Address line 1 Address line 2 City ST ZIP	Contact Telephone 1 Telephone 2 Fax Number	Tax Code Resale No Terms Cust Since
41ad Adams Company	95 North 12th Street Chicago, IL 60521	Terry Adams 708-555-1341 708-555-1342	 21-3300447 1% 10, Net 30 Days 7/5/96
42be Becker Brothers	233 Stanford Avenue Lombard, IL 60533	Alan Becker 708-555-1298 708-555-9876	 21-9834671 1% 10, Net 30 Days 7/5/96
43ca Carson Corporation	155 Roosevelt Road Chicago, IL 60521	Judy Wheeler 708-555-6543 708-555-6544	 21-2131548 1% 10, Net 30 Days 7/5/96
44du Dubin Enterprises	60 N. Broadway Burr Ridge, IL 60521	Barry Dubin 708-555-4811 708-555-4812	 21-9876329 1% 10, Net 30 Days 7/5/96
45fa Steven Faulker	760 Prospect Avenue Chicago, IL 60021	 708-555-9911 708-555-8716	IL Net 30 Days 7/5/96

Recording Sales

In PAW, all the information about a sale is recorded in a "Sales/Invoicing" window. Then, PAW takes the necessary information from the window and automatically journalizes the transaction in the sales journal. Only sales on account are recorded in this special journal. PAW also prepares sales invoices using information from the "Sales/Invoicing" window. As a matter of fact, the window itself looks like an invoice. Later, information from the "Sales/Invoicing" window will be used when cash receipts are recorded. For now, we will concentrate on recording sales.

As you will recall, PAW uses a perpetual inventory system. Therefore, every sale of merchandise on account requires the following:

- Record the sale:
   Debit Accounts Receivable for the **selling price.**
   Credit Sales for the **selling price.**

- Update the Merchandise Inventory and Cost of Sales accounts:
   Debit Cost of Sales for the **cost** of the units being sold.
   Credit Merchandise Inventory for the **cost** of the units being sold.

You probably observed that two new accounts are used to record this transaction. The Sales account is a very popular revenue account title used by merchandising businesses. The Cost of Sales account is used to keep a cumulative record of the cost of the units that have been sold. It has a normal balance on the debit side. As you will recall, Cost of Sales is subtracted from total revenues to determine a company's gross profit. Both the Sales and Cost of Sales accounts appear on the income statement and both are temporary accounts.

PAW records the sale and updates Merchandise Inventory and Cost of Sales in one journal entry. As you will recall, an entry with multiple debits and/or credits is called a compound journal entry.

For some practice in recording a sale of merchandise on account, let's use PAW to journalize the following transaction for TKT Products:

Dec. 2   Sold 70 hinges on account at $15.00 each to Dubin Enterprises, Invoice No. 2001; terms 1/10, n/30, $1,050. The cost of these hinges was $630.

As usual, we start by recording the information on a data entry sheet. This forces us to read the transaction carefully and organize the information before going to the "Sales/Invoicing" window.

DATA ENTRY SHEET TKT Products					
Date	Account ID	Reference	Trans Description	Debit Amt	Credit Amt
12/2/96	111		Accounts Receivable, Dubin Enterprises, Inv. No. 2001	1,050.00	
	501		Cost of Sales	630.00	
	411		Sales		1,050.00
	112		Merchandise Inventory		630.00

> **Comment**
>
> Observe that the sale is recorded at the full selling price ($1,050) even though TKT is offering Dubin Enterprises a 1 percent cash discount if the account is paid within 10 days. At this point in time, TKT does not know whether Dubin will take advantage of the discount. If Dubin pays within the discount period, the discount will be recorded when the cash is received.

Referring to the data entry sheet, follow these steps to journalize this sale of merchandise on account in the sales journal:

step 1: From the main menu, select Tasks, Sales/Invoicing.

step 2: In the Customer ID box, click on the magnifying glass icon. Select Dubin Enterprises. Your cursor is in the "Invoice #" box. Press the <Enter> key.

step 3: In the Date box, type **2** and press the <Enter> key.

step 4: Click on the "Quantity" column. Type **70** in the "Quantity" column. Press the <Enter> key.

step 5: In the "Item" column, click on the magnifying glass icon and select "hinges for cabinets." The description "hinges for cabinets" is automatically completed.

step 6: Observe that the "A/R Account" box displays "111." This is TKT Products accounts receivable account.

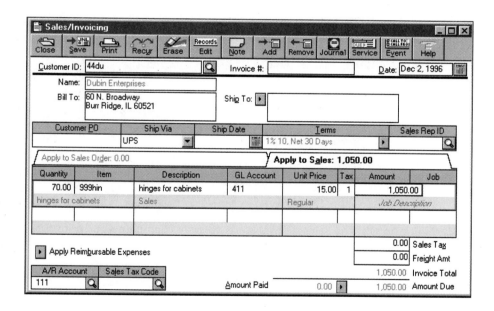

step 7: Click on the "Journal" icon to see the "Accounting Behind the Screens Sales Journal" window. Note the accounts debited and credited. Click on Ok to return to the "Sales/Invoicing" window.

Printing the Sales Invoice

When a sales invoice is printed, PAW automatically *saves* the related journal entry. Follow these steps to print the sales invoice:

step 1: Click on the Print icon.

step 2: The "Print Forms: Invoices/Credit Memo" window pops up. Highlight Invoice Plain Service.

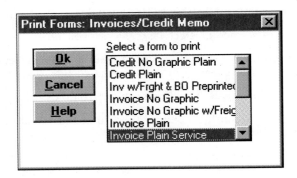

step 3: Click on Ok.

step 4: The "Print Forms: Invoice Plain Service" window pops up. Click on Real.

step 5: The "About to Print Invoices" window pops up. Type **2001** in the First invoice number box.

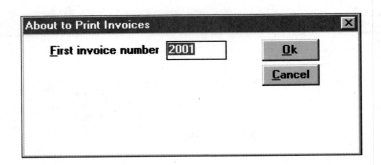

step 6: Click on Ok. The sales invoice starts to print. Compare your printout with Figure 10.3.

Figure 10.3

Invoice

Invoice Number:
2001

Invoice Date:
12/2/96

Page:
1

Voice:
Fax:

Sold To:
Dubin Enterprises
60 N. Broadway
Burr Ridge, IL 60521

Customer ID:44du

Customer PO	Payment Terms	Sales Rep ID	Due Date
	1% 10, Net 30 Days		1/1/97

Description	Amount
hinges for cabinets	1,050.00

Subtotal	1,050.00
Sales Tax	
Total Invoice Amount	1,050.00
Payment Received	0.00
TOTAL	1,050.00

Check No:

As we recorded information in the "Sales/Invoicing" window, you probably observed that PAW supplied some basic information about Dubin Enterprises such as its address and credit terms, as well as the unit price of the item being sold and the total amount of the sale. In a real situation, we would have previously stored basic information about our regular customers in PAW. Then, when recording transactions, this information is automatically supplied by PAW. In this textbook, the TKT Products company data contained this information.

Recording Sales Tax

objective 7
Use PAW to record sales to a
retail customer

A **wholesale business** sells merchandise to another business. A **retail business** sells merchandise to the end user (final customer). Many states and local municipalities levy a **sales tax** on retail sales. This tax is actually paid by the retail customer but the retail seller acts as a collection agent for the taxing authority. At the time of the sale, the seller charges the customer for the tax and later remits the cash to the appropriate taxing authority.

Once the seller has charged the customer for the sales tax, the tax becomes a liability (Sales Tax Payable) of the seller. The seller now owes the sales tax to the taxing authority. This liability must be recorded when the sale is recorded.

TKT Products is primarily a wholesale business, but it does have one retail customer. To demonstrate how a retail sale is recorded, let's use PAW to record the following transaction:

Dec. 3   TKT sold 3 kitchen cabinets on account at $450 each to Steven Faulker; Invoice No. 2002; terms net 30 days; $1,350. Because this is a retail sale, a 6 percent sales tax is applicable ($1,350 $\times$ .06 = $81). TKT's credit terms for all retail sales are net 30 days. The cost of these kitchen cabinets is $810.

In data entry sheet format, this transaction is recorded as follows:

DATA ENTRY SHEET TKT Products					
Date	Account ID	Reference	Trans Description	Debit Amt	Credit Amt
12/3/96	111		Accounts Receivable, Steven Faulker, Inv. No. 2002	1,431.00	
	501		Cost of Sales	810.00	
	411		Sales		1,350.00
	213		Sales Tax Payable		81.00
	112		Merchandise Inventory		810.00

Math Tip

Although PAW automatically calculates the sales tax on each retail sale, it is still important to understand how sales tax is computed.

$$\text{Sales Tax} = \text{Sale} \times \text{Tax Rate}$$
$$= \$1,350 \times 6\%$$
$$= \$1,350 \times .06$$
$$= \$81$$

Referring to the data entry sheet, we are now ready to journalize this retail sale on account in the sales journal and print Invoice No. 2002. (Remember, PAW automatically saves each transaction when the invoice is printed.)

step 1: From the main menu, select Tasks, Sales/Invoicing.

step 2: In the Customer ID box, click on the magnifying glass icon. Select Steven Faulker. Your cursor is in the "Invoice #" box. Press the <Enter> key.

step 3: In the Date box, type **3** and press the <Enter> key.

step 4: Click on the "Quantity" column. Type **3** in the "Quantity" column. Press the <Enter> key.

step 5: In the "Item" column, select kitchen cabinets.

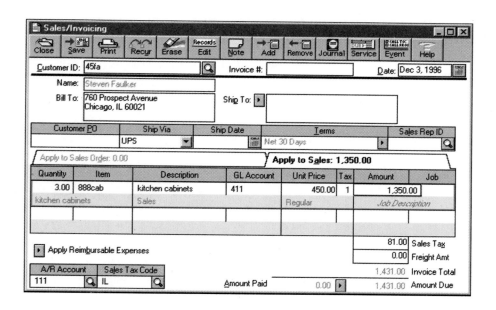

step 6: Click on the Print icon.

step 7: The "Print Forms: Invoices/Credit Memo" window pops up. Highlight "Invoice Plain Service."

step 8: Click on Ok.

step 9: The "Print Forms: Invoice Plain Service" window pops up. Click on Real.

step 10: The "About to Print Invoices" window pops up. In the First invoice number box, 2002 is shown.

step 11: Click on Ok. The sales invoice starts to print. Compare your printout with Figure 10.4 on page 294.

Figure 10.4

Invoice

Invoice Number:
2002

Invoice Date:
12/3/96

Page:
1

Voice:
Fax:

Sold To:
Steven Faulker
760 Prospect Avenue
Chicago, IL 60021

Customer ID:45fa

Customer PO	Payment Terms	Sales Rep ID	Due Date
	Net 30 Days		1/2/97

Description	Amount
kitchen cabinets	1,350.00

Check No:

Subtotal	1,350.00
Sales Tax	81.00
Total Invoice Amount	1,431.00
Payment Received	0.00
TOTAL	1,431.00

Recording Sales Returns and Allowances

objective 8
Use PAW to record sales returns

In Chapter 8, you learned about purchases returns and allowances. Now, we are ready to look at these transactions from the seller's point of view. To the seller, a return of merchandise from a customer is a sales return. An allowance granted by the seller to the customer for damaged but usable merchandise is a sales allowance. As in Chapter 8, we will focus our attention on returns since they are more common.

Whenever merchandise is returned on account, the seller must do two things:

- Record the sales return:
  Debit Sales Returns and Allowances for the **selling price.**
  If applicable, debit Sales Tax Payable for the related *sales tax.*
  Credit Accounts Receivable for the **selling price** (plus the *sales tax,* if it is a retail sales return).

- Update the Merchandise Inventory and Cost of Sales accounts:
    Debit Merchandise Inventory for the **cost** of the unit(s) returned.
    Credit Cost of Sales for the **cost** of the unit(s) returned.

When previously sold merchandise is returned, sales must be reduced. However, most businesses do not reduce the Sales account directly with a debit. Instead, most businesses record a **sales return** by debiting an account titled Sales Returns and Allowances. This account is known as a contra-revenue account or contra-sales account. On PAW's income statement, it is subtracted from sales in arriving at total revenues. Sales Returns and Allowances is a temporary account with a normal balance on the debit side.

Because sales returns have a negative impact on revenue, most businesses keep a careful watch over these types of transactions. The use of a minus sign in front of the invoice number alerts you to a sales return when examining the sales journal.

As noted earlier in Chapter 8, the seller prepares a credit memorandum to document each sales return. The word *credit* refers to the credit that reduces the customer's account receivable when this transaction is journalized. A copy of the credit memo is sent to the purchaser who uses it as a source document for the purchase return.

For some practice, let's use PAW to record the following sales return:

Dec. 4   Dubin Enterprises returned 10 of the hinges purchased on
          December 2 from TKT, Invoice No. 2001, $150. The cost of
          the returned hinges is $90.

In data entry sheet format, this sales return on account is recorded as follows:

DATA ENTRY SHEET TKT Products					
Date	Account ID	Reference	Trans Description	Debit Amt	Credit Amt
12/4/96	412		Sales Returns and Allowances	150.00	
	112		Merchandise Inventory	90.00	
	111		Accounts Receivable, Dubin Enterprises, Inv. No. 2001		150.00
	501		Cost of Sales		90.00

Referring to the data entry sheet, we are now ready to use PAW to journalize this transaction. Using the "Sales/Invoicing" window, we will record this sales return as a "negative" invoice by placing a minus sign before the invoice number (-2001) and the quantity (-10) as we enter the necessary information.

Follow these steps to journalize this sales return on account in the sales journal:

step 1: From the Tasks menu, click on Sales/Invoicing.

step 2: In the Customer ID box, select Dubin Enterprises.

step 3: Type **−2001** in the Invoice # box. (This is the invoice number with a minus sign in front of it.)

step 4: Type **4** in the Date box.

step 5: Type **−10** in the "Quantity" column. (This is the quantity with a minus sign in front of it.)

step 6: In the "Item" column, select hinges for cabinets.

step 7: Type **returned 10 hinges, Invoice No. 2001** in the "Description" column.

step 8: In the "GL Account" column, select Account No. 412, Sales Returns and Allowances.

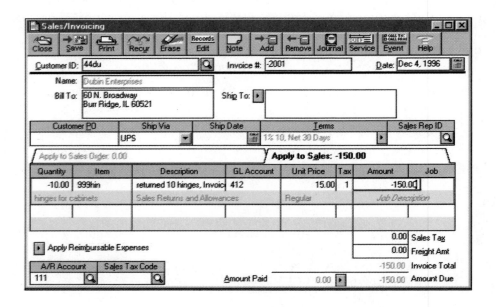

step 9: Click on the Save icon. By clicking on the Save icon, the "Sales/Invoicing" window is ready for the next transaction.

For additional practice, let's use PAW to record the following sales return from a retail customer:

Dec. 7 Steven Faulker, a retail customer, returns one of the kitchen cabinets purchased on December 3, Invoice No. 2002. The selling price of the cabinet was $450 plus 6 percent sales tax and the cost was $270.

In data entry sheet format, this retail sales return is recorded as follows:

		DATA ENTRY SHEET TKT Products			
Date	Account ID	Reference	Trans Description	Debit Amt	Credit Amt
12/7/96	412		Sales Returns and Allowances	450.00	
	213		Sales Tax Payable	27.00	
	112		Merchandise Inventory	270.00	
	111		Accounts Receivable, Steven Faulker, Inv. No. 2002		477.00
	501		Cost of Sales		270.00

Referring to the data entry sheet, we are now ready to use PAW to journalize this transaction. Using the "Sales/Invoicing" window, we will record this sales return as a "negative" invoice by placing a minus sign before the invoice number (−2002) and the quantity (−1). Then, in the "Item" column, select kitchen cabinets, type a description, and change the GL Account to 412 Sales Returns and Allowances. After completing the "Sales/Invoicing" window, compare your screen to the following:

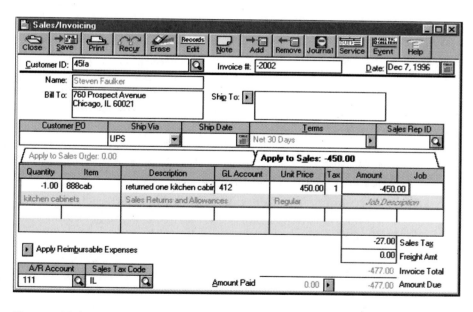

If your "Sales/Invoicing" window agrees with this one, click on the Save icon.

If your screen does *not* match it, make the necessary corrections, then click on the Save icon.

Additional TKT Products Transactions

Now you are ready to journalize the following additional TKT transactions for the month of December 1996. First, record the transactions on a data entry sheet, then use PAW to journalize them in the sales journal. If necessary, refer back to the appropriate steps given earlier in this chapter. As you journalize, you will notice a higher than normal number of returns. Again, this is meant to give you extra practice and does not reflect a normal pattern of sales and returns.

Since you will not be printing sales Invoice Numbers 2003 through 2007, they are not illustrated in this chapter. **Because you are not printing these invoices, you must click on the Save icon after each transaction.** Although the invoice number automatically advances when each invoice is saved, *the invoice number that PAW automatically generates may not be the correct number.* For example, positive Invoice No. 2003 would automatically be followed by positive Invoice No. 2004 and negative Invoice No. −2003 would automatically be followed by negative Invoice No. −2004. *Be sure to check the "Invoice #" box carefully and type in a corrected invoice number whenever necessary.*

Dec. 10 Sold 8 cabinet doors on account at $250 each to Adams Company; Invoice No. 2003; terms 1/10, n/30; $2,000. These cabinet doors cost $150 each, total cost $1,200. *Save Invoice No. 2003.*

   12 Adams Company returned 2 cabinet doors purchased on December 10, Invoice No. 2003, $500. The returned doors cost $300. *Save Invoice No. −2003.*

   14 Sold 5 tubes of wood glue on account at $8 each to Steven Faulker; Invoice No. 2004; terms net 30 days; $40 plus 6 percent sales tax. The tubes cost $4.80 each, total cost $24. *Save Invoice No. 2004.*

   15 Faulker returned 2 tubes of wood glue purchased on December 14, Invoice No. 2004, $16 plus sales tax. The returned tubes cost $9.60. *Save Invoice No. −2004.*

   18 Sold 20 kitchen cabinets on account at $450 each to Carson Corporation, Invoice No. 2005; terms 1/10, n/30; $9,000. The kitchen cabinets costs $270 each, total cost $5,400. *Save Invoice No. 2005.*

   21 Sold 2 cabinet doors on account at $250 each to Becker Brothers; Invoice No. 2006; terms 1/10, n/30; $500. The cabinet doors cost $150 each, total cost $300. *Save Invoice No. 2006.*

   23 Carson Corporation returned 4 kitchen cabinets purchased on December 18, Invoice No. 2005, $1,800. The returned cabinets cost $1,080. *Save Invoice No. −2005.*

   28 Sold 8 hinges for cabinets on account at $15 each to Steven Faulker; Invoice No. 2007; terms net 30 days; $120 plus 6 percent sales tax. The hinges cost $9 each, total cost $72. *Save Invoice No. 2007.*

Dec. 30   Faulker returned 2 hinges for cabinets purchased on December 28, Invoice No. 2007, $30 plus sales tax. The returned hinges cost $18. *Save Invoice No.* −*2007.*

Posting the Sales Journal

Follow these steps to post the sales journal:

objective 9
Post the sales journal

step 1:   From the main menu, select Tasks, System, then Post.

step 2:   Select the Sales Journal to post.

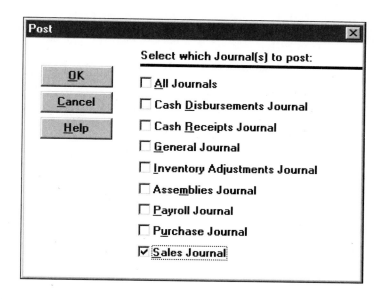

step 3:   Click on OK.

Printing the Sales Journal

Follow these steps to print the sales journal:

objective 10
Print the sales journal

step 1:   From the main menu, select Reports, then Accounts Receivable.

step 2:   In the Report List, highlight "Sales Journal." Then, make the selections to print.

Compare your sales journal with Figure 10.5 on pages 300–301. If you need to make any corrections, go back to the "Sales/Invoicing" window. Click on the Edit Records icon. The "Select Invoice" window displays. Click on the down arrow in the Status box. Select "Posted." The posted entries are listed on the screen. Make any needed corrections. *Save, post,* then *reprint* the sales journal. Again, compare your sales journal to Figure 10.5.

Figure 10.5

TKT Products
Sales Journal
For the Period From Dec 1, 1996 to Dec 31, 1996

Filter Criteria includes: Report order is by Invoice Date. Report is printed in Detail Format.

Date	Account ID	Invoice No	Line Description	Debit Amnt	Credit Amnt
12/2/96	411	2001	hinges for cabinets		1,050.00
	501		Cost of sales	630.00	
	112		Cost of sales		630.00
	111		Dubin Enterprises	1,050.00	
12/3/96	213	2002	IL: Illinois Sales Tax		81.00
	411		kitchen cabinets		1,350.00
	501		Cost of sales	810.00	
	112		Cost of sales		810.00
	111		Steven Faulker	1,431.00	
12/4/96	412	-2001	returned 10 hinges, Invoice No. 2001	150.00	
	501		Cost of sales		90.00
	112		Cost of sales	90.00	
	111		Dubin Enterprises		150.00
12/7/96	213	-2002	IL: Illinois Sales Tax	27.00	
	412		returned one kitchen cabinet, Invoice No. 2002	450.00	
	501		Cost of sales		270.00
	112		Cost of sales	270.00	
	111		Steven Faulker		477.00
12/10/96	411	2003	cabinet doors		2,000.00
	501		Cost of sales	1,200.00	
	112		Cost of sales		1,200.00
	111		Adams Company	2,000.00	
12/12/96	412	-2003	returned two cabinet doors, Invoice No. 2003	500.00	
	501		Cost of sales		300.00
	112		Cost of sales	300.00	
	111		Adams Company		500.00
12/14/96	213	2004	IL: Illinois Sales Tax		2.40
	411		wood glue		40.00
	501		Cost of sales	24.00	
	112		Cost of sales		24.00
	111		Steven Faulker	42.40	
12/15/96	213	-2004	IL: Illinois Sales Tax	0.96	
	412		returned two tubes of wood glue, Invoice No. 2004	16.00	
	501		Cost of sales		9.60
	112		Cost of sales	9.60	
	111		Steven Faulker		16.96
12/18/96	411	2005	kitchen cabinets		9,000.00
	501		Cost of sales	5,400.00	
	112		Cost of sales		5,400.00
	111		Carson Corporation	9,000.00	
12/21/96	411	2006	cabinet doors		500.00
	501		Cost of sales	300.00	
	112		Cost of sales		300.00
	111		Becker Brothers	500.00	

Figure 10.5 *(concluded)*

TKT Products
Sales Journal
For the Period From Dec 1, 1996 to Dec 31, 1996
Filter Criteria includes: Report order is by Invoice Date. Report is printed in Detail Format.

Date	Account ID	Invoice No	Line Description	Debit Amnt	Credit Amnt
12/23/96	412	-2005	returned four kitchen cabinets, Invoice No. 2005	1,800.00	
	501		Cost of sales		1,080.00
	112		Cost of sales	1,080.00	
	111		Carson Corporation		1,800.00
12/28/96	213	2007	IL: Illinois Sales Tax		7.20
	411		hinges for cabinets		120.00
	501		Cost of sales	72.00	
	112		Cost of sales		72.00
	111		Steven Faulker	127.20	
12/30/96	213	-2007	IL: Illinois Sales Tax	1.80	
	412		returned two hinges for cabinets, Invoice No. 2007	30.00	
	501		Cost of sales		18.00
	112		Cost of sales	18.00	
	111		Steven Faulker		31.80
		Total		**27,329.96**	**27,329.96**

Printing the Customer Ledger

Follow these steps to print the customer ledger:

step 1: From the main menu, select Reports, then Accounts Receivable.

step 2: Scroll down the Report List and highlight "Customer Ledgers." Then, make the selections to print. Compare your printout to Figure 10.6 on page 302.

objective 11
Print the customer ledger

Observe that the "Type" column in the customer ledger indicates that the posted information came from the sales journal, which is designated by SJ.

Figure 10.6

TKT Products
Customer Ledgers
For the Period From Dec 1, 1996 to Dec 31, 1996
Filter Criteria includes: Report order is by ID. Report is printed in Detail Format.

Customer ID Customer	Date	Trans No	Type	Debit Amt	Credit Amt	Balance
41ad Adams Company	12/10/96 12/12/96	2003 -2003	SJ SJ	2,000.00	500.00	2,000.00 1,500.00
42be Becker Brothers	12/21/96	2006	SJ	500.00		500.00
43ca Carson Corporation	12/18/96 12/23/96	2005 -2005	SJ SJ	9,000.00	1,800.00	9,000.00 7,200.00
44du Dubin Enterprises	12/2/96 12/4/96	2001 -2001	SJ SJ	1,050.00	150.00	1,050.00 900.00
45fa Steven Faulker	12/1/96 12/3/96 12/7/96 12/14/96 12/15/96 12/28/96 12/30/96	Balance Fwd 2002 -2002 2004 -2004 2007 -2007	SJ SJ SJ SJ SJ SJ	1,431.00 42.40 127.20	477.00 16.96 31.80	1,400.00 2,831.00 2,354.00 2,396.40 2,379.44 2,506.64 2,474.84

Backing Up Your Chapter 10 Data

objective 12
Back up your data

Be sure to back up your Chapter 10 data. You will need it when you begin Chapter 11. Follow these steps to back up your data:

step 1: Insert a blank formatted disk in drive A.

step 2: From PAW's main menu, select File, then Backup.

step 3: The "Destination" text box will display the last backup name that was typed. Type **a:\chap10.tkt** in the Destination text box.

step 4: Click on the Backup button. Your files begin to copy. When all the files have been saved to drive A, you are automatically returned to the main menu.

step 5: Click on File, Exit to exit PAW.

Chapter 10 Summary

The use of a trade discount allows the seller to change the selling price without reprinting the catalog. The actual selling price consists of the list price minus the trade discount. This discount does not appear in the accounts of the seller.

A customer ledger contains a separate account for each charge customer. The Accounts Receivable (control) account contains only summary information. The customer ledger provides the necessary detail.

TKT Products has chosen the first-in, first-out (FIFO) method to assign inventory costs. Under the FIFO method, the cost of the merchandise purchased first (first in) is assigned to the merchandise sold first (first out). The unsold units, or ending inventory, are assigned the last or remaining costs.

In PAW, all the information about a sale is recorded in a "Sales/Invoicing" window. Then, PAW takes the necessary information from the window and automatically journalizes the transaction in the sales journal. PAW also prepares sales invoices using information from the "Sales/Invoicing" window.

A wholesale business sells merchandise to another business. A retail business sells merchandise to the end user (final consumer). Many states and local municipalities levy a sales tax on retail sales. Once the seller has charged the customer for the sales tax, the tax becomes a liability (Sales Tax Payable) of the seller.

A return of merchandise from a customer is a sales return. Because sales returns have a negative impact on revenue, most businesses keep a careful watch over these types of transactions. The use of a Sales Returns and Allowances account, a contra account, makes it easier to monitor the volume of returns.

Demonstration Problem

Wong Imports sells a variety of products imported from Asia. It has both retail and wholesale customers. The state levies a 4 percent sales tax on retail sales. Wholesale credit terms are 2/10, n/30 and retail credit terms are net 30 days. Wong Imports completed the following selected transactions during May 1996:

May 1   Sold 6 oriental screens on account to Asian Accents, Invoice No. 342, $9,500. The screens cost $7,000.

       5   Sold 2 rosewood tables on account to Carol Lopez, Invoice No. 343, $900 plus sales tax. The tables cost $600.

       6   Asian Accents returned 2 oriental screens purchased on May 1, Invoice No. 342, $2,500. The returned screens cost $1,800.

       8   Sold 8 oriental fish bowls on account to Chang Gifts, Invoice No. 344, $800. The fish bowls cost $625.

     10   Carol Lopez returned one rosewood table purchased on May 5, Invoice No. 343, $450 plus sales tax. The table cost $300.

Instructions

1. Record these transactions on a data entry sheet. Leave the "Account ID" column blank.

2. How much is receivable from Asian Accents?

3. How much is receivable from Carol Lopez?

4. How much is receivable from Chang Gifts?

Solution to Demonstration Problem

1.

DATA ENTRY SHEET					
Wong Imports					
Date	Account ID	Reference	Trans Description	Debit Amt	Credit Amt
5/1/96			Accounts Receivable, Asian Accents, Inv. No. 342	9,500.00	
			Cost of Sales	7,000.00	
			Sales		9,500.00
			Merchandise Inventory		7,000.00
5/5/96			Accounts Receivable, Carol Lopez, Inv. No. 343	936.00	
			Cost of Sales	600.00	
			Sales		900.00
			Sales Tax Payable		36.00
			Merchandise Inventory		600.00
5/6/96			Sales Returns and Allowances	2,500.00	
			Merchandise Inventory	1,800.00	
			Accounts Receivable, Asian Accents, Inv. No. 342		2,500.00
			Cost of Sales		1,800.00
5/8/96			Accounts Receivable, Chang Gifts, Inv. No. 344	800.00	
			Cost of Sales	625.00	
			Sales		800.00
			Merchandise Inventory		625.00
5/10/96			Sales Returns and Allowances	450.00	
			Sales Tax Payable	18.00	
			Merchandise Inventory	300.00	
			Accounts Receivable, Carol Lopez, Inv. No. 343		468.00
			Cost of Sales		300.00

2. $7,000 ($9,500 − 2,500) is receivable from Asian Accents.

3. $468 ($936 − 468) is receivable from Carol Lopez.

4. $800 is receivable from Chang Gifts.

Glossary

contra-sales account　A debit-balance account that appears on the income statement as a subtraction from sales. Also referred to as a *contra-revenue account.* *295*

credit memorandum　A business document prepared by the seller containing information relevant to a sales return or allowance. The word *credit* refers to the credit that reduces the customer's account receivable.　*295*

customer ledger　A subsidiary ledger containing a separate account for each charge customer. This ledger supports or explains one general ledger account—the Accounts Receivable (control) account.　*283*

FIFO method　The cost of the merchandise purchased first (first in) is assigned to the merchandise sold first (first out). The ending inventory is assigned the last or remaining cost.　*285*

list price　A fixed price listed in a catalog. The list price minus a trade discount equals the selling price.　*282*

retail business　A business that sells merchandise to the end user (final customer).　*292*

sales allowance　A reduction in the price of previously sold merchandise. The seller "allows" for defective merchandise by reducing the price.　*294*

sales journal　A special journal used to record sales on account.　*288*

sales return　The return of previously sold merchandise to the seller.　*294*

sales tax　A tax on retail sales levied by a state or local municipality. It is paid by the retail customer but collected by the retail seller for the taxing authority. *292*

trade discount　A discount used by the seller to change the selling price of a product without having to reprint an entire catalog. The list price minus the trade discount equals the selling price.　*282*

wholesale business　A business that sells merchandise to another business. *292*

Self-Test

Select the best answer.

1. Sellers use trade discounts to
   a. change list prices without reprinting the catalog.
   b. change selling prices without reprinting the catalog.
   c. encourage charge customers to pay quickly.
   d. promote credit card sales.

2. The balance in the Accounts Receivable (control) account
   a. indicates the total amount receivable from all charge customers.
   b. should equal the total of the customer account balances in the customer ledger.
   c. is a summary figure.
   d. All of the above.

3. The entry to record a sale of merchandise on account requires a
   a. debit to the Accounts Receivable account.
   b. debit to the Cost of Sales account.
   c. credit to the Merchandise Inventory account.
   d. All of the above.

4. The entry to record a sales return requires a
    a. debit to the Sales account.
    b. debit to the Sales Returns and Allowances account.
    c. credit to the Sales Returns and Allowances account.
    d. None of the above.

5. The sales journal
    a. accommodates sales on account.
    b. accommodates sales returns on account.
    c. is a special journal.
    d. All of the above.

Answers to the self-test can be found after the cases at the end of this chapter.

Questions for Discussion

1. What is the difference between a wholesale business and a retail business?

2. How is a trade discount different from a cash discount?

3. What is the relationship between the Accounts Receivable (control) account and the customer ledger?

4. The sales journal accommodates what type(s) of transaction(s)?

5. Who levies, pays, and collects a sales tax?

6. What is the difference between a sales allowance and a sales return?

7. *a.* What is the normal balance (debit or credit) in the Sales Returns and Allowances account?
   b. Why is the Sales Returns and Allowances account referred to as a contra-sales account?

8. *a.* What is the purpose of the Cost of Sales account?
   b. Does it have a normal balance on the debit or credit side?
   c. Is it a temporary or permanent account?

9. Why is the Merchandise Inventory account credited every time a sale of merchandise is recorded?

Exercises

Exercise 10.1

Terminology
L.O. 1–11

Match the following terms with the definitions shown below:

1. Contra-sales account
2. Wholesale business
3. Credit memorandum
4. Trade discount
5. Customer ledger
6. Sales tax
7. List price
8. Sales return
9. Retail business
10. Sales journal

Definitions

a. A business that sells merchandise to another business.

b. A discount used by sellers to change the selling price of a product without having to reprint an entire catalog.

c. A tax on retail sales levied by a state or local municipality.

d. The return of previously sold merchandise to the seller.

e. A special journal used to record sales on account.

f. A business that sells merchandise to the final consumer.

g. A fixed price shown in a catalog.

h. A subsidiary ledger containing a separate account for each charge customer.

i. A business document prepared by the seller containing information relevant to a sales return or allowance.

j. A debit-balance account that is subtracted from sales to determine total revenue.

Exercise 10.2

Lane Products sells one unit of product RM-51 at a list price of $630 less a 10 percent trade discount.

Trade Discount
L.O. 1

a. Compute the trade discount.

b. What is the selling price?

Exercise 10.3

Gant Company uses the following journals:

Special Journals
L.O. 5, 7, 8

Sales journal

Purchases journal

Cash disbursements journal

General journal

Indicate in which journal each of the following transactions should be recorded:

1. Paid monthly rent.

2. Purchased supplies on account.

3. Sold merchandise on account.

4. Issued credit memo for merchandise returned by a charge customer.

5. Purchased merchandise on account.

6. Purchased merchandise for cash.

7. Received credit memo for merchandise returned on account to a vendor.

8. Paid creditor on account.

9. Recorded adjusting entry for expired insurance.

Exercise 10.4

Assuming the use of a customer ledger, record the following transactions on a data entry sheet:

Sale on Account; Return
L.O. 5, 8

Oct. 18 Sold merchandise on account to Bunny Corporation, Invoice No. 289, $500. The merchandise cost $410.

　　22 Bunny Corporation returned a portion of the merchandise purchased on October 18, Invoice No. 289, $140. The returned merchandise cost $105.

Exercise 10.5

Retail Sale; Return
L.O. 7, 8

Assuming the use of a customer ledger, record the following transactions on a data entry sheet:

June 17   Sold merchandise on account to William Johnson, Invoice No. 330, $230 plus 5 percent sales tax. The merchandise cost $225.

     20   William Johnson returned a portion of the merchandise purchased on June 17, Invoice No. 330, $175 plus sales tax. The returned merchandise cost $140.

Exercise 10.6

Customer Ledger
L.O. 2

Mendez Company's customer ledger appears as follows:

Mendez Company Customer Ledgers							
Filter Criteria includes: Report order is by ID.							
Vendor ID Vendor	Date	Trans No	Type	Paid	Debit Amt	Credit Amt	Balance
Archer Company	7/1/96 7/6/96	Balance Fwd.	SJ		145.00		270.00
Franzen Enterprises	7/1/96 7/18/96 7/20/96	Balance Fwd.	SJ SJ		220.00	105.00	740.00
Martino Corporation	7/1/96 7/2/96 7/15/96 7/20/96	Balance Fwd.	SJ SJ SJ		324.00 215.00	85.00	123.00
Trainor Company	7/1/96 7/8/96 7/14/96 7/15/96	Balance Fwd.	SJ SJ SJ		665.00 270.00	110.00	490.00

Instructions

a. Compute the balance for each customer's account.

b. The balance in the Accounts Receivable (control) account should be what amount?

Exercise 10.7

Entry from Invoice
L.O. 5

Using the following business document, record the transaction in data entry sheet format on the books of TKT Products:

```
TKT PRODUCTS                                    INVOICE NO. 765
2400 Main Street
Wheaton, IL 60187

Sold to:  Walton Company                 Date:   July 3, 1996
          3471 Avon Road
          Warren, Illinois 60169         Terms: Net 30 days
```

Quantity	Description	Unit Price	Total
5	WRJ-76 Cabinets	82.00	410.00
2	CMJ-76 Cabinets	57.00	114.00
			524.00

Exercise 10.8

Using the following business document, record the transaction in data entry sheet format on the books of TKT Products:

Entry from Credit Memo
L.O. 8

```
TKT PRODUCTS                          CREDIT MEMORANDUM NO. 62
2400 Main Street
Wheaton, IL 60187

Credit to:  Rose Corporation             Date:   March 12, 1996
            1550 Park Drive
            Glen Ellyn, Illinois 60137   Terms: Net 30 days
```

Your account is being credited as follows:		
1	#380 Hardware	$45.00

Problems—Set A

Problem 10.1A

Follow these steps to restore your ACS Products data from Chapter 9.

Restore Data
L.O. 4

step 1:   Start Windows, then PAW. Open ACS Products.

step 2:   Put your ACS Products backup disk in drive A.

step 3:   From the main menu, select File, then Restore.

step 4:   Type a:\acsdec.96a in the Source box. (Use the same file name that you used when you backed up in Chapter 9.)

step 5:   Click on the Restore button. Read the "Warning" screen, then click on OK. Restoring the files will take a few moments. When the files are restored, you are returned to the main menu.

step 6:   Remove disk from drive A.

step 7.   To be sure that your ACS Products data was properly restored, follow these steps to print the customer master file list:
   a. From the main menu, click on Reports, Accounts Receivable.
   b. Highlight the "Customer Master File List."
   c. Make the selections to print. Compare your printout to Figure 10.7 on page 310.

Figure 10.7

ACS Products
Customer Master File List

Filter Criteria includes: Report order is by ID.

Customer ID Customer	Address line 1 Address line 2 City ST ZIP	Contact Telephone 1 Telephone 2 Fax Number	Tax Code Resale No Terms Cust Since
55BU Burt Company	415 W. Gurley St. Chicago, IL 60021	Jan Underwood-Holmes 708-555-9212 708-555-9213	21-9871234 1% 10, Net 30 Days 7/6/96
66KR Kraus Corporation	7150 East Lincoln Drive Chicago, IL 60502	Richard Sims 708-555-9911 708-555-9912	21-9098097 1% 10, Net 30 Days 7/6/96
77SA Saxon Brothers	2344 North 44th Street Chicago, IL	Eula Saxon 708-555-3842 708-555-3491	21-9674320 1% 10, Net 30 Days 7/6/96
88WO Wong, Susan	742 Orchard Rd. Evanston, IL 60201	 708-555-3391 708-555-3916	IL Net 30 Days 7/6/96

Problem 10.2A

Data Entry Sheet
L.O. 5, 7, 8

ACS Products completed the following transactions during December 1996. A 6 percent sales tax is levied on retail sales.

Dec. 3   Sold 175 boxes of window cleaner on account to Burt Company; Invoice No. 3001; terms 1/10, n/30; $7,516.25. The cleaner cost $2,934.75.

     5   Burt Company returned 5 boxes of window cleaner purchased on December 3, Invoice No. 3001, $214.75. The returned window cleaner cost $83.85.

     8   Sold 50 packages of dust cloths on account to Kraus Corporation; Invoice No. 3002; terms 1/10, n/30; $647.50. The dust cloths cost $388.50.

     9   Sold 3 mop refills on account to Susan Wong; Invoice No. 3003; terms net 30 days; $65.85 plus sales tax. The refills cost $39.51.

   11   Sold 90 boxes of window cleaner on account to Saxon Brothers; Invoice No. 3004; terms 1/10, n/30; $3,865.50. The cleaner cost $1,509.30.

   15   Susan Wong returned 1 mop refill purchased on December 9, Invoice No. 3003; $21.95 plus sales tax. The returned mop refill cost $13.17.

   20   Sold 180 packages of dust cloths on account to Kraus Corporation; Invoice No. 3005; terms 1/10, n/30; $2,331.00. The dust cloths cost $1,398.60.

   22   Saxon Brothers returned 8 boxes of window cleaner purchased on December 11, Invoice No. 3004; $343.60. The returned cleaner cost $134.16.

   26   Sold 2 packages of dust cloths on account to Susan Wong; Invoice No. 3006; terms net 30 days; $25.90 plus sales tax. The dust cloths cost $15.54.

28   Sold 150 mop refills on account to Burt Company; Invoice No. 3007; terms 1/10, n/30; $3,292.50. The mop refills cost $1,975.50.

29   Susan Wong returned 1 package of dust cloths purchased on December 26, Invoice No. 3006, $12.95 plus sales tax. The returned dust cloths cost $7.77.

Instructions

Record these transactions on a data entry sheet.

Problem 10.3A

Referring to your data entry sheet from Problem 10.2A, use PAW to journalize the transactions in the sales journal. (Hint: Use the "Sales/Invoicing" window.) Print each sales invoice (Invoice Nos. 3001 through 3007). Do *not* print the negative sales invoices (sales returns).

Sales on Account; Sales Returns; Sales Invoices
L.O. 5–8

Problem 10.4A

After recording the ACS Products' transactions in the "Sales/Invoicing" window, you are ready to post the sales journal. Follow these steps:

Post the Sales Journal
L.O. 9

step 1:   From the main menu, select Ta*s*ks, S*y*stem, then *P*ost.

step 2:   Select the *S*ales Journal to post.

step 3:   Click on *O*K.

Problem 10.5A

Follow these steps to print the sales journal and customer ledger:

Print Sales Journal and Customer Ledger
L.O. 10, 11

step 1:   From the main menu, select *R*eports, then Accounts *R*eceivable.

step 2:   In the Report List, highlight "Sales Journal." Make the selections to print.

step 3:   Scroll down the Report List and highlight "Customer Ledgers." Make the selections to print.

step 4:   Close the "Select a Report" window.

Problem 10.6A

Your ACS Products data **must** be backed up. You will restore it in Chapter 11. Follow these steps:

Back Up
L.O. 12

step 1:   Insert a blank formatted disk in drive A.

step 2:   From PAW's main menu, select *F*ile, then *B*ackup.

step 3:   Type a:\acsdec.10a in the *D*estination text box.

step 4:   Click on the *B*ackup button. Your files begin to copy. When all the files have been saved to drive A, you are automatically returned to the main menu.

step 5:   Click on *F*ile, E*x*it to exit PAW.

Problems—Set B

Problem 10.1B

Restore Data
L.O. 4

Follow these steps to restore your LLS Products data from Chapter 9:

step 1:   Start Windows, then PAW. Open LLS Products.

step 2:   Put your LLS Products backup disk in drive A.

step 3:   From the main menu, select File, then Restore.

step 4:   Type **a:\llsdec.96b** in the Source box. (Use the same file name that you used when you backed up in Chapter 9.)

step 5:   Click on the Restore button. Read the "Warning" screen, then click on OK. Restoring the files will take a few moments. When the files are restored, you are returned to the main menu.

step 6:   Remove disk from drive A.

step 7:   To be sure that your LLS Products data was properly restored, follow these steps to print the customer master file list:
   a. From the main menu, click on Reports, Accounts Receivable.
   b. Highlight the "Customer Master File List."
   c. Make the selections to print. Compare your printout to Figure 10.8.

Figure 10.8

LLS Products
Customer Master File List

Filter Criteria includes: Report order is by ID.

Customer ID Customer	Address line 1 Address line 2 City ST ZIP	Contact Telephone 1 Telephone 2 Fax Number	Tax Code Resale No Terms Cust Since
05BU Budd Industries	799 Overland Avenue Wheaton, IL 60501	Budd Kurtz 708-555-1136 708-555-3012	21-9001572 2% 10, Net 30 Days 7/6/96
06KR Krim Products	4410 N. 40th Street Chicago, IL 60111	Michael O'Neil 708-555-9526 708-555-9804	21-8790138 2% 10, Net 30 Days 7/6/96
07RI Ritz Corporation	3160 Canyon Drive Chicago, IL 60212	Dana Held 708-555-1208 708-55-1209	21-4560912 2% 10, Net 30 Days 7/6/96
08SA Salley, John	1710 Walnut Street Matteson, IL 60443	 708-555-7808 708-555-8701	IL Net 30 Days 7/6/96

Problem 10.2B

Data Entry Sheet
L.O. 5, 7, 8

LLS Products completed the following transactions during December 1996. A 6 percent sales tax is levied on retail sales.

Dec. 4   Sold 160 compost buckets on account to Krim Products; Invoice No. 4001; terms 2/10, n/30; $3,200.00. The buckets cost $1,920.00

5   Sold 140 planters on account to Budd Industries; Invoice No. 4002; terms 2/10, n/30; $2,233.00. The planters cost $1,339.80.

8   Krim Products returned 15 compost buckets purchased on December 4, Invoice No. 4001, $300.00. The returned buckets cost $180.00.

11   Sold 6 topiary forms on account to John Salley; Invoice No. 4003; terms net 30 days; $119.70 plus sales tax. The forms cost $71.82.

12   Budd Industries returned 12 planters purchased on December 5, Invoice No. 4002, $191.40. The returned planters cost $114.84.

14   Sold 70 planters on account to Ritz Corporation; Invoice No. 4004; terms 2/10, n/30; $1,116.50. The planters cost $669.90.

16   John Salley returned 1 topiary form purchased on December 11, Invoice No. 4003, $19.95 plus sales tax. The returned form cost $11.97.

20   Sold 30 compost buckets on account to Krim Products; Invoice No. 4005; terms 2/10, n/30; $600.00. The buckets cost $360.00.

24   Sold 4 planters on account to John Salley; Invoice No. 4006; terms net 30 days; $63.80 plus sales tax. The planters cost $38.28.

28   John Salley returned 2 planters purchased on December 24, Invoice No. 4006, $31.90 plus sales tax. The returned planters cost $19.14.

Instructions

Record these transactions on a data entry sheet.

Problem 10.3B

Referring to your data entry sheet from Problem 10.2B, use PAW to journalize the transactions in the sales journal. (Hint: Use the "Sales/Invoicing" window.) Print each sales invoice (Invoice Nos. 4001 through 4006). Do *not* print the negative sales invoices (sales returns).

Sales on Account; Sales Returns; Sales Invoices
L.O. 5–8

Problem 10.4B

After recording the LLS Products' transactions in the "Sales/Invoicing" window, you are ready to post the sales journal. Follow these steps:

Post the Sales Journal
L.O. 9

step 1:   From the main menu, select Ta<u>s</u>ks, S<u>y</u>stem, then <u>P</u>ost.

step 2:   Select the <u>S</u>ales Journal to post.

step 3:   Click on <u>O</u>K.

Problem 10.5B

Follow these steps to print the sales journal and customer ledger:

Print Sales Journal and Customer Ledger
L.O. 10, 11

step 1:   From the main menu, select <u>R</u>eports, then Accounts <u>R</u>eceivable.

step 2:   In the Report List, highlight "Sales Journal." Make the selections to print.

step 3:   Scroll down the Report List and highlight "Customer Ledgers." Make the selections to print.

step 4:   Close the "Select a Report" window.

Problem 10.6B

Back Up
L.O. 12

Your LLS Products data **must** be backed up. You will restore it in Chapter 11. Follow these steps:

step 1: Insert a blank formatted disk in drive A.

step 2: From PAW's main menu, select File, then Backup.

step 3: Type a:\llsdec.10b in the Destination text box.

step 4: Click on the Backup button. Your files begin to copy. When all the files have been saved to drive A, you are automatically returned to the main menu.

step 5: Click on File, Exit to exit PAW.

Mini-Cases

Case 10–1

Your friend, Max Garfield, wants to have a catalog printed but he is concerned about the cost of printing and distribution every time he wants to change the selling price of an item. He asks if you have any suggestions.

Case 10–2

Pam Fortino, your new client, has always recorded sales returns by debiting the Sales account. How can you convince her that recording returns in a Sales Returns and Allowances account would be more helpful?

Case 10–3

You neighbor, Matthew Hoffman, owns his own business. Although he uses PAW, he records all sales transactions in the general journal and has his assistant type the invoices. Is there a better way to handle sales transactions?

A Case of Ethics

Sharon owns a wholesale business in a state that levies a sales tax on retail sales. Although she knows that some of her customers are retail customers, Sharon does not turn these customers away, nor does she charge them sales tax. She instructs employees not to ask any questions. "Sales are sales," says Sharon. "Why should I risk losing revenue so that the state can increase its revenues!" Comment.

Answers to Self-Test

1. *b*   2. *d*   3. *d*   4. *b*   5. *d*

Merchandising Business

Cash Receipts

LEARNING OBJECTIVES

After studying this chapter, you should be able to:

1. Compute sales discounts.

2. Restore data from the previous chapter.

3. Describe the Receipts Tasks.

4. Use PAW to record cash sales.

5. Use PAW to record receipts on account.

6. Post the cash receipts journal.

7. Print the cash receipts journal.

8. Print the customer ledger.

9. Back up your data.

In Chapter 10, you learned how to use PAW to record sales on account in a sales journal. In this chapter, you will learn to use PAW to record cash receipts in a cash receipts journal. But first, we will review cash discounts from the seller's point of view.

Sales Discounts

objective 1
Compute sales discounts

To encourage charge customers to pay quickly, a seller may offer the purchaser a cash discount. This is an amount that a customer may deduct from a bill if it is paid within a specified time known as the *discount period.* For example, credit terms of 1/15, n/30 indicate that a 1 percent discount may be deducted if the invoice is paid within 15 days of the invoice date or the full amount is due 30 days from the invoice date.

In Chapters 8 and 9, we focused on the purchaser's point of view. To the purchaser, the cash discount is a purchases discount. To the seller, the cash discount is a **sales discount.** In this chapter, we are going to concentrate on accounting for the seller. A lot of this discussion should sound familiar since we are looking at "the opposite side of the coin."

To demonstrate a sales discount, let's assume that on December 1, 1996, TKT Products sold 10 cabinet doors on account to Becker Brothers, Invoice No. 1998, terms 1/10, n/30, $2,500. The doors cost $1,500. In data entry sheet format, this transaction is recorded as follows:

DATA ENTRY SHEET TKT Products					
Date	Account ID	Reference	Trans Description	Debit Amt	Credit Amt
12/1/96	111		Accounts Receivable, Becker Brothers, Inv. No. 1998	2,500.00	
	501		Cost of Sales	1,500.00	
	411		Sales		2,500.00
	112		Merchandise Inventory		1,500.00

Observe that the account receivable and sale were recorded at $2,500 even though TKT has offered Becker a sales discount. Since TKT has no way of knowing whether Becker will take advantage of the discount, it will not be recorded until the cash is received.

Now, let's assume that on December 11, the last day of the discount period, TKT receives a check from Becker for the amount due on Invoice No. 1998. When recording this type of transaction, PAW automatically does the necessary arithmetic but it is still important for us to understand the process. With that in mind, let's review the following computations:

a. $2,500.00   Merchandise
        ×.01
      $ 25.00   Sales discount

b. $2,500.00   Accounts receivable
      −25.00   Less sales discount
     $2,475.00   Cash received

In data entry sheet format, this cash receipt is recorded as follows:

DATA ENTRY SHEET TKT Products					
Date	Account ID	Reference	Trans Description	Debit Amt	Credit Amt
12/11/96	110		Cash	2,475.00	
	413		Sales Discount	25.00	
	111		Accounts Receivable, Becker Brothers, Inv. No. 1998		2,500.00

You probably observed a new account was used in recording this transaction. The **Sales Discount** account is another example of a contra-sales or contra-revenue account. It is a temporary account with a normal balance on the debit side.

Comment

If an invoice includes the cost of merchandise plus transportation charges, the discount can be applied only to the cost of the merchandise. For example, if an invoice showed merchandise costing $500 plus transportation charges of $75, the discount could only be taken on the $500 cost of the merchandise. *Sales discounts do not apply to transportation charges.*

In this textbook, TKT's transportation terms are FOB shipping point, so the customer pays the carrier directly for transportation charges.

Now, we are ready to use PAW to record receipts of cash.

Restoring Data from Chapter 10

Your TKT Products data from Chapter 10 must be restored before you can use PAW to record cash receipts. Follow these steps to restore your data.

objective 2
Restore data from previous chapter

step 1:   Start Windows, then PAW. Open TKT Products.

step 2:   Place your Chapter 10 backup disk in drive A.

step 3:   From the main menu, select File, then Restore.

step 4:   Type a:\chap10.tkt in the "Source" box. (Use the same file name that you used when you backed up TKT in Chapter 10.)

step 5: Click on the Restore button. Read the "Warning" screen, then click on OK. When the files are restored, you are returned to the main menu.

step 6: Remove disk from drive A.

step 7: To be sure that your TKT data was restored properly, follow these steps to print TKT's customer master file list:
   a. From the main menu, click on Reports, Accounts Receivable.
   b. Scroll down the "Report List," then highlight "Customer Ledgers."
   c. Make the selections to print. Compare your printout with Figure 11.1.

Figure 11.1

TKT Products
Customer Ledgers
For the Period From Dec 1, 1996 to Dec 31, 1996
Filter Criteria includes: Report order is by ID. Report is printed in Detail Format.

Customer ID Customer	Date	Trans No	Type	Debit Amt	Credit Amt	Balance
41ad Adams Company	12/10/96	2003	SJ	2,000.00		2,000.00
	12/12/96	-2003	SJ		500.00	1,500.00
42be Becker Brothers	12/21/96	2006	SJ	500.00		500.00
43ca Carson Corporation	12/18/96	2005	SJ	9,000.00		9,000.00
	12/23/96	-2005	SJ		1,800.00	7,200.00
44du Dubin Enterprises	12/2/96	2001	SJ	1,050.00		1,050.00
	12/4/96	-2001	SJ		150.00	900.00
45fa Steven Faulker	12/1/96	Balance Fwd				1,400.00
	12/3/96	2002	SJ	1,431.00		2,831.00
	12/7/96	-2002	SJ		477.00	2,354.00
	12/14/96	2004	SJ	42.40		2,396.40
	12/15/96	-2004	SJ		16.96	2,379.44
	12/28/96	2007	SJ	127.20		2,506.64
	12/30/96	-2007	SJ		31.80	2,474.84

The Receipts Task

objective 3
Describe the Receipts Task

In PAW, the "Receipts" window is used to record inflows of cash from various sources. After all relevant information is recorded in the window, PAW automatically journalizes the entry in the cash receipts journal. All receipts of cash are recorded in the **cash receipts journal.** It is another example of a special journal. We will print out TKT Products' cash receipts journal later in this chapter. For now, let's focus on recording cash sales and receipts of cash on account.

Comment

At this point, you have been introduced to four special journals:

1. Purchase journal
2. Sales journal
3. Cash disbursements journal
4. Cash receipts journal

It is important to note that any transaction that does *not* fit into a special journal is recorded in the general journal. For example, adjusting entries do *not* fit into a special journal and are, therefore, recorded in the general journal.

Recording Cash Sales

TKT Products sometimes sells merchandise for cash. These are usually sales to retail customers. Because cash sales involve the receipt of cash, they are recorded in the cash receipts journal through the "Receipts" window. They are not recorded in the sales journal because they are not sales on account.

objective 4
Use PAW to record cash sales

To demonstrate, let's assume that on December 2 TKT sells 4 hinges for cash, Invoice No. 2000, $60 plus 6 percent sales tax. The cost of the hinges was $36.00. In data entry sheet format, this transaction is recorded as follows:

			DATA ENTRY SHEET TKT Products		
Date	Account ID	Reference	Trans Description	Debit Amt	Credit Amt
12/2/96	110		Cash	63.60	
	501		Cost of Sales	36.00	
	411		Sales		60.00
	213		Sales Tax Payable		3.60
	112		Merchandise Inventory		36.00

PAW automatically records this entry in the cash receipts journal based on the information you enter in the "Receipts" window.

Follow these steps to journalize this cash sale in the cash receipts journal:

step 1: From the Tasks menu, click on Receipts.

step 2: The "Select a Cash Account" window displays. Accept the default for "Cash" by clicking on Ok.

step 3: The "Deposit ticket ID" is highlighted. If not, click on the "Deposit ticket ID" box to highlight it. Type **12/2/96** in the "Deposit ticket ID" box. The transaction date is always entered in this box. Press the <Enter> key two times.

step 4: Type **Cash** in the "Name" box. Press <Enter>.

step 5: Type **Inv. 2000** in the "Reference" box. Press <Enter>.

step 6: Type **2** in the Date box. Press <Enter>.

step 7: Verify that "Cash" is displayed in the "Payment Method" box and that Account No. 110, Cash, is displayed in the "G/L Account" lookup box.

step 8: Make sure that the "Apply to Revenues" folder tab is selected. (PAW assumes you are going to apply the receipt to revenue, Sales Account No. 411, unless you select a customer with open invoices.)

step 9: Type **4** in the "Quantity" column. Press <Enter>.

step 10: Select "hinges for cabinets" as the inventory item.

step 11: Scroll down the screen or click on the "enlarge" window button.

step 12: Click on the magnifying glass icon in the "Sales Tax Code" lookup box (lower right of "Receipts" window). Select "Illinois Sales Tax." (Notice that $3.60 is automatically calculated in the Sales Ta<u>x</u> box.)

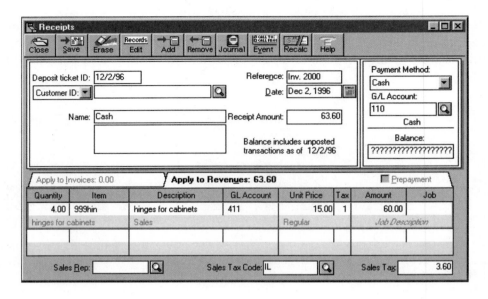

step 13: Click on the "<u>S</u>ave" icon. The "Receipts" window is ready for another transaction.

Recording Receipts on Account

objective 5
Use PAW to record receipts on account

In Chapter 10, you learned to use PAW to record sales on account. Through the Sales/Invoicing Task, PAW took the information from the "Sales/Invoicing" window and automatically journalized the transaction in the sales journal. In recording the sale, you specified the customer's name, invoice number, inventory item, and the description and price of the item being sold. PAW uses this information when cash is received from customers.

The following flowchart shows how the Sales/Invoicing Task and the Receipts Task work together in PAW.

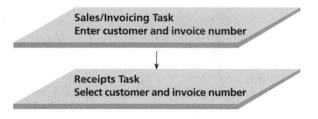

To demonstrate, let's return to TKT Products. As you will recall from Chapter 10, on December 2, TKT sold 70 hinges on account to Dubin Enterprises, Invoice No. 2001, terms 1/10, n/30, $1,050. Then, on December 4, Dubin returned 10 of the hinges, $150. Now, on December 7, TKT receives a check for $891 from Dubin Enterprises in full payment of Invoice No. 2001 less the sales discount.

Follow these steps to journalize this receipt of cash in the cash receipts journal:

step 1: If your "Receipts" window is not displayed, from the main menu select Tas<u>k</u>s, then <u>R</u>eceipts.

step 2: Highlight the "Deposit ticket ID" box. Type **12/7/96** in the "Deposit ticket ID" box. Remember to type the same date in the "Deposit ticket ID" box as the date of the transaction. Press <Enter>.

step 3: In the Customer ID lookup box, select Dubin Enterprises.

step 4: Type **Inv. 2001** in the Refer<u>e</u>nce box. Press <Enter>.

step 5: Type **7** in the <u>D</u>ate box. Press <Enter>.

step 6: In the "Payment Method" box, select "Check."

step 7: At the bottom of the window, the Apply to <u>I</u>nvoices folder tab is selected. Click on the pay box for Invoice No. −2001. Then click on the pay box for Invoice No. 2001. ***Please note that you must click on the negative invoice first.***

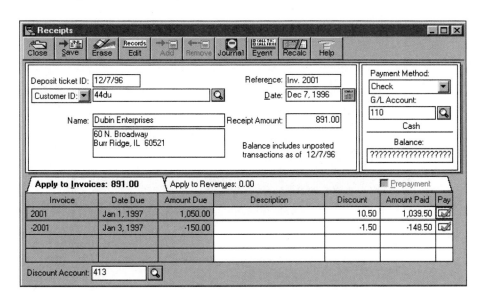

step 8: Click on the <u>S</u>ave icon to save this receipt. The "Receipts" window is ready for another transaction.

Additional TKT Products Transactions

Now you are ready to journalize the following additional TKT cash receipt transactions. Most of these transactions relate to TKT's December sales on account from Chapter 10. As you will recall, TKT's credit terms are 1/10, n/30 for wholesale customers and net 30 days for retail customers. As necessary, refer back to the appropriate steps given earlier in this chapter. **Be sure to save after journalizing each transaction.**

12/15/96	Received a check from Steven Faulker in payment of Invoice No. 1999; terms net 30 days; $1,400. (This check pays a November invoice that is shown as the December 1 balance forward in the customer ledger.)
12/20/96	Received a check from Adams Company in payment of Invoice No. 2003; dated 12/10/96; terms 1/10, n/30; less return on 12/12/96, $1,485.00.
12/21/96	Received a check from Steven Faulker in payment of Invoice No. 2002; dated 12/3/96; terms net 30 days; less return on 12/7/96, $954.00.
12/26/96	Received a check from Becker Brothers in payment of Invoice No. 2006; dated 12/21/96; terms 1/10, n/30; $495.00.
12/27/96	Received a check from Steven Faulker in payment of Invoice No. 2004; dated 12/14/96; terms net 30 days; less return on 12/15/96, $25.44. (Hint: Scroll down the "Apply to Invoices" table.)
12/28/96	Received a check from Carson Corporation in payment of Invoice No. 2005; dated 12/18/96; terms 1/10, n/30; less return on 12/23/96, $7,128.00.
12/29/96	Sold 2 tubes of wood glue for cash, Invoice No. 2008, $16.00 *plus sales tax.* The tubes cost $9.60. (Hint: Change the "Payment Method" to Cash.)
12/30/96	Sold 6 hinges for cash, Invoice No. 2009, $90.00 *plus sales tax.* The hinges cost $54.00.

objective 6
Post the cash receipts journal

Posting the Cash Receipts Journal

Follow these steps to post the cash receipts journal:

step 1: From the main menu, select Tas_k_s.

step 2: Select Sys_t_em, then _P_ost.

step 3: Select Cash _R_eceipts Journal.

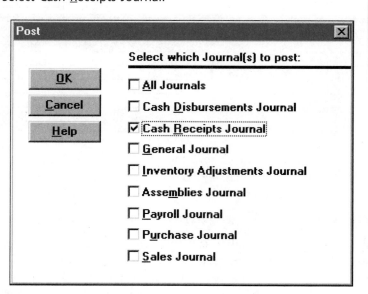

step 4: Click on _O_K.

Printing the Cash Receipts Journal

Follow these steps to print the cash receipts journal:

objective 7
Print the cash receipts journal

step 1: From the Reports menu, select Accounts Receivable.

step 2: Highlight "Cash Receipts Journal."

step 3: Make the selections to print.

Compare your printout to Figure 11.2 on page 324. If you need to make any corrections, go back to the "Receipts" window. Click on the "Edit Records" icon. The "Select Receipt" window displays. Click on the down arrow in the Status box. Select "Posted." The posted entries are listed on the screen. Make any needed corrections. *Save, post,* then *reprint* the cash receipts journal. Again, compare your cash receipts journal to Figure 11.2.

Figure 11.2

			TKT Products		
			Cash Receipts Journal		
			For the Period From Dec 1, 1996 to Dec 31, 1996		
			Filter Criteria includes: Report order is by Check Date. Report is printed in Detail Format.		

Date	Account ID	Transaction Ref	Line Description	Debit Amnt	Credit Amnt
12/2/96	213	Inv. 2000	IL: Illinois Sales Tax		3.60
	411		hinges for cabinets		60.00
	501		Cost of sales	36.00	
	112		Cost of sales		36.00
	110		Cash	63.60	
12/7/96	413	Inv. 2001	Discounts Taken	9.00	
	111		Invoice: 2001		1,050.00
	111		Invoice: -2001	150.00	
	110		Dubin Enterprises	891.00	
12/15/96	111	Inv. 1999	Invoice: 1999		1,400.00
	110		Steven Faulker	1,400.00	
12/20/96	413	Inv. 2003	Discounts Taken	15.00	
	111		Invoice: 2003		2,000.00
	111		Invoice: -2003	500.00	
	110		Adams Company	1,485.00	
12/21/96	111	Inv. 2002	Invoice: 2002		1,431.00
	111		Invoice: -2002	477.00	
	110		Steven Faulker	954.00	
12/26/96	413	Inv. 2006	Discounts Taken	5.00	
	111		Invoice: 2006		500.00
	110		Becker Brothers	495.00	
12/27/96	111	Inv. 2004	Invoice: 2004		42.40
	111		Invoice: -2004	16.96	
	110		Steven Faulker	25.44	
12/28/96	413	Inv. 2005	Discounts Taken	72.00	
	111		Invoice: 2005		9,000.00
	111		Invoice: -2005	1,800.00	
	110		Carson Corporation	7,128.00	
12/29/96	213	Inv. 2008	IL: Illinois Sales Tax		0.96
	411		wood glue		16.00
	501		Cost of sales	9.60	
	112		Cost of sales		9.60
	110		Cash	16.96	
12/30/96	213	Inv. 2009	IL: Illinois Sales Tax		5.40
	411		hinges for cabinets		90.00
	501		Cost of sales	54.00	
	112		Cost of sales		54.00
	110		Cash	95.40	
				15,698.96	15,698.96

Printing the Customer Ledger

objective 8
Print the customer ledger

As you will recall from Chapter 10, TKT Products has a customer ledger. PAW automatically updates the appropriate customer's account whenever a debit or credit to the Accounts Receivable account is journalized. Because most of the cash receipt transactions journalized in this chapter involved changes in Accounts Receivable, the customer balances have changed.

Follow these steps to print an up-to-date copy of the customer ledger.

step 1:   From the main menu, select Reports, then Accounts Receivable.

step 2:   Highlight "Customer Ledgers,"and then make the selections to print.

Compare your printout with Figure 11.3. Observe that the "Type" column in the customer ledger indicates that the posted information came from the sales journal (SJ) and the cash receipts journal (CRJ).

Figure 11.3

TKT Products
Customer Ledgers
For the Period From Dec 1, 1996 to Dec 31, 1996
Filter Criteria includes: Report order is by ID. Report is printed in Detail Format.

Customer ID Customer	Date	Trans No	Type	Debit Amt	Credit Amt	Balance
41ad	12/10/96	2003	SJ	2,000.00		2,000.00
Adams Company	12/12/96	-2003	SJ		500.00	1,500.00
	12/20/96	Inv. 2003	CRJ	15.00	15.00	1,500.00
	12/20/96	Inv. 2003	CRJ		1,500.00	0.00
42be	12/21/96	2006	SJ	500.00		500.00
Becker Brothers	12/26/96	Inv. 2006	CRJ	5.00	5.00	500.00
	12/26/96	Inv. 2006	CRJ		500.00	0.00
43ca	12/18/96	2005	SJ	9,000.00		9,000.00
Carson Corporation	12/23/96	-2005	SJ		1,800.00	7,200.00
	12/28/96	Inv. 2005	CRJ	72.00	72.00	7,200.00
	12/28/96	Inv. 2005	CRJ		7,200.00	0.00
44du	12/2/96	2001	SJ	1,050.00		1,050.00
Dubin Enterprises	12/4/96	-2001	SJ		150.00	900.00
	12/7/96	Inv. 2001	CRJ	9.00	9.00	900.00
	12/7/96	Inv. 2001	CRJ		900.00	0.00
45fa	12/1/96	Balance Fwd				1,400.00
Steven Faulker	12/3/96	2002	SJ	1,431.00		2,831.00
	12/7/96	-2002	SJ		477.00	2,354.00
	12/14/96	2004	SJ	42.40		2,396.40
	12/15/96	-2004	SJ		16.96	2,379.44
	12/15/96	Inv. 1999	CRJ		1,400.00	979.44
	12/21/96	Inv. 2002	CRJ		954.00	25.44
	12/27/96	Inv. 2004	CRJ		25.44	0.00
	12/28/96	2007	SJ	127.20		127.20
	12/30/96	-2007	SJ		31.80	95.40

Backing Up Your Chapter 11 Data

As noted previously, it is crucial to back up your TKT Products data. You will need it when you begin Chapter 12. Follow these steps to back up your data:

objective 9
Back up your data

step 1:   Insert a blank formatted disk in drive A.

step 2:   From PAW's main menu, select File, then Backup.

step 3:   The "Destination" text box will display the last backup name that was typed. Type **a:\chap11.tkt** in the Destination text box.

step 4:   Click on the Backup button. Your files begin to copy. When all the files have been saved to drive A, you are automatically returned to the main menu.

step 5:   Click on File, Exit to exit PAW.

Chapter 11 Summary

To encourage charge customers to pay quickly, a seller may offer the purchaser a cash discount. This is an amount that a customer may deduct from a bill if it is paid within a specified time known as the discount period. To the seller, the cash discount is a sales discount.

In PAW, the Receipts Task is used to record receipts of cash. When the customer's name and invoice number are recorded in the "Receipts" window, PAW is able to access the information previously recorded through the Sales/Invoicing Task and automatically journalize the receipt in the cash receipts journal. All receipts of cash are recorded in the cash receipts journal. It is another example of a special journal that can be viewed on our screen or printed out.

Whenever debits or credits to the Accounts Receivable account are journalized, PAW automatically updates the appropriate customer's account in the customer ledger.

Demonstration Problem

Avalos Company completed the following selected transactions during July 1996:

July 1 Sold merchandise for cash, Invoice No. 1735, $300 plus 4 percent sales tax. The merchandise cost $240.

2 Received a check from Bartel Company in payment of Invoice No. 1738, $450 less a 2 percent sales discount.

8 Received a check from Carolla Corporation in payment of Invoice No. 1742, $900 less a 2 percent sales discount.

12 Received a check from Gardner Associates in payment of Invoice No. 1743, $1,400 less a 1 percent sales discount.

16 Received a check from Avanti Enterprises in payment of Invoice No. 1746, $250.

19 Sold merchandise for cash, Invoice No. 1748, $560 plus 4 percent sales tax. The merchandise cost $490.

21 Received a check from Karrol Products in payment of Invoice No. 1747, $870 less a 1 percent sales discount.

28 Received a check from Mantel Company in payment of Invoice No. 1749, $725.

Instructions

Record these transactions on a data entry sheet. Leave the "Account ID" column blank.

Solution to Demonstration Problem

			DATA ENTRY SHEET Avalos Company		
Date	**Account ID**	**Reference**	**Trans Description**	**Debit Amt**	**Credit Amt**
7/1/96			Cash	312.00	
			Cost of Sales	240.00	
			Sales		300.00
			Sales Tax Payable		12.00
			Merchandise Inventory		240.00
7/2/96			Cash	441.00	
			Sales Discount	9.00	
			Accounts Receivable, Bartel Co., Inv. No. 1738		450.00
7/8/96			Cash	882.00	
			Sales Discount	18.00	
			Accounts Receivable, Carolla Corp., Inv. No. 1742		900.00
7/12/96			Cash	1,386.00	
			Sales Discount	14.00	
			Accounts Receivable, Gardner Assoc., Inv. No. 1743		1,400.00
7/16/96			Cash	250.00	
			Accounts Receivable, Avanti Enterprises, Inv. No. 1746		250.00
7/19/96			Cash	582.40	
			Cost of Sales	490.00	
			Sales		560.00
			Sales Tax Payable		22.40
			Merchandise Inventory		490.00
7/21/96			Cash	861.30	
			Sales Discount	8.70	
			Accounts Receivable, Karrol Products, Inv. No. 1747		870.00
7/28/96			Cash	725.00	
			Accounts Receivable, Mantel Co., Inv. No. 1749		725.00

Glossary

cash receipts journal   A special journal used to record all inflows of cash.   *318*

sales discount   The term used to describe a cash discount from the seller's point of view.   *316*

Self-Test

Select the best answer.

1. A cash discount
   a. encourages charge customers to pay quickly.
   b. is a purchases discount to the customer.
   c. is a sales discount to the seller.
   d. All of the above.

2. Every transaction in the cash receipts journal requires a
   a. debit to the Cash account.
   b. credit to the Cash account.
   c. debit to the Accounts Receivable account.
   d. None of the above.

3. The cash receipts journal accommodates
   a. only cash sales.
   b. only the receipt of payments on account.
   c. all inflows of cash.
   d. all outflows of cash.

4. A sales discount may be applied to
   a. merchandise only.
   b. merchandise plus transportation.
   c. transportation only.
   d. None of the above.

5. In PAW, inflows of cash are recorded in the
   a. "Sales/Invoicing" window.
   b. "Receipts" window.
   c. "Payments" window.
   d. All of the above.

Answers to the self-test can be found after the cases at the end of this chapter.

Questions for Discussion

1. a. What kind of account is the Sales Discount account?
   b. Is the normal balance on the debit or credit side?
   c. Is it a temporary or permanent account?

2. What is the difference between a cash discount and a sales discount?

3. The cash receipts journal accommodates what type(s) of transaction(s)?

4. Is a sales discount allowed on transportation charges?

5. In PAW, what is the purpose of the "Receipts" window?

6. How is the Sales/Invoicing Task related to the Receipts Task?

7. In which special journal are cash sales recorded?

8. How is the customer ledger related to the receipt of cash?

Exercises

Exercise 11.1

Match the following journals with the transactions shown below:

Special Journals
L.O. 4, 5

1. Sales journal
2. Purchase journal
3. Cash receipts journal
4. Cash payments journal
5. General journal

Transactions

a. Any transaction that does not fit into a special journal.
b. All payments of cash.
c. All purchases on account.
d. All sales on account.
e. All receipts of cash.

Exercise 11.2

Indicate in which window each of the transactions shown below should be recorded.

PAW Windows
L.O. 4, 5

"Purchases/Receive Inventory" window

"Payments" window

"Sales/Invoicing" window

"Receipts" window

1. Sold merchandise for cash.
2. Paid electric bill.
3. Purchased merchandise on account.
4. Sold merchandise on account.
5. Paid creditor on account.
6. Purchased merchandise for cash.
7. Issued a credit memo for merchandise returned by a charge customer.
8. Received a payment on account from a charge customer.
9. Returned merchandise on account to vendor.
10. Paid monthly rent.

Exercise 11.3

What do the following abbreviations in the "Type" column of the customer and vendor ledgers indicate?

Special Journals
L.O. 6, 8

1. SJ
2. CRJ
3. PJ
4. CDJ

Exercise 11.4

Sales Discount
L.O. 1

On October 1, Juarez Brothers sold merchandise on account to Johnson Enterprises; Invoice No. 864; terms 2/10, n/30; $1,800. The merchandise cost $1,500. Then, on October 5, Johnson returned a portion of the merchandise, $600. The cost of the returned merchandise was $450. On October 10, Juarez received a check from Johnson Enterprises in payment of Invoice No. 864.

What was the amount of the check? Be sure to show well-labeled computations.

Exercise 11.5

Receipt on Account
L.O. 1, 5

Record the following transactions in data entry sheet format:

February 1   Sold merchandise on account to Victor Moy Company; Invoice No. 384; terms 2/10, n/30; $480. The merchandise cost $415.

3   Victor Moy Company returned a portion of the merchandise purchased on February 1, Invoice No. 384, $150. The cost of the returned merchandise was $120.

9   Received a check from Victor Moy Company in payment of Invoice No. 384.

Exercise 11.6

Receipt on Account
L.O. 1, 5

Record the following transactions in data entry sheet format:

April 18   Sold merchandise on account to Wolf Associates; Invoice No. 987; terms 1/10, n/30; $872. The merchandise cost $760.

20   Wolf Associates returned a portion of the merchandise purchased on April 18, Invoice No. 987, $290. The cost of the returned merchandise was $240.

30   Received a check from Wolf Associates in payment of Invoice No. 987.

Exercise 11.7

Receipt on Account
L.O. 5

Record the following transactions in data entry sheet format:

August 9   Sold merchandise on account to Jill Marks, Invoice No. 589, terms net 30 days, $192 plus 5 percent sales tax. The merchandise cost $162.

12   Jill Marks returned a portion of the merchandise purchased on August 9, Invoice No. 589, $65 plus sales tax. The cost of the returned merchandise was $40.

28   Received a check from Jill Marks in payment of Invoice No. 589.

Exercise 11.8

If Patel Company receives Sorella's check on March 29, the check should be written for what amount? Show well-labeled computations.

Receipt on Account Using Invoice
L.O. 1, 5

PATEL COMPANY **2435 Hill Drive** **Plainfield, IL 60544**			**INVOICE NO. 9378**
Sold to: Sorella Company 8375 Park Avenue Chicago, IL 60647			Date: 3/19/96 Terms: 1/10, n/30 F.O.B.: Shipping point
Quantity	**Description**	**Unit Price**	**Total**
200	Model No. 437B Plus transportation charges	1.50	300.00 45.00
	Total amount due		345.00

Problems—Set A

Problem 11.1A

In Chapter 10, Problem Set A, you completed sales on account for ACS Products. Follow these steps to restore your data and print ACS's customer ledger:

Restore Data; Customer Ledger
L.O. 2, 8

step 1: Start Windows, then PAW. Open ACS Products.

step 2: Place your ACS Products backup disk in drive A.

step 3: From the main menu, select File, then Retore.

step 4: Type a:\acsdec.10a in the Source box. (Use the file name that you used in Chapter 10.)

step 5: Click on the Restore button. Read the "Warning" screen, then click on OK. Restoring the files will take a few moments. When the files are restored, you are returned to the main menu.

step 6: Remove disk from drive A.

step 7: To be sure that your ACS data was restored properly, from the main menu, click on Reports, then Accounts Receivable. Scroll down the Report List and highlight Customer Ledgers. Then, make the selections to print. Compare your printout to Figure 11.4 on page 332.

Figure 11.4

ACS Products
Customer Ledgers
For the Period From Dec 1, 1996 to Dec 31, 1996

Filter Criteria includes: Report order is by ID. Report is printed in Detail Format.

Customer ID Customer	Date	Trans No	Type	Debit Amt	Credit Amt	Balance
55BU Burt Company	12/3/96 12/5/96 12/28/96	3001 -3001 3007	SJ SJ SJ	7,516.25 3,292.50	 214.75 	7,516.25 7,301.50 10,594.00
66KR Kraus Corporation	12/8/96 12/20/96	3002 3005	SJ SJ	647.50 2,331.00		647.50 2,978.50
77SA Saxon Brothers	12/11/96 12/22/96	3004 -3004	SJ SJ	3,865.50	 343.60	3,865.50 3,521.90
88WO Wong, Susan	12/1/96 12/9/96 12/15/96 12/26/96 12/29/96	Balance Fwd 3003 -3003 3006 -3006	 SJ SJ SJ SJ	 69.80 27.45	 23.27 13.73	2,800.00 2,869.80 2,846.53 2,873.98 2,860.25

Problem 11.2A

Data Entry Sheet
L.O. 1, 3, 4, 5

ACS Products completed the following selected transactions during December 1996. ACS's credit terms are 1/10, n/30 for wholesale customers and net 30 days for retail customers.

12/10/96   Received a check from Susan Wong in payment of Invoice No. 3000; terms net 30 days; $2,800. (This check pays a November invoice that is shown as the December 1 balance forward in the customer ledger.)

12/13/96   Received a check from Burt Company in payment of Invoice No. 3001; dated 12/3/96; terms 1/10, n/30; less return on 12/5/96; $7,228.49.

12/18/96   Received a check from Kraus Corporation in payment of Invoice No. 3002; dated 12/8/96; terms 1/10, n/30; $641.02.

12/20/96   Received a check from Susan Wong in payment of Invoice No. 3003; dated 12/9/96; terms net 30 days; less return on 12/15/96; $46.53.

12/21/96   Received a check from Saxon Brothers in payment of Invoice No. 3004; dated 12/11/96; terms 1/10, n/30; less return on 12/22/96; $3,486.68.

12/26/96   Received a check from Kraus Corporation in payment of Invoice No. 3005; dated 12/20/96; terms 1/10, n/30; $2,307.69.

12/28/96   Received a check from Burt Company in payment of Invoice No. 3007; dated 12/28/96; terms 1/10, n/30; $3,259.58.

12/29/96   Sold 2 packages of dust cloths for cash, Invoice No. 3008, $25.90 *plus sales tax.* The dust cloths cost $15.54.

12/30/96   Sold 3 mop refills for cash, Invoice No. 3009, $65.85 *plus sales tax.* The mop refills cost $39.51.

Instructions

Record these transactions on a data entry sheet. In some cases, you will have to refer to ACS's Chapter 10 transactions.

Problem 11.3A

Referring to your data entry sheet from Problem 11.2A, use PAW's Receipts Task to journalize ACS's December transactions.

Receipts Task
L.O. 3, 4, 5

Problem 11.4A

Follow these steps to post and print the cash receipts journal:

Post and Print Cash Receipts Journal
L.O. 6, 7

step 1: From the Tasks menu, select System, then Post.

step 2: Select the Cash Receipts Journal for posting.

step 3: Click on OK.

step 4: From the Reports menu, select Accounts Receivable.

step 5: Highlight the "Cash Receipts Journal." Make the selections to print.

Problem 11.5A

Follow these steps to print the customer ledger:

Print Customer Ledger
L.O. 8

step 1: From the main menu, select Reports, then Accounts Receivable.

step 2: Scroll down the Report List and highlight "Customer Ledgers."

step 3: Make selections to print.

Problem 11.6A

Your ACS Products data **must** be backed up. You will restore it in Chapter 12. Follow these steps:

Back Up
L.O. 9

step 1: Insert a blank formatted disk in drive A.

step 2: From PAW's main manu, select File, then Backup.

step 3: Type a:\acsdec.11a in the Destination text box.

step 4: Click on the Backup button. Your files begin to copy. When all the files have been saved to drive A, you are automatically returned to the main menu.

step 5: Click on File, Exit to exit PAW.

Problems—Set B

Problem 11.1B

In Chapter 10, Problem Set B, you recorded sales on account for LLS Products. Follow these steps to restore your data and print LLS's customer ledger:

Restore Data; Customer Ledger
L.O. 2, 8

step 1: Start Windows, then PAW. Open LLS Products.

step 2: Place your LLS Products backup disk in drive A.

step 3: From the main menu, select File, then Restore.

step 4: Type a:\llsdec.10b in the Source box. (Use the same file name that you used in Chapter 10.)

step 5: Click on the Restore button. Read the "Warning" screen, then click on OK. Restoring the files will take a few moments. When the files are restored, you are returned to the main menu.

step 6: Remove disk from drive A.

step 7: To be sure that your LLS data was restored properly, from the main menu, click on Reports, then Accounts Receivable. Scroll down the Report List and highlight Customer Ledgers. Then, make the selections to print. Compare your printout to Figure 11.5.

Figure 11.5

LLS Products
Customer Ledgers
For the Period From Dec 1, 1996 to Dec 31, 1996
Filter Criteria includes: Report order is by ID. Report is printed in Detail Format.

Customer ID Customer	Date	Trans No	Type	Debit Amt	Credit Amt	Balance
05BU Budd Industries	12/5/96 12/12/96	4002 -4002	SJ SJ	2,233.00	191.40	2,233.00 2,041.60
06KR Krim Products	12/4/96 12/8/96 12/20/96	4001 -4001 4005	SJ SJ SJ	3,200.00 600.00	300.00	3,200.00 2,900.00 3,500.00
07RI Ritz Corporation	12/14/96	4004	SJ	1,116.50		1,116.50
08SA Salley, John	12/1/96 12/11/96 12/16/96 12/24/96 12/28/96	Balance Fwd 4003 -4003 4006 -4006	 SJ SJ SJ SJ	 126.88 67.63	 21.15 33.81	1,840.00 1,966.88 1,945.73 2,013.36 1,979.55

Data Entry Sheet
L.O. 1, 3, 4, 5

Problem 11.2B

LLS Products completed the following transactions during December 1996. LLS's credit terms are 2/10, n/30 for wholesale customers and net 30 days for retail customers.

12/9/96   Received a check from John Salley in payment of Invoice No. 4000; terms net 30 days; $1,840.00. (This check pays a November invoice that is shown as the December 1 balance forward in the customer ledger.)

12/14/96   Received a check from Krim Products in payment of Invoice No. 4001; dated 12/4/96; terms 2/10, n/30; less return on 12/8/96; $2,842.00.

12/15/96   Received a check from Budd Industries in payment of Invoice No. 4002; dated 12/5/96; terms 2/10, n/30; less return on 12/12/96; $2,000.77.

12/20/96   Received a check from John Salley in payment of Invoice No. 4003; dated 12/11/96; terms net 30 days; less return on 12/16/96; $105.73.

12/24/96   Received a check from Ritz Corporation in payment of Invoice No. 4004; dated 12/14/96; terms 2/10, n/30; $1,094.17.

12/26/96   Sold 4 planters for cash, Invoice No. 4007, $63.80 *plus sales tax.* The planters cost $38.28.

12/28/96   Received a check from Krim Products in payment of Invoice No. 4005; dated 12/20/96; terms 2/10, n/30; $588.00.

12/30/96   Sold 2 compost buckets for cash, Invoice No. 4008, $40 *plus sales*

Instructions

Record these transactions on a data entry sheet. In some cases, you will have to refer to LLS's Chapter 10 transactions.

Problem 11.3B

Referring to your data entry sheet from Problem 11.2B, use PAW's Receipts Task to journalize LLS's December transactions.

Receipts Task
L.O. 3, 4, 5

Problem 11.4B

Follow these steps to post and print the cash receipts journal:

Post and Print Cash Receipts Journal
L.O. 6, 7

step 1: From the Tasks menu, select System, then Post.

step 2: Select the Cash Receipts Journal for posting.

step 3: Click on OK.

step 4: From Reports menu, select Accounts Receivable.

step 5: Highlight the "Cash Receipts Journal." Make the selections to print.

Problem 11.5B

Follow these steps to print the customer ledger:

Print Customer Ledger
L.O. 8

step 1: From the main menu, select Reports, then Accounts Receivable.

step 2: Scroll down the Report List and highlight "Customer Ledgers."

step 3: Make selections to print.

Problem 11.6B

Your LLS Products data **must** be backed up. You will restore it in Chapter 12. Follow these steps:

Back Up
L.O. 9

step 1: Insert a blank formatted disk in drive A.

step 2: From PAW's main menu, select File, then Backup.

step 3: Type **a:\llsdec.11b** in the Destination text box.

step 4: Click on the Backup button. Your files begin to copy. When all the files have been saved to drive A, you are automatically returned to the main menu.

step 5: Click on File, Exit to exit PAW.

Mini-Cases

Case 11–1

Jennifer Kelsey uses PAW in her business; however, she never prints out a customer ledger. Instead, she keeps track of customer balances manually through the use of a hard copy invoice file. "I don't have time to learn how to do it using PAW," says Jennifer. Comment.

Case 11–2

Philip Cottam owns a small wholesale business. His credit terms are net 30 days. He complains to you that his accounts receivable collections are slow and revenues are down. He asks for your advice.

Case 11–3

Kathleen Coyne uses a manual accounting system in her business. She claims that computerized systems are too difficult to use. Using PAW's Receipts Task as an example, try to enlighten Kathleen.

A Case of Ethics

Matthew Hansen owns a small retail business and only accepts cash (currency and coin) from his customers. He records only half of his sales because he knows that cash is difficult to trace. "One sale for me and one sale for IRS," says Matthew. Since he offers customers good prices, they usually don't complain about paying cash or the lack of a receipt. "It's a win-win situation! My customers get bargain prices and I pay a lot less income tax." What is your opinion of this arrangement?

Answers to Self-Test

1. *d*   2. *a*   3. *c*   4. *a*   5. *b*

Payroll

Employee Earnings and Deductions

LEARNING OBJECTIVES

After studying this chapter, you should be able to:

1. Distinguish between an employee and an independent contractor.

2. Describe the various bases for employee compensation.

3. Compute total earnings.

4. Compute employee deductions.

5. Compute net pay.

6. Restore data from the previous chapter.

7. Add a Payroll Checking account.

8. Record an electronic funds transfer.

9. Print the employee list.

10. Record the payroll.

11. Print employees' paychecks.

12. Post the payroll journal.

13. Back up your data.

In previous chapters, when employees were paid, we simply debited Wages Expense and credited Cash, but that is only part of the story. The computation and recording of a payroll involve considerably more detail. In this chapter, you will study payroll accounting in greater depth.

Employees versus Independent Contractors

objective 1
Distinguish between an employee and an independent contractor

Two types of people perform services for a company. An **employee** works under the control and direction of the company; examples are secretaries, receptionists, bookkeepers, and managers. On the other hand, an **independent contractor** is hired by a company to do a specific job but does not work under the company's control or direction. The independent contractor is told what needs to be accomplished but not how to accomplish it. Examples might include doctors, lawyers, plumbers, and various types of repairers.

The difference between employees and independent contractors is an important legal and accounting distinction. Employees are on the company payroll, and employers are required by law to deduct certain payroll taxes from employee earnings. Independent contractors are not on the company payroll, and employers are not required to deduct payroll taxes from their fees. Based on this distinction, payroll accounting deals only with the relationship between employers and employees.

Employee Compensation

objective 2
Describe the various bases for employee compensation

The earnings of employees are frequently referred to as *compensation.* Although employees are usually paid in cash, compensation can take the form of meals, lodging, or property. TKT Products' employees are compensated in cash. Most compensation is based on wages, salary, piecework, or commissions.

Wages

TKT Products pays its employees based on the number of hours that they work. The earnings of employees who are paid on an hourly basis are referred to as **wages.** In most cases, a 40-hour week is considered a regular workweek for such employees. Hours worked through 40 are considered regular hours and are paid at a regular hourly rate. The wages paid for regular hours are known as **regular earnings.** Hours worked in excess of 40 in one workweek are considered overtime hours and are paid at an overtime rate per hour. The overtime rate is usually one and a half times the regular hourly rate and is frequently referred to as *time and a half.* In some instances, overtime on Sundays and holidays is paid at double or even triple the regular hourly rate. The wages paid for overtime hours are known as **overtime earnings.**

In small businesses, hourly workers keep a handwritten record of the number of hours they worked. In larger businesses, however, time clocks and computerized timekeeping systems are used. Assuming the use of a time clock, each worker has a time card that is punched as the worker comes and goes. TKT Products pays its employees every two weeks. Kevin

Barker's time cards for the first two weeks in December are shown in Figure 12.1.

Figure 12.1

TIME CARD

Employee: Barker, Kevin
Pay Period Ending: December 6, 1996

Day	In	Out	In	Out	Hours	
					Reg.	O.T.
M	7:55	12:01	12:59	5:00	8	
T.	7:59	12:00	1:00	5:01	8	
W	7:57	12:02	12:55	7:02	8	2
T	7:58	12:05	12:58	7:00	8	2
F	7:57	12:00	12:59	6:05	8	1
Total					40	5

TIME CARD

Employee: Barker, Kevin
Pay Period Ending: December 13, 1996

Day	In	Out	In	Out	Hours	
					Reg.	O.T.
M	7:55	12:01	12:59	5:00	8	
T	7:59	12:00	1:00	5:01	8	
W	7:57	12:02	12:55	6:02	8	1
T	7:58	12:05	12:58	6:00	8	1
F	7:57	12:00	12:59	5:05	8	
Total					40	2

Salary

Managerial, administrative, and professional employees (for example, engineers, accountants, or attorneys) are usually paid a fixed amount per week, month, or year. This amount is referred to as a **salary.** A salary is usually not tied to a specific number of hours worked, although basic salary is sometimes increased with overtime pay for hours worked in excess of 40 during one week.

Piecework

In some situations, employees are paid per unit produced. This used to be a common practice in the garment industry. Cutters and sewers were paid based on the number of garments made rather than on the number of hours worked. However, this is relatively uncommon in today's workplace.

Commissions

Employees involved in the sale of a product are often paid on a commission basis. Their earnings are equal to a percentage of their sales. Frequently, sales employees are paid through a combination of salary plus commission. Under such an arrangement, the employee is paid a base salary plus a commission on sales.

Understanding the Payroll Process

Preparing a payroll using PAW is extremely easy because PAW makes all the necessary computations. However, it is still important for you to understand *what* needs to be computed and *how* to compute it. Why? Because payroll accountants frequently have to answer questions about employee's paychecks. To respond to such questions, a basic knowledge of the payroll process and computations is an absolute necessity. On a personal level, this knowledge will help you better understand your own paycheck.

To demonstrate the payroll process and computations, let's compute Kevin Barker's earnings, deductions, and net pay. Later in the chapter, you will use PAW to record TKT's payroll.

Computation of Total Earnings

objective 3
Compute total earnings

To demonstrate the computation of total earnings, let's return to Kevin Barker's time cards as shown in Figure 12.1. Kevin is paid on an hourly basis and his regular hourly rate is $10. In this textbook, we will assume overtime to be hours worked in excess of 40 in one workweek. We will also assume that the overtime rate is one and a half times the regular hourly rate. Kevin's overtime rate per hour is computed as follows:

$$\text{Regular Hourly Rate} \times 1.5 = \text{Overtime Rate per Hour}$$
$$\$10 \qquad \times 1.5 = \qquad \$15$$

Looking back to Figure 12.1, we see that Kevin has worked a total of 87 (45 + 42) hours for the two weeks ended December 13. This means Kevin has worked 80 regular hours plus 7 overtime hours. Kevin's total earnings are computed as follows:

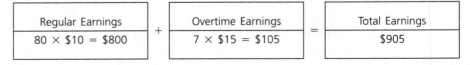

Regular Earnings		Overtime Earnings		Total Earnings
80 × $10 = $800	+	7 × $15 = $105	=	$905

Total earnings are often referred to as *gross pay*.

Deductions

Unfortunately, total earnings are not what employees actually take home. Various deductions must be subtracted from total earnings. In general, payroll deductions fall into two categories: required and voluntary. Employers are required by law to withhold federal income taxes and FICA taxes (social security and medicare) from the earnings of most employees. In some areas, withholding for state and city taxes may also be required. Voluntary deductions are for items such as U.S. savings bonds, insurance, union dues, charitable contributions, pension plans, and credit union savings and loan payments. Voluntary deductions are usually made at the employee's request or as the result of a labor agreement. Let's consider the required deductions more carefully.

objective 4
Compute employee deductions

Federal Income Tax

Since 1913, when the Sixteenth Amendment to the U.S. Constitution was passed, the federal government has been taxing the income of workers. However, only since 1943 have employers been required by law to withhold federal income tax from employees' earnings.

When hired, all employees must complete a Form W-4 for their employer. On this form, the employee indicates his or her name, address, social security number, marital status, and number of withholding allowances. Figure 12.2 shows Kevin Barker's Form W-4.

Figure 12.2

Form **W-4** Department of the Treasury Internal Revenue Service	**Employee's Withholding Allowance Certificate** ► **For Privacy Act and Paperwork Reduction Act Notice, see reverse.**	OMB No. 1545-0010 1996

1 Type or print your first name and middle initial *Kevin*	Last name *Barker*	**2** Your social security number 462 50 7534

Home address (number and street or rural route) *112 Underwood Court*	**3** ☐ Single ☒ Married ☐ Married, but withhold at higher Single rate. **Note:** *If married, but legally separated, or spouse is a nonresident alien, check the Single box.*
City or town, state, and ZIP code *Wheaton, IL 60187*	**4** If your last name differs from that on your social security card, check here and call 1-800-772-1213 for a new card . . . . ► ☐

5	Total number of allowances you are claiming (from line G above or from the worksheets on page 2 if they apply) .	**5**	*3*
6	Additional amount, if any, you want withheld from each paycheck	**6** $	
7	I claim exemption from withholding for 1996 and I certify that I meet **BOTH** of the following conditions for exemption:		

• Last year I had a right to a refund of **ALL** Federal income tax withheld because I had **NO** tax liability; **AND**
• This year I expect a refund of **ALL** Federal income tax withheld because I expect to have **NO** tax liability.

If you meet both conditions, enter "EXEMPT" here . . . . ► | **7** |

Under penalties of perjury, I certify that I am entitled to the number of withholding allowances claimed on this certificate or entitled to claim exempt status.

Employee's signature ► *Kevin Barker*   Date ► *November 30*, 19*96*

8	Employer's name and address (Employer: Complete 8 and 10 only if sending to the IRS)	**9** Office code (optional)	**10** Employer identification number

Cat. No. 10220Q

Comment A withholding allowance exempts a portion of an employee's earnings from income tax. In general, an employee is allowed one allowance for himself or herself, one for a spouse who does not claim an allowance, and one for each additional dependent.

In PAW, the information from each employee's W-4 is entered in a "Maintain—Employees/Sales Rep" window. In this textbook, that information has already been entered into your company data. Later PAW can access this information in determining each employee's income tax deduction.

The Internal Revenue Service allows employers to compute the federal income tax deduction using a formula or using withholding tables. For our purposes, it is a good idea to take a quick look at an example using an IRS withholding table. This will not only show us how to use the table, but it will also give us a greater appreciation of what PAW does for us.

A sample withholding table is shown in Figure 12.3. To use this table, you must know the length of the pay period, the employee's marital status, number of withholding allowances, and wages (total earnings) for the current pay period. Referring to Figure 12.3, let's determine Kevin Barker's federal income tax deduction for the pay period ending December 13, 1996.

Figure 12.3

MARRIED Persons—BIWEEKLY Payroll Period
(For Wages Paid in 1996)

If the wages are—		And the number of withholding allowances claimed is—										
At least	But less than	0	1	2	3	4	5	6	7	8	9	10
		The amount of income tax to be withheld is—										
$0	$250	0	0	0	0	0	0	0	0	0	0	0
250	260	1	0	0	0	0	0	0	0	0	0	0
260	270	3	0	0	0	0	0	0	0	0	0	0
270	280	4	0	0	0	0	0	0	0	0	0	0
280	290	6	0	0	0	0	0	0	0	0	0	0
290	300	7	0	0	0	0	0	0	0	0	0	0
300	310	9	0	0	0	0	0	0	0	0	0	0
310	320	10	0	0	0	0	0	0	0	0	0	0
320	330	12	0	0	0	0	0	0	0	0	0	0
330	340	13	0	0	0	0	0	0	0	0	0	0
340	350	15	0	0	0	0	0	0	0	0	0	0
350	360	16	1	0	0	0	0	0	0	0	0	0
360	370	18	3	0	0	0	0	0	0	0	0	0
370	380	19	4	0	0	0	0	0	0	0	0	0
380	390	21	6	0	0	0	0	0	0	0	0	0
390	400	22	7	0	0	0	0	0	0	0	0	0
400	410	24	9	0	0	0	0	0	0	0	0	0
410	420	25	10	0	0	0	0	0	0	0	0	0
420	430	27	12	0	0	0	0	0	0	0	0	0
430	440	28	13	0	0	0	0	0	0	0	0	0
440	450	30	15	0	0	0	0	0	0	0	0	0
450	460	31	16	2	0	0	0	0	0	0	0	0
460	470	33	18	3	0	0	0	0	0	0	0	0
470	480	34	19	5	0	0	0	0	0	0	0	0
480	490	36	21	6	0	0	0	0	0	0	0	0
490	500	37	22	8	0	0	0	0	0	0	0	0
500	520	39	25	10	0	0	0	0	0	0	0	0
520	540	42	28	13	0	0	0	0	0	0	0	0
540	560	45	31	16	1	0	0	0	0	0	0	0
560	580	48	34	19	4	0	0	0	0	0	0	0
580	600	51	37	22	7	0	0	0	0	0	0	0
600	620	54	40	25	10	0	0	0	0	0	0	0
620	640	57	43	28	13	0	0	0	0	0	0	0
640	660	60	46	31	16	2	0	0	0	0	0	0
660	680	63	49	34	19	5	0	0	0	0	0	0
680	700	66	52	37	22	8	0	0	0	0	0	0
700	720	69	55	40	25	11	0	0	0	0	0	0
720	740	72	58	43	28	14	0	0	0	0	0	0
740	760	75	61	46	31	17	2	0	0	0	0	0
760	780	78	64	49	34	20	5	0	0	0	0	0
780	800	81	67	52	37	23	8	0	0	0	0	0
800	820	84	70	55	40	26	11	0	0	0	0	0
820	840	87	73	58	43	29	14	0	0	0	0	0
840	860	90	76	61	46	32	17	2	0	0	0	0
860	880	93	79	64	49	35	20	5	0	0	0	0
880	900	96	82	67	52	38	23	8	0	0	0	0
900	920	99	85	70	55	41	26	11	0	0	0	0
920	940	102	88	73	58	44	29	14	0	0	0	0
940	960	105	91	76	61	47	32	17	2	0	0	0
960	980	108	94	79	64	50	35	20	5	0	0	0
980	1,000	111	97	82	67	53	38	23	8	0	0	0
1,000	1,020	114	100	85	70	56	41	26	11	0	0	0
1,020	1,040	117	103	88	73	59	44	29	14	0	0	0
1,040	1,060	120	106	91	76	62	47	32	17	3	0	0
1,060	1,080	123	109	94	79	65	50	35	20	6	0	0
1,080	1,100	126	112	97	82	68	53	38	23	9	0	0
1,100	1,120	129	115	100	85	71	56	41	26	12	0	0
1,120	1,140	132	118	103	88	74	59	44	29	15	0	0
1,140	1,160	135	121	106	91	77	62	47	32	18	3	0
1,160	1,180	138	124	109	94	80	65	50	35	21	6	0
1,180	1,200	141	127	112	97	83	68	53	38	24	9	0
1,200	1,220	144	130	115	100	86	71	56	41	27	12	0
1,220	1,240	147	133	118	103	89	74	59	44	30	15	0
1,240	1,260	150	136	121	106	92	77	62	47	33	18	3
1,260	1,280	153	139	124	109	95	80	65	50	36	21	6
1,280	1,300	156	142	127	112	98	83	68	53	39	24	9
1,300	1,320	159	145	130	115	101	86	71	56	42	27	12
1,320	1,340	162	148	133	118	104	89	74	59	45	30	15
1,340	1,360	165	151	136	121	107	92	77	62	48	33	18
1,360	1,380	168	154	139	124	110	95	80	65	51	36	21

As Kevin is paid bi-weekly and is married, the table in Figure 12.3 is appropriate to use in determining his deduction. Kevin's wages (total earnings, $905) are "at least $900, but not more that $920," and he has claimed three withholding allowances. Based on this information, the table indicates that $55 should be withheld from Kevin's earnings for federal income tax.

PAW uses the formula approach to compute each employee's deduction. The formula is provided by IRS and is stored within PAW. When formula results are not in even dollars, PAW automatically rounds to the nearest penny. Referring to Figure 12.3, you will observe that the table contains only even dollar amounts. Later in this chapter, when you use PAW to compute Kevin Barker's federal income tax deduction, you will notice that the amount is $54.55 instead of an even $55. Because the difference between the formula and table figures is small and due to rounding, either figure is acceptable to the IRS.

State Income Tax

As mentioned earlier, many states levy income taxes. The state of Illinois, where TKT Products is located, is one of those states. In addition to federal income tax, employers in such states are required to deduct state income tax from employees' paychecks. After entering the employee's name and the number of hours worked, PAW automatically computes the deduction using stored employee data and a formula supplied by the state.

In Kevin Barker's case, PAW will deduct $23.69 for state income tax.

FICA—Social Security Tax

Under the provisions of the Federal Insurance Contributions Act (FICA), both the employee and the employer must pay social security taxes. These taxes support a variety of programs that include pension, disability, and survivor's benefits for retired persons. You will study the employee's contribution in this chapter and the employer's contribution in Chapter 13.

Computation of the employee's social security contribution involves two things. One is a tax rate. The second is a limit on earnings that are subject to the tax during any one calendar year. This limit is commonly known as *maximum earnings.* Both the social security tax rate and the maximum are determined by the U.S. Congress and are subject to change. In recent years, changes have been frequent. In 1996, the social security tax rate was 6.2 percent on maximum earnings of $62,700.

Comment   Once an employee's cumulative earnings equal $62,700, additional earnings are not subject to social security tax for the remainder of the calendar year. However, on January 1 of the next year, earnings will again be subject to social security tax until the $62,700 limit is reached in that year. Since none of TKT's employees earned more than $62,700 in 1996, they all paid social security tax throughout the year.

The employee's social security tax deduction is computed by multiplying social security taxable earnings by the social security tax rate:

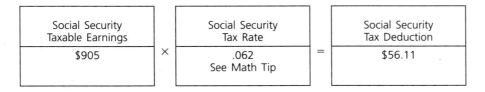

Social Security Taxable Earnings	×	Social Security Tax Rate	=	Social Security Tax Deduction

TOTAL EARNING LESS 62,700 @ 6.2% FICA

Let's demonstrate this computation by returning to Kevin Barker. As you will recall, Kevin's total earnings for the current pay period are $905. Because Kevin is a new employee, he has not accumulated any previous earnings this year. Therefore, all of Kevin's current earnings are subject to social security tax. His social security tax deduction is computed as follows:

Social Security Taxable Earnings	×	Social Security Tax Rate	=	Social Security Tax Deduction
$905		.062 See Math Tip		$56.11

Math Tip

To convert a percentage to a decimal:

step 1: Move the decimal point two places to the left.

step 2: Drop the percentage sign.

Example: 6.2% = .062

When necessary, round to the nearest penny following standard rounding rules:

- If the number in the third decimal place is 5 or more, add one penny.
  Example: $625 × .065 = $40.62**5** = $40.63

- If the number in the third decimal place is 4 or less, simply drop it.
  Example: $417 × .052 = $21.68**4** = $21.68

FICA—Medicare Tax

Medicare taxes support health care benefits for retired persons. Like the social security tax, the Federal Insurance Contributions Act (FICA) requires both the employee and the employer to pay medicare taxes. You will study the employer's contribution in Chapter 13.

Since 1991, the medicare tax has been computed and recorded separately from the social security tax. This is necessary because their rates and maximum earnings are different. Like social security, the medicare rate is determined by Congress and is subject to change. In 1996, the medicare tax applied to all earnings with no maximum earnings limit. The medicare tax rate is 1.45 percent on all earnings.

The employee's medicare tax deduction is computed by multiplying total earnings by the medicare tax rate.

Let's demonstrate the computation by returning to Kevin Barker. As you will recall, Kevin's total earnings for the current pay period are $905. Kevin's medicare tax deduction is computed as follows:

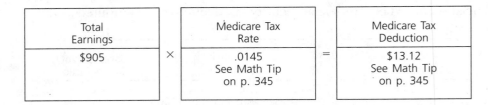

Voluntary Deductions

As mentioned earlier, voluntary deductions are usually made at the employee's request or as the result of a labor agreement. Let's assume that Kevin Barker's voluntary deductions include the following:

Health insurance	$10.50 per week × 2 = $21.00
Union dues	3.00 per week × 2 = $ 6.00

Total Deductions

Kevin Barker's total deductions for the two weeks ended December 13 are computed as follows:

Federal income tax (PAW)	$ 54.55
FICA—social security tax	56.11
FICA—medicare tax	13.12
State income tax	23.69
Health insurance	21.00
Union dues	6.00
Total deductions	$174.47

Computation of Net Pay

Kevin Barker's net pay for the two weeks ended December 13 is computed as follows:

Total Earnings	−	Deductions	=	Net Pay
$905		$174.47		$730.53

Net pay is also known as *take-home pay*. **Net pay** is the amount that actually appears on the face of the employee's paycheck.

Now that you can compute earnings, deductions, and net pay, you are ready to learn how to record TKT's payroll.

Restoring Data from Chapter 11

Follow these steps to restore your Chapter 11 data:

objective 6
Restore data from the
previous chapter

step 1:   Start Windows, then PAW. Open TKT Products.

step 2:   Place your Chapter 11 backup disk in drive A.

step 3:   From the main menu, select File, then Restore.

step 4:   Type **a:\chap11.tkt** in the Source box. (Use the same file name that you used when you backed up in Chapter 11.)

step 5:   Click on the Restore button. Read the "Warning" screen, then click on OK. When the files are restored, you are returned to the main menu.

step 6:   Remove disk from drive A.

step 7:   To make sure that you have restored your Chapter 11 data, print a trial balance. (Hint: From the main menu, select Reports, General Ledger, General Ledger Trial Balance, Print.) Compare your printout with the one in Figure 12.4.

Figure 12.4

TKT Products
General Ledger Trial Balance
As of Dec 31, 1996
Filter Criteria includes: Report order is by ID. Report is printed in Detail Format.

Account ID	Account Description	Debit Amt	Credit Amt
108	Change Fund	75.00	
109	Petty Cash	100.00	
110	Cash	13,722.53	
111	Accounts Receivable	95.40	
112	Merchandise Inventory	5,481.50	
113	Supplies	364.00	
114	Prepaid Insurance	900.00	
120	Truck	6,000.00	
121	Accumulated Depreciation		1,200.00
210	Accounts Payable		114.00
213	Sales Tax Payable		70.80
310	Dennis Taylor, Capital		10,000.00
320	Dennis Taylor, Drawing	4,500.00	
330	Retained Earnings		1,373.63
410	Fees Earned		40,047.00
411	Sales		14,226.00
412	Sales Returns and Allowances	2,946.00	
413	Sales Discount	101.00	
501	Cost of Sales	6,768.00	
610	Depreciation Expense	1,100.00	
611	FICA--Soc. Sec. Tax Expense	620.00	
612	FICA--Medicare Tax Expense	145.00	
613	FUTA Tax Expense	56.00	
614	SUTA Tax Expense	243.00	
615	Insurance Expense	492.00	
616	Rent Expense	7,200.00	
617	Repair Expense	644.00	
618	Service Charge Expense	165.00	
619	Supplies Expense	2,750.00	
620	Utilities Expense	2,563.00	
621	Wages Expense	10,000.00	
	Total:	**67,031.43**	**67,031.43**

Adding the Payroll Checking Account

objective 7
Add a Payroll Checking
Account

Most companies use a separate checking account for payroll. This means that cash must be transferred from the regular checking account to the payroll checking account, then individual employee paychecks are written on the payroll checking account.

TKT Products has decided to open a second checking account to be used solely for payroll purposes. On TKT's books, the new account will be titled Payroll Checking and it will be Account No. 107. This new account must be added to TKT's chart of accounts.

Follow these steps to add the Payroll Checking account:

step 1:   Select Maintain, Chart of Accounts. Type **107** in the Account ID box, then press <Enter>.

step 2:   Type **Payroll Checking** in the Description box, then press <Enter>. The Account Type displays "Cash."

step 3:   Click on Save.

step 4:   Print the Chart of Accounts and compare it to Figure 12.5.

Figure 12.5

TKT Products
Chart of Accounts
As of Dec 31, 1996
Filter Criteria includes: Report order is by ID. Report is printed with Accounts having Zero Amounts and in Detail Format.

Account ID	Account Description	Active?	Account Type
107	Payroll Checking	Yes	Cash
108	Change Fund	Yes	Cash
109	Petty Cash	Yes	Cash
110	Cash	Yes	Cash
111	Accounts Receivable	Yes	Accounts Receivable
112	Merchandise Inventory	Yes	Inventory
113	Supplies	Yes	Inventory
114	Prepaid Insurance	Yes	Other Current Assets
120	Truck	Yes	Fixed Assets
121	Accumulated Depreciation	Yes	Accumulated Depreciation
210	Accounts Payable	Yes	Accounts Payable
211	Wages Payable	Yes	Other Current Liabilities
213	Sales Tax Payable	Yes	Other Current Liabilities
214	Federal Income Tax Payable	Yes	Other Current Liabilities
215	FICA--Soc. Sec. Tax Payable	Yes	Other Current Liabilities
216	FICA--Medicare Tax Payable	Yes	Other Current Liabilities
217	State Income Tax Payable	Yes	Other Current Liabilities
220	FUTA Tax Payable	Yes	Other Current Liabilities
221	SUTA Tax Payable	Yes	Other Current Liabilities
223	Health Insurance Payable	Yes	Other Current Liabilities
224	Union Dues Payable	Yes	Other Current Liabilities
310	Dennis Taylor, Capital	Yes	Equity-doesn't close
320	Dennis Taylor, Drawing	Yes	Equity-gets closed
330	Retained Earnings	Yes	Equity-Retained Earnings
410	Fees Earned	Yes	Income
411	Sales	Yes	Income
412	Sales Returns and Allowances	Yes	Income
413	Sales Discount	Yes	Income
501	Cost of Sales	Yes	Cost of Sales
610	Depreciation Expense	Yes	Expenses
611	FICA--Soc. Sec. Tax Expense	Yes	Expenses
612	FICA--Medicare Tax Expense	Yes	Expenses
613	FUTA Tax Expense	Yes	Expenses
614	SUTA Tax Expense	Yes	Expenses
615	Insurance Expense	Yes	Expenses
616	Rent Expense	Yes	Expenses
617	Repair Expense	Yes	Expenses
618	Service Charge Expense	Yes	Expenses
619	Supplies Expense	Yes	Expenses
620	Utilities Expense	Yes	Expenses
621	Wages Expense	Yes	Expenses
622	Miscellaneous Expense	Yes	Expenses

Electronic Funds Transfer

An **electronic funds transfer** allows businesses and individuals to instruct banks to transfer funds by computer (electronically) from one bank account to another. Such transfers do not require the use of a check. Funds can be transferred electronically from one bank to another bank; this is usually referred to as a *wire transfer.* More commonly, funds are transferred from one account to another within the same bank.

TKT Products uses the Wheaton Valley Bank for both its regular and payroll checking accounts. Every two weeks, just before paychecks are issued, TKT electronically transfers cash from its regular checking account to its payroll checking account. To arrange the transfer, TKT simply calls the bank with instructions that include the amount of the transfer and the account numbers. Although this process does not involve a check, TKT must still record a general journal entry showing a decrease in Cash (Account No. 110) and a corresponding increase in Payroll Checking (Account No. 107).

To demonstrate, let's assume that on December 12, 1996, TKT electronically transfers $4,000 from Cash (Account No. 110) to Payroll Checking (Account No. 107). In data entry sheet format, this transaction is recorded as follows:

DATA ENTRY SHEET TKT Products					
Date	Account ID	Reference	Trans Description	Debit Amt	Credit Amt
12/12/96	107		Payroll Checking	4,000.00	
	110		Cash		4,000.00

Now, referring to the data entry sheet, let's use PAW to journalize this transaction in the general journal. We will also print and post this transaction.

step 1: From the main menu, select Tas**k**s, then **G**eneral Journal Entry.

step 2: Record the December 12, 1996, entry for the electronic funds transfer.

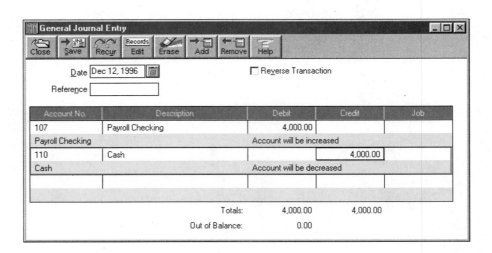

step 3: Print the General Journal for December 12, 1996. (Hint: Select Reports; General Ledger; General Journal; Print; From Dec 12; to Dec 12, OK; OK.)

Compare your screen to Figure 12.6.

Figure 12.6

TKT Products
General Journal
For the Period From Dec 12, 1996 to Dec 12, 1996

Filter Criteria includes: Report order is by Date. Report is printed with Accounts having Zero Amounts and with Truncated Transaction Descriptions and in Detail

Date	Account ID	Reference	Trans Description	Debit Amt	Credit Amt
12/12/96	107		Payroll Checking	4,000.00	
	110		Cash		4,000.00
		Total		**4,000.00**	**4,000.00**

step 4: Post the General Journal.

Printing the Employee List

Let's use PAW to print TKT's employee list. It will give us some basic information about TKT's employees.

objective 9
Print the employee list

Follow these steps to print the employee list:

step 1: From the main menu, select Reports, Payroll.

step 2: In the "Report List," the "Employee List" is highlighted.

step 3: Make the selections to print. Compare your screen to Figure 12.7 on page 352.

Referring to Figure 12.7, we can see that TKT has six employees and that all are paid on an hourly basis.

Figure 12.7

	TKT Products			
	Employee List			
Filter Criteria includes: Report order is by ID.				
Employee ID **Employee**	**Address line 1** **Address line 2** **City ST ZIP**	**SS No**	**Fed Filing Status**	**Pay Type**
11BAR Barker, Kevin	112 Underwood Wheaton, IL 60187	462-50-7534	Married	Hourly
12GRA Grant, Mary	23 East Avenue Lombard, IL 60148	207-99-6712	Single	Hourly
13HIL Hill, Charles	771 Holly Street Chicago, IL 60013	505-88-1122	Married	Hourly
14KAR Karr, James	4590 Waring Avenue Hinsdale, IL 60432	304-22-8791	Single	Hourly
15LAM Lamb, Carol	89341 N. Elm Street Burr Ridge, IL 60521	876-39-1234	Married	Hourly
16ROT Roth, Gary	616 North Citrus Avenue Chicago, IL 60181	466-27-1289	Married	Hourly

Recording the Payroll

objective 10
Record the payroll

As noted earlier, TKT Products pays it employees every two weeks. To record each biweekly payroll, an entry must be recorded for each employee. Time cards are the source document for each of these entries. To demonstrate how the December 13 payroll is recorded, let's begin with Kevin Barker. As you will recall, earlier in the chapter we computed the hours Kevin worked and his total earnings, deductions, and net pay. This information must be journalized in the payroll journal. Only payroll entries are recorded in the payroll journal. It is another example of a special journal. In Chapter 13, we will print out TKT's payroll journal.

In data entry sheet format, Kevin Barker's wages are recorded as follows:

			DATA ENTRY SHEET TKT Products		
Date	**Account ID**	**Reference**	**Trans Description**	**Debit Amt**	**Credit Amt**
12/13/96	621		Wages Expense	905.00	
	214		Federal Income Tax Payable		54.55
	217		State Income Tax Payable		23.69
	215		FICA—Soc. Sec. Tax Payable		56.11
	216		FICA—Medicare Tax Payable		13.12
	223		Health Insurance Payable		21.00
	224		Union Dues Payable		6.00
	107		Payroll Checking, Kevin Barker, Check No. 101		730.53

Now that we understand the manual process of recording Kevin's wages, we are ready to use PAW to record the payroll. It was necessary to study the manual payroll process in order to understand what PAW does "behind the scenes."

Through PAW's "Payroll Entry" window, we simply enter Kevin Barker's name, the number of regular and overtime hours worked, the date, and the Payroll Checking account number. That's it! Using that information, PAW automatically accesses Kevin's payroll information, makes the necessary computations, and journalizes the entry in the payroll journal.

To demonstrate how easy it is, let's use PAW to record Kevin Barker's December 13 payroll entry in the payroll journal:

step 1: From the main menu, select Ta_s_ks, Payroll _E_ntry. The "Payroll Entry" window displays. (You will notice that it looks like a paycheck.)

step 2: Click on the magnifying glass icon in the Emp_l_oyee ID field.

step 3: Select Kevin Barker, then click on Ok or press the <Enter> key.

step 4: In the _D_ate field, type **13** and press <Enter>.

step 5: In the "Cash Account" box, select Account No. 107, Payroll Checking. Click on Ok or press <Enter>.

step 6: In the Pay Period End field, type **13** and press <Enter>.

step 7: Accept the default for Weeks in the Pay Period (2) by pressing the <Enter> key.

step 8: Notice that the "Hours Worked" table already has 80.00 completed in the Regular Hours column. Type **7** in the Overtime Hours column. (Kevin worked 7 overtime hours this pay period.) Press the <Enter> key.

step 9: Notice that the employee deductions for Federal income tax, state income tax, social security, medicare, insurance and union dues are automatically entered in the "Employee/Employer Fields" table. The amount of Kevin's check, **$730.53**, is displayed in the "Dollars" field of the paycheck.

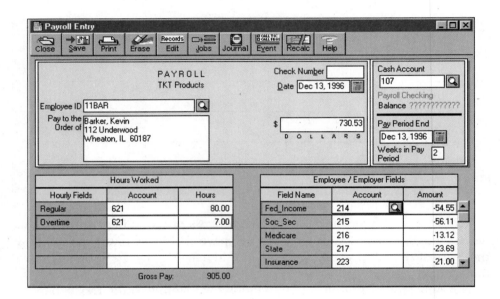

Printing the Paycheck

objective 11
Print employees' paychecks

After the payroll entry has been journalized, we are ready to print the employee's paycheck. Follow these steps to print Kevin Barker's paycheck:

step 1: Click on the Print icon. The "Print Forms: Payroll Checks" window pops up.

step 2: There are a number of choices available in the Select a form to print list. Highlight "PR Preprint 1 Stub" if you are using the working papers.

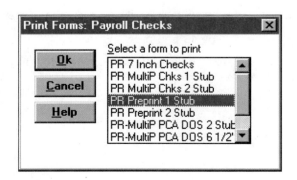

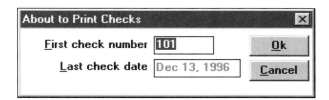

> *Comment*
>
> If you are printing on plain paper, the form you select is tied to the kind of printer you are using. For example, if you are using an HP DeskJet 520, the form that you should select is "PR MultiP Chks 2 Stub." You may need to make a different selection depending on your printer.

step 3: Click on <u>O</u>k.

step 4: The "Print Forms: PR Preprint 1 Stub" window pops up. Click on <u>R</u>eal.

step 5: The "About to Print Checks" window pops up. Type **101** in the <u>F</u>irst check number box.

step 6: Click on <u>O</u>k. Kevin Barker's paycheck begins to print.

Compare your printout to Figure 12.8.

Figure 12.8

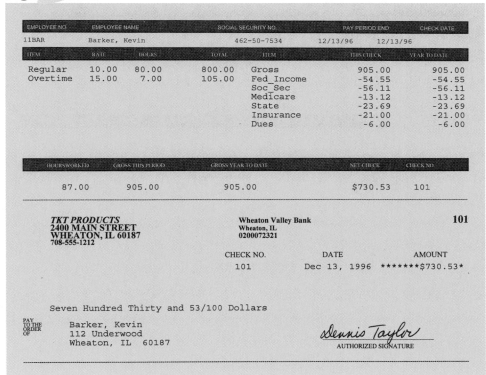

EMPLOYEE NO.	EMPLOYEE NAME	SOCIAL SECURITY NO.	PAY PERIOD END	CHECK DATE
11BAR	Barker, Kevin	462-50-7534	12/13/96	12/13/96

ITEM	RATE	HOURS	TOTAL	ITEM	THIS CHECK	YEAR TO DATE
Regular	10.00	80.00	800.00	Gross	905.00	905.00
Overtime	15.00	7.00	105.00	Fed_Income	-54.55	-54.55
				Soc_Sec	-56.11	-56.11
				Medicare	-13.12	-13.12
				State	-23.69	-23.69
				Insurance	-21.00	-21.00
				Dues	-6.00	-6.00

HOURS WORKED	GROSS THIS PERIOD	GROSS YEAR TO DATE	NET CHECK	CHECK NO.
87.00	905.00	905.00	$730.53	101

TKT PRODUCTS
2400 MAIN STREET
WHEATON, IL 60187
708-555-1212

Wheaton Valley Bank
Wheaton, IL
0200072321

101

CHECK NO.	DATE	AMOUNT
101	Dec 13, 1996	*******$730.53*

Seven Hundred Thirty and 53/100 Dollars

PAY
TO THE
ORDER
OF

Barker, Kevin
112 Underwood
Wheaton, IL 60187

Dennis Taylor
AUTHORIZED SIGNATURE

TKT's Other Employees

During the same two-week period, TKT Products' other employees worked the following hours:

Employee Name	Regular Hours	Overtime Hours	Check No.
Grant, Mary	80	2	102
Hill, Charles	80		103
Karr, James	80		104
Lamb, Carol	80	3	105
Roth, Gary	80		106

Let's use PAW to do the following: *Complete both steps for one employee before going on to the next employee.*

- Record a payroll entry for each employee.
- Print Check Nos. 102 through 106.

Compare your checks with those shown in Figure 12.9.

Figure 12.9

EMPLOYEE NO	EMPLOYEE NAME		SOCIAL SECURITY NO.	PAY PERIOD END	CHECK DATE
12GRA	Grant, Mary		207-99-6712	12/13/96	12/13/96

ITEM	RATE	HOURS	TOTAL	ITEM	THIS CHECK	YEAR TO DATE
Regular	10.50	80.00	840.00	Gross	871.50	10,871.50
Overtime	15.75	2.00	31.50	Fed_Income	-100.87	-1,244.94
				Soc_Sec	-54.03	-674.03
				Medicare	-12.64	-157.64
				State	-24.99	-311.19
				Insurance	-21.00	-273.00
				Dues	-6.00	-78.00

HOURS WORKED	GROSS THIS PERIOD	GROSS YEAR TO DATE	NET CHECK	CHECK NO.
82.00	871.50	10871.50	$651.97	102

TKT PRODUCTS
2400 MAIN STREET
WHEATON, IL 60187
708-555-1212

Wheaton Valley Bank
Wheaton, IL
0200072321

102

CHECK NO.	DATE	AMOUNT
102	Dec 13, 1996	******$651.97*

Six Hundred Fifty-One and 97/100 Dollars

PAY TO THE ORDER OF   Grant, Mary
23 East Avenue
Lombard, IL 60148

Dennis Taylor
AUTHORIZED SIGNATURE

Figure 12.9   *(continued)*

EMPLOYEE NO.	EMPLOYEE NAME		SOCIAL SECURITY NO.	PAY PERIOD END	CHECK DATE
13HIL	Hill, Charles		505-88-1122	12/13/96	12/13/96

ITEM	RATE	HOURS	TOTAL	ITEM	THIS CHECK	YEAR TO DATE
Regular	6.00	80.00	480.00	Gross	480.00	480.00
Overtime	9.00			Fed_Income	-5.51	-5.51
				Soc_Sec	-29.76	-29.76
				Medicare	-6.96	-6.96
				State	-12.09	-12.09
				Insurance	-21.00	-21.00
				Dues	-6.00	-6.00

HOURS WORKED	GROSS THIS PERIOD	GROSS YEAR TO DATE	NET CHECK	CHECK NO.
80.00	480.00	480.00	$398.68	103

TKT PRODUCTS
2400 MAIN STREET
WHEATON, IL 60187
708-555-1212

Wheaton Valley Bank
Wheaton, IL
0200072321

103

CHECK NO.	DATE	AMOUNT
103	Dec 13, 1996	*******$398.68*

Three Hundred Ninety-Eight and 68/100 Dollars

PAY TO THE ORDER OF

Hill, Charles
771 Holly Street
Chicago, IL   60013

Dennis Taylor
AUTHORIZED SIGNATURE

Figure 12.9   *(continued)*

EMPLOYEE NO.	EMPLOYEE NAME		SOCIAL SECURITY NO.	PAY PERIOD END	CHECK DATE
14KAR	Karr, James		304-22-8791	12/13/96	12/13/96

ITEM	RATE	HOURS	TOTAL	ITEM	THIS CHECK	YEAR TO DATE
Regular	8.75	80.00	700.00	Gross	700.00	700.00
Overtime	13.13			Fed_Income	-75.14	-75.14
				Soc_Sec	-43.40	-43.40
				Medicare	-10.15	-10.15
				State	-19.85	-19.85
				Insurance	-21.00	-21.00
				Dues	-6.00	-6.00

HOURS WORKED	GROSS THIS PERIOD	GROSS YEAR TO DATE	NET CHECK	CHECK NO.
80.00	700.00	700.00	$524.46	104

TKT PRODUCTS
2400 MAIN STREET
WHEATON, IL 60187
708-555-1212

Wheaton Valley Bank
Wheaton, IL
0200072321

104

CHECK NO.	DATE	AMOUNT
104	Dec 13, 1996	*******$524.46*

Five Hundred Twenty-Four and 46/100 Dollars

PAY TO THE ORDER OF

Karr, James
4590 Waring Avenue
Hinsdale, IL   60432

Dennis Taylor
AUTHORIZED SIGNATURE

Figure 12.9   *(continued)*

EMPLOYEE NO.	EMPLOYEE NAME			SOCIAL SECURITY NO.		PAY PERIOD END	CHECK DATE
15LAM	Lamb, Carol			876-39-1234		12/13/96	12/13/96

ITEM	RATE	HOURS	TOTAL	ITEM	THIS CHECK	YEAR TO DATE
Regular	9.00	80.00	720.00	Gross	760.50	760.50
Overtime	13.50	3.00	40.50	Fed_Income	-62.30	-62.30
				Soc_Sec	-47.15	-47.15
				Medicare	-11.03	-11.03
				State	-21.66	-21.66
				Insurance	-21.00	-21.00
				Dues	-6.00	-6.00

HOURS WORKED	GROSS THIS PERIOD	GROSS YEAR TO DATE	NET CHECK	CHECK NO.
83.00	760.50	760.50	$591.36	105

TKT PRODUCTS
2400 MAIN STREET
WHEATON, IL 60187
708-555-1212

Wheaton Valley Bank
Wheaton, IL
0200072321

105

CHECK NO.	DATE	AMOUNT
105	Dec 13, 1996	*******$591.36*

Five Hundred Ninety-One and 36/100 Dollars

PAY TO THE ORDER OF

Lamb, Carol
89341 N. Elm Street
Burr Ridge, IL 60521

Dennis Taylor
AUTHORIZED SIGNATURE

Figure 12.9   *(concluded)*

EMPLOYEE NO.	EMPLOYEE NAME			SOCIAL SECURITY NO.		PAY PERIOD END	CHECK DATE
16ROT	Roth, Gary			466-27-1289		12/13/96	12/13/96

ITEM	RATE	HOURS	TOTAL	ITEM	THIS CHECK	YEAR TO DATE
Regular	15.75	80.00	1,260.00	Gross	1,260.00	1,260.00
Overtime	23.63			Fed_Income	-122.51	-122.51
				Soc_Sec	-78.12	-78.12
				Medicare	-18.27	-18.27
				State	-35.49	-35.49
				Insurance	-21.00	-21.00
				Dues	-6.00	-6.00

HOURS WORKED	GROSS THIS PERIOD	GROSS YEAR TO DATE	NET CHECK	CHECK NO.
80.00	1260.00	1260.00	$978.61	106

TKT PRODUCTS
2400 MAIN STREET
WHEATON, IL 60187
708-555-1212

Wheaton Valley Bank
Wheaton, IL
0200072321

106

CHECK NO.	DATE	AMOUNT
106	Dec 13, 1996	*******$978.61*

Nine Hundred Seventy-Eight and 61/100 Dollars

PAY TO THE ORDER OF

Roth, Gary
616 North Citrus Avenue
Chicago, IL 60181

Dennis Taylor
AUTHORIZED SIGNATURE

Posting the Payroll Journal

Follow these steps to post the payroll journal:

objective 12
Post the payroll journal

step 1:   From the main menu, select Tasks, System, Post.

step 2:   Select the Payroll Journal.

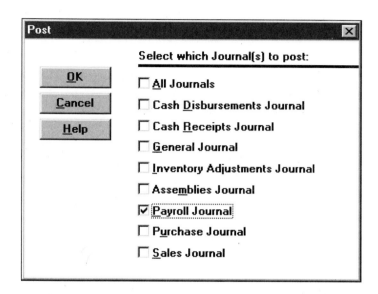

step 3:   Click on OK.

Additional Practice

As noted earlier, TKT Products pays its employees every two weeks. For additional practice, let's record TKT's December 27 payroll.

On December 26, TKT electronically transfers $4,000 from Cash (Account No. 110) to Payroll Checking (Account No. 107). In data entry sheet format, this transaction is recorded as follows:

DATA ENTRY SHEET TKT Products					
Date	Account ID	Reference	Trans Description	Debit Amt	Credit Amt
12/26/96	107		Payroll Checking	4,000.00	
	110		Cash		4,000.00

Now, referring to the data entry sheet, let's use PAW to journalize this transaction in the general journal:

step 1:   From the main menu, select Tas<u>k</u>s, then <u>G</u>eneral Journal.

step 2:   Record the December 26, 1996, entry for the electronic funds transfer.

step 3:   Print the General Journal for December 26, 1996. (Hint: Select <u>R</u>eports; <u>G</u>eneral Ledger; General Journal; Print; From Dec 26; to Dec 26, <u>O</u>K; OK.)

Compare your screen to Figure 12.10.

Figure 12.10

TKT Products
General Journal
For the Period From Dec 26, 1996 to Dec 26, 1996
Filter Criteria includes: Report order is by Date. Report is printed with Accounts having Zero Amounts and with Truncated Transaction Descriptions and in Detail

Date	Account ID	Reference	Trans Description	Debit Amt	Credit Amt
12/26/96	107		Payroll Checking	4,000.00	
	110		Cash		4,000.00
		Total		**4,000.00**	**4,000.00**

step 4:   Post the General Journal.

During the December 16 through 27 pay period, TKT's employees worked the following hours:

Employee Name	Regular Hours	Overtime Hours	Check No.
Barker, Kevin	80		107
Grant, Mary	80	1	108
Hill, Charles	80	2	109
Karr, James	80		110
Lamb, Carol	80		111
Roth, Gary	80	3	112

Based on this data, use PAW to:

- Record a payroll entry for each employee.
- Print Check Nos. 107 through 112.
- Post the payroll journal.

After completing the above, compare your checks with those shown in Figure 12.11. If you notice any mistakes, use the Edit Records icon to make the necessary changes; then, reprint the checks. A second printout of the checks will have "Duplicate" printed at the top.

Figure 12.11

EMPLOYEE NO.	EMPLOYEE NAME		SOCIAL SECURITY NO.	PAY PERIOD END		CHECK DATE
11BAR	Barker, Kevin		462-50-7534	12/27/96		12/27/96

ITEM	RATE	HOURS	TOTAL	ITEM	THIS CHECK	YEAR TO DATE
Regular	10.00	80.00	800.00	Gross	800.00	1,705.00
Overtime	15.00			Fed_Income	-38.80	-93.35
				Soc_Sec	-49.60	-105.71
				Medicare	-11.60	-24.72
				State	-20.54	-44.23
				Insurance	-21.00	-42.00
				Dues	-6.00	-12.00

HOURS WORKED	GROSS THIS PERIOD	GROSS YEAR TO DATE	NET CHECK	CHECK NO.
80.00	800.00	1705.00	$652.46	107

TKT PRODUCTS
2400 MAIN STREET
WHEATON, IL 60187
708-555-1212

Wheaton Valley Bank
Wheaton, IL
0200072321

107

CHECK NO.	DATE	AMOUNT
107	Dec 27, 1996	*******$652.46*

Six Hundred Fifty-Two and 46/100 Dollars

PAY
TO THE
ORDER
OF

Barker, Kevin
112 Underwood
Wheaton, IL 60187

Dennis Taylor
AUTHORIZED SIGNATURE

Figure 12.11 *(continued)*

EMPLOYEE NO.	EMPLOYEE NAME		SOCIAL SECURITY NO.	PAY PERIOD END		CHECK DATE
12GRA	Grant, Mary		207-99-6712	12/27/96		12/27/96

ITEM	RATE	HOURS	TOTAL	ITEM	THIS CHECK	YEAR TO DATE
Regular	10.50	80.00	840.00	Gross	855.75	11,727.25
Overtime	15.75	1.00	15.75	Fed_Income	-98.51	-1,343.45
				Soc_Sec	-53.06	-727.09
				Medicare	-12.41	-170.05
				State	-24.52	-335.71
				Insurance	-21.00	-294.00
				Dues	-6.00	-84.00

HOURS WORKED	GROSS THIS PERIOD	GROSS YEAR TO DATE	NET CHECK	CHECK NO.
81.00	855.75	11727.25	$640.25	108

TKT PRODUCTS
2400 MAIN STREET
WHEATON, IL 60187
708-555-1212

Wheaton Valley Bank
Wheaton, IL
0200072321

108

CHECK NO.	DATE	AMOUNT
108	Dec 27, 1996	*******$640.25*

Six Hundred Forty and 25/100 Dollars

PAY
TO THE
ORDER
OF

Grant, Mary
23 East Avenue
Lombard, IL 60148

Dennis Taylor
AUTHORIZED SIGNATURE

Figure 12.11 *(continued)*

EMPLOYEE NO.	EMPLOYEE NAME		SOCIAL SECURITY NO.	PAY PERIOD END	CHECK DATE
13HIL	Hill, Charles		505-88-1122	12/27/96	12/27/96

ITEM	RATE	HOURS	TOTAL	ITEM	THIS CHECK	YEAR TO DATE
Regular	6.00	80.00	480.00	Gross	498.00	978.00
Overtime	9.00	2.00	18.00	Fed_Income	-8.21	-13.72
				Soc_Sec	-30.88	-60.64
				Medicare	-7.22	-14.18
				State	-12.63	-24.72
				Insurance	-21.00	-42.00
				Dues	-6.00	-12.00

HOURS WORKED	GROSS THIS PERIOD	GROSS YEAR TO DATE	NET CHECK	CHECK NO.
82.00	498.00	978.00	$412.06	109

TKT PRODUCTS
2400 MAIN STREET
WHEATON, IL 60187
708-555-1212

Wheaton Valley Bank
Wheaton, IL
0200072321

109

CHECK NO.	DATE	AMOUNT
109	Dec 27, 1996	*******$412.06*

Four Hundred Twelve and 6/100 Dollars

PAY
TO THE
ORDER
OF

Hill, Charles
771 Holly Street
Chicago, IL 60013

Dennis Taylor
AUTHORIZED SIGNATURE

Figure 12.11 *(continued)*

EMPLOYEE NO.	EMPLOYEE NAME		SOCIAL SECURITY NO.	PAY PERIOD END	CHECK DATE
14KAR	Karr, James		304-22-8791	12/27/96	12/27/96

ITEM	RATE	HOURS	TOTAL	ITEM	THIS CHECK	YEAR TO DATE
Regular	8.75	80.00	700.00	Gross	700.00	1,400.00
Overtime	13.13			Fed_Income	-75.14	-150.28
				Soc_Sec	-43.40	-86.80
				Medicare	-10.15	-20.30
				State	-19.85	-39.70
				Insurance	-21.00	-42.00
				Dues	-6.00	-12.00

HOURS WORKED	GROSS THIS PERIOD	GROSS YEAR TO DATE	NET CHECK	CHECK NO.
80.00	700.00	1400.00	$524.46	110

TKT PRODUCTS
2400 MAIN STREET
WHEATON, IL 60187
708-555-1212

Wheaton Valley Bank
Wheaton, IL
0200072321

110

CHECK NO.	DATE	AMOUNT
110	Dec 27, 1996	*******$524.46*

Five Hundred Twenty-Four and 46/100 Dollars

PAY
TO THE
ORDER
OF

Karr, James
4590 Waring Avenue
Hinsdale, IL 60432

Dennis Taylor
AUTHORIZED SIGNATURE

Figure 12.11 *(continued)*

EMPLOYEE NO.	EMPLOYEE NAME	SOCIAL SECURITY NO.	PAY PERIOD END	CHECK DATE
15LAM	Lamb, Carol	876-39-1234	12/27/96	12/27/96

ITEM	RATE	HOURS	TOTAL	ITEM	THIS CHECK	YEAR TO DATE
Regular	9.00	80.00	720.00	Gross	720.00	1,480.50
Overtime	13.50			Fed_Income	-56.22	-118.52
				Soc_Sec	-44.64	-91.79
				Medicare	-10.44	-21.47
				State	-20.45	-42.11
				Insurance	-21.00	-42.00
				Dues	-6.00	-12.00

HOURS WORKED	GROSS THIS PERIOD	GROSS YEAR TO DATE	NET CHECK	CHECK NO.
80.00	720.00	1480.50	$561.25	111

TKT PRODUCTS
2400 MAIN STREET
WHEATON, IL 60187
708-555-1212

Wheaton Valley Bank
Wheaton, IL
0200072321

111

CHECK NO.	DATE	AMOUNT
111	Dec 27, 1996	*******$561.25*

Five Hundred Sixty-One and 25/100 Dollars

PAY TO THE ORDER OF

Lamb, Carol
89341 N. Elm Street
Burr Ridge, IL 60521

Dennis Taylor
AUTHORIZED SIGNATURE

Figure 12.11 *(concluded)*

EMPLOYEE NO.	EMPLOYEE NAME	SOCIAL SECURITY NO.	PAY PERIOD END	CHECK DATE
16ROT	Roth, Gary	466-27-1289	12/27/96	12/27/96

ITEM	RATE	HOURS	TOTAL	ITEM	THIS CHECK	YEAR TO DATE
Regular	15.75	80.00	1,260.00	Gross	1,330.89	2,590.89
Overtime	23.63	3.00	70.89	Fed_Income	-133.14	-255.65
				Soc_Sec	-82.52	-160.64
				Medicare	-19.30	-37.57
				State	-37.62	-73.11
				Insurance	-21.00	-42.00
				Dues	-6.00	-12.00

HOURS WORKED	GROSS THIS PERIOD	GROSS YEAR TO DATE	NET CHECK	CHECK NO.
83.00	1330.89	2590.89	$1,031.31	112

TKT PRODUCTS
2400 MAIN STREET
WHEATON, IL 60187
708-555-1212

Wheaton Valley Bank
Wheaton, IL
0200072321

112

CHECK NO.	DATE	AMOUNT
112	Dec 27, 1996	*****$1,031.31*

One Thousand Thirty-One and 31/100 Dollars

PAY TO THE ORDER OF

Roth, Gary
616 North Citrus Avenue
Chicago, IL 60181

Dennis Taylor
AUTHORIZED SIGNATURE

Backing Up Your Chapter 12 Data

objective 13
Back up your data

As usual, you must back up your TKT Products data. You will need it when you begin Chapter 13. Follow these steps to back up your data:

step 1:   Insert a blank formatted disk in drive A.

step 2:   From PAW's main menu, select File, then Backup.

step 3:   Type a:\chap12.tkt in the Destination text box.

step 4:   Click on the Backup button. Your files begin to copy. When all the files have been saved to drive A, you are automatically returned to the main menu.

step 5:   Click on File, Exit to exit PAW.

Chapter 12 Summary

The difference between employees and independent contractors is an important legal and accounting distinction. Employees work under the control and direction of an employer and are on the company payroll. Independent contractors are hired by a company to do specific jobs but do not work under the company's control or direction and are not on the company payroll. Payroll accounting deals only with the relationship between employers and employees.

The earnings of employees who are paid on an hourly basis are referred to as *wages*. Hours worked through 40 are considered regular hours and are paid at a regular hourly rate. Hours worked in excess of 40 in one workweek are usually considered overtime hours and are paid at an overtime rate per hour. The overtime rate is usually one and a half times the regular hourly rate. Total earnings equal regular earnings plus overtime earnings.

Payroll deductions fall into two general categories: required and voluntary. Employers are required to withhold state and federal income tax and FICA taxes (social security and medicare) from the earnings of most employees. Voluntary deductions are usually made at the employee's request or as the result of a labor agreement. They include deductions for such items as U.S. savings bonds, insurance, union dues, charitable contributions, pension plans, and credit union savings and loan payments.

Total earnings minus total deductions equal net pay. Net pay is also known as *take-home pay* and is the amount that appears on the face of the employee's paycheck.

| Total Earnings | − | Deductions | = | Net Pay |

To record the payroll, an entry for each employee must be recorded in the payroll journal. The employee's name, hours worked, and the Payroll Checking account number are entered through PAW's "Payroll Entry" window. Then, PAW automatically accesses the employee's payroll data, makes the necessary computations, and journalizes the entry in the payroll journal.

Paychecks are printed after each employee's payroll entry has been journalized.

Demonstration Problem

Susan Leung is married and claims four withholding allowances. Her total earnings at the end of the previous pay period amounted to $28,000. Susan is paid at an hourly rate of $12. She receives a paycheck every two weeks and is paid time and a half for overtime.

Instructions

1. Assuming Susan has worked a total of 86 hours during the pay period ending July 12 and has no voluntary deductions and that $30 is withheld for state income tax, compute the following:
   a. Regular earnings
   b. Overtime earnings
   c. Total earnings
   d. Federal income tax (using the table in Figure 12.3 on page 343).
   e. FICA—social security tax
   f. FICA—medicare tax
   g. Total deductions
   h. Net pay

2. In data entry sheet format, record Susan Leung's payroll entry for the pay period ending July 12, 1996. Leave the "Account ID" column blank. Assume that her employer uses a Payroll Checking account.

Solution to Demonstration Problem

1. a. $960.00 ($12 × 80)
   b. $108.00 ($18 × 6)
   c. $1,068.00 ($960 + 108)
   d. $65.00 (from tax table in Figure 12.3).
   e. $66.22 ($1,068 ×.062)
   f. $15.49 ($1,068 ×.0145)
   g. $176.71 ($30 + $65 + 66.22 + 15.49)
   h. $891.29 ($1,068 − $176.71)

2.

DATA ENTRY SHEET					
Date	Account ID	Reference	Trans Description	Debit Amt	Credit Amt
7/12/96			Wages Expense	1,068.00	
			Federal Income Tax Payable		65.00
			State Income Tax Payable		30.00
			FICA—Social Security Tax Payable		66.22
			FICA—Medicare Tax Payable		15.49
			Payroll Checking		891.29

Glossary

electronic funds transfer A transfer of cash from one account to another account without the use of a check. *350*

employee A person who works under the control and direction of an employer. *338*

independent contractor A person who is hired by a company to do a specific job but who does not work under the control or direction of the company. *338*

net pay Total earnings minus total deductions equal net pay; also known as *take-home pay.* *346*

overtime earnings The earnings for hours worked in excess of 40 in one workweek. The overtime rate per hour is usually one and a half times the regular hourly rate. *338*

payroll journal A special journal containing only payroll entries. *352*

regular earnings The earnings for 40 or fewer hours per workweek. *338*

salary A fixed amount per week, month, or year paid to managerial, administrative, and professional employees. *339*

total earnings Regular earnings plus overtime earnings equal total earnings; often referred to as *gross pay.* *340*

wages The earnings of an employee who is paid on an hourly basis. *338*

withholding allowance The exemption of a portion of an employee's earnings from income tax. *342*

Self-Test

Select the best answer.

1. Net pay equals
   a. regular earnings plus overtime earnings.
   b. total earnings minus deductions.
   c. taxable earnings minus deductions.
   d. None of the above

2. Which of the following involves both a rate and maximum earnings?
   a. Federal income tax
   b. FICA—social security
   c. State income tax
   d. FICA—medicare

3. When journalizing through the "Payroll Entry" window, you do *not* enter
   a. the employee's name.
   b. total earnings.
   c. hours worked.
   d. a date.

4. When payroll entries are recorded, which of the following accounts is credited?
   a. Payroll Checking
   b. Prepaid Wages
   c. Accounts Payable
   d. None of the above

5. In the journal entry to record the payroll, the debit to Wages Expense equals
   a. taxable earnings.
   b. total earnings.
   c. net pay.
   d. take-home pay.

Answers to the self-test can be found after the cases at the end of this chapter.

Questions for Discussion

1. What is the difference between an employee and an independent contractor?

2. Why must each newly hired employee complete a Form W-4 for his or her employer?

3. What is a withholding allowance?

4. Which taxes are employers required by law to withhold from employee earnings?

5. Which employee tax deduction involves both a rate and maximum earnings?

6. What is an electronic funds transfer?

7. How does PAW compute the deduction for federal income tax?

8. What is the relationship between the "Payroll Entry" window and the payroll journal?

Exercises

Exercise 12.1

Match the following terms with the definitions shown below:

Terminology
L.O. 1–8

1. Electronic funds transfer
2. Employee
3. Independent contractor
4. Net pay
5. Overtime earnings
6. Regular earnings
7. Salary
8. Total earnings
9. Wages
10. Withholding allowance

Definitions

a. Regular earnings plus overtime earnings equal total earnings; often referred to as *gross pay.*

b. A transfer of cash from one account to another account without the use of a check.

c. The exemption of a portion of an employee's earnings from income tax.

d. Total earnings minus total deductions; also known as take-home pay.

e. A person who works under the control and direction of an employer.

f. The earnings for 40 or fewer hours per workweek.

g. The earnings of an employee who is paid on an hourly basis.

h. A person who is hired by a company to do a specific job but who does not work under the control or direction of the company.

i. A fixed amount per week, month, or year paid to managerial, administrative, and professional employees.

j. The earnings for hours worked in excess of 40 in one workweek.

Exercise 12.2

Compute Total Earnings
L.O. 3

Donna Gillespie is married and claims two withholding allowances. Her total earnings at the end of the previous pay period amounted to $22,000. Donna is paid at an hourly rate of $15. She receives a paycheck every two weeks and is paid time and a half for overtime.

Instructions

Assuming that Donna has worked a total of 84 hours during the pay period ending September 13 and has no voluntary deductions and that $18 is withheld for state income tax, compute the following:

1. Regular earnings

2. Overtime earnings

3. Total earnings

Exercise 12.3

Compute Deductions
L.O. 4

Referring to the data given in Exercise 12.2, compute the following deductions for Donna Gillespie:

1. Federal income tax (using the tax table in Figure 12.3 on page 343).

2. FICA—social security tax.

3. FICA—medicare tax.

4. Total deductions. (Hint: Do not forget Donna's state income tax!)

Exercise 12.4

Compute Net Pay
L.O. 5

Referring to your data from Exercises 12.2 and 12.3, compute Donna Gillespie's net pay.

Exercise 12.5

Payroll Entry
L.O. 10

Referring to your data from Exercises 12.2 through 12.4, record Donna Gillespie's payroll entry for the pay period ending September 13, 1996. Record this entry in data entry sheet format leaving the "Account ID" column blank.

Exercise 12.6

Compute Total Earnings
L.O. 3

Patrick Riley is married and claims five withholding allowances. His total earnings at the end of the previous pay period amounted to $26,000. Patrick is paid an hourly rate of $14. He receives a paycheck every two weeks and is paid time and a half for overtime.

Instructions

Assuming that Patrick has worked a total of 82 hours during the pay period ending August 30, that $5 is withheld for union dues, and that $16 is withheld for state income tax, compute the following:

1. Regular earnings
2. Overtime earnings
3. Total earnings

Exercise 12.7

Referring to the data given in Exercise 12.6, compute the following deductions for Patrick Riley:

Compute Deductions
L.O. 4

1. Federal income tax (using the tax table in Figure 12.3 on page 343).
2. FICA—social security tax
3. FICA—medicare tax
4. Total deductions. (Hint: Do not forget Patrick's union dues and state income tax!)

Exercise 12.8

Referring to your data from Exercises 12.6 and 12.7, compute Patrick Riley's net pay.

Compute Net Pay
L.O. 5

Exercise 12.9

Referring to your data from Exercises 12.6 through 12.8, record Patrick Riley's payroll entry for the pay period ending August 30, 1996. Record this entry in data entry sheet format leaving the "Account ID" column blank.

Payroll Entry
L.O. 10

Exercise 12.10

On August 29, 1996, Turner Associates instructs its bank to electronically transfer $5,000 from its regular checking account to its payroll checking account. In data entry sheet format, record this transaction. Leave the "Account ID" column blank.

Electronic Funds Transfer
L.O. 8

Problems—Set A

Problem 12.1A

ACS Products uses a separate checking account for payroll. Follow these steps to restore your Chapter 11 data, add Account No. 107, Payroll Checking, and print a chart of accounts:

Restore Data; Payroll Checking Account; Chart of Accounts
L.O. 6, 7

step 1: Start Windows, then PAW. Open ACS Products.

step 2: Place your ACS Products backup disk in drive A.

step 3: From the main menu, select File, then Restore.

step 4: Type **a:\acsdec.11a** in the Source box. (Use the same file name that you used in Chapter 11.)

step 5: Click on the Restore button. Read the "Warning" screen, then click on OK. Restoring the files will take a few moments. When the files are restored, you are returned to the main menu.

step 6: Remove the disk from drive A.

step 7: Follow these steps to add Account No. 107, Payroll Checking:
a. From the main menu, select Maintain, Chart of Accounts.
b. In the Account ID box, type **107** and press <Enter>.
c. In the Description box, type **Payroll Checking** and press <Enter>.
d. The Account Type box displays "Cash." Click on the Save icon.

step 8: Follow these steps to print the chart of accounts:
a. From the main menu, select Reports, then General Ledger.
b. The "Chart of Accounts" is highlighted in the "Report List."
c. Make the selections to print. Compare your printout to Figure 12.12.

Figure 12.12

ACS Products
Chart of Accounts
As of Dec 31, 1996
Filter Criteria includes: Report order is by ID. Report is printed with Accounts having Zero Amounts and in Detail Format.

Account ID	Account Description	Active?	Account Type
107	Payroll Checking	Yes	Cash
108	Change Fund	Yes	Cash
109	Petty Cash	Yes	Cash
110	Cash	Yes	Cash
111	Accounts Receivable	Yes	Accounts Receivable
112	Merchandise Inventory	Yes	Inventory
113	Supplies	Yes	Inventory
114	Prepaid Insurance	Yes	Other Current Assets
120	Equipment	Yes	Fixed Assets
121	Accumulated Depreciation	Yes	Accumulated Depreciation
210	Accounts Payable	Yes	Accounts Payable
211	Wages Payable	Yes	Other Current Liabilities
213	Sales Tax Payable	Yes	Other Current Liabilities
214	Federal Income Tax Payable	Yes	Other Current Liabilities
215	FICA--Soc. Sec. Tax Payable	Yes	Other Current Liabilities
216	FICA--Medicare Tax Payable	Yes	Other Current Liabilities
217	State Income Tax Payable	Yes	Other Current Liabilities
220	FUTA Tax Payable	Yes	Other Current Liabilities
221	SUTA Tax Payable	Yes	Other Current Liabilities
223	Health Insurance Payable	Yes	Other Current Liabilities
224	Union Dues Payable	Yes	Other Current Liabilities
310	Joan Haywood, Capital	Yes	Equity-doesn't close
320	Joan Haywood, Drawing	Yes	Equity-gets closed
330	Retained Earnings	Yes	Equity-Retained Earnings
410	Cleaning Revenue	Yes	Income
411	Sales	Yes	Income
412	Sales Returns and Allowances	Yes	Income
413	Sales Discount	Yes	Income
501	Cost of Sales	Yes	Cost of Sales
610	Depreciation Expense	Yes	Expenses
611	FICA--Soc. Sec. Tax Expense	Yes	Expenses
612	FICA--Medicare Tax Expense	Yes	Expenses
613	FUTA Tax Expense	Yes	Expenses
614	SUTA Tax Expense	Yes	Expenses
615	Insurance Expense	Yes	Expenses
616	Rent Expense	Yes	Expenses
617	Repair Expense	Yes	Expenses
618	Service Charge Expense	Yes	Expenses
619	Supplies Expense	Yes	Expenses
620	Utilities Expense	Yes	Expenses
621	Wages Expense	Yes	Expenses
622	Miscellaneous Expense	Yes	Expenses

Problem 12.2A

Instructions

On December 12, ACS Products instructs First National Bank to electronically transfer $3,250 from its regular checking account (Account No. 110, Cash) to its payroll checking account (Account No. 107, Payroll Checking). Follow these steps to record this transaction:

Electronic Funds Transfer
L.O. 8

step 1: Use the "General Journal Entry" Task to journalize this transaction.

step 2: Print the General Journal for December 12, 1996.

step 3: Post the General Journal.

Problem 12.3A

Instructions

ACS Products has three employees. Follow these steps to print the employee list:

Employee List
L.O. 9

step 1: From the main menu, select Reports, Payroll.

step 2: In the "Report List," the "Employee List" is highlighted.

step 3: Make the selections to print the employee list.

Problem 12.4A

The table below shows the regular and overtime hours for each ACS employee for the two-week pay period ended December 13, 1996.

Payroll Entry, Checks, Post
L.O. 10–12

Employee Name	Regular Hours	Overtime Hours	Check No.
Reeves, Susan	80	2	1001
Wood, Kevin	80		1002
Yates, Denise	80		1003

Instructions

A. Follow these steps to journalize the payroll entry and print the paycheck for each employee. *Complete both steps for one employee before going on to the next employee.*

step 1: Use the "Payroll Entry" Task to record the payroll for the two-week period ending December 13, 1996.

step 2: Print the paycheck. Use the following check numbers:

    1001   Reeves
    1002   Wood
    1003   Yates

B. Post the payroll journal.

Problem 12.5A

On December 26, ACS Products electronically transfers $3,250 from its regular checking account (Account No. 110) to its payroll checking account (Account No. 107). Follow these steps to record this transaction:

step 1:   Use the "General Journal Entry" Task to journalize this transaction.

step 2:   Print the General Journal for December 26, 1996.

step 3:   Post the General Journal.

Problem 12.6A

The table below shows the regular and overtime hours for each ACS employee for the two-week pay period ended December 27, 1996.

Employee Name	Regular Hours	Overtime Hours	Check No.
Reeves, Susan	80		1004
Wood, Kevin	80	2	1005
Yates, Denise	80	1	1006

Instructions

A. Follow these steps to journalize the payroll entry and print the paycheck for each employee. *Complete both steps for one employee before going on to the next employee.*

step 1:   Use the "Payroll Entry" Task to record the payroll for the two week period ending December 27, 1996.

step 2:   Print the paycheck. Use the following check numbers:

> 1004   Reeves
> 1005   Wood
> 1006   Yates

B. Post the payroll journal.

Problem 12.7A

Your ACS Products data **must** be backed up. You will restore it in Chapter 13. Follow these steps:

step 1:   Insert a blank formatted disk in drive A.

step 2:   From PAW's main menu, select File, then Backup.

step 3:   Type a:\acsdec.12a in the Destination text box.

step 4:   Click on the Backup button. Your files begin to copy. When all the files have been saved to drive A, you are automatically returned to the main menu.

step 5:   Click on File, Exit to exit PAW.

Problems—Set B

Problem 12.1B

LLS Products uses a separate checking account for payroll. Follow these steps to restore your Chapter 11 data, add Account No. 107, Payroll Checking, and print a chart of accounts:

Restore Data; Payroll Checking Account; Chart of Accounts
L.O. 6, 7

step 1: Start Windows, then PAW. Open LLS Products.

step 2: Place your LLS Products backup disk in drive A.

step 3 From the main menu, select File, then Restore.

step 4: Type **a:\llsdec.11b** in the Source box. (Use the same file name that you used in Chapter 11.)

step 5: Click on the Restore button. Read the "Warning" screen, then click on OK. Restoring the files will take a few moments. When the files are restored, you are returned to the main menu.

step 6: Remove the disk from drive A.

step 7: Follow these steps to add Account No. 107, Payroll Checking:
a. From the main menu, select Maintain, Chart of Accounts.
b. In the Account ID box, type **107** and press <Enter>.
c. In the Description box, type **Payroll Checking** and press <Enter>.
d. The Account Type box displays "Cash." Click on the Save icon.

step 8: Follow these steps to print the chart of accounts:
a. From the main menu, select Reports, then General Ledger.
b. The "Chart of Accounts" is highlighted in the "Report List."
c. Make the selections to print. Compare your printout to Figure 12.13 on page 374.

Figure 12.13

LLS Products

Chart of Accounts

As of Dec 31, 1996

Filter Criteria includes: Report order is by ID. Report is printed with Accounts having Zero Amounts and in Detail Format.

Account ID	Account Description	Active?	Account Type
107	Payroll Checking	Yes	Cash
108	Change Fund	Yes	Cash
109	Petty Cash	Yes	Cash
110	Cash	Yes	Cash
111	Accounts Receivable	Yes	Accounts Receivable
112	Merchandise Inventory	Yes	Inventory
113	Supplies	Yes	Inventory
114	Prepaid Insurance	Yes	Other Current Assets
120	Equipment	Yes	Fixed Assets
121	Accumulated Depreciation	Yes	Accumulated Depreciation
210	Accounts Payable	Yes	Accounts Payable
211	Wages Payable	Yes	Other Current Liabilities
213	Sales Tax Payable	Yes	Other Current Liabilities
214	Federal Income Tax Payable	Yes	Other Current Liabilities
215	FICA--Soc. Sec. Tax Payable	Yes	Other Current Liabilities
216	FICA--Medicare Tax Payable	Yes	Other Current Liabilities
217	State Income Tax Payable	Yes	Other Current Liabilities
220	FUTA Tax Payable	Yes	Other Current Liabilities
221	SUTA Tax Payable	Yes	Other Current Liabilities
223	Health Insurance Payable	Yes	Other Current Liabilities
224	Union Dues Payable	Yes	Other Current Liabilities
310	Chris Canon, Capital	Yes	Equity-doesn't close
320	Chris Canon, Drawing	Yes	Equity-gets closed
330	Retained Earnings	Yes	Equity-Retained Earnings
410	Lawn Service Revenue	Yes	Income
411	Sales	Yes	Income
412	Sales Returns and Allowances	Yes	Income
413	Sales Discount	Yes	Income
501	Cost of Sales	Yes	Cost of Sales
610	Depreciation Expense	Yes	Expenses
611	FICA--Soc. Sec. Tax Expense	Yes	Expenses
612	FICA--Medicare Tax Expense	Yes	Expenses
613	FUTA Tax Expense	Yes	Expenses
614	SUTA Tax Expense	Yes	Expenses
615	Insurance Expense	Yes	Expenses
616	Rent Expense	Yes	Expenses
617	Repair Expense	Yes	Expenses
618	Service Charge Expense	Yes	Expenses
619	Supplies Expense	Yes	Expenses
620	Utilities Expense	Yes	Expenses
621	Wages Expense	Yes	Expenses
622	Miscellaneous Expense	Yes	Expenses

Problem 12.2B

Instructions

On December 12, LLS Products instructs Federated Bank & Trust to electronically transfer $3,250 from its regular checking account (Account No. 110, Cash) to its payroll checking account (Account No. 107, Payroll Checking). Follow these steps to record this transaction:

Electronic Funds Transfer
L.O. 8

step 1:   Use the "General Journal Entry" Task to journalize this transaction.

step 2:   Print the General Journal for December 12, 1996.

step 3:   Post the General Journal.

Problem 12.3B

Instructions

LLS Products has three employees. Follow these steps to print the employee list:

Employee List
L.O. 9

step 1:   From the main menu, select Reports, Payroll.

step 2:   In the "Report List," the "Employee List" is highlighted.

step 3:   Make the selections to print the employee list.

Problem 12.4B

Instructions

The table below shows the regular and overtime hours for each LLS employee for the two-week pay period ended December 13, 1996.

Payroll Entry, Checks, Post
L.O. 10–12

Employee Name	Regular Hours	Overtime Hours	Check No.
Taylor, Tom	80	1	1001
Dixon, Linda	80		1002
Perry, Karen	80		1003

Instructions

A. Follow these steps to journalize the payroll entry and print the paycheck for each employee. *Complete both steps for one employee before going on to the next employee.*

step 1:   Use the "Payroll Entry" Task to record the payroll for the two-week period ending December 13, 1996.

step 2:   Print the paycheck. Use the following check numbers:

       1001   Taylor
       1002   Dixon
       1003   Perry

B. Post the payroll journal.

Problem 12.5B

Electronic Funds Transfer
L.O. 8

On December 26, LLS Products electronically transfers $3,250 from its regular checking account (Account No. 110) to its payroll checking account (Account No. 107). Follow these steps to record this transaction:

step 1: Use the "General Journal Entry" Task to journalize this transaction.

step 2: Print the General Journal for December 26, 1996.

step 3: Post the General Journal.

Problem 12.6B

Entry, Checks, Post
L.O. 10–12

The table below shows the regular and overtime hours for each LLS employee for the two-week pay period ended December 27, 1996.

Employee Name	Regular Hours	Overtime Hours	Check No.
Taylor, Tom	80	1	1004
Dixon, Linda	80		1005
Perry, Karen	80		1006

Instructions

A. Follow these steps to journalize the payroll entry and print the paycheck for each employee. *Complete both steps for one employee before going on to the next employee.*

step 1: Use the "Payroll Entry" Task to record the payroll for the two-week period ending December 27, 1996.

step 2: Print the paycheck. Use the following check numbers:

1004   Taylor
1005   Dixon
1006   Perry

B. Post the payroll journal.

Problem 12.7B

Back Up
L.O. 13

Your LLS Products data **must** be backed up. You will restore it in Chapter 13. Follow these steps:

step 1: Insert a blank formatted disk in drive A.

step 2: From PAW's main menu, select File, then Backup.

step 3: Type a:\llsdec.12b in the Destination text box.

step 4: Click on the Backup button. Your files begin to copy. When all the files have been saved to drive A, you are automatically returned to the main menu.

step 5: Click on File, Exit to exit PAW.

Mini-Cases

Case 12–1

Sarah Falls, your company's receptionist, has requested that you treat her as an independent contractor for payroll purposes. "No payroll deductions would be the equivalent of a gigantic raise for me," says Sarah, "and it wouldn't cost you an extra penny!" Respond to Sarah's request.

Case 12–2

Felicia Stern, an employee, has come to see you about withholding for federal income tax. Felicia requests that you stop deducting federal income tax from her paycheck. She would prefer to pay the Internal Revenue Service directly on April 15 when she files her annual tax return. Respond to Felicia's request.

Case 12–3

Your friend, Pat Stahl, is self-employed. Pat's new accountant has complained that the company payroll is not being handled properly because there are no W-4 forms on file for any of the employees. The former accountant is now deceased, and Pat has no idea how the payroll was computed in the past. Knowing you are an accountant, Pat asks: "Why are these W-4s necessary?" Respond.

A Case of Ethics

Barbara and Joan work for the same company and are close friends. Barbara is a supervisor in the payroll department, and Joan is an administrative assistant to the marketing department manager. Joan arrives at lunch, enraged because she has just heard through the company grapevine that Ed, another administrative assistant, received a larger raise than she did. Joan asks Barbara to quietly check the payroll records to see if this is true. "I know it's against company policy, but I promise I won't tell a soul that you did this for me." What is your response to this situation?

Answers to Self-Test

1. *b*   2. *b*   3. *b*   4. *a*   5. *b*

Payroll
Employer Taxes and Other Responsibilities

13

LEARNING OBJECTIVES

After studying this chapter, you should be able to:

1. Compute the employer's payroll taxes.

2. Restore data from the previous chapter.

3. Record the employer's payroll tax expense.

4. Record tax payments.

5. Print Form 941.

6. Print Form 940-EZ.

7. Print a wage and tax statement (Form W-2) for each employee.

8. Print Transmittal of Wage and Tax Statements (W-3).

9. Back up your data.

10. Compute and record the premium for workers' compensation insurance.

In Chapter 12, you learned to record payroll taxes levied (imposed) on the employee. The employee pays these taxes out of his or her earnings through payroll deductions. These deductions appear as liabilities on the employer's balance sheet until the amounts are paid to the appropriate parties. In this chapter, we will focus our attention on payroll taxes levied on the employer. These taxes, paid by the employer, appear as expenses on the employer's income statement.

Employer's Payroll Taxes

objective 1
Compute the employer's
payroll taxes

Four payroll taxes are levied on the employer:

1. FICA—social security tax (employer's contribution)
2. FICA—medicare tax (employer's contribution)
3. Federal unemployment tax (FUTA)
4. State unemployment tax (SUTA)

Although these taxes are based on the total earnings of employees, they are paid by the employer. As discussed in Chapter 12, three of these taxes involve both a tax rate and a calendar-year limit on earnings subject to the tax, known as a *maximum*. The fourth, medicare, is levied on all earnings.

FICA—Social Security Tax

As you will recall, the **FICA—social security tax** supports a variety of programs that include pension, disability, and survivor's benefits for retired persons.

Equal amounts of FICA—social security tax are paid by the employee and the employer. In 1996, the FICA—social security tax rate is 6.2 percent on the first $62,700 earned by each employee. As discussed in Chapter 12, the employee's 6.2 percent contribution is deducted from total earnings when computing the employee's net pay. The employer must match each employee's contribution with an additional 6.2 percent contribution.

To demonstrate, let's return to Kevin Barker, one of TKT's employees. For the pay period ending December 13, Kevin's total earnings amounted to $905. Because Kevin was a new employee, his year-to-date earnings prior to December 13 were zero. Because Kevin was under the $62,700 maximum, all of his December 13 earnings were subject to social security tax. Through a FICA—social security tax payroll deduction, Kevin contributed $56.11 ($905 × .062). By law, TKT Products must also contribute $56.11 to match Kevin's contribution.

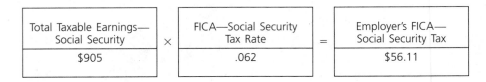

Total Taxable Earnings—Social Security		FICA—Social Security Tax Rate		Employer's FICA—Social Security Tax
$905	×	.062	=	$56.11

FICA—Medicare Tax

The **FICA—medicare tax** supports health care programs for retired persons. Equal amounts of medicare tax are paid by the employee and the employer. In 1996, the medicare rate was 1.45 percent on all employee earnings. The employer must match each employee's contribution with an additional 1.45 percent contribution.

Again, let's use Kevin Barker as an example. In Chapter 12, Kevin's payroll deductions included his FICA—medicare contribution of $13.12 ($905 × .0145). Remember that medicare has no earnings limit, so all earnings are subject to this tax. TKT products must contribute an additional $13.12.

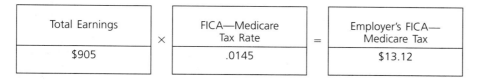

Total Earnings		FICA—Medicare Tax Rate		Employer's FICA—Medicare Tax
$905	×	.0145	=	$13.12

Federal Unemployment Tax (FUTA)

Unemployment taxes provide temporary financial support for unemployed workers. This is accomplished through a joint federal-state effort. Under the terms of the Federal Unemployment Tax Act (FUTA), the funds raised by the **federal unemployment tax** are used to cover the cost of administering the various state programs.

The federal unemployment tax is paid by the employer only. It is another example of a tax that involves both a rate and a maximum earnings limit. In 1996, the federal unemployment tax rate was .8 percent on the first $7,000 earned by each employee.

Again, let's return to Kevin Barker. Kevin had zero year-to-date earnings prior to December 13, so Kevin's total earnings of $905 are subject to federal unemployment tax. Remember, Kevin pays nothing because this is a tax levied on employers only. TKT Products' FUTA contribution is computed as follows:

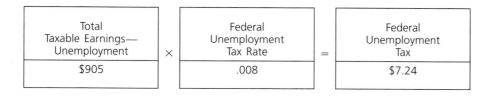

Total Taxable Earnings—Unemployment		Federal Unemployment Tax Rate		Federal Unemployment Tax
$905	×	.008	=	$7.24

Math Tip

A. To convert a percentage to a decimal:

step 1: Move the decimal point two places to the left.

step 2: Drop the percentage sign.

Example: .8% = .008

B. When necessary, round to the nearest penny following standard rounding rules:

- If the number in the third decimal place is 5 or more, add one penny.

- If the number in the third decimal place is 4 or less, simply drop it.

State Unemployment Tax (SUTA)

Under the terms of the State Unemployment Tax Act (SUTA), the funds raised by the **state unemployment tax** are used to pay unemployment benefits. Rates and benefits vary from state to state. In most states, this tax is paid by the employer only.

State unemployment tax is another example of a tax with both a rate and a maximum earnings limit. In this textbook, we are using the SUTA rate and maximum for the state of Illinois since that is where TKT Products is located. In 1996, the Illinois rate was 2.7 percent on the first $9,000 earned by each employee.

To demonstrate, let's consider how much state unemployment tax TKT has to pay for Kevin Barker. Since Kevin had zero year-to-date earnings prior to December 13, his total earnings of $905 are subject to state unemployment tax. Do not forget that Kevin pays nothing because this is a tax on employers only. TKT Products' SUTA contribution is computed as follows:

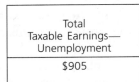
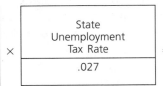
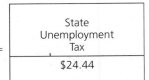

Total Taxable Earnings— Unemployment		State Unemployment Tax Rate		State Unemployment Tax
$905	×	.027	=	$24.44

Comment

If Kevin's year-to-date earnings prior to the December 13 pay period had been $9,000 or more, then TKT would *not* have to pay any more state unemployment tax on Kevin until the first pay period in January 1997.

Let's consider another scenario for Kevin. Let's assume Kevin's year-to-date earnings prior to the December 13 pay period had been $8,700. In this case, Kevin is under the maximum earnings limit. Not all of his total earnings of $905 would be subject to SUTA, but TKT would have to pay SUTA tax on $300 ($9,000 maximum − $8,700 YTD). The remaining $605 ($905 − $300) of Kevin's December 13 earnings would not be subject to this tax. TKT would not have to pay anymore state unemployment tax on Kevin until the first pay period in January 1997.

Although the dollar maximums are different for FICA—social security and for FUTA, the application of those maximums follows the same general pattern as SUTA.

Summary

TKT's payroll taxes for Kevin Barker are as follows:

FICA—social security tax . . . .$ 56.11

FICA—medicare tax 13.12

Federal unemployment tax 7.24

State unemployment tax 24.44

Total employer's payroll taxes $100.91

In our examples, we considered only one employee (Kevin Barker) and one pay period (December 13). Of course, TKT Products must compute these four employer payroll taxes for all of its employees and for every pay period.

Restoring Data from Chapter 12

As usual, your data from the previous chapter must be restored. Follow these steps to restore your Chapter 12 data:

objective 2
Restore data from the previous chapter

step 1: Start Windows, then PAW. Open TKT Products.

step 2: Place your Chapter 12 backup disk in drive A.

step 3: From the main menu, select File, then Restore.

step 4: Type **a:\chap12.tkt** in the Source box. (Use the same file name that you used when you backed up in Chapter 12.)

step 5: Click on the Restore button. Read the "Warning" screen, then click on OK. When the files are restored, you are returned to the main menu.

step 6: Remove disk from drive A.

Recording the Employer's Payroll Tax Expense

objective 3
Record the employer's payroll tax expense

The four payroll taxes levied on the employer represent four payroll tax expenses to the employer. The entry to journalize these expenses is recorded in the payroll journal. In data entry sheet format, the entry to record TKT's December 13 payroll tax expenses relating to Kevin Barker is shown below. Although these expenses have been incurred on December 13, TKT still owes these amounts to the various government agencies involved. Consequently, four liabilities must also be recorded in this entry.

\<td colspan="6" align="center"\>**DATA ENTRY SHEET**\<br\>**TKT Products**
Date	Account ID	Reference	Trans Description	Debit Amt	Credit Amt
12/13/96	611		FICA—Social Security Tax Expense	56.11	
	612		FICA—Medicare Tax Expense	13.12	
	613		FUTA Tax Expense	7.24	
	614		SUTA Tax Expense	24.44	
	215		FICA—Social Security Tax Payable		56.11
	216		FICA—Medicare Tax Payable		13.12
	220		FUTA Tax Payable		7.24
	221		SUTA Tax Payable		24.44

PAW automatically records the employer's payroll tax expense and related liabilities when each employee's payroll entry is recorded. Whenever you use the "Payroll Entry" window, PAW inserts these debits and credits into the payroll journal entry without any specific direction from you. In Chapter 12, as you recorded the payroll entry for each of TKT's employees, PAW recorded the related employer payroll tax expenses and liabilities. In other words, we do not have to make another journal entry because PAW has already done it for us. Sound too good to be true? Let's check it out by printing TKT's payroll journal.

Follow these steps to print the payroll journal:

step 1:   From the main menu, select Reports, then Payroll.

step 2:   In the "Report List," highlight "Payroll Journal."

step 3:   Make the selections to print.

Compare your payroll journal with Figure 13.1.

Observe that TKT's payroll journal shows each employee's complete payroll entry for both the December 13 and 27 pay periods. Be sure to look for the employer's payroll tax expenses and liabilities in Kevin Barker's December 13 entry. Did you see the employer's social security, medicare, FUTA, and SUTA expenses and liabilities that we computed earlier in this chapter? Did you also see Kevin Barker's matching social security and medicare contributions that we recorded in Chapter 12?

Figure 13.1

TKT Products
Payroll Journal
For the Period From Dec 1, 1996 to Dec 31, 1996
Filter Criteria includes: Report order is by Check Date. Report is printed in Detail Format.

Date Employee	GL Acct ID	Reference	Debit Amt	Credit Amt
12/13/96 Barker, Kevin	621	101	800.00	
	621		105.00	
	214			54.55
	215			56.11
	216			13.12
	217			23.69
	223			21.00
	224			6.00
	215			56.11
	216			13.12
	220			7.24
	221			24.44
	611		56.11	
	612		13.12	
	613		7.24	
	614		24.44	
	107			730.53
12/13/96 Grant, Mary	621	102	840.00	
	621		31.50	
	214			100.87
	215			54.03
	216			12.64
	217			24.99
	223			21.00
	224			6.00
	215			54.03
	216			12.64
	611		54.03	
	612		12.64	
	107			651.97
12/13/96 Hill, Charles	621	103	480.00	
	214			5.51
	215			29.76
	216			6.96
	217			12.09
	223			21.00
	224			6.00
	215			29.76
	216			6.96
	220			3.84
	221			12.96
	611		29.76	
	612		6.96	
	613		3.84	
	614		12.96	
	107			398.68

Figure 13.1   *(continued)*

TKT Products

Payroll Journal

For the Period From Dec 1, 1996 to Dec 31, 1996

Filter Criteria includes: Report order is by Check Date. Report is printed in Detail Format.

Date Employee	GL Acct ID	Reference	Debit Amt	Credit Amt
12/13/96	621	104	700.00	
Karr, James	214			75.14
	215			43.40
	216			10.15
	217			19.85
	223			21.00
	224			6.00
	215			43.40
	216			10.15
	220			5.60
	221			18.90
	611		43.40	
	612		10.15	
	613		5.60	
	614		18.90	
	107			524.46
12/13/96	621	105	720.00	
Lamb, Carol	621		40.50	
	214			62.30
	215			47.15
	216			11.03
	217			21.66
	223			21.00
	224			6.00
	215			47.15
	216			11.03
	220			6.08
	221			20.53
	611		47.15	
	612		11.03	
	613		6.08	
	614		20.53	
	107			591.36
12/13/96	621	106	1,260.00	
Roth, Gary	214			122.51
	215			78.12
	216			18.27
	217			35.49
	223			21.00
	224			6.00
	215			78.12
	216			18.27
	220			10.08
	221			34.02
	611		78.12	
	612		18.27	
	613		10.08	
	614		34.02	
	107			978.61

Figure 13.1 *(continued)*

TKT Products
Payroll Journal
For the Period From Dec 1, 1996 to Dec 31, 1996
Filter Criteria includes: Report order is by Check Date. Report is printed in Detail Format.

Date Employee	GL Acct ID	Reference	Debit Amt	Credit Amt
12/27/96	621	107	800.00	
Barker, Kevin	214			38.80
	215			49.60
	216			11.60
	217			20.54
	223			21.00
	224			6.00
	215			49.60
	216			11.60
	220			6.40
	221			21.60
	611		49.60	
	612		11.60	
	613		6.40	
	614		21.60	
	107			652.46
12/27/96	621	108	840.00	
Grant, Mary	621		15.75	
	214			98.51
	215			53.06
	216			12.41
	217			24.52
	223			21.00
	224			6.00
	215			53.06
	216			12.41
	611		53.06	
	612		12.41	
	107			640.25
12/27/96	621	109	480.00	
Hill, Charles	621		18.00	
	214			8.21
	215			30.88
	216			7.22
	217			12.63
	223			21.00
	224			6.00
	215			30.88
	216			7.22
	220			3.98
	221			13.45
	611		30.88	
	612		7.22	
	613		3.98	
	614		13.45	
	107			412.06

Figure 13.1 *(concluded)*

TKT Products
Payroll Journal
For the Period From Dec 1, 1996 to Dec 31, 1996
Filter Criteria includes: Report order is by Check Date. Report is printed in Detail Format.

Date Employee	GL Acct ID	Reference	Debit Amt	Credit Amt
12/27/96	621	110	700.00	
Karr, James	214			75.14
	215			43.40
	216			10.15
	217			19.85
	223			21.00
	224			6.00
	215			43.40
	216			10.15
	220			5.60
	221			18.90
	611		43.40	
	612		10.15	
	613		5.60	
	614		18.90	
	107			524.46
12/27/96	621	111	720.00	
Lamb, Carol	214			56.22
	215			44.64
	216			10.44
	217			20.45
	223			21.00
	224			6.00
	215			44.64
	216			10.44
	220			5.76
	221			19.44
	611		44.64	
	612		10.44	
	613		5.76	
	614		19.44	
	107			561.25
12/27/96	621	112	1,260.00	
Roth, Gary	621		70.89	
	214			133.14
	215			82.52
	216			19.30
	217			37.62
	223			21.00
	224			6.00
	215			82.52
	216			19.30
	220			10.65
	221			35.93
	611		82.52	
	612		19.30	
	613		10.65	
	614		35.93	
	107			1,031.31
			10,923.00	**10,923.00**

Tax Payments

Federal Income Tax and FICA Taxes

Both employer and employee FICA taxes (social security and medicare) and the amounts withheld from employees for federal income tax are paid together. Figure 13.2 shows a summary of deposit rules and due dates taken from *Circular E, Employer's Tax Guide.*

objective 4
Record tax payments

Figure 13.2

Summary of Deposit Rules for Social Security, Medicare, and Withheld Federal Income Tax	
Deposit Rules	**Deposit Due**
1. If at the end of the quarter, your total undeposited taxes for the quarter are less than $500:	1. No deposit is required. You may pay the taxes due to IRS with Form 941.
2. If total employment taxes during the lookback period were $50,000 or less, an employer must follow the monthly rule:	2. Taxes on payments made during a calendar month must be deposited by the 15th of the following month.
3. If total employment taxes during the lookback period were more than $50,000, an employer must follow the semiweekly rule:	3. Taxes on payments made on Wednesday, Thursday, and/or Friday must be deposited by the following Wednesday. Taxes on payments made on Saturday, Sunday, Monday, and/or Tuesday must be deposited by the following Friday.
4. If the total accumulated tax reaches $100,000 or more on any day during a deposit period:	4. Taxes must be deposited by the next banking day, whether the employer is a monthly or semiweekly depositor.

The lookback period referred to in Figure 13.2 consists of a previous four-quarter period—July 1 through June 30—determined as follows:

Lookback Period for Calendar Year 1996

Calendar Year 1996			
Jan.–Mar.	Apr.–June	July–Sept.	Oct.–Dec.

Lookback Period			
1994		**1995**	
July–Sept.	Oct.–Dec.	Jan.–Mar.	Apr.–June

New employers follow the monthly rules in making deposits because their tax liability for the lookback period is assumed to be zero. However, if a new employer's accumulated tax reaches $100,000 or more on any day during the month, the deposit must be made by the next banking day.

Comment

Circular E, Employer's Tax Guide, published by the Internal Revenue Service is available free of charge to all employers. This publication provides employers with a good source of basic payroll tax information. It discusses such information as tax rates, forms, due dates, payments, and so on. It also contains withholding tables for federal income tax, social security, and medicare.

In general, the larger the dollar amount, the sooner the amount must be paid. Most payments are deposited at a Federal Reserve Bank or some other authorized bank using deposit **Form 8109**, which is supplied by the Internal Revenue Service. A completed Form 8109 is shown in Figure 13.3.

Figure 13.3

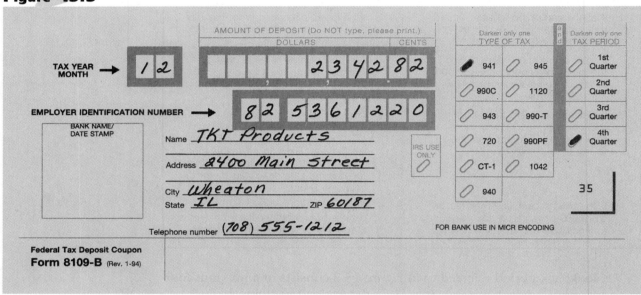

Comment

Just as each employee must have a social security number, every employer must have an employer identification number (EIN). This number must be included on all reports, forms, or correspondence submitted to the Internal Revenue Service (IRS) pertaining to payroll taxes. It is also required on all items submitted to the Social Security Administration (SSA).

Businesses whose total deposits of withheld income, social security, and medicare taxes exceeded $50,000 in calendar year 1995 must now deposit taxes due through electronic funds transfer. The Electronic Federal Tax Payment System (EFTPS), an electronic remittance processing system, must be used to make these deposits. Businesses that are not required to do so, may voluntarily make deposits by electronic funds transfer.

TKT Products owes the following amounts for social security and medicare (both employee and employer) and federal income tax.

Federal Income Taxes, Dec. 13 and 27 (employee): . . . . $ 830.90
Social Security Taxes, Dec. 13 and 27 (employee and employer) . 1,225.34
Medicare Taxes, Dec. 13 and 27 (employee and employer) 286.58
Total tax liability $2,342.82

These amounts are taken from TKT's ledger accounts as shown in Figure 13.4.

Figure 13.4

TKT Products
General Ledger
For the Period From Dec 1, 1996 to Dec 31, 1996
Filter Criteria includes: 1) IDs from 214 to 216. Report order is by ID. Report is printed in Detail Format.

Account ID Account Description	Date Reference	Jrnl	Trans Description	Debit Amt	Credit Amt	Balance
214 Federal Income Tax Payable	12/1/96		Beginning Balance			
	12/13/96 101	PRJ	Barker, Kevin		54.55	
	12/13/96 102	PRJ	Grant, Mary		100.87	
	12/13/96 103	PRJ	Hill, Charles		5.51	
	12/13/96 104	PRJ	Karr, James		75.14	
	12/13/96 105	PRJ	Lamb, Carol		62.30	
	12/13/96 106	PRJ	Roth, Gary		122.51	
	12/27/96 107	PRJ	Barker, Kevin		38.80	
	12/27/96 108	PRJ	Grant, Mary		98.51	
	12/27/96 109	PRJ	Hill, Charles		8.21	
	12/27/96 110	PRJ	Karr, James		75.14	
	12/27/96 111	PRJ	Lamb, Carol		56.22	
	12/27/96 112	PRJ	Roth, Gary		133.14	
			Current Period Change		830.90	-830.90
	12/31/96		**Ending Balance**			**-830.90**

Figure 13.4   *(continued)*

TKT Products
General Ledger
For the Period From Dec 1, 1996 to Dec 31, 1996
Filter Criteria includes: 1) IDs from 214 to 216. Report order is by ID. Report is printed in Detail Format.

Account ID / Account Description	Date / Reference	Jrnl	Trans Description	Debit Amt	Credit Amt	Balance
215	12/1/96		Beginning Balance			
FICA--Soc. Sec. Tax Payable	12/13/96 101	PRJ	Barker, Kevin		56.11	
	12/13/96 101	PRJ	Barker, Kevin		56.11	
	12/13/96 102	PRJ	Grant, Mary		54.03	
	12/13/96 102	PRJ	Grant, Mary		54.03	
	12/13/96 103	PRJ	Hill, Charles		29.76	
	12/13/96 103	PRJ	Hill, Charles		29.76	
	12/13/96 104	PRJ	Karr, James		43.40	
	12/13/96 104	PRJ	Karr, James		43.40	
	12/13/96 105	PRJ	Lamb, Carol		47.15	
	12/13/96 105	PRJ	Lamb, Carol		47.15	
	12/13/96 106	PRJ	Roth, Gary		78.12	
	12/13/96 106	PRJ	Roth, Gary		78.12	
	12/27/96 107	PRJ	Barker, Kevin		49.60	
	12/27/96 107	PRJ	Barker, Kevin		49.60	
	12/27/96 108	PRJ	Grant, Mary		53.06	
	12/27/96 108	PRJ	Grant, Mary		53.06	
	12/27/96 109	PRJ	Hill, Charles		30.88	
	12/27/96 109	PRJ	Hill, Charles		30.88	
	12/27/96 110	PRJ	Karr, James		43.40	
	12/27/96 110	PRJ	Karr, James		43.40	
	12/27/96 111	PRJ	Lamb, Carol		44.64	
	12/27/96 111	PRJ	Lamb, Carol		44.64	
	12/27/96 112	PRJ	Roth, Gary		82.52	
	12/27/96 112	PRJ	Roth, Gary		82.52	
			Current Period Change		1,225.34	-1,225.34
	12/31/96		**Ending Balance**			**-1,225.34**

Figure 13.4 *(concluded)*

TKT Products
General Ledger
For the Period From Dec 1, 1996 to Dec 31, 1996
Filter Criteria includes: 1) IDs from 214 to 216. Report order is by ID. Report is printed in Detail Format.

Account ID Account Description	Date Reference	Jrnl	Trans Description	Debit Amt	Credit Amt	Balance
216 FICA--Medicare Tax Payable	12/1/96		Beginning Balance			
	12/13/96 101	PRJ	Barker, Kevin		13.12	
	12/13/96 101	PRJ	Barker, Kevin		13.12	
	12/13/96 102	PRJ	Grant, Mary		12.64	
	12/13/96 102	PRJ	Grant, Mary		12.64	
	12/13/96 103	PRJ	Hill, Charles		6.96	
	12/13/96 103	PRJ	Hill, Charles		6.96	
	12/13/96 104	PRJ	Karr, James		10.15	
	12/13/96 104	PRJ	Karr, James		10.15	
	12/13/96 105	PRJ	Lamb, Carol		11.03	
	12/13/96 105	PRJ	Lamb, Carol		11.03	
	12/13/96 106	PRJ	Roth, Gary		18.27	
	12/13/96 106	PRJ	Roth, Gary		18.27	
	12/27/96 107	PRJ	Barker, Kevin		11.60	
	12/27/96 107	PRJ	Barker, Kevin		11.60	
	12/27/96 108	PRJ	Grant, Mary		12.41	
	12/27/96 108	PRJ	Grant, Mary		12.41	
	12/27/96 109	PRJ	Hill, Charles		7.22	
	12/27/96 109	PRJ	Hill, Charles		7.22	
	12/27/96 110	PRJ	Karr, James		10.15	
	12/27/96 110	PRJ	Karr, James		10.15	
	12/27/96 111	PRJ	Lamb, Carol		10.44	
	12/27/96 111	PRJ	Lamb, Carol		10.44	
	12/27/96 112	PRJ	Roth, Gary		19.30	
	12/27/96 112	PRJ	Roth, Gary		19.30	
			Current Period Change		286.58	-286.58
	12/31/96		**Ending Balance**			**-286.58**

On December 30, TKT Products paid these liabilities by issuing Check No. 1661 for $2,342.82 drawn on TKT's regular checking account (Cash, Account No. 110). This check was deposited at an authorized bank accompanied by the Form 8109 shown in Figure 13.3 on page 390.

Comment

Based on the deposit rules shown in Figure 13.2, TKT must deposit these taxes by January 15. While such deposits can be made any time before the deadline, most businesses wait until the last day. This allows them to use their cash for their own benefit as long as possible. TKT is making this deposit on December 30, 1996, because this textbook ends chronologically on December 31, 1996, and the authors wanted you to have an opportunity to journalize this transaction.

In data entry sheet format, this cash payment is recorded as follows:

			DATA ENTRY SHEET TKT Products		
Date	Account ID	Reference	Trans Description	Debit Amt	Credit Amt
12/30/96	214		Federal Income Tax Payable	830.90	
	215		FICA—Social Security Tax Payable	1,225.34	
	216		FICA—Medicare Tax Payable	286.58	
	110		Cash, Check No. 1661		2,342.82

Referring to the data entry sheet, we are ready to use PAW's Payments Task to journalize this transaction in the cash disbursements journal. We will also print Check No. 1661 and post the cash disbursements journal. Follow these steps:

step 1: From the main menu, select Tasks, Payments.

step 2: In the "Pay to the Order of" box, type **Wheaton Valley Bank** and press the <Enter> key two times.

step 3: In the Date box, type **30** and press <Enter>.

step 4: Click on the "Quantity" column. Type **1** and press <Enter> two times.

step 5: In the "Description" box, type **Federal Income Tax Payable** and press <Enter>.

step 6: In the "GL Account" column, select Account No. 214, Federal Income Tax Payable.

step 7: In the "Unit Price" column, type **830.90** and press the <Enter> key three times.

step 8: In the "Quantity" column, type **1** and press <Enter> two times.

step 9: In the "Description" box, type **FICA—Soc. Sec. Tax Payable** and press <Enter>.

step 10: In the "GL Account" column, select Account No. 215, FICA—Soc. Sec. Tax Payable.

step 11: In the "Unit Price" column, type **1225.34** and press the <Enter> key three times.

step 12: In the "Quantity" column, type **1** and press <Enter> two times.

step 13: In the "Description" box, type **FICA—Medicare Tax Payable** and press <Enter>.

step 14: In the "GL Account" column, select Account No. 216, FICA—Medicare Tax Payable.

step 15: In the "Unit Price" column, type **286.58** and press <Enter>.

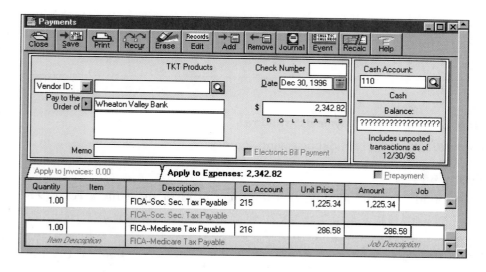

step 16: Make the selections to print Check No. 1661. If you are using the check form provided in the working papers, select form AP Preprint 1 Stub. Compare your printout to Figure 13.5 on page 396.

Figure 13.5

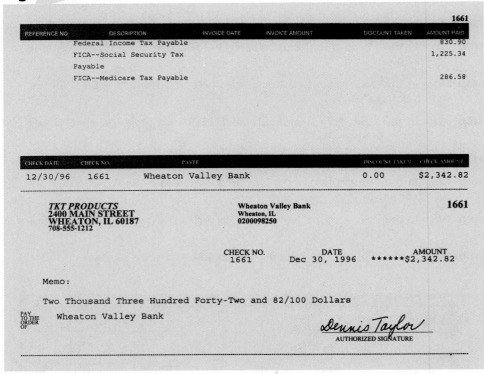

REFERENCE NO.	DESCRIPTION	INVOICE DATE	INVOICE AMOUNT	DISCOUNT TAKEN	AMOUNT PAID
	Federal Income Tax Payable				830.90
	FICA--Social Security Tax Payable				1,225.34
	FICA--Medicare Tax Payable				286.58

CHECK DATE	CHECK NO.	PAYEE	DISCOUNT TAKEN	CHECK AMOUNT
12/30/96	1661	Wheaton Valley Bank	0.00	$2,342.82

TKT PRODUCTS
2400 MAIN STREET
WHEATON, IL 60187
708-555-1212

Wheaton Valley Bank
Wheaton, IL
0200098250

1661

CHECK NO.	DATE	AMOUNT
1661	Dec 30, 1996	******$2,342.82

Memo:

Two Thousand Three Hundred Forty-Two and 82/100 Dollars

PAY
TO THE
ORDER
OF   Wheaton Valley Bank

Dennis Taylor
AUTHORIZED SIGNATURE

step 17: Close the "Payments" window.

step 18: Post the cash disbursements journal.

Form 941

At the end of each calendar quarter, the employer must file a Form 941.

Calendar Quarter	Form 941 Due Date
January 1–March 31	.April 30
April 1–June 30	.July 31
July 1–September 30	.October 31
October 1–December 31	.January 31

On Form 941, the employer shows the federal income tax (employee) and FICA tax liabilities (employer and employee) for the quarter, payments already deposited, and any resulting balance due or overpayment. Figure 13.6 shows a completed Form 941.

Figure 13.6

Form **941** (Rev. January 1996) Department of the Treasury Internal Revenue Service (O)	4141	**Employer's Quarterly Federal Tax Return** ▶ See separate instructions for information on completing this return. Please type or print.		

Enter state code for state in which deposits made . ▶ ☐ (see page 3 of instructions).

Name (as distinguished from trade name)	Date quarter ended	OMB No. 1545-0029
TKT Products Trade name, if any	Dec 31, 1996 Employer identification number	T
		FF
Address (number and street) 2400 Main Street Wheaton, IL 60187	82-5361220 City, state, and ZIP code	FD
		FP
		I
		T

If address is different from prior return, check here ▶ ☐

IRS Use

1 1 1 1 1 1 1 1 1 1   2   3 3 3 3 3 3   4 4 4
5 5 5   6   7   8 8 8 8 8   9 9 9   10 10 10 10 10 10 10 10 10 10

If you do not have to file returns in the future, check here ▶ ☐ and enter date final wages paid ▶
If you are a seasonal employer, see **Seasonal employers** on page 1 of the instructions and check here ▶ ☐

1	Number of employees (except household) employed in the pay period that includes March 12th ▶		
2	Total wages and tips, plus other compensation	**2**	9,881.64
3	Total income tax withheld from wages, tips, and sick pay	**3**	830.90
4	Adjustment of withheld income tax for preceding quarters of calendar year	**4**	
5	Adjusted total of income tax withheld (line 3 as adjusted by line 4—see instructions) . . .	**5**	830.90
6a	Taxable social security wages . . . . $ 9,881.64 × 12.4% (.124) =	**6a**	1,225.34
b	Taxable social security tips . . . . $ × 12.4% (.124) =	**6b**	
7	Taxable Medicare wages and tips . . . . . $ 9,881.64 × 2.9% (.029) =	**7**	286.58
8	Total social security and Medicare taxes (add lines 6a, 6b, and 7). Check here if wages are not subject to social security and/or Medicare tax. . . . . ▶ ☐	**8**	1,511.92
9	Adjustment of social security and Medicare taxes (see instructions for required explanation) Sick Pay $ _____ ± Fractions of Cents $ _____ ± Other $ _____ =	**9**	
10	Adjusted total of social security and Medicare taxes (line 8 as adjusted by line 9—see instructions)	**10**	1,511.92
11	**Total taxes** (add lines 5 and 10)	**11**	2,342.82
12	Advance earned income credit (EIC) payments made to employees, if any	**12**	
13	Net taxes (subtract line 12 from line 11). **This should equal line 17, column (d) below** (or line D of Schedule B (Form 941))	**13**	2,342.82
14	Total deposits for quarter, including overpayment applied from a prior quarter	**14**	2,342.82
15	**Balance due** (subtract line 14 from line 13). See instructions	**15**	0.00
16	**Overpayment,** if line 14 is more than line 13, enter excess here ▶ $ _____ and check if to be: ☐ Applied to next return **OR** ☐ Refunded.		

• All filers: If line 13 is less than $500, you need not complete line 17 or Schedule B.
• **Semiweekly schedule depositors:** Complete Schedule B and check here . . . . ▶ ☐
• **Monthly schedule depositors:** Complete line 17, columns (a) through (d), and check here. . . . . ▶ ☐

17	**Monthly Summary of Federal Tax Liability.**			
	(a) First month liability	**(b)** Second month liability	**(c)** Third month liability	**(d)** Total liability for quarter
			2,342.82	2,342.82

Sign Here

Under penalties of perjury, I declare that I have examined this return, including accompanying schedules and statements, and to the best of my knowledge and belief, it is true, correct, and complete.

Signature ▶ *Dennis Taylor*   Print Your Name and Title ▶ *Dennis Taylor, Owner*   Date ▶ *12-31-96*

For Paperwork Reduction Act Notice, see page 1 of separate instructions.   Cat. No. 17001Z   Form **941** (Rev. 1-96)

The heading of Form 941 includes the name of the owner, the name and address of the business, the date, and the employer's identification number. Use the following line-by-line description of Form 941 to enhance your study of Figure 13.6.

line	**1**	Number of employees during the pay period that includes March 12. (Line 1 in Figure 13.16 is blank because, in this textbook, we did not record any payrolls in the period that includes March 12.)
line	**2**	Total earnings subject to federal income tax withholding.
line	**3**	Total federal income tax withheld from the credit side of the Federal Income Tax Payable account.
line	**4**	Adjustment of withheld federal income tax. This line is used to correct withholding errors in earlier quarters of the same calendar year.
line	**5**	Adjusted total of federal income tax withheld: line 3 as adjusted by line 4.
line	**6a**	Total wages subject to social security tax. This amount is multiplied by 12.4 percent (6.2 percent from the employee plus 6.2 percent from the employer).
line	**6b**	Taxable social security tips. Employees must report to their employer all tips received. This amount is multiplied by 12.4 percent (6.2 percent from the employee plus 6.2 percent from the employer).
line	**7**	Taxable medicare wages and tips. All wages and tips are subject to medicare tax. This amount is multiplied by 2.9 percent (1.45 percent from the employee plus 1.45 percent from the employer).
line	**8**	Total social security and medicare taxes. This is the total of lines 6a, 6b, and 7. This amount should equal the credits in the FICA tax payable accounts.
line	**9**	Adjustment of social security and medicare taxes. This line is used to correct errors in social security and medicare taxes reported on an earlier return.
line	**10**	Adjusted total of social security and medicare taxes: line 8 as adjusted by line 9.
line	**11**	Total taxes: add lines 5 (income tax withheld) and 10 (social security and medicare).
line	**12**	Advance earned income credit (EIC) payments, if any. EIC payments to eligible employees are usually paid out of withheld income tax and employer and employee FICA taxes. TKT has no EIC payments.
line	**13**	Net taxes: subtract line 12 (EIC) from line 11 (total taxes). This amount should equal the total federal tax liability for the quarter as shown on line 17d at the bottom of the form.
line	**14**	Total deposits for the quarter. During the quarter, these deposits (amounts paid) were recorded with debits to the Federal Income Tax Payable account and the two FICA tax payable accounts.
line	**15**	Balance due: subtract line 14 (total deposits) from line 13 (net taxes). This amount is payable to the Internal Revenue Service.
line	**16**	An overpayment has been made if line 14 (total deposits) is more than line 13 (net taxes). The excess may be refunded or applied to next quarter's Form 941.

line 17   Monthly summary of federal tax liability. During the quarter, these amounts were credited to Federal Income Tax Payable and the two FICA tax payable accounts. This is a summary of the employer's tax liability, not deposits.

Comment

Referring to TKT's Form 941, as shown in Figure 13.6 on page 397, you will observe that PAW has printed out wages, federal income tax, FICA tax liabilities, and deposits that relate only to the month of December. That is the case because, in this textbook, we only journalized payroll transactions for one month. Because Form 941 is a quarterly form, PAW normally prints out cumulative figures covering a three-month period. For our purposes, however, using figures for only one month makes it easier for you to see the relationship between what you have recorded in December and where it appears on TKT's Form 941.

Using PAW to Print Form 941

PAW enables you to print out Form 941 with very little effort. At your request, PAW will automatically print out TKT's form with all the necessary information inserted. This is possible because PAW is programmed to know what goes on each line and is able to retrieve the necessary information from TKT's payroll data.

Follow these steps to print Form 941:

objective 5
Print Form 941

step 1:   From the main menu, select Reports, Payroll.

step 2:   Scroll down the "Payroll" Report List, then double-click on Federal Form 941. The file folder next to Federal Form 941 opens. A list of forms displays below the open folder for Federal Form 941.

step 3:   Highlight "FedForm 941 1996/1997." Click on the Print icon.

step 4:   In the Total deposits for quarter box, type **2342.82** and press <Enter>. Click on OK.

step 5:   At the "Print" window, click on OK.

Compare your printout with Figure 13.6 on page 397.

Comment

If you are using the actual form, you may need to adjust the alignment for printing. If alignment is required, select the Print icon, then click on "Align." Follow the instructions on the screen for making horizontal and vertical adjustments.

Federal Unemployment Tax (FUTA)

Due dates for the payment of federal unemployment tax vary according to amount. In general, if the accumulated liability at the end of a calendar quarter is more than $100, the tax payment is due by the last day of the month following the end of the calendar quarter (April 30, July 31, October 31, and January 31). If the accumulated liability is less than $100, it is not due until January 31 of the following calendar year. Again, *Circular E* provides the details. Deposit Form 8109, supplied by the IRS, is used to make the deposit at a Federal Reserve Bank or other authorized bank.

Employers must also file a **Form 940,** Employer's Annual Federal Unemployment Tax Return. This form is an annual summary of the liability incurred, payments already deposited, and any balance due or overpayment. Form 940 must be filed by January 31 of the following calendar year if there is any balance due; otherwise, it must be filed by February 10. TKT, like many employers, is able to file a simplified version of Form 940 known as **Form 940-EZ.** Figure 13.7 show TKT's completed Form 940-EZ.

Figure 13.7

Form **940-EZ**	Employer's Annual Federal Unemployment (FUTA) Tax Return	OMB No. 1545-1110

Department of the Treasury
Internal Revenue Service   (O)

		T	
		FF	
Name (as distinguished from trade name)	Calendar year	FD	
TKT Products	1996	FP	
Trade name, if any		I	
Address and ZIP code	Employer identification number	T	
2400 Main Street	82-5361220		

Wheaton, IL 60187

Follow the chart under **Who May Use Form 940-EZ** on page 2. If you cannot use Form 940-EZ, you must use Form 940 instead.

A Enter the amount of contributions paid to your state unemployment fund. (See instructions for line A on page 4.)▶ $ 243.00

B (1) Enter the name of the state where you have to pay contributions . . . . ▶ ....IL....

 (2) Enter your state reporting number as shown on state unemployment tax return. ▶ 21-6754633

If you will not have to file returns in the future, check here (see **Who Must File** on page 2) and complete and sign the return . . . . ▶ ☐

If this is an Amended Return, check here . . . . ▶ ☐

Part I   Taxable Wages and FUTA Tax

1	Total payments (including payments shown on lines 2 and 3) during the calendar year for services of employees	**1**	19,881.64
		Amount paid	
2	Exempt payments. (Explain all exempt payments, attaching additional sheets if necessary.) ▶ --------------	**2**	
3	Payments for services of more than $7,000. Enter only amounts over the first $7,000 paid to each employee. Do not include any exempt payments from line 2. Do not use your state wage limitation. The $7,000 amount is the Federal wage base. Your state wage base may be different	**3** 4727.25	
4	Total exempt payments (add lines 2 and 3)	**4**	4727.25
5	**Total taxable wages** (subtract line 4 from line 1) . . . . . . ▶	**5**	15154.39
6	**FUTA tax.** Multiply the wages on line 5 by .008 and enter here. (If the result is over $100, also complete Part II.)	**6**	121.23
7	Total FUTA tax deposited for the year, including any overpayment applied from a prior year (from your records)	**7**	56.00
8	**Amount you owe** (subtract line 7 from line 6). This should be $100 or less. Pay to "Internal Revenue Service." ▶	**8**	65.23
9	**Overpayment** (subtract line 6 from line 7). Check if it is to be: ☐ Applied to next return, or ☐ Refunded ▶	**9**	

Part II   Record of Quarterly Federal Unemployment Tax Liability (Do not include state liability.) Complete only if line 6 is over $100.

Quarter	First (Jan. 1 – Mar. 31)	Second (Apr. 1 – June 30)	Third (July 1 – Sept. 30)	Fourth (Oct. 1 – Dec. 31)	Total for year
Liability for quarter			56.00	65.23	121.23

Under penalties of perjury, I declare that I have examined this return, including accompanying schedules and statements, and, to the best of my knowledge and belief, it is true, correct, and complete, and that no part of any payment made to a state unemployment fund claimed as a credit was, or is to be, deducted from the payments to employees.

Signature ▶ *Dennis Taylor*   Title (Owner, etc.) ▶ *Owner*   Date ▶ *12-31-96*

DETACH HERE   Cat. No. 10983G   Form **940-EZ** (1995)

The name of the owner, the name and address of the business, the calendar year, and the employer identification number are included in the heading of Forms 940 and 940-EZ. Refer to the following line-by-line description of Form 940-EZ as you study Figure 13.7.

line A   Enter the dollar amount of state unemployment contributions from the debit side of the SUTA Tax Payable account. (Figure 13.11 on page *406* does not show the $243 debit shown on line A because Figure 13.11 displays only December activity. TKT's SUTA Tax Payable account was debited for a total of $243 prior to December 1.)

line B   Enter the name of the state in which the line A contributions were paid. Also enter the state reporting number from the state unemployment tax return. TKT's state of Illinois reporting number is 21-6754633.

Part I

line 1   Enter total wages paid from the debit side of the Wages Payable account.

line 2   Enter the amount of exempt payments. Exempt payments are payments that are not subject to tax. We do not have any exempt payments in our example.

line 3   On this line, enter the total wages paid during the calendar year that were *not* subject to unemployment tax. Mary Grant is TKT's only employee who has earned more than the $7,000 FUTA maximum. Mary's total 1996 earnings were $4,727.25 more than the $7,000 limit and, therefore, not subject to FUTA Tax. ($11,727.25 − 7,000 = $4,727.25)

line 4   Enter the total amount *not* subject to unemployment tax: add lines 2 and line 3.

line 5   Enter the total amount of wages subject to unemployment tax: subtract line 4 (amount not subject to tax) from line 1 (total wages).

line 6   Compute the FUTA tax by multiplying taxable wages (line 5) by .008.

line 7   Enter the total FUTA tax paid during the year from the debit side of the FUTA Tax Payable account.

line 8   Compute the amount owed: subtract line 7 (FUTA tax paid) from line 6 (FUTA tax). This amount should equal the credit balance in the FUTA Tax Payable account at year-end. **TKT will issue a check for $65.23 and submit it with Form 940-EZ.**

line 9   Compute an overpayment: subtract line 6 (FUTA tax) from line 7 (FUTA tax paid).

Part II

This part must be completed if the FUTA tax is more than $100. The total liability for the year must equal the total FUTA tax (line 6).

TKT's FUTA Tax Payable account is shown in Figure 13.8 on page 402.

Figure 13.8

TKT Products
General Ledger
For the Period From Dec 1, 1996 to Dec 31, 1996
Filter Criteria includes: 1) IDs from 220 to 220. Report order is by ID. Report is printed in Detail Format.

Account ID Account Description	Date Reference	Jrnl	Trans Description	Debit Amt	Credit Amt	Balance
220 FUTA Tax Payable	12/1/96		Beginning Balance			
	12/13/96 101	PRJ	Barker, Kevin		7.24	
	12/13/96 103	PRJ	Hill, Charles		3.84	
	12/13/96 104	PRJ	Karr, James		5.60	
	12/13/96 105	PRJ	Lamb, Carol		6.08	
	12/13/96 106	PRJ	Roth, Gary		10.08	
	12/27/96 107	PRJ	Barker, Kevin		6.40	
	12/27/96 109	PRJ	Hill, Charles		3.98	
	12/27/96 110	PRJ	Karr, James		5.60	
	12/27/96 111	PRJ	Lamb, Carol		5.76	
	12/27/96 112	PRJ	Roth, Gary		10.65	
			Current Period Change		65.23	-65.23
	12/31/96		**Ending Balance**			**-65.23**

On December 30, TKT issues Check No. 1662 to the Internal Revenue Service for $65.23 in payment of the FUTA tax that is still owed for 1996. This check will be submitted along with TKT's Form 940-EZ. Normally, such checks are submitted with a federal tax deposit coupon, Form 8109. However, since this payment is being submitted along with the Form 940-EZ, a Form 8109 is not required.

DATA ENTRY SHEET TKT Products					
Date	Account ID	Reference	Trans Description	Debit Amt	Credit Amt
12/30/96	220		FUTA Tax Payable	65.23	
	110		Cash, Check No. 1662		65.23

Referring to the data entry sheet, we are ready to use PAW's Payments Task to journalize this transaction in the cash disbursements journal. We will also print Check No. 1662 and post the cash disbursements journal.

Follow these steps:

step 1: From the main menu, select Tas<u>k</u>s, Pa<u>y</u>ments.

step 2: In the "Pay to the Order of" box, type **Internal Revenue Service** and press the <Enter> key two times.

step 3: In the <u>D</u>ate box, type **30** and press <Enter>.

step 4: Click on the "Quantity" column. Type **1** and press <Enter> two times.

step 5: In the "Description" box type **FUTA Tax Payable** and press <Enter>.

step 6: In the "GL Account" column, select Account No. 220, FUTA Tax Payable.

step 7: In the "Unit Price" column, type **65.23** and press <Enter>.

step 8: Click on the Print icon. Print Check No. 1662. If you are using the checks provided with the working papers, select Form AP Preprint 1 Stub. Compare your printout to the check shown in Figure 13.9.

Figure 13.9

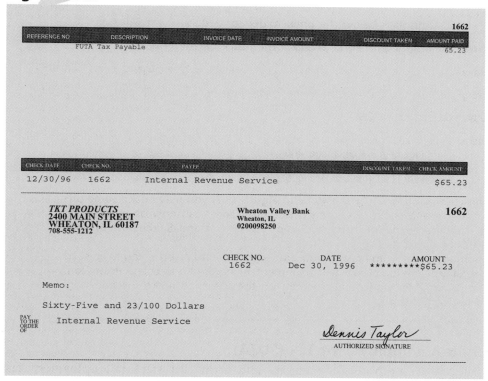

REFERENCE NO	DESCRIPTION	INVOICE DATE	INVOICE AMOUNT	DISCOUNT TAKEN	AMOUNT PAID
	FUTA Tax Payable				65.23

CHECK DATE	CHECK NO.	PAYEE	DISCOUNT TAKEN	CHECK AMOUNT
12/30/96	1662	Internal Revenue Service		$65.23

TKT PRODUCTS
2400 MAIN STREET
WHEATON, IL 60187
708-555-1212

Wheaton Valley Bank
Wheaton, IL
0200098250

1662

CHECK NO.	DATE	AMOUNT
1662	Dec 30, 1996	*********$65.23

Memo:

Sixty-Five and 23/100 Dollars

PAY
TO THE
ORDER
OF   Internal Revenue Service

Dennis Taylor
AUTHORIZED SIGNATURE

step 9: Close the "Payments" window.

step 10: **Post** the cash disbursements journal.

TKT is filing Form 940-EZ and making the FUTA tax payment on December 30 because this textbook ends chronologically on December 31, 1996, and the authors wanted you to have this practice. As noted in an earlier Comment, most businesses would wait until the January 31 deadline.

Using PAW to Print Form 940-EZ

objective 6
Print Form 940-EZ

At your request, PAW will automatically print out TKT's Form 940-EZ with all the necessary information inserted. As noted earlier, this is possible because PAW is programmed to know what goes on each line and is able to retrieve the necessary information from TKT's payroll data.

Follow these steps to print Form 940-EZ:

step 1:   From the main menu, select Reports, then Payroll.

step 2:   Scroll down the "Payroll" Report List, then double-click on Federal Form 940. The file folder next to Federal Form 940 opens. A list of forms displays below the open folder for Federal Form 940.

step 3:   Highlight "Form 940-EZ," then click on the Print icon.

step 4:   In the FUTA deposited for the year box, type **56** and press <Enter>.

step 5:   In the SUTA deposited for this year box, type **243** and press <Enter>.

step 6:   Click on OK.

step 7:   The "Print" window pops up. Click on OK. Compare your printout with Figure 13.7 on page 400.

Comment

In comparing your printout of Form 940-EZ to Figure 13.7, you may notice some differences on lines 4 and 5. Unfortunately, these differences can only be resolved by a relatively complicated design process. Except for lines 4 and 5, the rest of your form should print out correctly.

As noted in an earlier Comment, if you are using the actual form, you may need to adjust the alignment for printing. If alignment is required, select the Print icon, then click on "Align." Follow the instructions on the screen to make the necessary vertical and horizontal shifts.

State Unemployment Tax (SUTA)

Due dates, methods of payment, and forms for state unemployment tax (SUTA) vary from state to state. In Illinois, where TKT Products is located, businesses must file a quarterly Employer's Contribution and Wage Report. A check for the employer's quarterly tax is submitted along with this form.

Comment

Information about forms and procedures for your state are available from your state unemployment office.

Figure 13.10

STATE OF ILLINOIS Department of Employment Security
401 South State Street, Chicago, IL 60605

EMPLOYER'S CONTRIBUTION AND WAGE REPORT

Page No. 1 of 1   Pages
Do NOT include wage corrections for a prior quarter in this report.

Name: *TKT Products*
Address: *2400 Main Street*
City, State, Zip: *Wheaton, IL 60187*

21-675463	1996/4	12-31-96	PENALTY ($50 MIN.) (SEE 6B)	INTEREST DUE (SEE 6A)
ILLINOIS ACCOUNT NUMBER	YR. / QTR.	QUARTER ENDING		

Your Federal Employer Identification Number ➤ *82-536/2220*

CHANGE IN STATUS
If a change has occurred in the status of your business, complete form UI-50A.

1 ENTER **THE NUMBER OF COVERED WORKERS** earning wages during the pay period(s) including the 12th of each month of the quarter. Include workers who earned wages over $9000 and those on paid vacation or sick leave. Exclude workers on strike. If none, enter "0".

1ST MONTH *1*   2ND MONTH *1*   3RD MONTH *6*

2 TOTAL WAGES PAID for covered employment — *9,881.64*

3 LESS Wages in excess of $9000 per covered worker — IMPORTANT – SEE INSTRUCTIONS. *(871.50 + 855.75)* *1,727.25*

4 TAXABLE WAGES (line 2 minus line 3) — *8,154.39*

5A CONTRIBUTION DUE — Use this space if TOTAL WAGES (line 2) are less than $50,000 this quarter *(8,154.39 × .027)* *220.17*

5B CONTRIBUTION DUE — Use this space if TOTAL wages (line 2) are $50,000 or more this quarter.

6A Add Interest at 2% (.02) per month for late payment

6B Add Penalty for late filing ($50.00 minimum)

6C Add Previous Underpayment PLUS interest

6D Deduct Previous Overpayment

7 TOTAL PAYMENT DUE — MAKE CHECK PAYABLE TO: **"DIRECTOR OF EMPLOYMENT SECURITY"** (If Less than $1.00 – Send report only)   PENALTIES: SEE INSTRUCTIONS   *220.17*

I hereby certify that the information contained in this report and in all accompanying schedules is true and correct to the best of my knowledge and belief; and that no part of the contribution reported was or is to be deducted from workers' wages.

Signed *Dennis Taylor*
Title *Owner*
Telephone CODE AREA (*708*) *555-1212*
Date *12-30-96*

This report MUST be signed by owner, partner, or authorized officer. (See Instructions)

UI-340 (Rev. 1-95)   IL 427-0018   Stock No. 4601   *Printed on Recycled Paper*

Worker's Social Security Account Number 8.	NAME OF WORKER (Type or Print) 9.	TOTAL Wages Paid (Include Wages in Excess of $9,000) 10.	
000 : 00 : 0000		Dollars	Cents
462 : 50 : 7534	*Barker, Kevin*	*1,705*	*00*
207 : 99 : 6712	*Grant, Mary*	*1,727*	*25*
505 : 88 : 1122	*Hill, Charles*	*978*	*00*
304 : 22 : 8791	*Karr, James*	*1,400*	*00*
876 : 39 : 1234	*Lamb, Carol*	*1,480*	*50*
466 : 27 : 1289	*Roth, Gary*	*2,590*	*89*

11. Total Wages For This Quarter $ *9,881.64*

If more space is needed to list workers, use continuation sheets, Form UI-40A.

TKT's Employer's Contribution and Wage Report for the quarter ending December 31, 1996, is shown in Figure 13.10. Along with other information, it contains total wages paid during the quarter less exempt wages (over the $9,000 maximum), yielding taxable wages. The taxable wages are then multiplied by the tax rate (2.7 percent) to compute the contribution or payment due. TKT must also list each employee's name, social security number, and total wages paid during the quarter.

Referring to Figure 13.10, the total payment due is $220.17. This amount is equal to the balance in TKT's SUTA Tax Payable account (Account No. 221) which is shown in Figure 13.11.

Figure 13.11

TKT Products
General Ledger
For the Period From Dec 1, 1996 to Dec 31, 1996
Filter Criteria includes: 1) IDs from 221 to 221. Report order is by ID. Report is printed in Detail Format.

Account ID Account Description	Date Reference	Jrnl	Trans Description	Debit Amt	Credit Amt	Balance
221 SUTA Tax Payable	12/1/96		Beginning Balance			
	12/13/96 101	PRJ	Barker, Kevin		24.44	
	12/13/96 103	PRJ	Hill, Charles		12.96	
	12/13/96 104	PRJ	Karr, James		18.90	
	12/13/96 105	PRJ	Lamb, Carol		20.53	
	12/13/96 106	PRJ	Roth, Gary		34.02	
	12/27/96 107	PRJ	Barker, Kevin		21.60	
	12/27/96 109	PRJ	Hill, Charles		13.45	
	12/27/96 110	PRJ	Karr, James		18.90	
	12/27/96 111	PRJ	Lamb, Carol		19.44	
	12/27/96 112	PRJ	Roth, Gary		35.93	
			Current Period Change		220.17	-220.17
	12/31/96		**Ending Balance**			**-220.17**

On December 30, TKT issues Check No. 1663 to the Director of Employment Security in payment of the $220.17 SUTA tax due. In data entry sheet format, this SUTA tax payment is recorded as follows:

		DATA ENTRY SHEET TKT Products			
Date	Account ID	Reference	Trans Description	Debit Amt	Credit Amt
12/30/96	221		SUTA Tax Payable	220.17	
	110		Cash, Check No. 1663		220.17

Referring to the data entry sheet, we are ready to use PAW's Payments Task to journalize this transaction in the cash disbursements journal. We will also print Check No. 1663 and post the cash disbursements journal. Follow these steps:

step 1: From the main menu, select Ta<u>s</u>ks, Pa<u>y</u>ments.

step 2: In the "Pay to the Order of" box, type **Dir. of Employment Security** and press the <Enter> key two times.

step 3: In the <u>D</u>ate box, type **30** and press <Enter>.

step 4: Click on the "Quantity" column. Type **1** and press <Enter> two times.

step 5: In the "Description" box, type **SUTA Tax Payable** and press <Enter>.

step 6: In the "GL Account" column, select Account No. 221, SUTA Tax Payable.

step 7: In the "Unit Price" column, type **220.17** and press <Enter>.

step 8: Click on the Print icon. Print Check No. 1663. If you are using the checks provided with the working papers, select Form AP Preprint 1 Stub. Compare your printout with the check shown in Figure 13.12.

Figure 13.12

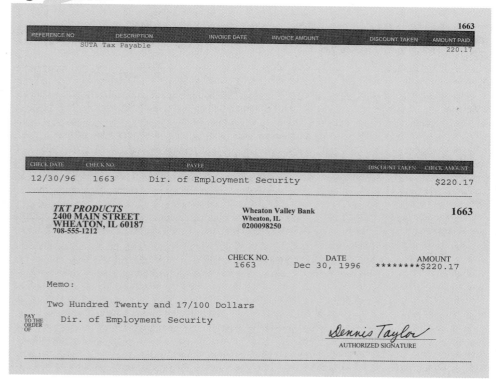

step 9: Close the "Payments" window.

step 10: **Post** the cash disbursements journal.

Wage and Tax Statement (Form W-2)

objective 7
Print a wage and tax statement (Form W-2) for each employee

In addition to providing information to the government, employers are required to provide each employee with an annual wage and tax statement. This information is reported on a **Form W-2,** which must be furnished to each employee by January 31. Form W-2 shows wages paid, federal and state income tax withheld, and social security and medicare taxes withheld during the preceding year. The employer submits a copy of each employee's W-2 form to the Social Security Administration. In addition, each employee attaches a copy of Form W-2 to his or her federal and state income tax returns.

To print W-2s for each of TKT's employees, follow these steps:

step 1: From the main menu, select Reports, Payroll.

step 2: Scroll down the Report List, then double-click on Federal Form W-2; scroll down, then highlight W-2 1996 Standard.

step 3: Make the selections to print. Compare your printout for Kevin Barker with Figure 13.13.

Figure 13.13

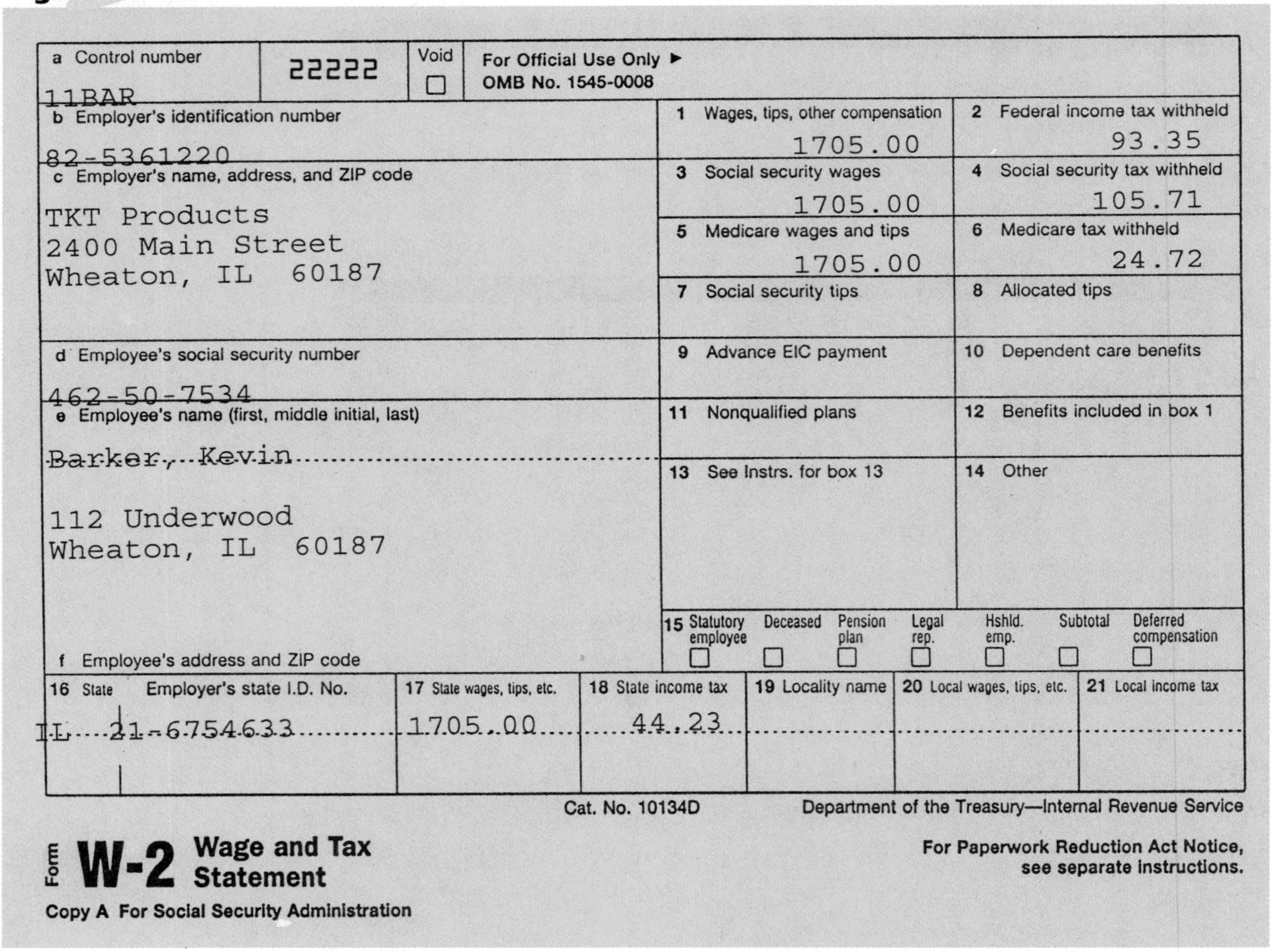

a Control number 22222 11BAR	Void ☐ For Official Use Only ► OMB No. 1545-0008
b Employer's identification number 82-5361220	1 Wages, tips, other compensation 1705.00
	2 Federal income tax withheld 93.35
c Employer's name, address, and ZIP code TKT Products 2400 Main Street Wheaton, IL 60187	3 Social security wages 1705.00
	4 Social security tax withheld 105.71
	5 Medicare wages and tips 1705.00
	6 Medicare tax withheld 24.72
	7 Social security tips
	8 Allocated tips
d Employee's social security number 462-50-7534	9 Advance EIC payment
	10 Dependent care benefits
e Employee's name (first, middle initial, last) Barker, Kevin 112 Underwood Wheaton, IL 60187	11 Nonqualified plans
	12 Benefits included in box 1
	13 See Instrs. for box 13
	14 Other
f Employee's address and ZIP code	15 Statutory employee ☐ Deceased ☐ Pension plan ☐ Legal rep. ☐ Hshld. emp. ☐ Subtotal ☐ Deferred compensation ☐

16 State	Employer's state I.D. No.	17 State wages, tips, etc.	18 State income tax	19 Locality name	20 Local wages, tips, etc.	21 Local income tax
IL	21-6754633	1705.00	44.23			

Cat. No. 10134D Department of the Treasury—Internal Revenue Service

Form **W-2** Wage and Tax Statement

For Paperwork Reduction Act Notice, see separate instructions.

Copy A For Social Security Administration

Transmittal of Wage and Tax Statements (Form W-3)

Form W-3, Transmittal of Wages and Tax Statements, is submitted to the Social Security Administration along with copies of each employee's Form W-2. Form W-3 summarizes the information shown on all the accompanying W-2s: total wages, total federal income tax withheld, total social security wages and amount withheld, and other information. This procedure allows the Social Security Administration to compare the W-2s and W-3 with information reported on the employer's quarterly 941 forms. Form W-3 is due on February 28, after the end of the calendar year. For practice, however, we will print TKT's Form W-3 now.

objective 8
Print Transmittal of Wage and Tax Statements (W-3)

Follow these steps:

step 1: From the main menu, select Reports, Payroll.

step 2: Scroll down the Report List, then double-click on Federal Form 940; highlight Form W-3. Click on the Print icon.

step 3: In the FUTA deposited for the year box, type **121.23** and press <Enter>.

step 4: Type **463.17** in the SUTA paid this year. Press <Enter>.

step 5: Make the selections to print. Compare your printout with Figure 13.14 on page 410.

Figure 13.14

DO NOT STAPLE

a Control number	33333	For Official Use Only ▶ OMB No. 1545-0008		

b Kind of Payer ▶	941 x☐ CT-1 ☐	Military ☐ Hshld. ☐	943 ☐ Medicare govt. emp. ☐	1 Wages, tips, other compensation 19881.64	2 Federal income tax withheld 1974.97

3   Social security wages   19881.64   4   Social security tax withheld   1232.67

c Total number of statements 6	d Establishment number

5   Medicare wages and tips   19881.64   6   Medicare tax withheld   288.29

e   Employer's identification number   82-5361220

7   Social security tips   8   Allocated tips

f   Employer's name   TKT Products

9   Advance EIC payments   10   Dependent care benefits

2400 Main Street
Wheaton, IL   60187

11   Nonqualified plans   12   Deferred compensation

13   Adjusted total social security wages and tips   19881.64

14   Adjusted total Medicare wages and tips   19881.64

g   Employer's address and ZIP code

h   Other EIN used this year

15   Income tax withheld by third-party payer

i   Employer's state I.D. No.   21-6754633

Under penalties of perjury, I declare that I have examined this return and accompanying documents, and, to the best of my knowledge and belief, they are true, correct, and complete.

Signature ▶   Title ▶   Date ▶

Telephone number   (   )

Form W-3 Transmittal of Wage and Tax Statements   Department of the Treasury Internal Revenue Service

Backing Up Your Chapter 13 Data

objective 9
Back up your data

As usual, you must back up your TKT Products data. You will need it when you begin Chapter 14. Follow these steps to back up your data:

step 1:   Place a blank formatted disk in drive A.

step 2:   From the main menu, select File, then Backup.

step 3:   Type **a:\chap13.tkt** in the Destination text box.

step 4:   Click on the Backup button. When all the files have been saved to drive A, you are automatically returned to the main menu.

step 5:   Click on File, Exit to exit PAW.

Workers' Compensation Insurance

Workers' compensation insurance protects workers in case of job-related illness or accident. Most states require employers to carry workers' compensation insurance. The employer usually has the option to contribute to a state insurance fund or acquire coverage from a state-approved private plan.

objective 10
Compute and record the premium for worker's compensation insurance

The employer normally pays the cost of this coverage. States assign insurance rates based on the level of risk. For example, a factory job would be assigned a higher rate because it involves greater risk than a clerical job. A company's accident history is also taken into consideration.

The premium is usually paid at the beginning of the year based on the estimated payroll for the year. To demonstrate, let's assume that in January TKT estimates its 1996 payroll will be $18,000 and the insurance rate is .25 percent. The estimated premium is computed as follows:

Estimated Payroll		Insurance Rate		Estimated Premium
$18,000	×	.0025	=	$45.00

Math Tip

As described earlier, .25 percent is converted to a decimal by (1) moving the decimal point two places to the left and (2) dropping the percentage sign.

$$.25\% = .0025$$

In data entry sheet format, the payment of this premium on January 10, 1996, is recorded as follows:

		DATA ENTRY SHEET			
		TKT Products			
Date	**Account ID**	**Reference**	**Trans Description**	**Debit Amt**	**Credit Amt**
1/10/96	114		Prepaid Insurance	45.00	
	110		Cash, Check No. 1664		45.00

In PAW, the Payments Task is used to journalize this transaction in the cash disbursements journal.

At year-end, when the actual payroll is known, the exact premium is computed. Continuing with our example, TKT's actual 1996 payroll amounts to $19,881.64. The additional premium is computed as follows:

step 1:

Actual Payroll $19,881.64	×	Insurance Rate .0025	=	Exact Premium $49.70

step 2:

Exact Premium $49.70	−	Estimated Premium $45.00	=	Additional Premium $4.70

The liability for the additional premium is recorded as part of the regular year-end adjustment for expired insurance. In data entry sheet format, it is recorded as follows:

DATA ENTRY SHEET TKT Products					
Date	**Account ID**	**Reference**	**Trans Description**	**Debit Amt**	**Credit Amt**
12/31/96	615	.	Insurance Expense	49.70	
	114		Prepaid Insurance		45.00
	212		Insurance Payable		4.70

In PAW, this adjusting entry is journalized through the "General Journal Entry" window. The additional premium is normally paid in January along with the following year's estimated premium.

If the exact premium turns out to be less than the estimated premium, the company receives a refund for the difference. Let's continue with our previous example but, this time, let's assume TKT's estimated premium was $55.

Estimated Premium $55.00	−	Exact Premium $49.70	=	Refund $5.30

In this case, the refund due is recorded as part of the year-end insurance adjustment. In data entry sheet format, it is recorded as follows:

DATA ENTRY SHEET TKT Products					
Date	Account ID	Reference	Trans Description	Debit Amt	Credit Amt
12/31/96	615		Insurance Expense	49.70	
	115		Refund Receivable	5.30	
	114		Prepaid Insurance		55.00

Comment

You probably noticed that we did not actually use PAW to record the workers' compensation insurance entries on the books of TKT Products. As this textbook follows a chronological pattern for The Kitchen Taylor and TKT Products, the journal entry to record the payment of the January premium should have been made in one of the early chapters. At that time, however, you were busy learning the basics and were not ready to deal with workers' compensation insurance. Because the January premium had not been recorded in PAW, it did not make sense to record the adjustment to the January entry in PAW. Instead, the authors chose to demonstrate the process and display the entries in data entry sheet format.

Chapter 13 Summary

Four payroll taxes are levied on the employer:

1. FICA—social security tax: Employer's contribution (6.2 percent of $62,700 maximum).
2. FICA—medicare tax: Employer's contribution (1.45 percent on all earnings).
3. Federal unemployment tax (FUTA). (.8 percent on $7,000 maximum).
4. State unemployment tax (SUTA) (2.7 percent on $9,000 maximum in Illinois).

All earnings are subject to medicare tax. The other three taxes involve both a tax rate and a calendar-year limit on earnings subject to the tax.

Matching amounts of FICA taxes are paid by both the employee and the employer. The employer's contributions are computed as follows:

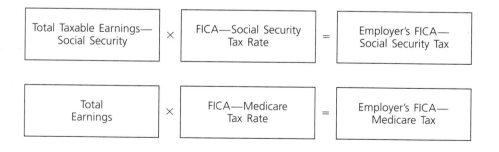

Federal unemployment tax is paid by the employer only. It is computed as follows:

State unemployment tax is paid by the employer only. It is computed as follows:

The employer's payroll taxes are recorded with debits to related expense accounts. The individual taxes are recorded as liabilities until they are paid. As the liabilities are paid, the liability accounts are debited and Cash is credited.

Both employer and employee FICA taxes (social security and medicare) and the amounts withheld from employees for federal income tax are paid together. The due dates vary according to the dollar amounts involved; *Circular E* provides the details. A Form 941 must be filed quarterly relative to these taxes and payments.

Due dates for the payment of federal unemployment tax also vary according to amount; again, *Circular E* provides details. A Form 940 or 940-EZ must be filed annually relative to this tax.

Due dates, methods of payment, and forms for the payment of state unemployment tax vary from state to state. Details are available at your state unemployment office.

Employers are required to provide each employee with an annual wage and tax statement. This information is reported on a Form W-2, which must be furnished to each employee by January 31. Form W-3 is submitted to the Social Security Administration along with copies of each employee's W-2. Form W-3 summarizes the information shown on the accompanying W-2 forms.

Most states require employers to carry workers' compensation insurance. The employer normally pays the cost of this coverage. An estimated premium is paid at the beginning of the year. At year-end, the exact premium is determined and the appropriate adjustment is recorded.

Demonstration Problem

The payroll records of Ricardo Company show the following information about Walter Watts for the pay period ending May 7, 1996:

Total earnings current pay period . . . .$ 475.00
Cumulative earnings previous pay period $6,800.00

Additional Data

FICA—social security tax: 6.2 percent on $62,700 maximum.
FICA—medicare tax: 1.45 percent on all earnings.
Federal unemployment tax: .8 percent on $7,000 maximum.
State unemployment tax: 2.7 percent on $9,000 maximum.

Instructions

1. Compute the following employer payroll taxes on Walter Watts for the pay period ending May 7, 1996:
   a. FICA—social security tax
   b. FICA—medicare tax
   c. Federal unemployment tax
   d. State unemployment tax
2. In data entry sheet format, record Ricardo Company's payroll tax expenses relating to Walter Watts for the pay period ending May 7, 1996. Leave the "Account ID" column blank.

Solution to Demonstration Problem

1. *a.* FICA—social security tax = $475 \times .062 = $29.45
   b. FICA—medicare tax = $475 \times .0145 = $6.89
   c. Federal unemployment tax = ($7,000 − 6,800 = $200) $\times$ .008 = $1.60
   d. State unemployment tax = $475 \times .027 = $12.83

2.

			DATA ENTRY SHEET Ricardo Company		
Date	Account ID	Reference	Trans Description	Debit Amt	Credit Amt
5/7/96			FICA—Social Security Tax Expense	29.45	
			FICA—Medicare Tax Expense	6.89	
			FUTA Tax Expense	1.60	
			SUTA Tax Expense	12.83	
			FICA—Social Security Tax Payable		29.45
			FICA—Medicare Tax Payable		6.89
			FUTA Tax Payable		1.60
			SUTA Tax Payable		12.83

Glossary

Circular E, Employer's Tax Guide   A publication of the Internal Revenue Service that discusses the tax rates, forms, due dates, payments, and so on. It also contains withholding tables for federal income tax, social security, and medicare.   *390*

employer identification number   A number assigned to a business by the Internal Revenue Service that must be included on all employer reports, forms, or correspondence submitted to the IRS.   *390*

federal unemployment tax (FUTA)   A tax that raises funds to cover the cost of administering the various state unemployment programs. This tax is paid by the employer only.   *381*

FICA—medicare tax   A tax that supports health care programs for retired persons. It is paid by both the employee and the employer.   *380*

FICA—social security tax A tax that supports a variety of programs including pension, disability, and survivor's benefits for retired persons. It is paid by both the employee and the employer. *380*

Form 940 An annual form, filed by the employer, summarizing the federal unemployment tax liability incurred, payments already deposited, and any balance due or overpayment. *400*

Form 940-EZ A simplified version of Form 940. *400*

Form 941 A quarterly form, filed by the employer, showing federal income tax (employee) and social security and medicare tax (employee and employer) liabilities, payments, and any resulting balance due or overpayment. *396*

Form 8109 A deposit form, supplied by the IRS, used to deposit all federal tax payments (federal income tax, FICA taxes, federal unemployment tax) at a Federal Reserve Bank or other authorized bank. *390*

Form W-2 An annual wage and tax statement, prepared by the employer, that must be furnished to each employee by January 31. This form shows wages paid, federal and state income tax withheld, and social security and medicare taxes withheld during the preceding calendar year. *408*

Form W-3 A transmittal form submitted to the Social Security Administration along with copies of each employee's W-2. It summarizes the information shown on the accompanying W-2s. *409*

state unemployment tax (SUTA) A tax that provides funds for paying state unemployment benefits. In most states, this tax is paid by the employer only. *382*

workers' compensation insurance Most states require that employers carry this insurance which protects workers in case of job-related illness or accident. The employer pays the cost of this coverage. *411*

Self-Test

Select the best answer.

1. Which of the following taxes is levied only on the employer?
   a. FICA—social security tax.
   b. FICA—medicare tax.
   c. Federal and state unemployment taxes.
   d. All of the above.

2. Which of the following employer payroll taxes does *not* have an earnings maximum?
   a. FICA—medicare tax.
   b. FICA—social security tax.
   c. Federal and state unemployment taxes.
   d. None of the above.

3. The entry to record the employer's payroll taxes includes
   a. a debit to Federal Income Tax Payable and credits to FICA—Social Security Tax Expense, FICA—Medicare Tax Expense, FUTA Tax Expense, SUTA Tax Expense.
   b. debits to FICA—Social Security Tax Expense, FICA—Medicare Tax Expense, FUTA Tax Expense, SUTA Tax Expense, and credits to various liability accounts.
   c. debits to various payroll tax-related expense accounts and a credit to Federal Income Tax Payable.
   d. debits to various payroll tax-related expense accounts and a credit to Wages Payable.

4. The entry to record the payment of the employer's payroll taxes should include
   a. a debit to the various payroll tax-related expense accounts and a credit to Cash.
   b. a debit to Federal Income Tax Payable and a credit to Cash.
   c. a debit to Wages Payable and a credit to Cash.
   d. debits to various tax-related liability accounts and a credit to Cash.

5. The workers' compensation premium is
   a. required in most states.
   b. normally paid by the employer.
   c. usually paid at the beginning of the year based on the estimated payroll.
   d. All of the above.

Answers to the self-test can be found after the cases at the end of this chapter.

Questions for Discussion

1. a. What are the four payroll taxes levied on the employer?
   b. What is the purpose of each tax?

2. A Form 8109
   a. is filed by whom?
   b. contains what information?
   c. is submitted along with what?

3. A Form 941
   a. is filed by whom?
   b. is filed how often?
   c. requires information about which tax(es)?

4. A Form 940 or 940-EZ
   a. is filed by whom?
   b. is filed how often?
   c. requires information about which tax(es)?

5. A Form W-2
   a. is prepared by whom?
   b. is prepared how often?
   c. contains what information?

6. A Form W-3
   a. is submitted to what government agency?
   b. is submitted along with what?
   c. summarizes what information?

7. a. What is the purpose of workers' compensation insurance?
   b. Who pays the premium?

8. What does *Circular E* contain? Describe its contents.

Exercises

Exercise 13.1

Match the following terms with the definitions shown below:

Terminology
L.O. 1–10

1. *Circular E*
2. Employer identification number

3. Federal unemployment tax

4. FICA—social security tax

5. Form 940

6. Form 941

7. Form W-2

8. Quarter

9. State unemployment tax

10. Workers' compensation insurance

Definitions

a. An annual wage and tax statement, prepared by the employer, that must be furnished to each employee by January 31. This form shows wages paid, federal and state income tax withheld, social security tax withheld, and medicare tax withheld during the preceding calendar year.

b. A time period consisting of three months.

c. Funds raised by this tax cover the cost of administering the various state unemployment programs. This tax is paid by the employer only.

d. Most states require that employers carry this insurance which protects workers in case of job-related illness or accident. The employer pays the cost of this coverage.

e. A quarterly form filed by the employer showing federal income tax (employee), social security tax (employee and employer), and medicare tax (employee and employer) liabilities, payments, and any resulting balance due or overpayment.

f. A number assigned by the Internal Revenue Service that must be included on all employer reports, forms, or correspondence submitted to the IRS.

g. A tax that raises funds to pay state unemployment benefits. This tax is paid by the employer only.

h. A tax that supports a variety of programs including pension, disability, and survivor's benefits for retired persons. It is paid by both the employee and the employer.

i. Employer's Tax Guide published by the Internal Revenue Service. It discusses tax rates, forms, due dates, payments, and so on. It also contains withholding tables for federal income tax, social security, and medicare.

j. An annual form filed by the employer summarizing the federal unemployment tax liability incurred, payments already deposited, and any balance due or overpayment.

Exercise 13.2

Compute Payroll Taxes
LO 1

The payroll records of Anton Company show the following information about Sarah Powell for the pay period ending June 14, 1996:

Total earnings current pay period . . . .$ 560.00
Cumulative earnings previous pay period $6,700.00

Additional Data

FICA—social security tax: 6.2 percent on $62,700 maximum.

FICA—medicare tax: 1.45 percent on all earnings.

Federal unemployment tax: .8 percent on $7,000 maximum.

State unemployment tax: 2.7 percent on $9,000 maximum.

Instructions

Compute the following employer payroll taxes on Sarah Powell for the pay period ending June 14, 1996:

1. FICA—social security tax

2. FICA—medicare tax

3. Federal unemployment tax

4. State unemployment tax

Exercise 13.3

Referring to your computations from Exercise 13.2, record Anton Company's payroll tax expense in relation to Sarah Powell for the pay period ending June 14, 1996. Record the entry in data entry sheet format leaving the "Account ID" column blank.

Record Payroll Taxes
L.O. 3

Exercise 13.4

On June 30, Martin Company's ledger shows the following selected account balances:

Record Payment of FIT and FICA Taxes
L.O. 4

FICA—Social Security Tax Payable	$1,625
FICA—Medicare Tax Payable	380
Federal Income Tax Payable	2,348
FUTA Tax Payable	210
SUTA Tax Payable	708
FICA—Social Security Tax Expense	5,890
FICA—Medicare Tax Expense	1,378
FUTA Tax Expense	760
SUTA Tax Expense	2,565
Wages Expense	95,000

In data entry sheet format, record the June 30 entry to record the payment of liabilities for social security, medicare, and federal income tax. Leave the "Account ID" column blank.

Exercise 13.5

Referring to the information given in Exercise 13.4, record the following transactions in data entry sheet format:

Record Payment of FUTA and SUTA Taxes
L.O. 4

a. The payment of the liability for federal unemployment tax.

b. The payment of the liability for state unemployment tax.

Exercise 13.6

The payroll records of Silver Enterprises show the following information on January 31, the end of their first month of operations:

Compute Payroll Taxes
L.O. 1

Employee	Cumulative Earnings
A	$3,520
B	2,690
C	6,250

Additional Data

FICA—social security tax: 6.2 percent on $62,700 maximum.
FICA—medicare tax: 1.45 percent on all earnings.
Federal unemployment tax: .8 percent on $7,000 maximum.
State unemployment tax: 2.7 percent on $9,000 maximum.

Compute the following January 31 account balances:

1. Wages Expense

2. FICA—Social Security Tax Expense

3. FICA—Medicare Tax Expense

4. FUTA Tax Expense

5. SUTA Tax Expense

Exercise 13.7

*Compute and Record
Estimated Workers'
Compensation
L.O. 10*

On January 6, Gentry Products estimates that its payroll for the coming year will total $160,000. The workers' compensation insurance rate assigned to Gentry is .35 percent.

a. Compute the estimated premium for workers' compensation insurance.

b. In data entry sheet format, record the payment of the estimated premium on January 6.

Exercise 13.8

*Compute and Record
Additional Workers'
Compensation Premium
L.O. 10*

On December 31, Gentry Products determines that its actual payroll for the past year amounts to $168,000. In reference to Exercise 13.7:

a. Compute the exact premium for workers' compensation insurance.

b. Compute the additional premium.

c. In data entry sheet format, record the liability for the additional premium as part of the regular December 31 adjustment for expired insurance.

Problems—Set A

Problem 13.1A

*Restore Data; Trial Balance
L.O. 2*

In Chapter 12, you recorded the payroll for ACS Products. Follow these steps to restore your Chapter 12 data and print a general ledger trial balance:

step 1: Start Windows, then PAW. Open ACS Products.

step 2: Place your Chapter 12 backup disk in drive A.

step 3: From the main menu, select File, then Restore.

step 4: Type a:\acsdec.12a in the Source box. (Use the same file name that you used in Chapter 12.)

step 5: Click on the Restore button. Read the "Warning" screen, then click on OK. Restoring the files will take a few moments. When the files are restored, you are returned to the main menu.

step 6: Remove disk from drive A.

step 7: From the main menu, select Reports, then General Ledger.

step 8: In the "Report List," highlight "General Ledger Trial Balance."

step 9: Make the selections to print.

Compare your printout to Figure 13.15.

Figure 13.15

ACS Products
General Ledger Trial Balance
As of Dec 31, 1996
Filter Criteria includes: Report order is by ID. Report is printed in Detail Format.

Account ID	Account Description	Debit Amt	Credit Amt
107	Payroll Checking	2,235.10	
108	Change Fund	30.00	
109	Petty Cash	50.00	
110	Cash	16,924.55	
111	Accounts Receivable	13.72	
112	Merchandise Inventory	2,578.89	
113	Supplies	490.95	
114	Prepaid Insurance	700.00	
120	Equipment	5,000.00	
121	Accumulated Depreciation		900.00
210	Accounts Payable		265.95
213	Sales Tax Payable		8.90
214	Federal Income Tax Payable		515.14
215	FICA--Soc. Sec. Tax Payable		695.10
216	FICA--Medicare Tax Payable		162.56
217	State Income Tax Payable		156.63
220	FUTA Tax Payable		31.80
221	SUTA Tax Payable		107.34
223	Health Insurance Payable		180.00
224	Union Dues Payable		60.00
310	Joan Haywood, Capital		7,500.00
320	Joan Haywood, Drawing	4,100.00	
330	Retained Earnings		1,937.00
410	Cleaning Revenue		42,000.00
411	Sales		17,836.25
412	Sales Returns and Allowances	593.25	
413	Sales Discount	170.94	
501	Cost of Sales	8,077.80	
610	Depreciation Expense	825.00	
611	FICA--Soc. Sec. Tax Expense	1,091.55	
612	FICA--Medicare Tax Expense	255.28	
613	FUTA Tax Expense	87.80	
614	SUTA Tax Expense	350.34	
615	Insurance Expense	460.00	
616	Rent Expense	7,500.00	
617	Repair Expense	406.00	
618	Service Charge Expense	198.00	
619	Supplies Expense	910.00	
620	Utilities Expense	1,702.00	
621	Wages Expense	17,605.50	
	Total:	**72,356.67**	**72,356.67**

Problem 13.2A

On December 30, 1996, ACS Products issues Check No. 1434 to First National Bank in payment of the liabilities for federal income tax withheld, social security, and medicare shown on their general ledger trial balance (refer to Problem 13.1A.)

FIT and FICA Taxes
L.O. 4

Instructions

1. Record this transaction in data entry sheet format.

2. Referring to your data entry sheet, use PAW's Payments Task to journalize this transaction in ACS's cash disbursements journal. Follow these steps:

step 1: From the main menu, select Tas<u>k</u>s, Pa<u>y</u>ments.

step 2: In the "Pay to the Order of" box, type **First National Bank** and press the <Enter> key.

step 3: In the <u>D</u>ate box, type **30** and press <Enter>.

step 4: Click on the "Quantity" column. Type **1** and press <Enter> two times.

step 5: In the "Description" box, type **Federal Income Tax Payable** and press <Enter>.

step 6: In the "GL Account" column, select Account No. 214, Federal Income Tax Payable.

step 7: In the "Unit Price" column, type **515.14** and press the <Enter> key three times. (Check this amount against your trial balance. Refer to Problem 13.1A.)

step 8: Enter the account data and amounts for social security and medicare as shown on ACS's trial balance in Problem 13.1A.

step 9: Make the selections to print Check No. 1434 in the amount of $1,372.80. If you are using the check forms from the working papers, select form AP Preprint 1 Stub.

Problem 13.3A

FUTA Tax
L.O. 4

On December 30, 1996, ACS Products issues Check No. 1435 to the Internal Revenue Service in payment of the FUTA tax liability shown on their general ledger trial balance (refer to Problem 13.1A). This check will accompany Form 940-EZ which will be prepared in Problem 13.5A.

Instructions

1. Record this transaction in data entry sheet format.

2. Referring to your data entry sheet, use PAW's Payments Task to journalize this transaction in ACS's cash disbursements journal. Follow these steps:

step 1: From the main menu, select Tas<u>k</u>s, Pa<u>y</u>ments.

step 2: In the "Pay to the Order of" box, type **Internal Revenue Service** and press the <Enter> key.

step 3: In the <u>D</u>ate box, type **30** and press <Enter>.

step 4: Click on the "Quantity" column. Type **1** and press <Enter> two times.

step 5: In the "Description" box, type **FUTA Tax Payable** and press <Enter>.

step 6: In the "GL Account" column, select Account No. 220, FUTA Tax Payable.

step 7: In the "Unit Price" column, type **31.80** and press <Enter>. (Check this amount against your trial balance. Refer to Problem 13.1A.)

step 8: Make the selections to print Check No. 1435. If you are using the check forms from the working papers, select form AP Preprint 1 Stub.

Problem 13.4A

On December 30, 1996, ACS Products issues Check No. 1436 to the Director of Employment Security in payment of the SUTA tax liability shown on their general ledger trial balance (refer to Problem 13.1A).

SUTA Tax
L.O. 4

Instructions

1. Record this transaction in data entry sheet format.

2. Referring to your data entry sheet, use PAW's Payments Task to journalize this transaction in ACS' cash disbursements journal. Follow these steps:

   step 1: From the main menu, select Tasks, Payments.

   step 2: In the "Pay to the Order of" box, type **Dir. of Employment Security** and press the <Enter> key.

   step 3: In the "Date" box, type **30** and press <Enter>.

   step 4: Click on the "Quantity" column. Type **1** and press <Enter> two times.

   step 5: In the "Description" box, type **SUTA Tax Payable** and press <Enter>.

   step 6: In the "GL Account" column, select Account No. 221, SUTA Tax Payable.

   step 7: In the "Unit Price" column, type **107.34** and press <Enter>. (Check this amount against your trial balance. Refer to Problem 13.1A.)

   step 8: Make the selections to print Check No. 1436. If you are using the check forms from the working papers, select form AP Preprint 1 Stub.

   step 9: **Post** the cash disbursements journal.

Problem 13.5A

1. Follow these steps to print Form 941:

941 and 940-EZ
L.O. 5, 6

   step 1: From the main menu, select Reports, then Payroll.

   step 2: Scroll down the "Payroll" Report List, then double-click on Federal Form 941.

   step 3: Scroll down, then highlight "FedForm 941 1996/1997." Click on the Print icon.

   step 4: Type **1372.80** in the Total deposits for quarter box. Make the selections to print.

2. Follow these steps to print Form 940-EZ:

   step 1: In the "Payroll" Report list, double-click on Federal Form 940. Scroll down the list, highlight Form 940-EZ.

   step 2: In the FUTA deposited for the year box, type **56** and press <Enter>.

   step 3: In the SUTA paid this year, type **243** and press <Enter>. Make the selections to print.

Problem 13.6A

W-2s and W-3
L.O. 7, 8

1. Follow these steps to print Form W-2s:

   step 1: From the main menu, select Reports, then Payroll.

   step 2: Scroll down the "Payroll" Report List, then double-click on Federal Form W-2.

   step 3: Highlight W-2 1996 Standard. Make the selections to print.

2. Follow these steps to print Form W-3:

   step 1: Scroll down the "Payroll" Report List, then double-click on Federal Form 940.

   step 2: Highlight Form W-3. In the FUTA deposited for the year box, type **87.80** and press <Enter>.

   step 3: In the SUTA paid this year, type **350.34** and press <Enter>. Make the selections to print.

Problem 13.7A

Back Up
L.O. 9

Your ACS Products data **must** be backed up. You will restore it in Chapter 14. Follow these steps:

step 1: Insert a blank formatted disk in drive A.

step 2: From PAW's main menu, select File, then Backup.

step 3: Type **a:\acsdec.13a** in the Destination text box.

step 4: Click on the Backup button. When all the files have been saved to drive A, you are automatically returned to the main menu.

step 5: Click on File, Exit to exit PAW.

Problems—Set B

Problem 13.1B

Restore Data; Trial Balance
L.O. 2

In Chapter 12, you recorded the payroll for LLS Products. Follow these steps to restore your Chapter 12 data and print a general ledger trial balance.

step 1: Start Windows, then PAW. Open LLS Products.

step 2: Place your Chapter 12 backup disk in drive A.

step 3: From the main menu, select File, then Restore.

step 4: Type **a:\llsdec.12b** in the Source box. (Use the same file name that you used in Chapter 12.)

step 5: Click on the Restore button. Read the "Warning" screen, then click on OK. Restoring the files will take a few moments. When the files are restored, you are returned to the main menu.

step 6: Remove disk from drive A.

step 7: From the main menu, select Reports, then General Ledger.

step 8: In the "Report List," highlight General Ledger Trial Balance.

step 9: Make the selections to print.

Compare your printout to Figure 13.16.

Figure 13.16

LLS Products
General Ledger Trial Balance
As of Dec 31, 1996
Filter Criteria includes: Report order is by ID. Report is printed in Detail Format.

Account ID	Account Description	Debit Amt	Credit Amt
107	Payroll Checking	2,189.14	
108	Change Fund	25.00	
109	Petty Cash	75.00	
110	Cash	3,824.24	
111	Accounts Receivable	33.82	
112	Merchandise Inventory	4,967.08	
113	Supplies	404.85	
114	Prepaid Insurance	590.00	
120	Equipment	5,000.00	
121	Accumulated Depreciation		900.00
210	Accounts Payable		242.85
213	Sales Tax Payable		14.13
214	Federal Income Tax Payable		560.24
215	FICA--Soc. Sec. Tax Payable		708.04
216	FICA--Medicare Tax Payable		165.60
217	State Income Tax Payable		162.08
220	FUTA Tax Payable		32.64
221	SUTA Tax Payable		110.16
223	Health Insurance Payable		180.00
224	Union Dues Payable		60.00
310	Chris Canon, Capital		7,000.00
320	Chris Canon, Drawing	4,600.00	
330	Retained Earnings		1,267.25
410	Lawn Service Revenue		38,000.00
411	Sales		7,436.80
412	Sales Returns and Allowances	543.25	
413	Sales Discount	133.16	
501	Cost of Sales	4,136.13	
610	Depreciation Expense	825.00	
611	FICA--Soc. Sec. Tax Expense	1,036.02	
612	FICA--Medicare Tax Expense	242.30	
613	FUTA Tax Expense	88.64	
614	SUTA Tax Expense	353.16	
615	Insurance Expense	550.00	
616	Rent Expense	7,140.00	
617	Repair Expense	466.00	
618	Service Charge Expense	182.00	
619	Supplies Expense	730.00	
620	Utilities Expense	1,995.00	
621	Wages Expense	16,710.00	
	Total:	**56,839.79**	**56,839.79**

Problem 13.2B

On December 30, 1996, LLS Products issues Check No. 1249 to Federated Bank & Trust in payment of the liabilities for federal income tax withheld, social security, and medicare shown on their general ledger trial balance (refer to Problem 13.1B.)

FIT and FICA Taxes
L.O. 4

Instructions

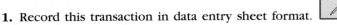

1. Record this transaction in data entry sheet format.
2. Referring to your data entry sheet, use PAW's Payments Task to journalize this transaction in LLS's cash disbursements journal. Follow these steps:

   step 1: From the main menu, select Tas**k**s, Pa**y**ments.

   step 2: In the "Pay to the Order of" box, type **Federated Bank & Trust** and press the <Enter> key.

   step 3: In the "**D**ate" box, type **30** and press <Enter>.

   step 4: Click on the "Quantity" column. Type **1** and press <Enter> two times.

   step 5: In the "Description" box, type **Federal Income Tax Payable** and press <Enter>.

   step 6: In the "GL Account" column, select Account No. 214, Federal Income Tax Payable.

   step 7: In the "Unit Price" column, type **560.24** and press the <Enter> key three times. (Check this amount against your trial balance. Refer to Problem 13.1B.)

   step 8: Enter the account data and amounts for social security and medicare as shown on LLS's trial balance in Problem 13.1B.

   step 9: Make the selections to print Check No. 1249 in the amount of $1,433.88. If you are using the check forms from the working papers, select form AP Preprint 1 Stub.

FUTA Tax
L.O. 4

Problem 13.3B

On December 30, 1996, LLS Products issues Check No. 1250 to the Internal Revenue Service in payment of the FUTA tax liability shown on their general ledger trial balance (refer to Problem 13.1B). This check will accompany Form 940-EZ which will be prepared in Problem 13.5B.

Instructions

1. Record this transaction in data entry sheet format.
2. Referring to your data entry sheet, use PAW's Payments Task to journalize this transaction in LLS's cash disbursements journal. Follow these steps:

   step 1: From the main menu, select Tas**k**s, Pa**y**ments.

   step 2: In the "Pay to the Order of" box, type **Internal Revenue Service** and press the <Enter> key.

   step 3: In the "**D**ate" box, type **30** and press <Enter>.

   step 4: Click on the "Quantity" column. Type **1** and press <Enter> two times.

   step 5: In the "Description" box, type **FUTA Tax Payable** and press <Enter>.

   step 6: In the "GL Account" column, select Account No. 220, FUTA Tax Payable.

   step 7: In the "Unit Price" column, type **32.64** and press <Enter>. (Check this amount against your trial balance. Refer to Problem 13.1B.)

   step 8: Make the selections to print Check No. 1250. If you are using the check forms from the working papers, select form AP Preprint 1 Stub.

Problem 13.4B

On December 30, 1996, LLS Products issues Check No. 1251 to the Director of Employment Security in payment of the SUTA tax liability shown on their general ledger trial balance (refer to Problem 13.1B).

SUTA Tax
L.O. 4

Instructions

1. Record this transaction in data entry sheet format.

2. Referring to your data entry sheet, use PAW's Payments Task to journalize this transaction in LLS's cash disbursements journal. Follow these steps:

   step 1: From the main menu, select Tas<u>k</u>s, Pa<u>y</u>ments.

   step 2: In the "Pay to the Order of" box, type **Dir. of Employment Security** and press the <Enter> key.

   step 3: In the "<u>D</u>ate" box, type **30** and press <Enter>.

   step 4: Click on the "Quantity" column. Type **1** and press <Enter> two times.

   step 5: In the "Description" box, type **SUTA Tax Payable** and press <Enter>.

   step 6: In the "GL Account" column, select Account No. 221, SUTA Tax Payable.

   step 7: In the "Unit Price" column, type **110.16** and press the <Enter> key.

   step 8: Make the selections to print Check No. 1251. If you are using the check forms from the working papers, select form AP Preprint 1 Stub.

   step 9: **Post** the cash disbursements journal.

Problem 13.5B

1. Follow these steps to print Form 941:

941 and 940-EZ
L.O. 5, 6

   step 1: From the main menu, select <u>R</u>eports, then Pa<u>y</u>roll.

   step 2: Scroll down the "Payroll" Report List, then double-click on Federal Form 941.

   step 3: Scroll down, then highlight "FedForm 941 1996/1997." Click on the Print icon.

   step 4: Type **1433.88** in the <u>T</u>otal deposits for quarter box. Make the selections to print.

2. Follow these steps to print Form 940-EZ:

   step 1: In the "Payroll" Report list, double-click on Federal Form 940. Scroll down the list, highlight Form 940-EZ.

   step 2: In the F<u>U</u>TA deposited for the year box, type **56** and press <Enter>.

   step 3: In the S<u>U</u>TA paid for the year box, type **243** and press <Enter>. Make the selections to print.

Problem 13.6B

1. Follow these steps to print Form W-2s:

W-2s and W-3
L.O. 7, 8

   step 1: From the main menu, select <u>R</u>eports, then Pa<u>y</u>roll.

   step 2: Scroll down the "Payroll" Report List, then double-click on Federal Form W-2.

   step 3: Highlight W-2 1996 Standard. Make the selections to print.

2. Follow these steps to print Form W-3:

> **step 1:** Scroll down the "Payroll" Report List, then double-click on Federal Form 940.
>
> **step 2:** Highlight Form W-3. Type **88.64** in the FUTA deposited for the year box.
>
> **step 3:** Type **353.16** in the SUTA paid this year. Make the selections to print.

Problem 13.7B

Back Up
L.O. 9

Your LLS Products data **must** be backed up. You will restore it in Chapter 14. Follow these steps:

step 1: Insert a blank formatted disk in drive A.

step 2: From PAW's main menu, select File, then Backup.

step 3: Type a:\llsdec.13b in the "Destination" text box.

step 4: Click on the Backup button. When all the files have been saved to drive A, you are automatically returned to the main menu.

step 5: Click on File, Exit to exit PAW.

Mini-Cases

Case 13–1

Your friend, Jack Kurz, operates his own business. All smiles, he tells you that one of his employees no longer wants to be part of the U.S. Social Security Program. "Isn't that great! Now I won't have to pay matching amounts for that employee," says Jack. Does he have cause for jubilation?

Case 13–2

Jacob Harvey, your new employer, does not want you to prepare W-2 forms for employees. "It's a waste of time and money! Let them use their check stubs," he says. Respond.

Case 13–3

Nelda Grant, your employer, is trying to reduce payroll costs without laying off any of her employees. "I just had a brainstorm!" Nelda tells you. "Since I'm paying half of my employees' HMO health insurance premiums, I don't need to pay a matching amount of FICA—medicare tax." Respond to Nelda's "brainstorm."

A Case of Ethics

Scott just started a new business and needs to hire several new employees. As with most new businesses, money is tight. He is planning to classify these new employees as independent contractors so he won't have to pay payroll taxes (social security, medicare, and state and federal unemployment) on them. "I'm 'small potatoes' to the government, so I doubt that I'll get caught," Scott says. "If I do, I'll just play dumb and say that I didn't understand the distinction between an employee and an independent contractor." What's your opinion of Scott's plan?

Answers to Self-Test

1. *c*   2. *a*   3. *b*   4. *d*   5. *d*

Merchandising Business

Month End

LEARNING OBJECTIVES

After studying this chapter, you should be able to:

1. Restore data from the previous chapter.

2. Account for unearned revenue.

3. Record adjustments for supplies, insurance, wages, and depreciation.

4. Print adjusting entries.

5. Post adjusting entries.

6. Replenish petty cash.

7. Reconcile the regular checking account.

8. Reconcile the payroll checking account.

9. Print the trial balance.

10. Back up your data.

In the last six chapters, you learned how to journalize and post the day-to-day transactions of a merchandising business using PAW's Purchases/Receive Inventory, Sales/Invoicing, Cash Payments, Cash Receipts, and Payroll Entry Tasks. In this chapter, you will continue with the accounting cycle for a merchandising business. Since the cycle for a merchandising business is the same as the cycle for a service business, many of the topics in this chapter will sound familiar. After restoring our data from Chapter 13, we will begin with how to record unearned revenue.

Restoring Data from Chapter 13

objective 1
Restore data from the previous chapter

The data you backed up at the end of Chapter 13 is your starting point for this chapter. Follow these steps to restore your Chapter 13 data:

step 1: Start Windows, then PAW. Open TKT Products.

step 2: Place your Chapter 13 backup disk in drive A.

step 3: From the main menu, select File, then Restore.

step 4: Type a:\chap13.tkt in the Source box. (Use the same file name that you used when you backed up in Chapter 13.)

step 5: Click on the Restore button. Read the "Warning" screen, then click on OK. When the files are restored, you are returned to the main menu.

step 6: Remove disk from drive A.

Unearned Revenue

Recording the Receipt of Cash

objective 2
Account for unearned revenue

Sometimes a business is paid in advance for a product or service to be delivered in the future. Although the cash has been received, the revenue cannot be recorded because it has not yet been earned. The receipt of a prepayment creates a liability for the seller because the seller now owes the customer the product or service.

To demonstrate, let's assume that on December 1, 1996, TKT Products receives a $5,400 prepayment from Adams Company for 12 kitchen cabinets to be delivered on December 31. Although TKT has received the cash, it has not earned the revenue because it has not yet provided the cabinets to Adams Company. This situation creates a liability for TKT Products because TKT now owes the cabinets to Adams Company.

In data entry sheet format, this transaction is recorded as follows:

		DATA ENTRY SHEET TKT Products			
Date	Account ID	Reference	Trans Description	Debit Amt	Credit Amt
12/1/96	110		Cash	5,400.00	
	212		Unearned Revenue		5,400.00

Referring to the data entry sheet, we are ready to use PAW's "Cash Receipts" window to journalize the receipt of this prepayment. Since Unearned Revenue is a new account, we will add that account to TKT's chart of accounts as we journalize.

Follow these steps to journalize the receipt of this prepayment in the cash receipts journal:

step 1: From the main menu, select Tasks, Receipts.

step 2: In the Deposit ticket ID box, type **12/1/96** and press <Enter>.

step 3: In the Customer ID box, select Adams Company.

step 4: In the Reference box, type **prepayment** and press <Enter>.

step 5: In the Date box, type **1** and press <Enter>.

step 6: Check that the "Payment Method" box displays "Check" and that the "G/L Account" box shows Account No. 110, Cash.

step 7: Click once on the Prepayment box. A check mark is placed in the box. Press <Enter>.

step 8: Click once on the "Description" column. Type **prepayment for 12 kitchen cabinets** and press <Enter>.

step 9: In the "GL Account" column, click on the magnifying glass icon. Click on the "New Records" icon. Add Account No. 212, Unearned Revenue. The Account Type is Other Current Liabilities. *Remember to click on the Save icon.*

step 10: Type **5400** in the "Amount" column.

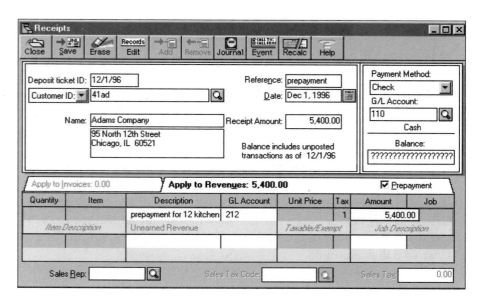

step 11: Click on the Save icon.

step 12: **Post** the Cash Receipts Journal.

Now, let's print out the cash receipts journal for December 1, 1996.

step 1: From the main menu, select Reports, then Accounts Receivable.

step 2: Highlight the Cash Receipts Journal.

step 3: Click on the Print icon. Click on the To calendar icon. Select December 1, 1996. Make the selections to print. Compare your printout to Figure 14.1.

Figure 14.1

TKT Products
Cash Receipts Journal
For the Period From Dec 1, 1996 to Dec 1, 1996
Filter Criteria includes: Report order is by Check Date. Report is printed in Detail Format.

Date	Account ID	Transaction Ref	Line Description	Debit Amnt	Credit Amnt
12/1/96	212	prepayment	prepayment for 12 kitchen cabinets		5,400.00
	110		Adams Company	5,400.00	
				5,400.00	5,400.00

Recording the Adjustment When the Revenue Is Earned

To continue with our example, let's assume that on December 31, TKT ships 12 kitchen cabinets to Adams Company, Invoice No. 2010, $5,400. The cabinets cost $3,240. Now the $5,400 in revenue has been earned because Adams has been provided with the cabinets. Accordingly, $5,400 must be removed from the Unearned Revenue account and transferred to the revenue account, Sales. Since revenue is being recorded, the Merchandise Inventory and Cost of Sales accounts also must be updated.

In data entry sheet format, this transaction is recorded as follows:

		DATA ENTRY SHEET			
		TKT Products			
Date	Account ID	Reference	Trans Description	Debit Amt	Credit Amt
12/31/96	212		Unearned Revenue	5,400.00	
	501		Cost of Sales	3,240.00	
	411		Sales, Inv. No. 2010		5,400.00
	112		Merchandise Inventory		3,240.00

Referring to the data entry sheet, we are now ready to journalize this transaction using PAW's "Sales/Invoicing" window. In addition to recording the revenue, this window automatically updates our Merchandise Inventory and Cost of Sales accounts.

Follow these steps to journalize this transaction in the sales journal:

step 1: From the main menu, select Tas<u>k</u>s, <u>S</u>ales/Invoicing.

step 2: In the <u>C</u>ustomer ID box, select Adams Company.

step 3: In the <u>I</u>nvoice # box, type **2010** and press <Enter>.

step 4: In the <u>D</u>ate box, type **31** and press <Enter>.

step 5: Click on the "Quantity" column, type **12** and press <Enter>.

step 6: In the "Item" column, select kitchen cabinets.

step 7: Click on the magnifying glass icon in the A/R Account box (lower left of screen). Select Account No. 212, Unearned Revenue. (Hint: Scroll down your screen or click on the "enlarge" button to go to the "A/R Account" lookup box.)

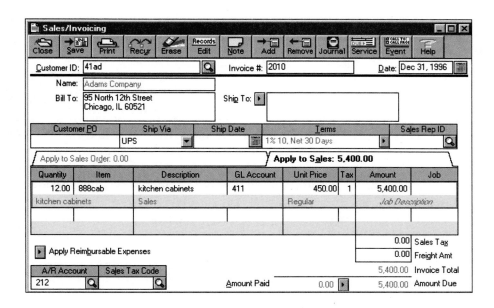

step 8: Click on <u>S</u>ave.

step 9: **Post** the Sales Journal.

Now, we are ready to print the sales journal for December 31, 1996. Follow these steps:

step 1: From the main menu, select <u>R</u>eports, Accounts <u>R</u>eceivable.

step 2: Highlight the Sales Journal. Click on the Print icon.

step 3: In the From box, click on the Calendar icon. Select 31 and press <Enter>. Make the selections to print. Compare your printout with Figure 14.2 on page 434.

TKT Products requires prepayments only if an order is exceptionally large or the customer has a poor credit record.

Figure 14.2

TKT Products
Sales Journal
For the Period From Dec 31, 1996 to Dec 31, 1996
Filter Criteria includes: Report order is by Invoice Date. Report is printed in Detail Format.

Date	Account ID	Invoice No	Line Description	Debit Amnt	Credit Amnt
12/31/96	411	2010	kitchen cabinets		5,400.00
	501		Cost of sales	3,240.00	
	112		Cost of sales		3,240.00
	212		Adams Company	5,400.00	
		Total		**8,640.00**	**8,640.00**

Recording Adjustments for Supplies, Insurance, Wages, and Depreciation

objective 3
Record adjustments

As you will recall, adjusting entries are really updating entries. The need to update exists because a few internal transactions have occurred but have not yet been recorded. It is acceptable to allow these internal transactions to go unrecorded on a daily basis, but we cannot prepare financial statements with incorrect account balances. Therefore, at the end of the accounting period, before preparing financial statements, we must adjust the accounts.

Although TKT Products is a merchandising business, you will observe that the adjustment process is the same as it was earlier when TKT was a service business.

The Adjustment for Supplies

TKT has determined that $135 worth of supplies has been used during December. Because the cost of the used supplies is no longer an asset, TKT must transfer $135 from the Supplies account to the Supplies Expense account.

In data entry sheet format, this adjustment for supplies is recorded as follows:

			DATA ENTRY SHEET **TKT Products**		
Date	Account ID	Reference	Trans Description	Debit Amt	Credit Amt
12/31/96	619		Supplies Expense	135.00	
	113		Supplies		135.00

The Adjustment for Insurance

TKT has determined that $210 of insurance has expired during December. Because the cost of the expired insurance is no longer an asset, TKT must transfer $210 out of the Prepaid Insurance account into the Insurance Expense account.

In data entry sheet format, this adjustment for insurance is recorded as follows:

			DATA ENTRY SHEET TKT Products		
Date	Account ID	Reference	Trans Description	Debit Amt	Credit Amt
12/31/96	615		Insurance Expense	210.00	
	114		Prepaid Insurance		210.00

The Adjustment for Wages

As you will recall from Chapters 12 and 13, Friday, December 27, was TKT's last payday in December. TKT's wages expense for the following Monday and Tuesday, December 30 and 31, amounts to $1,976. According to accrual-basis accounting, this expense has been incurred in 1996 and must be recorded in the Wages Expense account in 1996 even though it will not be paid until 1997. The resulting liability to TKT's employees is recorded in the Wages Payable account.

In data entry sheet format, this adjustment for wages is recorded as follows:

			DATA ENTRY SHEET TKT Products		
Date	Account ID	Reference	Trans Description	Debit Amt	Credit Amt
12/31/96	621		Wages Expense	1,976.00	
	211		Wages Payable		1,976.00

The Adjustment for Depreciation

On December 31, TKT records $1,200 of depreciation on the truck. Through an adjustment, $1,200 of used-up cost associated with the truck must be transferred to the Depreciation Expense account. The book value of the truck (cost minus accumulated depreciation) is reduced by increasing the contra-asset account, Accumulated Depreciation.

In data entry sheet format, this adjustment for depreciation is recorded as follows:

DATA ENTRY SHEET TKT Products					
Date	Account ID	Reference	Trans Description	Debit Amt	Credit Amt
12/31/96	610		Depreciation Expense	1,200.00	
	121		Accumulated Depreciation		1,200.00

Using PAW to Journalize the Adjusting Entries

Referring to the information recorded in data entry sheet format, we are now ready to use PAW's "General Journal Entry" window to record TKT's December 31, 1996, adjustments in the general journal.

Follow these steps:

step 1: From the main menu, select Tasks, General Journal Entry.

step 2: Type **31** in the Date box.

step 3: In the "Account No." column, click on the magnifying glass icon. Select Account No. 619, Supplies Expense.

step 4: In the "Description" column, type **Supplies Expense** and press <Enter>.

step 5: In the "Debit" column, type **135** and press <Enter> three times.

step 6: In the "Account No." column, click on the magnifying glass icon. Select Account No. 113, Supplies.

step 7: In the "Description" column, type **Supplies** and press <Enter> two times.

step 8: In the "Credit" column, type **135** and press <Enter>.

step 9: Click on the Save icon.

step 10: Repeat steps 2 through 9 to record the adjustments for insurance, wages, and depreciation using the appropriate account descriptions, account numbers, and amounts.

Printing the Adjusting Entries

objective 4
Print adjusting entries

Follow these steps to print the December 31 adjusting entries:

step 1: From the main menu, select Reports, General Ledger.

step 2: Highlight General Journal.

step 3: Click on the Print icon.

step 4: Click on the Calendar icon in the From box, then select 31.

step 5: Make the selections to print. Compare your printout with Figure 14.3.

Figure 14.3

TKT Products
General Journal
For the Period From Dec 31, 1996 to Dec 31, 1996
Filter Criteria includes: Report order is by Date. Report is printed with Accounts having Zero Amounts and with Truncated Transaction Descriptions and in Detai

Date	Account ID	Reference	Trans Description	Debit Amt	Credit Amt
12/31/96	619		Supplies Expense	135.00	
	113		Supplies		135.00
	615		Insurance Expense	210.00	
	114		Prepaid Insurance		210.00
	621		Wages Expense	1,976.00	
	211		Wages Payable		1,976.00
	610		Depreciation Expense	1,200.00	
	121		Accumulated Depreciation		1,200.00
		Total		3,521.00	3,521.00

Posting the Adjusting Entries

After the adjusting entries have been journalized, they must be posted to the general ledger. Follow these steps:

objective 5
Post adjusting entries

step 1: From the main menu, select Tasks, System, Post.

step 2: Click once on the box next to General Journal. A check mark is placed in the box.

step 3: Click on OK.

Replenishing Petty Cash

Some time ago, TKT established a $100 petty cash fund. Of course, petty cash has been replenished many times since then. As you will recall, the fund should always be replenished at the end of each month. This is necessary for the monthly financial statements to reflect up-to-date account balances. Remember, payments from the petty cash fund are not journalized until the fund is replenished.

objective 6
Replenish petty cash

On December 31, 1996, TKT's petty cash record contains the following information:

Payments:

Supplies	$12.50
Repair Expense	17.00
Miscellaneous Expense	30.00
Dennis Taylor, Drawing	10.00
Total payments	$69.50

Based on this information, TKT issues Check No. 1664 in the amount of $69.50 to replenish petty cash. This check will be made payable to "Cash." After the check is cashed, the $69.50 will be placed in the petty cash box bringing the fund up to $100, its full size.

In data entry sheet format, the replenishment of petty cash is recorded as follows:

DATA ENTRY SHEET TKT Products					
Date	Account ID	Reference	Trans Description	Debit Amt	Credit Amt
12/31/96	113		Supplies	12.50	
	617		Repair Expense	17.00	
	622		Miscellaneous Expense	30.00	
	320		Dennis Taylor, Drawing	10.00	
	110		Cash, Check No. 1664		69.50

Comment

Remember, replenishing petty cash does not change the fixed size of the fund. Therefore, the replenishment entry does *not* involve the Petty Cash account.

Using PAW to Journalize the Replenishment of Petty Cash

Referring to the data entry sheet, we are ready to use PAW's "Payments" window to journalize the replenishment of petty cash in the cash disbursements journal and print out the check. Follow these steps:

step 1:   From the main menu, select Tasks, Payments.

step 2:   In the "Pay to the Order of" box, type **Cash** and press <Enter> two times.

step 3:   In the Date box, type **31** and press <Enter>.

step 4:   In the "Quantity" column, type **1** and press <Enter> two times.

step 5:   In the "Description" column, type **Supplies** and press <Enter>.

step 6:   In the "GL Account" column, select Account No. 113, Supplies.

step 7:   In the "Unit Price" column, type **12.50** and press <Enter> three times.

step 8:   In the "Quantity" column, type **1** and press <Enter> two times.

step 9: In the "Description" column, type **Repair Expense** and press <Enter>.

step 10: In the "GL Account" column, select Account No. 617, Repair Expense.

step 11: In the "Unit Price" column, type **17** and press the <Enter> key three times.

step 12: Repeat steps 8 through 11 to record the rest of this entry. (Hint: Use the appropriate account descriptions, account numbers, and amounts.)

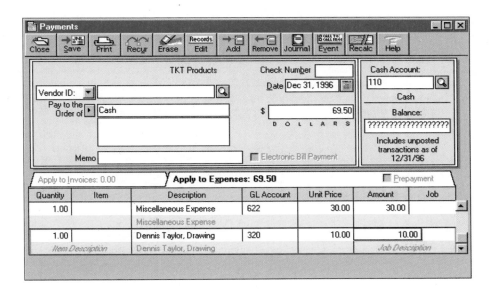

step 13: Click on the Print icon.

step 14: If you are using the working papers, insert Check No. 1664 into the printer. Select AP Preprint 1 Stub as the type of form to print. If you are *not* using the working papers, you may need to select another type of form to print. Remember, the forms are tied to the type of printer you are using.

step 15: Click on <u>O</u>k, then click on <u>R</u>eal.

step 16: The "About to Print Checks" window displays 1664. Click on <u>O</u>k.

step 17: Compare your printout with Figure 14.4 on page 440. Then, close the "Payments" window.

Figure 14.4

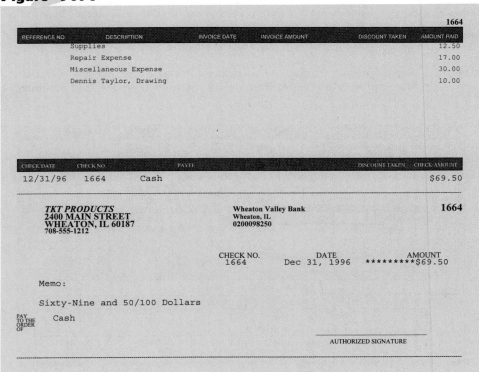

REFERENCE NO	DESCRIPTION	INVOICE DATE	INVOICE AMOUNT	DISCOUNT TAKEN	AMOUNT PAID
	Supplies				12.50
	Repair Expense				17.00
	Miscellaneous Expense				30.00
	Dennis Taylor, Drawing				10.00

CHECK DATE	CHECK NO.	PAYEE	DISCOUNT TAKEN	CHECK AMOUNT
12/31/96	1664	Cash		$69.50

TKT PRODUCTS
2400 MAIN STREET
WHEATON, IL 60187
708-555-1212

Wheaton Valley Bank
Wheaton, IL
0200098250

1664

CHECK NO.   DATE   AMOUNT
1664   Dec 31, 1996   *********$69.50

Memo:

Sixty-Nine and 50/100 Dollars

PAY TO THE ORDER OF   Cash

AUTHORIZED SIGNATURE

Now, let's look at this entry by printing out the cash disbursements journal for December 31, 1996. Follow these steps:

step 1: From the main menu, select Reports, Accounts Payable.

step 2: Scroll down the Report List. Highlight the Cash Disbursements Journal.

step 3: Click on the Print icon.

step 4: In the "From" box, select 31.

step 5: Make the selections to print. Compare your printout to Figure 14.5.

Figure 14.5

TKT Products
Cash Disbursements Journal
For the Period From Dec 31, 1996 to Dec 31, 1996
Filter Criteria includes: Report order is by Date. Report is printed in Detail Format.

Date	Check #	Account ID	Line Description	Debit Amount	Credit Amount
12/31/96	1664	113	Supplies	12.50	
		617	Repair Expense	17.00	
		622	Miscellaneous Expense	30.00	
		320	Dennis Taylor, Drawing	10.00	
		110	Cash		69.50
	Total			69.50	69.50

After comparing your printout with Figure 14.5, you need to post this journal entry. Follow these steps to post the cash disbursements journal:

step 1: From the main menu, select Tas<u>k</u>s, Sys<u>t</u>em, <u>P</u>ost.

step 2: Click once on the box next to Cash <u>D</u>isbursements Journal. A check mark is placed in the box.

step 3: Click on <u>O</u>K.

Preparing Two Bank Reconciliations

Back in Chapter 6, you learned how to use PAW to prepare a bank reconciliation. At that time, The Kitchen Taylor had only one checking account (Cash, Account No.110). TKT Products has two checking accounts. A regular checking account (Cash, Account No. 110) and a payroll checking account used only for employee paychecks (Payroll Checking, Account No. 107). This means that TKT receives two bank statements and must prepare two bank reconciliations—one for each account.

Reconciling the Regular Checking Account

On December 31, 1996, TKT's Cash account (Account No. 110) shows a balance of $8,424.81. The bank statement displayed in Figure 14.6 on page 442 shows an ending balance on December 31, 1996, of $9,294.81. To reconcile these two amounts, we must identify the reasons for the discrepancy. We begin this process by reviewing the bank statement for items that have not been recorded on TKT's books. Journal entries are required to update for these items.

objective 7
Reconcile the regular checking account

The bank statement shown in Figure 14.6 indicates that TKT must record a journal entry for service charges ($25). The other items shown on the bank statement (checks, deposits, and electronic funds transfers) do not require entries because they have already been recorded on TKT's books.

Figure 14.6

WHEATON VALLEY BANK				
Wheaton, Illinois				

TKT PRODUCTS			Statement Date: 12-31-96	
2400 Main Street			Account No. 0200098250	
Wheaton, Illinois 60187			12-1-96 to 12-31-96	

REGULAR CHECKING				
Previous Balance				14,405.63
10 Deposits (+)				17,859.00
10 Checks (−)				14,944.82
Electronic funds transfer (−)				8,000.00
Service Charges (−)				25.00
Ending Balance				9,294.81

DEPOSITS					
12-1-96	5,400.00	12-20-96	1,485.00	12-28-96	7,128.00
12-2-96	63.60	12-21-96	954.00	12-29-96	16.96
12-7-96	891.00	12-26-96	495.00		
12-15-96	1,400.00	12-27-96	25.44		

CHECKS (Asterisk * indicates break in check number sequence)				
		12-18-96	1650	3,175.20
		12-19-96	1651	1,633.50
		12-19-96	1652	600.00
		12-20-96	1653	265.00
		12-22-96	1654	117.60
		12-24-96	1655	65.00
		12-26-96	1656	5,821.20
		12-30-96	*1658	855.00
		12-30-96	*1661	2,342.82
		12-31-96	*1664	69.50

ELECTRONIC FUNDS TRANSFER				
		12-12-96	4,000.00	
		12-26-96	4,000.00	

In data entry sheet format, the service charges are recorded as follows:

DATA ENTRY SHEET					
TKT Products					
Date	**Account ID**	**Reference**	**Trans Description**	**Debit Amt**	**Credit Amt**
12/31/96	618		Service Charge Expense	25.00	
	110		Cash		25.00

Now, let's use PAW's "General Journal Entry" window to journalize and post this transaction. Follow these steps:

step 1: From the main menu, select Tas**k**s, **G**eneral Journal Entry.

step 2: Type **31** in the **D**ate box.

step 3: In the "Account No." column, click on the magnifying glass icon. Select Account No. 618, Service Charge Expense.

step 4: Type **Service Charge Expense** in the "Description" column.

step 5: In the "Debit" column, type **25** and press <Enter> three times.

step 6: In the "Account No." column, click on the magnifying glass icon. Select Account No. 110, Cash.

step 7: In the "Description" column, type **Cash** and press <Enter> two times.

step 8: In the "Credit" column, type **25** and press <Enter>.

step 9: Click on the **S**ave icon.

step 10: Post the General Journal. (Hint: Select Tas**k**s, **P**ost, put a check mark next to **G**eneral Journal, click on **O**k.)

Now, let's print out the Cash account (Account No. 110), so that we can determine the updated balance on December 31, 1996. Follow these steps:

step 1: Click on **R**eports, then **G**eneral Ledger.

step 2: On the Report List, highlight General Ledger.

step 3: Click on the Print icon.

step 4: In the "F**i**lter, Type From, To" table, click on the first row (General Ledger Account ID) of the "From" column. The magnifying glass icon is shown. Select Account No. 110, Cash.

step 5: In the "To" column, click on the magnifying glass icon. Select Account No. 110, Cash.

step 6: Click on **O**K.

step 7: The "Print" window pops up. Click on **O**K. The Cash account begins to print. Compare your printout with Figure 14.7 on page 444.

Figure 14.7

TKT Products
General Ledger
For the Period From Dec 1, 1996 to Dec 31, 1996
Filter Criteria includes: 1) IDs from 110 to 110. Report order is by ID. Report is printed in Detail Format.

Account ID Account Description	Date Reference	Jrnl	Trans Description	Debit Amt	Credit Amt	Balance
110 Cash	12/1/96		Beginning Balance			14,405.63
	12/1/96 prepayment	CRJ	Adams Company	5,400.00		
	12/2/96 Inv. 2000	CRJ	Cash	63.60		
	12/7/96 Inv. 2001	CRJ	Dubin Enterprises	891.00		
	12/12/96	GENJ	Cash		4,000.00	
	12/14/96 1650	CDJ	Kavan Manufacturing		3,175.20	
	12/15/96 Inv. 1999	CRJ	Steven Faulker	1,400.00		
	12/15/96 1651	CDJ	Avery Products		1,633.50	
	12/15/96 1652	CDJ	Jackson Rentals		600.00	
	12/17/96 1653	CDJ	Federal Freight		265.00	
	12/19/96 1654	CDJ	Franklin Products		117.60	
	12/20/96 Inv. 2003	CRJ	Adams Company	1,485.00		
	12/21/96 Inv. 2002	CRJ	Steven Faulker	954.00		
	12/21/96 1655	CDJ	Archer Plumbing		65.00	
	12/23/96 1656	CDJ	Kavan Manufacturing		5,821.20	
	12/26/96	GENJ	Cash		4,000.00	
	12/26/96 Inv. 2006	CRJ	Becker Brothers	495.00		
	12/26/96 1657	CDJ	Morton Trucking		382.00	
	12/27/96 Inv. 2004	CRJ	Steven Faulker	25.44		
	12/27/96 1658	CDJ	Saroya Corporation		855.00	
	12/28/96 Inv. 2005	CRJ	Carson Corporation	7,128.00		
	12/29/96 Inv. 2008	CRJ	Cash	16.96		
	12/29/96 1659	CDJ	Wheaton Supplies		125.00	
	12/30/96 Inv. 2009	CRJ	Cash	95.40		
	12/30/96 1660	CDJ	Fox Valley Power		198.00	
	12/30/96 1661	CDJ	Wheaton Valley Bank		2,342.82	
	12/30/96 1662	CDJ	Internal Revenue Service		65.23	
	12/30/96 1663	CDJ	Dir. of Employment Security		220.17	
	12/31/96	GENJ	Cash		25.00	
	12/31/96 1664	CDJ	Cash		69.50	
			Current Period Change	17,954.40	23,960.22	-6,005.82
	12/31/96		**Ending Balance**			**8,399.81**

In PAW, the "Account Reconciliation" feature makes it easy to complete our bank reconciliation. Follow these steps:

step 1: From the main menu, select Tas<u>k</u>s, then <u>A</u>ccount Reconciliation.

step 2: In the "Account to Reconcile" box, select Account No. 110, Cash.

step 3: Type **9294.81** in the "Statement Ending Balance" box. This is the ending balance on TKT's bank statement shown in Figure 14.6 on page 442.

step 4: In the "Checks and Credits" table, click on the box in the "Clear" column to place a check mark next to each check, electronic funds transfer, and service charge transaction that is shown on the bank statement in Figure 14.6.

step 5: In the "Deposits & Debits" table, place a check mark in the "Clear" column for each deposit that is listed on the bank statement shown in Figure 14.6.

step 6: Click on Ok.

Observe that the updated Cash account balance on December 31, 1996, is $8,399.81.

Follow these steps to print the account reconciliation report:

step 1: From the main menu, select Reports, Account Reconciliation.

step 2: In the Report List, highlight Account Reconciliation.

step 3: Click on the Print icon.

step 4: Make sure that Account No. 110 is shown as the GL Account ID.

step 5: Click on OK.

step 6: In the "Print" window, click on OK. The Account Reconciliation Report starts to print. Compare your printout to Figure 14.8.

Figure 14.8

TKT Products
Account Reconciliation
As of Dec 31, 1996
110 - Cash
Bank Statement Date: December 31, 1996

Filter Criteria includes: Report is printed in Detail Format.

Beginning GL Balance				14,405.63
Add: Cash Receipts				17,954.40
Less: Cash Disbursements				<15,935.22>
Add <Less> Other				<8,025.00>
Ending GL Balance				8,399.81
Ending Bank Balance				9,294.81
Add back deposits in transit				
	Dec 30, 1996	12/30/96	95.40	
Total deposits in transit				95.40
<Less> outstanding checks				
	Dec 26, 1996	1657	<382.00>	
	Dec 29, 1996	1659	<125.00>	
	Dec 30, 1996	1660	<198.00>	
	Dec 30, 1996	1662	<65.23>	
	Dec 30, 1996	1663	<220.17>	
Total outstanding checks				<990.40>
Add <Less> Other				
Total other				
Unreconciled difference				
Ending GL Balance				8,399.81

Reconciling the Payroll Checking Account

Reconcile the payroll checking account

We will now follow the same procedure to reconcile TKT's Payroll Checking account. On December 31, 1996, TKT's Payroll Checking account (Account No. 107) shows a balance of $302.60. The bank statement displayed in Figure 14.9 shows an ending balance on December 31, 1996, of $1,260.91. To reconcile these two amounts, we must review the bank statement for items that have not been recorded on TKT's books. As before, journal entries are required to update for these items.

Figure 14.9

WHEATON VALLEY BANK				
Wheaton, Illinois				
TKT PRODUCTS 2400 Main Street Wheaton, Illinois 60187			Statement Date: 12-31-96 Account No. 0200072321 12-1-96 to 12-31-96	
PAYROLL CHECKING				
Previous Balance				0.00
2 Deposits (+)				8,000.00
10 Checks (−)				6,724.09
Service Charges (−)				15.00
Ending Balance				1,260.91
DEPOSITS				
12-12-96	4,000.00	12-26-96	4,000.00	
CHECKS (Asterisk * indicates break in check number sequence)				
		12-14-96	101	730.53
		12-14-96	102	651.97
		12-16-96	103	398.68
		12-16-96	104	524.46
		12-17-96	105	591.36
		12-17-96	106	978.61
		12-28-96	107	652.46
		12-28-96	108	640.25
		12-30-96	*110	524.46
		12-30-96	*112	1,031.31

The bank statement shown in Figure 14.9 indicates that TKT must record a journal entry for service charges ($15). The other items shown on the bank statement (checks and deposits) do not require entries because they have already been recorded on TKT's books.

In data entry sheet format, the service charges are recorded as follows:

DATA ENTRY SHEET TKT Products					
Date	Account ID	Reference	Trans Description	Debit Amt	Credit Amt
12/31/96	618		Service Charge Expense	15.00	
	107		Payroll Checking		15.00

Now, let's use PAW's "General Journal Entry" window to journalize and post this transaction. Follow these steps:

step 1: From the main menu, select Tasks, General Journal Entry.

step 2: In the Date box, type **31** and press <Enter>.

step 3: In the "Account No." column, click on the magnifying glass icon. Select Account No. 618, Service Charge Expense.

step 4: In the "Description" column, type **Service Charge Expense** and press <Enter>.

step 5: In the "Debit" column, type **15** and press <Enter> three times.

step 6: In the "Account No." column, click on the magnifying glass icon. Select Account No. 107, Payroll Checking.

step 7: In the "Description" column, type **Payroll Checking** and press the <Enter> key two times.

step 8: In the "Credit" column, type **15** and press <Enter>.

step 9: Click on the Save icon.

step 10: Post the General Journal. (Hint: Select Tasks, Post, put a check mark next to General Journal, click on Ok.)

Now, let's print out the Payroll Checking account (Account No. 107), so that we can determine the updated balance on December 31, 1996. Follow these steps:

step 1: Click on Reports, then General Ledger.

step 2: On the Report List, highlight General Ledger.

step 3: Click on the Print icon.

step 4: In the "Filter, Type From, To" table, click on the first row (General Ledger Account ID) of the "From" column. The magnifying glass icon is shown. Select Account No. 107, Payroll Checking.

step 5: In the "To" column, click on the magnifying glass icon. Select Account No. 107, Payroll Checking.

step 6: Click on OK. Compare your screen to Figure 14.10 on page 448.

Figure 14.10

TKT Products
General Ledger
For the Period From Dec 1, 1996 to Dec 31, 1996
Filter Criteria includes: 1) IDs from 107 to 107. Report order is by ID. Report is printed in Detail Format.

Account ID Account Description	Date Reference	Jrnl	Trans Description	Debit Amt	Credit Amt	Balance
107 Payroll Checking	12/1/96		Beginning Balance			
	12/12/96	GENJ	Payroll Checking	4,000.00		
	12/13/96 101	PRJ	Barker, Kevin		730.53	
	12/13/96 102	PRJ	Grant, Mary		651.97	
	12/13/96 103	PRJ	Hill, Charles		398.68	
	12/13/96 104	PRJ	Karr, James		524.46	
	12/13/96 105	PRJ	Lamb, Carol		591.36	
	12/13/96 106	PRJ	Roth, Gary		978.61	
	12/26/96	GENJ	Payroll Checking	4,000.00		
	12/27/96 107	PRJ	Barker, Kevin		652.46	
	12/27/96 108	PRJ	Grant, Mary		640.25	
	12/27/96 109	PRJ	Hill, Charles		412.06	
	12/27/96 110	PRJ	Karr, James		524.46	
	12/27/96 111	PRJ	Lamb, Carol		561.25	
	12/27/96 112	PRJ	Roth, Gary		1,031.31	
	12/31/96	GENJ	Payroll Checking		15.00	
			Current Period Change	8,000.00	7,712.40	287.60
	12/31/96		**Ending Balance**			**287.60**

As noted earlier, PAW's "Account Reconciliation" feature makes it easy to complete our bank reconciliation. Follow these steps:

step 1: From the main menu, select Ta**s**ks, then **A**ccount Reconciliation.

step 2: In the "Account to Reconcile" box, select Account No. 107, Payroll Checking.

step 3: Type **1260.91** in the "Statement Ending Balance" box. This is the ending balance on TKT's bank statement shown in Figure 14.9 on page 446.

step 4: In the "Checks and Credits" table, click on the box in the "Clear" column to place a check mark next to each check and service charge transaction that is shown on the bank statement in Figure 14.9.

step 5: In the "Deposits & Debits" table, place a check mark in the "Clear" column for each deposit that is listed on the bank statement shown in Figure 14.9.

step 6: Click on OK.

Observe that the updated Payroll Checking account balance on December 31, 1996, is $287.60.

Follow these steps to print the account reconciliation report:

step 1: From the main menu, select **R**eports, Acc**o**unt Reconciliation.

step 2:   In the Report List, highlight Account Reconciliation.

step 3:   Click on the Print icon.

step 4:   In the GL Account ID box, select Account No. 107, Payroll Checking.

step 5:   Click on OK.

step 6:   In the "Print" window, click on OK. The Account Reconciliation Report starts to print. Compare your printout to Figure 14.11.

Figure 14.11

TKT Products
Account Reconciliation
As of Dec 31, 1996
107 - Payroll Checking
Bank Statement Date: December 31, 1996

Filter Criteria includes: Report is printed in Detail Format.

Beginning GL Balance			
Add: Cash Receipts			
Less: Cash Disbursements			<7,697.40>
Add <Less> Other			7,985.00
Ending GL Balance			287.60
Ending Bank Balance			1,260.91
Add back deposits in transit			
Total deposits in transit			
<Less> outstanding checks			
	Dec 27, 1996	109	<412.06>
	Dec 27, 1996	111	<561.25>
Total outstanding checks			<973.31>
Add <Less> Other			
Total other			
Unreconciled difference			0.00
Ending GL Balance			287.60

Printing the Trial Balance

Now that all of TKT's accounts are up to date, we are ready to print out the general ledger trial balance. Since it is prepared after the accounts have been adjusted, it is also known as an adjusted trial balance. Like all trial balances, its purpose is to check the overall equality of debits and credits in the general ledger.

objective 9
Print the trial balance

Follow these steps to print the general ledger trial balance:

step 1:   From the "Select a Report" window, highlight General Ledger.

step 2:   Highlight General Ledger Trial Balance, then make the selections to print.

Be sure to compare your printout with Figure 14.12 on page 450.

Figure 14.12

TKT Products
General Ledger Trial Balance
As of Dec 31, 1996

Filter Criteria includes: Report order is by ID. Report is printed in Detail Format.

Account ID	Account Description	Debit Amt	Credit Amt
107	Payroll Checking	287.60	
108	Change Fund	75.00	
109	Petty Cash	100.00	
110	Cash	8,399.81	
111	Accounts Receivable	95.40	
112	Merchandise Inventory	2,241.50	
113	Supplies	241.50	
114	Prepaid Insurance	690.00	
120	Truck	6,000.00	
121	Accumulated Depreciation		2,400.00
210	Accounts Payable		114.00
211	Wages Payable		1,976.00
213	Sales Tax Payable		70.80
217	State Income Tax Payable		273.38
223	Health Insurance Payable		252.00
224	Union Dues Payable		72.00
310	Dennis Taylor, Capital		10,000.00
320	Dennis Taylor, Drawing	4,510.00	
330	Retained Earnings		1,373.63
410	Fees Earned		40,047.00
411	Sales		19,626.00
412	Sales Returns and Allowances	2,946.00	
413	Sales Discount	101.00	
501	Cost of Sales	10,008.00	
610	Depreciation Expense	2,300.00	
611	FICA--Soc. Sec. Tax Expense	1,232.67	
612	FICA--Medicare Tax Expense	288.29	
613	FUTA Tax Expense	121.23	
614	SUTA Tax Expense	463.17	
615	Insurance Expense	702.00	
616	Rent Expense	7,200.00	
617	Repair Expense	661.00	
618	Service Charge Expense	205.00	
619	Supplies Expense	2,885.00	
620	Utilities Expense	2,563.00	
621	Wages Expense	21,857.64	
622	Miscellaneous Expense	30.00	
	Total:	**76,204.81**	**76,204.81**

Backing Up Your Chapter 14 Data

objective 10
Back up your data

It is important to back up your TKT Products data. As usual, you will need it when you begin the next chapter. Follow these steps to back up your Chapter 14 data.

step 1: Insert a blank formatted disk in drive A.

step 2: From PAW's main menu, select File, then Backup.

step 3: Type a:\chap14.tkt in the Destination text box.

step 4: Click on the Backup button. When all the files have been saved to drive A, you are automatically returned to the main menu.

step 5: Click on File, Exit to exit PAW.

Chapter 14 Summary

Sometimes a business is paid in advance for a product or service to be delivered in the future. Although the cash has been received, the revenue cannot be recorded because it has not yet been earned. The receipt of a prepayment creates a liability for the seller because the seller now owes the customer the product or service. This liability (Unearned Revenue) is eliminated and the revenue is earned when the product or service is provided to the customer.

Adjusting entries are updating entries. The need to update exists because a few internal transactions have occurred but have not yet been recorded. It is acceptable to allow these internal transactions to go unrecorded on a daily basis, but we cannot prepare financial statements with incorrect account balances. Therefore, at the end of the accounting period, before preparing financial statements, we must adjust the accounts. Commonly, adjustments are required for supplies, insurance, wages, and depreciation.

The petty cash fund should always be replenished at the end of each month. This is necessary for the monthly financial statements to reflect up-to-date account balances. This is the case because payments from the petty cash fund are not journalized until the fund is replenished.

A bank reconciliation must be prepared for each checking account. Since TKT has two checking accounts, two bank reconciliations must be prepared each month. To reconcile each account, we must identify the reasons for the discrepancy between the ending ledger account balance and the ending bank statement balance. We begin this process by reviewing the bank statement for items that have not been recorded on the books. Journal entries are required to update for these items. Then, an account reconciliation report is prepared using PAW's "Account Reconciliation" feature.

After all the accounts have been updated, a general ledger trial balance is printed out. Since it is prepared after the accounts have been adjusted, it is also known as an *adjusted trial balance*. Like all trial balances, its purpose is to check the overall equality of debits and credits in the general ledger.

Demonstration Problem

A. In data entry sheet format, record the following transactions on the books of Brown Company. Leave the "Account ID" column blank.

  2/5/96   Received a $1,000 prepayment from Dalton Associates for merchandise to be delivered at a later date.

  3/30/96 Brown Company shipped the merchandise to Dalton Associates, Invoice No. 324, $1,000. The merchandise cost $850.

B. In data entry sheet format, record adjustments based on the following information:

  12/31/96 Supplies used during December, $250.
            Insurance expired during December, $400.
            Wages expense incurred but not yet paid, $900.
            Depreciation on equipment, $600.

Solution to Demonstration Problem

A.

			DATA ENTRY SHEET Brown Company		
Date	Account ID	Reference	Trans Description	Debit Amt	Credit Amt
2/5/96			Cash	1,000.00	
			Unearned Revenue		1,000.00
3/30/96			Unearned Revenue	1,000.00	
			Cost of Sales	850.00	
			Sales, Inv. No. 324		1,000.00
			Merchandise Inventory		850.00

B.

			DATA ENTRY SHEET Brown Company		
Date	Account ID	Reference	Trans Description	Debit Amt	Credit Amt
12/31/96			Supplies Expense	250.00	
			Supplies		250.00
12/31/96			Insurance Expense	400.00	
			Prepaid Insurance		400.00
12/31/96			Wages Expense	900.00	
			Wages Payable		900.00
12/31/96			Depreciation Expense	600.00	
			Accumulated Depreciation		600.00

Glossary

unearned revenue   The liability to the customer created when cash has been received for a product or service to be delivered in the future. The seller now owes the customer the product or service.   *431*

Self-Test

Select the best answer.

   1. The Unearned Revenue account is
       a. a liability account.
       b. updated by removing the amount that has been earned and transferring it to a revenue account.
       c. updated with an entry that includes a debit to Unearned Revenue and a credit to Sales.
       d. All of the above.

2. Adjusting entries are also called
   a. updating entries.
   b. closing entries.
   c. trial balance entries.
   d. None of the above.

3. In PAW, which window is used to journalize adjusting entries?
   a. Sales/Invoicing
   b. Payroll Entry
   c. Payments
   d. General Journal Entry

4. In PAW, which window is used to journalize the entry to replenish petty cash?
   a. Sales/Invoicing
   b. Payroll Entry
   c. Payments
   d. General Journal Entry

5. In PAW, which feature is used for a bank reconciliation?
   a. Cash Reconciliation
   b. Account Reconciliation
   c. Check Reconciliation
   d. All of the above

Answers to the self-test can be found after the cases at the end of this chapter.

Questions for Discussion

1. *a.* What is unearned revenue?
   b. Why is unearned revenue a liability?

2. Why must the Supplies account be adjusted?

3. Why must the Prepaid Insurance account be adjusted?

4. Why is an adjustment for wages necessary?

5. In recording depreciation:
   a. What account is debited? On what statement does it appear? What information does its balance convey?
   b. What account is credited? On what statement does it appear? What information does its balance convey?

6. Why is the Petty Cash account not involved in the replenishment of petty cash?

7. In a bank reconciliation, what types of items require journal entries?

8. What is the purpose of an adjusted trial balance?

Exercises

Exercise 14.1

Terminology
L.O. 2–9

Match the following terms with the definitions shown below:

1. Adjusting entries.
2. Bank reconciliation.
3. Unearned revenue.
4. Bank statement.
5. Updating entries.
6. Book value.

Definitions

a. The liability to the customer created when cash has been received for a product or service to be delivered in the future.

b. A figure that represents cost minus accumulated depreciation.

c. Entries that update internal transactions that have occurred but have not yet been recorded (journalized).

d. A statement prepared by the bank showing account activity for a specified period of time.

e. Another term for adjusting entries.

f. The process of bringing the bank statement balance and the Cash account balance into agreement.

Exercise 14.2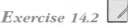

Unearned Revenue
L.O. 2

In data entry sheet format, record the following transactions on the books of Parker Enterprises. Leave the "Account ID" blank.

9/1/96   Received a $5,000 prepayment from Sawyer Company for merchandise to be delivered at a later date.

10/15/96   Parker Enterprises shipped the merchandise to Sawyer Company, Invoice No. 678, $5,000. The merchandise cost $4,200.

Exercise 14.3

Supplies Adjustment
L.O. 3

a. In data entry sheet format, record the adjustment for supplies used during December, $360.

b. If the balance in the Supplies account was $700 before adjustment, what is the balance in the Supplies account after adjustment?

Exercise 14.4

Insurance Adjustment
L.O. 3

a. In data entry sheet format, record the adjustment for expired insurance, $725.

b. If the balance in the Prepaid Insurance account was $1,500 before adjustment, what is the balance in the Prepaid Insurance account after adjustment?

Exercise 14.5

a. In data entry sheet format, record the adjustment for wages expense incurred but not yet paid, $1,800.

b. If the balance in the Wages Expense account was $24,000 before adjustment, what is the balance in the Wages Expense account after adjustment?

Wages Adjustment
L.O. 3

Exercise 14.6

a. In data entry sheet format, record the adjustment for depreciation on the truck, $900.

b. After the adjustment for depreciation, is the book value of the truck larger or smaller?

Depreciation Adjustment
L.O. 3

Exercise 14.7

Earlier in the year, Thompson Company established an $80 petty cash fund. On December 31, 1996, Thompson's petty cash record shows the following payments:

Petty Cash
L.O. 6

Supplies	$36.00
Delivery Expense	20.00
Miscellaneous Expense	15.00

In data entry sheet format, record the entry to replenish petty cash on December 31, 1996.

Exercise 14.8

Tiger Enterprises' December 31, 1996, bank statement shows the following:

Bank Reconcilation
L.O. 7, 8

Beginning balance	$8,100.00
Checks	− 6,000.00
Deposits	+ 7,500.00
Electronic funds transfers	− 1,000.00
Service charges	− 30.00
Ending balance	$8,570.00

In data entry sheet format, record the necessary reconciliation entry or entries based on the information shown on the bank statement.

Problems—Set A

Problem 14.1A

Follow these steps to restore your Chapter 13 ACS Products data and print a general ledger trial balance:

Restore Data; Trial Balance
L.O. 1, 9

step 1:   Start Windows, then PAW. Open ACS Products.

step 2:   Place your Chapter 13 backup disk in drive A.

step 3:   From the main menu, select File, then Restore.

step 4:   Type **a:\acsdec.13a** in the Source box. (Use the same file name that you used when you backed up in Chapter 13.)

step 5: Click on the Restore button. Read the "Warning" screen, then click on OK. When the files are restored, you are returned to the main menu.

step 6: Remove the disk from drive A.

step 7: To be sure your ACS data was restored properly, follow these steps to print the general ledger trial balance:
a. From the "Select a Report" window, highlight General Ledger.
b. Highlight General Ledger Trial Balance, then make the selections to print.

Compare your printout with Figure 14.13.

Figure 14.13

ACS Products
General Ledger Trial Balance
As of Dec 31, 1996

Filter Criteria includes: Report order is by ID. Report is printed in Detail Format.

Account ID	Account Description	Debit Amt	Credit Amt
107	Payroll Checking	2,235.10	
108	Change Fund	30.00	
109	Petty Cash	50.00	
110	Cash	15,412.61	
111	Accounts Receivable	13.72	
112	Merchandise Inventory	2,578.89	
113	Supplies	490.95	
114	Prepaid Insurance	700.00	
120	Equipment	5,000.00	
121	Accumulated Depreciation		900.00
210	Accounts Payable		265.95
213	Sales Tax Payable		8.90
217	State Income Tax Payable		156.63
223	Health Insurance Payable		180.00
224	Union Dues Payable		60.00
310	Joan Haywood, Capital		7,500.00
320	Joan Haywood, Drawing	4,100.00	
330	Retained Earnings		1,937.00
410	Cleaning Revenue		42,000.00
411	Sales		17,836.25
412	Sales Returns and Allowances	593.25	
413	Sales Discount	170.94	
501	Cost of Sales	8,077.80	
610	Depreciation Expense	825.00	
611	FICA--Soc. Sec. Tax Expense	1,091.55	
612	FICA--Medicare Tax Expense	255.28	
613	FUTA Tax Expense	87.80	
614	SUTA Tax Expense	350.34	
615	Insurance Expense	460.00	
616	Rent Expense	7,500.00	
617	Repair Expense	406.00	
618	Service Charge Expense	198.00	
619	Supplies Expense	910.00	
620	Utilities Expense	1,702.00	
621	Wages Expense	17,605.50	
	Total:	**70,844.73**	**70,844.73**

Problem 14.2A

Unearned Revenue
L.O. 2

1. On a data entry sheet, record the following ACS Products transactions:

12/5/96   Received a $4,295 prepayment from Saxon Brothers for 100 boxes of window cleaner to be shipped at a later date.

12/31/96   Shipped 100 boxes of window cleaner to Saxon Brothers, Invoice No. 3010, $4,295. The window cleaner cost $1,677.

2. *a.* Referring to your data entry sheet, use PAW's "Cash Receipts" window to journalize the December 5, 1996, transaction in the cash receipts journal. (Hint: Add Account No. 212, Unearned Revenue.)

   b. **Post** the cash receipts journal.

   c. Follow these steps to print the December 5, 1996, cash receipts journal:

     1) From the main menu, select <u>R</u>eports, then Accounts <u>R</u>eceivable.

     2) Highlight the Cash Receipts Journal.

     3) Click on the Print icon. Click on the From calendar icon, then select 5. Click on the To calendar icon, then select 5. Make the selections to print.

3. *a.* Referring to your data entry sheet, use PAW's "Sales/Invoicing" window to journalize the December 31, 1996, transaction in the sales journal.

   b. **Post** the sales journal.

   c. Follow these steps to print the December 31, 1996, sales journal:

     1) From the main menu, select <u>R</u>eports, then Accounts <u>R</u>eceivable.

     2) Highlight the Sales Journal.

     3) Click on the Print icon. Click on the From calendar icon, then select 31. Make the selections to print.

Problem 14.3A

1. In data entry sheet format, record the following ACS adjustments:

Adjust for Supplies, Insurance, Wages Depreciation
L.O. 3, 5

   12/31/96 Supplies used during December, $210.

           Insurance expired during December, $175.

           Wages expense incurred but not yet paid, $650.

           Depreciation on equipment, $500.

2. *a.* Referring to your data entry sheet, use PAW's "General Journal Entry" window to journalize ACS's December 31, 1996, adjustments in the general journal.

   b. **Post** the general journal. (You will print the general journal in Problem 14.7A.)

Problem 14.4A

Some time ago, ACS Products established a $50 petty cash fund. On December 31, ACS issued Check No. 1437, made out to "Cash," for $39 based on the following information from the petty cash record:

Petty Cash
L.O. 6

         Payments:

           Supplies . . . . $ 9.00

           Miscellaneous Expense. 12.00

           Joan Haywood, Drawing 18.00

           Total payments . . . . $ 39.00

Instructions

1. On a data entry sheet, record the entry to replenish petty cash on December 31, 1996.

2. Referring to your data entry sheet, use PAW's "Payments" window to journalize the replenishment of petty cash in the cash disbursements journal and print out Check No. 1437.

3. **Post** the cash disbursements journal.

4. Follow these steps to print the December 31, 1996, cash disbursements journal:
    a. From the main menu, select <u>R</u>eports, then Accounts <u>P</u>ayable.
    b. Highlight the Cash Disbursements Journal.
    c. Click on the Print icon. Click on the From calendar icon, then select 31. Make the selections to print.

Problem 14.5A

Reconcile regular account *L.O. 7*

On December 31, 1996, ACS Products' Cash account (Account No. 110), shows a balance of $19,668.61. The bank statement displayed in Figure 14.14 shows an ending balance on December 31, 1996, of $21,017.95. ACS uses this checking account for everything *except* employee paychecks.

Figure 14.14

FIRST NATIONAL BANK
Wheaton, Illinois

ACS PRODUCTS	Statement Date: 12-31-96
452 Mountain Drive	Account No. 0267018556
Evanston, Illinois 60187	12-1-96 to 12-31-96

REGULAR CHECKING

Previous Balance				16,429.00
9 Deposits (+)				24,092.44
10 Checks (−)				12,983.49
Electronic funds transfer (−)				6,500.00
Service Charges (−)				20.00
Ending Balance				21,017.95

DEPOSITS

12-1-96	4,295.00	12-20-96	46.53	12-29-96	27.45
12-10-96	2,800.00	12-21-96	3,486.68		
12-13-96	7,228.49	12-26-96	2,307.69		
12-18-96	641.02	12-28-96	3,259.58		

CHECKS (Asterisk * indicates break in check number sequence)

	12-14-96	1425	625.00	
	12-13-96	1426	4,108.65	
	12-15-96	1427	72.00	
	12-16-96	1428	1,903.65	
	12-19-96	1429	206.00	
	12-23-96	1430	2,465.19	
	12-30-96	1431	2,107.20	
	12-31-96	*1433	84.00	
	12-31-96	1434	1,372.80	
	12-31-96	*1437	39.00	

ELECTRONIC FUNDS TRANSFER

	12-12-96	3,250.00	
	12-26-96	3,250.00	

Instructions

1. *a.* After reviewing the bank statement in Figure 14.14, record the necessary entry or entries on a data entry sheet.
   b. Referring to your data entry sheet, use PAW's "General Journal Entry" window to journalize the transaction(s) in the general journal.
   c. **Post** the general journal. (You will print the general journal in Problem 14.7A.)

2. *a.* Use PAW's "Account Reconciliation" feature to complete the bank reconciliation.
   b. Print the account reconciliation report.

Problem 14.6A

On December 31, 1996, ACS Products' Payroll Checking account (Account No. 107) shows a balance of $2,235.10. The bank statement shown in Figure 14.15 shows an ending balance of $2,798.91. The previous balance is zero because ACS just opened this payroll checking account in December. ACS uses this account only for employee paychecks.

Reconcile Payroll Account
L.O. 8

Figure 14.15

FIRST NATIONAL BANK Wheaton, Illinois				
ACS PRODUCTS 452 Mountain Drive Evanston, Illinois 60187			Statement Date: 12-31-96 Account No. 0267998723 12-1-96 to 12-31-96	
PAYROLL CHECKING				
Previous Balance				0.00
2 Deposits (+)				6,500.00
5 Checks (−)				3,679.09
Service Charges (−)				22.00
Ending Balance				2,798.91
DEPOSITS				
	12-12-96	3,250.00		
	12-26-96	3,250.00		
CHECKS (Asterisk * indicates break in check number sequence)				
	12-16-96	1001	608.11	
	12-17-96	1002	772.30	
	12-18-96	1003	742.56	
	12-30-96	*1005	800.18	
	12-31-96	1006	755.94	

Instructions

1. *a.* After reviewing the bank statement in Figure 14.15 on page 459, record the necessary entry or entries on a data entry sheet.

   b. Referring to your data entry sheet, use PAW's "General Journal Entry" window to journalize the transaction(s) in the general journal.

   c. **Post** the general journal. (You will print the general journal in Problem 14.7A.)

2. *a.* Use PAW's "Account Reconciliation" feature to complete the bank reconciliation.

   b. Print the account reconciliation report.

Problem 14.7A

General Journal; Trial Balance
L.O. 9

1. Follow these steps to print ACS's December 31,1996, general journal.

   a. From the main menu, select Reports, General Ledger.

   b. Highlight General Journal.

   c. Click on the Print icon.

   d. Click on the Calendar icon in the From box, then select 31.

   e. Make the selections to print.

2. Print a December 31, 1996, general ledger trial balance for ACS Products. This is an adjusted trial balance.

Problem 14.8A

Back Up
L.O. 10

Your ACS Products data **must** be backed up. You will restore it in Chapter 15. Follow these steps:

step 1: Insert a blank formatted disk in drive A.

step 2: From PAW's main menu, select File, then Backup.

step 3: Type **a:\acsdec.14a** in the Destination text box.

step 4: Click on the Backup button. When all the files have been saved to drive A, you are automatically returned to the main menu.

step 5: Click on File, Exit to exit PAW.

Problems—Set B

Problem 14.1B

Restore Data; Trial Balance
L.O. 1, 9

Follow these steps to restore your Chapter 13 LLS Products data and print a general ledger trial balance:

step 1: Start Windows, then PAW. Open LLS Products.

step 2: Place your Chapter 13 backup disk in drive A.

step 3: From the main menu, select File, then Restore.

step 4: Type **a:\llsdec.13b** in the Source box. (Use the same file name that you used when you backed up in Chapter 13.)

step 5: Click on the Restore button. Read the "Warning" screen, then click on OK. When the files are restored, you are returned to the main menu.

step 6: Remove the disk from drive A.

step 7: To be sure your LLS data was restored properly, follow these steps to print the general ledger trial balance:

a. From the "Select a Report" window, highlight General Ledger.

b. Highlight General Ledger Trial Balance, then make the selections to print.

Compare your printout with Figure 14.16.

Figure 14.16

LLS Products
General Ledger Trial Balance
As of Dec 31, 1996
Filter Criteria includes: Report order is by ID. Report is printed in Detail Format.

Account ID	Account Description	Debit Amt	Credit Amt
107	Payroll Checking	2,189.14	
108	Change Fund	25.00	
109	Petty Cash	75.00	
110	Cash	2,247.56	
111	Accounts Receivable	33.82	
112	Merchandise Inventory	4,967.08	
113	Supplies	404.85	
114	Prepaid Insurance	590.00	
120	Equipment	5,000.00	
121	Accumulated Depreciation		900.00
210	Accounts Payable		242.85
213	Sales Tax Payable		14.13
217	State Income Tax Payable		162.08
223	Health Insurance Payable		180.00
224	Union Dues Payable		60.00
310	Chris Canon, Capital		7,000.00
320	Chris Canon, Drawing	4,600.00	
330	Retained Earnings		1,267.25
410	Lawn Service Revenue		38,000.00
411	Sales		7,436.80
412	Sales Returns and Allowances	543.25	
413	Sales Discount	133.16	
501	Cost of Sales	4,136.13	
610	Depreciation Expense	825.00	
611	FICA--Soc. Sec. Tax Expense	1,036.02	
612	FICA--Medicare Tax Expense	242.30	
613	FUTA Tax Expense	88.64	
614	SUTA Tax Expense	353.16	
615	Insurance Expense	550.00	
616	Rent Expense	7,140.00	
617	Repair Expense	466.00	
618	Service Charge Expense	182.00	
619	Supplies Expense	730.00	
620	Utilities Expense	1,995.00	
621	Wages Expense	16,710.00	
	Total:	**55,263.11**	**55,263.11**

Problem 14.2B

1. On a data entry sheet, record the following LLS Products transactions:

Unearned Revenue

L.O. 2

12/2/96   Received a $1,596 prepayment from Ritz Corporation for 80 topiary forms to be shipped at a later date.

12/31/96   Shipped 80 topiary forms to Ritz Corporation, Invoice No. 4009, $1,596. The topiary forms cost $957.60.

2. *a.* Referring to your data entry sheet, use PAW's "Cash Receipts" window to journalize the December 2, 1996, transaction in the cash receipts journal. (Hint: Add Account No. 212, Unearned Revenue.)

b. **Post** the cash receipts journal.

c. Follow these steps to print the December 2, 1996, cash receipts journal.
   1) From the main menu, select <u>R</u>eports, then Accounts <u>R</u>eceivable.
   2) Highlight the Cash Receipts Journal.
   3) Click on the Print icon. Click on the From calendar icon, then select 2. Click on the To calendar icon, then select 2. Make the selections to print.

3. a. Referring to your data entry sheet, use PAW's "Sales/Invoicing" window to journalize the December 31, 1996, transaction in the sales journal.
   b. **Post** the sales journal.
   c. Follow these steps to print the December 31, 1996, sales journal.
      1) From the main menu, select <u>R</u>eports, then Accounts <u>R</u>eceivable.
      2) Highlight the Sales Journal
      3) Click on the Print icon. Click on the From calendar icon, then select 31. Make the selections to print.

Problem 14.3B

Adjust for Supplies, Insurance, Wages, Depreciation
L.O.3, 5

1. In data entry sheet format, record the following LLS adjustments:

   12/31/96   Supplies used during December, $305.

   Insurance expired during December, $260.

   Wages expense incurred but not yet paid, $590.

   Depreciation on equipment, $450.

2. a. Referring to your data entry sheet, use PAW's "General Journal Entry" window to journalize LLS's December 31, 1996 adjustments in the general journal.
   b. **Post** the general journal. (You will print the general journal in Problem 14.7B.)

Problem 14.4B

Petty Cash
L.O. 6

Some time ago, LLS Products established a $75 petty cash fund. On December 31, LLS issued Check No. 1252, made out to "Cash," for $64 based on the following information from the petty cash record:

Payments:

Supplies	$ 7.00
Repair Expense	25.00
Miscellaneous Expense . . .	32.00
Total payments	$64.00

Instructions

1. On a data entry sheet, record the entry to replenish petty cash on December 31, 1996.

2. Referring to your data entry sheet, use PAW's "Payments" window to journalize the replenishment of petty cash in the cash disbursements journal and print out Check No. 1252.

3. **Post** the cash disbursements journal.

4. Follow these steps to print the December 31, 1996, cash disbursements journal:
   a. From the main menu, select <u>R</u>eports, then Accounts <u>P</u>ayable.
   b. Highlight the Cash Disbursements Journal.
   c. Click on the Print icon. Click on the From calendar icon, then select 31. Make the selections to print.

Problem 14.5B

On December 31, 1996, LLS Products' Cash account (Account No. 110), shows a balance of $3,779.56. The bank statement displayed in Figure 14.17 shows an ending balance on December 31, 1996, of $5,227.96. LLS uses this checking account for everything *except* employee paychecks.

Reconcile Regular Account
L.O. 7

Figure 14.17

FEDERATED BANK & TRUST Wheaton, Illinois				
LLS PRODUCTS 1823 King Drive Wheaton, Illinois 60221			Statement Date: 12-31-96 Account No. 0367418221 12-1-96 to 12-31-96	
REGULAR CHECKING				
Previous Balance				13,133.75
8 Deposits (+)				10,134.30
10 Checks (−)				11,508.09
Electronic funds transfer (−)				6,500.00
Service Charges (-)				32.00
Ending Balance				5,227.96
DEPOSITS				
12-2-96	1,596.00	12-20-96	105.73	
12- 9-96	1,840.00	12-24-96	1,094.17	
12-14-96	2,842.00	12-26-96	67.63	
12-15-96	2,000.77	12-28-96	588.00	
CHECKS (Asterisk * indicates break in check number sequence)				
		12-4-96	1240	595.00	
		12-7-96	1241	115.00	
		12-9-96	1242	97.00	
		12-14-96	1243	2,234.40	
		12-16-96	1244	2,344.65	
		12-20-96	1245	937.86	
		12-22-96	1246	215.00	
		12-29-96	1247	3,471.30	
		12-31-96	*1249	1,433.88	
		12-31-96	*1252	64.00	
ELECTRONIC FUNDS TRANSFER				
	12-12-96	3,250.00		
	12-26-96	3,250.00		

Instructions

1. *a.* After reviewing the bank statement in Figure 14.17 on page 463, record the necessary entry or entries on a data entry sheet.

   b. Referring to your data entry sheet, use PAW's "General Journal Entry" window to journalize the transaction(s) in the general journal.

   c. **Post** the general journal. (You will print the general journal in Problem 14.7B.)

2. *a.* Use PAW's "Account Reconciliation" feature to complete the bank reconciliation.

   b. Print the account reconciliation report.

Problem 14.6B

Reconcile Payroll Account
L.O. 8

On December 31, 1996, LLS Products' Payroll Checking account (Account No. 107) shows a balance of $2,189.14. The bank statement shown in Figure 14.18 shows an ending balance of $2,917.57. The previous balance is zero because LLS just opened this payroll checking account in December. LLS uses this account only for employee paychecks.

Figure 14.18

FEDERATED BANK & TRUST Wheaton, Illinois				
LLS PRODUCTS 1823 King Drive Wheaton, Illinois 60221			Statement Date: 12-31-96 Account No. 0367091234 12-1-96 to 12-31-96	
PAYROLL CHECKING				
Previous Balance				0.00
2 Deposits (+)				6,500.00
5 Checks (−)				3,554.43
Service Charges (−)				28.00
Ending Balance				2,917.57
DEPOSITS				
	12-12-96	3,250.00		
	12-26-96	3,250.00		
CHECKS (Asterisk * indicates break in check number sequence)				
	12-16-96	1001	596.96	
	12-17-96	1002	756.43	
	12-18-96	1003	802.04	
	12-30-96	1004	596.96	
	12-31-96	*1006	802.04	

Instructions

1. *a.* After reviewing the bank statement in Figure 14.18, record the necessary entry or entries on a data entry sheet.

   b. Referring to your data entry sheet, use PAW's "General Journal Entry" window to journalize the transaction(s) in the general journal.

   c. **Post** the general journal. (You will print the general journal in Problem 14.7B.)

2. *a.* Use PAW's "Account Reconciliation" feature to complete the bank reconciliation.

   b. Print the account reconciliation report.

Problem 14.7B

1. Follow these steps to print LLS's December 31,1996, general journal.

   a. From the main menu, select Reports, General Ledger.

   b. Highlight General Journal.

   c. Click on the Print icon.

   d. Click on the Calendar icon in the From box, then select 31.

   e. Make the selections to print.

2. Print a December 31, 1996, general ledger trial balance for LLS Products. This is an adjusted trial balance.

General Journal; Trial Balance
L.O. 9

Problem 14.8B

Your LLS Products data **must** be backed up. You will restore it in Chapter 15. Follow these steps:

Back Up
L.O. 10

step 1: Insert a blank formatted disk in drive A.

step 2: From PAW's main menu, select File, then Backup.

step 3: Type **a:\llsdec.14b** in the Destination text box.

step 4: Click on the Backup button. When all the files have been saved to drive A, you are automatically returned to the main menu.

step 5: Click on File, Exit to exit PAW.

Mini-Cases

Case 14–1

Molly Olson, owner of Scantech Products, is your new employer. Although Molly is a skilled computer engineer, her background in accounting is weak. Today, when you asked where the petty cash record was kept, Molly replied that it was a waste of time to keep track of individual petty cash payments. "We just write it off to Petty Cash Expense when we replenish the fund." Is it a waste of time?

Case 14–2

You friend, Annette Sammartino, owns a clothing store. She has recently begun accepting orders for custom-made dresses and suits. In these situations, Annette requires the customer to pay for the merchandise in advance. Upon receiving the cash, she locks it in the safe and makes no entry until the order is delivered to the customer four to six weeks later. Her accountant wants her to deposit the cash and to show this prepayment as a liability until the order is delivered to the customer. Annette doesn't understand why this is necessary. Explain.

Case 14–3

Your neighbor, Keith Donalds, is upset with his accountant. "Today he admitted that he doesn't keep the Supplies and Prepaid Insurance accounts up to date on a daily basis. Do you think I should fire him?" Respond.

A Case of Ethics

Beverly, the owner of a newly organized business, plans to apply for a business loan. She knows that the bank will carefully review the financial statements before making a decision on the loan. With this in mind, Beverly instructs her accountant to transfer everything in the Unearned Revenue account to Sales. "We've got to 'beef up' our net income if we're going to get that loan approved," says Beverly. Comment.

Answers to Self-Test

1. *d*   2. *a*   3. *d*   4. *c*   5. *b*

Merchandising Business

Year-End

LEARNING OBJECTIVES

After studying this chapter, you should be able to:

1. Describe the content and purpose of financial statements.

2. Restore data from the previous chapter.

3. Print the financial statements.

4. Record closing entries.

5. Use PAW to close the fiscal year.

6. Print a post-closing trial balance.

7. Back up your data.

8. Describe the accounting cycle.

In Chapters 1 through 7 of this textbook, you studied the accounting cycle for a service business. Then, in Chapter 8, you began studying the accounting cycle for a merchandising business. Although the basic cycle remained the same, you learned to integrate some new types of transactions into that cycle. In this chapter, you are going to complete the accounting cycle for a merchandising business by preparing financial statements, closing entries, and a post-closing trial balance.

Financial Statements

objective 1
Describe the content and purpose of financial statements

Up to this point, you have used PAW to journalize and post daily transactions for TKT Products, adjust the accounts at the end of the month, and reconcile the Cash and Payroll Checking accounts. The trial balance, displayed in Figure 15.1 was prepared at the end of Chapter 14 and shows TKT Products' account balances after adjustment on December 31, 1996.

Figure 15.1

TKT Products
General Ledger Trial Balance
As of Dec 31, 1996
Filter Criteria includes: Report order is by ID. Report is printed in Detail Format.

Account ID	Account Description	Debit Amt	Credit Amt
107	Payroll Checking	287.60	
108	Change Fund	75.00	
109	Petty Cash	100.00	
110	Cash	8,399.81	
111	Accounts Receivable	95.40	
112	Merchandise Inventory	2,241.50	
113	Supplies	241.50	
114	Prepaid Insurance	690.00	
120	Truck	6,000.00	
121	Accumulated Depreciation		2,400.00
210	Accounts Payable		114.00
211	Wages Payable		1,976.00
213	Sales Tax Payable		70.80
217	State Income Tax Payable		273.38
223	Health Insurance Payable		252.00
224	Union Dues Payable		72.00
310	Dennis Taylor, Capital		10,000.00
320	Dennis Taylor, Drawing	4,510.00	
330	Retained Earnings		1,373.63
410	Fees Earned		40,047.00
411	Sales		19,626.00
412	Sales Returns and Allowances	2,946.00	
413	Sales Discount	101.00	
501	Cost of Sales	10,008.00	
610	Depreciation Expense	2,300.00	
611	FICA--Soc. Sec. Tax Expense	1,232.67	
612	FICA--Medicare Tax Expense	288.29	
613	FUTA Tax Expense	121.23	
614	SUTA Tax Expense	463.17	
615	Insurance Expense	702.00	
616	Rent Expense	7,200.00	
617	Repair Expense	661.00	
618	Service Charge Expense	205.00	
619	Supplies Expense	2,885.00	
620	Utilities Expense	2,563.00	
621	Wages Expense	21,857.64	
622	Miscellaneous Expense	30.00	
	Total:	**76,204.81**	**76,204.81**

Periodically (usually monthly or yearly), the information contained in the accounts must be summarized in a format that is more helpful to users of financial data such as owners, creditors, or government agencies. Financial statements provide that format.

As you will recall from earlier chapters, there are three basic financial statements:

1. Income statement
2. Balance sheet
3. Statement of Cash Flow

Comment

In manual accounting systems, there is a fourth financial statement known as the statement of owner's equity. It is prepared after the income statement but before the balance sheet. The purpose of the statement of owner's equity is to update the owner's capital account for net income or loss and withdrawals by the owner.

	Beginning capital account balance
+	Net income (or minus net loss)
−	Withdrawals by the owner
	Ending capital account balance

The up-to-date capital account balance is then displayed as a single figure on the balance sheet. In PAW, however, a statement of owner's equity is not prepared because PAW updates capital for these items in the capital section of the balance sheet.

As a group, these statements present a financial picture of the business. It is important to understand that no single statement presents the whole picture. Each statement presents only a part of the total picture.

Let's review the purpose of each statement and their interrelationships. Then, we will use PAW to print TKT Products' financial statements.

Income Statement

The purpose of the income statement is to compute net income or loss for a specified period of time. Only revenue and expense accounts appear on the income statement because they are the only accounts needed to compute net income.

Since net income is a summary figure representing a combination of revenue earned and expenses incurred over a period of time, it is important that the date line reflect the period of time covered by the statement. It would be impossible, for example, to draw any valid conclusions about net income being "good" or "bad" without knowing whether the income statement reflected results for a month or a year.

In outline form, the income statement appears as follows:

	Total revenues
−	Cost of sales
	Gross profit
−	Total expenses
	Net income (loss)

Let's look at each section in greater detail.

Total Revenues

Revenues are selling prices. They represent how much the customer was charged when the merchandise was sold. In PAW, total revenues equal revenues (such as Fees Earned and Sales) minus the contra-revenue accounts (such as Sales Returns and Allowances and Sales Discount). What PAW calls total revenues is often referred to as *net revenue*.

Cost of Sales

The cost of sales represents how much the business paid to acquire the units that were sold during this accounting period. As you will recall, PAW automatically updates the balance in the Cost of Sales account each time a sale is recorded.

Gross Profit

Gross profit represents the difference between the cost and the selling price of the merchandise sold.

Expenses

Expenses incurred in the normal day-to-day operation of the business are called operating expenses. They are frequently subclassified into selling and general expenses. Selling expenses are directly related to the sale of merchandise. Examples include sales salaries expense and advertising expense. General expenses are more administrative in nature and are not directly related to the sale of the merchandise. Examples include office supplies expense, office salaries expense, and rent expense. PAW does not subclassify expenses on TKT Products' income statement.

Net Income (Loss)

The excess of all revenues over all expenses is called net income. An excess of expenses over revenue results in a net loss. This figure is often referred to as *the bottom line*.

Figure 15.2

TKT Products
Income Statement
For the Twelve Months Ending December 31, 1996

	Current Month		Year to Date	
Revenues				
Fees Earned	0.00	0.00	40,047.00	70.72
Sales	19,626.00	118.38	19,626.00	34.66
Sales Returns and Allowances	<2,946.00>	<17.77>	<2,946.00>	<5.20>
Sales Discount	<101.00>	<0.61>	<101.00>	<0.18>
Total Revenues	16,579.00	100.00	56,626.00	100.00
Cost of Sales				
Cost of Sales	10,008.00	60.37	10,008.00	17.67
Total Cost of Sales	10,008.00	60.37	10,008.00	17.67
Gross Profit	6,571.00	39.63	46,618.00	82.33
Expenses				
Depreciation Expense	1,200.00	7.24	2,300.00	4.06
FICA--Soc. Sec. Tax Expense	612.67	3.70	1,232.67	2.18
FICA--Medicare Tax Expense	143.29	0.86	288.29	0.51
FUTA Tax Expense	65.23	0.39	121.23	0.21
SUTA Tax Expense	220.17	1.33	463.17	0.82
Insurance Expense	210.00	1.27	702.00	1.24
Rent Expense	600.00	3.62	7,200.00	12.72
Repair Expense	82.00	0.49	661.00	1.17
Service Charge Expense	40.00	0.24	205.00	0.36
Supplies Expense	135.00	0.81	2,885.00	5.09
Utilities Expense	198.00	1.19	2,563.00	4.53
Wages Expense	11,857.64	71.52	21,857.64	38.60
Miscellaneous Expense	30.00	0.18	30.00	0.05
Total Expenses	15,394.00	92.85	40,509.00	71.54
Net Income	$ <8,823.00>	<53.22> $	6,109.00	10.79

TKT Products' Income Statement

Looking at TKT's income statement as shown in Figure 15.2 on page 471, you will observe that PAW automatically prints out figures for the current month and also cumulative figures for the year to date. For example, the bottom line shows that TKT had a net loss of ⟨$8,823⟩ for the month of December but net income of $6,109 for the year ending December 31, 1996.

In addition to dollar figures, you will observe that TKT's income statement also includes percentage of revenue columns for both the current month (December) and the year to date. The percentages shown next to each dollar amount indicate the relationship of each item to total revenues. For example, in the current month column, TKT's gross profit ($6,571) is 39.63 percent of total revenues ($16,579).

$$\frac{\text{Gross Profit}}{\text{Total Revenues}} = \frac{\$\ 6{,}571}{\$16{,}579} = .3963 = 39.63\%$$

PAW automatically makes these computations and prints them out on every income statement. This information is very useful in analyzing relationships between revenues and expenses and in making comparisons between different time periods and even different companies.

Balance Sheet

As its name implies, the balance sheet proves that the accounting equation is in balance as of a specified date. Unlike the income statement, the date line on the balance sheet indicates a specific day, not a period of time.

Only asset, liability, and owner's equity accounts are shown on this statement. As you will recall, the *terms* capital and *owner's equity* mean the same thing. Both terms are commonly used in financial statements. Referring to TKT Products' balance sheet shown in Figure 15.3, you will observe that PAW uses the term capital.

Let's take a closer look at each section.

Figure 15.3

TKT Products
Balance Sheet
December 31, 1996

ASSETS

Current Assets
Payroll Checking	$ 287.60	
Change Fund	75.00	
Petty Cash	100.00	
Cash	8,399.81	
Accounts Receivable	95.40	
Merchandise Inventory	2,241.50	
Supplies	241.50	
Prepaid Insurance	690.00	
Total Current Assets		12,130.81

Property and Equipment
Truck	6,000.00	
Accumulated Depreciation	<2,400.00>	
Total Property and Equipment		3,600.00

Other Assets

Total Other Assets	0.00
Total Assets	$ 15,730.81

LIABILITIES AND CAPITAL

Current Liabilities
Accounts Payable	$ 114.00	
Wages Payable	1,976.00	
Sales Tax Payable	70.80	
State Income Tax Payable	273.38	
Health Insurance Payable	252.00	
Union Dues Payable	72.00	
Total Current Liabilities		2,758.18

Long-Term Liabilities

Total Long-Term Liabilities	0.00
Total Liabilities	2,758.18

Capital
Dennis Taylor, Capital	10,000.00	
Dennis Taylor, Drawing	<4,510.00>	
Retained Earnings	1,373.63	
Net Income	6,109.00	
Total Capital		12,972.63
Total Liabilities & Capital		$ 15,730.81

Current Assets

Current assets consist of cash and other assets that will either be converted into cash or used up within one year. Examples include cash, accounts receivable, merchandise inventory, supplies, and prepaid insurance. On the balance sheet, assets are listed in liquidity order. By liquidity, we mean closeness to cash. A liquid asset is cash or an asset that can be quickly converted into cash. Because of this, current assets are listed before property and equipment on the balance sheet.

Property and Equipment

PAW lists assets that will last longer than a year under the property and equipment heading. *Plant assets* and *fixed assets* are common terms that mean the same thing as property and equipment. Examples of accounts in this category include automobiles, equipment, buildings, and land. TKT's truck and its related accumulated depreciation are listed under property and equipment on the balance sheet shown in Figure 15.3 on page 473.

Other Assets

The other assets category consists of investments and intangible assets such as patents, copyrights, and goodwill. These assets are complicated to account for and are usually studied in more advanced accounting courses. TKT Products does not have any assets in this category.

Current Liabilities

Current liabilities are debts that will become due within one year. They are normally paid out of current assets. Examples include accounts payable, wages payable, and unearned revenue.

Long-Term Liabilities

Long-term liabilities are debts that will become due and payable beyond one year. Common examples of long-term liability accounts are mortgage payable and bonds payable. At this time, TKT Products does not have any long-term liabilities.

Capital (Owner's Equity)

Total capital represents the net worth of a business: the difference between all a business owns (assets) and all it owes (liabilities). We can also think of capital or owner's equity as describing the rights of the owner to assets of the business. In PAW, total capital is computed as follows:

	Owner's capital account balance
−	Owner's drawing account balance
+	Retained earnings
+	Net income (or minus net loss)
	Total capital

To demonstrate, let's refer to the capital section of TKT's balance sheet as shown in Figure 15.3 on page 473.

In PAW, the owner's investments in the business are recorded in the owner's capital account. The balance in the Dennis Taylor, Capital, account represents Dennis's original $10,000 investment in the business. As he has not made any additional investments, the balance remains $10,000.

The $4,510 balance in the Dennis Taylor, Drawing, account represents the amount that Dennis withdrew for personal use during 1996. It is subtracted in arriving at total capital.

The $6,109 net income figure reflects TKT's net income for 1996. It is added in arriving at total capital.

We have saved the discussion of retained earnings for last because it is probably the most complex component of capital. To begin, let's repeat that net income (or loss) is a summary figure representing a combination of revenue and expense. As you will recall from earlier chapters, revenue, expense, and drawing accounts are temporary owner's equity accounts. They all have special relationships to total capital (+ or −). Let's quickly review those relationships. For the purposes of our review, let's consider net income and net loss rather than revenue and expense individually.

- Drawing *decreases* (−) total capital.
- Net income *increases* (+) total capital.
- Net loss *decreases* (−) total capital.

At year-end, drawing and net income or net loss are closed to the Retained Earnings account. Referring to TKT's balance sheet, the $1,373.63 balance in retained earnings represents the cumulative effect of drawing and net income or loss that has been closed to retained earnings in previous years. Because TKT is a relatively new business, the retained earnings balance represents only one previous year—1995. After the temporary accounts are closed at the end of 1996, the balance in TKT's Retained Earnings account will be $2,972.63 ($1,373.63 + $6,109.00 − $4,510.00). We will discuss this in more detail later in this chapter when we study the closing procedure for a merchandising business.

Statement of Cash Flow

The statement of cash flow describes the flow of cash in and out of the business during a specific period of time. It provides the answers to three important questions:

1. From where did cash receipts come?
2. For what were cash payments used?
3. What was the overall change in cash?

As you already know, TKT Products uses the accrual basis of accounting. Under the accrual basis, revenue is recorded when it is earned and expenses are recorded when they are incurred, regardless of whether the cash has been received or paid. Over the long run, the accrual basis is generally the most useful way to measure revenues and expenses. Over the short run, however, TKT Products must have sufficient cash to pay its bills as they come due.

When the accrual basis of accounting is used, the balance sheet and income statement provide little information about the flow of cash. It is possible that TKT Products might have net income but be short of cash, or have a net loss and have excess cash. Therefore, the information provided by the statement of cash flow is extremely useful.

Referring to Figure 15.4, you will observe that PAW automatically separates TKT Products' cash flows (both receipts and payments) into three basic groups: operating activities, investing activities, and financing activities.

Figure 15.4

TKT Products
Statement of Cash Flow
For the twelve Months Ended December 31, 1996

	Current Month	Year to Date
Cash Flows from operating activities		
Net Income	$ <8,823.00> $	6,109.00
Adjustments to reconcile net income to net cash provided by operating activities		
Accumulated Depreciation	1,200.00	2,400.00
Accounts Receivable	1,304.60	<95.40>
Merchandise Inventory	<2,241.50>	<2,241.50>
Supplies	8.50	<241.50>
Prepaid Insurance	210.00	<690.00>
Accounts Payable	<11.00>	114.00
Wages Payable	1,976.00	1,976.00
Sales Tax Payable	70.80	70.80
State Income Tax Payable	273.38	273.38
Health Insurance Payable	252.00	252.00
Union Dues Payable	72.00	72.00
Total Adjustments	3,114.78	1,889.78
Net Cash provided by Operations	<5,708.22>	7,998.78
Cash Flows from investing activities		
Used For		
Truck	0.00	<6,000.00>
Net cash used in investing	0.00	<6,000.00>
Cash Flows from financing activities		
Proceeds From		
Dennis Taylor, Capital	0.00	10,000.00
Used For		
Dennis Taylor, Drawing	<10.00>	<4,510.00>
Net cash used in financing	<10.00>	5,490.00
Net increase <decrease> in cash	$ <5,718.22> $	7,488.78
Summary		
Cash Balance at End of Period	$ 8,862.41 $	8,862.41
Cash Balance at Beginning of P	<14,580.63>	0.00
Net Increase <Decrease> in Cash	$ <5,718.22> $	8,862.41

The chart shown in Figure 15.5 includes some common types of operating, investing, and financing activities. Of course, TKT has not been involved in all the activities shown.

Figure 15.5

OPERATING ACTIVITIES

Cash received from:
Sale of goods and services
Interest received

Cash paid for:
Merchandise inventory
Operating expenses
Interest paid

INVESTING ACTIVITIES

Cash received from:
Sale of property and equipment
Sale of investments
Collection of principal on loans

Cash paid for:
Purchase of property and equipment
Purchase of investments
Lending money

FINANCING ACTIVITIES

Cash received from:
Investments by owner
Borrowing money

Cash paid for:
Withdrawals by owner
Repayment of principal on loans

In the summary section at the bottom of the statement of cash flow, PAW automatically computes the net increase or decrease in cash for the current month and also for the year to date. This is done by comparing the beginning cash balance (first day of the month or year) with the ending cash balance (last day of the month or year). A net increase is indicated if the ending balance is larger than the beginning balance. On the other hand, a net decrease is indicated if the ending balance is smaller than the beginning balance.

Comment

Although PAW makes it seem easy, the preparation of the statement of cash flow requires a lot of analysis. In an introductory course, such as this, our focus is on the general purpose and content of this important statement. A more detailed discussion of the statement of cash flow is usually included in more advanced accounting courses.

Interrelationship of the Financial Statements

Observe that the three financial statements shown in Figures 15.2, 15.3, and 15.4 are separate but related. The year-to-date net income figure ($6,109) is taken from the income statement and used on the balance sheet to update the capital section. Total cash of $8,862.41 (includes Payroll Checking, Change Fund, Petty Cash, and Cash accounts) as shown on the balance sheet is explained in detail on the statement of cash flow using information from both the income statement and the balance sheet.

As mentioned earlier, it is important to remember that no single statement tells the whole story. For example, the income statement indicates how much revenue a business has earned during a specific period of time, but it says nothing about how much of that amount has or has not been received in cash. For information about cash and accounts receivable, we have to look at the balance sheet and statement of cash flow.

Restoring Data from Chapter 14

objective 2
Restore data from the previous chapter

Before you can print financial statements, you must restore your data from Chapter 14. Follow these steps to restore your data:

step 1:   Start Windows, then PAW. Open TKT Products.

step 2:   Place your Chapter 14 backup disk in drive A.

step 3:   From the main menu, select File, then Restore.

step 4:   Type **a:\chap14.tkt** in the Source box. (Use the same file name that you used when you backed up in Chapter 14.)

step 5:   Click on the Restore button. Read the "Warning" screen, then click on OK. When the files are restored, you are returned to the main menu.

step 6:   Remove disk from drive A.

Printing the Financial Statements

objective 3
Print the financial statements

Now that you have reviewed their content and purpose, you are ready to print out TKT Products' income statement, balance sheet, and statement of cash flow.

Follow these easy steps:

step 1:   From the main menu, select Reports, then Financial Statements.

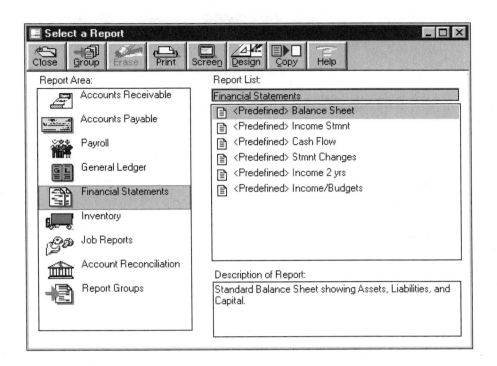

step 2:   Highlight <Predefined> Income Statement.

step 3:   Click on the Print icon. The <Predefined> Income Statement window displays.

Predefined refers to formats that PAW has established. Formats can be changed. For the purposes of this textbook, you will use the predefined formats.

Comment

step 4:   Click once on the check mark in the box next to "Show Zero Amounts" to deselect it.

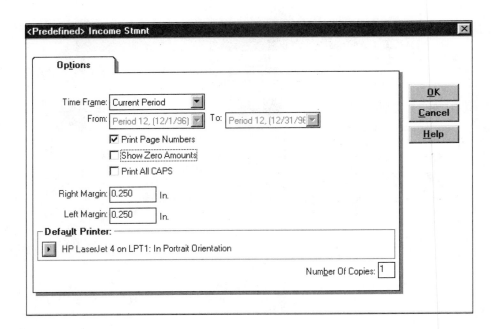

step 5:   Click on <u>O</u>K. When the "Print" window pops up, click on OK. The income statement starts to print. **Compare your printout with Figure 15.2 shown on page 471.**

step 6:   To print the balance sheet, highlight the <Predefined> Balance Sheet and make the selections to print. **Compare your printout with Figure 15.3 shown on page 473.**

step 7:   To print the statement of cash flow, highlight the <Predefined> Cash Flow, deselect "Show Zero Amounts," then make the selections to print. **Compare your printout with Figure 15.4 shown on page 476.**

Closing the Fiscal Year

objective 4
Record closing entries

In Chapter 7, we studied the closing procedure for a service business. In this chapter, we will use the same procedure to close the fiscal year for a merchandising business. Let's begin with a review of the closing procedure.

At the end of every fiscal year, the temporary owner's equity accounts (revenue, expense, drawing) must be closed to a permanent owner's equity account. In PAW, there are two permanent owner's equity accounts: the owner's capital account and the Retained Earnings account. PAW closes the temporary accounts to the Retained Earnings account.

In accounting for a merchandising business, we have added some new temporary accounts: Sales, Sales Returns and Allowances, Sales Discount, and Cost of Sales. The closing of these new accounts is integrated into Steps 1 and 2 of the usual three-step closing procedure. Let's review the three steps:

step 1:   Close all revenue accounts to the Retained Earnings account.

step 2:   Close all expense accounts and other debit-balance temporary accounts (such as Cost of Sales, Sales Returns and Allowances, and Sales Discount) to the Retained Earnings account.

step 3:   Close the owner's drawing account to the Retained Earnings account.

Each step in the closing procedure requires a journal entry. To demonstrate, let's return to TKT Products. Referring to the trial balance shown in Figure 15.1 on page 468 for the account titles and balances, TKT's closing entries are recorded as follows in data entry sheet format:

			DATA ENTRY SHEET TKT Products		
Date	Account ID	Reference	Trans Description	Debit Amt	Credit Amt
12/31/96	410		Fees Earned	40,047.00	
	411		Sales	19,626.00	
	330		Retained Earnings		59,673.00
12/31/96	330		Retained Earnings	53,564.00	
	412		Sales Returns and Allowances		2,946.00
	413		Sales Discount		101.00
	501		Cost of Sales		10,008.00
	610		Depreciation Expense		2,300.00
	611		FICA—Soc. Sec. Tax Expense		1,232.67
	612		FICA—Medicare Tax Expense		288.29
	613		FUTA Tax Expense		121.23
	614		SUTA Tax Expense		463.17
	615		Insurance Expense		702.00
	616		Rent Expense		7,200.00
	617		Repair Expense		661.00
	618		Service Charge Expense		205.00
	619		Supplies Expense		2,885.00
	620		Utilities Expense		2,563.00
	621		Wages Expense		21,857.64
	622		Miscellaneous Expense		30.00
12/31/96	330		Retained Earnings	4,510.00	
	320		Dennis Taylor, Drawing		4,510.00

Now, let's look at the Retained Earnings account after closing entries have been journalized and posted. The ending credit balance is now $2,972.63, computed as follows:

	Beginning retained earnings balance	$ 1,373.63 cr.
+	Revenues	59,673.00 cr.
−	Expenses	53,564.00 dr.
−	Drawing	4,510.00 dr.
	Ending retained earnings balance	$ 2,972.63 cr.

After closing entries have been journalized and posted, all the temporary accounts (revenue, expense, drawing) have *zero* balances. They are *closed*.

Using PAW To Close the Fiscal Year

In PAW, when you select "Close Fiscal Year," the closing entries are automatically journalized and posted. To demonstrate how easy it is, let's close TKT Products' fiscal year.

Follow these steps:

step 1: From the main menu, select Tasks, System, Close Fiscal Year.

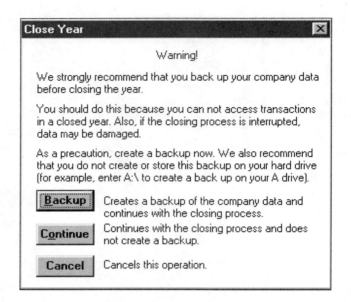

step 2: Click on Continue.

step 3: The next screen is a "Peachtree Accounting Question" window.

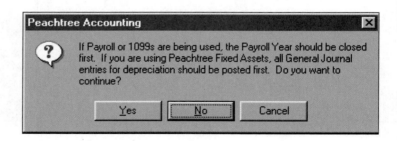

step 4: Read the question, then click on Yes.

step 5: The next window displays "Would you like to print your invoices or checks before continuing?"

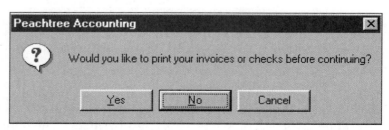

If this screen does *not* display, skip ahead to step 7.   ***Comment***

step 6:   Click on <u>N</u>o.

step 7:   The next window displays "Would you like to print your reports before continuing?"

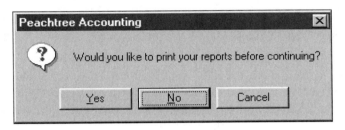

step 8:   Click on <u>N</u>o.

step 9:   The next window displays "You are closing to the retained earnings account: '330'."

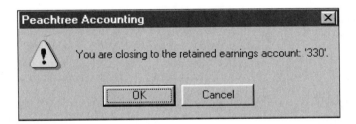

step 10:   Click on OK.

step 11:   The "Close Fiscal Year" window displays.

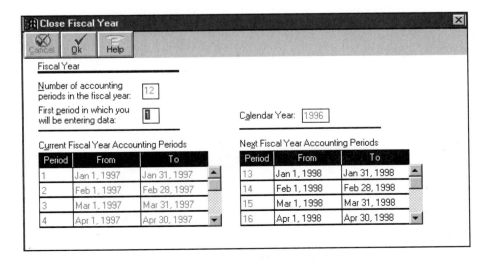

step 12:   Click on <u>O</u>k.

step 13:   The "Fiscal Year close completed; do you want to purge?" window displays.

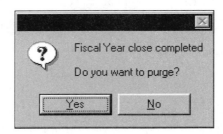

step 14:   Click on <u>N</u>o. You are returned to the main menu.

Printing the Post-Closing Trial Balance

objective 6
Print a post-closing trial
balance
Now that TKT's fiscal year is closed, we are ready to complete the accounting cycle by printing a post-closing trial balance. This provides a final check at year-end to prove that the debits in the general ledger equal the credits in the general ledger. The post-closing trial balance completes the basic accounting cycle for a merchandising business. We will review the steps in the accounting cycle at the end of this chapter. For now, follow these steps to print a post-closing trial balance.

step 1:   From the main menu, select <u>R</u>eports, <u>G</u>eneral Ledger, General Ledger Trial Balance.

step 2:   Make the selections to print the post-closing trial balance. Compare your printout to Figure 15.6.

Figure 15.6

TKT Products
General Ledger Trial Balance
As of Jan 31, 1997
Filter Criteria includes: Report order is by ID. Report is printed in Detail Format.

Account ID	Account Description	Debit Amt	Credit Amt
107	Payroll Checking	287.60	
108	Change Fund	75.00	
109	Petty Cash	100.00	
110	Cash	8,399.81	
111	Accounts Receivable	95.40	
112	Merchandise Inventory	2,241.50	
113	Supplies	241.50	
114	Prepaid Insurance	690.00	
120	Truck	6,000.00	
121	Accumulated Depreciation		2,400.00
210	Accounts Payable		114.00
211	Wages Payable		1,976.00
213	Sales Tax Payable		70.80
217	State Income Tax Payable		273.38
223	Health Insurance Payable		252.00
224	Union Dues Payable		72.00
310	Dennis Taylor, Capital		10,000.00
330	Retained Earnings		2,972.63
	Total:	**18,130.81**	**18,130.81**

You will notice that the post-closing trial balance is considerably shorter than previous trial balances. Since all the temporary accounts are closed, it only contains permanent accounts with existing balances. You will also observe that the post-closing trial balance is dated January 31, 1997. All the permanent account balances have been brought forward to the next accounting period—January 1 through 31, 1997.

Backing Up Your Chapter 15 Data

Be sure to back up your Chapter 15 data. Although this is the last chapter (yeah!), you may still need to access this data for error correction or testing purposes.

objective 7
Back up your data

Follow these steps:

step 1: Insert a blank formatted disk in drive A.

step 2: From the main menu, select File, then Backup.

step 3: Type **a:\chap15.tkt** in the Destination text box.

step 4: Click on the Backup button. When all the files have been saved to drive A, you are returned to the main menu.

step 5: Click on File, Exit to exit PAW.

The Accounting Cycle

You have now studied the basic accounting cycle twice—once for a service business and again for a merchandising business.

objective 8
Describe the accounting cycle

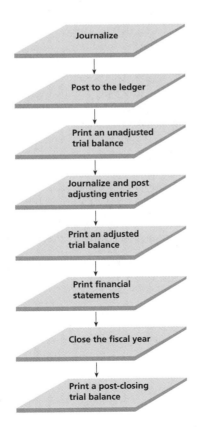

Journalize

↓

Post to the ledger

↓

Print an unadjusted trial balance

↓

Journalize and post adjusting entries

↓

Print an adjusted trial balance

↓

Print financial statements

↓

Close the fiscal year

↓

Print a post-closing trial balance

Whether accounting is done manually or on a computer, whether a business is large or small, wholesale or retail, the same basic accounting cycle is followed. It provides the basis for every business' accounting system.

Chapter 15 Summary

Periodically (usually monthly or yearly), the information contained in the accounts must be summarized in a format that is more helpful to users of financial data such as owners, creditors, or government agencies. Financial statements provide that format.

In PAW, three basic financial statements are prepared.

1. Income statement
2. Balance sheet
3. Statement of cash flow

As a group, these statements present a financial picture of the business. It is important to understand that no single statement presents the whole picture. Each statement presents only a part of the total picture.

The purpose of the income statement is to compute net income or loss for a specified period of time. Only revenue and expense accounts appear on the income statement.

As its name implies, the balance sheet proves that the accounting equation is in balance as of a specified date. Unlike the income statement, the date line on the balance sheet indicates a specific day, not a period of time. Only asset, liability, and owner's equity accounts are shown on the balance sheet.

The statement of cash flow describes the flow of cash in and out of the business during a specific period of time. This is important because under the accrual basis of accounting, the income statement and balance sheet provide very little information about the flow of cash. On the statement of cash flow, cash flows (both receipts and payments) are separated into three basic groups: operating activities, investing activities, and financing activities. In the summary section, the net increase or decrease in cash is computed.

At the end of every fiscal year, the temporary owner's equity accounts (revenue, expense, drawing) must be closed to a permanent owner's equity account. In PAW, there are two permanent owner's equity accounts: the owner's capital account and the Retained Earnings account. PAW closes the temporary accounts to the Retained Earnings account in three steps:

step 1: Close all revenue accounts to the Retained Earnings account.

step 2: Close all expense accounts and other debit-balance temporary accounts (such as Cost of Sales, Sales Returns and Allowances, and Sales Discount) to the Retained Earnings account.

step 3: Close the owner's drawing account to the Retained Earnings account.

Although each of these steps requires a journal entry, PAW automatically journalizes and posts the closing entries when "Close Fiscal Year" is selected.

After the temporary accounts have been closed, a post-closing trial balance is prepared. This provides a final check at year-end to prove that the debits in the general ledger equal the credits in the general ledger.

Demonstration Problem

On December 31, 1996, the end of the fiscal year, Dillon Company's adjusted trial balance contains the following accounts and balances:

Account Description	Debit Amt	Credit Amt
Cash	12,000.00	
Accounts Receivable	18,000.00	
Merchandise Inventory	25,000.00	
Supplies	600.00	
Prepaid Insurance	1,400.00	
Equipment	17,000.00	
Accumulated Depreciation		2,000.00
Accounts Payable		4,235.00
Wages Payable		3,100.00
Amy Dillon, Capital		15,000.00
Amy Dillon, Drawing	16,300.00	
Retained Earnings		31,298.00
Sales		135,000.00
Sales Returns and Allowances	7,000.00	
Sales Discount	500.00	
Cost of Sales	36,000.00	
Depreciation Expense	1,000.00	
FICA—Social Security Tax Expense	3,720.00	
FICA—Medicare Tax Expense	870.00	
FUTA Tax Expense	168.00	
SUTA Tax Expense	675.00	
Insurance Expense	1,800.00	
Rent Expense	14,700.00	
Supplies Expense	1,300.00	
Utilities Expense	2,600.00	
Wages Expense	30,000.00	

1. In data entry sheet format, record the closing entries. Leave the "Account ID" column blank.
2. After closing entries have been posted, what is the balance in the Retained Earnings account?

Solution to Demonstration Problem

1.

			DATA ENTRY SHEET Dillon Company		
Date	**Account ID**	**Reference**	**Trans Description**	**Debit Amt**	**Credit Amt**
12/31/96			Sales	135,000.00	
			Retained Earnings		135,000.00
12/31/96			Retained Earnings	100,333.00	
			Sales Returns and Allowances		7,000.00
			Sales Discount		500.00
			Cost of Sales		36,000.00
			Depreciation Expense		1,000.00
			FICA—Soc. Sec. Tax Expense		3,720.00
			FICA—Medicare Tax Expense		870.00
			FUTA Tax Expense		168.00
			SUTA Tax Expense		675.00
			Insurance Expense		1,800.00
			Rent Expense		14,700.00
			Supplies Expense		1,300.00
			Utilities Expense		2,600.00
			Wages Expense		30,000.00
12/31/96			Retained Earnings	16,300.00	
			Amy Dillon, Drawing		16,300.00

2. $49,665 ($31,298 + 135,000 − 100,333 − 16,300)

Glossary

cost of sales   A figure representing how much a business paid to acquire the units that were actually sold during an accounting period. *470*

current asset   Cash or an asset that will either be converted into cash or used up within one year. *474*

current liability   A debt that will become due within one year; normally paid out of current assets. *474*

general expenses   Operating expenses of a general or administrative nature not directly related to the sale of merchandise. *470*

gross profit   Represents the difference between the cost and selling price of the merchandise sold: total revenues minus cost of sales equals gross profit. *470*

liquidity   Closeness to cash. For example, accounts receivable are more liquid than land because they can be converted to cash more quickly. *474*

long-term liability   A debt that will become due and payable beyond one year. *474*

net income   The excess of all revenue over all expenses. Often referred to as *the bottom line.*   *470*

net loss   An excess of expenses over revenue. Often referred to as *the bottom line.*   *470*

operating expense   Expenses incurred in the normal day-to-day operation of the business; frequently subdivided into selling and general expenses.   *470*

property and equipment   A group of assets that will last longer than one year. Also known as *plant assets* or *fixed assets.*   *474*

selling expenses   Operating expenses directly related to the sale of merchandise. *470*

total capital   Represents the net worth of a business: the difference between all a business owns (assets) and all it owes (liabilities).   *474*

total revenues   Represent how much the customer was charged when the merchandise was sold.   *470*

Self-Test

Select the best answer.

1. On the income statement, the cost of sales represents the
   a. beginning balance in the Merchandise Inventory account.
   b. ending balance in the Merchandise Inventory account.
   c. cost of the merchandise sold during the accounting period.
   d. cost of the merchandise purchased during the accounting period.

2. Total revenues minus the cost of sales equals
   a. net income.
   b. gross profit.
   c. retained earnings.
   d. None of the above.

3. On a monthly balance sheet, total capital is
   a. increased by net income.
   b. decreased by net loss.
   c. decreased by drawing.
   d. All of the above.

4. In closing the fiscal year, retained earnings is
   a. increased by revenues.
   b. decreased by expenses.
   c. decreased by drawing.
   d. All of the above.

5. A post-closing trial balance
   a. is prepared after the fiscal year is closed.
   b. checks the overall equality of debits and credits in the ledger.
   c. completes the basic accounting cycle.
   d. All of the above.

Answers to the self-test can be found after the cases at the end of this chapter.

Questions for Discussion

1. What is the purpose of the income statement?

2. What types of accounts are shown on the income statement?

3. What is the purpose of the balance sheet?

4. What types of accounts are shown on the balance sheet?

5. What is the difference between current assets and property and equipment?

6. What is the difference between current liabilities and long-term liabilities?

7. What is the purpose of the statement of cash flow?

8. What is the purpose of closing the fiscal year?

9. What are the three steps in the closing process?

10. What is the purpose of a post-closing trial balance?

Exercises

Exercise 15.1

Terminology
L.O. 1–6

Match the following terms with the definitions shown below:

1. Current liability
2. Property and equipment
3. Cost of sales
4. Gross profit
5. Net income
6. Long-term liability
7. Current asset
8. Operating expenses
9. Total capital
10. Liquidity

Definitions

a. Represents the net worth of a business.

b. A group of assets that will last longer than one year.

c. Expenses incurred in the normal day-to-day operation of the business.

d. The excess of revenue over expenses.

e. A debt that will become due and payable beyond one year.

f. Closeness to cash.

g. Represents the difference between the cost and selling price of the merchandise sold.

h. A debt that will become due within one year.

i. Cash or an asset that will either be converted into cash or used up within one year.

j. A figure representing how much a business paid to acquire the units that were actually sold during an accounting period.

Exercise 15.2

Arrange the following steps in the accounting cycle in their proper order:

Accounting Cycle
L.O. 8

a. Post to the ledger.

b. Journalize and post adjusting entries.

c. Journalize.

d. Print the unadjusted trial balance.

e. Print the post-closing trial balance.

f. Print the financial statements.

g. Close the fiscal year.

h. Print the adjusted trial balance.

Exercise 15.3

Classify each of the accounts listed below as one of the following:

Financial Statements
L.O. 1

CA—current asset

PE—property and equipment

CL—current liability

LT—long-term liability

1. Supplies
2. Wages Payable
3. Cash
4. Unearned Revenue
5. Equipment
6. Prepaid Insurance
7. Land
8. Accounts Payable
9. Merchandise Inventory
10. Accounts Receivable

Exercise 15.4

Indicate on which statement the accounts listed below are shown:

Financial Statements
L.O. 1

IS—income statement

BS—balance sheet

1. Sales
2. Prepaid Insurance
3. Accounts Receivable
4. Sales Returns and Allowances
5. Unearned Revenue
6. Cash
7. Jeffrey Chan, Capital
8. Cost of Sales
9. FUTA Tax Payable
10. Accumulated Depreciation
11. FICA—Medicare Tax Expense
12. Sales Discount

Exercise 15.5

Income Statement
L.O. 1
On December 31, 1996, the end of the fiscal year, Fisher Products' adjusted trial balance contains the following accounts and balances:

Account Description	Debit Amt	Credit Amt
Cash	6,000.00	
Accounts Receivable	9,000.00	
Merchandise Inventory	12,500.00	
Supplies	300.00	
Prepaid Insurance	700.00	
Equipment	8,500.00	
Accumulated Depreciation		1,000.00
Accounts Payable		2,528.00
Wages Payable		1,600.00
Jeremy Fisher, Capital		12,000.00
Jeremy Fisher, Drawing	7,300.00	
Retained Earnings		35,650.00
Sales		89,000.00
Sales Returns and Allowances	7,100.00	
Sales Discount	625.00	
Cost of Sales	48,000.00	
Depreciation Expense	500.00	
FICA—Social Security Tax Expense	2,232.00	
FICA—Medicare Tax Expense	522.00	
FUTA Tax Expense	56.00	
SUTA Tax Expense	243.00	
Insurance Expense	900.00	
Rent Expense	10,800.00	
Supplies Expense	6,400.00	
Miscellaneous Expense	2,100.00	
Wages Expense	18,000.00	

From the above information, compute:

a. Total revenues

b. Gross profit

c. Total expenses

d. Net income

Exercise 15.6

From the information given in Exercise 15.5, compute:

Balance Sheet
L.O. 1

a. Total current assets

b. Total property and equipment

c. Total current liabilities

d. Total capital

Exercise 15.7

Referring to the information given in Exercise 15.5, record closing entries in data entry sheet format. Leave the "Account ID" column blank.

Closing Entries
L.O. 4

Exercise 15.8

Referring to the information given in Exercise 15.5 and your data entry sheet from Exercise 15.7, compute the balance in the Retained Earnings account after closing entries have been posted.

Closing Entries
L.O. 4

Problems—Set A

Problem 15.1A

In Chapter 14, you printed an adjusted trial balance for ACS Products. Follow these steps to restore your Chapter 14 data and print ACS's adjusted trial balance:

Restore Data; Trial Balance
L.O. 2

step 1:   Start Windows, then PAW. Open ACS Products.

step 2:   Place your Chapter 14 backup disk in drive A.

step 3:   From the main menu, select File, then Restore.

step 4:   Type **a:\acsdec.14a** in the Source box. (Use the same file name that you used when you backed up in Chapter 14.)

step 5:   Click on the Restore button. Read the "Warning" screen, then click on OK. When the files are restored, you are returned to the main menu.

step 6:   Remove disk from drive A.

step 7:   To be sure that your ACS data was restored properly, follow these steps to print the general ledger trial balance:
a. From the "Select a Report" window, highlight General Ledger.
b. Highlight General Ledger Trial Balance, then make the selections to print.

Compare your printout with Figure 15.7 on page 494.

Figure 15.7

ACS Products
General Ledger Trial Balance
As of Dec 31, 1996
Filter Criteria includes: Report order is by ID. Report is printed in Detail Format.

Account ID	Account Description	Debit Amt	Credit Amt
107	Payroll Checking	2,213.10	
108	Change Fund	30.00	
109	Petty Cash	50.00	
110	Cash	19,648.61	
111	Accounts Receivable	13.72	
112	Merchandise Inventory	901.89	
113	Supplies	289.95	
114	Prepaid Insurance	525.00	
120	Equipment	5,000.00	
121	Accumulated Depreciation		1,400.00
210	Accounts Payable		265.95
211	Wages Payable		650.00
213	Sales Tax Payable		8.90
217	State Income Tax Payable		156.63
223	Health Insurance Payable		180.00
224	Union Dues Payable		60.00
310	Joan Haywood, Capital		7,500.00
320	Joan Haywood, Drawing	4,118.00	
330	Retained Earnings		1,937.00
410	Cleaning Revenue		42,000.00
411	Sales		22,131.25
412	Sales Returns and Allowances	593.25	
413	Sales Discount	170.94	
501	Cost of Sales	9,754.80	
610	Depreciation Expense	1,325.00	
611	FICA--Soc. Sec. Tax Expense	1,091.55	
612	FICA--Medicare Tax Expense	255.28	
613	FUTA Tax Expense	87.80	
614	SUTA Tax Expense	350.34	
615	Insurance Expense	635.00	
616	Rent Expense	7,500.00	
617	Repair Expense	406.00	
618	Service Charge Expense	240.00	
619	Supplies Expense	1,120.00	
620	Utilities Expense	1,702.00	
621	Wages Expense	18,255.50	
622	Miscellaneous Expense	12.00	
	Total:	**76,289.73**	**76,289.73**

Problem 15.2A

Instructions

Print Financial Statements
L.O. 3

Print ACS Products' financial statements for the fiscal year ending December 31, 1996.

1. Print the income statement.

2. Print the balance sheet.

3. Print the statement of cash flow.

Problem 15.3A

Instructions

1. Referring to your ACS adjusted trial balance from Problem 15.1A, record closing entries in data entry sheet format.

2. Using PAW, close ACS's fiscal year ending December 31, 1996.

3. Print ACS Products' post-closing trial balance.

Closing Entries; Post-Closing Trial Balance
L.O. 4–6

Problem 15.4A

Your ACS Products data **must** be backed up. You may still need to access this data for error correction or testing purposes. Follow these steps:

Back Up
L.O. 7

step 1: Insert a blank formatted disk in drive A.

step 2: From PAW's main menu, select File, then Backup.

step 3: Type **a:\acsdec.15a** in the Destination text box.

step 4: Click on the Backup button. When all the files have been saved to drive A, you are automatically returned to the main menu.

step 5: Click on File, Exit to exit PAW.

Problems—Set B

Problem 15.1B

In Chapter 14, you printed an adjusted trial balance for LLS Products. Follow these steps to restore your Chapter 14 data and print LLS's adjusted trial balance:

Restore Data; Trial Balance
L.O. 2

step 1: Start Windows, then PAW. Open LLS Products.

step 2: Place your Chapter 14 backup disk in drive A.

step 3: From the main menu, select File, then Restore.

step 4: Type **a:\llsdec.14b** in the Source box. (Use the same file name that you used when you backed up in Chapter 14.)

step 5: Click on the Restore button. Read the "Warning" screen, then click on OK. When the files are restored, you are returned to the main menu.

step 6: Remove disk from drive A.

step 7: To be sure that your LLS data was restored properly, follow these steps to print the general ledger trial balance:
   a. From the "Select a Report" window, highlight General Ledger.
   b. Highlight General Ledger Trial Balance, then make the selections to print.

Compare your printout with Figure 15.8 on page 496.

Figure 15.8

LLS Products
General Ledger Trial Balance
As of Dec 31, 1996
Filter Criteria includes: Report order is by ID. Report is printed in Detail Format.

Account ID	Account Description	Debit Amt	Credit Amt
107	Payroll Checking	2,161.14	
108	Change Fund	25.00	
109	Petty Cash	75.00	
110	Cash	3,747.56	
111	Accounts Receivable	33.82	
112	Merchandise Inventory	4,009.48	
113	Supplies	106.85	
114	Prepaid Insurance	330.00	
120	Equipment	5,000.00	
121	Accumulated Depreciation		1,350.00
210	Accounts Payable		242.85
211	Wages Payable		590.00
213	Sales Tax Payable		14.13
217	State Income Tax Payable		162.08
223	Health Insurance Payable		180.00
224	Union Dues Payable		60.00
310	Chris Canon, Capital		7,000.00
320	Chris Canon, Drawing	4,600.00	
330	Retained Earnings		1,267.25
410	Lawn Service Revenue		38,000.00
411	Sales		9,032.80
412	Sales Returns and Allowances	543.25	
413	Sales Discount	133.16	
501	Cost of Sales	5,093.73	
610	Depreciation Expense	1,275.00	
611	FICA--Soc. Sec. Tax Expense	1,036.02	
612	FICA--Medicare Tax Expense	242.30	
613	FUTA Tax Expense	88.64	
614	SUTA Tax Expense	353.16	
615	Insurance Expense	810.00	
616	Rent Expense	7,140.00	
617	Repair Expense	491.00	
618	Service Charge Expense	242.00	
619	Supplies Expense	1,035.00	
620	Utilities Expense	1,995.00	
621	Wages Expense	17,300.00	
622	Miscellaneous Expense	32.00	
	Total:	**57,899.11**	**57,899.11**

Problem 15.2B

Instructions

Print Financial Statements
L.O. 3

Print LLS Products' financial statements for the fiscal year ending December 31, 1996.

1. Print the income statement.

2. Print the balance sheet.

3. Print the statement of cash flow.

Problem 15.3B

Instructions

1. Referring to your LLS adjusted trial balance from Problem 15.1B, record

   closing entries in data entry sheet format.

2. Using PAW, close LLS's fiscal year ending December 31, 1996.

3. Print LLS Products' post-closing trial balance.

Closing Entries; Post-Closing Trial Balance
L.O. 4–6

Problem 15.4B

Your LLS Products data **must** be backed up. You may still need to access this data for error correction or testing purposes. Follow these steps:

Back Up
L.O. 7

step 1: Insert a blank formatted disk in drive A.

step 2: From PAW's main menu, select File, then Backup.

step 3: Type **a:\llsdec.15b** in the Destination text box.

step 4: Click on the Backup button. When all the files have been saved to drive A, you are automatically returned to the main menu.

step 5: Click on File, Exit to exit PAW.

Mini-Cases

Case 15–1

Your new employer, Jennifer Crane, says that her previous accountant never prepared a statement of cash flow. "I can get all the information about cash that I need from the income statement and balance sheet," she says. Convince Jennifer that a statement of cash flow would be helpful.

Case 15–2

Your friend, John Marszalek, is about to complete the first fiscal year for his new business. John has a weak background in accounting and has asked you if anything special needs to be done at year end. Respond.

Case 15–3

Iris Becker, your neighbor, opened her new business one month ago. She is using PAW for the first time and is confused about having both current month and year-to-date columns on the income statement. "If PAW is going to print out the same figures in both columns every month, why clutter up the statement with duplicate information," asks Iris. Clarify this matter for Iris.

A Case of Ethics

Your friend, Don Wilcox, owns a muffler shop. Knowing that you have recently started working as an accountant for one of his competitors, Don has started asking you sensitive financial questions about your employer's business. You value Don's friendship but feel uncomfortable socializing with him now because of these questions. How should this situation be handled?

Answers to Self-Test

1. *c*   2. *b*   3. *d*   4. *d*   5. *d*

Comprehensive Review Problem 2

Covering Chapters 8–15

Part A

Flashtec was started by Sue Baxter in the spring of 1996. Flashtec sells a wide range of electronic business equipment such as fax machines, computers, printers, laminators, cash registers, and paper shredders. Flashtec is mainly a wholesale business, but it does have one retail customer. This review problem will focus on operations for December 1996.

Instructions to load the Flashtec company data and print the chart of accounts.

1. Start Windows. If you are running Windows 3.1*x*, choose File, ‾un in Program Manager. If you are running Windows 95, choose Start, Run.

2. Place the Company Data CD-ROM in drive D (or the appropriate drive for your CD-ROM).

3. Type **d:\setup.exe** in the dialog box. (This text assumes drive D is your CD-ROM drive. Use the appropriate drive letter if your CD-ROM is located in a different location.)

4. Click on the OK button. A screen pops up that says "One moment please. . . ."

5. The "Company Data to accompany College Accounting with Peachtree" window pops up. Click on Continue.

6. Accept the default for the "Path: C:\PEACHW" by clicking on Continue. (If Peachtree was installed in a different directory, type that location in the "Path" dialog box.)

7. The next screen, "Companies", shows the data that is included on the Company Data CD-ROM.

8. Since you are loading data for Flashtec only, click on the box next to Flashtec.

9. Click on Continue. A scale shows what percentage of the data has been copied. All files have been copied to the hard drive of your computer when the scale is completed. The "Success" window displays.

10. Click on OK. You are returned to Program Manager in Windows 3.1*x* or the desktop in Windows 95.

11. Remove the Company Data CD-ROM from drive D (or the appropriate drive for your CD-ROM).

12. Double-click on the Peachtree Accounting icon. At the "Presenting Peachtree Accounting" window, click on Open.

13. Click once on Flashtec to highlight it.

14. Click on Ok. The main menu for Flashtec displays.

15. Follow these steps to print Flashtec's chart of accounts.
    a. From the main menu, select Reports, then General Ledger. In the Report List, the "Chart of Accounts" is highlighted.
    b. On the icon bar, click on the Print icon. The "Chart of Accounts Filter" window displays.
    c. Click on OK and the "Print" window pops up.
    d. Click on OK and the chart of accounts starts to print. Compare your printout with Figure 15.9.

Figure **15.9**

Flashtec
Chart of Accounts
As of Dec 31, 1996

Filter Criteria includes: Report order is by ID. Report is printed with Accounts having Zero Amounts and in Detail Format.

Account ID	Account Description	Active?	Account Type
107	Payroll Checking	Yes	Cash
108	Change Fund	Yes	Cash
109	Petty Cash	Yes	Cash
110	Cash	Yes	Cash
111	Accounts Receivable	Yes	Accounts Receivable
112	Merchandise Inventory	Yes	Inventory
113	Supplies	Yes	Inventory
114	Prepaid Insurance	Yes	Other Current Assets
120	Equipment	Yes	Fixed Assets
121	Accumulated Depreciation	Yes	Accumulated Depreciation
210	Accounts Payable	Yes	Accounts Payable
211	Wages Payable	Yes	Other Current Liabilities
212	Unearned Revenue	Yes	Other Current Liabilities
213	Sales Tax Payable	Yes	Other Current Liabilities
214	Federal Income Tax Payable	Yes	Other Current Liabilities
215	FICA--Soc. Sec. Tax Payable	Yes	Other Current Liabilities
216	FICA--Medicare Tax Payable	Yes	Other Current Liabilities
217	State Income Tax Payable	Yes	Other Current Liabilities
220	FUTA Tax Payable	Yes	Other Current Liabilities
221	SUTA Tax Payable	Yes	Other Current Liabilities
223	Health Insurance Payable	Yes	Other Current Liabilities
310	Susan Baxter, Capital	Yes	Equity-doesn't close
320	Susan Baxter, Drawing	Yes	Equity-gets closed
330	Retained Earnings	Yes	Equity-Retained Earnings
410	Sales	Yes	Income
411	Sales Returns and Allowances	Yes	Income
412	Sales Discount	Yes	Income
501	Cost of Sales	Yes	Cost of Sales
610	Depreciation Expense	Yes	Expenses
611	FICA--Soc. Sec. Tax Expense	Yes	Expenses
612	FICA--Medicare Tax Expense	Yes	Expenses
613	FUTA Tax Expense	Yes	Expenses
614	SUTA Tax Expense	Yes	Expenses
615	Insurance Expense	Yes	Expenses
616	Rent Expense	Yes	Expenses
617	Repair Expense	Yes	Expenses
618	Service Charge Expense	Yes	Expenses
619	Supplies Expense	Yes	Expenses
620	Utilities Expense	Yes	Expenses
621	Wages Expense	Yes	Expenses
622	Miscellaneous Expense	Yes	Expenses

    e. On the icon bar, click on "Close." You are returned to the main menu.

    f. To exit PAW, select File, Exit.

Part B

Flashtec completed the following transactions during December 1996:

    Dec 1   Issued Check No. 3475 to Wheaton Plaza Properties for monthly rent, $820. This was a cash purchase.

Comment

PAW requires that you post the special journals between transactions. For example, before you can use the "Receipts" Task (cash receipts journal), you must post the cash disbursements journal.

While you are journalizing transactions, a "Peachtree Question" window pops up. It asks "All the Journals need to be posted! Post them all now?" In response to that question, click on Yes. Another window pops up which asks "All the journals will be posted!" Again, Click on Yes.

2   Sold 6 color printers for cash, Invoice No. 6845, $3,000 *plus 6 percent sales tax.* This merchandise cost $1,800.

3   Issued Check No. 3476 to Beltway to pay Invoice No. 906, $1,750. (This pays a November invoice which is shown as the December 1 balance forward in the vendor ledger.)

3   Sold 10 laminators on account to Carmen Products, Invoice No. 6846, terms 2/10, n/30, $2,600. This merchandise cost $1,200.

4   Issued Check No. 3477 to Koretke Brothers for supplies, $52.40. This was a cash purchase.

5   Issued Check No. 3478 to Jordon, Inc., to pay Invoice No. F832, $400. (This pays a November invoice which is shown as the December 1 balance forward in the vendor ledger.)

5   Purchased 13 fax machines from Wong Products Invoice No. W543, terms net 30 days, $1,300.

6   Sold 9 laminators for cash, Invoice No. 6847, $2,340 *plus 6 percent sales tax.* This merchandise cost $1,080.

9   Issued Check No. 3479 to Wong Products to pay Invoice No. W125, $800. (This pays a November invoice which is shown as the December 1 balance forward in the vendor ledger.)

9   Sold 25 fax machines on account to Frazer Associates, Invoice No. 6848, terms 2/10, n/30, $3,750. The merchandise cost $2,500.

10   Issued Check No. 3480 to Fox Valley Power for electric bill, $132. This was a cash purchase.

10   Received an $1,800 prepayment from Carmen Products for 4 electronic cash registers to be shipped at a later date.

11   Frazer Associates returned one fax machine, Invoice No. 6848, $150. The returned merchandise cost $100.

11   Received a check from Carmen Products in payment of Invoice No. 6846, $2,548.

12   Electronically transferred $1,950 from the regular checking account to the payroll checking account.

13   Based on the following information for the two-week pay period ending December 13, journalize the payroll entry and print the paycheck for each employee. *Remember to both journalize and print the check for one employee before going on to the next employee.* (Hint: Remember to click on the magnifying glass icon in the Cash Account box. Select Account No. 107, Payroll Checking.)

Employee Name	Regular Hours	Overtime Hours	Check No.
Alvarez, Alissa	80	4	1006
Dunaway, Kerry	80	2	1007

Comment

If you are using working papers, select PR Preprint 1 Stub R3 as the type of check to print.

If you are printing on plain paper, the form you select is tied to the kind of printer you are using. For example, if you are using an HP DeskJet 520, the form that you should select is "PR MultiP Chks 2 Stub R3." You may need to make a different selection depending on your printer.

13 Issued Check No. 3481 to Wong Products to pay Invoice No. W543.

14 Received a check from Warren Watkins in payment of Invoice No. 6840, $3,581.50. (This check pays a November invoice that is shown as the December 1 balance forward in the customer ledger.)

15 Received a check from Frazer Associates in payment of Invoice No. 6848, less return on 12/11/96, $3,528.

16 Purchased 6 color printers from Hunter Corporation, Invoice No. 5120, terms 2/10, n/30, $1,800.

16 Sold 5 computers on account to Carmen Products, Invoice No. 6849, terms 2/10, n/30, $9,000. This merchandise cost $5,000.

17 Issued Check No. 3482 to Archer Plumbing for a repair, $85. This was a cash purchase.

18 Issued Check No. 3483 to Myrtle Beach Bell for telephone service (Utilities Expense), $176.

19 Issued Check No. 3484 to Susan Baxter, a withdrawal for personal use, $450.

21 Returned one color jet printer purchased on December 16 from Hunter Corporation, Invoice No. 5120, $300.

23 Sold 9 laminators on account to Martin Brothers, Invoice No. 6850, terms 2/10, n/30, $2,340. The merchandise cost $1,080.

23 Purchased 2 computers from Beltway Company, Invoice No. 1081, terms net 30 days, $2,000.

24 Issued Check No. 3485 to Hunter Corporation to pay Invoice No. 5120, less 12/21/96 purchase return.

26 Electronically transferred $2,325 from the regular checking account to the payroll checking account.

26 Purchased 4 paper shredders from Ferris Enterprises, Invoice No. 8973, terms 1/10, n/30, $800.

27 Based on the following information for the two-week pay period ending December 27, journalize the payroll entry and print the paycheck for each employee. *Remember to both journalize and print the check for one employee before going on to the next employee.*

Employee Name	Regular Hours	Overtime Hours	Check No.
Alvarez, Alissa	80	1	1008
Dunaway, Kerry	80	3	1009

27   Sold 3 paper shredders on account to Warren Watkins, Invoice No. 6851, terms net 30 days, $1,200 *plus 6 percent sales tax.* The merchandise cost $600.

27   Purchased 10 fax machines from Wong Products, Invoice No. W589, terms net 30 days, $1,000.

28   Martin Brothers returned one laminator purchased on December 23, Invoice No. 6850, $260. The returned merchandise cost $120.

28   Sold 2 computers on account to Frazer Associates, Invoice No. 6852, terms 2/10, n/30, $3,600. The merchandise cost $2,000.

28   Issued Check No. 3486 to Rapid Freight for transportation charges relating to the purchase of merchandise, $235. This was a cash purchase.

30   Shipped 4 electronic cash registers to Carmen Products, Invoice No. 6853, $1,800. The electronic cash registers cost $1,200. Prepayment was received on December 10, 1996.

Instructions

1. Record these transactions on a data entry sheet. Number the data entry sheet pages.

2. Using your completed data entry sheet, journalize the transactions in the appropriate journals using PAW's Tasks feature.

3. **Post all the journals. (Hint: Click on Tasks, System, Post. "All Journals" is the default. Click on Ok.)**

4. Print the following journals using PAW's Reports feature:
   a. Purchase journal
   b. Cash disbursements journal
   c. Sales journal
   d. Cash receipts journal
   e. Payroll journal
   f. General journal

5. Proofread your journals. If necessary, make corrections using PAW's "Edit Records" icon. If you make any corrections, reprint the appropriate journals.

6. Print a general ledger trial balance. This is an unadjusted trial balance.

7. Make a backup. Use **a:\utb.fla** as the file name. (Hint: Remember to use a blank formatted disk when you back up.)

Part C

1. On December 30, 1996, Flashtec issued Check No. 3487 to **Valley National Bank** in payment of the liabilities for federal income tax withheld, social security, and medicare shown on Flashtec's unadjusted trial balance. Refer to Instruction B (6).

a. Record this transaction on a data entry sheet.

b. Referring to your data entry sheet, use PAW's Payments Task to journalize this transaction in Flashtec's cash disbursements journal and print Check No. 3487. If you are using the check forms from the working papers, select form AP Preprint 1 Stub.

2. On December 30, 1996, Flashtec issued Check No. 3488 to the **Internal Revenue Service** in payment of the FUTA tax liability shown on Flashtec's unadjusted trial balance. Refer to Instruction B (6). Flashtec will submit this check along with Form 940-EZ.

   a. Record this transaction on a data entry sheet.

   b. Referring to your data entry sheet, use PAW's Payments Task to journalize this transaction in Flashtec's cash disbursements journal and print Check No. 3488. If you are using the check forms from the working papers, select form AP Preprint 1 Stub.

3. On December 30, 1996, Flashtec issued Check No. 3489 to the **Director of Employment Security** in payment of the SUTA tax liability shown on Flashtec's unadjusted trial balance. Refer to Instruction B (6).

   a. Record this transaction on a data entry sheet.

   b. Referring to your data entry sheet, use PAW's Payments Task to journalize this transaction in Flashtec's cash disbursements journal and print Check No. 3489. If you are using the check forms from the working papers, select form AP Preprint 1 Stub.

4. **Post the cash disbursements journal.** You will print these journal entries in Part F.

Part D

1. Print Form 941.
   a. Type **965.35** in the Total deposits for quarter box.
   b. Make the appropriate selections to print Form 941.

2. Print Form 940-EZ.
   a. Type **56** in the FUTA deposited for the year box.
   b. Type **229.50** in the SUTA paid this year box.
   c. Make the appropriate selections to print Form 940-EZ.

3. Print Forms W-2.

4. Print Form W-3.
   a. Type **77.44** in the FUTA deposited for the year box.
   b. Type **315.36** in the SUTA paid this year box.
   c. Make the appropriate selections to print Form W-3.

Part E

Flashtec's accounts need to be adjusted based on the following December 31 data:

Supplies used during December, $705.

Insurance expired during December, $175.

Wages Expense incurred but not yet paid, $650.

Depreciation on equipment, $45.

1. Record the adjustments on a data entry sheet.

2. Referring to your data entry sheet, use PAW's "General Journal Entry" feature to journalize the December 31 adjustments in the general journal.

3. **Post the general journal.** (You will print the December 31 general journal in Part I.)

Part F

When Flashtec began operations, it established a $75 petty cash fund. On December 31, 1996, Flashtec issued Check No. 3490, made out to "Cash," for $35 based on the following information taken from the petty cash record:

Payments:

Supplies $15.00

Miscellaneous Expense 20.00

Total payments $35.00

1. On a data entry sheet, record the entry to replenish petty cash on December 31, 1996.

2. Referring to your data entry sheet, use PAW's "Payments" window to journalize the replenishment of petty cash in the cash disbursements journal and print Check No. 3490. If you are using the check forms from the working papers, select form AP Preprint 1 Stub R3.

3. **Post the cash disbursements journal.**

4. Print the cash disbursements journal for December 30 and 31, 1996. (Hint: Click on the Calendar icon in the "From" box. Then select 30.)

5. Print a general ledger trial balance. This is an adjusted trial balance.

Part G

Flashtec's Cash account (Account No. 110) has a December 31 balance of $10,397.25 as shown on the adjusted trial balance printed in Instruction F (5). The bank statement displayed in Figure 15.10 shows an ending balance on December 31, 1996 of $10,464.55. Flashtec uses this checking account for everything *except* employee checks.

Figure **15.10**

VALLEY NATIONAL BANK				
Wheaton, Illinois				

Flashtec			Statement Date: 12-31-96	
126 Elm Street			Account No. 0910065410	
Wheaton, Illinois 60187			12-1-96 to 12-31-96	

REGULAR CHECKING				
Previous Balance				6,332.40
6 Deposits (+)				17,117.90
14 Checks (−)				8,670.75
Electronic funds transfer (−)				4,275.00
Service Charges (−)				40.00
Ending Balance				10,464.55

DEPOSITS					
12-2-96	3,180.00	12-10-96	1,800.00	12-14-96	3,581.50
12-6-96	2,480.40	12-11-96	2,548.00	12-15-96	3,528.00

CHECKS (Asterisk * indicates break in check number sequence)				
	12-1-96	3475	820.00	
	12-3-96	3476	1,750.00	
	12-4-96	3477	52.40	
	12-5-96	3478	400.00	
	12-9-96	3479	800.00	
	12-10-96	3480	132.00	
	12-13-96	3481	1,300.00	
	12-17-96	3482	85.00	
	12-18-96	3483	176.00	
	12-19-96	3484	450.00	
	12-24-96	3485	1,470.00	
	12-28-96	3486	235.00	
	12-31-96	3487	965.35	
	12-31-96	*3490	35.00	

ELECTRONIC FUNDS TRANSFER			
	12-12-96	1,950.00	
	12-26-96	2,325.00	

1. *a.* After reviewing the bank statement in Figure 15.10 on page 505, record the necessary entry or entries on a data entry sheet.

   b. Referring to your data entry sheet, use PAW's "General Journal Entry" window to journalize the transaction(s) in the general journal.

   c. **Post the general journal.** (You will print the December 31 general journal in Part I.)

2. *a.* Use PAW's "Account Reconciliation" feature to complete the bank reconciliation.

   b. Print the account reconciliation report.

Part H

Flashtec's Payroll Checking account (Account No. 107) has a December 31 balance of $1,066.68 as shown on the adjusted trial balance printed in Instruction F(5). The bank statement displayed in Figure 15.11 shows an ending balance of $1,051.68. Flashtec only uses this account for employee paychecks.

Figure 15.11

VALLEY NATIONAL BANK Wheaton, Illinois				
Flashtec 126 Elm Street Wheaton, Illinois 60187			Statement Date: 12-31-96 Account No. 0063049211 12-1-96 to 12-31-96	
PAYROLL CHECKING				
Previous Balance				300.00
2 Deposits (+)				4,275.00
4 Checks (−)				3,508.32
Service Charges (−)				15.00
Ending Balance				1,051.68
DEPOSITS				
12-12-96	1,950.00	12-26-96	2,325.00	
CHECKS (Asterisk * indicates break in check number sequence)				
		12-13-96	1006	1,066.86
		12-13-96	1007	708.49
		12-27-96	1008	1,013.32
		12-27-96	1009	719.65

1. *a.* After reviewing the bank statement in Figure 15.11, record the necessary entry or entries on a data entry sheet.

   b. Referring to your data entry sheet, use PAW's "General Journal Entry" window to journalize the transaction(s) in the general journal.

   c. **Post the general journal.** (You will print the December 31 general journal in Part I.)

2. *a.* Use PAW's "Account Reconciliation" feature to complete the bank reconciliation.

   b. Print the account reconciliation report.

Part I

1. Print Flashtec's December 31, 1996 general journal. (Hint: Click on the Calendar icon in the "From" box. Then select 31.)

2. Print a December 31, 1996, general ledger trial balance for Flashtec.

Part J

1. Print the following items for the fiscal year ending December 31, 1996:
   a. Ask your instructor if it is necessary to print the general ledger. *Please note that it will take approximately 18 pages to print the entire general ledger.*
   b. Print customer ledgers.
   c. Print vendor ledgers.
   d. Print the income statement.
   e. Print the balance sheet.
   f. Print the statement of cash flow.

2. Make a backup. Use **a:\flashtec.dec** as the file name.

Part K

1. Referring to Flashtec's general ledger trial balance, printed in Instruction I (2), record closing entries on a data entry sheet.

2. Using PAW, close Flashtec's fiscal year ending December 31, 1996.

3. Print Flashtec's post-closing trial balance.

4. Be sure to back up your Flashtec data. You may need it for error correction or testing purposes. Use **a:\flashtec.end** as the file name.

Appendix A:

Installing Peachtree Accounting Software

This section gives you instructions for installing Peachtree Accounting for Windows software on an IBM-PC or compatible computer. *You may need to check with your instructor to see if Peachtree has already been installed in the classroom or computer lab.*

Using Antivirus Programs While Installing

Virus checking programs can interfere with the installation process for Peachtree Accounting for Windows. Before you begin to install, disable virus checking. Consult your antivirus software documentation for information. After Peachtree is installed you may resume use of your antivirus software.

Installing Peachtree on a Single Machine

If you are installing Peachtree on your home computer or on a single classroom computer (non-networked), you will need to follow these directions. *If a previous version of Peachtree is already installed on your computer, go directly to the "Upgrading" section of this appendix on page 514.*

step   1:   Turn on your computer and monitor.

step   2:   Start Windows.

step   3:   Place the CD labeled Peachtree Accounting for Windows, Release 5.0, Educational Version, into your CD-ROM drive.

step   4:   From the Program Manager, click on File, then click on Run. (In Windows 95, click on Start, then click on Run.)

step   5:   Type **d:\setup**. This text assumes that drive D is your CD-ROM drive. Use the appropriate letter if your CD-ROM drive is in a different location.

step   6:   Click on OK. After a few moments, the "Peachtree Accounting Release 5—Educational Version" appears.

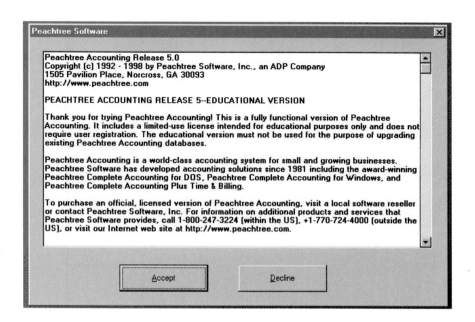

step   7:   Read the information on this screen. Click on Accept.

step   8:   The Peachtree Accounting "Installation-Welcome" window appears.

Custom

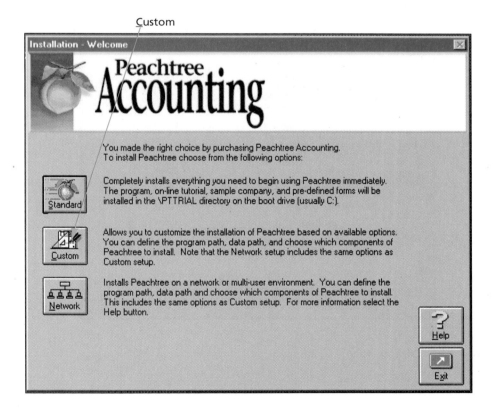

step   9:   Click on Custom. The "Custom Install Peachtree Accounting" window displays. Read the information explained on the "Custom Install Peachtree Accounting" window. Highlight PTTRIAL. Type **PEACHW**.

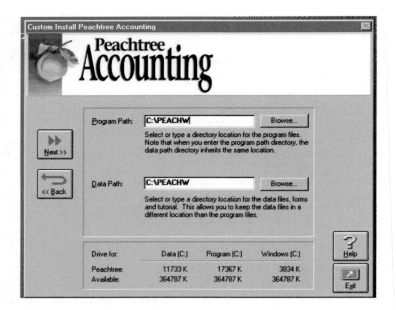

step 10: Click on <u>N</u>ext. A screen pops up that says "The directory C:\PEACHW does not exist. Do you want to create it?" Click on <u>Y</u>es.

step 11: The next screen says "This lets you install Peachtree and any of its components. . . ."

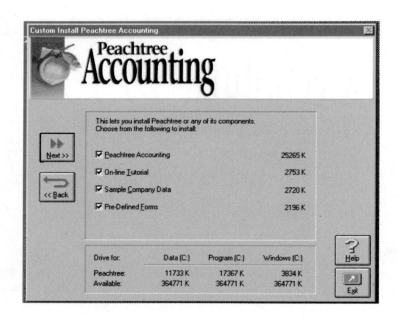

step 12: Click on <u>N</u>ext.

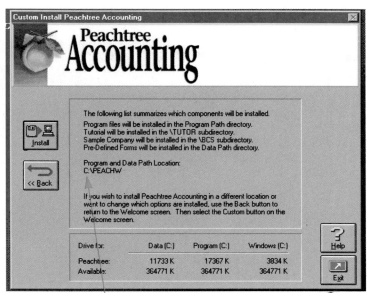

Program and Data Path Location: C:\PEACHW

step 13:   Click on Install. Peachtree starts to install. A scale at the bottom of the screen shows you what percentage of the program has been installed.

step 14:   The screen displays: "All of the files needed to use Peachtree have been successfully copied. . . ."

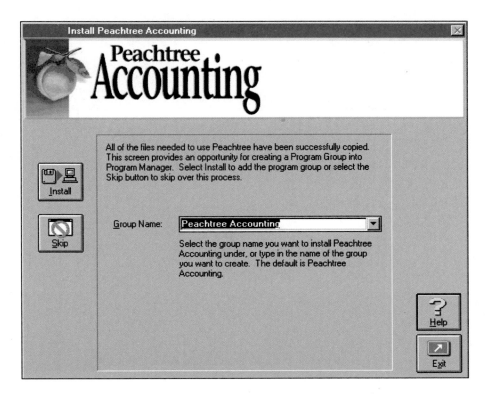

step 15:   Click on Install to create program icons.

step 16:   Remove the CD from your CD-ROM drive.

step 17:   Click on Begin.

step 18:   The "Presenting Peachtree Accounting" screen displays.

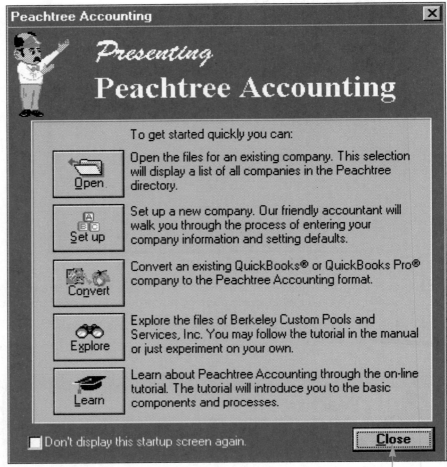

Close

step 19:   In the lower right corner of your screen, click on Close.

step 20:   From the menu at the top of your screen, click on File. Then click on Exit to exit Peachtree.

Your installation is complete.

Upgrading from a Previous Version of Peachtree Accounting for Windows

If you have a previous version of Peachtree Accounting for Windows installed, you should perform an upgrade installation.

Follow these steps to upgrade Peachtree Accounting for Windows:

step **1:**   Turn on the computer and start Windows.

step **2:**   Place the CD labeled Peachtree Accounting for Windows, Release 5.0, Educational Version, into your CD-ROM drive.

step **3:**   From the Windows Program Manager, click on <u>F</u>ile, then click on <u>R</u>un. (In Windows 95, click on Start, then click on <u>R</u>un.)

step **4:**   Type **d:\setup** and click on OK. This text assumes that drive D is your CD-ROM drive. Use the appropriate letter if your CD-ROM drive is in a different location.

Upgrade

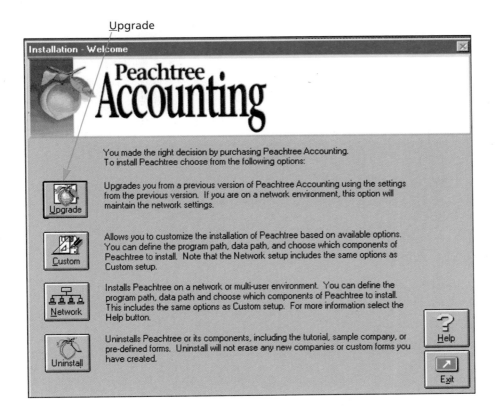

step **5:**   The Peachtree Accounting for Windows Detected window pops up. It states that "Setup has detected that you have an earlier release of Peachtree Accounting installed. To replace this Educational Version of Peachtree Accounting Release 5.0, select the Custom option and install to the location of your current version of Peachtree Accounting." Click on OK.

Comment

If you get an Information window saying "Setup has detected that you have already installed Peachtree Accounting Release 5.0," click on OK. The CD, Peachtree Accounting for Windows, Release 5.0, Batch 03, is packaged with the text. To check your version and batch of PAW, start Peachtree, open any company, then click on <u>H</u>elp, <u>A</u>bout. If you have an earlier batch of PAW 5.0 installed, check with your instructor on how to uninstall it.

step 6: Follow the instructions for Installing Peachtree on a Single Machine starting on page 510 with step 6.

Appendix B:

Loading The Kitchen Taylor Company Data

The directions shown below are for loading The Kitchen Taylor Company
Data onto the hard drive of your computer. Before you install this data,
make sure you have at least 6 MB of free disk space and that Microsoft
Windows is installed.

1. Start Windows. If you are running Windows 3.1*x*, choose <u>F</u>ile, <u>R</u>un in
   Program Manager. If you are running Windows 95, choose Start, <u>R</u>un.

2. Place the Company Data CD-ROM in drive D (or the appropriate
   drive for your CD-ROM).

3. Type **d:\setup.exe** in the dialog box. (This text assumes drive D is
   your CD-ROM drive. Use the appropriate drive letter if your CD-ROM
   is located in a different location.)

4. Click on the OK button. A screen pops up that says "One moment
   please. . . ."

5. The next screen displayed is shown below.

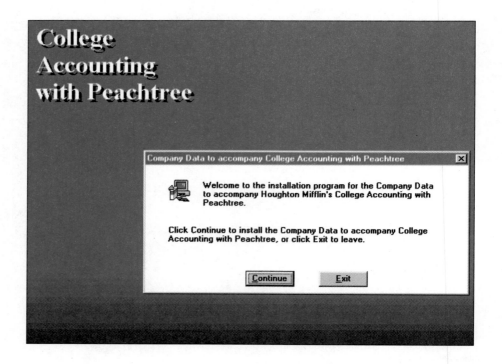

6. Click on <u>C</u>ontinue.

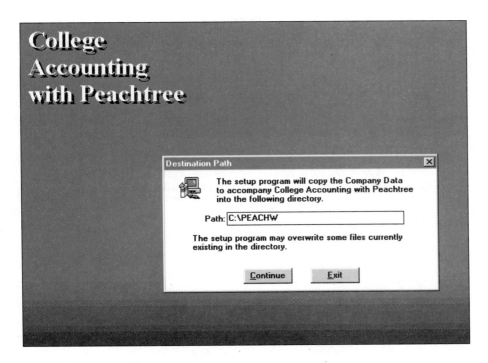

7. Accept the default for the "Path: C:\PEACHW" by clicking on <u>C</u>ontinue. (If Peachtree was installed in a different directory, type that location in the "Path" dialog box.)

8. The next screen, "Companies," shows the data that is included on the Company Data CD- ROM.

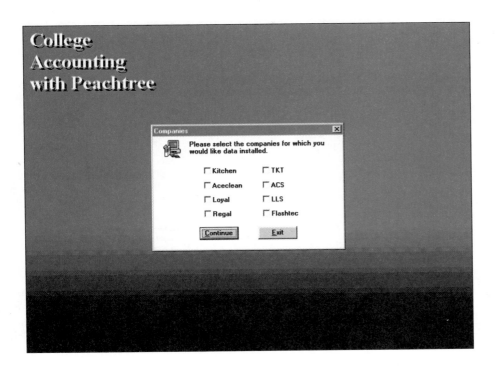

9. Since you are loading data for The Kitchen Taylor only, click on the box next to Kitchen.

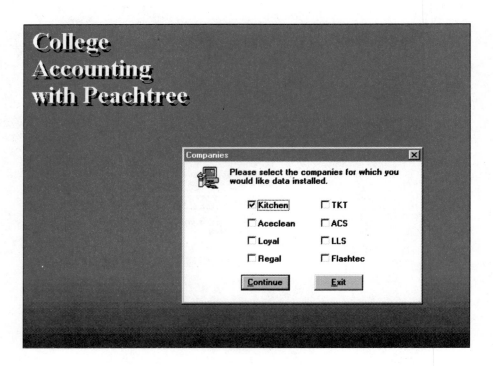

10. Click on Continue. A scale shows what percentage of the data has been copied. All files have been copied to the hard drive of your computer when the scale is completed. The "Success" window displays.

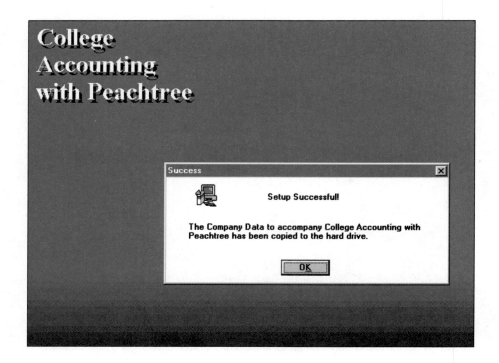

11. Click on O<u>K</u>. You are returned to Program Manager in Windows 3.1*x* or the desktop in Windows 95.

12. Remove the Company Data CD-ROM from drive D (or the appropriate drive for your CD-ROM).

To check that your company data was installed properly, do the following:

1. Double-click on the Peachtree icon.

2. At the "Presenting Peachtree Accounting" screen, click on <u>O</u>pen. The Kitchen Taylor should be shown in the Company <u>N</u>ame box.

Comment   Your screen may show other companies, as well as The Kitchen Taylor, listed in the "Company <u>N</u>ame" box. This is okay. Berkeley Custom Pools & Services, Inc. is Peachtree Software's sample company, so it automatically appears in your "Company <u>N</u>ame" box. In addition, if you are working in a computer lab at school, another student may have already installed other companies before you started using this computer.

3. Click once on The Kitchen Taylor to highlight it.

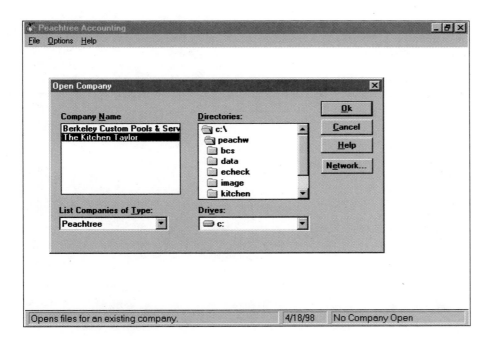

4. Click on Ok.

5. The "Convert Company Files" window pops up.

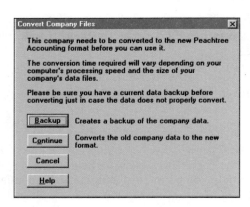

6. Click on Continue. A series of screens pop up. The program is converting your data for use with Peachtree Accounting for Windows, Release 5.0. The main menu for The Kitchen Taylor displays.

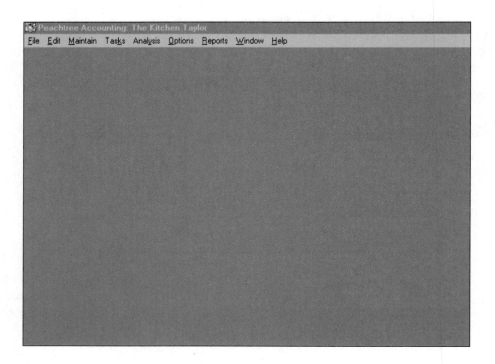

7. To exit Peachtree, click on File, then Exit.

Comment: *What if your setup failed?* If an error screen displays that says "Setup Failed!", attempt to install the Company Data again. If installation fails on the second attempt, contact Houghton Mifflin Software Support at 1-800-732-3223.

Index